THE *unofficial* GUIDE®
ᵀᴼ Universal Orlando®

2025

COME CHECK US OUT!

Supplement your valuable guidebook with tips, news, and deals by visiting our websites:

theunofficialguides.com
touringplans.com

Also, while there, sign up for The Unofficial Guide newsletter for even more travel tips and special offers.

Join the conversation on social media:

𝕏 @theUGSeries   theUnofficialGuides

theUnofficialGuides   theUnofficialGuides

TheUnofficialGuideSeries   theUnofficialGuides

Other Unofficial Guides

The Disneyland Story: The Unofficial Guide to the Evolution of Walt Disney's Dream

Universal vs. Disney: The Unofficial Guide to American Theme Parks' Greatest Rivalry

The Unofficial Guide to Disney Cruise Line

The Unofficial Guide to Disneyland

The Unofficial Guide to Las Vegas

The Unofficial Guide to Walt Disney World

The Unofficial Guide to Washington, D.C.

THE *unofficial* GUIDE®

TO Universal Orlando®

2025

SETH KUBERSKY *with* ALICIA STELLA,
BOB SEHLINGER & LEN TESTA

Every effort has been made to ensure the accuracy of this book, and its contents are believed to be correct at the time of publication. Nevertheless, please be aware that these contents are subject to change after publication, owing to numerous factors that influence the travel industry. The publishers therefore cannot accept responsibility for errors or omissions, for changes in prices and other information presented in this guide, or for the consequences of relying on this information. We strongly suggest that you confirm details when making your travel plans.

The authors' assessments of attractions and the like are subjective—they may not reflect the publisher's opinion or align with a reader's own experience. Readers are invited to write the publisher with ideas, comments, and suggestions for future editions.

The Unofficial Guides
An imprint of AdventureKEEN
2204 First Ave. S., Ste. 102
Birmingham, AL 35233

Cover design by Scott McGrew, with updates by Jonathan Norberg

Text design by Vertigo Design, with updates by Annie Long

For information on our other products and services or to obtain technical support, please contact us from within the United States at 800-678-7006 or by fax at 877-374-9016.

AdventureKEEN also publishes its books in a variety of electronic formats. Some content that appears in print may not be available in electronic formats.

ISBN 978-1-62809-160-1 (pbk.); ISBN 978-1-62809-161-8 (ebook)

Distributed by Publishers Group West

Manufactured in the United States of America

5 4 3 2 1

CONTENTS

List of Maps vii
About the Authors viii

Introduction 1
Why "Unofficial"? 1
Universal Orlando: An Overview 5
    COMPARISON OF ATTRACTIONS FOUND AT BOTH UNIVERSAL
      STUDIOS HOLLYWOOD AND UNIVERSAL ORLANDO 18
    UNIVERSAL LEXICON IN A NUTSHELL 19
    COMMON ABBREVIATIONS 19

PART 1 Planning Before You Leave Home 21
Gathering Information 21
    IMPORTANT UNIVERSAL ADDRESSES 23
    UNIVERSAL ORLANDO PHONE NUMBERS 24
Timing Your Visit 25
    UNIVERSAL ORLANDO CLIMATE 28
Allocating Money 32
    UNIVERSAL ORLANDO ADMISSIONS 33
Making the Most of Your Time and Money at Universal Orlando 42

PART 2 Accommodations 70
The Basic Considerations 70
Universal Orlando Resort Hotels 101 72
Universal Orlando Resort Hotel Services and Amenities 76
Universal Orlando Resort Hotel Profiles 83
Universal Orlando Vacation Packages 101
Off-Site Lodging Options 103
The Best Hotels Near Universal Orlando 110
    HOW THE HOTELS COMPARE 114
The 10 Best Hotel Values 118
    THE TOP 10 BEST DEALS 118

PART 3 Arriving and Getting Around 119
Getting There 119
Getting Oriented 133

PART 4 Universal Essentials 139
Money, Etc. 139
Packing the Essentials 141
Problems and Unusual Situations 142
Services 146
Universal Orlando for Guests with Special Needs 156

PART 5 Universal Orlando with Kids 167
It's a Small Universe, After All 167
About the Unofficial Guide Touring Plans 171
Stuff to Think About 171
Strollers 173
Lost Children 176
Universal, Kids, and Scary Stuff 178
     SMALL-CHILD FRIGHT-POTENTIAL TABLE 180–183
     POTENTIALLY PROBLEMATIC ATTRACTIONS FOR GROWN-UPS 185
     ATTRACTION HEIGHT REQUIREMENTS 186–187
Universal Characters 189
     CHARACTER-GREETING LOCATIONS 190–191
Babysitting 192

PART 6 Universal Studios Florida 193
Getting Oriented at Universal Studios Florida 193
Universal Studios Florida Attractions 197
Live Entertainment at Universal Studios Florida 224
Special Events at Universal Studios Florida 226
Universal Studios Florida Touring Plans 238

PART 7 Universal Islands of Adventure 242
Getting Oriented at Universal Islands of Adventure 243
Universal Islands of Adventure Attractions 244
Special Events at Universal Islands of Adventure 269
Universal Islands of Adventure Touring Plans 271

PART 8 Universal Epic Universe 273
Getting Oriented at Universal Epic Universe 273
Universal Epic Universe Attractions 276
Live Entertainment at Universal Epic Universe 287
Universal Epic Universe Touring Plans 288

PART 9 **Universal Volcano Bay 290**
Getting Oriented at Universal Volcano Bay 292
Universal Volcano Bay Attractions 295
Universal Volcano Bay Touring Strategy 300

PART 10 **Dining and Shopping at Universal Orlando 302**
  PLANT-BASED DINING AT UNIVERSAL 305
Character Meals 306
Fast Food in Universal Orlando's Parks 307
Universal Orlando Quick-Service Restaurant Mini-Profiles 317
Universal Orlando Full-Service Restaurant Profiles 339
  UNIVERSAL ORLANDO RESTAURANTS BY CUISINE 342–343
Dining near Universal Orlando 360
Shopping at Universal Orlando 361
Shopping near Universal Orlando 368

PART 11 **Universal Orlando CityWalk 370**
Arriving and Parking 371
Contacting CityWalk 371
CityWalk Clubs 371
CityWalk Entertainment 375

Appendix 379
Index 381
Touring Plans 395

LIST *of* MAPS

Universal Orlando 8–9
Hotels in the Universal & International Drive Areas 111
South Orlando 122–123
I-Drive Area Sneak Routes 124
Universal Studios Florida 194–195
Universal Islands of Adventure 246–247
Universal Epic Universe 274–275
Universal Volcano Bay 291
Universal Orlando CityWalk 372–373

ABOUT *the* AUTHORS

Seth Kubersky is the coauthor of *The Unofficial Guide to Disneyland* and *The Unofficial Guide to Las Vegas,* a contributor to *The Unofficial Guide to Walt Disney World,* and a regular contributor to the Unofficial Guides blog (**TheUnofficialGuides.com**). A resident of Orlando since 1996, Seth is a former employee of Universal Orlando's entertainment department. He covers arts and attractions for *Orlando Weekly, Attractions Magazine,* and other publications. You can find Seth online at SethKubersky.com and on social media (@skubersky).

Alicia Stella has been covering themed attractions since 2015, on both her website **OrlandoParkStop.com** and her YouTube channel **Theme Park Stop.** She specializes in reporting on new attraction development, and her work has been cited by *The New York Times, USA Today,* CNN, *The Today Show,* and more. Alicia lives in Central Florida with her wife, Jenn, and their daughter, Haley.

Bob Sehlinger is the author of *The Unofficial Guide to Walt Disney World* and *The Unofficial Guide to Las Vegas* and coauthor of *The Unofficial Guide to Walt Disney World with Kids* (with Liliane J. Opsomer). He has served as publisher of the Unofficial Guides series since its inception.

Len Testa is the coauthor of *The Unofficial Guide to Walt Disney World* and *The Unofficial Guide to Disney Cruise Line* (with Tammy Whiting and Erin Foster), as well as the webmaster of Touring Plans (**TouringPlans.com**). Len has also contributed to *The Unofficial Guide to Disneyland, The Unofficial Guide to Las Vegas,* and *The Unofficial Guide to Walt Disney World with Kids.*

INTRODUCTION

WHY "UNOFFICIAL"?

DECLARATION OF INDEPENDENCE

THE AUTHORS AND RESEARCHERS of this guide specifically and categorically declare that they are and always have been totally independent. The material in this guide originated with the authors and has not been reviewed, edited, or in any way approved by Universal Orlando or any other companies whose travel products are discussed.

The purpose of this guide is to provide you with the information necessary to tour with the greatest efficiency and economy and with the least hassle and stress. In this guide we represent and serve you, the consumer. If a restaurant serves bad food, a gift item is overpriced, or a certain ride isn't worth the wait, we can say so, and in the process we hope to make your visit more fun, efficient, and economical.

DANCE TO THE MUSIC

A DANCE HAS A BEGINNING and an end. But when you're dancing, you're not concerned about getting to the end or where on the dance floor you might wind up. In other words, you're totally in the moment. That's the way you should be on your Universal Orlando vacation.

You may feel a bit of pressure concerning your holiday. Vacations, after all, are very special events—and expensive ones to boot. So you work hard to make your getaway the best that it can be. Planning and organizing are essential to a successful Universal Orlando vacation, but if they become your focus, you won't be able to hear the music and enjoy the dance.

So think of us as your dancing coaches. We'll teach you the steps to the dance in advance, so that when you're on vacation and the music plays, you'll dance with effortless grace and ease.

A BETTER MOUSETRAP?

DIE-HARD DISNEY DEVOTEES may want to cover their mouse ears, because we are about to utter the ultimate blasphemy: it is possible to enjoy an awesome Orlando vacation without spending a single minute in Mickey's world. For much of the past half century, the notion of spending a holiday in Central Florida without seeing Walt Disney's sprawling wonderland seemed silly. While visitors might take a day or two out of their trip to explore independent attractions such as Sea-World, Busch Gardens, or Kennedy Space Center, the Magic Kingdom and its sister parks were seen by most as the area's main draw.

Much to the Mouse House's dismay, that situation is swiftly shifting. While Walt Disney World is in no danger of closing for lack of interest, its share of Orlando's lucrative tourism market has been steadily and significantly swinging in favor of an energetic upstart located a few miles up I-4: Universal Orlando Resort.

Originally opened in 1990 as a single theme park packed with advanced but unreliable attractions, Universal Orlando has matured into a full-service, fully immersive vacation destination with enough world-class activities to keep a family occupied for four days or more. **Universal Studios Florida,** a longtime rival of Disney's Hollywood Studios that draws its inspiration from movies and television, has been almost entirely overhauled since its debut, and it now houses one of the world's top collections of cutting-edge attractions. **Universal Islands of Adventure** debuted in 1999 as the most modern, high-tech theme park in the United States, featuring an all-star lineup of thrill rides that makes it the best park in town for older kids and young-at-heart adults.

Together, the two parks are home to the game-changing **Wizarding World of Harry Potter,** a meticulously imagined, multilayered experience that draws millions of Muggle fans from around the world to the hallowed halls of Hogwarts Castle and Gringotts' Wizarding Bank. Surrounding the two parks are six immaculately appointed on-site resort hotels; the elaborately themed **Volcano Bay** water park; and the **City-Walk** complex, full of restaurants, nightclubs, and entertainment options appealing to families and adults. And Universal Orlando has grown beyond the resort's original boundaries, opening a pair of value-priced resort hotels on the former site of the old Wet 'n Wild water park and constructing **Epic Universe**—a brand-new theme park complex with three additional hotels—near the Orange County Convention Center.

Universal Orlando's ascendancy is not about to bankrupt Walt Disney World, which is promising a multibillion-dollar expansion of its own, but Mickey's political battles and slow pace of post-pandemic expansion offer Universal an opportunity to usurp Disney's once-unquestioned domination. And those who approach Universal with open eyes will find that the resort can provide just as much magic and fantasy in its own fashion. Universal Orlando has an energy, pace, and attitude all its own that might appeal to the most adamant anti–amusement park person, and could even convert confirmed Disney customers. Instead of opting for the same old rat race, consider spending your next vacation playing Quidditch with Harry, saving New York with Spidey, and riding a runaway mine cart with Donkey Kong. You might just find yourself asking, "Mickey who?"

IT TAKES MORE THAN
ONE BOOK TO DO THE JOB RIGHT

WE'VE BEEN COVERING CENTRAL FLORIDA tourism for almost 40 years. We began by lumping everything into one guidebook, but that was when the Magic Kingdom and EPCOT were the only theme parks at Walt Disney World, at the very beginning of the boom that has made Central Florida one of the most visited tourist destinations on Earth. We currently have two titles that provide specialized information tailored to specific Central Florida visitors. Though some tips (such as arriving at the parks early) are echoed in both guides, most of the information in each book is unique.

The Unofficial Guide to Walt Disney World is the centerpiece of our Central Florida coverage because, well, Walt Disney World is the centerpiece of most Central Florida vacations. *The Unofficial Guide to Walt Disney World* is evaluative, comprehensive, and instructive—the ultimate planning tool for a successful Disney World vacation.

You already hold our in-depth guide dedicated to the attractions and amenities of the Universal Orlando Resort. Both of these guides are available at most bookstores and in digital editions.

THE DEATH OF SPONTANEITY

ONE OF OUR ALL-TIME favorite letters came from a man in Chapel Hill, North Carolina:

Your book reads like the operations plan for an amphibious landing: Go here, do this, proceed to Step 15. You must think that everyone is a hyperactive, type-A theme park commando. What happened to the satisfaction of self-discovery or the joy of spontaneity? Next you'll be telling us when to empty our bladders.

As it happens, Unofficial Guide researchers are a pretty existential crew who are big on self-discovery. But Universal Orlando—especially for first-time travelers—probably isn't the place you want to "discover" the spontaneity of needless waits in line or mediocre meals when you could be doing much better.

In many ways, Central Florida's theme parks are the quintessential system, the ultimate in mass-produced entertainment and the most planned and programmed environment anywhere. Lines for rides form in predictable ways at predictable times, for example, and you can either learn here how to avoid them or "discover" them on your own.

We aren't saying that you can't have a great time at Universal Orlando if you play it by ear, and enjoying the resort requires much less advance planning than an equivalent vacation at Walt Disney World. What we *are* saying is that you should think about what you want to do before you go. The time and money you save by planning will help you and your family have more fun.

THE SUM OF ALL FEARS

EVERY WRITER WHO EXPRESSES an opinion is accustomed to readers who strongly agree or disagree: it comes with the territory. Extremely troubling, however, is the possibility that our efforts to be objective have frightened some readers away from Universal Orlando or made others apprehensive.

For the record, if you love theme parks, Universal Orlando is as good as it gets—absolute nirvana. If you arrive without knowing a thing about the place and make every possible mistake, chances are about 90% that you'll have a wonderful vacation anyway. The job of a guidebook is to give you a heads-up regarding opportunities and potential problems. We're certain that we can help you turn a great vacation into an absolutely *superb* one.

THE UNOFFICIAL TEAM

THIS BOOK WAS WRITTEN by Seth Kubersky, building on decades of research from The Unofficial Guides by Bob Sehlinger, Len Testa, and the rest of the Unofficial team. Alicia Stella, of OrlandoParkStop.com, is our top source for updates on Epic Universe and other upcoming attractions. Derek Burgan, star blogger at TouringPlans.com, shares his "Saturday Six" lists and restaurant recommendations with us; Shelby Castle, of UniversalOrlandoVegans.com, offered plant-based food recommendations; and Jon Self supplied vital research for this guide's dining and off-site hotel reviews. Our prologue (see next page) is excerpted from Sam Gennawey's *Universal vs. Disney: An Unofficial Guide to American Theme Parks' Greatest Rivalry.*

Special thanks to Genevieve Bernard for her research assistance, proofreading, and patience. Holly Cross, Jenna Barron, and Emily Beaumont edited the project; Brian Cooper, Chris Eliopoulos, and Tami Knight drew the cartoons; Steve Jones and Cassandra Poertner created the maps; and Rich Carlson indexed the book; thanks go to each of them.

UPDATES AND BREAKING NEWS

LOOK FOR THESE at the Unofficial Guide website, **TheUnofficial Guides.com,** and at our sister website, **TouringPlans.com.** See page 21 for a complete description of these sites.

COMMENTS FROM READERS

MANY OF THOSE WHO USE The Unofficial Guides contact us to share comments or their own strategies for visiting Central Florida. We appreciate all such input, both positive and critical, and encourage our readers to continue writing. Readers' comments and observations are frequently incorporated into revised editions of The Unofficial Guides and have contributed immeasurably to their improvement. If you contact us, you can rest assured that we won't release your name and email address to any mailing lists, advertisers, or other third party.

Reader Survey

After your vacation, please fill out our reader survey by visiting theugseries.com/survey. Unless you instruct us otherwise, we will assume that you don't object to being quoted in a future edition.

How to Contact the Authors

Seth Kubersky and Bob Sehlinger c/o The Unofficial Guides
2204 First Ave. S, Ste. 102
Birmingham, AL 35233
info@theunofficialguides.com.

If you email us, please let us know where you're from. And remember, as travel writers, we're often out of the office for long periods of time, so forgive us if our response is slow.

UNIVERSAL ORLANDO:
An Overview

PROLOGUE: AMERICAN THEME PARKS' GREATEST RIVALRY

UNIVERSAL STUDIOS DIDN'T SET OUT to challenge The Walt Disney Company in the theme park business. The men who ran the Music Corporation of America (MCA) were quite happy with the industrial tour they created in 1964 at Universal City. The Universal Studio Tour took visitors behind the scenes of the largest and busiest back lot in Hollywood to show how motion pictures and television programs were manufactured. . . .

In 1979 MCA bought land in Orlando 10 miles north of Walt Disney World and later announced that it was going to build a motion picture and television production studio. The new studio would have also featured a tour just like the one in California. Lew Wasserman, MCA's legendary chief executive, knew better than to compete with Disney and its dominance with fantasy landscapes. He enjoyed the fact that the two Southern California tourist attractions complemented each other, and he was making money with minimal investment.

Everything changed just a few years later. In 1984 Disney hired Michael Eisner as its new chief executive officer and Frank Wells as president. Before Disney, Eisner had been president of Paramount Pictures, and Wells had been a well-respected executive at Warner Bros. Within two weeks of the Disney leadership change, MCA president and Wasserman's protégé, Sidney Sheinberg, sent a letter to his old friends proposing a meeting to discuss ideas that would be in the mutual interest of both companies.

It made sense to turn to Michael Eisner. While he was at Paramount, Sheinberg had shown him MCA's Florida plans with the hopes
of forming a partnership. Eisner liked what he saw. When nothing
came of the talks, Eisner blamed the impasse on powers higher up
the corporate food chain at Paramount's parent company, Gulf and
Western. Now that Eisner was in charge of Disney, Sheinberg thought
Eisner would be excited to become MCA's partner in Florida.

During the call, a confident Sheinberg suggested to Eisner, "Let's
get together on a studio tour in Orlando. We tried with your predecessors, but they were unresponsive. We think we can help you."[1] Much
to the surprise of the MCA executives, Eisner told his old friend,
"We're already working on something of our own."[2] . . .

Then, on February 7, 1985, Michael Eisner made headlines at his
first meeting with Walt Disney Productions shareholders. Before a
packed house at the Anaheim Convention Center, he announced that
Disney would soon start construction of a third theme park at Walt Disney World. The heart of Disney's park would be a real working production studio with two soundstages and a working animation studio. . . .

The men at MCA were livid. After reviewing Disney's plans, Sheinberg claimed that Eisner stole the idea he heard at the 1981 pitch at Paramount. For his part, Eisner claimed the presentation occurred "many,
many years" ago and added "when I arrived at [Disney], the studio tour
was already on the drawing boards and had been for many years."[3] . . .

A bitter Sheinberg replied, "You're going to have to work awfully
hard to convince me that [Eisner] didn't know about [MCA's plans].
That's ridiculous. . . . Disney announced it would do the theme park
and would have you believe it's been in the works since 1926—if you
believe in mice, you probably believe in the Easter Bunny also."[4] At
MCA, you do not get mad. You get even. This is how the greatest
rivalry in the theme park industry began.

A UNIVERSAL PRIMER

UNIVERSAL ORLANDO RESORT'S original campus is located on
roughly 735 acres inside the city of Orlando, about 8 miles northeast of
Walt Disney World (which actually lies within the municipalities of Lake
Buena Vista and Bay Lake). A new 750-acre expansion site sits a few
miles due south, near the Orange County Convention Center. When that
addition debuts in 2025, the entire resort will consist of three theme
parks—Universal Studios Florida, Universal Islands of Adventure, and
Universal Epic Universe—along with the Volcano Bay water park; 11
Loews-operated Universal hotels; and the CityWalk dining, nightlife,
and shopping complex.

Universal Studios Florida (USF) opened in June 1990. It debuted a
year after the similarly themed Disney–MGM Studios (now known as

1 Ellen Farly, "Behind the MCA-Disney War in Fla.," *The Los Angeles Times,* 23 April 1989.
2 Michael D. Eisner with Tony Schwartz, *Work in Progress: Risking Failure, Surviving Success* (New York: Hyperion, 1998).
3 Kathryn Harris, "Florida Fund may Invest in MCA Park," *The Los Angeles Times,* 20 May 1985.
4 Farly, "Behind the MCA-Disney War in Fla."

Disney's Hollywood Studios) but made almost four times the area of its facility accessible to visitors. USF's original attractions focused on characters and situations from familiar Universal films, from *Jaws* and *King Kong* to *Earthquake* and *E.T.* Unfortunately, while the opening-day rides incorporated state-of-the-art technology and lived up to their billing in terms of creativity and uniqueness, several lacked the capacity or reliability to handle the number of guests who frequent major Florida tourist destinations.

With only one theme park, Universal played second fiddle to Disney's juggernaut for almost a decade. Things began to change when Universal opened **Islands of Adventure (IOA)** in 1999. Adding a second park, along with the CityWalk nightlife complex and three on-site resort hotels, made Universal a legitimate two-day destination and provided Universal with enough critical mass to begin serious competition with Disney for tourists' time and money.

IOA opened to good reviews and sizable crowds, and it did steady business for the first few years. Ongoing competition with Disney, however, and a lack of money to invest in new rides eventually caught up with IOA. Attendance dropped from a high of 6.3 million visitors in 2004 to a low of 4.6 million in 2009, less than half that of Animal Kingdom, Disney's least-visited park in Orlando that year.

In the middle of this slide, Universal management made one bold bet: securing the rights in 2007 to build a Harry Potter–themed area within IOA. Harry, it was thought, was possibly the only fictional character extant capable of trumping Mickey Mouse, and Universal went all out to create a setting and attractions designed to be the envy of the themed-entertainment industry.

The first phase of **The Wizarding World of Harry Potter,** as the new land was called, opened at IOA in 2010 and was an immediate hit. Its headliner attraction, **Harry Potter and the Forbidden Journey,** broke new ground in its ride system and immersive storytelling. Families raced to ride the attraction, and IOA's attendance grew 28% in 2010 and another 28% in 2011.

Harry Potter single-handedly upended the power structure in Florida's theme parks. Emboldened by its success, Universal's new owner, Comcast—which acquired a majority stake in the NBCUniversal conglomerate in 2011 and purchased full ownership from General Electric in 2013—embarked on an unprecedented wave of expansions, rapidly adding new attractions and extensions, including **The Wizarding World of Harry Potter—Diagon Alley** at USF and additional on-site hotels.

While Disney responded to the Potter phenomenon by slowly building *Avatar* and *Star Wars* attractions, Universal struck additional blows by opening affordable on-site hotels, more acclaimed thrill rides, and Volcano Bay, its first highly themed on-site water park. Their boldest move of all is the 2025 opening of a massive second campus dubbed **Universal Epic Universe (EU),** which features even

continued on page 10

Universal Orlando

Water taxi stop
Bus stop
Walking path

Universal Islands of Adventure

Turkey Lake Road

← To Tampa & Walt Disney World

Universal Cabana Bay Beach Resort

Hollywood Way

Universal Volcano Bay

Universal Aventura Hotel

Loews Sapphire Falls Resort

International Drive

4

Loews Royal Pacific Resort

Endless Summer Surfside Inn & Suites

Universal Blvd.

400
4

American Way

400
4

435

Par

Endless Summer Dockside Inn & Suites

Kirkman Road

435

← To Universal Epic Universe

International Drive

Grand National Dr.

4

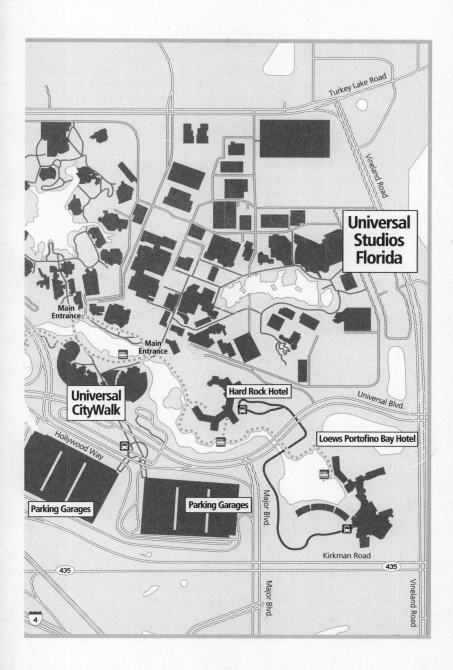

Turkey Lake Road

Vineland Road

Universal Studios Florida

Main Entrance

Main Entrance

Hard Rock Hotel

Universal CityWalk

Universal Blvd.

Loews Portofino Bay Hotel

Hollywood Way

Parking Garages

Parking Garages

Major Blvd.

Kirkman Road

435

435

Major Blvd.

Vineland Road

4

continued from page 7

more Potter attractions, plus family-friendly Nintendo and Dream-Works franchises.

The gamble seems to be paying off for Universal. The Themed Entertainment Association estimated that IOA's attendance nearly equaled Disney's Hollywood Studios' in 2023, with both it and USF besting Animal Kingdom. COVID-caused closures resulted in revenue plummeting at all theme parks during 2020, but Universal Orlando moved more aggressively than its competitors to bring visitors back, returning to pre-pandemic attendance levels by 2021, and breaking all-time records by 2022, although crowds have softened across Central Florida since their post-pandemic peak.

Disney and Universal officially downplay their fierce competition, pointing out that any new theme park or attraction makes Central Florida a more marketable destination. Behind closed doors, however, the two companies share a Pepsi-versus-Coke rivalry that keeps both working hard to gain a competitive edge. The good news is that all this translates into better and better attractions for you to enjoy.

THE UNIVERSAL DIFFERENCE

IN MANY WAYS, UNIVERSAL ORLANDO will never achieve parity with Walt Disney World. It's minuscule compared to the 27,000-odd acres of Walt Disney World and will still be significantly smaller even after Universal's 750-acre expansion property is fully developed. And while guest service at Universal is generally exceptional by industry standards, there's something special about the "Disney Way" that some visitors will inevitably prefer. But in the areas where it *can* compete with Disney—namely, in theme park design and attraction quality—Universal has pulled even, if not ahead.

Even hard-core Disney fans, such as this Moncton, Nebraska, reader, are beginning to pay attention:

> *I'm a huge fan of all things Disney, so it pains me a little to say that the highlight of our most recent trip was actually Universal Orlando. Not because Disney World isn't spectacular—it always is—but because Universal's themed Harry Potter experience is by far the most immersive I've ever had. Disney has to be a little nervous.*

A reader from Toronto, Canada, wrote:

> *Reluctantly, I agree the Disney magic is fading. Attention to detail has deteriorated, and bus transport is often (but not always) slow and problematic. Tired hotel rooms (at deluxe prices) are badly in need of refurbishment. It was a stark contrast to the seamless experience we had at Universal's on-site moderate hotel.*

From a family in Dublin, Ireland:

> *We went from a week in Disney to a stay in Universal. Overall, I think we enjoyed Universal better. The parks are more enjoyable to*

walk around. The detail on the sets is so elaborate—it makes for a much better experience strolling around than in Disney, where, apart from EPCOT, you seem to spend time running from ride to ride.

A woman from Noblesville, Indiana, says:

This was the first non-Disney theme park that I felt could have been a Disney-owned theme park. It was clean and well themed, with fun rides and wonderful team members. I truly enjoyed Universal as much (and in some ways more) than my trips to Disney World.

A Lake Frederick, Virginia, family agrees:

After being loyal to Disney for years, my family wanted to visit The Wizarding World. I was really impressed with Universal! Everyone we talked to was very nice. It was even more pleasant than dealing with Disney people—pretty surprising. We thoroughly enjoyed our time at Universal and can't wait to go back!

This reader from Boise, Idaho, is also joining Universal's parade:

This was my first time to Universal Orlando (I'm a Disney girl), and I have to say I'm a convert! Universal definitely has a different vibe than Disney, but I love how close together everything is! And their Mardi Gras festival was WONDERFUL!

A mom of tweens from Ellicott City, Maryland, compared the two resorts' signature cinematic lands and gave the nod to Universal:

Batuu [at Star Wars Galaxy's Edge] is cool and beautiful, but the cast members seemed lost, somewhat uncertain of their roles, and not at all up to the standard of the immersive experience we had at The Wizarding World of Harry Potter. They would have done better taking a cue from their neighbor down the street. The completely immersive Wizarding World blows Batuu out of the galaxy.

And as guests come to grips with alterations to the traditional Walt Disney World experience, more Mickey loyalists are taking a look at Universal, like this local from Apopka, Florida:

You could say I've been a die-hard Disney fan since birth—I even have the same birthday as Walt Disney. But with the pandemic and downsizing at WDW, I wanted to look elsewhere for entertainment. Not only was I pleasantly surprised at what Universal Orlando has to offer, but it surpasses Disney in many ways. I'm almost ashamed to say that I had only gone to Universal Orlando when it first opened [in 1990] and never returned—it was all about Disney for me and my family. Now that I live in Central Florida, and with all the changes at Disney that I'm not happy with, I actually bought a Preferred Annual Pass for Universal Orlando.

Another hard-core Disney fan from Reston, Virginia, was driven to visit Universal after a "mercenary" vacation with Mickey:

I had an absolute blast [at Cabana Bay], and for a fraction of what I spent on a similar length of stay at WDW (at Pop Century) just 16 months ago. On every single day of my 6 days at the resort I over-heard at least one conversation in which an admitted WDW hard-core was prepared to spend at least some of that Disney cash at UOR instead. I won't say that WDW needs to be panicked, but they absolutely need to be paying attention. When Epic Universe opens it's going to get even sportier.

A frequent visitor from Taos, New Mexico, adds:

Having been to Universal and Disney dozens of times, we find that we're now much bigger fans of Universal compared to Disney. In the postpandemic era, we feel that Disney is doing everything possible to annoy guests while Universal is doing everything right.

Finally, this father from Rigby, Idaho, cuts to the chase:

Universal was less crowded and less expensive, and frankly, the rides were more fun and appropriate for all but the youngest of kids. EVERYONE, all ages, far preferred Universal over Disney World. That wasn't true 25 years ago, when our then-younger and smaller family first visited these places—but it is certainly true now.

To be fair, we also get occasional missives that dissent from our praise for Universal's product, such as this one from a multigenerational matriarch in New York City:

Universal's attractions were indeed state of the art, and the Harry Potter areas were amazing, but I didn't feel that magic that I did when we visited Disney three years ago. I don't know if my expectations were too high, or if it was because we were with a more diverse group age-wise, or what. Overall, I have no burning desire to return anytime soon, unlike with Disney, when I couldn't wait to go back.

Or this, from a mother of two in Arlington, Virginia:

Some of the rides were super impressive and fun, but too much of it was screen-based, and there was very little that all four of us could handle (and therefore do together). I'm sure my teens would like to return, but I'll let them save that for their school band trips; as a family it's WDW all the way.

Another mother from Rochester, Minnesota, said:

Universal was rougher around the edges than Disney. We had ticket issues almost every day. It wasn't as clean in the parks. We hated that they allowed everyone to run to rides at rope drop.

And a visitor from Brooklyn, New York, opined:

I went to Universal with an open mind and reasonable expectations. Aside from the Harry Potter experiences, I was surprised at how underwhelming and just plain bad so much of Universal is compared to Disney. It's maybe what Disney would be like if it was commissioned by a company who makes malls.

MOUSE JABS

THERE'S NOTHING WRONG with a little friendly competition, and we've seen plenty of examples of the No. 2 brand poking a little fun at the No. 1 brand. Pepsi and Coke, Marvel and DC, Burger King and McDonald's, and . . . Universal and Disney? While you won't find any references to Universal at Walt Disney World, Derek Burgan—author of the weekly "Saturday Six" column on TouringPlans.com—has cataloged a whole bunch of funny jabs that Universal has made at the Mouse House down the street.

5. Men in Black Alien Attack The entire attraction is a spoof on Disney's iconic pavilions from the 1964–1965 New York World's Fair, like Carousel of Progress and Ford's Magic Skyway.

4. The Simpsons Ride You'll see giant posters outside referencing The Jungle Cruise and Pirates of the Caribbean, and the preshow is filled with nods to Disney attractions, including The Haunted Mansion, *The Hall of Presidents,* and even *Kitchen Kabaret.*

3. Dudley Do-Right's Ripsaw Falls Keep an eye out for the movie posters making fun of such films as *Star Wars* and *Three Men and a Baby,* which was the first hit of former Disney CEO Michael Eisner's reign.

2. Duff Brewery The Seven Duffs are pretty much the exact opposites of Disney's lovable Seven Dwarfs. The topiaries of Dizzy, Tipsy, Sleazy, Queasy, Surly, Edgy, and Remorseful make some of the best photo ops in the park.

1. Jurassic Park River Adventure In a twist on Walt Disney's most famous quote, the narrator of Jurassic Park's queue video says, "I hope we never lose sight of one thing—that it all started with a mosquito."

This father from Lawrenceville, New Jersey, was especially critical of Universal's high-energy atmosphere:

The Marvel area was loud and unpleasant to spend time in. City-Walk was a frenetic nightmare after leaving the parks; trying to find somewhere to eat was crazy. All the noise, blaring music, and GIANT TV screens were not at all easy to take after our day in the parks. Like some ADHD torture chamber.

A handful of readers have criticized this book for mentioning Disney at all, including this online reviewer:

If I wanted a book about Disney, I would have purchased a book about Disney. I'm going to Universal; I don't care about what Disney does or offers.

In our defense, the majority of first-time Universal visitors (and hence, our readers) have previously been to Walt Disney World or another Disney attraction. Disney's product practically defines *theme park* in the public imagination, even among people who have never visited a Disney park, and its Florida resort sets the standard against which the entire industry is judged, not only in Orlando but around the world. So we point out parallels between Disney and Universal where appropriate only to give you a clearer picture of what to expect from your visit and how to spend your time.

We see the four Universal parks and the six Disney World parks (including water parks) as rough equals, and every one is world-class. Both Universal and Disney have splendid on-site hotels, with Universal offering more perks to its guests. There will always be those who miss the indescribable "magic" for which Disney World is famous. But here are five important arenas in which we think Universal currently has an advantage in the Orlando theme park wars:

MORE ADULT   If there's one distinguishing element that most separates Universal from Disney, it's the distinctly adult attitude that informs the resort's attractions and ambience. While Walt wanted a park that appealed equally to parents and their children, the majority of entertainment in today's Walt Disney World focuses on themes and characters catering to little kids. (That's not to say that there aren't plenty of adults who enjoy singing "Let It Go" at the top of their lungs, but the less said about that the better.) The same goes for most Disney rides, which emphasize visual charm over physical intensity; aside from the half dozen "mountains," you could probably take a nap on any given WDW attraction.

Universal, on the other hand, sets its sights slightly higher demographically, with a much higher proportion of attractions aimed at tweens, teens, and young (and young-at-heart) adults. Many of Universal's properties are based on PG-13 or R-rated movies; even its animated ambassadors, such as *Despicable Me*'s Minions, are a bit edgier than Mickey and friends. Don't try to fall asleep on Universal's simulators and scream machines, which range in intensity from pleasantly discombobulating to, "Dear Lord, what have I done?"

This parent from the Dallas area agrees:

> *Universal is PG-13 regarding its rides, while Disney is PG. Universal's rides are amazing, while Disney's seem dated. We might not have noticed if we had visited Disney first. The thrill rides were the most important experience for my teens, who tremendously enjoyed their time on their own at Universal.*

Universal offers the CityWalk nightlife venue, just outside the park gates, for those with the energy to make a night of it; WDW's closest equivalent, the sprawling Disney Springs complex, is far more family focused. And observant audience members will also notice that the scripts at Universal have a subversively snarky, postmodern spin that flies over youngsters' heads but serves as a welcome antidote to pixie-dusted perfection. After all, as the host in *Universal Orlando's Horror Make-Up Show* jokes, "This isn't Disney. We don't have to be nice to kids!"

All this isn't to imply that there's nothing for wee tykes to enjoy at Universal; on the contrary, the playgrounds in USF's DreamWorks Land, IOA's Seuss Landing and Jurassic Park, and EU's Isle of Berk are as good as any at WDW, and Universal's child-swap policy is arguably more user-friendly than Disney's. But rather than spending the day focused on fulfilling their offspring's fantasies, parents at Universal get to realize some of their own along the way.

MORE ADVANCED   Universal has been technologically ascendant for several years, introducing revolutionary motion systems and special effects in both rides and theater performances. As a dad from Mount Desert Island, Maine, wrote us:

Our family toured both Disney and Universal, beginning our stay at Disney. The difference in ride quality and technology was striking. It would've been difficult to go the other way (Universal to Disney), as the rides at Disney seemed dated and carnival-like by comparison.

A father from Conway, Arkansas, agrees, adding:

Magic Kingdom and EPCOT are full of old technology and uninteresting rides. New attractions are badly needed, especially to keep up with Universal.

While Disney relies conservatively on a combination of highly detailed themed areas, beloved characters, and inspiration from classic animated features (that many young people under age 16 have never seen), Universal takes more technological swings for the fences.

Granted, Disney parks do have their share of high-tech attractions—particularly Pandora's Avatar Flight of Passage, which outdoes Universal simulators in sheer gee-whiz factor—and not all Universal attractions approach the creative genius of Harry Potter and the Forbidden Journey or Escape from Gringotts. But while guests at both Disney and Universal report high levels of satisfaction, it's the next-gen technology manifested in Universal's headliners that delivers true "Wow!" moments. Plus, the lush lands of the new Epic Universe park—along with the earlier The Wizarding World of Harry Potter areas at IOA and USF—clearly demonstrate that Universal can create exquisitely detailed and totally immersive themed areas.

MORE CURRENT   Doc Brown's time-traveling DeLorean from *Back to the Future* may be parked at USF, but Orlando's real time machine is found at Walt Disney World's theme parks. The Magic Kingdom's recent top attractions are either reskins of aging rides (Tiana's Bayou Adventure, formerly Splash Mountain) or inspired by intellectual properties that date from the 1930s (Seven Dwarfs Mine Train) through the 1980s (TRON Lightcycle/Run)—and much of its older inventory is even more old-fashioned. Disney's Hollywood Studios' *Star Wars* expansion is set during the sequel films, but its most recognizable icons (like Chewbacca and the *Millennium Falcon*) date to the 1970s. EPCOT has finally swept away its detritus of dated celebrities in favor of Pixar and Marvel intellectual properties, and Animal Kingdom's DinoLand is targeted for redevelopment, but any all-new attractions are still years away.

Universal, on the other hand, has been relentlessly aggressive about constantly updating its lineup with currently relevant characters. The best example of this is its Wizarding World of Harry Potter, the first phase of which debuted while the record-breaking film franchise was still in theaters. Potter is still relevant, thanks to video games and the upcoming television series, while Marvel's superheroes, *Despicable Me*'s Minions, and the *Fast & Furious* family remain hot box office commodities. And the 2025 opening of Epic Universe adds globally popular characters from *How to Train Your Dragon* and Super Mario Brothers to the mix.

The downside to Universal's obsession with staying on the cultural cutting edge is a sense of impermanence that prevents the resort from retaining its rich history. Disney's blessing of size allows it to preserve the type of long-in-the-tooth attractions that space-squeezed Universal often sacrifices for the next generation. As a result, repeat visitors to WDW develop a sense of nostalgia over a lifetime of revisiting beloved rides, whereas those returning to Universal after a long absence are more likely to be befuddled; for a fun (and dangerous) drinking game, stand outside Diagon Alley and take a sip every time someone asks, "Where's Jaws?"

MORE COMPACT   While the lack of available elbowroom hurts Universal in some ways, it's a huge advantage in others. Anyone who has stayed on-site at WDW (especially in a hotel not serviced by the monorail) can testify how arduous navigating Mickey's vast transportation system can be. Taking the Disney bus to Animal Kingdom sometimes seems to take longer than an actual African safari, and if you want to transfer from Disney Springs to a theme park, you'd better pack a lunch.

At Universal, on the other hand, you can go your whole vacation without ever taking a ride (other than the amusement kind) because everything is within easy walking distance. Even the most remote hotel room on the original campus is only a 20- or 25-minute walk from the park gates, which are themselves separated by only a few hundred yards, making park-hopping at Universal a no-brainer. And Epic Universe makes it even easier, with a luxury hotel integrated into the theme park's central hub. If your feet do get tired, a fleet of water taxis and colorful buses is available to transport you, usually with much less waiting than their WDW equivalents. As one reader put it:

> What we appreciated about USF and IOA more than Disney is how compact the entire area is. It was incredibly easy to park in one of the large garages and walk to the theme parks. And they are so close together that you can easily walk from one park to another.

In fact, if Universal Orlando closely compares to any Disney resort, it is not Walt Disney World but Disneyland in California. Both properties boast multiple first-rate theme parks in close proximity to each other, with an adjoining entertainment complex and nearby hotels for easy pedestrian access. If you've ever enjoyed the Disneyland Resort's intimacy, in contrast to Disney World's overwhelming scale, you'll feel right at home at Universal Orlando.

MORE MANAGEABLE   Universal's smaller scale also has both logistical and psychological benefits. Walt Disney World is so vast that there is no way to do it all, even if you were to stay for weeks. For some travelers, that overabundance of options creates anxiety and a fear of missing out or not getting your money's worth. Universal has plenty to occupy your attention—you could stay for a week without getting bored—but the list of choices is much more manageable.

More important, once you choose what you want to do at Universal, you can generally just go ahead and do it without jumping through the hoops currently in place at Disney World. Disney's **Lightning Lane** line-cutting service, which replaced its old FastPass+ service, no longer requires guests to book rides months in advance. But whereas FastPass+ was free (if inconvenient), Lightning Lane is not; after paying up to $39 per day for **Lightning Lane Multi Pass** access, you can reserve up to three rides per day in advance from a select list. Reservations open seven days before your hotel stay for on-site guests, or three days out for everyone else, and return times for popular rides sell out swiftly. You have to pay a separate **Lightning Lane Single Pass Selection** fee to jump the line at certain headliner attractions, the cost of which varies from $10 to $25 each depending on crowd levels.

On the other hand, Universal's **Express Pass** covers all participating attractions (except for a few that don't offer Express at all), and you can use it whenever you want without needing reservations. The **Express Unlimited Pass** lets you ride each attraction as many times as you like per day (the base pass limits you to one ride per day on any participating attraction). Both the base and Unlimited Express Passes are available for a single park or both USF and IOA (Volcano Bay and certain special events have their own Express Passes that must be booked separately). Finally, **free Express Passes** are available for Universal Premier Pass holders and guests of select Signature Collection hotels—Lightning Lane costs extra for all Walt Disney World guests. (Express Pass policies for Epic Universe were not announced yet at press time.)

Universal Express was a big hit with this Texas family:

Universal's inclusion of the Express Pass [is] genius. My girls couldn't stop raving about the pass. They had gotten spoiled going to any ride and using the Express Pass with less than 10 minutes of wait time.

Likewise, WDW may have many more table-service restaurants inside and outside its parks, but good luck getting a seat in a popular eatery without booking your table months in advance. At Universal, on the other hand, walk-ups are often accommodated, or you can simply make a reservation with your smartphone a few days (or even hours) before you want to eat. Universal clearly comes out ahead on ease of use, as this Bellingham, Washington, reader found:

The Express Pass was a "can't live without" over the weekend—and the whole experience was definitely cheaper and more laid-back than Disney. No penalty for last-minute canceling or changing dining reservations . . . we just woke up in the morning and decided what to do.

SHOULD I GO TO UNIVERSAL ORLANDO IF I'VE SEEN UNIVERSAL HOLLYWOOD?

UNIVERSAL STUDIOS HOLLYWOOD (USH) in California shares much in common with its younger sibling in Orlando, including several headliner attractions. So is it worth visiting UOR if you've already done USH? In a word, "Absolutely!"

The Hollywood park is primarily a working movie studio with a park bolted on, making it less than cohesive as a themed attraction. There's nothing in Orlando that can compare to USH's justly famous Studio Tour, though some of its sights (the King Kong encounter and the *Fast & Furious* segment) have stand-alone analogues on the East Coast. USH is also home to America's first Super Nintendo Land, although the version opening in 2025 with Orlando's Epic Universe is far larger. But aside from the tram tour, a *Secret Life of Pets* dark ride, and the *WaterWorld* stunt show, the bulk of USH's limited lineup consists of virtual clones of attractions found in Orlando, only in less immersive environments. USH's CityWalk complex is larger than Orlando's, and offerings include copies of several unique restaurants that originated in Orlando, along with a number of familiar chains.

USH is looking better than ever, thanks to an ambitious multiyear expansion plan, which renovated three-quarters of the park during the last decade and will bring new attractions, amenities, and production facilities—including a high-speed *Fast & Furious* roller coaster and new on-site hotels—to the California complex in the coming years. But even with USH's Wizarding World open, it only reproduces the Hogsmeade area from IOA; for the full Diagon Alley and Hogwarts Express experience, Orlando continues to be your only option.

The bottom line is that USH makes a fine daylong diversion from a Disneyland vacation, but it is not yet big enough by itself to build a trip around. Universal Orlando, on the other hand, has nearly everything USH has, plus a whole lot more.

Comparison of Attractions Found at Both
UNIVERSAL STUDIOS HOLLYWOOD and **UNIVERSAL ORLANDO**
Despicable Me Minion Mayhem USH has an elaborate interactive exterior and much higher capacity; the ride itself is the same at both parks.
Flight of the Hippogriff Track layout and queue look about the same, but USH's ride feels much smoother.
Harry Potter and the Forbidden Journey The USH version boasts scarier animatronics and enhanced lighting and scenery, but it's essentially the same ride.
Jurassic Park River Adventure USH's version was rethemed in 2019 to the *Jurassic World* franchise, with new dinosaurs and special effects. IOA's drop is slightly taller, but otherwise the rides are similar.
Revenge of the Mummy—The Ride Much longer with better effects at USF.
The Simpsons Ride Ride is about the same at both parks, but USH has a less claustrophobic queue and an on-ride photo op.
Transformers: The Ride–3D About the same at both parks.

UNIVERSAL-SPEAK POCKET TRANSLATOR AND GUIDE TO COMMON ABBREVIATIONS

UNIVERSAL ORLANDO (like Walt Disney World) has its own somewhat peculiar language. The table on the facing page lists some terms and abbreviations that you're likely to bump into, both in this guide and in the larger Universal (and Disney) community.

UNIVERSAL LEXICON IN A NUTSHELL

ATTRACTION Ride or show

AUDIENCE Crowd

BACKSTAGE Behind the scenes, out of view of customers

CHARACTER Cartoon or movie character impersonated by an employee
- **Animated Character** A character who wears a head-covering costume (Scooby-Doo, the Minions, the Simpsons)
- **Face Character** A "celebrity" character who doesn't wear a head-covering costume (Doc Brown, Marilyn Monroe, and the like)

COSTUME Work attire or uniform

DARK RIDE Indoor ride

DAY GUEST Any customer not staying at a Universal resort

EARLY PARK ADMISSION (EPA) Morning hour at Universal's theme parks for eligible guests (*Early Entry* or *Extra Magic Hour* in Disney-speak)

EXPRESS Universal's paid services for skipping attraction standby queues; similar to Disney's Lightning Lane

GENERAL PUBLIC Same as day guest

GREETER Employee positioned at an attraction entrance

GUEST Customer

ON-SITE One of the Loews-operated resort hotels located on Universal Orlando property

ONSTAGE In full view of customers

PRESHOW Entertainment at an attraction before the feature presentation

QUICK-SERVICE RESTAURANT Counter-service or fast food–style restaurant

RESORT GUEST A customer staying at a Universal resort hotel

ROLE A team member's job

TEAM MEMBER Employee (*cast member* in Disney-speak)

TECHNICAL REHEARSAL Opening a park or attraction before its stated opening date (*soft opening* in Disney-speak)

COMMON ABBREVIATIONS

AP Annual pass	**TM** Team member
EPA Early Park Admission	**UOAP** Universal Orlando Annual Pass
EU Universal Epic Universe theme park	**UOR** Universal Orlando Resort
I-DRIVE International Drive (major Orlando thoroughfare)	**USF** Universal Studios Florida theme park
	UX or UEx Universal Express
IOA Universal Islands of Adventure theme park	**VB** Volcano Bay
	WWoHP Wizarding World of Harry Potter

UPCOMING AT UNIVERSAL ORLANDO RESORT

ALTHOUGH EPIC UNIVERSE is brand-new in 2025, additions to the park are already underway, including a possible Super Nintendo World expansion and more dining options.

At Islands of Adventure, Poseidon's Fury was permanently closed in 2023, and the neighboring *Eighth Voyage of Sindbad Stunt Show* remains shuttered since 2018, fueling speculation that Hyrule from Nintendo's Zelda games may replace The Lost Continent in 2027 or beyond.

STELLA SAYS

FIND ADDITIONAL PREVIEWS of upcoming experiences and Easter egg trivia from Orlando Park Stop's Alicia Stella in "Stella Says" sidebars throughout this guide.

At Universal Studios Florida, Hollywood Rip Ride Rockit, Fast & Furious: Supercharged, and The Simpsons Ride are all rumored to be ripe for removal in the near future. *Fear Factor Live* was also slated for demolition, but plans to replace the stadium with a Harry Potter virtual reality ride were abandoned. Likewise, an expansion of Volcano Bay that would add sliding capacity to the water park has been anticipated for several years, with no progress at press time.

PART 1

PLANNING *Before* YOU LEAVE HOME

■ GATHERING INFORMATION

IN ADDITION TO READING THIS GUIDE, we recommend that you visit **our website** (theunofficialguides.com), which is dedicated to news about our guidebooks and also has a blog with posts from Unofficial Guide authors. You can also sign up for the **"Unofficial Guide Newsletter,"** containing even more travel tips and special offers.

Our sister website, **Touring Plans** (touringplans.com), offers essential tools for planning your trip and saving you time and money. At the Touring Plans blog (blog.touringplans.com), you'll find breaking news for Universal Orlando Resort (UOR) and Universal theme parks worldwide. The site also offers computer-optimized touring plans for Universal Studios Florida (USF) and Islands of Adventure (IOA), with Epic Universe (EU) plans arriving soon, along with complete dining menus, including wine lists, for every food cart, stand, kiosk, counter-service restaurant, and sit-down restaurant in the resort.

Another really popular part of Touring Plans is the **Crowd Calendar,** which shows crowd projections for USF and IOA for every day of the year. Look up the dates of your visit, and the calendar will not only show the projected wait times for each day but will also indicate for each day which theme park will be the least crowded. Historical wait times are also available, so you can see how crowded the parks were last year for your upcoming trip dates.

Much of the content on Touring Plans—including the menus and resort photos and videos—is completely free for anyone to use. Access to part of the site, most notably the Crowd Calendar, premium touring plans, and in-park wait times, requires a small subscription fee (owners of this book's current edition get a substantial discount). This nominal charge helps keep the site online and costs less than lunch at the Leaky Cauldron restaurant in Diagon Alley. Plus, Touring Plans offers a 45-day money-back guarantee.

UNIVERSAL ONLINE

THOUGH SOME DISNEY-CENTRIC SITES cover Universal in some (usually minimal) way, independent sites dedicated to Universal Orlando are much rarer. Of these sites, we recommend **MouseSavers** (mousesavers .com) for hotel and admission bargains.

For the latest Universal updates and rumors, **Orlando Park Stop** (orlandoparkstop.com) features breaking news from Unofficial Guide contributor Alicia Stella. Also, try **Orlando Informer** (orlandoinformer .com), **Parkscope** (parkscope.net), **Rix Flix** (youtube.com/rixflix), and the message boards at **Inside Universal** (insideuniversal.net). For crowd projections and touring tips, check **Touring Plans.** The **Thrills Taste Travels blog** (thrillstatetravels.com) features dining reviews and handy links to all of UOR's restaurants. Four more reliable websites that cover Central Florida attractions, including Universal Orlando, are **Attractions Magazine** (attractionsmagazine.com), **Theme Park Insider** (themeparkinsider.com), **Screamscape** (screamscape.com), and **Orlando Theme Park News** (orlandoparksnews.com). Theme park developments, along with general Orlando-area news, are also available at the websites for the **Orlando Sentinel** (orlandosentinel.com), the **Orlando Business Journal** (bizjournals.com /orlando), and **Orlando Weekly** magazine (orlandoweekly.com). For insider information on attractions, new technologies, and changes in the parks, check **Jim Hill Media** (jimhillmedia .com). Finally, there's the official **Universal Orlando website** (universalorlando.com). The official **Discover Universal blog** (blog.discoveruniversal.com) produces podcasts and vlogs with behind-the-scenes interviews and trip-planning advice directly from Universal. Annual passholders may want to join the official **UOAP Facebook group** (uoapfb.com), which is a rich source of both breaking news and petty griping.

unofficial **TIP**
You'll need the Universal app to place mobile dining orders and set up your TapuTapu account before visiting Volcano Bay, so be sure to install it before you arrive at UOR.

UNIVERSAL MOBILE APP Universal phased out printed park maps and show schedules in favor of a free app for Apple (iOS 15.0+) and Android (ver. 8.0+) devices that displays wait times, performance times, and interactive maps inside the parks, using the resort's free Wi-Fi (connect to "Universal" and accept the terms to access). Park admission can also be purchased through the app and stored in a digital wallet, along with a virtual credit card for contactless payments.

unofficial **TIP**
Lines is the only Universal app that shows you both posted and actual wait times.

We also recommend **Lines,** Touring Plans' mobile app, available for Apple devices at the iTunes Store (search for "TouringPlans") and for Android devices at the Google Play Store. Owners of other phones can use the web-based version at m.touringplans.com. The app is free to download, but you'll need to log in with a paid Touring Plans subscription to access most of its features.

The web-based touring plans, menus, Crowd Calendar, and other tools are available in Lines, which provides continuous real-time updates on wait times at Universal Orlando. Using in-park staff and updates sent in by readers, Lines shows you current wait times at every attraction in every park, as well as estimated actual waits for these attractions for the rest of today. For example, Lines will tell you that the posted wait for Harry Potter and the Escape from Gringotts is 60 minutes, and that based on what they know about how Universal manages Gringotts's queue, the actual time you'll probably wait in line is 48 minutes.

You can update the touring plans when you're in the parks too. The ability to redo your plan allows you to recover from any situation while still minimizing your waits for the rest of the day. Lines also has an online chat feature, where folks can ask questions and give travel tips. Hundreds of "Liners" interact every day in discussions that stay remarkably on-topic for an internet forum.

As long as you have that smartphone handy in the parks, we and your fellow Unofficial Guide readers would love it if you could report on the actual wait times you get while you're there. Run Lines, log in to your user account, and click **+time** in the upper right corner to help everyone out. We'll use that information to update the wait times for everyone in the park and make everyone's lives just a little bit better.

BEST UNIVERSAL PODCASTS   The best podcast devoted to Universal is **"UUOP: The Unofficial Universal Orlando Podcast"** (uuopodcast.com), which features regular reports from this book's author on "all the little things" that are new around the resort; incidentally, the podcast is based not in Orlando but the United Kingdom. Seth also co-hosts a weekly podcast for **Attractions Magazine** (see page 22) that frequently focuses on Universal. **"Orlando Tourism Report"** (orlandotourismreport

---

IMPORTANT UNIVERSAL ADDRESSES

- **THEME PARKS & CITYWALK PARKING GARAGE ADDRESS**   6000 Universal Blvd., Orlando, FL 32819   **GPS COORDINATES: N28° 28.439′ W81° 27.737′**
- **GUEST SERVICES & CORPORATE OFFICES**
  Universal Orlando Resort, 1000 Universal Studios Pl., Orlando, FL 32819
- **HARD ROCK HOTEL**   5800 Universal Blvd., Orlando, FL 32819
- **LOEWS PORTOFINO BAY HOTEL**   5601 Universal Blvd., Orlando, FL 32819
- **LOEWS ROYAL PACIFIC RESORT**   6300 Hollywood Way, Orlando, FL 32819
- **LOEWS SAPPHIRE FALLS RESORT**   6601 Adventure Way, Orlando, FL 32819
- **UNIVERSAL AVENTURA HOTEL**   6725 Adventure Way, Orlando, FL 32819
- **UNIVERSAL CABANA BAY BEACH RESORT**   6550 Adventure Way, Orlando, FL 32819
- **UNIVERSAL ENDLESS SUMMER RESORT, DOCKSIDE INN & SUITES**
  7125 Universal Blvd., Orlando, FL 32819
- **UNIVERSAL ENDLESS SUMMER RESORT, SURFSIDE INN & SUITES**
  7000 Universal Blvd., Orlando, FL 32819
- **UNIVERSAL HELIOS GRAND HOTEL**   8505 Kirkman Road, Orlando, FL 32819
- **UNIVERSAL STELLA NOVA RESORT**   4500 Epic Blvd., Orlando, FL 32819
- **UNIVERSAL TERRA LUNA RESORT**   5500 Epic Blvd., Orlando, FL 32819

UNIVERSAL ORLANDO PHONE NUMBERS	
Universal Orlando Main Information	☎ 407-363-8000
Guest Relations	☎ 407-224-4233
Online Ticket Store Assistance	☎ 407-224-7840
Annual Passholder Support and Renewals	☎ 866-727-7438
FlexPay (Annual Pass Monthly Payments)	☎ 888-535-3972
Merchandise	☎ 888-762-0820
Vacation Packages	☎ 877-801-9720
Vacation Packages, Deaf or Hard of Hearing (TDD)	☎ 800-447-0672
On-Site Hotel Reservations	☎ 888-273-1311
Meeting Attendees/Individual Call-In for Group Blocks	☎ 866-360-7395
Universal In-Park Dining and Character Meals	☎ 407-224-3663
Universal Resort Dining and Character Meals	☎ 407-503-3463
Mandara Spa at Portofino Bay	☎ 407-503-1244
Hard Rock Hotel	☎ 407-503-2000
Loews Portofino Bay Hotel	☎ 407-503-1000
Loews Royal Pacific Resort	☎ 407-503-3000
Loews Sapphire Falls Resort	☎ 407-503-5000
Universal Aventura Hotel	☎ 407-503-6000
Universal Cabana Bay Beach Resort	☎ 407-503-4000
Universal Endless Summer Resort, Dockside Inn & Suites	☎ 407-503-8000
Universal Endless Summer Resort, Surfside Inn & Suites	☎ 407-503-7000
Universal Helios Grand Hotel	☎ 888-430-4999
Universal Stella Nova Resort	☎ 888-273-1311
Universal Terra Luna Resort	☎ 888-273-1311

.com) covers local attraction news, and the **Orlando ParkStop Podcast** (orlandoparkstop.com) is your first stop for hot rumors. And for news and in-depth interviews with ride designers and executives from theme parks around the world, check out **"The Season Pass"** (seasonpasspodcast.com), **"The Coaster101 Podcast"** (coaster101.com /podcast), and "**CoasterRadio.com**" (coasterradio.com).

BEST UNIVERSAL SOCIAL MEDIA FEEDS   If you prefer your Universal news and rumors in 280-character bites or 30-second reels, follow The Unofficial Guides at **@TheUGSeries** on X and **@TheUnofficialGuides** on Instagram and Threads, along with the following prolific park posters: **@universalorl, @parkscope, @insideuniversal, @themepark, @themeparks, @attractions, @horrornightsorl, @aliciastella, @scott gustin, @orlandoparkstop, @orlandoinformer, @thrillgeek, @richobj, @bioreconstruct, @derekburgan, @pastorjonself, @touringplans,** and **@skubersky.**

TIMING YOUR VISIT

TRYING TO REASON WITH THE TOURIST SEASON

CENTRAL FLORIDA THEME PARKS and attractions are traditionally busiest the last week or so of December and the first few days of January. Next busiest—if not busier—is the spring break period from mid-March through the week of Easter. Following those are Thanksgiving week and the weeks of Mardi Gras and Presidents' Day in February. June and July, when summer vacation is at its peak, used to be packed, but attendance in those months has dipped sharply, no doubt due in part to soaring temperatures.

The least busy time is from the middle of August through the beginning of October. Next slowest are the weeks in mid-January after the Martin Luther King Jr. holiday weekend up to Presidents' Day in February. The weeks after Thanksgiving and before Christmas are less crowded than average, as is mid-April–mid-May, between spring break and Memorial Day.

unofficial **TIP**
Though crowds have grown in September and October as a result of promotions aimed at the international market and families without school-age children, these months continue to be good ones for touring.

Late February, March, and early April are dicey. Crowds ebb and flow according to spring break schedules and the timing of Mardi Gras and Presidents' Day weekend. Besides being asphalt-melting hot, late July normally brings throngs of South American tourists on their winter holiday.

THE DOWNSIDES OF OFF-SEASON TOURING

THOUGH WE STRONGLY RECOMMEND going to Universal Orlando in the fall, winter, or spring, there are a few trade-offs. The parks often close early during the off-season, either because of low crowds or special events such as the Halloween and Rock the Universe events at Universal Studios Florida. Be especially wary of Gradventure and Grad Bash all-night events for graduating students each April and May, which crowd the parks with teens and tweens during the afternoon, and close them to regular guests by dinnertime. This drastically reduces touring hours. Even when crowds are small, it can be challenging to see everything at USF or IOA between 9 a.m. and 6 p.m. Early closing also usually means no evening entertainment. And because these are slow times, some rides and attractions may be closed; all of Volcano Bay is closed on select weekdays during the fall and winter off-season. Finally, Central Florida temperatures fluctuate wildly during late fall, winter, and early spring; daytime highs in the 40s and 50s aren't uncommon.

Given the choice, however, smaller crowds, bargain prices, and stress-free touring are worth risking cold weather or closed attractions. Touring in fall and other off periods is so much easier that our research team, at the risk of being blasphemous, would advise taking children out of school for an Orlando visit.

Most readers who have tried Central Florida's attractions at various times agree. A New Hampshire parent writes:

> *I took my grade-school children out of school for a few days to go during a slow time and would highly recommend it. We communicated with the teachers about a month before traveling to seek their preference for whether classwork and homework should be completed before, during, or after our trip. It's so much more enjoyable to be [in Orlando] when your children can experience rides and attractions . . . rather than standing in line. And traveling at a time of year when it's not unbearably hot makes such a difference as well. I would be hard-pressed to go during a hot or busy time ever again.*

There's another side to this story, and we've received some well-considered letters from parents and teachers who don't think taking kids out of school is such a hot idea. From a father in Fairfax, Virginia:

> *My wife and I are disappointed that you seem to be encouraging families to take their children out of school to avoid the crowds [in Orlando] during the summer months. My wife is an eighth-grade teacher of chemistry and physics. She has parents pull their children, some honor roll students, out of school for vacations, only to discover when they return that the students are unable to comprehend the material. Parents' suspicions about the quality of their children's education should be raised when children go to school for 6 hours a day yet supposedly can complete this same instruction with less than an hour of homework each night.*

A Martinez, California, teacher offers this compelling analogy:

> *There are a precious 180 days for us as teachers to instruct our students, and there are 185 days during the year for [vacation]. I have seen countless students during my 14 years of teaching struggle to catch up the rest of the year due to a week of vacation during critical instructional periods.*

But a teacher from Penn Yan, New York, sees things differently:

> *I've read the comments from teachers saying that they all think it's horrible for a parent to take a child out of school for a vacation. As a teacher and a parent, I disagree. If a parent takes the time to let us know a child is going to be out, we help them get ready for upcoming homework the best we can. If the child is a good student, why shouldn't they go have a wonderful experience with their family? I also don't understand when teachers say they can't get something together for the time the student will be out. We all have to plan ahead, and we know what we are teaching days, if not weeks, in advance. Take 20 minutes out of your day and set something up. Learn to be flexible!*

BE UNCONVENTIONAL Orlando's Orange County Convention Center (OCCC) hosts some of the largest conventions and trade shows in the world. Hotel rooms anywhere around International Drive can be hard to find (and expensive) when there's a big convention. You can check the convention schedule at the OCCC for the next six months at events.occc.net.

DON'T FORGET AUGUST Kids go back to school pretty early in Florida (and in many other places too). This makes mid- to late August a good time to visit Universal Orlando for families who can't vacation during the fall. A New Jersey mother of two school-age children spells it out:

> The end of August is the PERFECT time to go (just watch out for hurricanes; it's the season). There were virtually no wait times, 20 minutes at the most.

A mom from Rapid City, South Dakota, agrees:

> School starts very early in Florida, so our mid-August visit was great for crowds but not for heat.

And from a family from Roxbury, New Jersey:

> I recommend the last two weeks of August for anyone traveling there during the summer. We have visited twice during this time of year and have had great success touring the parks.

Though we recommend off-season touring, we realize it's not possible for many families. We want to make it clear, therefore, that you can have a wonderful experience regardless of when you go. Our advice, irrespective of season, is to arrive early at the parks and avoid the crowds by using one of our touring plans. If attendance is light, kick back and forget the touring plans.

WE'VE GOT WEATHER! Long before theme parks, tourists visited Florida year-round to enjoy the temperate tropical and subtropical climates. The best weather months are generally November through March. Fall and winter are usually dry, whereas spring and summer are wet. December, January, and February vary, with daytime high temperatures sometimes sliding from springlike down into the low 50s. May is hot but mostly tolerable. June, July, August, and September are the warmest and wettest months. Rain, usually in the form of scattered thunderstorms, is possible at any time. An entire day of rain is unusual, but midafternoon downfalls occur regularly during the summer. These squalls, with lightning and gale-force winds, can temporarily shutter attractions but typically disperse in under an hour. Immediately after a storm is an ideal time to experience rides with little wait, especially at Volcano Bay.

Although everybody talks about Orlando's heat, it can also get quite cold here on rare occasions. You're never going to see real snow sticking to Hogwarts Castle, and during even the most frigid Florida winter, you'll spot Midwesterners walking around wearing shorts. But be aware that the temperatures have been known to drop low enough to keep the water park closed and confound operations of some theme park attractions, as this reader from Baltimore discovered:

UNIVERSAL ORLANDO CLIMATE											
JAN	FEB	MAR	APR	MAY	JUN	JUL	AUG	SEP	OCT	NOV	DEC
Average Daily Max Heat Index (Temperature + Humidity)											
72°F	75°F	81°F	92°F	106°F	119°F	121°F	120°F	111°F	96°F	79°F	75°F
Average Daily Temperature											
62°F	64°F	68°F	74°F	79°F	82°F	84°F	83°F	82°F	77°F	69°F	65°F
Average Rainfall per Month											
2.1"	1.9"	2.5"	2.2"	2.7"	6.1"	6.0"	6.6"	5.5"	2.4"	1.2"	1.6"
Number of Days of Rain per Month											
4	4	5	6	12	13	14	11	5	3	4	

Source: climate-data.org

*Some of the big thrill rides in Universal (including The Incredible
Hulk Coaster, Hollywood Rip Ride Rockit, and Hagrid's Magical
Creatures Motorbike Adventure) have trouble in cold weather (I am
guessing because of outdoor tracks). We happened to be there during
the coldest days of the year in January but didn't know this would
be an issue. There were a couple of days that Hulk and Hollywood
Rip Ride Rockit didn't operate at all.*

SUMMER TEMPERATURES CAN FEEL LIKE 120°F Did you know that
air temperature is measured in the shade? So, if your phone's weather
app says it's 95°F in Orlando, it's warmer if you're standing in the
sun, and hotter still if you're wearing dark-colored clothing. Florida's
notorious humidity makes the heat feel worse because it prevents
your perspiration from evaporating to cool you off. The heat index
expresses the combined effect of heat and humidity as a temperature
reading we can understand. During summer at Universal Orlando,
you'll commonly see heat index values of 110°F or above—and we've
measured highs of up to 122°F. How hot is that? A steak cooked rare
is considered done at 130°F. If you aren't used to it, don't discount the
impact of Orlando's humidity even after the peak of summer, says this
couple from Syracuse, New York:

*We chose September for our trip because of the low crowd levels. We
managed to avoid hurricanes, but goodness, was it hot and humid.
Being from upstate New York (where we are settling in to a lovely
autumn this time of year), we were melting by 8:30 in the morning.
I think we'll try early December next time!*

HOW MUCH TIME TO ALLOCATE

PRIOR TO THE DEBUT OF THE WIZARDING WORLDS, some
visitors found that they could see everything of note at both Universal
parks within a single day. Not anymore: Touring any one of Universal's
theme parks, including one meal and a visit to the Wizarding World,
takes at least 8–10 hours.

For that reason, we recommend devoting **a minimum of a full day
to each Universal Orlando theme park,** especially if this is your first
visit. Three days is ideal for visiting USF and IOA, particularly with a

Park-to-Park Pass, as it will allow you to fully explore each park and revisit your favorite attractions. Plan to devote another full day to Epic Universe when it opens in 2025, and add an extra day to your trip if you want to enjoy Volcano Bay water park. An on-site stay of four or more days will allow you to sample the parks in smaller bites while taking full advantage of the resort's other amenities.

Some Universal Orlando attractions don't open until 10 a.m. or later, while most of the theater attractions don't schedule performances until 11 a.m. or after. This means that early in the day, all park guests are concentrated among the limited number of attractions in operation.

As a postscript, you won't have to worry about any of this if you use our Universal Orlando touring plans. We'll keep you one jump ahead of the crowd and make sure that any given attraction is running by the time you get there.

unofficial **TIP**
Get to the park with your admission already purchased at least 30–45 minutes before official opening time. Arrive 45–60 minutes before official opening time if you need to buy admission. Be aware that you can't do a comprehensive tour of both Universal theme parks in a single day.

SELECTING THE DAY OF THE WEEK FOR YOUR VISIT

WHEN READERS ASKED, "What is the best day to visit Universal Orlando?," we used to reply that Sunday was the least crowded day at the resort (presumably because people are starting their vacations at Walt Disney World [WDW]), followed by Monday and Saturday, and that Thursday was the most crowded. However, there are too many other variables—including weather and special events—to make this a reliable rule of thumb. Most recently, Saturdays and Mondays have seen the biggest crowds, while Wednesdays and Thursdays have been the least busy.

The best way to know which day to visit Universal Orlando is with the **Touring Plans Crowd Calendar** at theugseries.com/crowd_cal. No matter which day you visit, arriving early and following a touring plan makes a much bigger difference than what day of the week it is.

INTEGRATING A UNIVERSAL ORLANDO VISIT WITH A WDW VACATION

WHILE UNIVERSAL ORLANDO has recently made strides in convincing visitors to make UOR their primary destination, for many travelers a stop at Universal is a side trip in their Walt Disney World–centric vacation. If you are devoting the bulk of your Orlando holiday to Disney but still want to make a detour to Universal, you have three primary options:

unofficial **TIP**
Check TouringPlans .com's Crowd Calendars for both WDW and UOR, and visit WDW on the days it will be less busy because crowds can make a bigger difference there than at UOR.

THE DAY TRIP Most Disney guests who want to sample Universal take a single day out of their vacation to visit Universal's parks. This solution is simplest for guests with their own cars, but taxis and rideshare services are readily available too (see page 130). The day trip has a couple of drawbacks: the per-day cost can be high, especially if you want to visit multiple UOR theme parks, and (depending on transportation arrangements) you may be unable to arrive before rope drop (essential for optimal touring) or have to depart before closing time.

THE WDW-UOR-WDW SANDWICH   An increasing number of guests take a night or two out of the middle of their WDW trip and stay on property at Universal. Again, transportation can be handled through a private car or rideshare. This method allows you to explore Universal over the course of two or three days and enjoy the perks of staying on-site, such as Early Park Admission to The Wizarding World. The main drawback is that you must check in and out (and back in again) at your Disney hotel, or pay for nights in a WDW bed that you won't be using.

THE SPLIT TRIP   The best option if you want to divide your vacation roughly equally between Disney and Universal is a split trip, where you stay at one resort for the first half of your visit, then transfer to the other for the remainder. Look into the three-way transportation offered by outfits such as **Quicksilver** (see page 129).

If possible, this reader from upstate New York suggests saving your Universal visit for last to diminish disappointment:

> *We visited Universal Orlando first and were blown away by the technology of the rides and the quality of the attractions, especially in the Harry Potter sections. When we got to Disney, we had fun, but we weren't nearly as impressed. We enjoyed the attractions, but some of them seemed dated and a little less than spectacular.*

A mom from Missouri City, Texas, reported a similar experience:

> *For families planning a combined UOR/Disney trip, especially for those who like thrill rides but whose kids are older and the Disney magic may not be as exciting as it used to be, I recommend going to WDW parks before UOR. For my 13-year-old, it seemed like the Disney rides were too tame after having done two days first at UOR. He specifically called out Space Mountain for not being as thrilling as he remembered.*

WHICH PARK TO VISIT?

UNIVERSAL ORLANDO'S THEME PARKS are all spectacular, so if you can only visit one, you can't really go wrong. Obviously, as the new kid on the block, Epic Universe will be the big draw when it opens in 2025—and for many years to come. To choose between the two older parks, if you've visited Universal since 2010, when the first Wizarding World opened, but have not yet seen Diagon Alley, you'll want to go to Universal Studios Florida; if you've experienced Harry Potter and the Escape from Gringotts but not Hagrid's Magical Creatures Motorbike Adventure and the Jurassic World VelociCoaster, go to Islands of Adventure. For those who have never been to Universal Orlando, or at least not in over a decade, the decision is down to what type of attractions you prefer. If you are a fan of simulators, screen-based experiences, and live shows, then USF is right for you. If you prefer big outdoor roller coasters and wild water rides, IOA is your destination. EU eschews both extreme thrills and simulated motion in favor of family-friendly adventures through physical environments. Of course, if you are a Harry Potter devotee, you're going to have to visit all three parks to get the full Wizarding World experience. Incidentally, USF is the better park to visit during inclement weather, due to its larger percentage of indoor attractions. Finally, waterslide enthusiasts will want to spend at least one full day of their vacation at Volcano Bay.

ARRIVAL- AND DEPARTURE-DAY ACTIVITIES

GUESTS STAYING AT UNIVERSAL'S on-site resorts can take advantage of all provided theme park perks—including early admission and free Express Passes—from dawn on their arrival day until midnight on their day of departure. However, that requires using a full day's park admission for what may be only a few hours of entertainment, depending on your travel plans. Here are some suggestions on how to spend that spare half-day at the start or end of your vacation:

- Explore Universal's resort hotels using the **garden walking paths** and **free water taxis.**

- Relax at your **hotel pool** if the weather is clear, or spend some quarters inside the **game room** if it's inclement.

- Knock down some pins at **Cabana Bay Beach Resort's Galaxy Bowl** (see page 349).

- Play a round at **Hollywood Drive-In Mini-Golf,** or catch a first-run flick at the **Universal Cinemark** at CityWalk (see pages 378 and 375, respectively).

- Take the free **Vibe tour** of musical memorabilia at the **Hard Rock Cafe** (see page 349).

- Enjoy a **luau dinner show** at the Royal Pacific (see page 359).

- Drive to the nearby **Fun Spot America** amusement park (5700 Fun Spot Way; ☎ 407-363-3867; fun-spot.com) for a few laps around the multilevel go-kart tracks, then ride the White Lightning and Freedom Flyer roller coasters.

- Indulge in some retail therapy at the **Orlando Premium Outlets** shopping mall on International Drive (see page 369).

- Try Universal's **Great Movie Escape Room** in CityWalk (see page 376) or an independent escape-room game on International Drive, like **The Bureau** (5400 International Dr., Suite B; ☎ 407-337-7856; thebureauorlando .com), which features performers from Universal Orlando, or **The Escape Game** (8145 International Dr., Suite 511; ☎ 407-501-7222; theescapegame .com/orlando).

- Visit the **Icon Park** complex (iconorlando.com) on International Drive, home to an enormous observation wheel, as well as a wax museum and an aquarium. After closing their show in CityWalk during the pandemic, the **Blue Man Group** returned to Orlando in late 2024, opening a new 500-seat theater at Icon Park's Universal Boulevard entrance, not far from Epic Universe. Or try **Dezerland Park** (dezerlandpark.com/orlando) on I-Drive's north end, with a massive automobile museum and indoor go-karts.

OPERATING HOURS

THE UNIVERSAL ORLANDO WEBSITE publishes preliminary park hours up to six months in advance, but schedule adjustments can happen at any time, including on the day of your visit. Check theugseries .com/unihrs or call ☎ 407-363-8000 for the exact hours before you arrive. Off-season, parks may be open as few as 8 hours (9 a.m.–5 p.m.). At busy times (particularly holidays), they may operate 8 a.m.–10 p.m., while 9 a.m.–9 or 10 p.m. was the standard summer schedule in 2024.

Volcano Bay opens at 10 a.m. (9 a.m. in the summer) and closes between 5 and 8 p.m., depending on the season; the park is closed on select weekdays (typically Tuesdays and Wednesdays, or Wednesdays and Thursdays) during the late fall–winter off-season. It's a shame that Volcano Bay is so rarely open past dusk, as it was designed for nighttime operation, with the majestic waterfalls cascading down the park's centerpiece transforming into blazing lava after sunset. If the park is open late during your visit, even if you exit during the afternoon, try to return during the closing hours to experience Volcano Bay's beauty at twilight.

Universal's website publishes its official operating hours, but on most days, the parks actually open earlier. If the official hours for the theme parks are 9 a.m.–9 p.m., for instance, turnstiles for the park (or parks) participating in Early Park Admission will open between 7:45 a.m. and 8 a.m., and the one not offering early entry may still open its gates as early as 8:45 a.m.

Queues to attractions usually close to new guests at exactly the park's official closing time; if you're already in line at closing, you will be permitted to stay as long as it takes for you to ride, barring any technical malfunctions. (Exceptions are popular brand-new rides, which may close their queue before the rest of the park if the estimated wait significantly exceeds the time remaining in the operating day.) The main gift shops near the front of each park remain open 30 minutes to an hour after the rest of the park has closed.

ALLOCATING MONEY

UNIVERSAL ORLANDO TICKETS

UNIVERSAL OFFERS TICKETS good for one to five days of admission to its theme parks. The **1-Day Base Ticket** includes entry to one theme park per day. If you buy a 2-Day Base Ticket, you can visit IOA on one day and USF on the next. You may *not* use a 2-Day Base Ticket to visit multiple parks in one day, but you can exit and return to the same park on the same day, in case you want to head back to your hotel for a nap.

Note: At press time, tickets to Epic Universe can **only** be purchased through third-party agents as part of a vacation package, in conjunction with a 2-Day or longer ticket to IOA and USF. Only 1-Day tickets are available for EU, and none permit park-hopping between EU and the original parks (unless you use up two days worth of tickets on one day). Pricing and availability for standalone tickets and annual passes to Epic Universe will be announced prior to the park opening.

If you want to visit both USF and IOA on the same day, purchase the **Park-to-Park** option, which allows you to move freely between both original parks on the same day. On the main campus, it takes about 12–15 minutes to walk from the entrance of one park to the next, or you can take the 4-minute Hogwarts Express trip between The Wizarding Worlds. Free bus transportation between the parking hub and Epic Universe takes about 15 minutes. Be aware that you *must* have Park-to-Park admission to ride the Hogwarts Express train between IOA and USF; you can upgrade single-park tickets at Guest

UNIVERSAL ORLANDO ADMISSIONS *(online prices, includes tax)*		
TICKET TYPE	**ADULTS**	**CHILDREN (Ages 3–9)**
1-Day Single-Park (USF/IOA)	$127–$190	$121–$185
1-Day Volcano Bay	$85–$96	$80–$91
1-Day Park-to-Park (USF/IOA)	$185–$249	$180–$244
2-Day Single-Park (USF/IOA)	$248–$372	$238–$361
2-Day Park-to-Park (USF/IOA)	$312–$436	$301–$425
2-Day Park-to-Park (USF/IOA/VB)	$355–$473	$344–$462
3-Day Single-Park (USF/IOA)	$273–$404	$262–$393
3-Day Single-Park (USF/IOA/VB)	$315–$441	$305–$430
3-Day Park-to-Park (USF/IOA)	$337–$468	$326–$457
3-Day Park-to-Park (USF/IOA/VB)	$379–$505	$368–$494
4-Day Single-Park (USF/IOA)	$290–$420	$279–$409
4-Day Single-Park (USF/IOA/VB)	$343–$468	$332–$457
4-Day Park-to-Park (USF/IOA)	$359–$489	$348–$478
4-Day Park-to-Park (USF/IOA/VB)	$412–$537	$401–$526
5-Day Single-Park (USF/IOA)	$309–$436	$298–$425
5-Day Single-Park (USF/IOA/VB)	$373–$494	$362–$484
5-Day Park-to-Park (USF/IOA)	$383–$510	$373–$500
5-Day Park-to-Park (USF/IOA/VB)	$447–$569	$437–$558
2-Park Seasonal Annual Pass	$453	$453
2-Park Power Annual Pass	$506	$506
2-Park Preferred Annual Pass	$671	$671
2-Park Premier Annual Pass	$964	$964
3-Park Seasonal Annual Pass	$559	$559
3-Park Power Annual Pass	$623	$623
3-Park Preferred Annual Pass	$788	$788
3-Park Premier Annual Pass	$1,166	$1,166

Services or at the King's Cross (USF) or Hogsmeade (IOA) train stations. (See the next section for more about Park-to-Park admission.)

All single and multiday Universal Orlando tickets are date-specific, and prices can vary significantly depending on the date you select during purchase for its first use. Examine Universal's online ticket pricing calendar carefully, because during certain seasons you may save some dollars by buying multiday passes with start dates a couple of days before your arrival.

Admission to **Volcano Bay** water park costs $85–$96 per day for adults ($5 cheaper for kids ages 3–9) depending on the season; Florida residents can save up to $10 on select days during the off-season. Volcano Bay access can be added to multiday Base and Park-to-Park tickets to make them into 3-Park passes, with pricing depending on ticket length and starting date.

unofficial **TIP**
Universal Orlando does not require advance reservations to visit its parks, but the turnstiles may temporarily close on rare occasions if the capacity limit is reached. On-site hotel guests, reentering guests, and those with date-specific tickets are granted admission priority over multiday ticket holders and annual passholders if the parks approach their capacity limit.

A 1-Day Single-Park Base Ticket to Universal is on par cost-wise with tickets at the Disney parks, but multiday tickets can be much more expensive at Disney, where, for example, a 5-Day Park Hopper costs at least 50% more than UOR's equivalent 5-Day/2-Park Park-to-Park pass.

All multiday tickets expire five to eight days after their first use, depending on pass type and length. Kids under age 3 are admitted for free, but tickets for kids ages 3–9 are discounted only $5–$10 from the adult prices, despite the large number of rides with height requirements at Universal. Prices listed in the table below are what you'll pay online, including 6.5% sales tax; gate prices for multiday tickets are $21 higher.

Park-to-Park: Worth the Price?

Many readers ask us if it's really worth the extra expense for Park-to-Park access, often phrased as "Why spend so much more just to ride a train?" For visits of one or two days, you can easily make do with a base ticket, but we strongly suggest Park-to-Park admission for anyone who is **(a)** visiting Universal Orlando for three or more days, **(b)** staying at an on-site hotel, or **(c)** a big Harry Potter fan. If you fall into one or more of those categories, here are four key reasons why it doesn't pay to skimp on Park-to-Park access:

1. Hogwarts Express is among Universal Orlando Resort's top-rated attractions in our reader surveys, and we consider it not to be missed.

2. The Early Park Admission perk included with on-site hotel stays is usually valid at only one theme park; with park-hopping privileges, you can take advantage of early entry but spend the rest of the day elsewhere.

3. Park-to-Park access allows you to visit Volcano Bay in the early morning and evening when it's pleasant, and spend the crowded middle part of the day in another park.

4. During inclement weather, Park-to-Park access lets you hop over to USF when most of the other parks' outdoor attractions are shut down.

If you're anxious to trim admission costs, consider reducing your pass length by a day while keeping the Park-to-Park option. If you're staying for four days/three nights, a 3-Day Ticket—rather than a 4-Day—allows you to use your arrival or departure half-day to explore alternative attractions (as suggested on page 31).

UNIVERSAL ORLANDO ANNUAL PASSES

UNIVERSAL ORLANDO offers some of the best deals on annual passes in town, not only for locals but also for anyone visiting UOR more than four days out of the year. The entry-level **2-Park Seasonal Annual Pass** costs about the same as a peak 5-Day Park-to-Park Ticket, and the top-of-the line **3-Park Premier Annual Pass** is about the price of two peak 5-Park, 3-Day Park-to-Park Tickets. The 3-Park Premier Annual Pass is also about 25% cheaper than Walt Disney World's Incredi-Pass (which is currently the only WDW annual pass available for new purchases, unless you are a DVC member or Florida resident), and while Disney has several more parks included in its annual passes, Universal throws in some great perks (depending on pass level) to compensate. Annual pass options for Epic Universe were not yet available at press time.

Universal annual passes include Park-to-Park admission to USF and IOA, including special events that don't require a separate ticket, such as Mardi Gras (except Seasonal Pass holders on concert nights), Grinchmas, and Universal's Holiday Parade, as well as discounts on those that cost extra, such as Halloween Horror Nights and Rock the Universe.

Any annual pass can be purchased with access to all three parks, including Volcano Bay, for about the price of one or two single-day passes to the water park. Current 2-Park Pass holders can upgrade to 3-Park access midyear by paying the difference, but no prorated discounts are given. All annual passholders except 3-Park Premier are blocked from entering Volcano Bay during select dates; see below for details.

Annual passes can be scanned into your wallet inside Universal's app and stored as a QR code that may be used for admission and benefits (including Express after 4 p.m. for Premier Pass holders), but you should keep your physical pass and ID on hand for verification.

A **UOAP lounge** in the Toon Lagoon section of IOA is open to all annual passholders daily, 11 a.m.–4 p.m. The lounge doesn't offer free snacks, but it does have air-conditioning, phone-charging ports, and the opportunity to purchase exclusive passholder merchandise and bottled Coke products. During peak seasons, operations may be extended from park opening until closing.

All annual passholders receive 10%–15% off food and non-alcoholic beverages at most resort hotel locations; select locations do not honor discounts during special events and holidays. See theug series.com/UOAPPerks for details. Passholders also receive 10% off

VIP tours, up to 40% off room rates at on-site hotels, up to 30% off Budget and Avis rental-car base rates and free upgrades, 15% off regular or private admission to Universal's Great Movie Escape, $3 off evening admission for yourself and one guest at Universal Cinemark, $1 off daily Coca-Cola Freestyle souvenir cup refills, and other discounts as detailed below. Here are the four types of Universal annual passes:

Seasonal Pass

- Valid for one year, but with about 8 weeks of block-out dates, including spring break, July, Thanksgiving, and Christmas week at USF and IOA, and all concert nights at USF only; Volcano Bay block-out dates are over spring break and June–mid-August
- No free parking
- 10% off food and nonalcoholic beverages at most resort hotel locations; no food or merchandise discounts at parks or CityWalk
- 10% off gate prices for additional multiday park tickets

Power Pass

- Valid for one year, but with about three weeks of block-out dates at USF and IOA, including spring break and Christmas week; Volcano Bay block-out dates are before 4 p.m. June–mid-August
- 50% discount on self-parking (after the first visit)
- 10% off food and nonalcoholic beverages at most resort hotel locations; no food or merchandise discounts at parks or CityWalk
- 15% off gate prices for additional multiday park tickets

Preferred Annual Pass

- Valid 365 days at USF and IOA; Volcano Bay block-out dates are before 4 p.m. July–August
- Early Park Admission up to 1 hour before official opening to USF and/or IOA and VB; not valid on mornings listed at theugseries.com/uoapepa, including spring break, Thanksgiving, Christmas week, and peak summer season
- Free standard self-parking; discounted Prime self-parking and valet parking (after the first visit)
- 10% off all Universal-owned in-park restaurants and merchandise, including outdoor carts (excluding alcohol); 10%–15% off food and merchandise at select CityWalk and most resort hotel locations
- 15% off gate prices for additional multiday park tickets
- 10% off My Universal Photos (excluding packages)
- Additional discounts at CityWalk and the resort hotels

Premier Annual Pass

- Valid 365 days at all parks
- Early Park Admission 1 hour before official opening to USF and/or IOA and VB; valid 365 mornings per year
- Free Prime self-parking and valet parking (after the first visit; when available)
- 15% off all Universal-owned in-park restaurants and merchandise, including outdoor carts (excluding alcohol); 10%–15% off food and merchandise at select CityWalk and most resort hotel locations

- Free Universal Express at USF and IOA after 4 p.m. every day (one time per participating attraction
- One free Halloween Horror Nights ticket (valid select off-peak nights only)
- 15% off gate prices for additional multiday park tickets
- 15% off My Universal Photos (excluding packages)
- Additional discounts at CityWalk and the resort hotels

unofficial **TIP**
Visit universalorlando
.com/web/en/us/tickets
-packages/annual-
passes/hotel-guide
to search Universal's
online hotel inventory
for available annual
passholder discounts.

In addition, all annual passholders get periodic emails with announcements of special limited-time perks, such as exclusive merchandise offers and menu items, private parking toll lanes and entrance turnstiles, free buttons and magnets, or passholder-only events during Passholder Appreciation Days, held in the off-season; see theugseries .com/uniappdays for details. And if you can't handle the cost of a pass in one big bite, Universal's FlexPay service will (after a substantial down payment) split the remaining bill into interest-free monthly payments. Be aware that you'll have to pay off your balance in full before upgrading your pass tier. After the initial yearlong payment contract is complete, FlexPay will automatically renew on a month-to-month basis with a significantly higher monthly payment. FlexPay customers do not get the 20% renewal discount offered to paid-in-full passholders, but they may be eligible for bonus months during seasonal sales promotions. Annual pass pricing and benefits change regularly, so visit theugseries.com/uorannualpass for the latest offers.

So should you buy a Universal Orlando annual pass, and if so, which one? If you are making only one trip to Universal within the year, are staying off-site, and are planning to spend four days or fewer in the parks, then you should stick with standard tickets. If, however, you plan to spend five or more days at Universal's parks, anticipate returning to Universal within the year, or want to stay at an on-site hotel for even one night, then it's well worth your while to run the numbers on an annual pass. Even if you live out of state, Universal's annual passes may entice you to become a repeat visitor, like this family from Taos, New Mexico:

> The annual pass is an incredible bargain, and when you combine it with a stay at one of the resorts that include an Express Pass, it makes for a reasonably priced and super-fun short getaway.

As for which one to buy, first double-check the current Seasonal and Power Pass block-out dates at theugseries.com/uoapblockout to ensure they don't conflict with your trip. If only the first portion of your visit overlaps with the block-out period, it's possible to buy multiday tickets, then apply their full value to annual passes by upgrading them at Guest Services before they expire. Even if you're in the clear, at least one member of your party will want to pick up at least a Power Pass for its 50% parking discount if you're driving to the resort; four days of self-parking at $32 per day adds up to $128, which is about double the difference in price between the Seasonal and Power Passes. After factoring in the block-out dates and lack of discounts, the Seasonal Pass is a poor value for most guests, and the Preferred Pass surpasses the Power Pass in parking savings alone if you visit at least 12 times a year. (Note that free or discounted parking only applies after your first visit; you must first activate your annual pass at a park gate before receiving free parking.)

If—and only if—you take advantage of all its amenities, the Premier Annual Pass is an excellent value. You can easily get your money's worth in free valet parking alone, and the free Universal Express after 4 p.m. is especially useful when the parks are open late. (See the Universal Express section on page 57 for more details.) The free Halloween Horror Nights pass isn't valid on most nights in October and can't be upgraded or transferred to another person, which limits its value if you are also planning to buy a Frequent Fear Pass. *Note:* Starting in 2025, Premier Pass holders will need to make an advance online reservation to use their free Halloween Horror Nights ticket.

BUYING ADMISSION TO UNIVERSAL ORLANDO

ONE OF OUR BIG GRIPES ABOUT UNIVERSAL is that there are never enough ticket windows open in the morning to accommodate the crowds. That means guests wait in long ticket lines during the peak holiday and summer seasons just to reach a sales window before they can enjoy more waits at the turnstiles and attractions. You can purchase Volcano Bay tickets at the Volcano Bay bus stop inside the parking structure or at the park entrance. However, we strongly recommend buying your admission in advance. Passes are available directly from Universal at universalorlando.com or by phone at ☎ 800-711-0080; at the concierge desks or attraction box offices of many Orlando-area hotels (including the DoubleTree across Kirkman Road from the resort entrance); and at Universal's gift shops inside Orlando International Airport.

You can also buy single or multiday admission directly through the Universal mobile app, which will display a bar code that serves as your ticket, avoiding the need for paper altogether. Prices for passes purchased through the app are the same as on Universal's website.

SAVING MONEY ON ADMISSION TO UNIVERSAL ORLANDO

UNIVERSAL'S ADMISSION DISCOUNTS change too rapidly to comprehensively cover in this guide. The best online clearinghouse for keeping up with the latest available offers is **MouseSavers** (see theugseries .com/unideals).

Ticket Savings Direct from Universal Orlando

Universal offers discounts when you purchase passes online at universalorlando.com, including $21-per-ticket discounts on all multiday tickets, plus other time-limited specials. Universal no longer offers shipping of actual tickets for online orders. Tickets purchased online can be printed at home or sent to your mobile device and used at the turnstiles without the need to exchange them at a box office, or they can be retrieved using the credit card with which they were purchased from automated will-call kiosks outside each park; look for the ATM-like terminals to the right of the Guest Services window at USF, or to the left of Toothsome Chocolate Emporium outside IOA. Annual passes cannot be retrieved from an automated kiosk but must be picked up at a ticket booth, Guest Services window, or hotel Vacation Services desk. Tickets purchased online (including annual passes) do not begin expiring until first activated at a park entrance.

Universal offers a best-price guarantee: if you buy park tickets through Universal's website and then find them cheaper online within seven days, Universal Orlando will give you a gift card (good at restaurants and shops around the resort) refunding the price difference. The price guarantee is only on regular admission tickets (not Express or special-event tickets) available to the general public from US-based websites, and it excludes time-share promotions, group rates, or other special discounts. To claim your refund, call ☎ 800-644-4678 or send an email to guestservices@universalorlando.com.

Florida (and sometimes Georgia) residents can take advantage of an ever-changing array of price breaks, often tied to a fast-food chain or soft drink promotion. Local resident tickets may expire weeks or months after first use, unlike regular multiday tickets, which expire after a week. These specials require valid photo ID proving residency to redeem, so don't try using one if you aren't eligible. Current annual passholders get a modest 10%–15% price break when buying additional multiday tickets at the gate, which may add up to double or triple the standard online discount. Visit theugseries.com/unitix to see the locals' latest discounts.

Active-duty and retired members of the U.S. Armed Forces should visit universalorlando.com/military for exclusive deals on tickets and hotel packages. In 2024, eligible military service members could purchase a Military Freedom Pass Promotional Ticket, which was valid for admission through December 20, 2024, with two weeks of block-outs around Christmas and Easter; the pass starts at $210 for 2-park access, with 3-park upgrades available. Universal Orlando tickets are available at most base Leisure Travel offices, as well as at Shades of Green resort at Walt Disney World, but you need to show military ID at a Universal ticket window to activate them. A typical military discount vacation package includes four nights of accommodations in an on-site or partner hotel and a 3-Park Freedom Pass Ticket.

Universal Orlando periodically offers online-only specials that are usually superior to any other available discount. For example, in summer 2024 Universal sold 5-Day Tickets for the price of a 3-Day Ticket. These tickets have to be used before a certain expiration date, and block-out days may apply, but the savings can be substantial.

Ticket Savings from Third-Party Vendors

The lowest possible prices on electronically delivered Universal tickets that we're aware of are through **Tripster** (☎ 888-590-5910; tripster .com) and **Undercover Tourist** (☎ 800-846-1302; undercovertourist .com), ticket wholesalers that sell multiday tickets for Universal (as well as tickets to many other attractions around the country) for 2%–20% less than Universal's website. Undercover Tourist offers the best savings on 3-Park Park-to-Park tickets, while Tripster has the lowest prices on 2-Park and Base Tickets. All tickets are brand-new and delivered to you electronically, just like those direct from Universal, but mandatory handling fees nibble into the advertised savings.

We also recommend **Orlando Ticket Connection** (☎ 855-473-7987; orlandoticketconnection.com), which undercuts Universal's online prices on multiday Base Tickets by 1%–4% and on Park-to-Park Passes by 4%–6%. Even though it doesn't discount quite as deeply as its competitors, Orlando Ticket Connection advertises all its prices inclusive of tax and electronic delivery, and it will typically match or beat the short-term deals Universal offers on its own website. Orlando Ticket Connection gets high marks for customer service from readers like this one:

> *I ordered tickets for SeaWorld and Universal Orlando from Orlando Ticket Connection late on Thursday night (around midnight), and at 9:08 on Friday morning I received my tickets by email. It was quick, and they were actual tickets that you take directly to the turnstile. I used them both at the parks today and had no problems whatsoever. I would order tickets from them again without a second thought.*

Universal doesn't offer ticket discounts to **AAA** or **CAA** members at the gate, but some regional offices sell discounted passes to members in advance; prices vary by area. The closest **Auto Club South** office to Universal Orlando is at 110 South Orlando Avenue in Winter Park; call ☎ 407-647-1033 for hours and directions. AAA South members can buy discounted tickets, annual passes, and vacation packages online at aaa.com/universal.

Costco Wholesale sometimes sells discounted Universal Orlando tickets to members. If you are visiting UOR from the United Kingdom, check out **Attraction Tickets** (attractiontickets.com) for good deals on 14-day tickets.

OTHER DISCOUNTS AT UNIVERSAL ORLANDO

UNIVERSAL ORLANDO PROVIDES DISCOUNTS on dining, entertainment, and lodging to members of many travel organizations, including automobile clubs such as AAA and CAA. Discounts are also available to Universal Orlando annual passholders. This section is a guide to finding the best discounts for members of these groups and the general public.

Resorts

All annual passholders (including Seasonal and Power Pass holders) receive discounts of up to 40% on resort lodging, depending on availability. If you're staying at a Universal resort for two or more days, you may save enough on lodging to offset the cost of an annual pass for the adult booking the room. Similar (and sometimes superior) seasonal Florida resident discounts are detailed at theugseries.com/uniflres.

AAA members can book on-site rooms and vacation packages at a modest discount, usually 5%–10%. Packages may include $25–$50 activity credit that can be used for vacation add-ons. You must call AAA or Loews directly to get the discount; it cannot be applied online.

Check **MouseSavers** (mousesavers.com), which lists seasonal and specialized discounts for Universal's resorts, such as discounts available to residents of certain states.

Dining

See pages 35–37 for discounts offered to annual passholders.

If you're visiting during late August–early October, several Universal resort hotel restaurants participate in **Orlando's Magical Dining,** when you can order three courses from special prix fixe menus for only $40 or $60; visit magicaldining.com for details. A similar $35 promotion called **Bite30** (bite30.com) is offered in June and early July at some upscale restaurants near Universal, although none on property.

Entertainment and Other Discounts

Preferred Pass holders receive 10% off services at Portofino Bay's **Mandara Spa,** and Premier Pass holders save 20% (Monday–Thursday only; some services excluded). Discounted Mandara Spa packages are also regularly offered at mandaraspa.com/offers.

Preferred and Premier Pass holders receive discounts on an 18-hole round at **Hollywood Drive-In Golf** for up to five players; Preferred Pass holders save 10%, while Premier Pass holders save 15%.

All annual passholders save $3 off adult admission to any **Universal Cinemark** movie showing after 6 p.m. for themselves and one guest.

All annual passholders save 15% on regular or private admission to **Universal's Great Movie Escape.**

Preferred and Premier Pass holders get a $5 discount on **Classic Albums Live** concert tickets at the Hard Rock Live box office.

All annual passholders (including Seasonal Pass holders) get 10% off inflatable **pool tubes and cabana rentals** at Cabana Bay Beach Resort.

All annual passholders can save up to 30% off base car-rental rates and get a free upgrade at **Budget** and **Avis.**

Finally, you *might* save money at Universal by booking a package with tickets and lodging through **Universal Orlando Vacations** (☎ 877-801-9720; universalorlandovacations.com), the official travel company of Universal Orlando Resort. It advertises packages with attractive-sounding rates, like "bundle and save up to $200," but you must take full advantage of every package component (including food or photos you may not want) to realize a modest 5% discount over buying each component separately. For a full break-down of Universal Orlando Vacation bundles, see page 101.

MAKING *the* MOST *of* YOUR TIME *and* MONEY *at* UNIVERSAL ORLANDO

THE CARDINAL RULES FOR SUCCESSFUL TOURING

MANY VISITORS DON'T HAVE three or four days to devote to Universal Orlando. Some are en route to other destinations or are visiting Universal as a sideline to their Disney World vacation. For these visitors, efficient touring is a must.

Even the most time-effective touring plan won't allow you to com-prehensively cover more than one Universal theme park in one day. Plan to allocate an entire day to each park. An exception to this is when the parks close at different times, allowing you to tour one park until closing and then proceed to another.

One-Day Touring

A comprehensive tour of *multiple* Universal Orlando theme parks in one day is virtually impossible. A comprehensive one-day tour of USF *or* IOA is possible but requires knowledge of the park, good planning, good navigation, and plenty of energy and endurance. Seeing all of Epic Universe in a day will also be a challenge, given its size and expected popularity. One-day touring leaves little time for sit-down meals, pro-longed browsing in shops, or lengthy breaks. One-day touring can be fun and rewarding, but allocating at least three full days to enjoy the two theme parks is preferable.

We provide one-day plans for each Universal park, plus one- and two-day plans for those with Park-to-Park access. We also provide tour-ing advice for Volcano Bay, though due to the water park's use of Vir-tual Line technology, a step-by-step touring plan isn't possible. Guests with three days should use our comprehensive two-day, two-park plan, followed by one of our specialized one-day plans; guests with more than three days can try multiple specialized one-day plans, or spend their additional days at leisure exploring without an itinerary. Even if you're on a relaxed schedule, following a touring plan can still enhance your trip, according to this reader from Rockford, Michigan:

> We had four days to explore Universal. We followed the two-day Park-to-Park plan the first day, and it worked amazingly! It allowed us to get so much in that we could relax the rest of the trip and see and do everything we wanted, plus repeat rides everyone liked.

Successfully touring a Universal Orlando theme park in one day hinges on three rules:

1. Determine in Advance What You Really Want to See

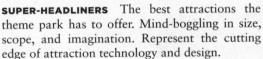

Which attractions appeal to you most? Which ones would you like to experience if you have time left? What are you willing to forgo?

To help you set your touring priorities, we describe the theme parks and their attractions in detail in Parts 6, 7, and 8. In each description, we include the author's evaluation of the attraction and the opinions of UOR guests expressed as star ratings. Five stars is the highest rating.

Finally, because attractions range from midway-type rides and walk-through exhibits to high-tech extravaganzas, we have developed a hierarchy of categories to pinpoint an attraction's magnitude:

SUPER-HEADLINERS The best attractions the theme park has to offer. Mind-boggling in size, scope, and imagination. Represent the cutting edge of attraction technology and design.

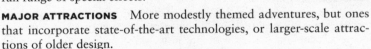

HEADLINERS Multimillion-dollar, themed, full-scale adventures and theater presentations. Modern in technology and design and employing a full range of special effects.

MAJOR ATTRACTIONS More modestly themed adventures, but ones that incorporate state-of-the-art technologies, or larger-scale attractions of older design.

MINOR ATTRACTIONS Midway-type rides, small theater presentations, and elaborate walk-through attractions.

DIVERSIONS Exhibits, both passive and interactive. Includes playgrounds, video arcades, and street theater.

Though not every attraction fits neatly into these descriptions, the categories provide a comparison of size and scope. Remember: bigger and more elaborate doesn't always mean better or more popular. Flight of the Hippogriff, a kiddie coaster in IOA's Hogsmeade, sometimes attracts a longer line than the larger Harry Potter and the Forbidden Journey. Likewise, for many young children, no attraction, regardless of size, surpasses One Fish, Two Fish, Red Fish, Blue Fish, a simple Seussian spinner.

2. Arrive Early! Arrive Early! Arrive Early!

This is the single most important key to efficient touring and avoiding long lines. First thing in the morning, there are no lines and fewer people. The same four rides you experience in 1 hour in the early morning can take as long as 3 hours after 10:30 a.m. Besides that, the parks are now open as few as 8 hours per day in the off-season. Factoring in meals and breaks, that leaves as little as 6–6½ hours to see the park. Eat breakfast before you arrive; don't waste prime touring time sitting in a restaurant.

The earlier a park opens, the greater your advantage: most vacationers won't rise early and get to a park before it opens. Fewer people are willing to make an 8 a.m. opening than a 9 a.m. opening. If you visit during midsummer, arrive at the turnstile 30–45 minutes before you are eligible to enter. During holiday periods, arrive 45–60 minutes early. If you won't take our word for it, listen to this couple from New Orleans:

> Your advice to get to the parks 30 minutes before they open (we did not have early admission) was spot on. We could pretty much get on almost any ride with little to no wait until about 10:30–11 a.m. each day we were there.

3. Avoid Bottlenecks

Helping you avoid bottlenecks is what *The Unofficial Guide* is about. This involves being able to predict where, when, and why bottlenecks occur. Concentrations of hungry people create gridlocks at restaurants during lunch and dinner; concentrations of people moving toward the exit near closing time cause gift shops en route to clog; concentrations of visitors at new and popular rides, and at rides slow to load and unload, create logjams and long lines.

Our solution for avoiding bottlenecks: touring plans for all three parks. We also provide detailed information on rides and performances, enabling you to estimate how long you may have to wait in line and allowing you to compare rides for their crowd capacity. All touring plans are in the back of this book, following the index. Plans for Universal Studios Florida begin on page 395; for Islands of Adventure, on page 399; and for Epic Universe, on page 413. One- and two-day touring plans covering both USF and IOA are provided for those with Park-to-Park admission, as are one-day plans devoted to Epic Universe.

WHAT'S A QUEUE?

THOUGH IT'S NOT COMMONLY USED in the United States, *queue* (pronounced "cue") is the universal English word for a line, such as one in which you wait to cash a check at the bank or to board a ride at a theme park. Queuing theory, a mathematical area of specialization within the field of operations research, studies and models how lines work. Because the *Unofficial Guide* draws heavily on this discipline, we use some of its terminology. In addition to the noun, the verb *to queue* means "to get in line," and a *queuing area* is "a waiting area that accommodates a line."

TOURING PLANS:
WHAT THEY ARE AND HOW THEY WORK

MINIMIZING OUR READERS' WAITS in line has been a top priority. We know from our research and that of others that theme park patrons measure overall satisfaction based on the number of attractions they're able to experience during a visit: the more attractions, the better. Thus, we developed and offered our readers field-tested touring plans that allow them to experience as many attractions as possible with the least amount of waiting in line.

Our touring plans have always been based on theme park traffic flow, attraction capacity, the maximum time a guest is willing to wait, walking distance between attractions, and waiting-time data collected at every attraction in every park, every day of the year.

The *Unofficial Guide* touring plan program contains patented algorithms that allow it to quickly analyze tens of millions of possible plans in a very short time. The program can analyze standby wait times and estimate the time saved by using Universal Express Passes. The software can also schedule rest breaks throughout the day and estimate walking times to meals if you specify a preferred restaurant. Numerous other features are available, many of which we'll discuss in the next section.

Over the years, this research has been recognized by the travel industry and academia, having been cited by such diverse sources as *The New York Times, USA Today, Travel Weekly, Bottom Line, Money, Operations Research Forum,* CBS News, Fox News, the BBC, the Travel Channel, *The Dallas Morning News,* and *The Atlanta Journal-Constitution.* The methodology behind our touring plans was also used as a case study in the 2010 book *Numbers Rule Your World* by Kaiser Fung, professor of statistics at New York University.

We get a ton of reader mail—98% of it positive—commenting on our touring plans. From an Edmonds, Washington, family who used one of our touring plans for IOA:

> *It worked like a charm! I've always wondered how it feels to follow your plans, not ever having seen the park before, and now I know— it was easy!*

Another reader reports:

> *We didn't have early entry and got there 30 minutes before the official opening time of 9 a.m. and walked on the first three rides on the plan. We spent two days at both parks and got on everything twice. Never waited more than 45 minutes.*

And from a Fruit Cove, Florida, family:

We found the touring plans extremely helpful. When we followed the plans exactly, we were able to experience all rides with little to no wait.

Customize Your Touring Plans

The attractions included in our touring plans are the best and most popular as determined by our expert team and reader surveys. If you've never been to Universal Orlando, we suggest using the plans in this book. They'll ensure that you see the best Universal attractions with as little waiting in line as possible.

If you're a returning visitor, your favorite attractions may be different. One way to customize the plans is to go to touringplans.com or use the Lines app to create personalized versions. Tell the software the date, time, and park you've chosen to visit, along with the attractions you want to see. The plan will tell you, for your specific travel date and time, the exact order in which to visit the attractions to minimize your waits in line. Lines also supports child swap (see page 187) on thrill rides. Besides rides, you can schedule shows, meals, breaks, character greetings, and more. You can even tell Lines how fast you plan to walk, and whether or not you'll be using Universal Express, and it will make the necessary adjustments.

Alternatively, some changes are simple enough to make on your own. If a plan calls for an attraction in which you're not interested, simply skip it and move on to the next one. You can also substitute similar attractions in the same area of the park. If a plan calls for, say, riding Cat in the Hat and you'd rather not, but you would enjoy the Caro-Seuss-el (which is not on the plan), then go ahead and substitute that for Cat. As long as the substitution is a similar attraction— substituting a show for a ride won't work—and is pretty close by the attraction called for in the touring plan, you won't compromise the plan's overall effectiveness. If all else fails and you need some extra hand-holding, Seth provides **personalized tour-planning services** for all Universal parks; visit his website (sethkubersky.com) or email skubersky@gmail.com for pricing and details.

OVERVIEW OF THE TOURING PLANS

OUR TOURING PLANS are step-by-step guides for seeing as much as possible with a minimum of standing in line, and without needing Universal Express Passes. They're designed to help you avoid crowds and bottlenecks on any day of the year. The plans will save you time on days when attendance is lighter (see "Trying to Reason with the Tourist Season," page 25), but on those days, they won't be as critical to successful touring.

What You Can Realistically Expect from the Touring Plans

Though we present one-day, two-park plans for Universal Orlando, USF and IOA together have more attractions than you can reasonably expect to see in one day, as does Epic Universe all by itself. You can either experience both of The Wizarding Worlds in depth, or hit highlights of the parks' non-Potter parts, but not both in a single visit. Because our two-day plan for USF and IOA is the most comprehensive, efficient, and relaxing, we strongly recommend it over the one-day, two-park plans. But if you must cram your visit to both original parks into a single day, the one-day plans will allow you to see as much as is humanly possible.

Variables That Affect the Success of the Touring Plans

The plans' success will be affected by how quickly you move from ride to ride; when and how many refreshment and restroom breaks you take; when, where, and how you eat meals; and your ability (or lack thereof) to find your way around. Smaller groups almost always move faster than larger groups, and parties of adults generally cover more ground than families with young children. Child swap (see page 187), also known as rider swap, baby swap, or switching off, inhibits families with little ones from moving as expeditiously as possible among attractions.

Plus, some folks simply cannot conform to the plans' "early to rise" conditions, as this reader from Cleveland Heights, Ohio, recounts:

> *Our touring plans were thrown totally off by one member who could not be on time for opening. Even in October, this made a huge difference in our ability to see attractions without waiting.*

And a family from Centerville, Ohio, says:

> *The toughest thing about your touring plans was getting the rest of the family to stay with them. Getting them to pass by attractions to hit something across the park was no easy task.*

If you have young children, the appearance of a cartoon character (especially one of the Trolls or Minions) can stop a touring plan in its tracks, and even adults will detour to snap a selfie with Optimus Prime or the Hogwarts Express conductor. While some characters stroll the parks, it's more common that they assemble in a specific location where families queue up for photos. Meeting characters isn't as popular a pastime at Universal as at Disney, but it can still burn valuable touring time. If your kids collect character selfies, you need to anticipate these interruptions by including character greetings when creating your online touring plans, or else negotiate some understanding with your children about when you'll stop for photos.

Some things are beyond your control. Chief among these are the manner and timing of bringing a particular ride to capacity. For example, Harry Potter and the Escape from Gringotts, an indoor roller coaster in USF, may begin operation with four or five trains running, and then add two to five more as needed. If the waiting line builds rapidly before operators go to full capacity (as frequently happens at IOA's Forbidden Journey), you could have a long wait, even in early morning.

A variable that can give your touring plans a boost is the singles line (see page 63), as this English reader explains:

We used the touring plans to the letter and found that not only did they work, but they also worked even better in conjunction with single-rider queues. The only rides we queued up for normally were ones with a 20-minute-or-less queue time and wet rides.

Another variable is your arrival time for a theater show. You'll wait from the time you arrive until the end of the presentation in progress. Thus, if a show starts every 30 minutes and you arrive 1 minute after it has begun, your wait will be 29 minutes. Conversely, if you arrive just before the next show begins, your wait will be only a minute or two.

While we realize that following the touring plans isn't always easy, we nevertheless recommend continuous, expeditious touring until around noon. After that, breaks and diversions won't affect the touring plans significantly.

What to Do if You Lose the Thread

We suggest sticking to the plans religiously, especially in the mornings, if you're visiting during busy times. The consequence of touring spontaneity in peak season is hours of standing in line. When using the plans, however, relax and always be prepared for surprises and setbacks. If unforeseen events interrupt a plan:

1. If you're following a touring plan in the Lines app (touringplans.com /lines), just press OPTIMIZE when you're ready to start touring again. Lines will figure out the best possible plan for the remainder of your day.

2. If you're following a printed touring plan, skip a step on the plan for every 20 minutes' delay. For example, if you lose your wallet and spend an hour hunting for it, skip three steps and pick up from there.

3. Forget the plan and organize the remainder of the day using the standby wait times listed in the Lines app.

Even if you aren't strictly following a touring plan, remember to refresh the Lines app after a detour, as a father of three from Sydney, Australia, advises:

When using Lines and seeing what the attraction wait times are, make sure to refresh it first so you can see the up-to-date wait times, not the wait times from 2 hours ago when you last refreshed it. I may have been guilty of not doing this, as I took the family from one side of the park to the other to go to Transformers, and then waited 40 minutes for the ride when I told everyone it was a 15-minute line. Or it might have been the two restroom stops on the way?

Clip-Out Touring Plans

For your convenience, the touring plans combine itineraries with numbered maps. Select the plan appropriate for your party, and get familiar with it. Then clip the pocket version from the back of this guide and carry it with you as a quick reference at the theme park.

Will the Plans Continue to Work Once the Secret Is Out?

Yes! First, all the plans require that a patron be there when a park opens. Many Universal Orlando patrons simply won't get up early while on vacation. Second, less than 2% of any day's attendance has been exposed to the plans—too few to affect results. Last, most groups tailor the plans, skipping rides or shows according to taste.

Why Do I Need a Touring Plan If I Have Universal's Smartphone App?

You might imagine that the availability of real-time wait times inside Universal Orlando's free app would obviate your need for a touring plan. But in fact, it has the exact opposite effect, as this mom from Athens, Georgia, explains:

> I believe the touring plans are even more important now that everyone has a wait-time app from the park on their phone. I would see 10-minute wait times pop up on the Universal app, and if we happened to walk past those rides on our way to another ride, the line would jump up to 20 minutes or more. People are just chasing the shortest lines, but then everyone goes to that ride and the lines increase. We did do this for a few hours when we went to the park late in the day and instantly regretted it.

How Frequently Are the Touring Plans Revised?

We revise them every year, and updates are always available at touring plans.com. Be prepared for surprises, though: opening procedures and showtimes may change, for example, and you can't predict when an attraction might break down.

Tour Groups on Steroids

We've discovered that tour groups of up to 200 people sometimes use our plans. Unless your party is as large as that tour group, this development shouldn't alarm you. Because tour groups are big, they move slowly and have to stop periodically to collect stragglers. The tour guide also has to accommodate the unpredictability of five dozen or so bladders. In short, you should have no problem passing a group after the initial encounter.

"Bouncing Around"

Some readers object to crisscrossing a theme park, as our touring plans sometimes require. A woman from Decatur, Georgia, told us she "got dizzy from all the bouncing around." Believe us, we empathize.

We've worked hard over the years to eliminate the need to crisscross a theme park in our touring plans. (In fact, our customized software can minimize walking instead of waiting in line, if that's important to you.) Occasionally, however, it's possible to save a lot of time in line with a few extra minutes of walking.

The reasons for this are varied. Sometimes a park is designed intentionally to require walking. In USF, for example, the most popular attraction (Harry Potter and the Escape from Gringotts in Diagon Alley) is placed at the farthest corner from the front gate, so guests are more evenly distributed throughout the day. Epic Universe takes this tactic to the extreme, placing each land's headliner ride as far as possible from the central hub, which you must return to before exploring the next area. Other times, you may be visiting just after a new attraction has opened that everyone wants to try. In that case, a special trip to visit the new attraction may be required earlier in the day than normal to avoid longer waits later. And live shows, especially at USF, sometimes have performance schedules so at odds with each other (and the rest of the park's schedule) that orderly touring is impossible.

If you want to experience headliner attractions in one day without long waits, you can see those first (which requires crisscrossing the park), use Universal Express and single-rider lines (if available), or hope to squeeze in visits during parades and the last hour the park is open (which may not work).

If you have two days to visit USF and IOA, use the two-day touring plan (see pages 409–412). This spreads the popular attractions over two mornings and works great even when the parks close early.

Touring Plan Rejection

Some folks don't respond well to the regimentation of a touring plan. If you encounter this problem with someone in your party, roll with the punches, as this Maryland couple did:

> The rest of the group was not receptive to the use of the touring plans. I think they all thought I was being a little too regimented about planning this vacation. Rather than argue, I left the touring plans behind as we ventured off to the parks. You can guess the outcome. We took videos and watched them when we returned home. About every 5 minutes or so, there's a shot of us all gathered around a park map trying to decide what to do next.

This Syracuse, New York, couple compromised by following a plan until early afternoon, but then taking a break:

> Getting there prior to park opening, touring consistently until about 2 p.m., and then leaving for a nap and a swim was a huge hit with my fiance, who had never been to Disney or Universal before. Sometimes we didn't even need to go back to the park at night because we had accomplished everything we wanted to in the 6 hours or so that we had been in the park.

Finally, a Connecticut woman alleges that the plans are incompatible with some readers' bladders, as well as their personalities:

> When you write those plans next year, can you schedule bathroom breaks in there too? You expect us to be at a certain ride at a certain

time and with no stops in between. The schedules are a problem if you are a laid-back, slow-moving, careful detail noticer. What were you thinking when you made these schedules?

Before you injure your urinary tract, feel free to deviate from the touring plan as necessary to heed the call of nature. If you're using a customized plan in Lines, you can build in as many breaks (bathroom or otherwise) as you like, and the optimizer will plan around them.

WHAT TO EXPECT WHEN YOU ARRIVE AT THE PARKS (ROPE DROP)

BECAUSE MOST TOURING PLANS ARE BASED ON being present when the theme park opens, you need to know about opening procedures. Universal Orlando's on-site resort transportation to the parks via buses and water taxis begins 2 hours before official opening, or 1 hour before Early Park Admission (see page 53). Guests staying on-site during peak periods will want to catch the first ride of the morning (or start walking around the time it leaves) to be the first into The Wizarding World during the early-entry period. Off-season visitors should arrive at the gates 15–30 minutes before Early Park Admission (EPA) begins.

The parking facilities also open 2 hours before official opening, but on days of exceptional attendance (like the grand opening of a new attraction), parking has opened as early as 3 a.m. If you are driving to the resort and aren't eligible for EPA, plan to arrive at the Universal parking tollbooths 45–60 minutes prior to official opening. If you need to purchase park admission, add another 15 minutes to that. At the original campus, it takes approximately 10–15 minutes to walk from the parking garage to the parks' entrance turnstiles, so you should arrive at the turnstiles 30–45 minutes before the park opens.

Lines tend to be evenly distributed at each turnstile, but if you see a shorter line, get in it. There are secondary turnstiles to the far left of IOA's entrance and to the far right behind the guest relations windows at USF. When open, these relatively hidden entrances usually have short waits.

Universal's turnstiles use photo validation (aka facial recognition), instead of finger biometrics, which snaps your picture when using your ticket for the first time. This process may also be completed at designated terminals outside the park entrance or ahead of time through the smartphone app. On follow-up visits, guests scan their passes, then look into a screen-mounted camera until their image is identified. The process takes about 2 seconds (far quicker than Disney's MagicBands), but guests can opt out and choose to display photo IDs instead. If using paper tickets, you'll also be asked to sign your pass, so you don't mix it up with those of other family members.

Rope Drop at Universal Studios Florida

USF team members select a "first family" from the early risers at the turnstiles each morning and usher them in a few minutes early to open the park with an old-fashioned movie clapboard. It's a cute moment worth catching if you can.

On the rare occasions when USF opens for EPA, resort guests walk straight toward Revenge of the Mummy and are escorted to The Wizarding World via San Francisco. Day guests are restricted to the front of the park, where Despicable Me Minion Mayhem opens to all guests 10–15 minutes before the official opening.

On days when USF does not officially offer EPA, the gates will usually open 10 minutes before the official opening time, with Despicable Me Minion Mayhem typically running for all early guests. Guests can enter the Harry Potter and the Escape from Gringotts queue before official opening, but the ride may not begin running until park opening (or a few minutes before) on non-EPA mornings.

Most of the crowd will head for The Wizarding World of Harry Potter's Gringotts ride, which usually sees its longest waits between opening and early afternoon. Despicable Me and Villain-Con, both located a short distance past the entrance, also attract large crowds, as do Transformers: The Ride–3D and Hollywood Rip Ride Rockit (which may not start running until 15 minutes after park opening). A smaller number of visitors will head for Revenge of the Mummy, but except for DreamWorks Land, all the attractions along the east side of the lagoon—including The Simpsons Ride, E.T. Adventure, and Men in Black Alien Attack—are inaccessible until 10 a.m.

Rope Drop at Islands of Adventure

IOA's gates also open up to 15 minutes before the official opening time. On days when EPA isn't offered, most entering guests turn counterclockwise through Seuss Landing and make a beeline for Hogsmeade or the VelociCoaster as soon as the park is open. A smaller number of guests will head clockwise for The Incredible Hulk Coaster (which may allow guests to ride a few minutes before the official opening time) and then continue through Toon Lagoon to Skull Island and Jurassic Park.

When EPA is offered at IOA, eligible guests may head to Hogsmeade and the VelociCoaster as soon as the gates open, walking counterclockwise through Seuss Landing and Lost Continent. Guests without EPA privileges can still enter early but will be held in the Port of Entry and Seuss Landing. Marvel Super Hero Island's attractions may open to all guests up to 15 minutes before the official park opening time. If IOA officially opens an hour after USF, only guests eligible for EPA may ride the Hogwarts Express during IOA's early-entry hour.

Unless you have early entry, our advice is to see Marvel Super Hero Island and Reign of Kong first and save The Wizarding World until later in the day.

Rope Drop at Epic Universe

Details on EPA and rope drop procedures at EU were not yet available, but guests at the Helios Grand Hotel, which is integrated into the rear of the park, are expected to have a leg up on everyone else in the mornings, especially when heading into the Wizarding World.

Rope Drop at Volcano Bay

Arrival at Volcano Bay is complicated by the fact that there is no parking at the water park itself, so all guests must be bused in from the main parking garage or resorts. Hotel guests and annual passholders with early-entry privileges begin arriving at the turnstiles up to an hour before EPA begins, but distribution of the mandatory TapuTapu wrist-

unofficial **TIP**
Decorative planters keep lines from forming at Volcano Bay's center turnstiles, making the outside lines longer. Squeeze through to the middle lanes for quicker entry.

bands doesn't begin until moments before early entry starts. Day guests not eligible for EPA aren't bussed over until about 15 minutes prior to the regular opening time. Queues can become chaotic prior to park opening, so ask a team member exactly which turnstiles will be operating. Upon entering, most bolt for the lockers and beach chairs, with all the prime spots around the wave pool usually snapped up within an hour of opening. Long lines for guests trying to rent cabanas also immediately form at the concierge hut closest to the entrance. All slides start the day with "Ride Now" status, but queues can build swiftly, and Virtual Line waits for popular slides may exceed an hour by 11 a.m.

EARLY PARK ADMISSION (EARLY ENTRY)

THE MOST VALUABLE PERK available for free to all Universal on-site resort hotel guests is Early Park Admission (EPA, also sometimes referred to as early entry), which grants entry to The Wizarding World of Harry Potter in IOA or USF 1 hour before the general public. Select attractions at Epic Universe will open early for all on-site guests; details are not yet available. Thirty minutes to an hour of early entry is also offered every morning at the Volcano Bay water park. In addition to guests staying at on-site hotels, guests holding certain designated vacation packages—purchased through Universal Orlando Vacations (☎ 877-801-9720; universalorlandovacations.com) and including both accommodations at an off-site Universal partner hotel *and* theme park admission—are allowed in early. Premier Pass holders can take advantage of EPA at IOA or USF on any morning it is offered, as can Preferred Pass holders on select days (block-outs apply).

Which park you may enter on any particular day, and which attractions will be operating, are at Universal's discretion and will vary with the attendance seasons. The turnstiles to the park(s) participating in early entry will open 60–75 minutes before the official opening time, depending on crowd levels; gates typically open 5 minutes prior to the early entry hour. Both hotel and day guests will be admitted to the park, and each EPA-eligible guest (including children) will need to show their own room key or annual pass to pass beyond the park's entry plaza during the early admission hour. Guests not eligible for EPA will be held in an alternate area to await the official opening time.

During EPA, most attractions, shops, and restaurants in the participating Wizarding World area should be open, along with select attractions outside the Harry Potter area. Attractions offer standby queues
during EPA (along with single-rider lines and child swap, where available), but Express Passes are valid only during regular operating hours.

Most of the feedback we get about EPA at Universal is extremely
positive, like this comment from a multigenerational family of seven:

> *Early entry to the park was a game changer and gave us enough time
> to do everything we wanted to do by noon. This allowed us to go
> back to the hotel and rest. (Best idea ever!)*

However, because EPA crowds are concentrated in The Wizarding
World, it can quickly become overcrowded, particularly on days when
only one park participates. This comment from a Carbondale, Illinois,
reader reflects a common criticism of Universal's early entry:

> *I wasn't a fan of the early admission at Universal. Most of the rides
> are not open, and you are shuttled back to Harry Potter with every-
> one else. The early admission did not seem like a perk.*

EPA at IOA can be especially harried thanks to Hagrid, whose popular Motorbike Adventure attracts hour-long waits within minutes of
opening. Early birds at the head of the queue can be on and off his
adventure well before the park officially opens, but only if the ride
begins running on time; if Hagrid's is having technical difficulties during
early entry and you aren't already within sight of the boarding station,
bail out of line and try again later in the day. Similarly, the Forbidden
Journey ride doesn't open until 30 minutes after early entry begins, and
it typically operates only about 25% of its ride vehicles during EPA,
which makes the queue move maddeningly slow. If the queue is backed
up beyond the talking portraits, you may want to enjoy the other attractions and save Forbidden Journey until afternoon, lest you spend most
of the hour inching through Hogwarts's boarding area.

If you aren't near the front of the pack when the turnstiles open,
but you're eligible for Express access, you may be better off riding participating headliners like VelociCoaster and Gringotts just as EPA ends,
according to this reader from Natick, Massachusetts:

> *The early-entry hour was a bit disappointing because it was soooo
> crowded in Diagon Alley. It was absolute gridlock in the wand shop
> from the moment the park opened. We waited about half an hour
> for Gringotts during that first hour. Then immediately afterward, at
> 9 a.m., when we could use Express, we walked right onto Gringotts.*

Instead, guests with Universal Express Passes may want to use the
early-entry hour to enjoy Ollivanders and the interactive wand effects,
as this mom from Dallas suggests:

> *If your kids want to cast every spell and wander around Hogsmeade
> and Diagon Alley for hours, do that first thing in the morning, espe-
> cially if you have Express Passes to ride the other rides.*

Universal publishes its EPA calendar several months in advance at theugseries.com/uniepa, but procedures seem to change often and arbitrarily with no warning. Ask at your hotel's front desk to find out what opening procedures are in effect during your visit.

IOA-Only Early Park Admission

During most off-peak times, only IOA (and not USF) will admit eligible guests for EPA. IOA-only EPA was in effect during most of 2024. The following attractions should be available during IOA-only EPA:

• Flight of the Hippogriff	• Hogwarts Express (*only if USF is open*)
• Hagrid's Magical Creatures Motorbike Adventure	• Jurassic World VelociCoaster
• Harry Potter and the Forbidden Journey	• Ollivanders Wand Shop

No matter which park offers EPA, the **Hogwarts Express** does not provide a shortcut around the rope-drop rush. The first train from Hogsmeade Station should depart shortly after both parks have opened their gates for the day. The first trainload of guests riding from IOA will enter Diagon Alley a few minutes after the first guests entering through USF's front gates. Likewise, the day's first train riders coming from USF will find themselves standing in line for Hogsmeade's attractions behind the crowd that came straight into IOA. Early-entry guests at IOA are held at the VelociCoaster until the park's official opening time, at which point they may proceed through Jurassic Park to any other attraction.

USF-Only Early Park Admission

During exceedingly rare off-peak periods, EPA may be confined to USF. The following attractions should be available during USF-only EPA:

• Despicable Me Minion Mayhem	• Ollivanders Wand Shop (*seasonally*)
• Harry Potter and the Escape from Gringotts	

The **Hogwarts Express** train from King's Cross Station will not begin running to The Wizarding World of Harry Potter—Hogsmeade in IOA until both parks have opened their gates to guests. The first trainload of guests riding from USF will enter Hogsmeade shortly after the first guests entering through IOA's front gates.

Two-Park Early Park Admission
(Peak Season)

Universal guarantees early admission to only one park per day, but during the busiest times of the year—primarily the week between Christmas and New Year's—Universal offers EPA to The Wizarding Worlds at both USF (Diagon Alley) and IOA (Hogsmeade).

When both parks are scheduled to open at the same time, Hogwarts Express will begin running when EPA starts. The following attractions should be available during peak season early entry:

UNIVERSAL STUDIOS FLORIDA

• Despicable Me Minion Mayhem	• Hogwarts Express (*only if IOA is open*)
• Harry Potter and the Escape from Gringotts	• Ollivanders Wand Shop

ISLANDS OF ADVENTURE

• Flight of the Hippogriff	• Hogwarts Express (*only if USF is open*)
• Hagrid's Magical Creatures Motorbike Adventure	• Jurassic World VelociCoaster
• Harry Potter and the Forbidden Journey	• Ollivanders Wand Shop

Volcano Bay Early Park Admission

In addition to the early entry offered at the theme parks, Volcano Bay also opens 30 minutes–1 hour early every morning for all on-site resort hotel guests and select annual passholders, with many of its attractions operating. The following attractions should be available during early entry:

• Honu & ika Moana Raft Slides	• Ohyah & Ohno Drop Slides
• Ko'okiri Body Plunge	• Waturi Wave Pool
• Krakatau Aqua Coaster	

Pathways around the park's south side don't open until early entry is over, so you must either turn right at the main lagoon or cut through the volcano's caverns to reach the Krakatau Aqua Coaster during EPA. While EPA is a wonderful luxury in The Wizarding World, at the water park it's an absolute necessity. Because the park closes when it reaches capacity, which on busy days may be within hours of the official opening time, early admission is the only way to be guaranteed admittance to Volcano Bay, much less have a chance to enjoy most of the slides.

During the early-entry hour, most, if not all, of the slides are kept at "Ride Now" status, allowing guests to take advantage of the relatively short lines. During peak season, using EPA is just about the only way to experience all the slides in one day without purchasing an Express Pass, as one woman from Stamford, Connecticut, found:

> You are only able to get the "Ride Now" signs if you come for early admission. The moment the park opens to the public, the waiting times for the attractions increase fast. If you don't have early-admission privileges, you may be able to do three or four rides during the day, as waiting times longer then 100 minutes are typical. We came at 7:30 and did the rides we wanted, then left in the afternoon.

Off-site guests who aren't eligible for early entry should still try to get to the parking garage at least 30–60 minutes before official opening, so they can get through security and board the first bus of day guests to the park. If you aren't able to arrive that early, save yourself a lot of frustration and skip Volcano Bay until you can. Alternatively, use a multiday Park-to-Park Ticket to sample some slides in the late afternoon (preferably post-rainstorm) after spending the morning in USF or IOA.

To prevent overcrowding, Universal caps attendance inside Volcano Bay at a maximum of 8,000–10,000 guests, a limit that can be reached within hours after opening during the peak summer period. When the park approaches maximum capacity, Universal first restricts day visitors, then on-site guests. The park usually reopens its gates as guests depart in the afternoon, but no refunds or rain checks are issued if you are refused entry after capacity is reached.

Annual Passholder Early Park Admission

Premier Pass holders may use EPA at USF or IOA on any day of the year, while Preferred Pass holders can enter USF or IOA early on most days (see theugseries.com/apearly for details). Three-Park Premier and Preferred Pass holders can take advantage of EPA at Volcano Bay on those same days without having to stay on-site, and Power and Seasonal Pass holders can sometimes use EPA on select dates during the off-season.

UNIVERSAL EXPRESS

THIS SYSTEM ALLOWS GUESTS to "skip the line" and experience an attraction via a special queue with little or no waiting. Guests approach the marked Universal Express entrance at participating attractions, present their Universal Express Pass to the greeter for scanning, and proceed to ride with a significantly reduced wait—usually 20% or less of the posted standby time, or no more than a 15- to 20-minute wait. If a ride that accepts Universal Express is using a Virtual Line instead of a standby queue, Express users will be able to enter the attraction whenever they like without a prearranged return time. At shows, you can produce your pass for priority seating 15 minutes before showtime, but that's less of a perk because Universal's large theaters rarely fill up.

Though Disney's **Lightning Lane** line-jumping service and Universal Express both let guests bypass the typical waits, there are several major differences between them:

1. While neither Lightning Lane nor Express is free, Universal Premier Pass holders and guests of some Universal resort hotels get special Express Passes at no extra charge (see pages 37 and 59). At the time of this writing, Disney resort guests and annual passholders receive no equivalent perk.

2. Lightning Lane requires you to reserve the rides you want to experience during a given day on the Disney mobile app, and you can book up to three rides at a time. In contrast, Universal Express involves no advance planning—simply visit any eligible operating attraction whenever you choose, no return-time windows required.

3. Access to Lightning Lanes is covered under the $25–$39-per-person daily Lightning Lane Multi Pass fee at most participating attractions, but scheduling the top one or two headliners in each Disney park requires paying a separate Single Pass charge, which may vary with demand. In contrast, nearly all attractions at Universal (with a couple of exceptions, noted on the following page) accept Express across the board, with no extra charges for the headliners.

A reader from Taos, New Mexico, experienced both services and returned with this review:

Universal's Express Pass is far superior to Disney's Lightning Lanes. Yes, it's much more expensive, but the ability to get on most rides at any time and do a favorite ride multiple times with the Unlimited add-on is worth the extra cost, especially during peak periods.

It's worth noting that, while almost all the Express queues are themed, in a few cases—Revenge of the Mummy and Men in Black Alien Attack at USF; Doctor Doom's Fearfall and Skull Island: Reign of Kong at IOA—they sacrifice significant scenic elements and story setups that the regular standby line sees. We recommend experiencing these attractions using the standard queue for your first time, if time permits. Express Pass users at Harry Potter and the Forbidden Journey and Escape from Gringotts rides get to see nearly all of the same scenery as standby guests, and none of the parks' other Express queues skip anything important.

Finally, be aware that **Hagrid's Magical Creatures Motorbike Adventure** wasn't yet accepting Express Passes at press time. **Pteranodon Flyers** at IOA, a slow-loading children's ride with limited capacity, also does not accept Universal Express. Neither do the **Ollivanders** Wandkeeper presentations in the Wizarding Worlds. Pricing and availability for Universal Express at Epic Universe was not yet released; although all rides and indoor shows there are designed to accommodate the service, it may not be offered until months (or longer) after the grand opening. Further, all of the Express types (including the free passes for resort guests) are valid only during regular operating hours and not during separately ticketed events. Separate Express Passes are available at an additional cost for special events such as Rock the Universe and Halloween Horror Nights.

Universal Express and Express Unlimited for Purchase

The basic **Universal Express Pass** allows one person one ride on each attraction at USF or IOA that participates in Universal Express. (Note that for single-use Express, each Hogwarts Express station counts as a separate attraction, so you can ride the train once in each direction.) Holders of the top-of-the-line Premier Pass get free single-use Universal Express access at USF and IOA every day from 4 p.m. until park closing. A **Universal Express Unlimited Pass** grants an unlimited number of rides on any participating attraction. The number of Express Passes is limited each day, and they can sell out. Passes are available up to eight months in advance through Universal's app and at theugseries.com/uorexpress. You'll need to know when you plan on using it, though, because prices vary depending on the date.

Universal Express Pass prices range from $96 for a one-park, single-use pass during slow seasons to $415 for a two-park Unlimited Pass on a holiday. Incidentally, the online calendar of Express Pass prices is a great indicator of how crowded Universal will be on any given day; the more expensive the passes, the more packed the park will be.

STELLA SAYS

BE ON THE LOOKOUT in the official app for a new type of paid single-use Express Pass that Universal might be testing during your visit. You may be able to purchase à la carte–style ride reservations for select attractions (similar to Disney's Individual Lightning Lanes) through the app's attraction detail page by selecting an available time that best suits you; payment is via the credit card stored in your app's wallet. These reservations could save you time waiting in line for your most anticipated ride, without having to dish out the full price for Unlimited Express.

You can also buy Universal Express at the theme parks' ticket windows, just outside the front gates, but it's faster to do so inside the parks—Express Passes are sold at the large stores near the front of each park, from freestanding podiums in the streets, and in most major gift shops. When the park is open late, Universal sometimes sells an unadvertised Express Pass valid after 4 p.m. only for about $60; ask at any Express sales location for details.

Universal Express Unlimited for Resort Guests

Registered guests at Universal's Hard Rock, Portofino Bay, and Royal Pacific resort hotels receive Unlimited Express passes at no extra charge. Simply present your room key card for admission through any Universal Express attraction entrance inside USF or IOA. These Express passes are not valid at Epic Universe or Volcano Bay, and at press time they are not provided to guests at Helios Grand, Sapphire Falls, or any other hotels.

Unlimited Universal Express for eligible resort guests is available at USF and IOA from the moment of check-in until park closing time on the day of checkout. And even though check-in time at Universal's on-site hotels isn't until 4 p.m., guests can retrieve room keys and Express Passes as early in the morning as they are able to arrive, and guests may drop their luggage in the lobby and head to the parks until their room is ready. Therefore, a single night's stay on-site yields two full days of Universal Express access. This perk far surpasses any benefit accorded to guests of Disney resorts; combined with the hour of Early Park Admission to The Wizarding World, it helps make touring Universal Orlando a remarkably low-stress experience for on-site guests, even during peak attendance periods.

unofficial **TIP**
Express Passes for Universal resort guests are not valid at Volcano Bay or during Halloween Horror Nights.

A father from Snellville, Georgia, did the math and discovered that it was cheaper for his family to stay at a Universal resort than buy Universal Express:

The benefits of staying on-property are worth it, with early entry to The Wizarding World and Express Unlimited privileges at both parks. We got a room at the Royal Pacific Resort for $349 on a Saturday night, which allowed us to use Universal Express Saturday and Sunday. The room cost $43.63 per person per day, while an [à la *carte] Express Pass this same weekend would have cost $56 per person per day, and we still would have had to pay for a hotel.*

Universal Express at Volcano Bay

Universal Express Passes valid at Volcano Bay are sold on select days inside the park at the concierge stands or in advance online. Volcano Bay's basic Universal Express Passes cost $21–$138 (depending on the season). These are valid for one ride each on select slides, which include the Krakatau Aqua Coaster and the Honu and ika Moana slides but exclude the Kala and Tai Nui body slides, Ohyah and Ohno drop slides, and Ko'okiri Body Plunge. A **1-Day Universal Express Plus Pass** costs $53–$181 for a single trip down every slide in the park; no unlimited usage Express option is available. Express allows you to act as if participating attractions say "Ride Now," but even though you won't need a TapuTapu return time, you'll still experience some waiting before your slide.

Is Universal Express Worth It?

No matter when you use it, Universal Express will significantly reduce the amount of time you spend waiting in queues at Universal Orlando. But whether or not that time saving is worth it depends on the season you visit, hours of park operation, and crowd levels.

During busy periods, Universal Express users should wait no more than 15–20 minutes for a ride, even when the standby wait is well over an hour. That's a significant time savings and may make the difference between seeing all your favorite headliners in a single day or going home disappointed.

During slow periods, Express users should experience little to no wait at most attractions and can practically walk on to most rides. However, the standby waits will typically top out between 15 and 30 minutes at these times, making the total minutes saved with Express much less impressive.

Universal Express is *not* mandatory for enjoying the parks (as we've heard some claim), just so long as you show up bright and early with a well-organized agenda. If you want to sleep in and arrive at a park after opening, Express is an effective, albeit expensive, way to avoid long lines at the headliner attractions, especially during holidays and busy times. If, however, you arrive at least 30 minutes before park opening and you use our touring plans (see pages 395–416), you should experience the lowest possible waits.

If you aren't eligible for free Express Passes, we encourage you to try the touring plans first, but if waits for rides become intolerable, you can always buy Express in the parks (provided they haven't sold out, an infrequent occurrence).

A New York mom questioned the value of the investment:

Universal Express was neither necessary nor consistently effective. By arriving at park opening, we were able to see many attractions right away without needing the passes at all. The passes helped on about *three attractions between the two parks—a poor return for an investment of $156, but it was like life insurance: good to have just in case.*

On the other hand, this Kansas City family thought very highly of the Express Unlimited Passes included in their Royal Pacific stay:

The free Express Pass you get by staying at one of the top resorts is a lifesaver. We never waited in line more than 15 minutes, and it was usually closer to 5. For my roller coaster–loving family, this was great. We didn't have a scheduled time to ride anything like at Disney, so we could stray from our plan and re-ride The Incredible Hulk Coaster or Hollywood Rip Ride Rockit over and over again.

And this mom from Massachusetts agreed:

Universal Express did not disappoint. We walked on to every ride we wanted to, and we could easily and immediately re-ride our faves with no wait. I would definitely either stay at Royal Pacific or spring for Universal Express on my next trip. It was wonderful to have that flexibility with our kids. We could wait to ride Gringotts the first day, until our 8-year-old had worked up the nerve. Then we could spontaneously ride again—right away with no wait!

Finally, you'll want to devise a convenient way to keep track of your pass, as this Endicott, New York, reader suggests:

The paper Express Passes were not nearly as user friendly as Disney's MagicBands. The lanyard was a lifesaver, or we surely would have lost something.

Universal will happily sell you a souvenir lanyard with a plastic pouch, so you can proudly wear your admission around your neck for all to see. Universal's lanyards start at around $14 for a basic one and come in a variety of character themes, including the colors of each Hogwarts house, for $16; the ticket pouch costs an extra $9–$11, depending on the style. You can also pick up equally usable and far cheaper (though less magical) versions at your local office supply store.

How Universal Express Affects Crowd Conditions at Attractions

Guests using Universal Express don't have to modify their touring behavior in any way; simply visit any attraction at will and enjoy the shorter waits. However, the Express effect can be somewhat less salutatory for guests without Express. The standby and Express queues at each attraction meet up shortly before the boarding area, and attendants are supposed to merge them so that Express guests wait 15 minutes or less, without the standby guests' wait being inflated beyond the estimate posted outside.

Typically, this means about half of each ride's capacity is dedicated to Express guests, which ordinarily keeps both queues flowing smoothly. The catch is that, because Universal Express guests (unlike users of Disney's Lightning Lane) don't schedule ride times in advance, the number of them waiting in a queue at any given time is highly variable and unpredictable, as one Highlands Ranch, Colorado, reader pointed out:

> *If everyone holding an Express Pass decides to use it at the same time on the same ride, wait times can get very long, making the pass seem less of a bargain.*

As a result, an unexpected backlog of Express guests—either because of a sudden influx of pass users or a temporary technical breakdown that pauses the line—can force Universal to increase the ratio of Express to standby, slowing non-Express guests' progress to a crawl.

While that's great news for Universal Express users, this can dramatically affect crowd movement (and touring-plan usage) for those without it, as a woman from Yorktown, Virginia, writes:

> *People in the Express line were let in at a rate of about 10 to 1 over the regular-line folks. This created bottlenecks and long waits for people who didn't have the Express privilege.*

If you encounter this situation while waiting standby, simply grit your teeth and take some deep yoga breaths; the situation normally clears up quickly, and your total wait should still be approximately as originally advertised. And if you can't beat 'em, join 'em, like this reader from Doylestown, Pennsylvania:

> *On the third day we finally bought Express Passes because we were miserable standing in lines for so long and watching Express Pass holders pass us again and again and again. It made a huge difference, and next time, we will absolutely stay on-site for the early admission hours and Express Pass benefits.*

VIRTUAL LINES

UNIVERSAL HAS INTRODUCED another line-skipping service, but unlike the aforementioned Express options, Virtual Line is completely free for all park guests, regardless of hotel or ticket type. With Virtual Lines guests may claim time slots for certain rides on a first-come, first-served basis and can experience the attraction with a minimal wait after returning during their assigned hour. The service is mandatory for most slides at **Volcano Bay,** where it's tied to the **TapuTapu** wristbands; see page 292 for a detailed explanation. Virtual Line has also been implemented in the past at Race Through New York Starring Jimmy Fallon, Fast & Furious: Supercharged, and Revenge of the Mummy in USF and at Hagrid's Magical Creatures Motorbike Adventure and Pteranodon Flyers in IOA, but it was no longer offered for any of those attractions at press time. Virtual Line is also sometimes used during special events, such as to select volunteer float riders for the Mardi Gras parade, and it could potentially be used to control access to attractions, restaurants, or entire lands inside Epic Universe.

The method and usefulness of Virtual Lines vary depending on the attraction; log into the Universal smartphone app and check the main menu to see if the service is being offered during your visit. If it is available, you should be able to select the number of guests in your party and receive a confirmation screen displaying a QR code with a return time. When your Virtual Line time arrives, you'll have 30 minutes to proceed to the attraction with your QR code in hand. There may be an initial queue outside the ride for guests needing mandatory lockers; once past the locker logjam, you may still wait 20 minutes or more before boarding the attraction.

The Virtual Line system is activated only after the park officially opens for the day, so Early Park Admission visitors can go directly to the standby queue. Additional return times are released periodically throughout the day, so if you try to get in the Virtual Line and receive a message that it's "temporarily at capacity," keep refreshing the app or check back a little later. On less-busy days, Virtual Line passes will not be available until standby wait times build later in the day, if at all. You don't need to be inside a theme park to join a Virtual Line, but your phone's GPS must register that you are inside the geofence surrounding Universal's property. That means you can access the Virtual Line system from the parking garage, CityWalk, or even your on-site hotel room, but not from off-site hotels (except a few nearby properties along Major Boulevard) or your home.

Finally, if something goes wrong and your ride is unavailable when your return time arrives—due to technical difficulties, weather delays, or the like—your Virtual Line pass should automatically convert to a free one-time-use Express Pass, valid anytime until the end of that operating day at the original attraction (assuming it starts running again) or select other rides.

SINGLE-RIDER LINES

ANOTHER TIME-SAVING OPTION available to all Universal Orlando guests without extra charge is the single-rider (or singles) line. Several attractions at USF, IOA, and EU have this special line for guests traveling alone, or at least willing to be temporarily separated from their companions. Single riders wait in a separate queue and are slipped into vacant seats left by large groups without (theoretically) impacting the other lines. Singles lines are a useful option for those unable or unwilling to cough up the dough for Universal Express Passes, as this reader from Portland, Connecticut, points out:

unofficial **TIP**
Hagrid's Magical Creatures Motorbike Adventure offers a single-rider entrance, but it rarely saves much time.

> *Single-rider lines are the key to enjoying the parks. While you may miss some of the theming of the queue areas, it's a terrific trade-off to saving 45 minutes per ride. If on a budget, it's a great alternative to the Universal Express Pass granted to guests of the deluxe resorts.*

The singles line is often just as fast as the Express line, especially at attractions that seat three or four guests per row. However, because the speed of the singles line is highly dependent on the flow of odd-numbered parties through the other queues, the wait time can be extremely unpredictable on rides with two-by-two seating. At some times we've walked onto Forbidden Journey via the singles line when the standby wait time was more than an hour; at others we've stood longer in Hagrid's Magical Creatures Motorbike Adventure's singles line than the posted standby wait.

Single-rider lines open at the discretion of the ride attendants and may temporarily close if crowds are very light (because they aren't needed) or very heavy (when the singles queue becomes filled to capacity). In the latter case, try hanging around the entrance for 15 or 20 minutes, which is usually how long it takes for the singles line to shrink enough to be reopened.

Also note that some queues (particularly those of Forbidden Journey and Escape from Gringotts) are attractions in themselves and should be experienced during your first ride. Even so, we generally recommend using the singles line whenever possible—it will decrease your overall wait and leave more time for repeat rides or just ambling around the parks.

Singles lines are usually available at the following attractions:

UNIVERSAL STUDIOS FLORIDA

• Fast & Furious: Supercharged	• Men in Black Alien Attack
• Harry Potter and the Escape from Gringotts	• Revenge of the Mummy
• Hollywood Rip Ride Rockit	• Transformers: The Ride–3D

ISLANDS OF ADVENTURE

• The Amazing Adventures of Spider-Man	• The Incredible Hulk Coaster
• Doctor Doom's Fearfall	• Jurassic Park River Adventure
• Hagrid's Magical Creatures Motorbike Adventure	• Jurassic World VelociCoaster
• Harry Potter and the Forbidden Journey	• Skull Island: Reign of Kong

UNIVERSAL EPIC UNIVERSE

• Curse of the Werewolf	• Mine-Cart Madness
• Harry Potter and the Battle at the Ministry	• Monsters Unchained: The Frankenstein Experiment
• Mario Kart: Bowser's Challenge	• Stardust Racers

In addition, Universal intermittently offers single-rider access at **Dudley Do-Right's Ripsaw Falls** in IOA and at **The Simpsons Ride** and **E.T. Adventure** in USF.

VIP TOURS

FOR THE ULTIMATE no-expenses-spared Universal Orlando experience, book a VIP tour of one or both parks. VIP guests are given the red-carpet treatment at both parks and never have to worry about waiting in line. And don't worry if you aren't a genuine VIP—or even a social media pseudo-celebrity—because at Universal, anyone can be treated like the rich and famous . . . but it'll cost you.

Universal offers two types of VIP tours: **nonexclusive** and **private.** On nonexclusive tours, your party of up to 6 guests will be paired with other guests to form a group of up to 12. Nonexclusive tours depart hourly starting at 8:30 a.m. and last 5–7 hours. Your guide will whisk you onto a minimum of 8–10 attractions based on group consensus. On a nonexclusive tour, you're at Universal's mercy as to whom you might be paired up with, but you can indicate your interests to your guide upon arrival: if, say, you're a party of thrill-seeking adults and you're matched with a family of small children, ask if you can swap before your group gets moving.

Private tours give you free rein to set your start time and make your own itinerary because the guide is dedicated to only your party for a full 8 hours. Private tours are mandatory if your party has seven or more members. You can even ride your favorite ride over and over all day, if you like.

Either way, your VIP experience begins with free valet parking and a complimentary hot buffet breakfast in USF's Cafe La Bamba (for tours starting before 11 a.m.). In addition to backdooring you into rides—bypassing even the Universal Express queues—and getting you reserved seating at shows, VIP tour guides are fonts of trivia about the history and operations of the parks and can even grant

unofficial **TIP**
At the time of this writing, the only way to cut the line at Hagrid's Magical Creatures Motorbike Adventure is on a VIP tour.

backstage access to see how some of the magic is done, like a glimpse underneath Revenge of the Mummy's ride track or inside Transformer's high-tech control booth.

Nonexclusive two-park VIP tours include a complimentary quick-service midday meal, while private VIP tour guests receive two full-service meals inside the theme parks or at CityWalk, along with a three-day My Universal Photos package (valid starting on their first tour day). At the end of the tour, your souvenir VIP lanyard serves as an Express Unlimited Pass for the rest of the day and offers discounts on food and merchandise.

Perhaps most important, VIP tours are the quickest way to skip the queues at the headlining Harry Potter attractions during peak times, when even the Express entrances can be overwhelmed; during the height of Diagon Alley's opening summer, when guests were waiting more than 4 hours just for Gringotts, Bob and Len were able to experience everything in both Wizarding Worlds (including lunch and ice cream) plus other park highlights in a little more than 5 hours.

Of course, this kind of star treatment doesn't come cheap. A 7-hour one-day nonexclusive tour of both parks starts at $277 and is typically $300–$450. However, during peak pricing times (July and the weeks around Christmas and Easter), that rate jumps as high as $554. Five-hour tours of a single park are sometimes available, but they don't include lunch and only cost $11–$21 less than the two-park tours.

Private-tour pricing approaches "if you have to ask, you can't afford it" territory, starting at $4,150 for a day in both parks; one-park exclusive tours are available during off-peak periods on special request, but you will only save a couple hundred dollars off the two-park price. That flat rate is good for one to five guests; additional guests (up to a total of 10) cost another $425 each for a two-park tour. During peak times (Christmas and spring break), those base prices increase to $6,388, plus $612 for each additional guest. Finally, if you splurge on the ultimate two-day, two-park private tour, you'll be poorer by $7,700 ($11,300 during peak periods).

Before you break out your credit card, there's one final catch: the aforementioned prices are on top of admission, which is required and not included with any VIP tour.

Whether the VIP tours are worth it depends largely on your net worth and your tolerance for any type of wait. Having taken them many times over the years, we can say that the experience is a dream come true for theme park junkies (who will get their money's worth in insider info alone), as well as anyone allergic to rubbing elbows with unwashed hordes. If you were already planning to pony up for Express Unlimited Passes, the extra couple hundred per person (depending on the season) could seem a bargain in the heat of summer. For most visitors, a stay at a luxury on-site hotel (that includes free Express Unlimited) is probably a more economical investment, but no one we know who has taken a VIP tour has regretted it, even if it may forever ruin the regular park-going experience for you.

Nonexclusive tours can be booked online through an interactive calendar with availability and pricing at theugseries.com/univip, but private tours must be reserved by phone (☎ 866-346-9350). In either case, book early, because VIP tours can fill up quickly at busier times.

Note that all of the previously mentioned tours are offered only during regular daytime operating hours. Different VIP tours with their own pricing may be available during separately ticketed special events such as Halloween Horror Nights (see page 232).

FREE BEHIND-THE-SCENES TOURS

IF YOU WANT TO FEEL LIKE A VIP BUT CAN'T AFFORD THE FARE, Universal generously offers unpublicized free backstage tours at several attractions to any guest who inquires (subject to staff availability). Simply ask a greeter outside the attraction if a tour is available; your best odds are during mid-morning (around 10 a.m.) or in late afternoon (around 4 p.m.) on days of moderate attendance. For details on these "secret" behind-the-scenes experiences, read the following attraction descriptions in Part Six (for USF) and Part Seven (for IOA):

UNIVERSAL STUDIOS FLORIDA FREE TOURS	ISLANDS OF ADVENTURE FREE TOURS
Fast & Furious: Supercharged garage tour	Doctor Doom's Fearfall villains tour
Harry Potter and the Escape from Gringotts bank tour	Harry Potter and the Forbidden Journey castle tour
Men in Black Alien Attack immigration tour	The Incredible Hulk Coaster gamma tour
Race Through New York Starring Jimmy Fallon studio tour	Jurassic Park Discovery Center nursery tour
Revenge of the Mummy production tour	Jurassic World VelociCoaster facilities tour
	Skull Island: Reign of Kong temple tour

TECHNICAL REHEARSALS

TECHNICAL REHEARSALS, or soft openings as they are commonly called, are when Universal uses its paying guests as guinea pigs and allows them to preview an attraction that isn't yet ready for prime time. Technical rehearsals may be held anywhere from a few weeks to a few days before a new ride officially opens, but they are never preannounced or guaranteed; frontline employees may be instructed to deny that any opening is possible until the moment they open the queue. In exchange for bragging rights that they were the first inside a hot new attraction, technical rehearsal participants must accept the possibility of waiting a long time without ever getting to ride, as the soft opening may end at any moment.

For theme park aficionados who live in the area, technical rehearsals can be both a blessing and a curse. Some folks stood in front of Diagon Alley for more than 30 consecutive days waiting for a soft opening, and even then the Gringotts ride never had a public preview before grand opening. Similar scenes occurred at IOA in the spring of 2019 before Hagrid's Magical Creatures Motorbike Adventure opened, as fans waited fruitlessly for days, fueled by rumors on social media. On the other hand, the Jurassic World VelociCoaster and Villain-Con Minion Blast both hosted several weeks of all-day technical rehearsals, giving tens of thousands a chance to ride long before opening day. Unless you're a local with lots of time on your hands, or you're on an extended vacation and obsessed with a particular about-to-open attraction, avoid spending your valuable time waiting for a ride that may or may not open. Instead, enjoy everything else the parks have to offer, and keep your ears open—and an eye on the Unofficial Guides social media feeds (@theunofficialguides)—just in case.

UNIVERSAL ORLANDO INSIDER HACKS

WANT TO CRUISE THROUGH the Universal Orlando Resort like a local instead of bumbling about like the typical tourist? Then take advantage of these insider tips, tricks, and hacks to make your vacation friction-free:

- Save time and money by **buying tickets in advance online** instead of at the gate (see page 38).

- Keep your park admission and hotel key card on a **lanyard** around your neck instead of in your pocket, especially if you'll be pulling it out frequently for Universal Express.

- Arrive after 6 p.m. or see a matinee movie to get **free self-parking** (see page 134).

- Download the Universal mobile app in advance, and use its **Mobile Ordering** feature where available instead of standing in line at a quick-service dining location (see page 310).

- **Child swap** lets parents experience thrill rides without splitting up the family or waiting in line twice (see page 187).

- If you don't mind sitting separately from your party, the **single-rider line** is a huge time-saver (see page 63).

- Ask about **free backstage tours** at select theme park attractions (see page 66).

- Save on snacks with **refillable cups and popcorn buckets** (see page 313).

- If you're interested in buying on-ride pictures, consider investing in a **My Universal Photos** package (see page 152).

- Always ask about available **food and merchandise discounts** if you have an annual pass (see pages 35–37).

- Visit IOA's **private UAOP lounge** for annual passholders (see page 35) or USF's **Visa cardholder lounge** (see page 140).

QUIET SPOTS AROUND UNIVERSAL ORLANDO

UNLIKE DISNEY'S PARKS, which are bathed in soothing background music that is carefully curated to create a relaxing ambience, Universal insists on blasting high-energy soundtracks at full volume through every available speaker. When you're lucky, you'll only be exposed to one stirring orchestral score at a time; if you linger too long in spots where competing sound systems overlap, you could quickly lose your sanity. That's not to mention the attractions themselves, which frequently feature explosions and other earsplitting sound effects played at decibel levels that would make Spinal Tap shudder.

Fortunately, there are at least a few spots in each park where you can find a respite from the racket. At Universal Studios Florida, take a rest on the artificial lawn at Music Plaza, in Gramercy Park and Sting Alley in the New York section, at waterfront seating in front of Diagon Alley's London facade and behind Springfield's Duff Gardens, in the courtyard of the closed *Fear Factor Live* stadium, and (during daytime) in the Central Park viewing area for the lagoon show. In Islands of Adventure, escape to the lagoon-side plaza at the far end of Port of Entry, Captain America Diner's rear patio in Marvel Super Hero Island, the walkways surrounding Me Ship, The Olive in Toon Lagoon, the outdoor seating behind Hogsmeade's Three Broomsticks, the pathways around Mythos Restaurant in The Lost Continent, and Sneech Beech in Seuss Landing. Epic Universe puts the "park" back in theme park, with lush landscaping and inviting benches throughout the expansive hub. Volcano Bay has quiet areas in the back corners beside Taniwha Tubes and Honu ika Moana; each of the resort hotels has at least one garden area and a cozy corner off the main lobby; and the landscaped walking paths linking the entire resort are serene outside the hours around park opening and closing.

QUITTING TIME

BECAUSE THE DAY PARKING for the original Universal theme parks and the CityWalk shopping, dining, and entertainment complex is consolidated in the same parking structures, chaos can ensue on days when both parks close at the same time, resulting in an epic flood of humanity heading to the garages.

An Orlando woman, obviously very perturbed, comments:

> Both Universal Studios and Islands of Adventure share the same parking lot. IT MAKES NO SENSE for the two theme parks to close at the same time. I cannot even explain the amount of people. It was insane at closing (and other people were coming IN to go to City-Walk, so it was SUCH a big mess)!

If you're unlucky enough to find yourself in such a situation, we suggest taking a side trip to CityWalk and sitting out the stampede with a snack or drink. If you haven't yet exited the park, you can try lingering inside the gates as long as possible, browsing the shops that remain open past closing time. Security guards will eventually gently shoo you out, but not until most of the parking mess has cleared. Epic Universe may allow guests to hang out in the Celestial Park hub after the themed lands close, enjoying the full-service restaurants and bars found there, following the nightly fountain show.

PART 2

ACCOMMODATIONS

The BASIC CONSIDERATIONS

WHILE YOU'LL SURELY HAVE FUN inside Universal's parks wherever you spend the night, your choice of hotel is critical to the overall success of your vacation. Visitors to Universal face the basic question of whether to stay inside the resort—where room rates range from around $115 on an off-season weeknight at a Value Inns and Suites resort to more than $700 per night for a peak-season Signature Collection property—or outside Universal, where rooms are as low as $80 a night. Affordability and easier access to non-Universal attractions must be weighed against the convenience and comfort of staying on property.

Universal Orlando currently operates eight on-site resorts for a total of 9,000 rooms. Former NBCUniversal CEO Stephen Burke said the resort could someday support up to 20,000 rooms, and **Epic Universe** will open with the 500-room Helios Grand hotel attached to the rear of the new theme park's central hub, as well as a pair of 750-room hotels— the Stella Nova and Terra Luna Resorts—right across the street from its main entrance, bringing Universal's total inventory up to 11,000 rooms.

Compared with the more than 30,000 rooms Walt Disney World has spread across nearly 30 hotels, your choice of an on-site hotel at Universal is a lot simpler, but you may find limited room availability during busy times. On the other hand, Universal's hotels—all operated by the highly regarded **Loews** chain—boast service and amenities equal to or better than the competition, and usually at a lower cost. Universal's upscale properties are often priced like Disney's Moderates, and its value-priced resorts outshine Disney's All-Star and Pop Century hotels. You should also consider the superior benefits granted to Universal's on-site guests, a couple of which can make the difference between a marvelous vacation and a miserable one.

Whether you decide to stay on-site or off, this chapter will help you get a grip on the multitude of lodging options in the Universal Orlando area and find the property that fits your family's needs.

THE TAX MAN COMETH

SALES AND LODGING TAXES can add a chunk of change to the cost of your hotel room. Cumulative tax in Orange County, which includes the Universal Orlando area and International Drive, is 12.5% on nightly hotel rates and in-room amenities like rollaways and microwaves. A 6.5% tax is applied to parking, dining, and other incidentals. Room rates listed in this chapter are before taxes; all other prices are tax inclusive, unless otherwise noted.

BENEFITS OF STAYING ON-SITE AT UNIVERSAL ORLANDO

UNIVERSAL OFFERS PERKS to get park visitors into its hotels. All guests at any Universal Orlando Resort on-site hotel can take advantage of the following:

- **Early Park Admission to The Wizarding Worlds and Volcano Bay** up to 1 hour before the public (see page 53)
- **The ability to charge in-park purchases** to your room key
- **Free package delivery to your room** for items purchased in the parks
- **Free transportation to the parks and CityWalk,** plus free scheduled transportation to SeaWorld and Aquatica (see page 131)
- **Pool-hopping privileges** to use any hotel's recreational facilities (excluding Endless Summer Resort)
- **Free Wi-Fi in all hotel rooms and public areas** (faster speeds available for a fee)

In addition, every guest staying at Portofino Bay, Hard Rock, or Royal Pacific (but not Helios Grand at press time) receives the following benefits:

- **Free Universal Express Unlimited Passes** for both USF and IOA (see page 59)
- **Priority seating at select restaurants** in the parks and CityWalk

All these benefits are available from the moment you arrive until midnight on the day you check out. Even if your room won't be ready until the afternoon, you can register at your hotel as early in the morning as you like, leaving your bags and retrieving your Express Passes (if eligible) in time for the Early Park Admission hour. Then linger at the resort after your checkout time, taking advantage of your pool privileges until late in the evening.

The most valuable of these perks is admission to The Wizarding World of Harry Potter and Volcano Bay up to 1 hour before the general public each morning, along with the Universal Express Unlimited Passes for guests of select Signature Collection hotels. It's hard to put a dollar value on the Early Park Admission, but two-park Universal Express Unlimited Passes are sold to the general public for $144–$415 per day, per person, including tax, depending on the time of year you visit. Universal says the pass is "an average value of $199.99 (plus tax) per person, per day," which works out to $852 per day for a family of four. One night at Universal's Royal Pacific hotel costs anywhere from

$536 to $987, including tax, depending on the season. If you were planning on staying at a comparable off-site deluxe hotel anyway, staying at the Royal Pacific gets your family two days of Universal Express Unlimited at no additional cost. During busy season, this can be a huge boon for parties of four or five, though be aware that an additional $62-per-night fee (taxes included) applies to each adult beyond the first two staying in the room at hotels offering free Express. If you are traveling solo or as a couple, or are visiting at a slow time of year, calculate the cost of staying at one of the cheaper hotels and buying Express Passes on arrival if they turn out to be necessary.

Having stayed at each of Universal's hotels, we think a sometimes-overlooked benefit is the ability to walk to the parks from your hotel. And it's not just the convenience—the walkways are pretty and almost serene at night, if you can ignore the roars from The Incredible Hulk Coaster. This Dallas-area family found foot accessibility to the parks to be Universal's biggest advantage over Walt Disney World's on-site resort hotels:

> *The simple convenience of being able to walk everywhere whenever you wanted was definitely worth the expense. Disney's shuttle and parking systems are extensive. We tried the bus, but it gets bogged down by the stops. Driving your own vehicle meant parking and then using a tram to get to the gate. You can't hop from park to park quickly. At Universal, with one parking area, everything was easily and quickly reachable. The girls could enjoy the park early (with little wait time), walk back to the hotel to nap, and then go back to the park or CityWalk. They felt very grown up being on their own without us adults to slow them down. This was inconvenient at Disney due to the transport time.*

Combine the resorts' walkability with Express Unlimited access from the luxury hotels, and the result is the perfect recipe for rejuvenation, according to this reader from San Antonio, Texas:

> *I can't remember how long it's been since we had such a relaxing vacation. That's right—I said it was relaxing, and I credit the hotel location and Express Pass. We got up whenever we wanted and went to whatever park we wanted. It was a 5-minute walk to the front gates of USF. We got tired, we took a nap. We felt too hot, we took a dip in the pool. It was heavenly.*

UNIVERSAL ORLANDO RESORT HOTELS 101

UNIVERSAL CURRENTLY HAS EIGHT RESORT HOTELS, with three more opening soon. The 750-room **Portofino Bay Hotel** is a gorgeous property set on an artificial bay and themed like an Italian coastal town. The 650-room **Hard Rock Hotel** is an ultracool "Hotel California" replica, and the 1,000-room, Polynesian-themed **Royal Pacific**

Resort is sumptuously decorated and richly appointed. All three of the aforementioned hotels are on the pricey side. The retro-style **Cabana Bay Beach Resort,** Universal's largest hotel, has 2,200 moderately priced rooms, plus a bowling alley and lazy river not seen at comparable Disney resorts. The Caribbean-styled **Sapphire Falls Resort** offers 1,000 rooms priced between Royal Pacific and the **Aventura Hotel,** a 600-room property that sits next to Sapphire Falls and across from the similarly priced Cabana Bay; Aventura is a Miami-style modern highrise with a Y-shaped glass tower and rooftop lounge. **Endless Summer Resort,** Universal's first value-priced option, consists of the 750-room **Surfside Inn and Suites** and the 2,050-room **Dockside Inn and Suites** and resides just down the road from the rest of the resort. The upscale 500-room **Helios Grand Hotel** abuts the rear of Epic Universe, and the **Stella Nova and Terra Luna Resorts** (each with 750 moderately priced rooms) sit across the street; all three open in 2025.

Before you make any decisions, understand these basics regarding Universal Orlando Resort hotels.

UNIVERSAL ORLANDO RESORT HOTEL POLICIES

Resort Classifications

Universal's hotels fall into three categories. The original campus's three most expensive on-site hotels—**Portofino Bay Resort, Hard Rock Hotel,** and **Royal Pacific Resort**—are called **Signature Collection resorts,** and their perks include Universal Express Unlimited at USF and IOA, priority restaurant seating, and water taxi transportation to CityWalk. **Sapphire Falls Resort** is also labeled a **Signature Collection resort;** it's a AAA Four Diamond–awarded hotel, just like the aforementioned properties, and it offers water taxi service but lacks free Universal Express and priority restaurant seating. Likewise, the luxurious new **Helios Grand Hotel** is also part of the Signature Collection, despite not including free Express or priority seating at press time. However, it does offer the unprecedented perk of direct pedestrian access into Epic Universe.

Stella Nova Resort, Terra Luna Resort, and the **Aventura Hotel** represent the **Prime Value hotels. Cabana Bay Beach Resort** and **Endless Summer Resort** are designated as **Value Inns and Suites.** Cabana Bay and Aventura have bus and pedestrian access to the attractions (including Volcano Bay), but neither is connected to the water taxi system. Endless Summer, Terra Luna, and Stella Nova (which has a walking path to Epic Universe) are all serviced by buses. Regardless of classification, all on-site Universal guests enjoy amenities that surpass any other value-priced hotels in the area.

Seasonal Rates

Universal uses so many adjectives—*Value, Regular, Summer, Holiday,* and *Peak*—to describe its seasonal calendar that it's hard to keep up. Plus, Universal also changes the price of its hotel rooms with the day of the week, charging more for the same room on Friday and Saturday nights. Each Universal hotel profile (see pages 83–101) includes the lowest rack (nondiscounted) rate (Value season) and the highest rack rate (Holiday season). These prices are for a weeknight stay in a basic room with a standard view, usually of a "garden" or parking lot; upgrades to pool or bay views start at $25–$50. Rates include a maximum of two adults per room, plus any children up to the room's capacity; additional adults each incur a $62-per-night surcharge (taxes included) at Signature Collection hotels, $23 at Prime Value, and $17 at Value Inns and Suites. Rack rates do not include taxes or parking, but no hidden resort fees are tacked on at Universal's hotels.

unofficial **TIP**
Newly purchased annual passes may be used to secure hotel discounts even before they are first activated at the park gates, as long as you show them upon checkout.

Discounts

Universal hotel rack rates are just the starting point, and most clever visitors can save substantially on their stay with a little legwork because Universal frequently offers sizable percentage-off deals to fill its rooms.

Start by reviewing the resort discount information in Part One (see page 41); then visit universalorlando.com and click on "Places to Stay," then "Special Offers" to view the latest deals. Next, go to theugseries.com/uorhotel aph (for annual passholders) or theugseries.com/uorhotelflo (for Florida residents) and select your travel dates to see available discounts. You don't have to prove eligibility for these discounts, but you will need to show appropriate identification upon check-in.

If you're staying multiple nights, Universal's **Stay More, Save More** pricing structure kicks in. Stays at any on-site hotel room of four to seven nights save 10%–25% during Holiday, Peak, and Summer seasons, and stays of three to seven nights save 10%–30% during Regular and Value seasons.

Making Reservations

The easiest way to book a room at Universal Orlando is online through universalorlando.com, or by phone at ☎ 888-273-1311. If you are attending a meeting or event, call ☎ 866-360-7395 for your group block room.

Cancellations

A credit card deposit equal to one night's room rate (plus tax) is required when booking. Cancellations made six or more days prior to check-in receive a full refund. Cancellations five or fewer days before check-in forfeit the deposit. However, Universal's severe-weather cancellation policy says that if you are unable to travel to Orlando due to an "active named storm impacting your travel," you can reschedule your vacation or receive a full refund. This applies only for rooms, park tickets, or vacation packages booked directly with Loews and Universal; if you use a third-party reseller, you'll need to check its cancellation policy. Guests purchasing packages directly from **Universal Vacations** may cancel for any reason with optional travel protection (see page 103).

Check-In and Checkout

Check-in time at all Universal hotels is 4 p.m., and checkout is 11 a.m.; if you ask nicely, you can usually get a noon checkout for free. Remember that all on-site hotel benefits—including Express Unlimited Passes (for guests of select Signature Collection hotels) and Early Park Admission—begin the first morning of your stay and last until midnight after you check out. So even if you can't get into your room, you can preregister as early as you like, leave your luggage, grab your Express Passes (at the participating hotels), and hit the parks at rope drop.

Lines to check in during midafternoon can be long, especially at Cabana Bay. If possible, fill out the online pre-check-in form in advance to speed the process once you arrive, and check in early (you can leave your bags at the luggage stand and receive a text when your room is ready) or late. Checkout can be done at the front desk, through the interactive TV, or via express with your bill emailed to you.

Note that upon checking in, you'll be asked to preauthorize your credit card for $200 per day, so you can use your hotel room key for charges around the resort. You may request to change this authorization amount, or you may decline it entirely if you don't wish to make charges to your room account.

Age Requirements

The minimum age to book a hotel room at Universal Orlando is 21, and valid ID is required at check-in. At least one guest staying in the room must be age 21 or older.

Accessibility

All Universal Orlando hotels have wheelchair-accessible public areas and offer designated accessible rooms for mobility-, sight-, and/or hearing-impaired guests. Accessibility features include 36-inch-wide entry doors, peepholes at 3½ feet from the floor, closets with rods at 48 inches high, toilets with hand bar, and roll-in shower stalls or combination shower/tubs with adjustable showerheads. Sight- and hearing-impaired features include Braille room numbers, closed-captioned TVs, smoke detectors with lights, and Hearing-Impaired Kits, including a TDD-relay service that may be used in any guest room. CPAP users can purchase distilled water from the front desk for about $5 per gallon.

Pets

Loews "loves pets" and is one of the few luxury chains to allow cats and dogs in its rooms. It even has a special (and expensive) room service menu for four-legged guests. There are some restrictions, starting with a $100 flat fee per stay for a maximum of two pets per guest room. Guests will be assigned a pet-friendly room category on arrival, which includes garden- and bay-view rooms at the Portofino Bay and standard rooms at the Royal Pacific and Sapphire Falls. Club rooms don't participate in the pet program, nor do any of the Prime Value or Value Inns and Suites properties, such as Cabana Bay Beach Resort, Aventura Hotel, Stella Nova Resort, Terra Luna Resort, and Endless Summer Resort.

The Pets Unleashed program at Hard Rock Hotel also costs $100 for stays of up to one week and includes a "sWAG bag" with a shirt for your pet and customized "pet tracks" Spotify playlists. A percentage of the pet fee is donated to local animal shelters. There is a maximum of two pets (up to 50 pounds total) per guest room. Hard Rock's pet program gets two paws up (and a wagging tail) from Derek Burgan's pup Bacini.

Dogs may be walked only in designated areas and are prohibited in the pool/lounge and restaurant areas. No pets (except properly trained service animals) are allowed into CityWalk or the theme parks, and Universal's kennel facilities are permanently closed. Arrangements must be made with housekeeping for room cleaning, a special door tag must be displayed to alert staff to your pet's presence, and there is a $10-per-hour "time out" fee if your pet is found unattended. If other guests complain about your pet's behavior, you may be asked to board it off-site. You must also provide current vaccination records from a licensed veterinarian on request. Read the full Loews Loves Pets policy at theugseries.com/loewspetsrpr.

Smoking

All Universal Orlando Resort hotels are smoke-free. Smoking is permitted only outdoors in designated locations. If you light up in your room, you'll be burned with a $250 cleaning fee.

UNIVERSAL ORLANDO RESORT HOTEL SERVICES *and* AMENITIES

DINING

TO KEEP YOU FED, every Universal on-site hotel has multiple restaurants, a spot for coffee and grab-and-go snacks, and at least two bars. The Signature Collection properties each have sit-down restaurants, including one family-friendly eatery, while Cabana Bay has a counter-service food court, as well as table-service munchies in the bowling alley. Aventura Hotel has an upscale food court with international dishes and a rooftop bar that serves small plates. The Signature Collection hotels also have 24-hour room service menus, while the Value Inns and Suites and Prime Value properties offer pizza delivery to the rooms noon–midnight.

The primary downside to staying on-site at Universal is the cost of food at the Signature Collection hotels' restaurants, which seem to be priced as if everyone staying at the hotels is on a corporate expense account. Fortunately, many good, cheaper restaurant choices are within a few minutes' drive of the hotels on **Major Boulevard, International Drive,** and **Sand Lake Road.** Hotel guests also have easy access to **CityWalk,** which has some cheaper choices for dining.

POOLS AND RECREATION

SWIMMING IS MANY GUESTS' NO. 1 priority (after the parks, of course), so you'll find some of Orlando's best pools at Universal's hotels. Each resort has at least one themed swimming facility. The main pool is the more active, family-centric one, where you'll find playground equipment and organized activities, both for kids (water-based games and contests) and adults (free smoothies and cool towels). Several resorts have a waterslide, and Cabana Bay has a lazy river. On most nights (weather permitting) a PG or PG-13 "dive-in" movie is projected on an outdoor screen, with the *Despicable Me,* DreamWorks, and *Transformers* flicks in heavy rotation.

The secondary pools at Portofino Bay are usually slightly more sedate and attract a more adult clientele. All pools are staffed with trained lifeguards during operating hours (which vary seasonally, typically 8 a.m.–10 p.m.) and have adjacent hot tubs, changing facilities, and drink services. Towels are free with resort ID, and hotel guests (excluding those at Endless Summer) are free to pool-hop from one resort to another; ask at the front desk for a keycard to access another hotel's pool security gate.

Each hotel's main pool (except those at Stella Nova and Terra Luna, Endless Summer, and Aventura) has **private cabanas** for rent, which start around $100 per day. Aside from providing shade and cushioned lounge chairs, cabanas come with ceiling fans, TVs, a refrigerator, free soft drinks, food and drink delivery, and a personal safe. Reserve a cabana by calling ☎ 407-503-4175 at Cabana Bay, ☎ 407-503-5200 ext. 35235 at Sapphire Falls, ☎ 407-503-3235 at Royal Pacific, ☎ 407-503-2236 at Hard Rock, or ☎ 407-503-1200 at Portofino Bay. Same-day cancellations incur a 50% penalty fee. You'll also find a variety of recreational activities around the pools, from a bocce court at Portofino Bay to a croquet lawn at the Royal Pacific; free equipment can be checked out to play.

KIDS' ACTIVITIES AND KIDS' SUITES

THE LOEWS LOVES KIDS PROGRAM means that there's always something at the hotel to keep the rug rats occupied when your family isn't in the parks. Free lending libraries of games and sports equipment are available at every hotel, and a schedule of supervised activities is offered at each main pool (or indoors on rainy days). The Minions (or other Universal characters) make regular meet and greet appearances at

BEST ON-SITE HOTEL ROOMS FOR FAMILIES

WHEN TOURING PLANS contributor Derek Burgan was growing up, his family vacationed at cheap off-site motels, which may have once been used as prisons (judging by the size of the rooms). Now that Derek's in charge of booking his family's trips, he pretty much always stays on-site. Here are six of his favorite family-friendly rooms on Universal property.

6. Jurassic World Kids' Suite (Loews Royal Pacific Resort) A kids' suite at Universal hotels is basically comprised of two separate living areas: a main bedroom for adults and an ultra-themed bedroom for kids. The adult's bedroom has a king-size bed, a love seat, a desk area, and the suite's bathroom. The attached room is for the kids and has two twin beds modeled as gyrospheres from Jurassic World. Every inch of the room is themed to the film series, with one of my favorite things being a detailed map of Isla Nublar.

5. Family Suite (Cabana Bay Beach Resort) After a lifetime spent in standard hotel rooms, the two things I appreciate most now are theming and—maybe more important—space. I love my family, but after a week of them in a standard hotel room, I'm ready to lose my mind. The family suites at Cabana Bay Beach Resort are the perfect combination of theming, space, and even something my parents would have appreciated ... VALUE. Walking into a family suite is like walking out of a time machine into a simpler era. The entire theme of Cabana Bay is built around family vacations of years past, and the retro design aesthetic of the rooms is my jam.

4. Family Suite (Endless Summer Dockside Inn & Suites) Speaking of value, you can't go wrong with the amount of space you get at Endless Summer when booking a family suite. With Dockside having the best food court at any theme park Value resort, great pool bars, and a rate of under $200 a night (usually under $150 for Florida residents), this hotel may be good option for families considering a Disney vacation too.

3. Future Rock Star Suite (Hard Rock Hotel) In general, standard hotel room size, even at Disney Deluxe resorts, is under 350 square feet. The Jurassic World Kids' Suite is 670 square feet, while the family suites at Cabana Bay Beach Resort and Endless Summer are 430-440 square feet. The Future Rock Star Suite at Hard Rock Hotel is a whopping 800 square feet! The main bedroom includes a king-size bed for the adults along with a living room, while the kids' room has two twin beds and a fun area for the family to rock out.

2. Despicable Me Kids Suite (Loews Portofino Bay Hotel) We've taken our kiddos to every themed suite at Disney and Universal, and while they loved each of the rooms at Art of Animation, the Despicable Me suite at Universal blew their minds and is something they remember in detail years later. Everything about the room, including the bank vault–like door to enter, is brilliant. The "bomb beds" are incredible, and everyone in the family will love the Minion theming.

1. Volcano View Room (Cabana Bay Beach Resort) When I was growing up, Disney would often show ads featuring guests looking out their hotel windows into the nearby Cinderella Castle. The ads made it seem like the castle was so close you could almost touch it. Reality slapped me in the face when my parents actually took me to Walt Disney World and I realized I had fallen victim to some clever marketing magic. There were no hotels THAT close. Years later, the Universal Orlando Resort delivered on that promise of a (water) theme park right outside your window when they added the two towers to Cabana Bay. Gazing out at the Krakatau volcano from your standard room or family suite is pure serenity.

Cabana Bay Beach Resort on Friday evenings. In addition, every hotel (except Aventura) has an arcade with video games; Cabana Bay's Game-O-Rama is the biggest.

If you want to go all out and amaze the kids, reserve one of the elaborately decorated **Kids' Suites.** Portofino Bay's Despicable Me suites look like Gru's laboratory, with missile-shaped beds and vaultlike doors. Royal Pacific's Jurassic World suites have appropriately dinosaurian decor, while Helios Grand's suites boast Berk-inspired dragon designs. The Hard Rock's Future Rock Star suites give kids a pint-size stage to shred on. Aventura's and Sapphire Falls's Kids' Suites have a separate kids' room with TV and child-size furniture but no whimsical theming. All the Kids' Suites have separate bedrooms for the kids that only open on the parents' room (not the hallway). You'll get some extra privacy but pay a hefty price with the resort's highest room rates (outside the outrageous presidential suites). Note that you must have at least one minor in your party to reserve a Kids' Suite. Cabana Bay and Endless Summer don't offer Kids' Suites, but they do have Family Suites, without the private kids' quarters, for a much lower cost.

PARKING

UNIVERSAL'S SIGNATURE COLLECTION hotels all charge a $35-per-night self-parking fee ($45 for valet) for registered guests; day guests pay $53 for self-parking over 30 minutes ($11 for 5–30 minutes) and $50 for valet. **Cabana Bay** and Prime Value properties charge $24 for overnight guests (self-parking only), and **Endless Summer** charges $20 ($80 for RVs); all bill $53 per day for day visitors. Note that unlike Universal's parking garages, Loews Hotels' posted parking rates don't include sales tax; prices listed here include taxes. All Loews on-site hotels offer free **electric vehicle charging stations** with paid parking (subject to availability).

Most of the hotels' table-service restaurants (including **Bice** and **Mama Della's** at Portofino, **Jake's** and **Islands Dining Room** at Royal Pacific, **Strong Water Tavern** and **Amatista Cookhouse** at Sapphire Falls, and **Bar 17 Bistro** at Aventura) will validate diners for free self-parking or discounted valet parking; **The Palm** at Hard Rock Hotel offers complimentary valet. You must spend at least $40 on food or beverages to receive parking validation. There are no annual pass discounts on parking at the hotels. The hotels don't charge for another night until midnight, so you can leave your car in the lot long past your checkout time without paying extra.

UNIVERSAL VACATION PLANNING CENTER

LOEWS STAFF have no authority over park tickets or anything else involving the attractions, so if you ask the front desk or concierge about park admission and the like, you'll be directed to the Universal Orlando Vacation Planning Center. Typically located in the main hotel lobby, the Vacation Planning Center can help you purchase park tickets (or pick up ones you preordered), as well as arrange for Universal Express Passes, dining reservations, off-site transportation, and other amenities. The Vacation Planning Center in each hotel is usually open daily, 7 a.m.–8 p.m.

INTERNET

ALL UNIVERSAL ORLANDO HOTELS offer free Wi-Fi in their public areas and guest rooms for up to four devices. The service is somewhat spotty but good enough for email and social media, with download and upstream speeds averaging 20mbps. If you plan to stream 4K videos or upload large photos, you may want to pay $15 per 24 hours for **Premium Plus Internet,** which affords higher bandwidth of around 100mbps on up to eight devices.

BUSINESS CENTERS

EACH OF THE SIGNATURE COLLECTION HOTELS has a fully equipped business center offering computers with printers, copy and fax services, and mail facilities through FedEx and UPS. The business centers at **Portofino Bay, Royal Pacific,** and **Sapphire Falls** are open Monday–Friday, 7 a.m.–5:30 p.m. (closed Saturday and Sunday). **Hard Rock Hotel**'s business center is open 24-7, and the others may be accessed during off-hours by contacting the front desk. Fees apply for certain services such as copying and faxing. **Aventura Hotel** and **Endless Summer Resort** have no business center, but their lobbies have touchscreens for printing airline boarding passes.

CRIBS AND ROLLAWAY BEDS

COMPLIMENTARY CRIBS ARE AVAILABLE in all rooms. Rollaway beds can be requested at Signature Collection hotels on a first-come, first-serve basis for $39; this fee is in addition to any nightly charges for having more than two adults in the room. Only one rollaway per room is allowed, and they are not available at Prime Value hotels or Value Inns and Suites.

MICROWAVES AND REFRIGERATORS

ALL HOTEL ROOMS INCLUDE small refrigerators, and the Family Suites at Cabana Bay and Endless Summer have kitchenettes with a microwave and sink. Microwaves are available for rent in rooms that don't include them on a first-come, first-serve basis for $17 each per day.

TRANSPORTATION AND CAR RENTAL

ALL OF UNIVERSAL'S HOTELS OFFER free transportation via bus and/or water taxi to CityWalk and the parks, as well as well-lit landscaped walking paths connecting the resorts. Water taxis depart from each of the main campus's Signature Collection hotels every 15–20 minutes, while the buses from the Prime Value and Value Inns and Suites resorts run almost continuously. Either transportation method takes about 15 minutes to reach the park entrances, while walking takes between less than 5 minutes from the Hard Rock Hotel to 15 or 20 minutes from Cabana Bay and Portofino Bay. There is also continuous bus service between the original campus's parking hub and Epic Universe, as well as direct connections from the hotels to Volcano Bay.

Free daily transportation for hotel guests to SeaWorld and Aquatica is available from the parking garage hub (see page 131).

Another free bus from Universal's parking hub to **Busch Gardens Tampa** is available to anyone holding a paid park ticket; visit busch gardens.mears.com or call ☎ 800-221-1339 for details. Paid taxi or rideshare services are your best option for getting to Walt Disney World or the airport. If you want to rent a car, **Avis** rental-car service desks operate inside each hotel daily, 8 a.m.–4 p.m.; call ☎ 407-503-3156 for information and reservations.

FITNESS CENTERS AND MANDARA SPA

IF YOU WANT TO STAY IN SHAPE while vacationing, every Universal hotel has a well-appointed fitness center filled with the latest in exercise equipment. The expansive Jack LaLanne–themed workout room at **Cabana Bay Beach Resort,** as well as the somewhat smaller workout rooms in the other hotels, are free for all hotel guests to use.

Whether you're staying at a Universal hotel or not, you may book services at Portofino Bay's **Mandara Spa,** which is attached to the hotel's fitness center. Access to the spa's shower and sauna facilities is free for club-level guests or anyone purchasing spa services.

Universal Orlando's Mandara Spa features luxurious, state-of-the-art massage and sauna facilities amid an Asian ambience, despite its location in an Italy-themed resort. We like the contrast, though, and find it slightly exotic. Waiting areas are decorated in comforting earth tones; treatment rooms feature silk-draped ceilings and decorative lighting. Changing and bathroom areas are spacious and clean, but they also include less-than-subtle advertisements for products sold on premises.

The emphasis on tranquility extends to the stellar spa services, which include free self-heating oil for massages. Men and women enjoy separate steam and sauna facilities; the hot tub is unisex. The Portofino's sand-bottom pool is conveniently located near the entrance to the spa, as are nail services. The fitness center is still on the other side of the glass wall, however, so you may feel a bit like that doggy in the window.

We rate the Mandara Spa at Portofino Bay as a four-star experience, just behind the spas at Disney's Grand Floridian, the Waldorf Astoria, and the Four Seasons and equivalent to the spas at the Ritz-Carlton, Disney's Saratoga Springs, and Gaylord Palms. Prices range from $120 (plus tax and tip) for a 30-minute reflexology foot rub to $540 for a 90-minute couple's massage package. Hair salon, nail care, waxing, and makeup services are also on the menu. A 20% automatic gratuity applies to all services, and Preferred and Premier Annual Pass holders can save 10%–20% on services (Monday–Thursday only). Visit mandaraspa.com/offers for money-saving monthly specials. Purchase of most massages and treatments also includes access to the fitness center for the day. Call ☎ 407-503-1244 or visit theugseries.com/mand_spa to view the price list and make a reservation.

LAUNDRY

ALL THE HOTELS offer self-service laundries. (Portofino Bay's is located on the second floor of the west wing.) Machines take credit cards only and cost $4 per load to wash, and the same to dry; detergent or softener costs $2. At all the Signature Collection hotels, you can also avail yourself of valet laundry, dry cleaning, quick pressing, and shoeshines, with express same-day service available daily, 9 a.m.–6 p.m.; pricing and instructions can be found inside your closet.

CLUB LEVEL

THE FOUR TOP HOTELS each offer club-level rooms or suites that allow access to an exclusive lounge, where you'll find a free Continental breakfast, afternoon snacks, hot and cold evening hors d'oeuvres with free beer and wine, and after-dinner desserts. Club-level guests also get free fitness center access, discounted poolside cabana rentals, personal concierge service, evening turndown service, and other luxurious touches. **Hard Rock Hotel**'s **Rock Royalty Lounge** and **Royal Pacific**'s **Royal Club Lounge** are on the seventh floor, while **Helios Grand Hotel**'s club lounge is on the ninth level, and **Portofino Bay**'s **Portofino Club Lounge** is in the lobby; all are open daily, 7 a.m.–9:30 p.m. Most of our readers who stay in a club-level room seem happy with their choice, like this family from Kansas City:

> We stayed on the club level of the Royal Pacific. Absolutely worth the money. It not only includes breakfast every morning but also includes sodas all day and cocktails in the evening with heavy appetizers, which we usually made a meal out of. There was always a salad and then something hot. One night it was beef stew, then fried rice, and then chicken potpie. And if you weren't full, they put out dessert 8–9 p.m. This ended up saving us money, and we were usually tired from the day, so just walking down the hall was fabulous.

This family from St. Louis also felt that the club level's cost was money well spent:

> Club level was only $40 more, and we easily had this covered with breakfast and dinner that we didn't eat out, along with soda and water taken into the park. For a family of four, it was well worth it. When my son became ill, the concierge service connected us with an urgent care that stayed open late. Amazing service.

As did this family from Babylon:

> We stayed at Portofino Bay club level and the combo of the Express Pass with the club level food and drink offerings made this feel like a real vacation. We felt like the club level more than paid for itself. We had our breakfast and dinner covered every night and bought lunch in the parks.

And this family of five from Minnetonka, Minnesota, made the most of their club level stay:

> Having five of us, the ability to eat breakfast and dinner (via heavy apps) each day in the club and utilizing the Express Passes were complete game changers and huge savings! The convenience of the

hotel's location was also amazing. We easily came back each day for a break after lunch in the park.

WEDDINGS

THERE IS NO DEDICATED WEDDING PAVILION at Universal (yet), but each hotel has facilities for staging fairy-tale ceremonies, large or small. Intimate weddings with 50 or fewer guests start at $1,800 for a simple ceremony, and $110 per guest for a 1-hour cocktail reception with alcohol, hors d'oeuvres, and a cake. A Signature wedding for more than 50 guests starts at $3,000–$4,500 for the ceremony and $180-plus per plate for a dinner reception. (Prices don't include a 25% service charge and 6.5% tax.) To Universal's credit, it doesn't quote an hourly rate for having Minions attend your bachelorette party, but this is Orlando: money talks. Visit theugseries.com/uniwed to download brochures with pricing and menus, and start planning your Universal union today.

UNIVERSAL ORLANDO RESORT HOTEL PROFILES

Hard Rock Hotel Orlando ★★★★

5800 Universal Blvd. Orlando
☎ 407-503-2000 or 888-273-1311
hardrockhotelorlando.com

Rate per night $555–$960. **Pool** ★★★★. **Fridge in room** Yes. **Shuttle to parks** Yes (Universal, SeaWorld, Aquatica). **Maximum number of occupants per room** 5 (2 queens) or 4 (king). **Comment** Pets welcome (2/room, $100/stay). **Survey results** 95% of *Unofficial Guide* readers would stay here again; 91% would recommend this resort to a friend.

STRENGTHS	WEAKNESSES
• Steps away from the theme parks	• Expensive
• Includes Unlimited Express Passes	• Smaller standard rooms than Disney's deluxe hotels
• Fun theme for rock-loving families	• Can be noisy, especially near the main pool

FOR YOUNGER ADULTS AND FAMILIES with older kids, the Hard Rock Hotel is the hippest place to lay your head. Opened in 2001, it is the closest resort to Universal's theme parks. The exterior has a California Mission theme, with white stucco walls, arched entryways, and rust-colored roof tiles. Inside, the lobby is a tribute to rock-and-roll style, all marble, chrome, and stage lighting. The lobby's walls are decorated with enough concert posters, costumes, and musical instruments to start another wing of Cleveland's Rock and Roll Hall of Fame. Exhibits include outfits from Lady Gaga and Rihanna, and QR codes near each artifact let you take a self-guided memorabilia tour via your smartphone.

The eight floors hold 650 rooms, including 29 suites, with the rooms categorized into standard, deluxe, and Rock Royalty club-level tiers. Standard rooms are 375 square feet, slightly larger than rooms at Disney's Moderate resorts and a bit smaller than most Disney Deluxe rooms. They feature light-gray walls and linens and colorful retro-inspired accents, such as mirrors marked with the heights of famous rock stars. The style looks more bubblegum pop than hard rock, but the brighter look is a bit more soothing after you stumble back from a fatiguing day in the parks.

Standard rooms are furnished with two queen beds, with plush, comfortable linens and more pillows than you'll know what to do with. Rooms also include a TV, a refrigerator, a coffee maker, and a Bluetooth alarm clock with USB charging ports.

A six-drawer dresser and separate closet with sliding doors ensure plenty of storage space. In addition, most rooms have a reading chair and a small desk with two chairs. An optional rollaway bed, available at an extra charge, allows standard rooms to sleep up to five people.

Each room's dressing area includes a sink and hair dryer. The bathroom is probably large enough for most adults to get ready in the morning while another person gets ready in the dressing area.

Guests staying in standard rooms can choose from one of three views: standard, which can include anything from walkways and parking lots to lawns and trees; garden view, which includes the lawn, trees, and (in some rooms) the waterway around the resort; and pool view, which includes the Hard Rock's expansive pool.

A step up from standard rooms are deluxe rooms. Deluxe rooms with king beds are around 400 square feet and can accommodate up to three people with an optional rollaway bed rental. These rooms feature a U-shaped sitting area in place of the second bed, and the rest of the amenities are the same as in standard rooms. Deluxe queen rooms are 500 square feet and can hold up to five people using a rental rollaway.

For families, each 800-square-foot **Future Rock Star Suite** features an authentic piece of music memorabilia, along with a simulated stage inside the separate kids' bedroom. Or you can really live like The King in the 2,000-square-foot **Graceland Suite,** which comes complete with a baby grand piano and fireplace.

Situated in the middle of the resort's C-shaped main building, the 12,000-square-foot zero-entry pool includes a 250-foot waterslide (the longest at any Universal hotel), a sand beach, and underwater speakers so you can hear the music while you swim. Adjacent to the pool are a fountain play area for small children, a sand volleyball court, hot tubs, and a poolside bar. The entire pool area is lined with tall palm trees, and private cabanas are available for rent. The Hard Rock also has a small, functional fitness center, but for spa services you'll have to go to the **Mandara Spa** at Universal's nearby Portofino Bay. The Hard Rock also has a business center and video arcade.

On-site dining includes **The Kitchen,** a casual full-service restaurant open for breakfast, lunch, and dinner that serves American food such as burgers, steaks, and salads. **The Palm Restaurant** is an upscale steakhouse available for dinner only. There is also an **Emack & Bolio's** ice cream shop and grab-and-go marketplace on the lower level; the stylish **Velvet Bar** in the lobby for drinks after dark and periodic Velvet Sessions rock-and-roll cocktail parties (visit hardrockhotels.com/orlando/velvet-sessions.aspx for the schedule and to purchase tickets); and the **BeachClub** bar and grill by the pool. And, of course, the **Hard Rock Cafe** is just a short distance away at CityWalk. Oenophiles will want to keep an eye on theugseries .com/hrhwineriffs for announcements about periodic **Wine Riffs** events ($186 per person plus gratuity, including valet parking), which pair five courses of vino and victuals with a carefully curated soundtrack.

Guests can also stream a free personalized playlist at music.hardrock hotels.com and swap their room key card for a free souvenir guitar pick at checkout. If all that musical immersion puts you in the mood to jam, you can borrow a Crosley turntable with a stack of vinyl records or 1 of 20 Fender guitars—including Stratocasters, Telecasters, and even bass guitars—with amp and headphones for free (after a $1,000 credit card deposit) through the hotel's **Sound of Your Stay** program; ask the front desk for details. Alternatively, investigate the **Rock Om** in-room yoga program (hardrockhotels.com/orlando/soundbody.aspx), featuring free mats and on-demand instructional videos, if you yearn to achieve a state of zen.

With its comfy rooms and killer location, Hard Rock Hotel is so popular with families that, during certain seasons when school is out of session, it can command a higher nightly rate than the fancier Portofino Bay. While not exactly cheap, Hard Rock is a good value compared to, say, Disney's Yacht & Beach Clubs. What you're paying for at the Hard Rock is a short walk to the theme parks and Universal Express Unlimited first, and the room second.

While the hotel can get a bit loud, especially in areas facing the pool, it gets high marks from families with teenagers, like this Texas parent with two daughters, ages 15 and 17:

> One word: "WOW!" My group loved it! We splurged for a club room. My teenagers liked the club lounge . . . allowing them to pop in for food whenever they wanted. The beds were super comfortable, soft instead of firm mattresses. The pool was a big hit with the girls. We all liked the convenience of being so close to walk to the parks.

Loews Portofino Bay Hotel ★★★★½

5601 Universal Blvd. Orlando
☎ 407-503-1000 or 888-273-1311
loewshotels.com /portofino-bay-hotel

Rate per night $531–$984. **Pools** ★★★★. **Fridge in room** Yes. **Shuttle to parks** Yes (Universal, SeaWorld, Aquatica). **Maximum number of occupants per room** 5 (2 queens) or 3 (king). **Comment** Pets welcome (2/room, $100/stay). **Survey results** 91% of *Unofficial Guide* readers would stay here again; 90% would recommend this resort to a friend.

STRENGTHS	WEAKNESSES
• Universal's most luxurious resort	• Expensive, especially for dining
• Includes Unlimited Express Passes	• Buildings are being refurbished
• Full-service spa and multiple pools	• Farthest Premier hotel from the theme parks

IF YOU WANT THE ULTIMATE European-style, spare-no-expense on-site experience, look no further than the Portofino Bay Hotel. Universal's top-of-the-line hotel evokes the Italian seaside city of Portofino, complete with a man-made Portofino Bay past the lobby. To Universal's credit, the layout, color, and theming of the guest room buildings are a good approximation of the architecture around the harbor in the real Portofino (Universal's version has fewer yachts, though).

The front of the Portofino continues the theme, with Vespa-like scooters parked around a burbling fountain. Deep-green tapestries hang from the sand-colored porte cochere, which is flanked by narrower recessed arches. It's a convincing transition from the nearby parking deck.

Inside, the lobby is decorated with pink-marble floors, white wood columns, and arches. The space is both airy and comfortable, with side rooms featuring seats and couches done in bold reds and deep blues.

Most guest rooms are 450 square feet and have either one king or two queen beds. King rooms sleep up to three people with an optional rollaway bed; the same option allows queen rooms to sleep up to five. Two room-view types are available: garden rooms overlook the landscaping and trees (many of these are the east-facing rooms in the resort's east wing; others face one of the three pools); bay-view rooms face either west or south and overlook Portofino Bay, with a view of the piazza behind the lobby too. Rooms in the west wing are closest to the water taxi dock and resort walking paths. A small number of rooms have working balconies; you can't reserve one in advance but may upgrade at check-in if one is available.

Rooms come furnished with a 42-inch TV, a small refrigerator, a coffee maker, and an alarm clock with USB charging ports. Other amenities include a small desk with two chairs, a comfortable reading chair with lamp, a chest of drawers, and a standing closet. Beds are large and comfortable. You'll have a hard time in the morning convincing yourself that getting out of them and going to a theme park is the best option you have.

Guest bathrooms in Portofino Bay's deluxe and club-level rooms are the best on Universal property. We've seen smaller New York apartments! The shower has an adjustable spray nozzle that varies the water pulses to simulate everything from monsoon season in the tropics to the rhythmic thumps of wildebeest hooves during migrating season.

Portofino Bay has three pools, the largest of which is the **Beach Pool,** on the west side of the resort. The Beach Pool has a zero-entry design and a waterslide themed after a Roman aqueduct, plus a children's play area, hot tubs, and a poolside bar and grill. We like the naturalistic Mediterranean seaside feel of the Beach Pool, but it can be a bit too authentic for some guests, like this mom from St. Louis:

> *The biggest disappointment about Portofino Bay was actually the main pool. The kids felt that it was dirty with the sand, and it was nearly impossible to find chairs in the afternoon due to many being "reserved" with towels.*

Two smaller, quieter pools sit at the far end of the east wing and to the west of the main lobby. The **Villa Pool** has private cabana rentals for that Italian Riviera feeling and a bocce ball court with free equipment for that Jersey Shore feeling, while the smaller **Hillside Pool**, tucked behind the east wing, is the most secluded. Rounding out the luxuries are the full-service **Mandara Spa;** a complete fitness center with weight machines, treadmills, and more; a business center; and a video arcade.

On-site dining includes three sit-down restaurants serving Italian cuisine, plus a deli that doubles as a pizzeria, as well as a café serving coffee and gelato. Visit the café during "dolce hour," 3–5 p.m. daily, for discounted scoops. A waterfront bar rounds out the food offerings at Portofino. The Portofino has 10 separate convention meeting rooms and is a popular destination for small to midsize groups. Perhaps because Universal figures that most guests have an expense account, some of the food prices go well beyond what we'd consider reasonable, even for a theme park hotel.

While we think Portofino Bay has some of Universal's best rooms, certain areas are starting to show their age, and the entire facade is undergoing a major refurbishment now through July 2025. Even so, the prices put it on par with the Ritz-Carlton, something its good points can't quite justify. On the other hand, the Ritz isn't a short walk from Harry Potter, and the Portofino is significantly cheaper than the hotels along Disney's monorail, as this Shelby, North Carolina, reader remarked:

> We stayed at Portofino Bay for three nights before transferring to Disney's Contemporary Resort, and we liked the Portofino much better for half the price!

If you can't swing a stay here, at least take a free sunset water taxi ride to the harbor for **Musica della Notte,** the free mini-concert of romantic operatic pop tunes belted from Portofino's bayside balconies daily at sunset (weather permitting). Four times each year, Harbor Nights are held on the plaza, with free-flowing wine, heavy hors d'oeuvres, and live music. Tickets are $84 for standing-only general admission and $116 for VIP admission with reserved seating and private food stations. The experience is like attending an upscale wedding without having to bring a gift, and it makes for a wonderfully romantic date night. See theugseries.com /pbhharbornights for details on the next date.

Loews Royal Pacific Resort   ★★★★

6300 Hollywood Way
Orlando
☎ 407-503-3000 or
888-273-1311
loewshotels.com
/royal-pacific-resort

Rate per night $458–$650. **Pool** ★★★★. **Fridge in room** Yes. **Shuttle to parks** Yes (Universal, SeaWorld, Aquatica). **Maximum number of occupants per room** 5 (2 queens) or 3 (king). **Comments** Pets welcome (2/room, $100/stay). **Survey results** 94% of *Unofficial Guide* readers would stay here again; 87% would recommend this resort to a friend.

STRENGTHS	WEAKNESSES
• Cheapest hotel with Express included	• Still pricey considering the room size
• Lush South Pacific landscaping and luau	• Balinese buildings clash with contemporary decor.
• Pleasant walk or boat ride from the parks	• Rooms facing IOA's roller coasters can be noisy

A FAVORITE OF BOTH YOUNG FAMILIES and solo travelers, the Royal Pacific Resort is the least expensive and most relaxing of Universal's top hotels. You may be tempted, as we were initially, to write off the Royal Pacific, which opened in 2002, as a knockoff of Disney's Polynesian Village Resort. There are indeed similarities, but the Royal Pacific is attractive enough, and has enough strengths of its own, for us to recommend that you try a stay there to compare for yourself.

The South Seas–inspired theming is both relaxing and structured, but it strains somewhat against the colder contemporary elements installed during a 2020 refurbishment. Guests enter the lobby from a walkway two stories above an artificial stream that surrounds the resort. Once inside, you're struck by the enormous amount of light coming in from the windows and three-story A-frame roof. Contrasting with the structure's warm natural woods, industrial sheets of textured steel studded with small flowerlike objects line the lobby, which wraps around an enormous outdoor fountain filled with frolicking elephant statues.

The Royal Pacific's 1,000 guest rooms are spread among three Y-shaped wings attached to the resort's main building. Standard rooms are 335 square feet and have one king or two queen beds. The beds, fitted with 300-thread-count sheets, are very comfortable.

The rooms feature modern monochrome wall treatments and carpets, accented with boldly colored floral graphics. Rooms include a flat-panel TV, a refrigerator, a coffee maker, and an alarm clock with an iPhone docking port, plus several USB-equipped power outlets. Other amenities include a small desk with two chairs, a comfortable reading chair, a chest of drawers, and a large closet.

As at the Hard Rock, rooms at the Royal Pacific have a dressing area with sink, separated from the rest of the room by a wall. Adjacent to the dressing area is the bathroom, with a shower and toilet. While they're acceptable, the bathroom and dressing areas at the Royal Pacific are our least favorite in the upscale Universal resorts.

The Royal Pacific also offers themed rooms for kids with its **Jurassic World Kids' Suites**. These 370-square-foot two-room suites have a door connecting the kids' room to the main hotel room, but only the main room has a door out to the hallway. The kids' room has two twin beds with headboards that look like Gyrospheres, as well as a wall-size mural of dinosaurs.

Some standard-view rooms overlook the Royal Pacific's green landscape, while others see the parking lot or nearby roads. Water-view rooms facing the pool or lagoon are also available, many of which have a great look at Hogwarts Castle. Guests in north- and west-facing rooms in Tower 1 are closest to the walking path to the park but also closest to the attractions at Islands of Adventure (IOA); you can hear the roar from IOA's Incredible Hulk Coaster throughout the day and night. East-facing rooms in Towers 1 and 2 are exposed to traffic noise from Universal Boulevard and, more distantly, I-4. Quietest are south-facing pool-view rooms in Tower 1 and south-facing rooms in Tower 3, which are also nearest to the water taxi dock. Tower 2 is the most remote from amenities and transportation.

Like the Hard Rock Hotel, the Royal Pacific's zero-entry pool includes a sand beach, volleyball court, play area for kids, hot tub, and cabanas for rent, plus a poolside bar and grill. Designed to look like a cross between a tropical island and cruise ship pool (complete with faux exhaust tower and observation deck), the swimming complex pool is huge; it does not, however, have a waterslide. Lounge chairs line most of the walkway around the pool, and portable folding umbrellas provide shade where the palm trees and lush green plants can't. For the full island experience, the

Wantilan Luau is held every Saturday night year-round; see the review on page 359.

The Royal Pacific includes a 5,000-square-foot fitness facility, with free weights and machines, treadmills, stair-climbers, elliptical machines, and exercise bikes, plus separate lockers, dressing areas, and sauna rooms for men and women. The Royal Pacific's expansive convention facilities cover more than 132,000 square feet and connect to the Sapphire Falls Resort via an air-conditioned bridge. A business center and video arcade round out the on-site amenities.

On-site dining includes a full-service restaurant, three bars, and a luau. **Islands Dining Room** is open daily for breakfast; à la carte options range from steel-cut oatmeal and custom omelets to more exotic eye-openers like Tahitian French toast l'orange. At dinner, Islands serves better-than-average international cuisine. Another breakfast option is the grab-and-go **Tuk Tuk Market** in the lobby, which also serves Starbucks coffee, hot sandwiches, and gelato. **Jake's American Bar** serves a casual sit-down menu for lunch and dinner, along with late-night bar snacks. Several casual bar areas—including Jake's American Bar, the **Orchid Court Lounge & Sushi Bar,** and the poolside **Bula Bar & Grille** with neighboring ice cream stand—are located in the resort.

Though they're nice, the rooms alone aren't worth the rates, but adding in Universal Express Unlimited and a short walk to the parks makes it the best deal among Universal's top hotels.

Loews Sapphire Falls Resort ★★★★

6601 Adventure Way
Orlando
☎ 407-503-5000 or
888-273-1311
loewshotels.com
/sapphire-falls-resort

Rate per night $245–$305. **Pool** ★★★★. **Fridge in room** Yes. **Shuttle to parks** Yes (Universal, SeaWorld, Aquatica). **Maximum number of occupants per room** 5 (2 queens) or 4 (king). **Comment** Pets welcome (2/room, $100/stay). **Survey results** 91% of *Unofficial Guide* readers would stay here again; 90% would recommend this resort to a friend.

STRENGTHS	WEAKNESSES
• Cheapest hotel with water taxi to CityWalk	• Unlimited Express Passes aren't included.
• Massive main pool and free saunas	• Caribbean theming is too subtle in some spots.
• Strong Water Tavern is an *Unofficial Guide* favorite.	• Standard rooms are a bit small and bland.

SAPPHIRE FALLS RESORT brings a sunny Caribbean island vibe to the moderate market with its 1,000 rooms (including 77 suites), which opened in summer 2016. Sandwiched between Royal Pacific and Aventura Hotel—both physically and price-wise—Sapphire Falls sports most of the amenities of Universal's fancier hotels, including water taxi transportation to the parks, with the crucial exception of complimentary Express Passes.

Rather than replicating the stereotypical pastel palette seen at Disney's Caribbean-themed hotel, Sapphire Falls' designers went with a cooler blue-and-white color scheme for the exterior. The lobby continues the modern reinterpretation of island aesthetics with a playful hanging sculpture of wicker beach balls and a massive floor-to-ceiling window providing a postcard-perfect view of the rear lagoon, with the towers of Doctor

Doom's Fearfall posing in the background. Public spaces fuse seemingly ancient structures—such as a stunning stone silo, complete with authentic-looking mill equipment—with clean contemporary architecture and colorful images of today's West Indies. Although some transitional areas feel underthemed, we truly appreciate Sapphire Falls Resort's casually sophisticated vibe, which hits a sweet spot between the family-friendly freneticism of Cabana Bay and the elegance of Universal's more upscale hotels.

Water figures heavily at Sapphire Falls, whose namesake waterfalls form the scenic centerpiece of the resort. The 16,000-square-foot main pool boasts 3,500 square feet of sand on which to set your lounger, as well as a 100-foot waterslide, children's play areas, fire pits, a hot tub, and cabanas for rent. There are two zero-entry points near the middle of the pool on opposite sides, which allow you to pretend to walk across the water. Although billed as the largest pool on Universal property, its organic shape and 4.5-foot maximum depth make it better suited for wading than swimming laps, and there's no secondary quiet pool if you aren't into reggae-flavored rock.

A well-equipped fitness room just off the pool holds saunas in both changing rooms, along with spa-style lockers and showers that are free for all guests to use. Table tennis (free to use) and a pool table (nominal fee per game) are available outside near the small arcade.

On the lower level, **Amatista Cookhouse** offers à la carte or buffet American breakfast, followed by table-service Caribbean food for lunch and dinner. **Drhum Club Kantine** serves tapas-style small plates, sandwiches, and massive bowls of alcohol near the pool bar's fire pit. **New Dutch Trading Co.,** an island-inspired grab-and-go marketplace, has ice cream, coffee, hot entrées and sandwiches, refillable Coke Freestyle cups, and packaged snacks. **Strong Water Tavern,** in the lobby, offers rum tastings and freshly made ceviche, and a **Universal Studios Store** in the lobby sells sundries and resort souvenirs.

The rooms range from 321 square feet in a standard queen or king to 529 square feet in the 36 **Kids' Suites,** and up to 1,936 square feet in the 15 **Presidential Suites,** which are appointed with charmingly rustic light fixtures and are sizable enough to live in long-term. All rooms include a 49-inch TV, an alarm clock with iPhone dock, in-wall USB charging ports, a minifridge, and a coffee maker. The rooms are aesthetically acceptable but a bit antiseptic, aside from a garishly colored mirror frame and metallized photos above the beds, and they are barely bigger than the standard Cabana Bay rooms. We like these rooms a bit better than those at Aventura, but they're more expensive too. The layout is perfectly functional, but there are some odd design quirks, such as a sliding door to the toilet that doesn't latch; don't plan on doing your business in private if you have inquisitive kids.

Sapphire Falls also contains nearly 115,000 square feet of meeting space and a business center. Covered walkways connect to a parking structure, which in turn connects to the meeting facilities at Royal Pacific, making the sister properties ideal for conventions. That also leads us to our main critique of Sapphire Falls: outside of the lobby and pool, the public areas feel a little like a standard convention hotel.

Water taxi transportation to Sapphire Falls takes only a few minutes longer than sailing to Royal Pacific, though boats may be delayed by traffic congestion under the bridge between the hotels and CityWalk. A pedestrian pathway to the parks starts near the boat dock, joining up with the Royal Pacific garden path near that hotel's convention center entrance. If you want to walk from Sapphire Falls to Cabana Bay, note that there's no pedestrian crosswalk at the heavily trafficked intersection that separates the two hotels; instead, walk to the corner of Hollywood Way and use the garden bridge to cross over Adventure Way, or use the path between Aventura and Volcano Bay to walk beneath the busy road.

Sapphire Falls occupies an interesting spot in Universal's hotel spectrum, appealing to people turned off both by the midcentury aesthetics of Cabana Bay (or Aventura's ultramodernism) and the higher price tags of the resort's other properties. If water taxi transportation is important to you, but Express Unlimited access is not, Sapphire Falls is your spot. Otherwise, search for photos online to see if you like the resort's look, and carefully compare the rates to both Cabana Bay and Aventura Hotel for the time of your planned visit.

Universal Aventura Hotel ★★★½

6725 Adventure Way
Orlando
☎ 407-503-6000
or 888-273-1311
loewshotels.com
/universals-aventura-hotel

Rate per night Standard rooms, $205–$250; Kids' Suites, $327–$501. **Pools ★★★. Fridge in room** Yes. **Shuttle to parks** Yes (Universal, SeaWorld, Aquatica). **Maximum number of occupants per room** 4 (2 queens or king with pullout) or 5 (Kids' Suites). **Comment** Pets not permitted. **Survey results** 81% of *Unofficial Guide* readers would stay here again; 83% would recommend this resort to a friend.

STRENGTHS	WEAKNESSES
• Short walk from Volcano Bay or CityWalk	• Ultramodern design lacks charm.
• Stunning views from rooftop bar	• Smallest standard rooms and pool at a Universal hotel
• Smart-home technology in each room	• Touchscreen controls can be clunky and confusing.

SQUEEZED NEXT TO THE LUSHLY TROPICAL Sapphire Falls and across the street from the colorfully retro Cabana Bay, Universal Aventura Hotel may seem a bit underthemed in comparison to its neighbors. But if you've ever seen the luxury skyscrapers lining Miami's waterfronts, this 16-story Y-shaped tower will make you feel right at home with its ultramodern curvilinear glass-covered design (which looks suspiciously similar to a giant fidget spinner).

From the sleek, spacious lobby to the streamlined guest rooms, Aventura embodies that trendy aesthetic that Universal describes as "simplified style" but cynics might describe as IKEA stark; if you've ever stayed in a European micro-hotel, Aventura's rooms will feel familiar. Standard rooms start at a minuscule 238 square feet—about 22 square feet smaller than Disney's All-Star Resorts—for a king room with a pullout couch, while the standard room (with two queen beds), at 314 square feet, is a smidgen smaller than those at Sapphire Falls next door. Deluxe rooms, available with two queen beds or a single king, have a little more elbow-room at 395 square feet but still sleep a maximum of four. Because the deluxe rooms are located at the ends of the hotel's wings, you'll wake up to a dramatic 180-degree view.

If you need more room, 16 **Kids' Suites** are available; at 575 square feet, they have space for six, including a separate interior room with two twin beds and a play area with a pullout couch but no special theming. Unusu-ally, room upgrades are priced not based on direction of view but altitude: "skyline" rooms on the topmost floors charge an extra $30 per night for panoramic views of the City Beautiful from one side of the tower or of Universal Orlando from the others. Odd-numbered rooms XX01–XX15 and even-numbered rooms XX30–XX44 face I-4 and International Drive; odd-numbered rooms XX31–XX45 and even-numbered rooms XX50–XX64 face Cabana Bay and Volcano Bay; and even-numbered rooms XX00–XX14 and odd-numbered rooms XX51–XX65 face toward Sapphire Falls and IOA.

All of the hotel's rooms share the same minimalist design scheme, fea-turing faux-hardwood tile floors and a monochromatic palette with a noticeable absence of color or artwork. Floor plans are oddly shaped, owing to the hotel's curved footprint, but floor-to-ceiling windows and translucent dividers between the bed and bath help the rooms feel more spacious. The beds are passable, though not plush, and all of the electron-ics work. However, the shower curtain doesn't extend far enough down, resulting in a wet floor every time.

In addition to the standard amenities, such as separate vanity and toilet areas, a minifridge, a coffee maker, and a 43-inch TV, Aventura's rooms integrate smart home technology. Not only are USB plugs pre-installed in the power outlets for recharging your digital devices, but every room also includes a tablet that you can use to adjust the air-conditioning, tune the TV, or even order a pizza and clean towels. If you have a Chromecast-compatible device or subscribe to Netflix or Ama-zon Prime, you can stream your own videos on the TV set. The iPad integration is innovative but also annoying if you need to use the sink in the middle of the night; thankfully, there are still physical switches for illuminating the toilet.

The pool at Aventura Hotel is also in the chic South Floridian style, with a compact crescent-shaped main pool surrounded by white decks and strategically placed palm trees. There's a splash pad and underwater speakers (all the better to hear the dive-in movies) for the kids, and a fire pit and hot tub for the grown-ups; anyone with a couple of bucks can enjoy the Foosball and pool tables. Rainy-day recreation includes a free fitness room and a Universal Studios Store.

Aventura Hotel doesn't have a full-service restaurant, but that doesn't mean you'll starve. Along with the de rigueur **Starbucks** in the lobby, you'll also find **Urban Pantry,** a fast-casual food hall serving international entrées like ramen, artisanal pizza, and rotisserie chicken, plus a rooftop bar that serves craft cocktails and small plates. There are two additional bars, in the lobby and at the pool, but you'll want to take the dedicated elevator up to **Bar 17 Bistro** on the rooftop for its million-dollar views of Volcano Bay's namesake peak and the surrounding city.

Like Cabana Bay, Aventura lacks direct water taxi service to CityWalk, though you can easily walk over to Sapphire Falls and use its boats. Bus service delivers guests to the parking hub, and there is direct pedestrian access to all three parks, including a dedicated sidewalk past the pool to Volcano Bay. Reader reactions to Aventura have been decidedly mixed compared to other Universal resorts, with this comment from a Portland, Connecticut, father being fairly representative:

> The room itself was very, very small. Go for the deluxe room for any sort of extra space if you have more than two in your party. Nothing about Aventura screamed Universal or Florida. NOTHING. The lobby was as sterile as an office building, and about as colorful.

On the other hand, the property does have its fans among millennials, like this woman from Bellingham, Washington:

> I need to put in a good word for Aventura Hotel, because I had zero issues on my stay there. It is absolutely geared toward a specific genre of traveler, but I fell perfectly into that niche group: single young adult, no children. Yes, the room was small, but for just myself it was perfectly adequate. Plus, the hotel never seemed crowded, Urban Pantry had great food, and the buses ran very close together, which I really appreciated.

Aventura and Cabana Bay both include Early Park Admission but not Universal Express, and their rack rates are similar. So the choice between them might come down to whether your preferred style is cutting-edge cool or vibrant vintage. That said, we think Cabana Bay is a better option overall.

Universal Cabana Bay Beach Resort ★★★½

6550 Adventure Way
Orlando
☎ 407-503-4000 or
888-273-1311
loewshotels.com
/cabana-bay-hotel

Rate per night Standard rooms, $205–$250; suites, $263–$315. **Pools** ★★★★½. **Fridge in room** Yes. **Shuttle to parks** Yes (Universal, SeaWorld, Aquatica). **Maximum number of occupants per room** 4 (2 queens) or 6 (suites). **Comments** Character greeting in lobby on Friday. Pets not permitted. **Survey results** 87% of *Unofficial Guide* readers would stay here again; 83% would recommend this resort to a friend.

STRENGTHS	WEAKNESSES
• Marvelous midcentury modern vibe	• Issues with maintenance and upkeep in some rooms
• Exclusive amenities like a lazy river and bowling alley	• Long waits for check-in during peak times
• Some rooms have spectacular views of Volcano Bay.	• Volcano Bay's noise can intrude in tower rooms.

IF YOU'RE OBSESSED WITH VINTAGE 1950s and 1960s designs, and with finding a good value (we're guilty on both accounts), you may just fall in love with Cabana Bay Beach Resort. The midcentury modern aesthetic starts with the neon signage that welcomes you outside and continues inside with lots of windows, bright colors, and period-appropriate lighting and furniture. The designers were inspired by classic seaside hotels such as the doo-wop Caribbean Motel in Wildwood Crest, New

Jersey, and the original Americana Hotel in Bal Harbour, Florida. We think the resort would be right at home in the deserts of Palm Springs or Las Vegas, while our British friends say the decor reminds them of Butlin's Bognor Regis resort circa 1985.

Whatever Cabana Bay reminds you of, we think it is an excellent choice for price- and/or space-conscious families visiting Universal. Kids love the two large and well-themed pools (one with a lazy river), the amount of space they have to run around in, the vintage cars parked outside the hotel lobby, and the video arcade. Adults will appreciate the sophisticated kitsch of the decor, the multiple lounges, and the on-site Starbucks.

The hotel's closest competitor in the Orlando area is Disney's Art of Animation Resort, and the two share many similarities. Both have standard rooms and Family Suites. At 430 square feet per suite, Cabana Bay suites are about 135 square feet smaller than comparable suites at Art of Animation and have only one bathroom. We found them well appointed for two to four people per room (though not for the six Loews claims as its capacity). Rates for the suites are significantly cheaper than Art of Animation's. Standard rooms are only 300 square feet but can frequently be had for around $25–$50 a night less than Disney's cheapest rooms.

Each **Family Suite** has a small bedroom with two queen beds and a 40-inch TV, divided from the living area and kitchenette by a sliding screen; a pullout sofa in the living area offers additional sleeping space and a second 40-inch TV. The bath is divided into three sections: toilet, sink area, and shower room with additional sink; all are separated by doors, so three people can theoretically get ready at once. Retro theming even extends to the toiletries, which include the fondly remembered Zest and VO5 brands. The kitchenette has a microwave, coffee maker, and minifridge. A bar area allows extra seating for quick meals, and a large closet has enough space to store everyone's luggage. Built-in USB charging outlets for your devices are a thoughtful touch. Standard rooms have the same two queen beds but without the living area, kitchenette, or three-way bathroom. Instead, they get a minifridge with coffee maker and an average-size single bathroom.

Cabana Bay's rooms are divided among five long structures and two towers, arranged around two pool courtyards and connected in the center by the lobby facilities. The **Castaway, Thunderbird,** and **Starlight** (designated buildings 1, 2, and 3, respectively, each proudly identified in glowing neon script) are motel-style structures with exterior entrances surrounding the Cabana Courtyard. The **Continental** (building 4) and **Americana** (buildings 5 and 6) frame the Lazy River Courtyard and have hotel-style interior hallways. At the far end of the Continental and Americana buildings, Universal built the **Bayside** (building 7) and **Beachside** (building 8) expansion towers with 400 additional guest rooms, 20 of which are expansive 772-square-foot two-bedroom suites with stunning views of the Volcano Bay water park; be warned that guests in these rooms may struggle to sleep in once the park's conch horn begins blowing at park opening. Buildings 4 (rooms XX00–XX21) and 5 (rooms XX00–XX24) are closest to the bus loop and cafeteria, while some north-facing rooms in building 2 have a view of Hogwarts Castle.

Cabana Bay's two large pools both have artificial beaches and zero-entry sloping bottoms. The **Cabana Courtyard Pool** is more active, with a splash-pad playground and 100-foot waterslide wrapped around a central diving tower (which you can't actually dive off of, for safety reasons). The **Lazy River Courtyard** is a little more laid-back, with classic rock music (as opposed to the Top 40 usually played around the Cabana Courtyard) and a lushly landscaped circular stream in which to relax. Flotation toys ($10–$18) are provided unpackaged and preinflated, but they can be exchanged for an uninflated packaged tube before departure (during pool operating hours). Cabana Bay even sells watertight cups at the pool bar, so you can sip your cocktail while circulating in the lazy river.

Indoor recreational options include the **Game-O-Rama** arcade (well stocked with late-model machines and classic carnival-style redemption games) and the 10-lane **Galaxy Bowl,** modeled after the Hollywood Star Lanes featured in *The Big Lebowski.* Bowling, which is open to non-hotel guests, costs $22 per person (up to six bowlers; $20 before 5 p.m. Monday–Friday), for 45–75 minutes of play with shoe rental; socks must be worn and can be purchased for $4–$7. Reservations are strongly recommended and may be made up to two weeks in advance at ☎ 407-503-4230, in person at Galaxy Bowl during operating hours, or through Resy.com (for parties of three or more bowlers). Lane time can be in demand, especially on rainy days.

Other diversions include poolside table tennis and billiards, as well as a large **Jack LaLanne Fitness Center** with free access. An activity room with board games and beanbag chairs opens on rainy days. Finally, outdoor movies are shown nightly near both pools, and the food court sells s'mores kits to roast over the gas-fueled fire pits.

In addition to the lobby's full-service **Starbucks,** the cavernous cafeteria-style **Bayliner Diner** food court serves breakfast, lunch, and dinner, with Coke Freestyle dispensers and giant screens in the seating area showing 1960s TV clips. **Swizzle Lounge** in the lobby, two pool bars (both with attached counter-service grills), in-room pizza delivery, and table-service snacks and sandwiches at the Galaxy Bowl round out the on-site dining options. The **Universal Studios Store** is the largest hotel store in the resort and stocks candy and clothes exclusive to Cabana Bay. The hotel is especially festive during the Halloween season, when exclusive Horror Nights photo ops and drink specials are offered

Colorful buses head to the parks' main parking hub from outside Cabana Bay's food court. The bus service is amazingly efficient; we've never waited more than 5 minutes for one to arrive, and the total transit time to the attractions is usually less than 15 minutes. It takes about the same amount of time to walk to CityWalk along the landscaped garden walkway, which passes the Sapphire Falls Resort before joining the walking path to Royal Pacific. And with an exclusive on-site entrance into Volcano Bay just for Cabana Bay guests, rolling out of bed just in time for early admission at the water park is a breeze; request the Bayside tower or Americana building 6 for the shortest walk.

Day guests who want to check out Cabana Bay should take the bus there from the parking hub, because the garden walk's gate requires a key card for hotel access. Take care when driving into and out of the hotel's driveway on Adventure Way. If you miss the entrance, or make a right when exiting, you'll find yourself on a one-way road to I-4 West toward Disney, and you won't be able to correct course until the FL 528 expressway.

We've received rave reviews of Cabana Bay from our readers, like this mom from Putney, Vermont:

> *I LOVED the hotel. I usually share a standard room with my two children, but after trying the (very reasonably priced) Family Suites, I don't think I can go back! We each had our own bed, and it was wonderful. The pullout bed was hard but perfect for my back. The theming of the hotel is so fun. The kids loved the lazy river. The food court is fun too.*

A mother from Overland Park, Kansas, adds:

> *We loved Cabana Bay. It had something for all of my kids (oldest is 17, youngest is 5), so everyone was happy. My husband and I even got some time while the kids were swimming each night to sit at the poolside bar and fire pit to wind down. Our kids didn't need us to entertain them in the pool area because there was so much to do. My 5- and 13-year-olds both enjoyed the waterslide. I loved the layout of the hotel and the quick ride to places like CityWalk (by far our favorite Orlando experience) and the parks.*

And a dad from Colorado Springs, Colorado, raves:

> *The hotel was great! We took the bus, and it was very convenient and fast, getting us there well before the park opened. Our second day, we walked to Sapphire Falls and took the boat to the parks, then walked back to Cabana Bay that night. The hotel gift shop was great too. It had some items you couldn't find in the parks.*

The biggest complaint we hear about Cabana Bay is that wait times to check in during the midafternoon are often excessive. Also, as the hotel enters its second decade, many of the furnishings are showing noticeable wear, and on a recent stay we were forced to repeatedly relocate into different rooms due to maintenance issues, which put a damper on our longtime love for Cabana Bay. In addition, housekeeping services can sometimes be inconsistent in comparison to the pricier Loews properties—particularly if you don't depart your room before Early Park Admission begins, as this traveler from the Netherlands learned:

> *Our room was cleaned only two out of the five nights we were there. Mistakes can be made, but when we talked to the staff about it, their attitude was very unfriendly; they blamed us for leaving our room so "late" (at latest around 9 a.m.!)*

Universal Endless Summer Resort ★★★½

Surfside Inn & Suites
7000 Universal Blvd.
Orlando
☎ 407-503-7000 or
888-430-4999
loewshotels.com
/surfside-inn-and-suites

Dockside Inn & Suites
7125 Universal Blvd.
Orlando
☎ 407-503-8000 or
888-430-4999
loewshotels.com
/dockside-inn-and-suites

Rate per night Standard rooms, $161-$193; suites, $210-$253. **Pools** ★★★. **Fridge in room** Yes. **Shuttle to parks** Yes (Universal, SeaWorld, Aquatica). **Maximum number of occupants per room** 4 (two queens) or 6 (suites). **Comment** Pets not permitted. **Survey results** *Surfside:* 92% of *Unofficial Guide* readers would stay here again, and 86% would recommend this resort to a friend. *Dockside:* 88% of *Unofficial Guide* readers would stay here again, and 87% would recommend this resort to a friend. These are the #1 and #2 highest-rated value-priced resorts at both Universal Orlando and Walt Disney World.

STRENGTHS	WEAKNESSES
• Room rates undercut inferior off-site motels.	• Soft goods aren't up to Loews's usual standards.
• Quick and convenient bus service to CityWalk	• Long walk across busy roads to main campus
• Affordably priced food courts and pool bars	• No table service dining or special amenities

FOR ANYONE WHO FONDLY REMEMBERS the eponymous 1966 seminal surfing documentary, the phrase *Endless Summer* conjures images of pristine oceans, epic waves, and limitless freedom. Universal Endless Summer Resort, a 2,800-room complex of value-priced rooms completed in 2020, is built along an inland lake that was previously home to the Wet 'n Wild water park, so the only waves it has ever known were artificial. But the resort does offer liberation of a sort, both from the traditional boundaries of Universal's property and from the limitation that park-owned hotels must always cost more than their off-site competition.

Endless Summer Resort actually comprises two sibling hotels, which sit across from each other on Universal Boulevard. **Surfside Inn and Suites,** located to the south on the land originally occupied by Wet 'n Wild's attractions, opened in summer 2019 with 750 rooms (360 standard and 390 two-bedroom suites) along the shoreline surrounding a surfboard-shaped pool. **Dockside Inn and Suites,** situated on the north side of the street in the water park's former parking lot, boasts a substantial 2,050 rooms (937 standard and 1,113 suites), supported by a separate lobby and two organically shaped pools; it opened in late 2020, after COVID-19 delayed its debut by several months. Both properties share a similar sunny aesthetic, with colorful images of seaside fun etched into the hotels' multistory cement towers. Between the two, we think Surfside has a slight edge owing to its smaller, more manageable size, but Dockside has a few improved amenities and food options.

Despite sporting Universal's Value Inn and Suites label, the 313-square-foot standard room with two queen beds is roughly the same size as the rooms at the Prime Value locations. They're also about the size of a Disney Moderate hotel room, but at (or under) Disney Value prices. And they aren't cheap from an aesthetic perspective either, as long as you appreciate the shabby chic look popular at vintage beachside hotels. In this modernized reinterpretation of a hippie hangout, the floors and furniture resemble reclaimed driftwood, and the tie-dyed curtains and vibrant wall art recall the summer of love. Thankfully, unlike the bohemian beach shacks of yore, at Endless Summer all the modern amenities are included: separate vanity and toilet areas, minifridge, convenient soda can holder, 43-inch TV, smart-home controls for the temperature, and built-in high-amperage USB-C charging outlets. Room soundproofing is excellent, which is a surprise at this price, and there are plenty of under-shelf hooks on which to hang things, though only a handful of drawers for stowing your clothes. Our biggest nitpick is the poor quality of the soft goods; foam pillows and polyblend bath towels should be outlawed.

A little more than half the rooms at each Endless Summer complex are 440-square-foot suites with three queen beds, one bathroom, and a kitchenette complete with sink, microwave, low-end coffee maker, and kitschy picnic table for dining alfresco indoors. That's about 65–80 square feet smaller—and one less bathroom than—Disney's Family Suites, but a little roomier than the pricier Family Suites at Cabana Bay. We also like that Endless Summer's suites have a separate private bedroom with a second 49-inch TV for the third bed (as opposed to a pullout sofa), though we prefer Cabana Bay's split toilet/shower setup.

Endless Summer's lobbies, which display colorful surfboard signage and provide wicker swings on which to lounge, aren't as architecturally impressive as those at the upscale hotels, but the whole atmosphere is warmer and cozier than at Aventura or Sapphire Falls. The pools feature small splash pads for the kids and hold organized family activities like bingo and hoop contests, but they are unusually shallow (maximum depth 4 feet) and lack waterslides. Unfortunately, Endless Summer guests are forbidden from crashing the pool at the other resorts. Each hotel also includes a surprisingly well-stocked free fitness room with internet-enabled treadmills that have interactive touchscreens, plus a **Universal Studios Store** and a video arcade. Full-service dining isn't offered, but cafeteria-style food courts, lobby and pool bars, **Starbucks** cafés, and pizza delivery are all available.

Because Endless Summer is on the opposite side of International Drive and I-4 from Universal Orlando's main campus, walking to the parks from there isn't practical, so a fleet of free buses is provided, servicing both the parking hub (from which you walk to CityWalk and the theme parks) and direct to Volcano Bay and Epic Universe. The ride to the parking hub from here is actually slightly shorter than the one from Cabana Bay; travel time is barely 5 minutes each way, and the entire trip (including walking and waiting to depart) takes about 15 minutes. At Surfside Inn, tower 1 is closest to the bus stop; the hotel's hallways are seemingly endless, and it can be quite a hike to the rooms most distant from the lobby. That problem is magnified at the massive Dockside Inn; rooms in the south wing of tower 1 are most convenient to the lobby and bus stop.

Endless Summer compares favorably with Disney's moderate hotels, but it can cost hundreds of dollars less, particularly when discounts are applied for staying four or more nights. Even at full rack rate, the hotel's competitive pricing undercuts many of its independent I-Drive neighbors, whose aging amenities will struggle to compete with Universal's 800-pound gorilla. Cost-conscious visitors should think twice before booking an off-site hotel that doesn't offer Early Park Admission and easy transportation now that Endless Summer is open, and many readers—like this Taos, New Mexico, couple—find they prefer it over Disney's competing properties:

> *The Endless Summer Dockside and Surfside resorts are a much better value than the "Value" resorts at Disney. We stayed in a three-queen suite at Dockside and couldn't believe how spacious and comfortable it was, with enough room for a sweet little picnic table big enough for four. And it cost $50–$70 less than a tiny*

room at Pop Century. We'll be spending much more of our Orlando vacation time at Universal from now on.

Universal Helios Grand Hotel ★★★★½

Rate per night TBD. **Pools** ★★★. **Fridge in room** Yes. **Shuttle to parks** Yes (Universal, SeaWorld, Aquatica). **Maximum number of occupants per room** 5 (2 queens) or 3 (king). **Comments** Pets welcome (2/room, $100/stay). **Survey results** Too new to rate.

8505 S. Kirkman Road
Orlando
☎ 888-430-4999
loewshotels.com
/helios-grand-hotel

STRENGTHS	WEAKNESSES
• Universal's newest luxury resort	• Expensive, especially for dining
• Direct access to Epic Universe and views of the park	• Smallish rooms for the price
• Rooftop bar and nighttime show-viewing area	• Less impressive pool than other resorts

REDEFINING THE TOP TIER for Universal Orlando hotels, the Universal Helios Grand Hotel is the resort's new luxury option. Located at the back of the Epic Universe theme park, Helios Grand is Universal Orlando's first hotel that is actually connected to a theme park. Resort guests can use a special entrance to walk directly into Epic Universe from the lobby, without having to travel all the way to the park's front entry.

This 500-room hotel offers mostly 325-square-foot double-queen-bed rooms, with only a handful of 340-square–foot rooms appointed with a single king-size bed. Plus, there are 14 545-square-foot dragon-themed family suites and two 1,500-square-foot presidential suites. All rooms include 55-inch TVs, tablet-based environmental controls, and 300-thread-count linens, and most feature incredible views overlooking Epic Universe, which is this hotel's claim to fame. Ten stories tall, with a rooftop bar and fireworks viewing area on the highest level, the Helios Grand was meant to be seen by parkgoers inside of Epic Universe as much as it was designed to offer breathtaking views of it.

Intended to act as Epic's equivalent of Cinderella Castle at Disney's Magic Kingdom, Helios Grand is stunningly beautiful as viewed from within the central areas of Epic Universe. It serves as the backdrop for the nightly fireworks and lagoon show, and is lit up like the sun at night, a nod to its namesake, Helios, the Greek personification of the sun. The exterior is adorned with ornate decoration inspired by celestial forms and constellations, and the interior's elegant style could be described as ultra-modern Mediterranean.

Its pool is perhaps no more impressive than the other Universal resorts (including Prime Value offerings), and quarters can be somewhat cramped. Much like staying in the original rooms of Walt Disney World's Contemporary Resort, you are paying for proximity to the park and the view over room size. But boy, what a view!

While guests are never far from the many offerings within the Epic Universe theme park for a bite, Helios Grand itself offers a couple of dining locations, including the grab-and-go **Aurora Market** and the full-service **Flora Taverna** with outdoor seating overlooking the park. The hotel features three bars: one in the lobby, **Lotus Lagoon** by the pool, and **Bar Helios** at roof level with spectacular views of the park's nighttime fireworks. Also located on the rooftop level, a private ballroom can be rented for private functions. A **Universal Studios Store** in the lobby has toiletries, as well as souvenirs, plus there's a game room, a fitness center, and a business center.

Note: Helios Grand guests do not get free Express passes or priority restaurant seating at press time.

4500 and 5500
Epic Blvd., Orlando
☎ 888-273-1311
loewshotels.com
/stella-nova-resort
loewshotels.com
/terra-luna-resort

Universal Stella Nova and Terra Luna Resorts
★★★½

Rate per night $134–$225. **Pools** ★★★. **Fridge in room** Yes. **Shuttle to parks** Yes (Universal, SeaWorld, Aquatica). **Maximum number of occupants per room** 4 (2 queens). **Comments** Pets not permitted. **Survey results** Too new to rate.

STRENGTHS	WEAKNESSES
• Universal's newest value-priced resort	• No on-site table service dining
• Easy access to Epic Universe	• Close to Epic Universe, but much farther from the other parks
• Affordably priced quick-service dining and convenient pizza delivery	• Not very close to CityWalk, or even most I-Drive restaurants

DESCRIBED BY THE COMPANY as the new gateway entrance to the Universal Orlando Resort, the Terra Luna and Stella Nova Resorts sit a couple of miles south of the original Universal Orlando parks. What they lack in proximity to USF, IOA, and Volcano Bay, they more than make up for by being located directly in front of Epic Universe. Of course, bus transportation is available to all the parks, as well as CityWalk, but you could just walk across the street from Stella Nova and be at Epic Universe's front door—which for a Prime Value hotel, is quite a perk.

Stella Nova officially opens January 21, 2025, and Terra Luna opens February 25, 2025. Technically two separate hotels, divided from each other by Kirkman Road, both resorts offer 750 reasonably priced double-queen bed rooms. Styled after galaxies, each hotel is plastered with shiny—and highly reflective—colorful tiles. While their exteriors appear quite colorful, the lobbies are understated and modern, with a sea of molded white architecture, contemporary wood accents, and only small pops of color, a design motif that Universal refers to as "fresh."

Both resorts offer large pools, with a hot tub, kids' splash pad area, poolside bar and grill, as well as the usual fitness center, arcade, Universal Studios Store, and quick-service dining options. Unlike other newer hotels at Universal Orlando, these two do not include a Starbucks (although you will find two of them inside the Epic Universe theme park nearby). The lobbies each include one quick-service restaurant offering three meals daily, as well as a grab-and-go pickup location. Neither resort offers a full-service restaurant, one of their biggest downsides. But you can order pizza directly to your room, just like at other Prime Value hotels, which is convenient and easy.

Rooms are comparable to the standard rooms at Cabana Bay. They feature nearly the same square footage, two queen beds to sleep up to 4, and similar amenities like a coffee maker and minifridge. Simply replace Cabana Bay's retro decor with Stella Nova and Terra Luna's outer space–inspired theme, complete with spaceship-style curved windows: think *Star Trek* meets Holiday Inn.

Universal promotes rooms at Stella Nova and Terra Luna starting slightly cheaper than Cabana Bay, which is impressive for brand-new hotels. These two hotels are well suited for guests looking to spend time at the new Epic Universe theme park. The older hotels, located closer to Universal Studios Florida and Islands of Adventure, may be what you're looking for if you plan to only spend a single day (or no days) at Epic Universe, just for the time-saving convenience of travel alone. However, you are only a 15-minute complimentary shuttle bus ride away from the other parks (similar to the trip between Walt Disney World's All-Star Resorts and the Magic Kingdom), which doesn't seem too much of a sacrifice if the room rates are good.

UNIVERSAL ORLANDO VACATION PACKAGES

UNIVERSAL FREQUENTLY OFFERS VACATION packages including hotel accommodations and park tickets via its in-house travel company, **Universal Orlando Vacations.** You can book a package yourself by calling ☎ 877-801-9720 or by visiting universalorlandovacations.com, or you can contact your preferred travel agent. Universal Orlando Vacations booked more than 45 days in advance require only a $50-per-person deposit (airfare fully due at time of booking) that is fully refundable until 45 days out; after that, the penalty is $200 per package, though some event tickets may be nonrefundable.

Universal Orlando Vacations also handles group sales; if you want to organize a family reunion at Cabana Bay, call ☎ 800-224-4489 and choose option 3, or visit res.universalorlandovacations.com/group/groups.aspx.

Universal advertises its packages with enticing taglines like, "The Wizarding World from only $149 a night!," along with offers of up to $1,000 in dining gift cards (valid for food and drinks at most resort restaurants). You have to do the math, though, because it's difficult for package purchasers to save money over buying à la carte unless they fully exploit every included component.

Here's an example. A Wizarding World of Harry Potter Vacation Package in late 2024 offered a family of four (two adults and two kids under age 10) these components:

1. Five nights at a Universal on-site hotel (or off-site partner hotel)
2. Five days of Park-to-Park admission to USF and IOA
3. Breakfast at Three Broomsticks (one per person)
4. Breakfast at Leaky Cauldron (one per person)

5. Photography session at Shutterbutton's in Diagon Alley, including souvenir DVD in a collectible tin and one exclusive designed 8-by-10-inch photo print

6. An ice-cream flight from Florean Fortescue's, with your choice of four scoops in a Honeydukes cooler tote.

7. Early Park Admission to The Wizarding World of Harry Potter and Volcano Bay 1 hour before the general public

At Endless Summer Resort, the package started at $2,268.54, including tax, during the value season (late August–September). There were significant restrictions, including block-out dates, and the stay had to occur on Sunday–Thursday nights to qualify for that low rate; weekend nights were more expensive.

Here's the first thing to recognize: the last item—early admission to The Wizarding World—is automatically given to everyone who stays at a Universal resort and purchases a theme park ticket, so it doesn't have any value by itself. As for the "special" flight at Florean Fortescue's, anyone can purchase the same ice-cream scoops for $32, and the Honeydukes tote is of nominal worth.

There are only four remaining components to price: the hotel, tickets, the Shutterbutton's session, and the breakfasts at the Three Broomsticks and Leaky Cauldron. We checked Universal's website for the cost of the other components using various dates and ensured those dates would also qualify for the aforementioned package. Here's a typical cost per component:

- $535.80 for five nights at Endless Summer Resort during value season
- $1,503.74 for 5-Day, 2-Park Park-to-Park Tickets from universalorlando.com
- $ 138.36 for breakfast for four at the Three Broomsticks and Leaky Cauldron, including tax
- $85.19 for the Shutterbutton's DVD, including tax
- $31.91 for four scoops of Florean Fortescue's ice cream, including tax

The total cost if you bought each component separately is $2,295.01, which means that buying the vacation package saves you about $26. If, however, you were to forgo the ice cream, breakfasts, and Shutterbutton's video, you'd save more than $225 by buying separately. You can still reserve breakfast in The Wizarding World through your hotel's Vacation Planning Center without a package, or even just walk up to the restaurants on many mornings. Unless you're certain that you want the breakfasts and DVD, you're better off having lunch at the Leaky Cauldron with the money you'll save by buying each item of the package separately, as this anonymous reader discovered to their dismay:

> I'm still kicking myself for purchasing the entire package: flights, transfers, meal plan, etc. I was a total sucker and had a good time adding up the numbers for our meals and realizing it was virtually impossible to spend enough money to break even.

Even if it won't save you money, there are a few reasons why you may still want to book a Universal Orlando Vacations package. The first is if you can't afford to stay on-site but still want Early Park Admission to

The Wizarding World and Volcano Bay. Booking a room at a Universal-area partner hotel as part of a package through Universal Orlando Vacations is the *only* way to get guaranteed early entry to the Harry Potter attractions and the water park, other than staying in an on-site hotel.

Another reason is if you're attending a special event at Universal Orlando that offers exclusive experiences for package buyers. For example, the now-discontinued Celebration of Harry Potter fan convention held an after-hours party in The Wizarding World just for vacation-package purchasers. Occasionally, packages are offered with truly unique perks: before the openings of Hogsmeade and Diagon Alley, a limited number of package holders were allowed into the new Wizarding Worlds weeks before the general public, and similar early-bird offers could be available at Epic Universe. These rare opportunities are only for the diehards because uncontrollable technical delays can always preempt previews without refunds.

If you opt to book through Universal Orlando Vacations, be sure to pay very close attention during the confirmation process, as a mom of three from Arlington, Virginia, explains:

> We did not get the package we thought we were getting because we didn't catch the omission when the phone attendant confirmed our travel plans. When we called back about it, they went back to the recording transcripts and said that because we had not caught the omission then, it was our fault, and they didn't have to reinstate that portion of the package. I was miffed.

Guests purchasing packages directly from Universal Vacations can add optional travel protection for $55 per person (ages 3 and older), allowing them to cancel for any reason up to 24 hours prior to departure, and receive a full refund and/or air travel credit. Just be aware that, in case of a cancellation, Universal Vacations may take a while to refund your payments, as was the case with this reader from Drummond, Wisconsin:

> When it was announced that the parks would be closed, I called Universal to cancel the trip and was told that the credit back to my account would take four to six weeks to process. Not having received the credit (after seven weeks and multiple calls), I'm frustrated with the process and the uncertainty of whether I'll actually receive the refund. I'll certainly never consider booking with Universal again.

OFF-SITE LODGING OPTIONS

SELECTING AND BOOKING A HOTEL

LODGING COSTS IN ORLANDO vary incredibly. If you shop around, you can find a clean motel with a pool for as low as $80 a night. Because of hot competition, discounts abound, particularly for AAA and AARP members. If you want to be near Universal Orlando, there are two primary areas to consider:

1. UNIVERSAL ORLANDO AREA In the triangular area bordered by I-4 on the southeast, Vineland Road on the north, and Turkey Lake Road on the west are Universal Orlando and the hotels most convenient to it. Running north–south through the middle of the triangle is Kirkman Road, which connects to I-4. On the east side of Kirkman are a number of independent hotels and restaurants. Universal hotels, parks, and CityWalk are west of Kirkman. Traffic in this area is not nearly as congested as on nearby International Drive, and there are good interstate connections in both directions.

2. INTERNATIONAL DRIVE AREA This area, about 5 minutes from Universal, parallels I-4 on its eastern side and offers a wide selection of hotels and restaurants. Prices range from around $100 to $450 per night. The chief drawbacks of this area are its terribly congested roads, countless traffic signals, and inadequate access to I-4 West. While International's biggest bottleneck is its intersection with Sand Lake Road, the mile between Kirkman and Sand Lake Roads is almost always gridlocked.

Regarding traffic on International Drive (known locally as I-Drive), a conventioneer from Islip, New York, weighed in with this:

> *We wasted huge chunks of time in traffic on International Drive. Our hotel was in the section between Sand Lake Road and Universal Boulevard. There are practically no left-turn lanes in this section, so anyone turning left can hold up traffic for a long time.*

Traffic aside, a man from Ottawa, Ontario, sings the praises of his I-Drive experience:

> *International Drive is the place to stay in Orlando. Your description of this location failed to point out that there are several discount stores, boutiques, restaurants, miniputts, and other entertainment facilities all within walking distance of remarkably inexpensive accommodations and a short drive away from the attractions.*

I-Drive hotels are listed on the **Visit Orlando** website: visitorlando .com/places-to-stay (click "International Drive Area").

HOTEL SHOPPING

OTAS **Online travel agencies** (**OTAs**) sell travel products from a wide assortment of suppliers, often at deep discounts. These sites include such familiar names as **Travelocity, Orbitz, Priceline, Expedia,** and **Hotels.com.**

The better-known OTAs draw a lot more web traffic than a given hotel's (or even hotel chain's) website. Most hotels offer some sort of "lowest-price guarantee" on their websites, offering to match or beat a price seen elsewhere for the same reservation.

MORE POWER TO THE SHOPPER OTAs are a powerful tool for obtaining the best rates for the hotel of your choice. It's why we tell you to shop the web for the lowest price available and then call your travel agent or the hotel itself to ask if they can beat it. Any savvy reservationist knows that selling you the room directly will both cut the hotel's cost and improve gross margin. If the reservationist can't help you, ask to speak to their supervisor. (We've actually had to explain hotel economics to more than a few clueless reservation agents.)

As for travel agents, they have clout based on the volume of business they send to a particular hotel or chain and can usually negotiate a rate even lower than what you've found online. Even if the agent can't beat the price, they can often obtain upgrades, preferred views, free breakfasts, and other deal sweeteners. When we bump into a great deal on the web, we call our agent. Often she can beat the deal or improve on it, perhaps with an upgrade. *Reminder:* Except for special arrangements agreed to by you, the fee or commission due to your travel agent will be paid by the hotel.

THE SECRET   When we're really hungry for a deal, there are a number of sites we always check out:

OUR FAVORITE ONLINE HOTEL RESOURCES	
HOTELCOUPONS.COM	Self-explanatory
ORLANDOVACATION.COM	Great rates for condos and home rentals
VISITORLANDO.COM	Good info; not user-friendly for booking

We scour these sites for great hotel deals that meet our criteria (location, quality, price, and amenities). If we find a hotel that fills the bill, we check it out at other websites and comparative travel search engines such as **Kayak** (kayak.com), **Hotels.com,** and **Trivago** (trivago .com). Your initial shopping effort should take about 15–20 minutes, faster if you can zero in quickly on a particular hotel.

Next, call the hotel or have your travel agent call. Start by asking about specials. If there are none, or if the hotel can't beat the best price you've found on the internet, share your findings and ask if the hotel can do better. Sometimes you'll be asked for proof of the rate you've discovered online—to be prepared for this, go to the site and enter the dates of your stay, plus the rate you've found to make sure it's available. If it is, print the page or take a screenshot of this information and have it handy for your travel agent or for when you call the hotel. (*Note:* Always call the hotel's local number, not its national reservations number.)

We've also had great results using **HotelTonight.com**'s free smartphone app around the country and in Europe. If you don't mind not knowing where you'll rest your head until a few days (or even hours) in advance, you can score tremendous savings on properties near Universal, though not on-site.

AIRBNB   This service (airbnb.com) connects travelers with owner-hosted alternative lodging all over the world, from spare bedrooms in people's homes to private apartments, vacation homes, and even live-in boats.

We find Airbnb less useful in Orlando for a couple of reasons. First, Orlando has an enormous supply of vacation-home rentals and hotel rooms, which keeps prices down for lodging around Universal

Orlando. Second, Universal's incentives for staying on-property are hard to beat. That said, Kissimmee appears to be a rapidly growing market for Airbnb. If you find a good property this way, let us know.

IS IT WORTH IT?   You might be asking yourself if it's worth all this effort to save a few bucks. Saving $10 on a room may not sound like a lot, but if you're staying six nights, that adds up to $60. Unusually juicy deals—deep discounts predicated by who-knows-what circumstances that add up to big money—are available every day, and with a little perseverance, you'll find them. Happy hunting!

CONDOMINIUMS AND VACATION HOMES

BECAUSE CONDOS TEND TO BE part of large developments (frequently time-shares), amenities such as swimming pools, playgrounds, game arcades, and fitness centers often rival those found in the best hotels. Generally, condo developments don't have restaurants, lounges, or spas. In a condo, if something goes wrong, there will be someone on hand to fix the problem. Vacation homes rented from a property-management company likewise will have someone to come to the rescue, though responsiveness tends to vary vastly from company to company. If you rent directly from an owner, correcting problems is often more difficult, particularly when the owner doesn't live in the same area as the rental home.

In a vacation home, all the amenities are contained in the home (though in planned developments, there may be community amenities available as well). Depending on the specific home, you might find a small swimming pool, hot tub, two-car garage, family room, game room, and even a home theater. Features found in both condos and vacation homes include full kitchens, laundry rooms, TVs, DVD players, and frequently stereos. Interestingly, though almost all freestanding vacation homes have private pools, very few have backyards. This means that, except for swimming, the kids are pretty much relegated to playing in the house.

Time-share condos are clones when it comes to furniture and decor, but single-owner condos and vacation homes are furnished and decorated in a style that reflects the owner's taste. Vacation homes, usually one- to two-story houses in a subdivision, very rarely afford interesting views (though some homes overlook lakes or natural areas), while condos, especially the high-rise variety, sometimes offer exceptional ones.

How the Vacation Home Market Works

In the Orlando area just prior to the pandemic, there were more than 26,000 rental homes, including stand-alone homes, single-owner condos (that is, not time-shares), and town homes. The same area had about 128,000 hotel rooms. Some owners deal directly with renters, while others enlist the assistance of a property-management company.

Incredibly, about 700 property-management companies operate in the Orlando market. Most of these are mom-and-pop outfits that manage an inventory of 10 homes or fewer (probably fewer than 70 companies oversee more than 100 rental homes).

Some homes are made available to wholesalers, vacation packagers, and travel agents. A wholesaler or vacation packager will occasionally drop its rates to sell slow-moving inventory, but more commonly the cost to renters is higher than when dealing directly with owners or management companies: because most wholesalers and packagers sell their inventory through travel agents, both the wholesaler/packager's markup and the travel agent's commission are passed along to the renter. These costs are in addition to the owner's cut and/or the fee for the property manager.

Along similar lines, logic may suggest that the lowest rate of all can be obtained by dealing directly with owners, thus eliminating middlemen. Though this is sometimes true, it's more often the case that property-management companies offer the best rates. With their marketing expertise and larger customer base, these companies can produce a higher occupancy rate than the owners themselves can. What's more, management companies, or at least the larger ones, can achieve economies of scale not available to owners regarding maintenance, cleaning, linens, and even acquiring furniture and appliances (if a house is not already furnished). The combination of higher occupancy rates and economies of scale adds up to a win–win situation for owners, management companies, and renters alike.

Location, Location, Location

The best vacation home is one that is within easy commuting distance of the parks. If you plan to visit Walt Disney World and SeaWorld in addition to the Universal parks, you'll want something just southwest of Universal Orlando (between Walt Disney World and Orlando).

Zoning laws in Orange County—which also includes most of Orlando, Universal Studios, SeaWorld, Lake Buena Vista, and the International Drive area—allow short-term rentals of homes and single-owner condos only in a few predominantly tourist-oriented areas. Practically all of the vacation-rental homes in Orange County are in the **Floridays** and **Vista Cay** developments.

By our reckoning, about half the rental homes in Osceola County and all the rental homes in Polk County are too far away for commuting to be practical. You might be able to save a few bucks by staying farther out, but the most desirable homes to be found are in **Vista Cay** and in developments no more than 10 miles south of Universal's main entrance, from west of John Young Parkway to east of the FL 429 Western Beltway.

To get the most from a vacation home, you need to be close enough to commute in 20 minutes or less to your Orlando destination. This will allow for naps, quiet time, swimming, and dollar-saving meals you prepare yourself.

Shopping for a Vacation Home

There are three main types of websites in the home-rental game: those for property-management companies, which showcase a given company's homes and are set up for direct bookings; individual owner sites; and third-party listings sites, which advertise properties available through different owners and sometimes management companies as well. Sites in the last category will usually refer prospective renters to an owner's or management company's site for reservations.

We've found that most property-management sites are not very well designed and will test your patience to the max. You can practically click yourself into old age trying to see all the homes available or figure out where on earth they are. Nearly all claim to be "just minutes from Universal [or Disney]." (By that reasoning, we should list Bob's home; it's also just minutes from Universal . . . 570 minutes, to be exact!)

Many websites list homes according to towns (such as Clermont, Lake Buena Vista, Windermere, and Winter Garden) or real estate developments (including Eagle Pointe, Floridays, Golden Oaks, and Vista Cay) in the general Universal area, none of which you're likely to be familiar with. The information that counts is the distance of a home or condo from Universal; for that, you often must look for something like "4 miles from Universal" embedded in the home's description.

The best websites provide the following:

- Numerous photos and in-depth descriptions of individual homes to make comparisons quick and easy
- Overview maps or text descriptions that reflect how far specific homes or developments are from your Orlando destination
- The ability to book the specific rental home of your choice on the site
- An easy-to-find phone number for bookings and questions

The best sites are also easy to navigate, let you see what you're interested in without your having to log in or divulge any personal information, and list memberships in such organizations as the Better Business Bureau and the Florida Vacation Rental Managers Association (visit fvrma.org for the association's code of ethics).

Recommended Websites

After checking out dozens upon dozens of sites, here are the ones we recommend. All of them meet the criteria listed above. (For the record, we elected not to list some sites that met our criteria but whose homes are too far away from the Orlando-area attractions.)

Florida Dream Homes (floridadreamhomes.com) has a good reputation for customer service and has photos of and information about the homes in its online inventory.

Vacation Rentals by Owner (vrbo.com) is a nationwide vacation-homes listings service that puts prospective renters in direct contact with owners. The site is straightforward and always lists a large number of rental properties in Celebration, Disney's planned community situated about 15–20 minutes from the Universal theme parks. A similar listing service is **Vacation Rentals 411** (vacationrentals411.com).

The website for **Visit Orlando** (visitorlando.com) is the place to go if you're interested in renting a condo at a time-share development (click on "Places to Stay" at the site's home page). You can call the developments directly, but going through this website allows you to bypass sales departments and escape their high-pressure invitations to sit through sales presentations. The site also lists hotels, vacation homes, and campgrounds. For all types of accommodations, you can sort by distance from where you'll spend your touring time. Distance-sorting categories include Universal, Walt Disney World, the Orange County Convention Center, and downtown Orlando, among others.

Making Contact

Once you've found a vacation home you like, check around the website for a frequently asked questions (FAQ) page. If there's not an FAQ page, here are some of the things you'll want to check out on the phone with the owner or rental company.

1. How close is the property to my vacation destination?
2. Is the home or condominium that I see on the internet the one I'll get?
3. Is the property part of a time-share development?
4. Are there any specials or discounts available?
5. Is everything included in the rental price, or are there additional charges? What about taxes?
6. How old is the house or condo that I'm interested in? When was it last refurbished?
7. What is the view from the property?
8. Is the property near any noisy roads?
9. What is your smoking policy?
10. Are pets allowed? This consideration is as important to those who want to avoid pets as to those who want to bring them.
11. Is the pool heated?
12. Is there a fenced backyard where children can play?
13. How many people can be seated at the main dining table?
14. Is high-speed internet access available?
15. Are linens and towels provided?
16. How far are the nearest supermarket and drugstore?
17. Are childcare services available?
18. Are restaurants nearby?
19. Is transportation to the parks provided?
20. Will we need a car?
21. What is required to make a reservation?
22. What is your change/cancellation policy?
23. When is checkout time?

24. What will we be responsible for when we check out?
25. How will we receive our confirmation and arrival instructions?
26. What are your office hours?
27. What are the directions to your office?
28. What if we arrive after your office has closed?
29. Whom do we contact if something goes wrong during our stay?
30. How long have you been in business?
31. Are you licensed by the state of Florida?
32. Do you belong to the Better Business Bureau and/or the Florida Vacation Rental Managers Association?

We frequently receive letters from readers extolling the virtues of renting a condo or vacation home. This endorsement by a family from Ellington, Connecticut, is typical:

> *Our choice to stay in a vacation home was based on cost and sanity. Our children don't want to share the same bed. We've also gotten tired of turning off the lights at 8 p.m. and lying quietly in the dark waiting for our children to fall asleep. With this in mind, we needed a condo/suite layout. We decided on the Sheraton Vistana Resort, located on FL 535. We had a two-bedroom villa with a full kitchen, living room, three TVs, and a washer/dryer. I packed for half the trip and did laundry almost every night. The facilities offered a daily children's program and several pools, kiddie pools, and playscapes. We had a 5- to 10-minute drive to most attractions, including SeaWorld, Disney, and Universal.*

The BEST HOTELS *near* UNIVERSAL ORLANDO

IN THIS SECTION, we compare hotels in two main areas outside Universal Orlando (see page 104) with those inside the resort. Additional hotels can be found in Lake Buena Vista and along the I-4 corridor, at the intersection of US 27 and I-4, on US 441 (Orange Blossom Trail), and in downtown Orlando. Most of these require more than 30 minutes of commuting to the Orlando-area attractions and thus are not included in this book. We also haven't rated lodging along US 192.

WHAT'S IN A ROOM?

EXCEPT FOR CLEANLINESS, STATE OF REPAIR, and decor, travelers pay little attention to hotel rooms. There is, of course, a clear standard of quality and luxury that differentiates Motel 6 from Holiday Inn, Holiday Inn from Marriott, and so on. Many guests, however, fail to appreciate that some rooms are better engineered than others. Making the room usable to its occupants is an art that combines both form and function.

Decor and taste are important. No one wants to stay in a room that's dated, garish, or ugly. But beyond decor, how "livable" is the room? In

Hotels in the Universal & International Drive Areas

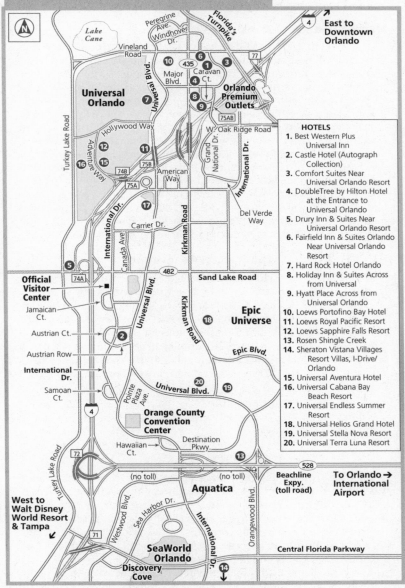

HOTELS
1. Best Western Plus Universal Inn
2. Castle Hotel (Autograph Collection)
3. Comfort Suites Near Universal Orlando Resort
4. DoubleTree by Hilton Hotel at the Entrance to Universal Orlando
5. Drury Inn & Suites Near Universal Orlando Resort
6. Fairfield Inn & Suites Orlando Near Universal Orlando Resort
7. Hard Rock Hotel Orlando
8. Holiday Inn & Suites Across from Universal
9. Hyatt Place Across from Universal Orlando
10. Loews Portofino Bay Hotel
11. Loews Royal Pacific Resort
12. Loews Sapphire Falls Resort
13. Rosen Shingle Creek
14. Sheraton Vistana Villages Resort Villas, I-Drive/Orlando
15. Universal Aventura Hotel
16. Universal Cabana Bay Beach Resort
17. Universal Endless Summer Resort
18. Universal Helios Grand Hotel
19. Universal Stella Nova Resort
20. Universal Terra Luna Resort

Orlando, for example, we've seen some beautifully appointed rooms that aren't well designed for human habitation. Even more than decor, your room's details and design elements are the things that will make you feel comfortable and at home.

HOW TO GET THE ROOM YOU WANT

MOST HOTELS WON'T GUARANTEE a specific room when you book but will post your request on your reservations record and try to accommodate you. Our experience indicates that if you give them your first, second, and third choices, you'll probably get one of the three.

When speaking to the reservationist or your travel agent, be specific. If you want a room overlooking the pool, say so. Similarly, be sure to clearly state preferences such as a particular floor, a corner room, a room close to restaurants, a room away from elevators and ice machines, a nonsmoking room, a room with a balcony, or any other preference. If you have a list of preferences, type it up in order of importance, and email or fax it to the hotel or to your travel agent; keep your request as brief and specific as possible. Be sure to include your own contact information and, if you've already booked, your reservation confirmation number. If it makes you feel better, call back in a few days to make sure that your preferences were posted to your reservations record.

unofficial **TIP**
Request a renovated room at your hotel—these can be much nicer than the older rooms.

About Hotel Renovations

Most hotels more than five years old refurbish 10%–20% of their guest rooms each year. This incremental approach minimizes disruption of business but makes your room assignment a crapshoot. You might luck into a newly renovated room or be assigned a threadbare room. Some hotels will guarantee an updated room when you book, so you should ask. Before you begin to shop for a hotel, take a hard look at this letter we received from a couple in Hot Springs, Arkansas:

> We canceled our room reservations to follow the advice in your book [and reserved a hotel highly rated by The Unofficial Guide]. We wanted inexpensive but clean and cheerful. We got inexpensive but dirty, grim, and depressing. I really felt disappointed in your advice and the room. It was the pits. That was the one real piece of information I needed from your book!

Needless to say, this letter was as unsettling to us as the bad room was to our reader. Our integrity as travel journalists, after all, is based on the quality of the information we provide to our readers. When we rechecked the hotel that our reader disliked so intensely, we discovered that our review was correctly representative but that he and his wife had unfortunately been assigned to one of a small number of threadbare rooms scheduled for renovation.

The key to avoiding disappointment is to do some snooping around in advance. We recommend that you check out the hotel's website to see a standard guest room photo before you book. Be forewarned, however, that some hotel chains use the same guest room photo for all hotels in the chain, and that the guest room in a specific property may not resemble the photo on the website. When you or your travel agent call, ask how old the property is and when the guest room you are being assigned was last renovated. If you arrive and are assigned a room inferior to that which you had been led to expect, demand to be moved to another room.

ROOM RATINGS

OVERALL STAR RATINGS		
★★★★★	Superior rooms	Tasteful and luxurious by any standard
★★★★	Extremely nice rooms	What you'd expect at a Hyatt Regency or Marriott
★★★	Nice rooms	Holiday Inn or comparable quality
★★	Adequate rooms	Clean, comfortable, and functional without frills—like a Motel 6

TO EVALUATE PROPERTIES FOR THEIR QUALITY, tastefulness, state of repair, cleanliness, and size of their standard rooms, we have grouped the hotels and motels into classifications denoted by stars—the overall star rating. Star ratings in this guide apply only to Orlando-area properties and don't necessarily correspond to ratings awarded by Frommer's, Forbes, AAA, or other travel critics. Because stars have little relevance when awarded in the absence of recognized standards of comparison, we have tied our ratings to expected levels of quality established by specific American hotel corporations.

If you used an earlier edition of this guide, you will notice that we've revamped the way we review hotels. In the years since we began publishing, the internet has utterly upended the art of researching hotel rooms, with websites such as TripAdvisor now providing crowd-sourced ratings of hundreds more properties than our team could possibly properly investigate. Instead of attempting to appear comprehensive by filling pages with superficial statistics, we've focused on crafting a curated collection of properties across a range of price points, and supplied succinct details on what sets each one apart from its competition. Our recommendations take into consideration not only room quality but also location, services, recreation, and amenities. Just because a hotel isn't listed here doesn't necessarily mean it's a bad bet for bedding down, but the properties profiled on the following pages are all places that we can personally vouch for.

Best Western Plus Universal Inn   ★★½

5618 Vineland Rd. Orlando
☎ 407-226-9119 or 800-780-7234
bestwestern.com

Rate per night $97–$126. Pool ★★. Fridge in room Yes. Shuttle to parks Yes (Universal, Aquatica, SeaWorld). Maximum number of occupants per room 4. Comments Free parking. No pets allowed.

A GOOD OPTION FOR A NO-FRILLS STAY, this budget motel is within a reasonable walking distance to Universal Orlando, although it's not as close as other off-site hotels. The rooms are basic (though King beds are available), and despite recent renovations it's suitable solely as a place to sleep and shower. However, you get a microwave in all rooms

HOW THE HOTELS COMPARE

HOTEL	PAGE	OVERALL QUALITY RATING	POOL RATING	COST
Loews Portofino Bay Hotel	85	★★★★½	★★★★	$531–$984
Sheraton Vistana Villages Resort Villas, I-Drive/Orlando	117	★★★★½	★★★★	$125–$249
Universal Helios Grand Hotel	99	★★★★½	★★★	TBD
DoubleTree by Hilton Hotel at the Entrance to Universal Orlando	115	★★★★	★★★★	$114–$209
Hard Rock Hotel Orlando	83	★★★★	★★★★	$555–$960
Loews Royal Pacific Resort	87	★★★★	★★★★	$458–$650
Loews Sapphire Falls Resort	89	★★★★	★★★★	$245–$305
Rosen Shingle Creek	117	★★★★	★★★★	$189–$323
Castle Hotel (Autograph Collection)	114	★★★½	★★★	$159–$229
Drury Inn & Suites Near Universal Orlando Resort	115	★★★½	★★★	$137–$173
Fairfield Inn & Suites Orlando Near Universal Resort	116	★★★½	★★★	$130–$189
Holiday Inn & Suites Across from Universal	116	★★★½	★★★½	$131–$197
Hyatt Place Across from Universal Orlando	116	★★★½	★★★	$139–$178
Universal Aventura Hotel	91	★★★½	★★★	$205–$250
Universal Cabana Bay Beach Resort	93	★★★½	★★★★½	$205–$250
Universal Endless Summer Resort	96	★★★½	★★★	$161–$193
Universal Stella Nova and Terra Luna Resorts	100	★★★½	★★★	$134–$225
Comfort Suites Near Universal Orlando Resort	115	★★★	★★★	$127–$144
Best Western Plus Universal Inn	113	★★½	★★	$97–$126

and continental breakfast every morning. Plus, Miller's Ale House and several fast-food places are nearby, as is Walgreens for supplies. The combination of nearby food options, in-room amenities, free parking, and basic complimentary breakfast will assist in saving money. On the downside, the shuttle service has repeatedly proved unreliable, so for the best experience we recommend using other transportation if you stay here.

Castle Hotel (Autograph Collection)   ★★★½

8629 International Dr.
Orlando
☎ 407-345-1511 or
855-696-4727
castlehotelorlando.com

Rate per night $159–$229. Pool ★★★. Fridge in room Yes. Shuttle to parks Yes (Universal, SeaWorld). Maximum number of occupants per room 4. Comments Pets welcome (2/room, 40-pound limit, $150 non-refundable fee for first pet and $50 for second pet). $25 daily self-parking fee, $35 valet.

YOU CAN'T MISS THIS ONE: it's the only castle on I-Drive and is part of Marriott's Autograph Collection. Inside you'll find the royal purples and opulent antler fixtures have been displaced by more modern decor in cooler colors, but Renaissance tapestries still hang behind the lobby desk.

The 214 rooms and suites also sport a streamlined reinterpretation of the royal treatment, featuring soothing pale pastels and gold-leaf accents. All rooms are fairly large and well equipped with a flatscreen TV, free high-speed Wi-Fi , coffee maker, minifridge, iron and board, hair dryer, and safe. The Guild Restaurant & Bar off the lobby serves breakfast, lunch, and dinner, with drinks until 11 p.m. You can also walk next door to BJ's Restaurant & Brewhouse or Café Tu Tu Tango (an *Unofficial* favorite). The heated circular pool is 5 feet deep and features a fountain in the center, a poolside bar, and a hot tub. There's no separate kiddie pool. Other amenities include a fitness center, gift shop, lounge, valet laundry service and facilities, and guest services desk with park passes for sale and babysitting recommendations.

Comfort Suites Near Universal Orlando Resort ★★★

5617 Major Blvd. Orlando
☎ 407-363-1967; choicehotels.com

Rate per night $127–$144. **Pool** ★★★. **Fridge in room** Yes. **Shuttle to parks** Yes (Universal only). **Maximum number of occupants per room** 5. **Comments** Pets welcome ($50 per stay, maximum of 2 pets, 75 pounds total). No parking or resort fees.

THIS ALL-SUITES HOTEL does not qualify as lavish, but it's clean with several perks. Guests enjoy a complimentary hot breakfast, free parking, and no resort fees. The suites are reasonably sized. The quality of the lobby, pool, and common areas is what you'd expect from this hotel brand. The limited shuttle service to Universal Orlando Resort works well, or guests can take a 20-minute walk to the parks. Overall, this property provides good value for larger groups simply needing a place to sleep.

DoubleTree by Hilton Hotel at the Entrance to Universal Orlando ★★★★

5780 Major Blvd. Orlando
☎ 407-351-1000; hilton.com

Rate per night $114–$209. **Pool** ★★★★. **Fridge in room** Yes. **Shuttle to parks** Yes (Universal only). **Maximum number of occupants per room** 4. **Comments** Pets welcome ($75 nonrefundable fee). $31/day self-parking, $40/day valet.

THIS PROPERTY OFFERS numerous conference/meeting spaces within the 742-room complex. It has the best overall rooms and amenities of properties in the Kirkman Road area. You'll find on-site dining options galore, including the table-service American Grill with a full-service bar; the counter-service Pizza, Burgers, & More; Sunshine Cafe, serving breakfast; a gelato shop; and an in-lobby Starbucks. Of course, cookies are available at the front desk by request anytime. In addition to fitness and business centers, the pool area features numerous relaxing areas, and laundry services are available. The DoubleTree is located a walkable distance from Universal Orlando, a Walgreens, and local restaurants; it also offers the most reliable shuttle service of off-site hotels to Universal Orlando. Because it's a popular convention hotel, prices vary drastically depending on the time of year.

Drury Inn & Suites Near Universal Orlando Resort ★★★½

7301 W. Sand Lake Rd. Orlando
☎ 407-354-1101; druryhotels.com

Rate per night $137–$173. **Pools** ★★★. **Fridge in room** Yes. **Shuttle to parks** Yes (Universal only). **Maximum number of occupants per room** 5. **Comments** Pets welcome (2/room, 80-pound combined limit, $50/day fee). No parking or resort fees.

AN EXCELLENT OPTION when visiting Universal Orlando with a car, this eight-floor hotel has 238 rooms with some suites that sleep six. It's located within 2 miles of Universal Orlando and has a grocery and many dining options nearby. Rooms on the higher floors afford better views and quality; if possible, request a corner room, as they're more spacious. The rooms themselves are ordinary in style, but all have a microwave, and the hotel has a 24-hour business center and a fitness area. A lobby soft-drink machine is available for guests most of the day. Visitors looking to save on food will appreciate the full breakfast buffet and light dinner (with limited alcoholic beverages) served daily.

Fairfield Inn & Suites Orlando Near Universal Orlando Resort ★★★½

5614 Vineland Rd.
Orlando
☎ 407-581-5600
marriott.com

Rate per night $130–$189. **Pools** ★★★. **Fridge in room** Yes. **Shuttle to parks** Yes (Universal only). **Maximum number of occupants per room** 4. **Comments** Free parking. No pets allowed.

THIS IS THE CLOSEST MARRIOTT HOTEL to Universal Orlando for those wishing to earn points or use rewards. Guests can also purchase vacation packages to earn in-park discounts and early park admission. Rooms are comfortable, with pillow-top beds and high-speed Wi-Fi, and suites with sleeper sofas are available for larger groups. Universal Orlando is a 15-minute walk, or you can use the partner hotel shuttle service. Free parking and complimentary hot breakfast each morning help guests save some vacation money. Several nearby dining options are another perk.

Holiday Inn & Suites Across from Universal ★★★½

5916 Caravan Ct.,
Orlando
☎ 407-351-3333
hiuniversal.com

Rate per night $131–$197. **Pool** ★★★½. **Fridge in room** Yes. **Shuttle to parks** Yes (Universal, SeaWorld, and Aquatica: free; Disney: $12/person). **Maximum number of occupants per room** 4–10. **Comments** Pets welcome (2/room, 65-pound limit, $100 fee per stay). $25/day self-parking. $18/night resort fee.

THIS 10-FLOOR HOTEL offers the shortest walking distance to Universal Orlando of any off-site hotel. Of its 390 rooms, 134 are suites, which come with a microwave, sleeper sofa, and dining area; suites that sleep 6 offer great value, and some suites even accommodate up to 10. Every room has a Keurig coffee maker, and business travelers will enjoy the portable desk. Guests may use an indoor hallway to access the TGI Fridays restaurant next door, which offers a reasonably priced breakfast buffet (kids under 12 eat free there with a paid adult hotel guest), but the hotel offers few other food options. The outdoor pool is clean and heated. Other amenities include a business center, a Budget car rental, an arcade, on-site children's activities, and Bark Avenue, a fenced area where dogs can run wild.

Hyatt Place Across from Universal Orlando ★★★½

5976 Caravan Ct.
Orlando
☎ 407-351-0627
hyatt.com

Rate per night $139–$178. **Pools** ★★★. **Fridge in room** Yes. **Shuttle to parks** Yes (Universal, SeaWorld, Aquatica). **Maximum number of occupants**

per room 4. **Comments** Pets welcome (2/room, 50-pound limit for 1/75-pound combined limit for 2, $75–$175 fee). $18/day self-parking.

A UNIVERSAL ORLANDO PARTNER HOTEL, HYATT PLACE is within walking distance of Universal Orlando and offers discount packages with special guest perks. The 150-room property features spacious rooms with Hyatt Grand Beds, and each room has a "Cozy Corner" with a sleeper sofa. Complimentary grab-and-go or hot breakfast is provided every morning, and other food and beverage options are available 24 hours a day. Guests may use digital check-in, and there's also an on-site fitness center.

Rosen Shingle Creek ★★★★

9939 Universal Blvd. Orlando
☎ 407-996-9939 or 866-996-6338
rosenshinglecreek.com

Rate per night $189–$323. **Pools** ★★★★. **Fridge in room** Yes. **Shuttle to parks** Yes (Universal, SeaWorld, Discovery Cove, Aquatica). **Maximum number of occupants per room** 4. **Comment** Pets welcome (1/room, $150 nonrefundable fee + additional $50/night). $28/day self-parking; $40/day valet. Additional $50/night after 7 nights.

BEAUTIFUL ROOMS (east-facing ones have great views) and excellent restaurants distinguish this mostly meeting- and convention-oriented resort. The pools, which are large and lovely, include a lap pool, a family pool, and a kiddie wading pool. There's an 18-hole golf course on-site, as well as a spa and an adequate fitness center.

Though a video arcade will gobble up your kids' pocket change, the real kicker, especially for the 8-years-and-up crowd, is a natural area encompassing lily ponds, grassy wetlands, Shingle Creek, and an adjacent cypress swamp. Running through the area is a nature trail complete with signs to help you identify wildlife. Great blue herons, wood storks, coots, egrets, mallard ducks, anhingas, and ospreys are common, as are sliders (turtles), chameleons, and skinks (lizards).

If you stay at Shingle Creek and plan to visit the theme parks, you'll want a car. Shuttle service is limited, departing and picking up at rather inconvenient times and stopping at three other hotels before delivering you to your destination.

Sheraton Vistana Villages Resort Villas, I-Drive/Orlando ★★★★½

12401 International Dr. Orlando
☎ 407-238-5000
marriott.com

Rate per night $125–$249. **Pool** ★★★★. **Fridge in room** Yes. **Shuttle to parks** No. **Maximum number of occupants per room** 6 (2-bedroom suite). **Comments** Free parking. No pets allowed.

THIS IS ONE OF TWO SHERATON VISTANA properties in Orlando that are favorites of *Unofficial Guide* readers (the other is the Sheraton Vistana Resort Villas in Lake Buena Vista). The 1,100-square-foot, two-bedroom villas are the rooms to get. Suites have fully equipped kitchens and a washer and dryer. All rooms have a private balcony or patio. The resort has two pools, including one zero-entry for kids; a fitness center; and a business center. The Vistana Villages are about a 20-minute drive to Universal Orlando.

The 10 BEST HOTEL VALUES

IN THE CHART BELOW, we look at the best combinations of quality and value in a hotel. A reader wrote to complain that he had booked one of our top-ranked rooms in terms of value and had been very disappointed in the room. We noticed that the room the reader occupied had an overall quality rating of ★★½. Remember that the list of top deals is intended to give you some sense of value received for dollars spent. A ★★½ room at $100 may have the same value as a ★★★★ room at $150, but that doesn't mean the rooms will be of comparable quality. Regardless of whether it's a good deal, a ★★½ room is still a ★★½ room.

	The Top 10 Best Deals		
	HOTEL	**OVERALL QUALITY**	**COST**
1	Sheraton Vistana Villages Resort Villas, I-Drive/ Orlando	★★★★½	$125–$249
2	DoubleTree by Hilton Hotel at the Entrance to Universal Orlando	★★★★	$114–$209
3	Drury Inn & Suites Near Universal Orlando Resort	★★★½	$137–$173
4	Hyatt Place Across from Universal Orlando	★★★½	$139–$178
5	Holiday Inn & Suites Across from Universal	★★★½	$131–$197
6	Fairfield Inn & Suites Orlando Near Universal Resort	★★★½	$130–$189
7	Universal Endless Summer Resort	★★★½	$161–$193
8	Universal Stella Nova and Terra Luna Resorts	★★★½	$134–$225
9	Comfort Suites Near Universal Orlando Resort	★★★	$127–$144
10	Best Western Plus Universal Inn	★★½	$97–$126

PART 3

ARRIVING *and* GETTING AROUND

▌ GETTING THERE

DIRECTIONS TO UNIVERSAL ORLANDO

UNIVERSAL ORLANDO IS LOCATED within Orlando city limits, a short distance from I-4 and Florida's Turnpike. You can access the resort's main campus from **I-4 East** by taking Exit 75A and turning left at the top of the ramp onto Universal Boulevard. From **I-4 West,** use Exit 74B and then turn right onto Hollywood Way. Entrances are also located off **Kirkman Road** to the east, **Turkey Lake Road** to the west, and **Vineland Road** to the north.

To reach Epic Universe from the original resort, drive south on Kirkman Road directly into the expansion property. **Universal Boulevard** connects the International Drive area to Universal via an overpass bridging I-4, and also stretches south to Epic Universe. **Grand National Drive** extends across another I-4 overpass that connects Major Boulevard on the east side of Universal with International Drive's northernmost end. Turkey Lake and Vineland Roads are particularly good alternatives when I-4 is gridlocked. See pages 122–123 and 124 for maps of the area.

Signs for Universal's hotels and theme parks are easy to find and read as soon as you've left the interstate. Once on Universal property, follow the signs to the parking garage or your hotel.

Tolls

Tolls from the airport to Universal on the **Beachline Expressway (FL 528)** are $2.50 each way. If you take FL 417 to I-4 in the Disney area, you'll need $4.50 each way. Bring a few dollars in quarters if your car doesn't have a **SunPass** or **E-Pass** transponder because many exits have no human toll-takers to accept bills. **Uni** (formerly known as E-ZPass), available in Florida and 18 other states on the East Coast, works at many toll locations in Orlando; bring your transponder from home if you have one (visit cfxway.com/uni for a list of participating toll systems or to purchase a transponder). Only a transponder or pay-by-plate is accepted along Florida's Turnpike north of Orlando. You can also pick up a free E-Pass transponder at Orlando International Airport and return it to a drop box before departing. Go to **Visitor Toll Pass** (visitor tollpass.com) and download the Visitor Toll Pass smartphone app to reserve your pass, which can save you 80% versus paying tolls through your car rental company.

FROM ORLANDO INTERNATIONAL AIRPORT (MCO)   From FL 528/ Beachline Expressway (a toll road), head west for about 9 miles until Exit 3, then bear right onto John Young Parkway northbound, and make a left on Destination Parkway to reach Epic Universe. To reach Universal's original campus, continue a few more miles on FL 528 to I-4. Bear right and go east 2 miles on I-4 East to Exit 75A, marked UNIVERSAL/INTERNATIONAL DRIVE. Make a left at the end of the exit ramp.

FROM WALT DISNEY WORLD   Go east on I-4, take Exit 72 to FL 528 East, then take Exit 2 onto northbound Universal Boulevard to reach Epic Universe. For the main Universal Orlando Resort, continue on I-4 East to Exit 75A (marked UNIVERSAL/INTERNATIONAL DRIVE), and make a left at the end of the exit ramp.

FROM DAYTONA BEACH, SANFORD INTERNATIONAL AIRPORT (SFB), AND ORLANDO   Head west on I-4 through Orlando. Take Exit 74B toward Universal Orlando's main campus, or take Exit 75B onto Kirkman Road south toward Epic Universe.

FROM MIAMI, FORT LAUDERDALE, AND SOUTHEASTERN FLORIDA Head north on Florida's Turnpike to Exit 259, and merge onto I-4 West toward Tampa. Take Exit 74B toward Universal Orlando's main campus, or Exit 75B toward Epic Universe.

FROM TAMPA AND SOUTHWESTERN FLORIDA   Take I-75 North to I-4. Go east on I-4, then follow the directions above from Walt Disney World.

FROM FLORIDA'S TURNPIKE SOUTH   Take Exit 259 to merge onto I-4 West toward Tampa; then take Exit 74B toward Universal Orlando's main campus or Exit 75B toward Epic Universe.

FROM I-10   Take I-10 East across Florida to I-75 South at Exit 296A/ Tampa; then take Florida's Turnpike (toll road) southbound at Exit 328 (on the left) toward Orlando. Take Exit 259 to merge onto I-4 West toward Tampa; then take Exit 74B toward Universal Orlando's main campus or Exit 75B toward Epic Universe.

FROM I-75 SOUTH   Take I-75 South onto Florida's Turnpike via Exit 328 (on the left) toward Orlando. Take Exit 259 to merge onto I-4 West toward Tampa, and then take Exit 74B toward Universal Orlando's main campus or Exit 75B toward Epic Universe.

FROM I-95 SOUTH   Take Exit 260B to merge onto I-4 West, and then take Exit 74B toward Universal Orlando's main campus or Exit 75B toward Epic Universe.

Universal Orlando Exits off I-4

West to east, seven I-4 exits serve Universal Orlando.

Exit 72 (Beachline Expressway) connects to FL 528 toward the airport, south of Epic Universe. This is a toll road, but there is no fee if you take Exit 2 for Universal Boulevard. Turn left at the light to head north to reach Universal's expansion property, including the Helios Grand Hotel and the Stella Nova and Terra Luna Resorts.

Exit 74A (Sand Lake Road) serves the southern edge of Universal's original property, with access to the main resort from Turkey Lake Road, which lies just west of the exit. This exit also provides access to Epic Universe and the attractions on the southern end of International Drive, heading toward the Orange County Convention Center, as well as Restaurant Row on West Sand Lake Road. This exit can get quite congested with I-Drive traffic.

Exit 74B (Adventure Way), accessible only from I-4 West, serves as the primary entrance to Universal's main campus from that direction. The exit ramp leads directly to the Cabana Bay and Sapphire Falls Resorts. Make a right at the light past the hotels to reach the Universal parking garage. Note that you can't return to I-4 East via this exit.

Exit 75A (Universal Boulevard/International Drive) serves as the primary entrance to the original Universal Orlando Resort for visitors coming from Walt Disney World on I-4 East. Make a left at the end of the ramp into Universal property, and the parking garage will be ahead on your right. Make a right off this exit to take Universal Boulevard south across International Drive to the Endless Summer Resort hotels and Epic Universe; it then parallels that busy road, making it a perfect bypass to south International Drive and the convention center.

Exit 75B (Kirkman Road) leads drivers from I-4 East to Kirkman Road on the east side of Universal Orlando. Bearing right on this ramp leads southbound on Kirkman Road toward International Drive and Epic Universe. To enter Universal's main property, stay in the left lane to Kirkman Road northbound, then turn left at the first traffic signal onto Major Boulevard. This is the closest exit to the Portofino Bay and Hard Rock Hotels, as well as most off-site hotels within walking distance.

Exit 75B-A (Kirkman Road/International Drive) is the exit from I-4 West to Kirkman Road just south of Universal. Stay to the right after Florida's Turnpike to take Exit 75. Bear left when the exit ramp splits for 75B to Kirkman Road southbound, toward Epic Universe and attractions on north International Drive; then turn right onto International Drive, and right again onto Universal Boulevard, to reach the Universal Orlando Resort parking garage. Your second option is to

continued on page 125

South Orlando

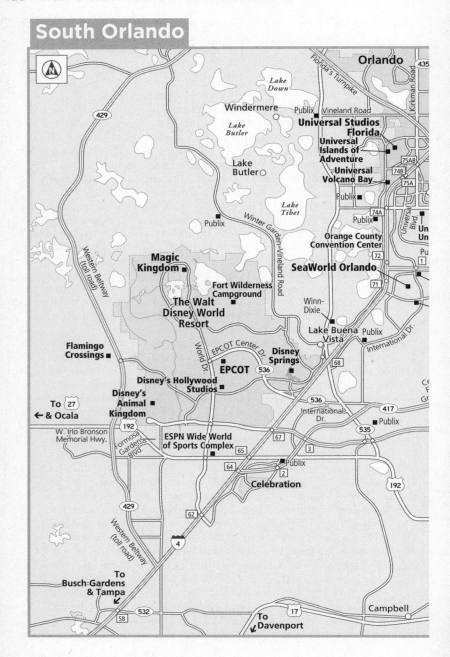

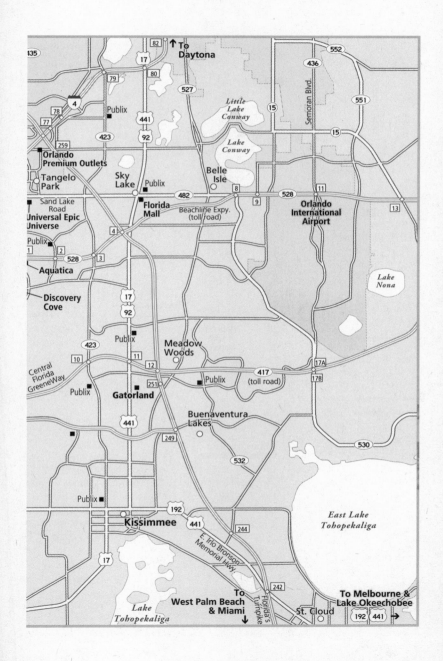

I-Drive Area Sneak Routes

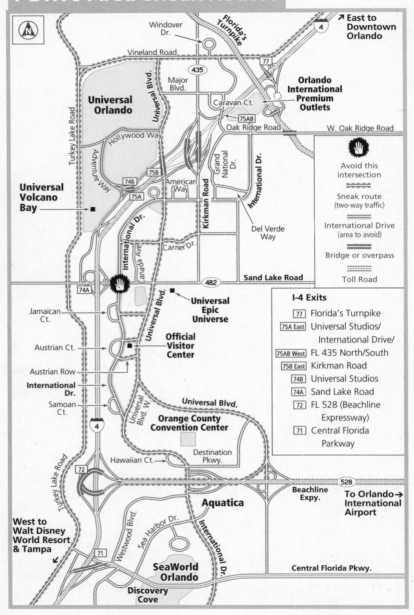

continued from page 121

stay right on Exit 75A to Kirkman Road northbound; you can't make a left turn directly into the resort, but you can make a right at the first intersection onto Major Boulevard, followed by a U-turn at Grand National Drive back toward Universal. (The Kirkman Road exit from I-4's express lanes deliver you directly to Grand National near Major, where you can make a left toward the resort.) For a third alternative, take the second left off Kirkman onto Vineland Road, and then turn left onto Universal Boulevard to enter the main resort from the north.

Exit 78 (Conroy Road/Millenia) is an option for westbound drivers when traffic is backed up approaching Florida's Turnpike. Make a right off the exit, and then make an immediate left onto Vineland Road. Universal Boulevard will be your second left after crossing Kirkman Road.

THE I-4 BLUES

OVER MANY YEARS OF COVERING Orlando's attractions, we've watched I-4 turn from a modern interstate highway into a parking lot. The greatest congestion used to be between the Universal Orlando–International Drive area and downtown Orlando, but the section to the southwest serving the Disney World exits has become the new choke point, seemingly irrespective of the time of day. If you're going from Walt Disney World toward Universal Orlando (east), the jam usually breaks up after you've passed the FL 535 exit. As you head west toward Tampa, traffic calms down after the US 192 interchange, but then gets congested again going past the ChampionsGate golf community.

Ameliorating (or complicating) the situation, the long-delayed "I-4 Ultimate" renovations have finally wrapped up on a 21-mile stretch of I-4, from FL 434 in the northeast to Kirkman Road in the southwest, but construction work on subsequent "I-4 Beyond the Ultimate" projects between Sand Lake Road and Lake Buena Vista promises to cause headaches through 2028 and beyond. Lane and exit ramp closures frequently occur between 10 p.m. and 6 a.m., which can snarl night owls exiting from CityWalk or early birds arriving before Early Park Admission.

In 2022, new tolled express lanes opened on I-4 from Kirkman Road (near Universal Orlando) east to FL 434. Usage starts at $0.50 per segment, or $3.50 to drive westbound for the entire distance; electronic toll transponders or pay-by-plate is required to use these limited-access lanes. If you use these express toll lanes westbound, take the left-hand Kirkman Road via Grand National exit, turn right at the stoplight to head north on Grand National. Then turn left onto Major Boulevard and cross Kirkman Road into Universal Orlando's main property, or make a left onto Kirkman southbound to Epic Universe. (See the second route described on page 121 for Exit 75B-A.)

Real-time road conditions are available at i4exitguide.com/i-4-traffic, and an interactive map showing all active construction projects in

Florida can be found at data.fdot.gov/road/projects. Info about construction in Orlando and the tourist areas is available at **Central Florida Roads** (cflroads.com), a Florida Department of Transportation website. For information and current conditions on area toll roads, check with the **Central Florida Expressway Authority** (cfxway.com).

On long road trips, we always use a GPS device that's smart enough to accept traffic updates and route us around delays. **TomTom** GPS units, for example, have an accessory cable that picks up traffic signals from HD radio broadcasts. If you have a smartphone, the free mobile app **Waze** (waze.com; iOS and Android) also does the trick.

If I-4 traffic becomes intolerable, it's pretty easy to commute from the Universal Orlando–International Drive area to Walt Disney World via **Turkey Lake Road,** connecting to Palm Parkway and FL 535 on the northwest side of I-4, or the southernmost section of I-Drive, which connects to FL 536 on the southeast side of the interstate.

SNEAK ROUTES

WE'RE CONSTANTLY LOOKING for ways to avoid traffic snarls. For some roads and areas, there are no alternative routes. For others, we've discovered sneak routes. These suggestions will not only help you avoid congestion, but they're also great ways to discover local restaurants outside the theme park orbit.

International Drive (I-Drive) is by far the most difficult area to navigate without long traffic delays. Most hotels on I-Drive are between **Kirkman Road** to the north and **FL 417 (Central Florida GreeneWay)** to the south. Between Kirkman Road and FL 417, three major roads cross I-Drive: From north to south on I-Drive, the first is **Universal Boulevard.** Next is **Sand Lake Road** (FL 482), pretty squarely in the middle of the hotel district. Finally, the **Beachline Expressway (FL 528)** connects I-4 and the airport. The southern third of I-Drive can be accessed via **Central Florida Parkway,** connecting I-4 and Palm Parkway with the Sea-World area of I-Drive, and by **Daryl Carter Parkway,** connecting Palm Parkway with the Orlando Vineland Premium Outlets.

I-Drive is a mess for a number of reasons: scarcity of left-turn lanes, long multidirectional traffic signals, and, most critically, limited access to westbound I-4. From the Orange County Convention Center south to the Beachline Expressway and FL 417/Central Florida GreeneWay, getting on westbound I-4 is easy, but in the stretch where the hotels are concentrated (from Kirkman to about a mile south of Sand Lake), the only way most visitors know to access I-4 westbound is to slog through the gridlock of the I-Drive–Sand Lake Road intersection en route to the I-4–Sand Lake Road interchange. A combination of a long, long traffic signal, a sea of motorists, and a scarcity of turn lanes makes this about as much fun as a root canal.

To travel between the main Universal campus and the northernmost end of International Drive (near the outlet mall), use the **Grand National Drive** overpass between Oak Ridge Road and Major Boulevard. If your hotel is north of Sand Lake, access **Kirkman Road** by going north on I-Drive (in the opposite direction of the heaviest traffic) to the Kirkman Road intersection and turning left, or by cutting over to Kirkman via eastbound Carrier Drive. You can also go north on **Universal Boulevard,** which parallels I-Drive to the east. After you cross I-4 onto Universal property, stay right and follow the signs for the parking garage, or take two left turns to reach I-4 westbound.

If your hotel is south of Sand Lake Road but north of Austrian Court, use **Austrian Row** or **Jamaican Court** to cut over to Universal Boulevard. If your hotel is south of Austrian Court, continue south until you intersect the **Beachline Expressway (FL 528)**; then take the Beachline west to I-4 (no toll). Universal's dedicated lanes along Kirkman Road are the best way to reach Epic Universe from the north, with Universal Boulevard and Destination Parkway offering alternative entrances along the property's southern edge.

SECURITY AT ORLANDO INTERNATIONAL AIRPORT (MCO)

unofficial **TIP**
We recommend arriving at MCO 90 minutes–2 hours before you're scheduled to depart.

THIS AIRPORT HANDLED A RECORD 57.7 million passengers in 2023, more than it saw prior to the COVID-19 pandemic. It isn't unusual to see lines from the checkpoints snaking out of the terminal and into the main shopping corridor and food court. Airport officials sometimes actually shut down moving sidewalks to use them for more queuing space. A number of passengers have reported missing their flights even when they arrived at the airport 90 minutes before departure, and showing up 3 hours before your flight is officially advised. Most waits to clear security are less than 30 minutes on average, but there can be substantial fluctuations, with peak waits exceeding an hour. For current security wait times, check the **Greater Orlando Aviation Authority** website (orlandoairports .net) or download the free MCO mobile app. To shorten your wait at security, make a free reservation at mco.whyline.com.

Guests with hidden disabilities such as autism may request a Sunflower Lanyard from the Main Terminal Information Booths on Level 3, which identifies them to airport employees as needing special attention; see orlandoairports.net/site/uploads/Hidden_Disabilities_Flyer.pdf for details. If you require preferential treatment going through security, you can request assistance from TSA Cares at tsa.gov/contact-center /form/cares or by calling ☎ 855-787-2227.

ALTERNATIVE AIRPORTS

A SHORT DISTANCE NORTHEAST of Orlando is **Sanford International Airport (SFB**; orlandosanfordairport.com). Small, convenient, and easily accessible, it's low hassle compared with the huge Orlando International Airport (MCO) and its block-long security-checkpoint lines.

The primary domestic carrier serving Sanford International is **Allegiant Air** (☎ 702-505-8888; allegiantair.com), with service from large and small airports throughout the eastern and midwestern United States.

A reader from Roanoke, Virginia, uses Sanford frequently, writing:

The 45-minute drive to [Orlando] is more than made up for by avoiding the chaos at Orlando International, and it's stress-free.

The downside is that Sanford is 35 miles from Universal Orlando. A one-way taxi ride will cost over $100 with tip, and a ride-hailing service will charge about $40 or more.

A handful of readers, like this couple from White Township, New Jersey, prefer flying into Tampa instead:

We've found that flying from Newark to Tampa instead of Orlando saves us money and our sanity. It means significantly lower fares, fewer children on the plane, and shorter security lines.

(Note that it's an 84-mile drive from Tampa International Airport to Universal Orlando—about an hour and 20 minutes.)

GETTING TO UNIVERSAL ORLANDO FROM MCO

YOU HAVE FIVE OPTIONS FOR GETTING from Orlando International Airport to Universal Orlando:

1. TAXI   Mears Transportation Group (☎ 407-422-2222; mearstransportation.com) maintains a near-monopoly on taxi service in Central Florida and operates multiple brands—**Yellow Cab, Checker Cab,** and **City Cab**—with identical rates. Taxis carry four to eight passengers (depending on vehicle type); rates vary according to distance. If your hotel is on Universal property, or nearby on International Drive or Major Boulevard, your fare will be about $60–$70, plus tip. You can download the Mears Taxi app for Apple or Android to estimate the cost of your trip, but it's buggy, so don't rely on it to hail your ride. Look for cabs on the lowest level at Terminals A and B, or on level 6 at Terminal C.

2. SHUTTLE SERVICE   Universal offers **SuperStar Shuttle** airport transfers only to on-site guests who book their stay through a Universal Vacations package. The shuttle costs $39 per adult, $36 per child ages 3–9 round-trip (kids under age 3 ride free); one-way costs $23 for adults and $21 for kids; all prices include tax. Guests arriving between 7 a.m. and 8 p.m. are welcomed at the Hotel Transportation Desk on the first floor of the airport terminal, where they receive a preprinted packet containing any tickets purchased with their vacation package; those with earlier or later flights will need to call ☎ 407-254-0299 for pickup. SuperStar service will not deliver luggage to your room, so you'll need to retrieve it from baggage claim yourself before checking in, and you'll have to provide your own child car seats. SuperStar airport transfers can be added to an existing Universal Vacations reservation by calling ☎ 800-407-4275; for more information, visit theugseries.com/unishuttle or call ☎ 866-604-7557 (daily, 8 a.m.–5:30 p.m.).

A reader from Exton, Pennsylvania, wasn't impressed with Universal's shuttle service:

The SuperStar Shuttle (which costs extra, although we were staying on-site) was a dark spot on an otherwise great trip. After our arrival in Orlando, we waited over an hour to get picked up. The first shuttle was too small to fit all of the people waiting for it. Why does Universal require advance reservations with flight arrival times if it won't be prepared for the amount of people it needs to transport?

Another dissatisfied SuperStar customer from Tulsa, Oklahoma, had this to say:

The Universal desk at the airport was very slow and disorganized. The shuttle from the airport to Cabana Bay was a rough ride, it took over 30 minutes for it to show up, it felt like the bus had no shocks, and it about jarred my neck.

For the same price, Universal Vacations also offers a "Take Two Transfer" van service from Quick Transportation that takes guests from a Walt Disney World hotel to Universal Orlando, and then to the airport (or the reverse). However, it doesn't include a full round-trip like Quicksilver's three-way service described below; call ☎ 888-784-2522 or ☎ 407-354-2456 for more information.

When using any shared-transportation service, you might have to wait at the airport until a vehicle fills. Once underway, the shuttle will probably stop several times to discharge passengers before reaching your hotel. Because shuttles make several pickups, they ask you to leave for the airport at the end of your vacation much earlier than you'd depart if you were taking a cab or returning a rental car.

3. TOWN CAR SERVICE   Like a taxi, a town car service will transport you directly from the airport to your hotel. The driver will usually be waiting for you in your airline's baggage-claim area. If saving time and hassle is worth the money, book a town car.

Each town car service we surveyed offers large, well-appointed late-model sedans, such as the Lincoln Town Car series, or limousines. These hold four persons; trunks easily hold golf bags. Some services also offer roomier luxury SUVs and vans for an extra fee. To reserve a child's car seat, call ahead.

Tiffany Towncar Service (☎ 888-838-2161 or 407-370-2196; tiffanytowncar.com) provides a prompt, clean ride. The round-trip fee to the Universal area in a town car is $190 plus tip; one-way is $95. Tiffany charges an extra $20 for pickups before 6 a.m. or after 10 p.m. but offers a free 20-minute stop at a supermarket en route to your hotel with a round-trip booking.

Quicksilver Tours & Transportation (☎ 888-GO-TO-WDW [468-6939] or 407-299-1434; quicksilver-tours.com) offers 8-person limos and 10-person vans in addition to 4-person town cars. Round-trip in a town car from MCO to the Universal area and back (with a free 20-minute grocery stop on the way) is $230; round-trip in a van costs $285; the round-trip limo rate is $420. Pickups cost $20 more between 8:30 and 11 p.m. and $35 more between 11 p.m. and 7 a.m. Quicksilver also offers a three-way trip from the airport to Walt Disney World, then to Universal Orlando, and finally back to the airport, starting at $335—perfect for those splitting their vacation between the two resorts.

Mears Transportation Group (☎ 407-423-5566; mearstransporta tion.com) also offers 3-passenger town car, 5-passenger SUV, or 8-passenger luxury van service from MCO to Universal for $106–$133; the return trip costs $89–$115.

4. RENTAL CARS Short- and long-term rentals are available, although selection has diminished and prices are inflated due to a shortage of cars. Most companies allow drop-off at certain hotels or subsidiary locations in the Universal area if you don't want the vehicle for your entire stay. Likewise, at any time during your stay, you can pick up a car at those hotels and locations. Check **MouseSavers** (mousesavers.com) for rental-car discount codes.

The preferred routes to Universal Orlando—as well as Walt Disney World, International Drive, and US 192—all involve toll roads. Some roads require exact change to enter or exit via automated gates, and manned tollbooths will not accept any denomination bill higher than $20. So before you leave the airport, make sure you're armed with at least $5 in quarters and some lower-denomination currency if you don't have a toll transponder (see page 119).

5. RIDE-HAILING SERVICES This somewhat-controversial option is represented in Orlando by the companies **Uber** and **Lyft.** You start by downloading a service's app to your smartphone (Apple or Android) and registering an account with a form of payment. When you want to hail a ride, the app shows you what available drivers are nearby and estimates the time and cost to your destination. You can follow your car's progress via GPS and add an optional gratuity through the app.

A four-passenger UberX or Lyft from the airport to Universal will cost about $40 (versus more than $60 for a traditional taxi), and UberX will provide a car seat for a few dollars more; a five-passenger UberXL or Lyft XL is around $50. Pickups for most rideshares are on the airport's second level, the same as where passengers are picked up by family and friends. Luxury rideshares like Uber Black use the Express Pickup Tunnel near the rental car desks on level one.

unofficial **TIP**
We recommend Lyft over Uber. While both companies offer about the same service at about the same cost, Uber tacks on an extra fee for pickups at Universal's parking hub.

GETTING TO UNIVERSAL ORLANDO FROM WALT DISNEY WORLD

DRIVING FROM WALT DISNEY WORLD to Universal Orlando along I-4 takes about 15 minutes with light traffic, or as much as 40 minutes during rush hour. If you're staying at Walt Disney World and you don't have a car, taxis, along with **Uber** and **Lyft**, are readily available between the resorts. A one-way taxi ride is about $45–$50 (plus tip), depending on which Disney hotel you are leaving from, and a luxury black sedan costs around $30 more. A rideshare will cost at least one-third less, and you can usually get picked up from any WDW hotel in less than 15 minutes. Taxis, as well as shuttle vans and buses, drop off at and pick up from the lower level of Universal's main parking hub, from which you can walk to CityWalk and the parks; rideshare and private cars use a designated drop-off on the garage's roof (see below). *Note:* **Mears Transportation** no longer offers a shuttle bus service between the resorts.

This family of five from Texas shares its positive experience getting to Universal from WDW via taxi:

> *It worked out cheaper for us to get a cab for five people than to hire a service or to rent a car for two days and pay for parking. We just walked to the front of our resort (Port Orleans Riverside), they hailed a waiting cab/van, and off we went. At the end of the day at Universal, we walked to the cab drop-off and pickup, got right into a cab, and headed back to our resort.*

UNIVERSAL PARTNER HOTEL CONNECTOR SHUTTLE

UNIVERSAL OFFERS FREE scheduled transportation to SeaWorld and Aquatica for its on-site hotel guests via the Universal Partner Hotel Shuttle (sometimes referred to as the **SuperStar Shuttle,** and not to be confused with the paid Super Star airport shuttle service previously discussed). Departure and return times are limited and are based on regular park operating hours.

Typically there is one outbound trip to SeaWorld and Aquatica in the morning at 10 a.m. and up to three returning runs in the evening. The shuttle picks up all guests at Universal's parking garage hub; no reservations or boarding passes are required, but check with your hotel's Vacation Planning Center 24 hours in advance if you have accessibility needs (such as a wheelchair or service animal). As with other free shuttles that service multiple hotels, your free ride may cost you valuable park time with its roundabout route; rope-drop enthusiasts may want to rely on ride hailing or rental cars instead.

OFF-SITE-HOTEL SHUTTLES

MANY INDEPENDENT HOTELS AND MOTELS near Universal Orlando provide free shuttle buses to the parks. Some properties participate in the same Universal Partner Hotel Shuttle program that services SeaWorld and Aquatica for Universal's on-site hotel guests, while others operate their own transportation. The shuttles are fairly carefree, depositing you at the parking garages' central hub and saving you parking fees. The rub is that they might not get you there as early as you desire—a critical point if you take our touring advice—or be available when you wish to return to your lodging. Each service is different; check details before you make reservations.

Some shuttles go directly to Universal, while others stop at other hotels en route. This can be a problem if your hotel is the second or third stop on the route. During periods of high demand, buses frequently fill up at the first stop, leaving little or no room for passengers at subsequent stops. Before booking, inquire how many hotels are on the route and the sequence of the stops. The hotels are often so close together that you can easily walk to the first hotel on the route and board there. Similarly, if there's a large hotel nearby, it might have its own dedicated bus service that is more efficient. Use it instead of the service provided by your hotel. The majority of Universal-area shuttles work on a fixed schedule, typically with three or four departures in the morning and a similar or smaller number of returns around closing. Knowing exactly when a bus will depart makes it easier to plan your day.

At closing or during a hard rain, more people will be waiting for the shuttle than it can hold, and some will be left behind. Most shuttles return for stranded guests, but they may wait 20 minutes to more than an hour.

If you're depending on shuttles, leave the park at least 45 minutes before closing. If you stay until closing and don't want the hassle of the shuttle, take a cab or request a rideshare. Cab stands, along with pickup/drop-off for guests and rideshares, are located on the fifth floor roof of the northern parking garage, in the Jurassic Park section (see page 136), and at each on-site hotel.

I-RIDE TROLLEY

TROLLEY-SHAPED BUSES, known as the **I-Ride Trolley** (☎ 407-248-9590; internationaldriveorlando.com/iride-trolley), offer cheap, convenient transportation servicing the International Drive area. The trolley circulates from the Orlando Vineland Premium Outlets on the south side of town to the hotels near Universal on Major Boulevard, with stops at SeaWorld and the Orange County Convention Center along the way. Trolleys run 8 a.m.–10:30 p.m., and typically circulate every 30–45 minutes; you can track their progress at buswhere.com/iridetrolley.

A single one-way fare costs $2 for adults ($1 for kids ages 3–9; 25¢ for seniors age 65 and older) and must be paid in cash using exact change. You can prepurchase unlimited ride passes for 1 day ($6) to 14 days ($20) at the website or at participating hotels and attractions in the I-Drive area.

The only issue with the trolley is that it doesn't stop at Universal Orlando—the closest stops are near Endless Summer Surfside Inn (marked R6 and G5 on the trolley route map) and east of the DoubleTree hotel at the corner of Grand National Drive and Major Boulevard (stop G4). From there you can walk to the Universal parks (see below).

WALKING TO UNIVERSAL ORLANDO FROM YOUR HOTEL

UNIVERSAL ORLANDO'S MAIN CAMPUS has a number of nearby off-site hotels within walking distance of the parks. The closest off-site hotels to Universal are along **Major Boulevard** near the intersection with

Kirkman Road, at the eastern entrance to Universal property. The DoubleTree hotel on this corner isn't much farther from Universal's parks than the on-site Portofino Bay. To reach the parks from this area, cross Kirkman at Major using the pedestrian bridge at the northeast corner, and follow the sidewalks to Universal Boulevard. Cross Universal Boulevard and turn left, and then walk to the escalators leading up to City-Walk from the valet parking circle. You should be able to walk the 0.5 mile from the DoubleTree to CityWalk in about 15 minutes.

Farther away, but still within walking distance of the original parks, are the hotels and motels on **I-Drive** near Universal Boulevard, adjacent to Universal Endless Summer Resort. This route requires walking north along Universal Boulevard, over the I-4 overpass, and into the bus and taxi parking loop on the lower level of the parking hub. While there are sidewalks and pedestrian traffic signals the entire way, this is at least a 0.75-mile walk alongside busy traffic, and we don't recommend it for families with young children.

There are also a handful of off-site hotels close to Epic Universe along Universal Boulevard near the convention center, but they are quite a hike from the park entrance.

THE PUBLIC TRANSPORTATION ALTERNATIVE

SOME OFF-SITE HOTEL SHUTTLES don't operate early enough to get you to the parks before opening. An alternative is the **LYNX** public bus system, which costs $2 (exact change required) for a single one-way fare, with discounted all-day, weekly, and monthly passes available for advance purchase online.

If you're staying in downtown Orlando, you can take the LYNX #21 or #40 bus from the central bus station to Universal's parking garage. To reach Walt Disney World, take LYNX #40 from Universal and transfer at Grand National Drive onto #8 (or the I-Ride Trolley from Kirkman and Major) to SeaWorld, and then transfer to LYNX #50 to the Magic Kingdom's Transportation and Ticket Center. The buses begin running daily hours before the parks open to accommodate commuting employees, but service to Universal is limited after 8 p.m. on Fridays, weekends, and holidays. Precise hours of service vary depending on where along the route you are. Use the online trip planner at golynx .com or call ☎ 407-841-LYNX (5969) for travel information.

◼️ GETTING ORIENTED

PARKING AT UNIVERSAL ORLANDO

UNIVERSAL'S MAIN CAMPUS IS HOME to two massive multistory parking garages, holding a combined total of 20,000 cars. Guests going to Epic Universe can park in the main campus's garage and take free bus transportation to the new park, or they can use the expansion's dedicated surface lot off Destination Parkway. The same parking rates and policies apply at both facilities. Signs route you from each of the resort entrances to the parking structures.

The primary toll plaza is situated between the two parking garages and accessed from Hollywood Way at Universal Boulevard; a secondary set of tollbooths, at the southern end of the garages, is used on busier days. To avoid congestion at the toll plazas, arrive an hour before park opening or at least 3 hours afterwards. Also try not to pull in right before 6 p.m., when idling cars awaiting free parking clog the toll lanes.

The two rectangular garages lie along a north–south axis, with the pedestrian walkways leading to the theme parks running along the west, or long, side of each building. Sections are named for classic Universal movies and characters found in the parks: Jurassic Park, King Kong, and Jaws in the north garage, and E.T., Spider-Man, and Cat in the Hat in the south structure. The first numeral following the section name tells you on which deck level you are located, and the remaining numbers specify the row. So if a sign tells you that you're on King Kong 409, you're in the King Kong section on the fourth floor in row nine. We strongly recommend taking a photo of the name and number of your section, level, and row.

Guests driving to Universal Orlando's attractions have three parking options:

SELF-PARKING Parking in the main garage or lot costs $32 for cars and $42 for RVs, trailers, and other large rigs. Regular parking in the garage is free for everyone after 6 p.m., except on Halloween Horror Nights when a fee is charged until midnight. Parking is free for Preferred and Premier Annual Pass holders, and half-price for Power Pass holders. You can also get free self-parking if you buy two or more matinee tickets for any movie starting 11 a.m.–6 p.m. at the Universal Cinemark; show your parking receipt at the box office for reimbursement. Self-parking is valid all day, so if you want to leave the resort and return in the evening, retain your receipt (even if you got free parking with your annual pass) and show it at the parking booths for free reentry.

PRIME SELF-PARKING For $60 ($50 during slower seasons), you will be parked closer to the gate in Epic Universe's lot or on the garages' central level in the closest available section to the central hub. These spots are supposed to be the second closest to the parks, after the handicapped parking section. However, we've scored spaces just as good or better using the regular parking, especially when we've arrived before 10:30 a.m. Because the garages are two-thirds as wide as they are long, the farther your parking place is from the west side, the worse it will be. This is why Prime parking in the garages is often not as close as regular parking—with the former, you'll be closer to the covered walkways to the parks, but if your particular space is toward the east side of the garage, you'll end up farther away than a guest who chose regular parking and was assigned a space closer to the west side of the structure.

An advantage of Prime parking, however, is that you'll park faster because the ratio of cars choosing Prime to regular is about 1 to 13. If you pick Prime, a piece of paper will be tucked under your windshield wiper at the tollbooth, and you'll be asked to turn your hazard blinkers on before following signs to the Prime parking section. Prime parking is free for Premier Annual Pass holders and costs $18 ($28 during peak season) for Preferred Pass holders or those with prepaid standard parking. Cars rented from **Avis** and **Budget** at Orlando International Airport include vouchers for a free upgrade to Prime with paid standard parking.

VOLCANO BAY PARKING   There is no dedicated guest parking at Volcano Bay itself. Instead, visitors pay the usual rates to park at the main campus on the first level of the southern parking structure used by other Universal theme park guests. Stay in the marked lanes, which are usually on the far right, when approaching the parking garage tollbooths and follow the signs for Volcano Bay parking.

unofficial **TIP**
Forgo valet parking if you're headed to Volcano Bay because you'll have to backtrack through the parking hub in order to reach the buses.

Note that parking for oversize vehicles is on the same ground level as Volcano Bay parking, so you may save time by using the Volcano Bay tollbooth lanes to get there.

VALET PARKING   In addition to the self-parking garages, valet parking is available at CityWalk for $32 for a visit of up to 2 hours or $75 for longer than that ($42 for 2-plus hours if arriving after 6 p.m., except during Halloween Horror Nights and other special events). The entrance to the valet parking circle is on Universal Boulevard, across the street from the parking garages' taxi/bus loop. The valet loop also has electric-vehicle charging stations (two Tesla 80-amp chargers, plus two Clipper Creek 48-amp chargers) that are free to use while using valet parking. After dropping off your car, ascend the escalator adjacent to the miniature-golf course, and turn right to enter the CityWalk complex.

Premier Pass holders valet-park for free (tip not included); Preferred Pass holders can valet for 50% off. If you don't carry cash, you can charge a tip for the valet on a credit card at the window, even if your parking is complimentary. On July 4, December 31, and Mardi Gras concert or Halloween event nights, Premier Pass holders are charged $42 ($52 for Preferred) if they don't pick up from valet before 7 p.m. And be warned that the valet circle closes 30 minutes after CityWalk shuts down; leave your car at valet overnight, and you'll have to pay a $90 nondiscountable fee in the morning.

Dropping off your car is usually quick, and our favorite unadvertised feature of the valet circle is its private security checkpoint, which usually has little wait. But beware that retrieving your car at the end of the evening can sometimes take up to half an hour, especially after a concert or special event in CityWalk or the parks. Automated kiosks to the right of the valet windows can cut the wait, when they are working properly. Scan your parking ticket and annual pass or credit card for priority vehicle retrieval, and double-check your receipt for accidental overcharges.

Guest Drop-Off/Pickup

If you aren't parking at the resort but only dropping off or picking up passengers, stay left when approaching the main Universal Orlando parking garage tollbooths and follow signs to the guest drop-off/pickup located on the fifth floor roof of the northern parking garage, in the Jurassic Park section. Epic Universe also has its own designated location for drop-offs. No parking fee is required to access the drop-off areas. These are also the designated locations for rideshare vehicles like Uber or Lyft, and the best spot to pick up departing guests at the end of the day. Some guests try to use the valet parking circle for this purpose, but it is officially prohibited.

Another option is to drop off at the lobby of the **Hard Rock Hotel,** which is a short walk from Universal Studios Florida's front gates if you cut through the pool. Note, however, that you can't backtrack through the pool at the end of the day without a resort key card. Conversely, the entrance into Epic Universe from the **Helios Grand Hotel** is exclusively for hotel guests, but anyone can exit the park through the hotel lobby and get picked up there after closing.

Speaking of the hotels, don't attempt to save money by parking at one of the resorts. Unless you are eating at a hotel restaurant that validates, off-site guests are charged a hefty fee for parking at the hotels.

Note that Uber tacks on an additional $4 fee for all trips originating from the parking garage pickup area; you can avoid this surcharge by using Lyft instead, or by departing from one of the resort hotels.

SECURITY SCREENINGS AT UNIVERSAL ORLANDO

CENTRAL FLORIDA'S THEME PARKS use uniformed and undercover security to screen and monitor guests entering their parks. Guests arriving at Universal Orlando must either pass through a full-body scanner or be screened with a hand-held detection wand, and also submit any bags for inspection, before continuing on to CityWalk and the parks.

On busy days, the crowd queuing for inspection in the parking garage rotunda may appear mind-boggling at first glance, but fortunately there is a phalanx of scanning machines, and Universal's security team could teach the TSA a thing or two about courtesy and efficiency. If you really hate to start your day with waiting, arrive extra early, or opt for valet parking, which has its own dedicated screening checkpoint. Guests staying at the resort hotels will be inspected before boarding the water taxis, and additional security screens pedestrians on the pathways near Margaritaville Orlando Resort and Hard Rock Hotel.

Volcano Bay guests get screened at a dedicated security checkpoint on the garage's bottom floor before boarding special shuttle buses that transport them along dedicated lanes to the water park's entrance. Hotel guests (and day guests on slower days) are screened by security upon arriving at Volcano Bay's bus stop. The process is not particularly pleasant and can be time-consuming, so arrive on Universal property 45–60 minutes before you want to actually get to Volcano Bay.

We've rarely experienced a serious issue with Universal's security procedures, but some guests, like this reader from Waipahu, Hawaii, found their efforts intrusive:

> Security checks at the hotel prior to getting on the boat shuttle are the most thorough I've been through—more than TSA. I encountered an employee who was overzealous in her checks and left me feeling very uncomfortable, and I heard others comment the same.

FINDING YOUR WAY AROUND

THERE ARE NO PARKING TRAMS at Universal's main campus, so depending on where in the garage your car is parked, you'll have an 8- to 20-minute hike to the theme park entrances. From the garages, moving sidewalks deliver you first to the central hub between the two garages. In this area, you'll find wheelchair rentals, a snack and souvenir stand, and escalators leading down to bus and taxi parking. To proceed to CityWalk and the parks, you'll need to pass through the aforementioned security screening checkpoint. To reach Volcano Bay, follow signs to park on the lowest level of the south garage, where you'll find ticket booths, security screenings, and dedicated shuttle buses that will transport you to and from the water park.

Upon exiting the parking structure, you'll pass Universal Cinemark on your right and Starbucks (always open early for that essential morning caffeine jolt) on your left before reaching CityWalk's central plaza. From here, you walk straight toward the lighthouse to reach the main entrance of Islands of Adventure, or bear right at the Coca-Cola kiosk toward the big globe for Universal Studios Florida's front gate.

If parking at Epic Universe, guests can simply walk straight to the park's entrance plaza, where you'll pass through a similar security screening before approaching the main gates.

TRANSPORTATION BETWEEN UNIVERSAL RESORTS AND PARKS

UNIVERSAL ORLANDO OFFERS **water taxi service** at its main campus between each of its Signature Collection hotels and the two original theme parks. The boat service uses a dock in CityWalk near the bridge to Universal Studios Florida as a hub, which is great if you're going from one of the hotels to a theme park. If you're traveling between hotels for a meal, however, you'll need to switch boats. Boats depart about every 15–20 minutes, from 1 hour before Early Park Admission begins until 1 hour after CityWalk shuts down; allow 20–25 minutes for each leg of your journey by boat.

Universal's main campus also offers a **shuttle bus service** that circulates every 20–30 minutes between its four Signature Collection hotels and the parking garage, from which you may walk to City-Walk, USF, or IOA. The bus is sometimes faster than transferring between boats for getting from one resort to another at dinnertime; tell the driver your destination when boarding. In addition, colorful character-covered buses run continuously between Cabana Bay Beach Resort and Aventura Hotel and the parking hub, with separate routes servicing the Endless Summer Resort and the hotels at Epic Universe. All of Universal's theme park–bound buses run until 15 minutes after CityWalk closes, and they drop off near the same spot, at the base of the escalator leading up to the security checkpoint.

All of the hotels have free buses directly to **Epic Universe,** except Helios Grand, which has an exclusive park entrance. All of the hotels—except for Cabana Bay and Aventura, which provide pedestrian access to the water park—also offer free shuttle buses directly to **Volcano Bay.**

unofficial **TIP**
Don't try to park at Cabana Bay or Aventura and walk to Volcano Bay if you aren't a registered guest. Day visitors are charged $51 for self-parking, and key cards are inspected at the hotel entrance.

Finally, walking from most resort hotels (except Endless Summer) to one of the theme parks takes a maximum of about 15–20 minutes using the resort's beautifully landscaped (though frustratingly winding) garden pathways. **Helios Grand Hotel** has an exclusive entrance directly into Epic Universe, and **Hard Rock Hotel** is the closest to the original parks, being only steps away from Universal Studios Florida's front gates, while **Portofino Bay** and **Cabana Bay** are the farthest. To walk between Portofino and Cabana Bay takes 30–40 minutes.

You'll find more about Universal Orlando transportation in Part Two (see page 80).

LEAVING UNIVERSAL ORLANDO

AT THE END OF YOUR VISIT, retrace your steps to your vehicle and follow directional signage to depart the resort. From the south garage, you have little option but to follow the arrows to I-4 or International Drive. If you exit the north garage onto Universal Boulevard, you can reach I-4 by turning right onto Major Boulevard and then right onto Kirkman Road. Stay right at the fork for I-4 West, or reach I-4 East by bearing left at the fork toward International Drive, then taking the I-4 on-ramp on your right. Alternatively, continue on Major Boulevard to Grand National and use the I-4 Express entrance to bypass frequent backups between Kirkman and the turnpike. When leaving Epic Universe, follow signs south onto FL 528 West towards I-4 West if headed to Disney, or go north on Kirkman Rd. for the original Universal Orlando campus and I-4 East. Practice deep breathing if you're departing with the masses at park closing on a crowded day, because the backups on the parking garages' exit ramps may induce road rage.

PART 4

UNIVERSAL ESSENTIALS

MONEY, ETC.

ATMS AND BANKING SERVICES

BANKING AT UNIVERSAL ORLANDO is limited to ATMs, which are marked on the park maps. There are a handful of ATMs in each theme park, plus two in CityWalk, one in each hotel, and one at Volcano Bay. Most major banking networks are accepted.

The closest full-service bank to Universal Orlando is **Regions** at the corner of Kirkman and Vineland Roads (5401 S. Kirkman Road).

USF ATM LOCATIONS	IOA ATM LOCATIONS
• Outside the park entrance to the right of the Guest Services window • Hollywood near First Aid and Lost and Found • New York outside the arcade • Outside Diagon Alley to the right of King's Cross Station • Restrooms near the London waterfront	• Outside the park entrance, to the right of the Guest Services window • Jurassic Park by the exit of Jurassic Park River Adventure • Hogsmeade outside The Three Broomstick
CITYWALK ATM LOCATIONS	**VOLCANO BAY ATM LOCATIONS**
• Between Starbucks and Cold Stone Creamery • Between Universal's Great Movie Escape and Fat Tuesday	• Outside Volcano Bay, to the right of the main entrance

CHECKS

UNIVERSAL ORLANDO ACCEPTS ONLY personal checks that are preprinted, drawn on US banks, and made out for the exact amount of the purchase, and they are accepted only at the front gate. Valid photo identification is required, and your check will be submitted to an online verification system.

Traveler's checks in US currency are accepted throughout the resort but must be signed by the bearer in front of the cashier and be presented with photo ID.

Business checks, cashier's checks, and school checks are accepted only if they are preprinted, drawn on US banks, made out for the exact amount of purchase, and presented with photo ID.

CREDIT CARDS

AMERICAN EXPRESS, DINERS CLUB, **Discover, MasterCard,** and **Visa** are accepted throughout Universal Orlando; the hotels also accept **Japan Credit Bureau** and **Carte Blanche** cards. Most point-of-sale registers at Universal have chip scanners and offer tap-to-pay transactions for mobile devices, such as **Apple Pay** and **Google Pay.**

The **Universal Rewards Plus Visa Signature** card gives 4% back on purchases at Universal, 2% on other travel and dining purchases, and 1% on everything else. There is a $99 annual fee, but you get a $300 credit for spending $1,000 during your first three billing cycles. It also includes 0% financing on Universal vacation packages; a free one-day/one-park ticket each year if you spend $6,000; and access to a new cardholder lounge near the front entrance of Universal Studios Florida with free bottled water, snacks, and charging stations. The **Universal Rewards Visa** has no annual fee, but you only get $150 statement credit and 2% back on Universal purchases (1% on everything else) and no lounge access, though you can use exclusive viewing sections for some parades and nighttime shows. Special incentives—like free Express passes, up to $200 in Universal gift cards, and Freestyle drink cups—are offered if you get instant approval at one of the sign-up kiosks located in the theme parks and parking hub, or visit theugseries.com /unirewardvisa to apply from home.

Universal Pay is a feature in the free Universal Orlando app's wallet that allows guests to charge purchases around the resort to a credit card simply by scanning a secure QR code. You can set up individual spending limits for each member of your party; transactions are quicker than using a physical card or even tap-to-pay. The only catch is that it works at only Universal-owned locations, not third-party vendors.

CURRENCY EXCHANGE

EXCHANGE YOUR EUROS, KRONER, OR ZLOTYS for good old American greenbacks—the only form of cash accepted at Universal Orlando—at either theme park's **Guest Services** window or any hotel front desk. There may be a daily limit on how much you can exchange (around $500), and a nominal transaction surcharge applies.

A LICENSE TO PRINT MONEY

AVAILABLE EXCLUSIVELY at the Gringotts Money Exchange shop in USF's Diagon Alley, **Gringotts Wizarding Bank Notes** come in $10 or $20 denominations, and there is no extra fee to exchange your Muggle money for some. The bank notes can be redeemed virtually anywhere on Universal Orlando property (even for valet parking) at a one-for-one exchange rate. While you won't lose any money on Wizarding currency as long as you spend it before you leave the resort, most guests (intentionally or unintentionally) take them home as souvenirs, making a healthy profit for Universal's goblin accountants.

Credit card–style **Universal Orlando** gift cards with various designs are also sold, with values from $10 up to $500, and accepted throughout the resort; you can buy them at universalorlando.com/web/en/us /gift-cards/purchase.html, and reload them in the parks with no fees or expiration.

SALES TAX

A COMBINED STATE AND LOCAL SALES TAX of 6.5% applies to all purchases made at Universal Orlando. Hotels also charge a 6% Orange County occupancy tax, for a total of 12.5%. All prices listed in this book include tax, unless otherwise noted.

PACKING *the* ESSENTIALS

WHAT SHOULD I BRING?

IN ADDITION TO THE BASICS that you would bring along on any vacation—casual clothing, comfortable footwear, bathing attire, necessary medications and toiletries—you'll want to stock up on the following before your Universal Orlando visit:

- Small bottles of hand sanitizer and sunscreen
- Cell phone backup battery or charger with cord and plug (see page 147)
- Lanyard for tickets and hotel key card (see page 61)
- Zip-top plastic bags, to protect electronics and wallets on water rides
- A hat with brim and sunglasses (even during the winter)
- Pocket-size umbrella and/or poncho, especially during summer and hurricane season (see page 146)
- Refillable water bottle (if you aren't purchasing unlimited Freestyle drinks; see page 313)

WHAT SHOULD I *NOT* BRING?

BY THE SAME TOKEN, Universal strictly enforces restrictions on the kinds of items guests are allowed to bring into its parks. Obviously, any form of weapon or illegal substance is prohibited, as is clothing with "offensive language or content" or that "represents someone as emergency personnel." You are also disallowed from entering with large duffel bags, folding chairs, beach umbrellas, or hard-sided coolers.

Packing picnics is officially prohibited, but you may bring bottled water and small snacks, along with baby food and any medically necessary nutritional items, as long as they are nonalcoholic, are not in glass containers, and are stored in a soft-sided cooler or bag no bigger than 8½ x 6 x 6 inches. Also, there are no on-site facilities for refrigerating or reheating food you bring into the parks.

Be aware that all items are subject to inspection before you enter CityWalk or Epic Universe, so come prepared to open your bags at the security checkpoint. Here are some items you'll definitely want to leave behind:

- Alcohol, controlled substances (including medical cannabis), and illegal drugs
- Weapons, including knives, firearms, and explosives
- Glass containers or glassware
- Large or hard-sided coolers
- Food that requires refrigerating or reheating (bottled water and small snacks are OK)
- Drones, hoverboards, and Segways (except as ADA mobility devices)

PROBLEMS *and* UNUSUAL SITUATIONS

ATTRACTION CLOSURES

FIND OUT IN ADVANCE what attractions are scheduled to be closed for repair during your visit. For complete refurbishment schedules, check **Universal's** official operating calendar (theugseries.com/unihrs) or **Touring Plans'** Universal Orlando closures page (touringplans.com /universal-orlando/closures), or use the mobile app Lines.

Universal's attractions are technically complex, so it's almost inevitable that you will experience some unscheduled downtime during your visit. If a ride is temporarily closed, ask the attendants outside if there is an estimated reopening time (usually they can't tell you) and continue with your touring, returning later if possible. If a ride stops running while you're already in the queue, decide whether to stay based on how long the posted wait was when you entered and how much time you've already invested. Most "brief operational delays" are resolved in about 15 minutes, but there are no guarantees.

If a ride halts unexpectedly while you're on it, remain calm and rest assured that Universal has extremely safe evacuation procedures for every contingency. Stay seated and listen for announcements, and be patient because employees may need to evacuate ride vehicles one at a time in a specific order. On the plus side, you may get an exclusive backstage view of how the ride operates, and you should be offered either an immediate reride (if the attraction resumes operating) or a return ticket to let you skip the standby line later on.

GASOLINE

THERE IS ONE **Mobil** gas station on Universal property. It's on the west side of the main resort, adjacent to the corporate offices and employee parking lot. The address is 5981 Turkey Lake Road. From the guest parking garages, take Hollywood Way west to Turkey Lake Road; turn right, and the station will be ahead on your right.

If you drive a Tesla or other electric vehicle, **charging stations** are available at Universal's valet parking circle and in the self-parking garages of all on-site resort hotels. There is no additional fee for charging beyond what you'll pay for parking.

CAR CARE

UNIVERSAL ORLANDO OFFERS free vehicle assistance—including battery jumps—to guests parked in its parking facilities. Raise your car's hood (if possible) and flag down a parking attendant, or use one of the security call boxes located in each parking section.

If you have more-serious car trouble, the nearest repair facility is the **Universal Service Center,** inside the Mobil station above (5989 Turkey Lake Road; ☎ 407-345-4860; universalservicecenter.net).

CELL PHONE SNAFUS

CELL PHONE SERVICE CAN BE SPOTTY at Universal Orlando, especially on days of high attendance. A woman from Leawood, Kansas, tells it like it is:

> *In our group, we were using three different carriers, and we all had problems sending and receiving texts and calls.*

The problem of signal strength is compounded by crowd noise and the ambient music played throughout the parks. Even if you have a decent signal, it can be challenging to find some place quiet enough to have a conversation. When possible, opt for texting.

Data speeds can be especially sluggish when the park is packed with guests trying to Instagram over 5G. Luckily, Universal's Wi-Fi is free

unofficial **TIP**
Wi-Fi coverage inside Volcano Bay has greatly improved, but cell service (especially AT&T) is still inconsistent inside the park. We suggest that you put away your phone and bring a book for the beach.

and fairly stable throughout the theme parks and CityWalk; you can even get decent reception inside Gringotts' vaults. In your phone's Wi-Fi settings, choose "Universal" from the list of available networks; then input an email address and accept the user agreement before opening your browser or social media apps. You may have to log in again every day or so.

LOST AND FOUND

IF YOU LOSE (OR FIND) SOMETHING in USF, go to the **Lost and Found** counter, to the right of the main gate as you enter. At Islands of Adventure (IOA) and Epic Universe (EU), Lost and Found is near stroller rental to the left of the park's entrance. At Volcano Bay, visit **Guest Services** at the front of the park. If you discover your loss after you've left the park(s), visit theugseries.com/uorlostandfound to submit a report with **Chargerback,** an automated service that will notify you of your item's status. If you need to talk to a live person, call ☎ 407-224-4233 and press 5, then 4.

It's best not to lose anything in the first place, but if you do, there is hope: we've had an excellent track record with Universal's Lost and Found, which has recovered errant hats and keys for us over the years.

MEDICAL MATTERS

HEADACHE RELIEF Sample sizes of some over-the-counter medications are available free from the **First Aid Stations** (see page 148 for locations). Aspirin and other sundries are sold at the **Universal Studios Store** in USF, at **Islands of Adventure Trading Company** in IOA, at **Other Worlds Mercantile** in EU, and at **Krakatoa Katy's** in Volcano Bay. Over-the-counter meds are stored behind the counter, so you must ask an employee for them.

ILLNESSES REQUIRING MEDICAL ATTENTION Off property, the closest walk-in clinic is **AdventHealth Centra Care Dr. Phillips** (8014 Conroy Windermere Road; ☎ 407-291-8975; centracare.adventhealth.com/urgent-care/dr-phillips). The clinic is open Monday–Saturday, 8 a.m.–8 p.m., and Sunday, 8 a.m.–5 p.m. Centra Care also operates a 24-hour physician house call service and runs a free shuttle (call ☎ 407-938-0650 to arrange pickup).

The Medical Concierge (☎ 855-932-5252; themedicalconcierge .com) has board-certified physicians available 24-7 for house calls to your hotel room. It offers in-room X-rays and IV therapy service, as well as same-day dental and specialist appointments. It also rents medical equipment. Insurance receipts, insurance billing, and foreign-language interpretation are provided. Walk-in clinics are available. You can also inquire about transportation arrangements.

DOCS (Doctors on Call Service; ☎ 407-399-3627; doctorson callservice.com) offers 24-hour house call service. All physicians are certified by the American Board of Medical Specialties. A father of two from O'Fallon, Illinois, gives them a thumbs-up:

> *My wife's cold developed into an ear infection that required medical attention, and DOCS was able to respond in 40 minutes. The doctor had medicine with him and was very professional and friendly.*

In case of a life-and-death emergency, the nearest fully equipped ER is at **Dr. Phillips Hospital** (9400 Turkey Lake Road; ☎ 407-351-8500).

DENTAL NEEDS Call **Watson Dental Care** (5979 Vineland Road, #205; ☎ 407-351-3213; dentistorlandoflorida.com).

PRESCRIPTION MEDICINE The nearest pharmacy is **Walgreens** (☎ 407-248-0315) at 5501 Kirkman Road, in the shopping plaza across from the main resort. (*Note:* Google indicates an AdventHealth at 1000 Universal Studios Plaza, but that's a backstage clinic for Universal employees only.) **Turner Drugs** (☎ 407-828-8125; turnerdrug .com) charges $15 to deliver a prescription to a Universal hotel's front desk ($7.50 for Disney hotels).

Sergeant Blisterblaster's Guide To Happy Feet

1. ON YOUR FEET! You can easily log 5–10 miles a day at the Universal Orlando parks, and a reader told us she clocked 13.5 (more than a half-marathon!), so shape up beginning a month or two before your visit. Start with short walks around the neighborhood, and gradually increase your distance until you can do 6 miles without CPR.

2. A-TEN-SHUN! No walking in flip-flops, loafers, or sandals. Wear well-constructed, broken-in running or hiking shoes with a pair of socks (such as Smartwool or Coolmax) that wicks perspiration away from your feet; antifungal powder is optional.

3. WHO DO YOU THINK YOU ARE? JOHN WAYNE? Don't be a hero. Take care of a foot problem the minute you notice it. Carry a small foot-emergency kit (including gauze, antibiotic ointment, moleskin, and blister bandages) or visit Universal First Aid for supplies if a problem arises. If you develop a hot spot in the same place every time you walk (a clue!), cover it with a blister bandage before you set out.

4. BITE THE BULLET! Check your kids' feet (and your own) several times a day for hot spots, and cover any you find ASAP with a blister bandage. If a blister develops, air out and dry the foot, clean the area with antibiotic ointment, and place a blister bandage over the blister. Don't cover the hot spot or blister with adhesive bandages; they'll slip and wad up. Moleskin can still be useful for lining the roughened inner surface of shoe heels and toes to prevent further foot damage.

RAIN

unofficial TIP
Raingear isn't always displayed in shops, so you may have to ask for it.

WEATHER BAD? Go to the parks anyway. The crowds are lighter, and most attractions and waiting areas are under cover. Showers, especially during warmer months, can be intense but are usually short and frequently occur in the late afternoon around 4 p.m.

Rainy-Day Touring

When it comes to deciding which park to visit, we think USF is an excellent wet-weather choice—almost all of its headliner attractions (except Hollywood Rip Ride Rockit) are indoors.

While the many outdoor attractions at IOA and EU can operate in a moderate downpour, they must shut down when lightning is in the vicinity and may require safety inspections before restarting. Hagrid's Magical Creatures Motorbike Adventure in particular is notorious for taking up to an hour to reopen after a storm clears. That leaves Harry Potter and the Forbidden Journey, The Amazing Adventures of Spider-Man, Reign of Kong, and Cat in the Hat as virtually the only rides at IOA that can operate during severe weather. At EU, each land has one major ride that is fully enclosed, plus a couple more that may close in bad weather.

Volcano Bay will let you keep swimming in a moderate rain, but as soon as lightning is detected in the vicinity, everyone must get out of the water. Many guests will flee when a downpour starts, but you should find some shelter and stay put. (Hey, you came here to get wet, right?) Once the weather clears, you'll have the slides to yourself, making poststorm summer afternoons the best time to enjoy the water park without crowds.

Raingear

Ponchos are $14 for adults, $12 for children; umbrellas cost $20–$27. All ponchos sold at Universal Orlando are made of clear plastic (though ones sold within The Wizarding World have a special insignia), so picking out somebody in your party on a rainy day can be tricky. Stores such as Target sell inexpensive solid-color ponchos that will make your family bright beacons in a plastic-covered sea of humanity.

unofficial **TIP**
To keep your head and face as dry as possible, we recommend wearing a cap under the poncho hood.

A Wilmington, North Carolina, mom thinks high-quality raingear is worth the investment:

> It rained every day on our trip, driving many people out of the parks and leaving others looking miserable in their ponchos. Meanwhile, we hardly noticed the rain from inside our high-end rain jackets as we walked right on to many of the attractions.

Some unusually heavy rain precipitated (no pun intended) dozens of reader suggestions for dealing with soggy days. The best came from this Memphis, Tennessee, mom:

1. *Raingear should include ponchos and umbrellas. When rain isn't beating down on your ponchoed head, it's easier to ignore.*
2. *Buy blue ponchos at Walgreens. We could keep track of each other more easily because we had blue ponchos instead of clear ones.*
3. *If you're using a stroller, bring a plastic sheet or extra poncho to protect it from rain. (Ponchos cover only single strollers.) Carry a towel in a plastic bag to wipe off your stroller after experiencing an attraction during a rainfall.*

HOW TO LODGE A COMPLAINT WITH UNIVERSAL

YOU'LL USUALLY FIND Universal folks highly responsive to guests' issues. **Guest Services** at the front of each Universal park will be happy to listen to any complaints and will be even happier to pass along praise for any exceptional employees you encounter. Minor problems are often addressed with a sincere apology and a pass to skip an attraction queue; on the other hand, a more global gripe, or one beyond an on-site manager's ability to resolve, is likely to founder in the labyrinth of Universal bureaucracy. To contact Guest Services after your trip, call ☎ 877-589-4783 or ☎ 407-224-4233, or send an email to GuestServices@Universal Orlando.com.

SERVICES

CELEBRATION BUTTONS

CELEBRATING A BIRTHDAY, ANNIVERSARY, honeymoon, engagement, or Bat Mitzvah at Universal? Or just celebrating the fact that it's your first visit to the parks? Stop by Guest Services for a free celebration button to wear during your special day. Buttons come in "It's My

Birthday!" and more generic "I'm Celebrating!" varieties. At a minimum, you'll have employees (and fellow guests) shouting you warm
wishes all day long. If you're lucky, you might find yourself treated to
preferred seating, a special meet and greet, or other unexpected perks,
as this Endicott, New York, reader happily discovered:

> *A birthday button earned many greetings, two free desserts, and a
> free drink.*

CELL PHONE CHARGING

THE ANNUAL PASSHOLDER AND VISA LOUNGES discussed previously stock charging adapters for most Apple and Android devices
(including Micro USB and Lightning). Aside from these locations, however, Universal Orlando has no other designated phone-charging stations in the parks, so pack a power cable and wall plug if you want to
steal juice from accessible outlets you find along the way.

If you prefer to charge on the go, we use **Anker** external batteries
for our devices, available at Amazon.

Another energy option is the **FuelRod,** a precharged battery pack
sold from automated kiosks scattered around the parks, CityWalk,
and the resort hotels. You can find higher-capacity batteries online for
less than the $35 FuelRod—the advantage is that whenever a FuelRod
runs out of power, you can simply stop and swap it for a full one at
any FuelRod kiosk on Universal property. Kiosks can be found in the
following locations:

USF FUELROD LOCATIONS	IOA FUELROD LOCATIONS
• Today Cafe restrooms	• Mulberry Street Store in Seuss Landing
• New York Palace Arcade	• Jurassic Park River Adventure restrooms
• Fast & Furious Custom Gear store	• Marvel Super Hero Island restrooms
• MIB Gear store	• Port of Entry restrooms
CITYWALK FUELROD LOCATIONS	**RESORT HOTEL FUELROD LOCATIONS**
• Guest Services	• Resort hotel gift shops

The downside: whereas similar kiosks on Disney property provide
free unlimited swaps, the ones at Universal charge $3 per exchange,
although you can sign into the FuelRod app for a $5 credit; "founders"
who purchased one before October 26, 2019, get lifetime free swaps.
Universal's kiosks dispense upgraded FuelRods with USB-C ports and
more capacity than the originals; if your older battery is rejected as
"invalid," call the phone number on the kiosk and they'll swiftly dispense you a brand-new kit.

This power-hungry family from Marlborough, Connecticut,
became confirmed FuelRod fans:

> *Between using the app, taking pictures, and everything else we use
> our phones for, batteries drain fast. FuelRod was our best find ever.
> Yes, we all have portable chargers, but they never seem to be with
> you and charged when you really need them. For our family of 4 (2
> adults, 2 teens), FuelRod was super convenient. We used it to charge*

our phones while on a ride or in a show, and then we'd swap it out for a freshly charged one and hand it off to the next person in need of power. I don't know how we would have made it through each day without it.

You can save money by buying FuelRods outside the resort—they're available in a two-pack for $40 from Amazon, or in airports and malls for about $30 each, and all are compatible with Universal's kiosks. Search online for a code to get a discount off your initial purchase.

FIRST AID

EACH UNIVERSAL PARK has a **Walgreens**-sponsored first aid center. In USF, it's on **Canal Street** behind Louie's Italian Restaurant, on the border between New York and San Francisco. In IOA, it's in the **Lost Continent** near The Mystic Fountain; look for the red cross behind the kebab house. There are two first aid centers at EU in **Celestial Park**—one to the right of the front entrance and another in the rear between the Wizarding World of Harry Potter and Helios Grand Hotel. In all parks, the **Family Services** nursing facilities and companion restroom are right next to First Aid. **Volcano Bay**'s First Aid is just inside the park entrance, and **CityWalk**'s First Aid is near Guest Services, at the end of the hallway behind Cold Stone Creamery.

Guests who use the service are generally very positive about it; Seth once sought treatment for a minor flesh wound and was patched up in a matter of minutes.

GROCERIES

EACH UNIVERSAL RESORT hotel has a shop or food court selling sundries, snacks, and grab-and-go breakfast foods. While their locations make them convenient, the selection is poor, and you'll find the prices higher and more frightening than Doctor Doom's Fearfall. For more down-to-earth prices, try **Publix,** north of Universal at the intersection of Kirkman and Conroy Roads (4606 S. Kirkman Road; ☎ 407-293-7673), or for fancier fare visit **Whole Foods,** southwest of Universal on Sand Lake Road near I-4 (8003 Turkey Lake Road; ☎ 407-355-7100).

If you don't have a car or you just don't feel like going to the supermarket, there are several services that will deliver your groceries. **GardenGrocer.com**, the area's longest-running delivery service, offers daily delivery (8 a.m.–4 p.m.) to Universal and surrounding hotels through their easy-to-use website. Delivery costs $15 (free for orders over $200) and must be arranged 48 hours in advance. **MagicalVaca tionServices.com** features preselected grocery packages, but also sells items like autograph books and Harry Potter candy. Delivery costs $25–$30 ($10 additional for alcohol) and isn't available on Sundays or Wednesdays. **VacationGroceryDeliveryFL.com** promises the lowest prices on groceries and stroller rentals, but you must pay $25 plus 5% in delivery and service fees ($30 plus 10% on alcohol) and an automatic 10% gratuity; they recommend booking at least 2–3 weeks in advance. **WeGoShop.com** takes your typed shopping list to the grocery store you request, buys at market rates, and delivers to your on-site Universal resort. WeGoShop charges on a sliding scale, from $21 for up to a $50 grocery bill, to 15% of the total for bills over $300; a $3 fuel surcharge is levied on all orders. **Instacart.com** will deliver to Universal-area hotels from Publix, Aldi, Costco, and numerous other stores. Delivery fees start at $3.99 with a $35 minimum, and free offers are often available. Their Publix Quick Delivery option delivers items within 30 minutes, with no prebooking required. Finally, Amazon Prime subscribers can order groceries through **Amazon Fresh** (fresh.amazon.com) for free 2-hour delivery on orders over $100; or **Whole Foods Market** (wholefoods.amazon.com), which charges $5–$10 for 2-hour delivery. For all these services, you must be present for delivery, because Universal's hotel bellhops can't hold your groceries, and a 10–20% tip is considered customary.

LOCKERS

WHEN WE VISIT THE UNIVERSAL PARKS, we try to pare down our gear to a bare minimum and bring only those necessities that fit comfortably in our pockets: admission, ID, a credit card or cash, and a cell phone. Many guests keep their tickets handy in a lanyard pouch (readily available around the resort for around $15 and up), and Seth swears by cargo shorts with zippered pockets, for function if not fashion.

But many guests—especially those accompanying young children or those with special needs—find that they simply can't travel that light. When your burden becomes too much to bear, make a beeline for a bank of lockers and lighten your load.

Universal Orlando's lockers are automated and use a computerized locking system. The locker banks are easy to find, and each bank has a small touch screen in the center; hold your physical admission ticket up to the bar code scanner below the screen. If you're using the mobile app to store your admission, ask a locker attendant for a bar code that will work with the scanners.

After you scan your ticket (and swipe your credit card for paid lockers), a nearby locker will pop open for you. Place your stuff (except for your ticket!) in the indicated locker, and press the illuminated button to lock it after you've closed the door. When you're ready to retrieve your belongings, return to the same kiosk and scan your ticket again. The locker should relinquish its contents; if you have any trouble, find a nearby employee to assist.

By default, only the ticket originally used to secure a locker can reopen it, but paid lockers let you attach additional tickets, thus giving other members of your party access. Look for a freestanding assistance kiosk near the lockers, and follow the instructions on the screen.

Universal Orlando Resort offers three types of lockers, described as follows.

Paid All-Day Lockers

These lockers charge one flat rate for a full day and can be opened and relocked as many times as you like during your visit using your ticket. All-day lockers in the theme parks come in two categories: "large" (about 12 inches wide by 13 inches high by 16.9 inches deep) for $15 per day, or the roomier family size (about 12 inches wide by 16.25 inches high by 16.9 inches deep) for $20 per day. Lockers inside **Volcano Bay** cost $14, $20, or $25 per day, depending on size, and are controlled with the TapuTapu wristbands. Volcano Bay has four locker facilities arrayed around the park's perimeter, plus one outside the entrance; see page 294 for details.

All-day lockers can be found in the following locations:

UNIVERSAL STUDIOS FLORIDA ALL-DAY LOCKERS
• Next to the Studio Audience Center inside the front gate (regular size)
• Behind the restrooms near the Studio Audience Center (family size)
• Near the exit turnstiles, next to wheelchair and stroller rental (regular size)

ISLANDS OF ADVENTURE ALL-DAY LOCKERS
• Inside the front gate near wheelchair and stroller rental (regular and family size)

EPIC UNIVERSE ALL-DAY LOCKERS
• Inside the front gate to the left (regular and family size)

Free and Discounted Short-Term Lockers

Universal enforces a mandatory locker system at its big thrill rides. Lockers outside these attractions come in two varieties. Small lockers (14 inches wide by 5.5 inches high by 16.9 inches deep) are free for an amount of time that varies with the length of the standby line—if the wait in line is 30 minutes, for example, and the ride itself lasts 10 minutes, you get 40 minutes plus a small cushion of about 15 minutes. The lockers then cost $3 for each 30 minutes after that, with a $20 daily maximum ($25 maximum at Escape from Gringotts only).

The free lockers, which are arranged horizontally, are too small to store souvenir soda cups standing up (look for vertical lockers at some rides, or empty your drink before stowing it) and are barely large enough for a few cell phones and wallets, as this reader from Brooklyn, New York, was frustrated to find:

> I wish I had known how SMALL the mandatory lockers at Universal are. I was very frustrated trying to fit my bag into the lockers, which are seemingly designed to fit only a small backpack or purse.

A limited number of larger lockers (12 inches wide by 13 inches high by 16.9 inches deep) are available, but they cost $3 during the posted wait time and an additional $3 per 30 minutes after, up to a daily maximum of $25. That adds up to the price of an all-day locker after only five attractions, so you may want to weigh that cost before walking too far from the park entrance, as this reader from Nof Ayalon, Israel, advises:

We had a medium-size backpack and struggled to stuff it into the lockers. When I reached Men in Black Alien Attack, I decided enough is enough and went to the park entrance to store our knapsack. I only later realized that I picked the farthest point in the park to do this.

Free short-term lockers are at the following attractions:

UNIVERSAL STUDIOS FLORIDA FREE SHORT-TERM LOCKERS
• Harry Potter and the Escape from Gringotts • Hollywood Rip Ride Rockit • Men in Black Alien Attack • Revenge of the Mummy

ISLANDS OF ADVENTURE FREE SHORT-TERM LOCKERS
• Hagrid's Magical Creatures Motorbike Adventure • Harry Potter and the Forbidden Journey • The Incredible Hulk Coaster • Jurassic World VelociCoaster

EPIC UNIVERSE FREE SHORT-TERM LOCKERS
• Monsters Unchained: The Frankenstein Experiment • Stardust Racers • Harry Potter and the Forbidden Journey

On most of the aforementioned rides, all bags, purses, and other objects too large to be secured in a pocket must be placed in a free locker during your ride; wallets, phones, and compact cameras are generally permitted, as are small hip belts or fanny packs that can be securely fastened and tucked beneath a shirt. Cross-body bags worn across the chest (rather than around the waist) cannot be taken on rides that require lockers.

Universal strictly enforces a "no loose items" policy at **The Incredible Hulk Coaster, Jurassic World VelociCoaster, Hollywood Rip Ride Rockit,** and **Stardust Racers.** At these rides, guests are required to undergo an airport-style security screening—complete with walk-through metal detectors and electronic scanning wands—to ensure that no phones, keys, or even spare change enters the queue. You should be permitted to hold on to your prescription eyeglasses and ticket lanyard. At Hulk and Rockit, this safety check occurs before entering the queue, but VelociCoaster and Stardust Racers feature double-sided locker systems just before the boarding station, allowing you to hold onto your smartphone through most of the line.

If a ride breaks down while you're in line and you exceed your free usage period through no fault of your own, a locker attendant can override the charge on request. You may need to be firm to avoid paying an overage fee, as this reader found:

Watch out for the Men in Black lockers. We went over our allotted time because of ride issues, but the [attendant] kept insisting we had to pay. Only after standing our ground did the attendant finally check with others and confirm that there were ride issues.

When you want to ride a thrill ride but don't want to bother with a locker, you can use the child-swap area (where available; see page 187) as a bag swap and leave a nonrider with your belongings. This is especially useful for the Harry Potter rides because the free lockers are too small to hold some longer wand boxes from Ollivanders, and the locker banks for Hagrid's and Gringotts are frequently overcrowded.

Paid Short-Term Lockers

Universal does not enforce mandatory locker usage on its water rides, but it does conveniently (or capitalistically) provide paid short-term lockers outside each attraction that is likely to soak you and your belongings. The short-term paid lockers come in the same two sizes as the free and discounted ones and operate identically. The difference is that the smaller ones cost $5 for the first 90 minutes and the larger ones are $6; both cost $3 for each additional half hour after that, with a $25 daily maximum.

Paid short-term lockers are located only at IOA at the following attractions:

ISLANDS OF ADVENTURE PAID SHORT-TERM LOCKERS
• Dudley Do-Right's Ripsaw Falls   • Jurassic Park River Adventure
• Popeye & Bluto's Bilge-Rat Barges

PACKAGE DELIVERY

FREE PACKAGE DELIVERY is available from stores in the theme parks and CityWalk to Universal Orlando's hotels for on-site guests only. Purchases made before 5 p.m. will be delivered to your hotel's front desk or luggage services between 9 a.m. and 4 p.m. the following day, so you can't use it on your checkout day. On-site and off-site guests alike can also pay for FedEx shipping of souvenirs direct to home; personal items and food (except for select packaged treats like Chocolate Frogs) may not be mailed. Ask the cashier for pricing and details when checking out.

If you get home and realize you missed an essential souvenir, shop for Universal Orlando tchotchkes online at shop.universalorlando.com.

MY UNIVERSAL PHOTOS (MUP)

WHILE SOME GUESTS still find their point-and-shoot or smartphone sufficient for documenting their vacation, Universal (in partnership with Colorvision's Amazing Pictures) has capitalized on advancing digital photo and social media technology with its My Universal Photos program. All the images captured during your day by Universal—either by roving paparazzi near the park entrances, at organized character meet and greets, or inside attractions—can be collected on plastic cards (distributed free from every photo location) and retrieved at the end of the day at the photography shops at the front of the parks: **On Location** at USF, **DeFotos Expedition Photography** at IOA, **Lens Flare** at Epic Universe, or **Krakatau Katy's** and **Waturi Marketplace** at Volcano Bay.

Photos can be purchased individually, but that quickly gets expensive, at $26 for a single 5-by-7-inch print or a digital download. The MUP daily packages are a better value, offering 1, 3, or 30 days of unlimited digital photos and a souvenir lanyard to hold your MUP card. With a MUP package, you receive discounts on online photo products and additional prints ($2 for 4-by-6-inch; $10 for 5-by-7-inch or 8-by-10-inch). MUP packages are available for all three parks and include all street photographers, on-ride still images, and even unique photo ops such as E.T.'s flying bicycle.

Digital images can be downloaded at myuniversalphotos.com for sharing via email or social media; they download at a resolution good enough for printing, though not for poster-size enlargements.

To use the MUP package, simply present your card to every Universal photographer you approach, or at the photo counters at the exits of rides. Ride photos can be edited to zoom in on your party, and some photographers can set up special effects shots.

Universal also has automated MUP kiosks at the exits of select attractions, including **Men in Black Alien Attack, Revenge of the Mummy, The Amazing Adventures of Spider-Man,** and **The Incredible Hulk Coaster,** letting you register your photos without waiting in line, though MUP team members are still available at some rides to help find and edit your photos if you don't want to use the self-service stations. You get two cards per MUP package, in case your party splits up, and any additional images you get on other photo cards can be added to your MUP account at any photo service center. The service

MY UNIVERSAL PHOTOS LOCATIONS

UNIVERSAL STUDIOS FLORIDA

- Park entrance
- Transformers meet and greet
- E.T. Toy Closet
- Men in Black Alien Attack on-ride photo
- Revenge of the Mummy on-ride photo
- Illumination Theater Meet & Greet
- DreamWorks Land meet and greets

- Hollywood Rip Ride Rockit on-ride photo
- Minions meet and greet at Super Silly Stuff
- Back to the Future car automated photo op
- Roaming photographers during Halloween Horror Nights and other events (seasonal)
- Troll's Trollercoaster on-ride photo

ISLANDS OF ADVENTURE

- Park entrance
- The Incredible Hulk Coaster on-ride photo
- The Amazing Adventures of Spider-Man on-ride photo
- Dudley Do-Right's Ripsaw Falls on-ride photo
- Jurassic Park spinosaurus automated photo op
- Jurassic Park River Adventure on-ride photo

- Jurassic World VelociCoaster on-ride photo
- Harry Potter and the Forbidden Journey on-ride photo
- Hagrid's Magical Creatures Motorbike Adventure on-ride photo
- Raptor Encounter
- Grinch meet and greet during Grinchmas (seasonal)

EPIC UNIVERSE

- Park entrance
- Harry Potter and the Battle at the Ministry on-ride photo
- Hiccup's Wing Gliders on-ride photo
- Mine-Cart Madness on-ride photo

- Monsters Unchained: The Frankenstein Experiment on-ride photo
- How to Train Your Dragon meet and greet
- Dark Universe monsters meet and greet

VOLCANO BAY

- Park entrance
- Krakatau Aqua Coaster on-ride photo
- Ohyah & Ohno Drop Slides on-ride photo
- Tonga and Raki of Taniwha Tubes on-ride photo

- Honu and ika Moana on-ride photo
- Punga Racers on-ride photo
- Volcano, Family, and Hug a Mo Selfie Station automated photo ops

centers can also help retrieve any attraction photos you forgot to pick up after exiting, as long as you can remember what time you rode.

In addition to on-ride pictures and wandering photogs, you'll find a few automated photo ops scattered around the parks, including the **Back to the Future** car in USF, the **Jurassic Park spinosaurus** in IOA, and several selfie stations at **Volcano Bay**. Scan your MUP card (or TapuTapu wristband) at the kiosk, then pose at the designated spot while the camera counts down to the flash.

If you prepurchase your MUP package online at theugseries.com /uniphotos or theugseries.com/myuniphoto, it won't begin expiring until you activate it at the photography shop near the front of each park. Once activated, MUP packages are valid for the purchased number of consecutive days. Online prices (including tax) are $96 for 1 day, $117 for 3 days, and $149 for 30 days. A full year of MUP service costs $170 and is sometimes discounted for annual passholders. A one-day photo pass valid only at Volcano Bay is $53; all other packages are valid in all three parks. Finally, a package combining a three-day MUP package with a video session at **Shutterbutton's** in Diagon Alley (see page 213) costs $170 online. MUP packages cost $11–$22 more if purchased inside the park.

If buying ride and character photos is important to you, you'll save money buying a package versus buying à la carte; if not, the freedom of unlimited snapshots may seduce you. That said, there are some deficits and gotchas to MUP that you should be aware of before buying.

For starters, MUP photographers can be found at each park's entrance, and occasionally at impromptu character greetings, but they aren't on every corner. You can sometimes find an exceptional Universal photographer who will spend time posing with your family in various locations, but you're equally likely to encounter a meet and greet where the photog has gone mysteriously MIA. You certainly shouldn't leave your camera at home expecting that MUP will be able to capture all your vacation memories.

Second, if you want to purchase any photos, you must do so (or buy and activate a MUP package) before you leave the park—once you exit at the end of the day, any photos not paid for or connected to an active MUP account will be erased. Likewise, if a photographer asks you to pose pointing or with your empty palm extended, you should stop by the photo store before leaving to have characters edited into the image; otherwise you'll look pretty silly in the shots. Even if you didn't take any "magic" photos, you should still review your pictures from the day on your phone or at a photo center before you leave, because images occasionally get mysteriously lost on the way to your account.

Finally, all digital photos in The Wizarding Worlds are included with MUP, but if you want a physical picture from the Forbidden Journey, Battle at the Ministry, or Escape from Gringotts ride, you must get your photo printed at those attractions. All other attraction pictures may be printed at any photo-service location. The chart on page 153 lists where you can always find MUP locations throughout Universal's parks.

RELIGIOUS SERVICES

THE CLOSEST CHURCHES TO UNIVERSAL ORLANDO are the nondenominational **God's House Orlando** (9501 Satellite Blvd., Ste 106; ☎ 407-851-6500; godshouseorlando.com) and the enormous **First Baptist Orlando** (3000 John Young Pkwy.; ☎ 407-425-2555; first orlando.com). The nearest Catholic Mass is held at **Holy Family Catholic Community** at 5125 S. Apopka-Vineland Road (☎ 407-876-2211; holy familyorlando.org), and the nearest synagogue is **Southwest Orlando Jewish Congregation** at 11200 S. Apopka-Vineland Road (☎ 407-239-5444; sojc.org).

For a list of religious services in the area, check allears.net/btp/church .htm and wdwinfo.com/tips_for_touring/churchservices.htm. Christian visitors may also be interested in the **Rock the Universe** religious-music weekend, held in late January (see page 226).

SMOKING

SMOKING OR VAPING TOBACCO is prohibited at the Universal Orlando Resort outside of a few designated areas. There is only one location where smoking or vaping is permitted inside each park: in USF's Central Park behind the Back to the Future train, on the lower lagoon landing in IOA's Port of Entry, and next to the Wave Village East lockers at Volcano Bay. Smoking sections are also found outside each park exit, at each resort hotel, and in CityWalk near Hard Rock Cafe, Red Coconut Club, and the Cineplex. Marijuana in any form is also prohibited on Universal property.

UNIVERSAL VACATION SERVICES

THROUGHOUT THE PARKS, you'll spot stands marked VACATION SER-VICES, staffed by chatty team members who will ask you where you're from as you pass. Most guests hurry by, assuming—correctly—that these outposts serve as sales pitches for time-shares. But Universal's Vacation Services actually serves other useful functions. In addition to selling Universal Orlando gift cards and Universal Express Passes, they can help you book dining reservations and answer other general questions handled by Guest Services, so if you need assistance, stop by one of these locations before you trek back to the front of the park. However, the satellite Vacation Services booths can't issue disability assistance passes (see page 164), so you must retrieve those at the parks' main guest service locations.

WINE, BEER, AND LIQUOR

ALCOHOL IS WIDELY AVAILABLE by the pint, glass, or shot through-out Universal's parks, hotels, and CityWalk. You can also buy wine by the bottle in the resort's table-service restaurants and some hotel shops. Note that while you can walk freely with a drink within the parks or

CityWalk, due to liquor-license laws, you may not pass from CityWalk into a park or hotel (or vice versa) with an open container in hand.

Wine and beer are also sold off property in grocery stores, convenience stores, and liquor stores. The best range of adult beverages is sold by **Grand Liquors** at 5601 International Drive (☎ 407-751-4517). The **Walgreens** across Kirkman Road from Universal also has a decent, if slightly expensive, liquor selection.

The minimum age to drink or buy booze in Florida is 21, and anyone who looks 30 or younger should plan to present government-issued photo ID (valid driver's license or passport) when purchasing. At CityWalk you'll be tagged with a paper bracelet while drinking to take home as a hair-snagging reminder of your debauched revels.

UNIVERSAL ORLANDO *for* GUESTS *with* SPECIAL NEEDS

UNIVERSAL ORLANDO STRIVES to accommodate every visitor in accordance with the Americans with Disabilities Act (ADA). The resort offers a free **"Rider's Guide for Rider Safety & Guests with Disabilities,"** describing each attraction's restrictions and requirements in detail at theugseries.com/uniada. You can download the booklet for each of the three parks in PDF format before your visit (which we highly recommend) or get printed copies at Guest Services, at resort front desks, or at wheelchair-rental locations inside the parks. The limitations you'll face at Universal Orlando, and the accommodations you can take advantage of, will vary according to the nature of your special needs.

MOBILITY RESTRICTIONS

UNIVERSAL ORLANDO IS FAIRLY FRIENDLY for nonambulatory guests to navigate, and the resort has repaved some bumpy streets (such as the uneven paving stones in USF's San Francisco and New York districts) to be more comfortable for wheelchair users.

Universal provides close(r)-in parking for disabled visitors; ask for directions when you pay your parking fee. These spots are on the main level of each parking garage, nearest to the central hub. You'll still have a substantial trip to CityWalk and the parks from even the best handicapped parking spot.

The entire Universal Orlando Resort transportation system is also disabled-accessible. Water taxis have roll-on ramps for easy boarding, and bus routes are served by vehicles with wheelchair lifts that can accommodate all but the largest motorized scooters.

Shopping, dining, and restroom facilities at the parks, CityWalk, and hotels are generally ADA compliant for wheelchair access. Some fast-food queues and shop aisles (especially in The Wizarding World of Harry Potter) are too narrow for wheelchairs; at these locations, ask a team member for assistance. All shows and performances (including parades) also have designated disability sections for guests in wheelchairs and their parties.

In addition, attraction queues in the theme parks (with the exception of **Pteranodon Flyers** in IOA) are fully wheelchair accessible, so you can enjoy the full preshow experience. Alternative routes are provided wherever necessary—these include elevators to bypass stairs at **Harry Potter and the Escape from Gringotts, Revenge of the Mummy,** and **Men in Black Alien Attack,** along with accessible boarding areas such as the stationary loading stations at **Harry Potter and the Forbidden Journey** and **Mine-Cart Madness.** You can take advantage of the accessible elevators even if you aren't in a wheelchair. Be sure to read the specific instructions posted outside each attraction, and bring your needs to the attention of the first attendant you see.

At **Volcano Bay,** only the **Krakatau Aqua Coaster** and **Maku Puihi Round Raft Rides** have elevators; for the other slides, you must be able to climb stairs to the top.

Strollers are not normally permitted inside most attractions, so if your child's stroller doubles as their wheelchair, swing by Guest Services for a special pass that will allow you to roll it through queues.

Except for the Hogwarts Express trains, Universal ride vehicles are unable to accommodate electric convenience vehicles (ECVs) or motorized wheelchairs, although a handful of rides have special cars that can carry a manual wheelchair. At these rides, guests can transfer from their powered chair to a nonmotorized one that will be provided at each applicable attraction. Be aware that nearly all Universal attractions (including some indoor theater shows) require you to transfer from your ECV to a manual wheelchair before you enter the queue, since it's almost impossible to navigate switchbacks in a motorized scooter.

Even if an attraction doesn't accommodate wheelchairs of any kind, nonambulatory guests may ride if they can transfer from their wheelchair to the ride's vehicle. Be aware, though, that Universal staff are neither trained nor permitted to assist with transfers—guests must be able to board the ride unassisted or have a member of their party help them. Either way, members of the nonambulatory guest's party will be permitted to ride with them.

Regarding Universal's accessibility for the mobility impaired, a reader from upstate New York wrote:

> My husband used a scooter throughout our trip because, though he can walk short distances, he has leg weakness and balance problems. Whenever we approached a ride or attraction at Universal, the employees were always very attentive and willing to help. When he was using the scooter, they guided him to accessible areas, and when he chose to walk into attractions (with an obvious gait issue), they always very politely showed him the easiest route (avoiding stairs or steep ramps, opening the unused roped-off queuing areas to avoid having to walk around them) or offered wheelchair transport.

And a woman from Regina, Saskatchewan, added:

We found that Universal Studios had better disability access to the rides for wheelchair users. They had escorts to show you the way to the back doors of the rides and elevators. Disney World only pointed the way and then you had to push up steep ramps to get to the ride.

Nonetheless, navigating Universal Orlando can be daunting for solo travelers in manual wheelchairs, as this Morristown, New Jersey, visitor shared:

None of the three parks are wheelchair friendly, with a lot of long uphill areas to battle, and the terrain is not smooth. As well, many of the lines to attractions have long inclines to deal with. When asked, most staff members will decline helping, as they are instructed not to. I found myself asking others in line for help more than I liked. I don't believe Universal considers how physically demanding navigating these parks can be for someone in a wheelchair. Not all of us come with someone to push!

Wheelchair and ECV Rentals

Any guest may rent a wheelchair, with no proof of medical need required. Most rides, shows, attractions, restrooms, and restaurants accommodate the nonambulatory disabled. If you're in a park and you need assistance, go to Guest Services. *Note:* Because almost all attraction queues are wheelchair accessible, using a wheelchair doesn't automatically entitle you to skip the standby line or shorten your wait.

Wheelchairs rent for $15 per day (tax included) with a fully refundable $50 deposit (cash or credit card) required. Standard wheelchairs are available at the central parking hub before you reach CityWalk (or just outside CityWalk's cinema) and inside each park near the front gates.

A limited number of ECVs are available for rent to guests 18 and older on a first-come, first-served basis at EU, USF, and IOA (not Volcano Bay). Easy to drive, they give nonambulatory guests tremendous freedom and mobility. ECVs cost $75 per day (tax inclusive), with no deposit required. An upgraded model with a sunshade is $95. ECVs are popular and tend to sell out by midmorning on peak days, so arrive early or reserve one elsewhere (see below). ECVs are available only inside the parks; you may rent a standard wheelchair at the parking hub and upgrade to an ECV once you reach the park.

A reader from Newbury, Ohio, found the entire ECV rental process to be user-*un*friendly:

You have to fill out paperwork to rent a wheelchair to get to the ECV rental area, where you have to fill out more paperwork to get the ECV, after traversing a long distance through the entrance terminal, over a long bridge, and through CityWalk. You can't use the ECVs in lines for the attractions, which doesn't matter, I guess, because most attractions are too turbulent for handicapped, older, or larger guests!

If you need an ECV to travel around the resort hotels or CityWalk, consider renting one from a third-party company such as **Buena Vista**

Rentals (buenavistascooters.com), **Best Price Mobility** (bpmobility
.com), **Scooter Bug** (scooterbug.com/orlando), or **Apple Scooter**
(applescooter.com). All four are "preferred vendors" authorized to
deliver a scooter and all necessary accessories to your Universal on-
site resort hotel. Third-party ECV rentals run about $30–$55 per
day (depending on features, weight capacity, and length of rental)—a
worthwhile investment for this reader from Middletown, Delaware:

> We rented an ECV for my mother-in-law and doubled the time
> we spent in the parks, and she enjoyed the day with dignity. The
> rental is worth it for the long haul from the parking lot to Diagon
> Alley alone. The staff on Hogwarts Express are phenomenal with
> getting the ECV to the queue and helping with embarking and dis-
> embarking the train.

Finally, those who normally rent ECVs may want to forgo them
in favor of manual wheelchairs during evening special events, when
the streets are especially dark and densely crowded, as this Illinois
reader notes:

> Taking an ECV during Halloween Horror Nights became more of
> a hassle than a help. You can't take the ECV inside the haunted
> houses—you have to park it at the entrance, sometimes far away
> from the entrance of the house you just came out of, and then you
> have to backtrack to get your ECV and then go back to where you
> exited. It was a pain in the posterior.

MISSING AND PROSTHETIC LIMBS

ALL GUESTS MUST BE ABLE to hold themselves upright and continuously grasp a safety restraint with at least one extremity to experience
most rides. Guests with prosthetic limbs may ride with them securely
attached on most rides. Those with prosthetic arms or hands may need
to demonstrate that they can grip the safety restraints. All prosthetic limbs
need to removed before riding **Jurassic World VelociCoaster** (both natural
legs must at least terminate below the knee), **Pteranodon Flyers** (both
natural legs must extend to the edge of your seat or terminate below the
knee), or **Hollywood Rip Ride Rockit** (must have one full natural leg and
one natural leg that extends to the edge of the seat or terminates below
the knee). Consult the "Rider's Guide" (see page 156) for details.

CASTS AND BOOTS

IF YOUR ARM OR LEG is in a plaster cast or walking boot because
of a broken bone, you should still be able to board the rides, provided
you can fit comfortably inside the safety restraints. The only exception
is **The Incredible Hulk Coaster,** as one young boy from Baltimore, Maryland, was distraught to discover:

> Our first ride was The Incredible Hulk Coaster. [All my] kids, except
> my son, came back ecstatic. He was in tears; he had a hard cast
> on his arm, and he wasn't allowed on the ride. We were crushed.
> Thankfully, [Hulk] was the only ride that didn't allow it.

FAMILY RESTROOMS

IF A MEMBER OF YOUR PARTY needs help using the restroom, check the digital park map for designated family or companion facilities, which are large enough for two adults to access. Family restrooms in **USF** are near the front of the park near the Studio Audience Center, in Springfield outside Fast Food Boulevard, in San Francisco across from Richter's Burger Co., at First Aid behind Louie's Italian Restaurant in New York, and outside Mel's Drive-In across from the Transformers gift shop. In **IOA,** the family restrooms are found at Guest Services near the entrance and at First Aid in Lost Continent. In **Epic Universe,** family restrooms can be found at most bathroom locations throughout each land, as well as at the First Aid stations to the right of the front entrance, outside the Helios Grand Hotel near the Wizarding World, and inside the child swap rooms of every participating ride. In **Volcano Bay,** family restrooms are at First Aid, under the Ohyah and Ohno slides, and near the entrance to Honu ika Moana.

SERVICE ANIMALS

SERVICE ANIMALS ARE WELCOME at Universal Orlando, and the Signature Collection Loews hotels accommodate nonservice pets as well. Working companion animals are allowed inside all Universal restaurants, retail locations, attraction queues, and most other locations throughout the resort. Specific guidelines for each attraction are posted at the queue entrance and listed in the "Rider's Guide." For attractions where service animals cannot safely enter, portable kennels are provided.

When nature calls, service-animal relief areas are marked on the app's digital park map; tap the magnifying glass icon on the top right corner and type "relief" to search for them. There are three designated animal-walking areas in **USF** (behind the NBC Media Center in Hollywood, in New York near the firehouse, and outside the Coke kiosk between Men in Black Alien Attack and The Simpsons Ride); three in **IOA** (Marvel Super Hero Island near Storm Force Accelatron, Lost Continent behind the Mystic Fountain, and Seuss Landing behind One Fish, Two Fish, Red Fish, Blue Fish); one in the north parking garage; and two in **CityWalk** (near the IOA lighthouse and outside the former Blue Man Group theater). **Volcano Bay**'s service-animal relief areas are near Honu ika Moana and next to Maku Puihi.

DIETARY RESTRICTIONS

UNIVERSAL ORLANDO RESTAURANTS work very hard to accommodate guests' special dietary needs. If properly informed, Universal's chefs can prepare food that is vegetarian or vegan; kosher or halal; or dairy-free, gluten-free, or nut-free. When you make a dining reservation, either online at theugseries.com/unidinres or by phone (☎ 407-224-FOOD [3663] for restaurants in the parks and CityWalk, or ☎ 407-503-DINE [3463] for hotel dining), you'll be asked about food allergies and the like. The host or hostess and your server will also ask about this and send the chef out to discuss the menu; if you're not asked, just talk to your server when you're seated.

Kosher and Halal table-service meals ($91 plus tip) must be ordered by emailing food.allergy@universalorlando.com at least 4–5 days in advance, and they can be delivered to any table-service restaurant where you have a reservation. Religious accommodation meals are made fresh to order and include an entrée paired with salad and dessert, such as beef kefta with spinach salad and strawberry cake, or chicken picatta with Caesar salad and chocolate mousse. The closest off-property Glatt Kosher restaurant to Universal Orlando is Kosher Grill (5615 International Dr.; ☎ 407-392-2292; koshergrillorlando .com), which delivers Mediterranean and American dishes certified by the Orthodox Rabbinate of Central Florida; special Shabbat dinners must be ordered via phone by Thursday evening.

At counter-service restaurants, ask to see the menu book with ingredient and allergen info. For those avoiding animal products, plant-based proteins like Beyond Burgers and Gardein Chick'n are now featured on most menus. Even the Wizarding World, which was previously the one place that did not get high marks for dietary accommodation, now offers additional vegan options, including a plant-based vegetable curry, mushroom-jackfruit pie, vegan Butterbeer topping, and meatless shepherd's pasty. Vegans can also find an array of plant-based pastries at Voodoo Doughnut; see page 305 for a list of recommended plant-based snacks and entrées. In general, guests on restricted diets will find many more options at Universal's table-service eateries.

Vegans ordering fried foods will want to enquire about the oil being used. For example, the french fries served at Burger Digs in Islands of Adventure are cooked in their own vegetable oil, but the onion rings are made in the same deep fryer as the chicken.

Be aware also that Universal Orlando does not have separate kitchen facilities in which to prepare allergen-free foods, so there is always a slight possibility of inadvertent allergen contamination before or during preparation. You're welcome to bring your own food into the resort, as long as you let security know you have a dietary issue and follow the restrictions on items permitted inside the parks (no glass containers nor large or hard coolers).

For more information, email your specific dietary requests to food .allergy@universalorlando.com and visit theugseries.com/uoallergies.

HEARING IMPAIRMENT

GUEST SERVICES AT THE PARKS provides free assistive-technology devices with a refundable deposit (depending on the device) to hearing-impaired guests. Hearing-impaired guests can benefit from amplified audio on many attractions, and closed-captioning is available on request for queue video monitors; select shows offer reflective captioning as well. Guest Services can also provide a printed script to many of the attractions for you to peruse.

In addition, Universal provides complimentary sign language interpretations of live shows at the theme parks on select days. There are typically only two or three interpreted performances per day in each park, so check the show schedule in the Universal app as soon as you arrive and plan your visit accordingly; additional American Sign Language–interpreted performances can be arranged for free if you email signlanguageservices@universalorlando.com at least two weeks in advance. Even if you don't understand sign language, it's well worth seeing for how animated and expressive the interpreters are—they truly steal the show.

While we're on the subject of sound, Universal loves to assail its guests with multiple overlapping background tracks, all cranked up to 11 for maximum impact. Even if you didn't have a hearing problem before arriving at Universal Orlando, the overwhelming amplification employed by many of the resort's attractions may leave your eardrums ringing. A reader from Bellingham, Washington, writes:

> You mention in the book that Universal is loud. I didn't really notice this the last time I was there, likely because I was alone. But my gosh, trying to yell over the noise and music to my hearing-impaired mom—even with her hearing aids—was so frustrating.

VISION IMPAIRMENT

PARK INFORMATION GUIDES, restaurant menus, and attraction scripts are available at Guest Services in large print and embossed Braille. Some rides can accommodate guests with white canes (a collapsible cane is recommended), while at others an attendant will hold the cane and return it to the guest immediately at the unload area.

Visitors with 20/20 vision may still feel impaired when entering many of Universal's murky, under-illuminated attraction queues. Be especially careful when transitioning from bright sunshine into the dimly lit lines leading to the Mummy, King Kong, and Wizarding World rides, as this unfortunate reader from Southington, Connecticut, warns:

> I took a painful shot "down below" in Forbidden Journey from a divider I didn't see. My wife had to hold my shoulder or belt because she couldn't see at all in many queues.

LARGER GUESTS

THRILL-SEEKING GUESTS OF SIZE may discover that several of Universal's rides are unable to accommodate them. The Harry Potter headliners are the most notorious for excluding plus-size riders, although both have certain seats—the outside seats on Harry Potter and the Forbidden Journey, along with rows three and six on Harry Potter and the Escape from Gringotts—that fit a fairly wide variety of body shapes. Likewise, the Hulk coaster at IOA has designated seats with double seat belts designed for bigger guests, and the back rows at Revenge of the Mummy offer extra legroom.

In all cases, these safety restrictions are based less on weight than torso circumference; some guests with large chests (40 inches or more) who would not otherwise be considered overweight may find the restraint harnesses challenging to lock properly. Before getting in line for any attraction, check out the sample ride vehicle at the entrance, and discuss your concerns with the attraction's greeter. Many test seats are discreetly tucked behind walls of greenery, so ask if you don't immediately spot it. A reader from Oakbrook, Illinois, pleaded with us to impress this point:

> *Let people know that they may not fit on Universal rides because the seating on several of their rides is not conducive to everyone. Even if you are not that big, you may not be able to ride because of your body shape, especially the rides that have over the head harnesses. I was very surprised (and majorly disappointed) that I could not go on either Harry Potter ride because my body shape (which is not out of the ordinary and pretty normal) did not make the "clicks."*

POTENTIALLY PROBLEMATIC RIDES FOR LARGER GUESTS

UNIVERSAL STUDIOS FLORIDA

Despicable Me Minion Mayhem (lap bar; request back row or stationary)	E.T. Adventure (lap bar; request bench seat)
Harry Potter and the Escape from Gringotts (lap bar; request row 3 or 6)	Hollywood Rip Ride Rockit (lap bar; request row 1 or 4)
Race Through New York Starring Jimmy Fallon (seatbelt; request extender)	Revenge of the Mummy (lap bar; request back row)
The Simpsons Ride (lap bar)	Transformers: The Ride-3D (lap bar)
Trolls Trollercoaster (lap bar; request solo seat)	

ISLANDS OF ADVENTURE

The Amazing Adventures of Spider-Man (lap bar)	Caro-seuss-el (seatbelt; request bench seat)
The Cat in the Hat (lap bar; request solo seat)	Doctor Doom's Fearfall (chest restraint)
Dudley Do-Right's Ripsaw Falls (lap bar; request ADA seat)	Flight of the Hippogriff (lap bar; request solo seat)
Hagrid's Magical Creatures Motorbike Adventure (lap bar; request motorbike)	Harry Potter and the Forbidden Journey (chest restraint; request end seat)
The High in the Sky Seuss Trolley Train Ride! (lap bar; request solo seat)	The Incredible Hulk Coaster (chest restraint; request two-buckle seat in row 1, 4, 5, or 8)
Jurassic Park River Adventure (lap bar)	Jurassic World VelociCoaster (lap bar)
One Fish, Two Fish, Red Fish, Blue Fish (seatbelt; request solo seat)	Popeye and Bluto's Bilge-Rat Barges (seatbelt; request extender)
Pteranodon Flyers (seatbelt)	

EPIC UNIVERSE

Constellation Carousel (seatbelt; request bench seat)	Curse of the Werewolf (lap bar)
Dragon Racer's Rally (chest restraints)	Harry Potter and the Battle at the Ministry (lap bar)
Hiccup's Wing Gliders (lap bar)	Mario Kart: Bowser's Challenge (lap bar)
Mine-Cart Madness (lap bar)	Monsters Unchained: The Frankenstein Experiment (chest restraint)
Stardust Racers (lap bar)	Yoshi's Adventure (lap bar)

At Volcano Bay, most body slides and raft rides have weight limits posted on each attraction's information sign. Every queue has a scale built into the ground (either at the base of the steps for body slides or at the top for raft slides) that is discreetly checked by an attendant to ensure compliance. Guests weighing more than 300 pounds will find themselves excluded from several slides. Some rafts have an overall weight limit, so even parties of four or more average-size adults may struggle to squeeze everyone into some multirider rafts.

OXYGEN TANKS AND CONCENTRATORS

FOR SAFETY REASONS, oxygen tanks are prohibited on most moving attractions at Universal Orlando, except for **Hogwarts Express, Villain-Con Minion Blast,** and **Despicable Me Minion Mayhem** (stationary seating only). Oxygen tanks are also permitted inside all shows and playgrounds, and portable oxygen concentrators are allowed on most rides as long as they don't interfere with the safety restraints.

NONAPPARENT DISABILITIES

WE RECEIVE MANY LETTERS from readers whose traveling companion or child requires special assistance but who, unlike a person in a wheelchair, is not visibly disabled. Autism, for example, makes it very difficult or impossible for someone with the disorder to wait in line for more than a few minutes or in queues surrounded by a crowd. Guests with extreme sensitivity to sound, light, or touch, or those unable to stand still for a significant length of time, may struggle with many of the standard theme park experiences.

A trip to Universal Orlando can be nonetheless positive and rewarding for guests with autism and similar conditions. And while any theme park vacation requires planning, a little extra effort to accommodate persons with special needs will pay large dividends.

Our first suggestion is to visit Universal's cognitive disabilities page at theugseries.com/UOCognitive and download a PDF of its comprehensive planning guide. It gives detailed sensory and safety information on every attraction, as well as tips about quieter places in the parks.

Next, you'll want to familiarize yourself with the following programs Universal offers to make your visit go more smoothly. Many variations on the AAP and GAP services described below are available, depending on the guest's needs, and they are not detailed anywhere online. There is currently no app-based version of Universal's accommodation services like Disney's DAS, and the registered guest with special needs must be present every time an alternative entry is requested or redeemed.

Universal has partnered with **International Board of Credentialing and Continuing Education Standards (IBCCES)** on an online Accessibility Card registration process, which guests requesting accommodations (or their guardian) should complete at least 48 hours prior to visiting the park. Go to **accessibilitycard.com** and fill out the registration form, which requires providing the contact information for a healthcare or education professional who will verify your needs and uploading supporting documentation such as a doctor's statement or Individualized Education Plan. Once your application is approved, you can download your digital IBCCES Accessibility Card (IAC), and a Universal employee will contact you regarding your needs. They'll give you a case number that you can take to Guest Services upon arrival and pick up your accommodation pass; if you don't receive your call, dial ☎ 407-224-4233 and press 5, then 4, but be prepared for a long wait on hold. The registration with IBCCES is valid for a full year and is also accepted by other area attractions like SeaWorld and Legoland.

Universal's Attractions Assistance Pass (AAP)

This pass is designed to accommodate guests who can't wait in regular standby lines. You must first register with IBCCES and have your interview before you can obtain an AAP at Guest Services of the first park you visit. Because all Volcano Bay guests are eligible to use the Virtual Line system, no AAPs are available at the water park. AAPs are good for parties of up to six people, but all members of your party who will use the service must have their admission tickets scanned at Guest Services. The same card is valid in the theme parks for the length of your vacation, or up to 14 days for annual passholders; hold onto your AAP for faster renewals.

AAPs can be used at any attraction, even if it doesn't have a Universal Express entrance. Present the card to a team member at the attraction you want to ride. If the ride's standby wait time is less than 30 minutes, you'll usually be immediately allowed into the Universal Express entrance. If the standby time is longer than 30 minutes, the team member will enter on the AAP the attraction name, time of day, wait time, and a return time for you to come back to ride. The return time will be based on the current wait time, so if you get to The Amazing Adventures of Spider-Man at 12:20 p.m. and the standby time is 40 minutes, your return time will be 40 minutes later, at 1 p.m.

You may return at the specified time or at any time thereafter, but you can't get another AAP return time until you've used or forfeited the first. When you return, you'll be given access to the Universal Express line, where you should face a wait of 15–20 minutes or less.

A Gold version of the AAP is also available that allows users to be escorted directly to the boarding area when their return time arrives, instead of waiting in the Express line; ask guest services about it if you are unable to tolerate the abbreviated queue.

Universal's Guest Assistance Pass (GAP) Entry Cards

If the AAP doesn't meet your family's needs, Universal makes a small number of these cards available on a strictly limited basis. Basically, a GAP Entry Card is identical to a One-Day, Two-Park Universal Express Unlimited Pass and provides immediate entry to any attraction's Universal Express queue, regardless of the standby wait. Like the Universal Express Pass, GAP Entry is valid only at attractions that offer Universal Express, which excludes Pteranodon Flyers and Hagrid's Magical Creatures Motorbike Adventure, so you'll still want an AAP for those attractions.

If you want a GAP because long standby lines make the AAP unworkable for your party, be prepared to endure some additional scrutiny on top of the usual IBCCES registration. If you get turned down, you can always purchase a regular Universal Express Pass (where available).

Finally, while visiting Universal Studios Florida, you may want to take advantage of the designated "quiet room" located behind the Studio Audience Center at the front of the park. This specially designed space, which features soothing decor and tactile toys, is available for 30-minute breaks on a first-come, first-served basis.

FRIENDS OF BILL W.

FOR INFORMATION ON THE NEAREST **Alcoholics Anonymous** meetings to Universal Orlando (held daily), visit cflintergroup.org or call ☎ 407-260-5408 for additional information. For information on **Al-Anon/Alateen** meetings in the area, visit al-anonorlando.org or call ☎ 407-896-4929.

INTERNATIONAL VISITORS

UNIVERSAL ORLANDO PROVIDES digital park maps in Spanish and Portuguese as PDF files (scan the QR codes posted near the park entrance to download them), and maintains special websites designed for visitors from Brazil, Latin America, and the United Kingdom. Click the language box at the top-right of the universalorlando.com menu bar to see the international options.

PART 5

UNIVERSAL ORLANDO *with* KIDS

IT'S *a* SMALL UNIVERSE, AFTER ALL

UNIVERSAL ORLANDO RESORT has positioned itself as an edgier, more adult alternative to the Mouse. Even Disney diehards will admit that UOR sports more attractions aimed at older teens and young adults than Walt Disney World currently does. But the commonly heard rejoinder is that there's "nothing" for little kids to do at Universal's parks.

That stereotype has seeds of truth. While the Magic Kingdom can claim more than a dozen rides with no height restrictions, Universal Studios Florida and Islands of Adventure combined have only five rides that accommodate kids less than 34 inches tall, and Epic Universe only offers two rides with no minimum height requirement. Plus, as popular as Universal characters like the Minions and SpongeBob are with the single-digit set, it's tough to compete with the multibillion-dollar marketing machine behind Mickey's menagerie. But numbers alone don't tell the tale because a vacation at UOR can actually be a better experience for the youngest visitors (and therefore the family members around them) than the equivalent WDW escape.

For starters, while Universal lacks many moving attractions for tots, it makes up for it with the best themed playgrounds in town, as this family from Lancaster, Pennsylvania, learned:

> We were concerned about the big rides at Universal leaving our youngest child (age 5) bored. In actuality, she had a blast at [DreamWorks Land], Seuss Landing, and Camp Jurassic. Even the older kids joined her to play at these areas whenever we got back together.

Second, without theme park reservations and Advanced Dining Reservations to worry about, a stay at UOR requires much less pre-planning, which means less damage to your day when the inevitable toddler tantrum derails your carefully laid touring plans. Universal's parks are more compact than Magic Kingdom and EPCOT, which means that little legs won't tire as quickly. Also, on any given day, the crowds are likely to be lighter at UOR, welcome news for anyone shoving a stroller through the streets. Finally, it's far easier to travel from Universal's on-site hotels to its parks and back, a key benefit when heading back to your room for that essential midday nap.

Ideally, your kids should be at least 42 inches tall to experience the bulk of the parks' dark rides and simulators, or 54 inches tall to brave the biggest roller coasters. But traveling to UOR with a toddler, or even infant, can be equally rewarding, as long as you know what you're getting into and prepare thoroughly. The biggest danger is in dealing with a child who's barely under the minimum for something they'll "just die" without riding, so read up on height requirements (see pages 185–187) in advance to avoid disappointment on the day. Some attractions offer special certificates to kids who are just under the minimum height, promising an expedited ride once they're tall enough.

When you're planning a UOR vacation with young children, consider the following:

AGE Though UOR's color and festivity excite all children (with specific attractions that delight toddlers and preschoolers), and there's no admission fee for those under 3 years old, Universal's entertainment is generally oriented to older children and adults. Children should be a fairly mature 8 years old to appreciate USF and Epic Universe, and a bit older to tackle the thrill rides in IOA, as this reader recommended:

> Wait to visit until your children are tall enough, brave enough, and/ or interested enough to ride at least most of the rides. USF and IOA have a much different vibe from the Disney parks. If your children can't or won't ride most of the rides, it will just be a waste of money.

Tweens 8–12 years old are perhaps the ideal age for family compatibility and togetherness at Universal Orlando. This "tweenage" group is old enough, tall enough, and sufficiently stalwart to experience, understand, and appreciate practically all Universal attractions. Moreover, they are developed to the extent that they can get around the parks on their own steam without being carried or collapsing. Best of all, they are still young enough to enjoy being with Mom and Dad. From our experience, ages 10–12 are better than 8–9, though what you gain in maturity is at the cost of that irrepressible, wide-eyed wonder so prevalent in the 8- and 9-year-olds. Note that Universal considers all kids ages 3–9 as children for pricing purposes, regardless of height or ability to experience rides.

WHEN TO VISIT Avoid the hot, crowded summer months, especially if you have preschoolers. Go in October, November (except Thanksgiving), early December, January, February, or May. If you have children of varied ages and they're good students, take the older ones out of school and visit during the cooler and less congested off-season.

Take advantage of the resort's free Wi-Fi to virtually homeschool from your hotel, and arrange special assignments relating to the educational aspects of Universal Orlando. If your children can't afford to miss school, take your vacation as soon as the school year ends. Alternatively, try late August before school starts. Please understand that you don't have to visit during one of the more ideal times of year to have a great vacation.

A Peterborough, England, woman agrees:

unofficial **TIP**
Coupled with a sense of humor and a little preparedness on your part, our touring plans and tips for families ensure a super experience at any time of year.

> *We visited at the end of August, and we expected that the crowds would be almost unbearable. However, we were surprised to find that because most local schools were back in session, we could walk on most headliner rides up until late afternoon, and even then there was only a short wait— some rides at Universal Studios didn't even open until 11 a.m. because we were visiting on a low-attendance day! We'd recommend that more people go this time of year, especially those people whose children don't return to school until later.*

BUILD NAPS AND REST INTO YOUR ITINERARY The parks are huge; don't try to see everything in one day. Tour in the early morning and return to your hotel around 11:30 a.m. for lunch, a swim, and a nap. Even during off-season, when crowds are smaller and the temperature is more pleasant, the size of the parks will exhaust most children younger than age 8 by lunchtime. Return to the park in the late afternoon or early evening and continue touring. A family from Texas underlines the importance of naps and rest:

> *Probably the most important tip your guide gave us was going to the hotel to swim and regroup during the day. The parks became unbearable by noon—and so did my husband and boys. The hotel was an oasis that calmed our nerves! After about 3 hours of playtime, we headed out to [the other park] for dinner and a cool evening of fun.*

Regarding naps, this mom doesn't mince words:

> *For parents of small kids: Take the book's advice, get out of the park, and take the nap, take the nap, TAKE THE NAP! Never in my life have I seen so many parents screaming at, ridiculing, or slapping their kids. (What a vacation!) [The parks can be] overwhelming for kids and adults.*

If you plan to return to your hotel at midday and want your room made up, let housekeeping know.

WHERE TO STAY The time and hassle involved in commuting to and from the theme parks will be less if your hotel is on Universal property. It's hard to overemphasize how convenient it is to commute between your room and the parks when staying at the top Loews resorts, and even the value-priced Cabana Bay is just a 15-minute stroller push away from IOA's front gates. A number of off-site hotels along Major Boulevard and International Drive (see pages 110–118) are also within walking distance, but you may not feel comfortable crossing busy roads with small kids in tow.

BE IN TOUCH WITH YOUR FEELINGS   When you or your kids get tired and irritable, call a time-out. Trust your instincts. What would feel best? Another ride, an ice cream break, or going back to the room for a nap?

LEAST COMMON DENOMINATORS   Someone is going to run out of steam first, and when they do, the whole family will be affected. Sometimes a snack break will revive the flagging member. Other times, however, it's better to return to your hotel. Pushing the tired or discontented beyond their capacity will spoil the day for them—and you. Energy levels vary. Be prepared to respond to members of your group who poop out. *Hint:* "We've driven a thousand miles to take you to Harry Potter and now you're ruining everything!" is not an appropriate response.

BUILDING ENDURANCE   Though most children are active, their normal play activities usually don't condition them for the exertion required to tour an Orlando park. Start family walks four to six weeks before your trip to get in shape. A mother from Wescosville, Pennsylvania, reports:

> *We had our 6-year-old begin walking with us a bit every day one month before leaving—when we arrived [in Orlando], her little legs could carry her, and she had a lot of stamina.*

From a Middletown, Delaware, mom:

> *You recommended walking for six weeks prior to the trip, but we began months in advance. My husband lost 10 pounds, and we met a lot of neighbors! We wouldn't have made it without you—thanks!*

SETTING LIMITS AND MAKING PLANS   To avoid arguments and disappointment, establish guidelines for each day and get everybody committed. Include the following:

1. Wake-up time and breakfast plans
2. When to depart for the park
3. What to take with you
4. A policy for splitting the group or for staying together
5. What to do if the group gets separated or someone is lost
6. What you want to see, including plans in the event an attraction is closed or too crowded
7. A policy on what you can afford for snacks
8. How long you plan to tour in the morning and what time you'll return to your hotel to rest
9. When you'll return to the park and how late you'll stay
10. Dinner plans
11. A policy for buying souvenirs, including who pays: the parents or the kids
12. Bedtimes

BE FLEXIBLE   Any day at Universal Orlando includes surprises; be prepared to adjust your plan. Listen to your intuition, and take advantage of the Lines app's optimization tool to update your itinerary after any unexpected detours.

ABOUT *the* UNOFFICIAL GUIDE TOURING PLANS

PARENTS WHO USE OUR TOURING PLANS are often frustrated by interruptions and delays caused by their young children. Here's what to expect:

1. CHARACTER ENCOUNTERS CAN WREAK HAVOC WITH THE TOURING PLANS.   Many children will stop in their tracks whenever they see a cartoon character like Shrek or Scooby-Doo. Attempting to haul your child away before they have satisfied their curiosity is likely to cause anything from whining to a full-scale revolt. Either go with the flow or specify a morning or afternoon for photos. Luckily, queues for characters at Universal aren't nearly as long as at Disney World.

2. OUR TOURING PLANS CALL FOR VISITING ATTRACTIONS IN A SEQUENCE, OFTEN SKIPPING ATTRACTIONS ALONG THE WAY.   Children don't like to skip anything! If something catches their eye, they want to see it right then. Some kids can be persuaded to skip attractions if parents explain their plans in advance. Other kids flip out at skipping something, particularly in Seuss Landing and The Wizarding Worlds.

3. IF YOU'RE USING A STROLLER, YOU WON'T BE ABLE TO TAKE IT INTO ATTRACTIONS OR ONTO RIDES.   You'll need to leave your stroller (personal or rented) outside each attraction, unless you have a special pass indicating a medical need (see page 157). An exception is the Hogwarts Express train, which provides transportation between the parks and accommodates personal strollers; rentals will be swapped for free at the stations. Well-marked stroller parking is available throughout the parks.

4. YOU PROBABLY WON'T FINISH THE TOURING PLAN.   Varying hours of operation, crowds, your group's size, your children's ages, and your stamina will all affect how much of the plan you'll complete. Tailor your expectations to this reality, or you'll be frustrated.

While our touring plans allow you to make the most of your time at the parks, it's impossible to define what *most* will be. It differs from family to family. If you have two young children, you probably won't see as much as two adults will. If you have four children, you probably won't see as much as a couple with only two children.

STUFF *to* THINK ABOUT

BLISTERS AND SORE FEET   In addition to wearing comfortable shoes, bring along some blister bandages if you or your children are susceptible to blisters. These bandages (which are also available at First Aid, if you didn't heed our warnings) offer excellent protection, stick well, and won't sweat off. Remember, a preschooler may not say anything about a blister until it's already formed, so keep an eye on things during the day. For an expanded discussion, see pages 144–145.

OVERHEATING, SUNBURN, AND DEHYDRATION These are the most common problems of younger children at Universal. Use sunscreen. Apply it on children in strollers, even if the stroller has a canopy. To avoid overheating, stop for rest regularly in the shade, in a restaurant, or at a show with air-conditioning.

unofficial **TIP**
Keep little ones well covered in sunscreen and hydrated with fluids. Don't count on hydrating young children with soft drinks and stops at water fountains. Carry refillable bottles of water. Bottles with screw caps are sold across the resort for about $4–$6. *Remember:* Excited kids may not tell you when they're thirsty or hot.

FIRST AID If you or your children have a medical problem, go to a First Aid Station (see page 148). They're friendlier than most doctor's offices and are accustomed to treating everything from paper cuts to allergic reactions. And if your kid just needs some rehydration and a short nap, they can provide a quiet cot.

CHILDREN ON MEDICATION Some parents of hyperactive children on medication discontinue or decrease the child's dosage at the end of the school year. If you have such a child, be aware that Universal Orlando might overstimulate them. Consult your physician before altering your child's medication regimen.

HEARING PROTECTION Children (and adults) who are especially sensitive to loud sounds may be driven right up the wall by Universal's high-decibel attractions. Consider bringing disposable foam earplugs or noise-canceling headphones.

GLASSES AND SUNGLASSES If your kids (or you) wear them, attach a strap to the frames so the glasses will stay on during rides and can hang from the child's neck while indoors.

THINGS YOU FORGOT OR RAN OUT OF Raingear, diapers, baby formula, sunburn treatments, memory cards, and other sundries are sold at the parks and at CityWalk. If you don't see something you need, ask if it's in stock. Basic over-the-counter meds are often available free in small quantities at the First Aid Stations in the parks.

INFANTS AND TODDLERS AT THE THEME PARKS All Universal parks have centralized **Family Services** facilities for infant and toddler care adjacent to the First Aid Stations. Everything necessary for changing diapers, preparing formula, and warming bottles and food is available. Supplies are for sale, and rockers and special chairs for nursing mothers are provided. In **USF,** Family Services is in Hollywood, near Lost and Found, and on **Canal Street,** behind Louie's Italian Restaurant, on the border between New York and San Francisco. In **IOA,** Family Services is in **Port of Entry** near Guest Services and in **The Lost Continent** near The Mystic Fountain (look for the red cross behind the

STROLLERS **173**

kebab house). In **Epic Universe**, Family Services is to the right of the front entrance and in Celestial Park between the Wizarding World and Helios Grand Hotel. In **Volcano Bay**, Family Services is immediately on your left as you enter the park. Dads are welcome at the centers and can use most services. In addition, most men's restrooms in the resort have changing tables.

RUNNING OUT OF GAS Hikers preparing for a challenging ascent—such as the 5,000-foot climb from the Colorado River to the rim of the Grand Canyon—are often advised to mix an electrolyte-replacement powder in their water and eat an energy-boosting snack at least twice every hour. While there's not much ascending to do at Universal, battling the heat, humidity, and crowds contributes to pooping out, especially where kids are concerned. Limiting calorie consumption to mealtimes just won't get it, as an experienced and wise grandma points out:

> *Children who get cranky during a visit often do so from all that time and energy expended without food. Feed them! A snack at any price goes a long way to keeping the little ones happy and parents sane. Oh, and the security people are very nice about you taking snacks or drinks in, but DO NOT bring glass containers!*

STROLLERS

STROLLERS ARE AVAILABLE for rent inside Epic Universe, USF, and IOA (but not Volcano Bay), to the left of the parks' front gates as you enter. A double stroller rental costs $40 (tax included) per day, with no deposit required. If you leave the park and return, or switch parks during the day, you can get another stroller for free by showing your receipt.

Strollers are a must for infants and toddlers, but we've seen many sharp parents rent strollers for somewhat older children—the stroller spares parents from having to carry kids when they sag, and it provides a convenient place to tote water and snacks.

A family from Tulsa, Oklahoma, recommends renting a stroller:

> *We rented a [stroller] for baggage room or in case the older child got tired of walking.*

But a New Lenox, Illinois, family advocates not leaving anyone out:

> *If your kids are 8 or under, rent strollers for all of them! An 8-year-old will fit in a stroller, and you can*

fit up to four kids in two doubles. My husband suggested getting a stroller for our 6-year-old and the two "babies" (ages 4 and 3). The kids didn't get nearly as tired because they could be seated whenever they wanted.

However, a McKean, Pennsylvania, reader thinks the situation has gotten out of hand:

Please tell parents that their children don't have to be in strollers if a) they're old enough to vote, b) they've served in the armed services, and/or c) they have kids of their own. It's gotten really ridiculous— this last visit we saw more 10-plus-year-olds in strollers than sub-10-year-olds. Strollers add congestion, especially with parents using them to blast through crowds like child-first battering rams. I never knew walking was bad for you.

A Charleston, West Virginia, mom recommends a backup plan:

Strollers are not allowed in lines for rides, so if you have a small child (ours was 4) who needs to be held, you might end up holding him a long time. If I had it to do over, I'd bring along some kind of child carrier for when he was out of the stroller.

The regular rental strollers are too large for all infants and many toddlers, and they are made of hard plastic with no padding; a limited number of infant-size strollers are sometimes available. If you plan to rent a stroller for your infant or toddler, bring pillows, cushions, or rolled towels to buttress them in. Bringing your own stroller is permitted. Your stroller is unlikely to be stolen, but mark it with your name.

STROLLER-RENTAL OPTIONS   Several Orlando companies are able to undercut the parks' prices, provide more comfortable strollers, and deliver them to your hotel. Most of the larger companies offer the same stroller models (the Baby Jogger City Mini Single, for example), so the primary differences between the companies are price and service.

To rate stroller companies, we had *Unofficial Guide* researchers rent the same strollers from each company, use the strollers in the parks, and return them. Our evaluation covers the overall experience, from the ease with which the stroller was rented to the delivery of the stroller, its condition upon arrival, and the return process.

Kingdom Strollers (☎ 407-271-5301; kingdomstrollers.com) topped our list, getting top marks for website ease of use, stroller selection, condition, and overall service. The stroller was also much easier to use than Universal's standard model, had more storage, and had an easier-to-use braking system. A rental of one to three nights costs $60; four to seven nights is $80. That makes the break-even point for choosing Kingdom Strollers over Universal at two days. At Universal's on-site resorts, you'll want to confirm your stroller delivery with the bell services manager on arrival. Alternatively, you can arrange to pick up and return your stroller at Orlando International Airport in Terminal A, Level 1, at the Wrap 'N Fly service counter, near the USO lounge (daily, 5 a.m.–7 p.m.).

We also recommend **Orlando Stroller Rentals, LLC** (☎ 800-281-0884; orlandostrollerrentals.com), which charges $55–$65 for one to three nights and $75–$85 for four to seven nights, depending on the model. Their excellent website allows you to easily compare the features of different strollers. It also does not require you to be present to drop off and pick up your stroller (they deliver and pick up from the hotel luggage stand) and is more flexible about arranging a meeting time.

STROLLER WARS   Sometimes strollers disappear while you're enjoying a ride or show. Universal staff will often rearrange strollers parked outside an attraction. This may be done to tidy up or to clear a walkway. Don't assume your stroller is stolen because it isn't where you left it. It may be neatly arranged a few feet away—or perhaps more than a few feet away, as this Skokie, Illinois, dad reports:

> *The stroller reorganizations while you're on rides are a bit unnerving. More than once, our stroller was moved out of visible distance from the original spot. On one occasion, it was moved to a completely different stroller-parking area near another ride, and no sign or team member was around to advise where. We had to track down a team member, and she had to call in to find out where it had been moved. Be prepared for this.*

unofficial **TIP**
Don't try to lock your stroller to a fence, post, or anything else at Universal. You'll get in big trouble.

Sometimes, however, strollers are taken by mistake or ripped off by people not wanting to spend time replacing one that's missing. Don't be alarmed if yours disappears. You won't have to buy it, and you'll be issued a new one.

While replacing a stroller is no big deal, it's inconvenient. Through our own experiments and readers' suggestions, we've developed a technique for hanging on to a rented stroller: affix something personal (but expendable) to the handle. Evidently, most strollers are pirated by mistake (they all look alike) or because it's easier to swipe someone else's than to replace one that has disappeared. Because most stroller "theft" results from confusion or laziness, the average pram pincher will hesitate to haul off a stroller containing another person's property. We tried several items and concluded that a bright, inexpensive scarf or bandanna tied to the handle works well as identification. A sock partially stuffed with rags or paper works even better (the weirder and more personal the object, the greater the deterrent). A multigenerational family from Utah went a step further:

> *We decorated our stroller with electrical tape to make it stand out, and my son added a small cowbell to make it clang if moved.*

STROLLERS AS LETHAL WEAPONS   A middle-aged couple from Brunswick, Maine, lobbies for a temporary stroller ban:

> *As an over-45 couple, we couldn't believe the number and sizes of strollers and those ubiquitous scooters. You had to be constantly vigilant or you would have your foot run over or path slowed down by*

*them. We've decided that one day a week, in one theme park, there
should be a "no wheels" day.*

You'd be surprised at how many people are injured by strollers
pushed by parents who are driving aggressively or in a hurry. Given
the number of strollers, pedestrians, and tight spaces, mishaps are
inevitable on both sides. A simple apology and a smile are usually the
best remediation.

LOST CHILDREN

THOUGH IT'S AMAZINGLY EASY to lose a child (or two) in the
parks, it usually isn't a serious problem: Universal employees are
schooled in handling the situation. If you lose a child in the resort,
report it to the nearest Universal employee, and then check at Guest
Services. Paging isn't used, but in an emergency, an all-points bulletin
can be issued throughout the park(s) via internal communications.

Iron on or sew a label into each child's shirt that states their name,
your name, the name of your hotel, and your cell phone number.
Accomplish the same thing by writing the information on a strip of
masking tape.

An easier and trendier option is a temporary tattoo with your
child's name and your phone number. Unlike labels, ID bracelets, or
wristbands, the tattoos cannot fall off or be lost. Temporary tattoos
last about two weeks, won't wash or sweat off, and are not irritating
to the skin. They can be purchased online from new.safetytat.com.
Special tattoos are available for children with food allergies or cognitive impairment such as autism.

A Kingston, Washington, reader recommends recording vital info
for each child on a plastic key tag or luggage tag and affixing it to the
child's shoe. This reader also snaps a photo of the kids each morning
to document what they're wearing. A mother from Rockville, Maryland, reported a strategy one step short of a cattle brand:

*Traveling with a 3-year-old, I was very anxious about losing him.
I wrote my cell phone number on his leg with a permanent marker
and felt much more confident that he'd get back to me quickly if he
became lost.*

One way to better keep track of your family is to buy each person
a Universal uniform—in this case, the same brightly and distinctively
colored T-shirt. A Yuma, Arizona, family tried this with great success:

*We all got the same shirts (bright red), so we could easily spot
each other in case of separation (VERY easy to do). It was a lifesaver when our 18-month-old decided to get out of the stroller and
wander off. No matter what precautions you try, it seems there are*

always opportunities to lose a child, but the recognizable shirts helped tremendously.

HOW KIDS GET LOST

CHILDREN GET SEPARATED from their parents every day at Universal Orlando under remarkably similar (and predictable) circumstances:

1. PREOCCUPIED SOLO PARENT   The party's only adult is preoccupied with something like buying refreshments, reading a map, or using the restroom. Junior is there one second and gone the next.

2. THE HIDDEN EXIT   Sometimes parents wait on the sidelines while two or more young children experience a ride together. Parents expect the kids to exit in one place and the youngsters pop out elsewhere. Exits from some attractions are distant from entrances. Know exactly where your children will emerge before letting them ride by themselves.

3. AFTER THE SHOW   At the end of many shows and rides, a Universal staffer announces, "Check for personal belongings and take small children by the hand." When dozens, if not hundreds, of people leave an attraction simultaneously, it's easy for parents to lose their children unless they have direct contact.

4. RESTROOM PROBLEMS   Mom tells 6-year-old Tommy, "I'll be sitting on this bench when you come out of the restroom." Three possibilities: One, Tommy exits through a different door and becomes disoriented (Mom may not know there's another door). Two, Mom decides she also will use the restroom, and Tommy emerges to find her gone. Three, Mom pokes around in a shop while keeping an eye on the bench but misses Tommy when he comes out.

If you can't find a companion- or family-accessible restroom, make sure there's only one exit. Designate a distinctive meeting spot and give clear instructions: "I'll meet you by this flagpole. If you get out first, stay right here." Have your child repeat the directions back to you.

5. PARADES   There are many parades and shows at which the audience stands. Children tend to jockey for a better view. By moving a little this way and that, your child can quickly put distance between you before either of you notices.

6. MASS MOVEMENTS   Be on guard when huge crowds disperse after fireworks or a parade, or at park closing. With 20,000–40,000 people at once in an area, it's very easy to get separated from a child or others in your party. Use extra caution after the evening lagoon shows in USF and Epic Universe, or the nighttime light display in Hogsmeade. Plan where to meet in the event you get separated.

7. CHARACTER GREETINGS   When the Universal characters appear, children can slip out of sight.

UNIVERSAL, KIDS, *and* SCARY STUFF

THOUGH THERE'S PLENTY FOR YOUNGER children to enjoy at the Universal parks, most major attractions can potentially make kids under age 8 wig out. To be frank, they freak out a fairly large percentage of adults as well. On average, Universal's rides move more aggressively and feature more intense (some would say assaultive) audiovisual effects than their Disney counterparts. There are attractions with menacing mummies, exploding insects, and man-eating dinosaurs—not to mention demonic soul-sucking Dementors and fire-breathing dragons. And while Walt Disney World rides always end on a happy note, Universal is equally as apt to send you out with a final scare or snarky parting shot, which is less likely to soothe shaken nerves. Universal also sets surprisingly strict minimum height requirements for some kid-centric rides, ruling out attractions such as Cat in the Hat and The High in the Sky Seuss Trolley Train Ride! for the infants who might enjoy them most.

You can reliably predict that a visit to UOR will, at one time or another, send a young child into system overload. Be sensitive, alert, and prepared for almost anything, even behavior that is out of character for your child. Most children take Universal's macabre trappings in stride, and others are easily comforted by an arm around the shoulder or a squeeze of the hand. Parents who know that their children tend to become upset should take it slow and easy, sampling milder adventures like Yoshi's Adventure or the E.T. Adventure, gauging reactions, and discussing with the children how they felt about what they saw. If your child has difficulty coping with the cartoon creatures in Despicable Me Minion Mayhem and Men in Black Alien Attack, you should think twice before exposing them to the photo-realistic Lord Voldemort in Harry Potter and the Escape from Gringotts, as this reader from Finstadjordet, Norway, wrote us to emphasize:

> Please remember: children are different. My 8-year-old boy found Revenge of the Mummy a bit scary and a bit fun, but he was super-scared on both Harry Potter rides because they seemed "too real" compared to the other rides. It can be difficult to tell in advance what will scare your child, but try to read your child while waiting in line. Universal has excellent child-swap systems; if in doubt, use them.

Sometimes young children will rise above their anxiety in an effort to please their parents or siblings. This doesn't necessarily indicate a mastery of fear, much less enjoyment. If children leave a ride in apparently good shape, ask if they would like to go on it again (not necessarily now but sometime). The response usually will indicate how much they actually enjoyed the experience.

Evaluating a child's capacity to handle the visual and tactile effects of UOR requires patience, understanding, and experimentation. Each of us has our own demons. If a child balks at or is frightened by a ride, respond constructively. Let your children know that lots of people, adults and children, are scared by what they see and feel. Help them understand it's OK if they get frightened and that their fear doesn't lessen your love or respect. Take pains not to compound the discomfort by making a child feel inadequate; try not to undermine self-esteem, impugn courage, or ridicule. Most of all, don't induce guilt by suggesting the child's trepidation might be ruining the family's fun. It's also sometimes necessary to restrain older siblings' taunting.

A visit to UOR is more than an outing or an adventure for a young child. It's a testing experience, a sort of controlled rite of passage. If you help your little one work through the challenges, the time can be immeasurably rewarding and a bonding experience for you both.

THE FRIGHT FACTOR

WHILE EACH YOUNGSTER IS DIFFERENT, following are seven attraction elements that alone or combined could push a child's buttons and indicate that a certain attraction isn't age appropriate for that child:

1. NAME OF THE ATTRACTION   Young children will naturally be apprehensive about something called Skull Island, Curse of the Werewolf, or *Horror Make-Up Show.*

2. VISUAL IMPACT OF THE ATTRACTION FROM OUTSIDE   Doctor Doom's Fearfall, Dudley Do-Right's Ripsaw Falls, The Incredible Hulk Coaster, Jurassic Park River Adventure, Jurassic World VelociCoaster, Reign of Kong, and Hollywood Rip Ride Rockit look scary enough to give adults second thoughts, and they terrify many young children. The same goes double for Stardust Racers, Mine-Cart Madness, and everything inside Dark Universe at Epic Universe.

3. VISUAL IMPACT OF THE INDOOR-QUEUING AREA   The dark forest inside E.T. Adventure, the Gothic manor of Monsters Unchained: The Frankenstein Experiment, and the castle dungeon of Harry Potter and the Forbidden Journey can frighten children, and the creepy creatures lurking inside Skull Island: Reign of Kong's temple ruins may induce an emergency undergarment change.

4. INTENSITY OF THE ATTRACTION   Some attractions inundate the senses with sights, sounds, movement, and even smell to create a total sensory experience. A Johnston, Iowa, mom describes the situation well:

> *The 3-D and 4-D experiences are way too scary for even a very brave 5-year-old girl. The shows that blew things on her, shot smells in the air, had bugs flying, etc. scared the bejabbers out of her.*

5. VISUAL IMPACT OF THE ATTRACTION   Sights in various attractions range from falling fish to flying bats, from grazing dinosaurs to gory body parts. What one child calmly absorbs may scare the bejabbers out of another the same age.

continued on page 184

SMALL-CHILD FRIGHT-POTENTIAL TABLE

This table provides a quick reference to identify attractions to be wary of, and why. It relates specifically to kids ages 3–7. It represents a generalization, and all kids are different. On average, children at the younger end of the range are more likely to be frightened than children in their sixth or seventh year. For more information about ride elements that may induce sensory overload, download Universal's planning guide for cognitive accessibility at theugseries.com/UOcognitive.

UNIVERSAL STUDIOS FLORIDA

MINION LAND

• **DESPICABLE ME MINION MAYHEM** Universal's mildest simulator motion-wise, but the huge images and loud soundtrack may startle preschoolers. Stationary benches are available in the front row to avoid the moving seats. Child swap available (see page 187).

• **VILLAIN-CON MINION BLAST** Physically, this ride is as mild as the airport's moving sidewalk, but chaotic cartoon screens may overwhelm small kids and sensitive adults.

NEW YORK

• **HOLLYWOOD RIP RIDE ROCKIT** The tallest roller coaster at Universal, with loud music to cover your screams. May terrify guests of any age. Child swap available (see page 187).

• **RACE THROUGH NEW YORK STARRING JIMMY FALLON** Moderate simulator motion, intense 3-D imagery, loud sounds, and the comedy stylings of Jimmy Fallon may disturb younger kids (and adults who remember Johnny Carson). Child swap available (see page 187).

• **REVENGE OF THE MUMMY** Very intense roller coaster in the dark with angry mummies, bugs, and fireballs. May frighten guests of any age. Child swap available (see page 187).

• **TRANSFORMERS: THE RIDE-3D** Intense, bloodlessly violent virtual reality simulator may frighten younger children and deafen guests of any age. Child swap available (see page 187).

SAN FRANCISCO

• **FAST & FURIOUS: SUPERCHARGED** Parental guidance suggested for intense simulated street-racing action with blasts of fog, loud noises, and improper use of turn signals. The actual motion of the vehicle is very mild. Child swap available (see page 187).

THE WIZARDING WORLD OF HARRY POTTER—DIAGON ALLEY

• **HARRY POTTER AND THE ESCAPE FROM GRINGOTTS** Visually intimidating with intense 3-D effects and brief moments of moderately fast roller coaster motion. Less frightening than Harry Potter and the Forbidden Journey but may still rattle some riders. Child swap available (see page 187).

• **HOGWARTS EXPRESS: KING'S CROSS STATION** Brief encounter with Dementors may scare some preschoolers; otherwise, not frightening.

• **OLLIVANDERS** Loud bells and lightning may bother some sensitive kids.

WORLD EXPO

• **MEN IN BLACK ALIEN ATTACK** Dark ride with spinning cars and comical aliens may frighten some preschoolers. Child swap available (see page 187).

SPRINGFIELD: HOME OF THE SIMPSONS

• **KANG & KODOS' TWIRL 'N' HURL** Dumbo-style midway ride. A favorite of many young children. Child swap available (see page 187).

• **THE SIMPSONS RIDE** Extremely intense visually, with USF's strongest simulated motion. May frighten many adults as well as kids. Child swap available (see page 187).

DREAMWORKS LAND

• **DREAMWORKS IMAGINATION CELEBRATION** Toddlers may be briefly startled by the giant puppets and video effects; otherwise, not frightening in any respect.

• **PO'S KUNG FU TRAINING CAMP** Not frightening in any respect, but your kids may get soaked.

• **SHREK'S SWAMP** Not frightening in any respect, unless you have a fear of talking donkeys.

• **TROLLS TROLLERCOASTER** A beginner's roller coaster; safe for all but the most timid tykes. Child swap available (see page 187).

HOLLYWOOD

• *ANIMAL ACTORS ON LOCATION!* Not frightening in any respect, unless you have an animal phobia.

• *THE BOURNE STUNTACULAR* Intense action-movie fight choreography, including live gunfire and loud explosions, may startle viewers of all ages.

• *CINESATIONAL: A SYMPHONIC SPECTACULAR* Oversize images of dinosaurs and monsters, accompanied by loud fireworks, may startle small children.

• **E.T. ADVENTURE** Dark ride with simulated flight and psychedelic creatures. A little intense for a few preschoolers, but the end is all happiness and harmony. Child swap available (see page 187).

• **UNIVERSAL MEGA MOVIE PARADE** Floats featuring giant Stay-Puft Marshmallow Man and T. Rex figures may intimidate small kids; otherwise, not frightening in any respect.

• *UNIVERSAL ORLANDO'S HORROR MAKE-UP SHOW* Gory props and film clips, presented educationally and humorously, may wig out wee ones, but most children seem to handle it disturbingly well. Interestingly, very few families report problems with this show.

ISLANDS OF ADVENTURE

MARVEL SUPER HERO ISLAND

• **THE AMAZING ADVENTURES OF SPIDER-MAN** Immersive 3-D effects and spinning simulator movement may frighten younger kids, but most take the comic book mayhem in stride. Technically similar to Transformers at USF but significantly less intense. Child swap available (see page 187).

• **DOCTOR DOOM'S FEARFALL** Visually intimidating to all guests, with an intense launch and brief weightlessness. The actual plummeting is less protracted than on WDW's Tower of Terror. Child swap available (see page 187).

• **THE INCREDIBLE HULK COASTER** Very intense looping roller coaster with a high-speed launch. This is a scary roller coaster by any standard. Child swap available (see page 187).

• **STORM FORCE ACCELATRON** Teacups-type midway ride can induce motion sickness in all ages, though most kids seem to love it. Child swap available (see page 187).

TOON LAGOON

• **DUDLEY DO-RIGHT'S RIPSAW FALLS** Visually intimidating from outside, with several intense, potentially drenching plunges. A toss-up, to be considered only if your kids like water-flume rides. Child swap available (see page 187).

• **ME SHIP,** *THE OLIVE* Not frightening in any respect.

• **POPEYE & BLUTO'S BILGE-RAT BARGES** Potentially frightening and certainly soaking for guests of all ages. Most younger children handle it well. Child swap available (see page 187).

SKULL ISLAND

• **SKULL ISLAND: REIGN OF KONG** The ride vehicle's motion is fairly mild, but don't let the low minimum height fool you: the visuals of mutant bugs are pretty gross, and the queue is even more frightening, with sections that resemble a haunted house. Child swap available (see page 187).

JURASSIC PARK

• **CAMP JURASSIC** Some preschoolers may be spooked by the dark caves and dinosaur sounds; guests who are afraid of heights should avoid the net climb.

• **JURASSIC PARK DISCOVERY CENTER** Not frightening in any respect.

• **JURASSIC PARK RIVER ADVENTURE** Visually intimidating boat ride with life-size dinosaurs and an intense flume finale. May frighten and dampen guests of any age. Child swap available (see page 187).

• **JURASSIC WORLD VELOCICOASTER** An extremely intense roller coaster featuring multiple high-speed launches, stomach-lurching loops, and close encounters with rapacious raptors. Child swap available (see page 187).

continued on next page

SMALL-CHILD FRIGHT-POTENTIAL TABLE *(continued)*

ISLANDS OF ADVENTURE *(continued)*

JURASSIC PARK *(continued)*

• **PTERANODON FLYERS** A short, slow suspended roller coaster. Frightens some children who are scared of heights.

• **RAPTOR ENCOUNTER** The velociraptor makes loud, growling noises and sudden, snapping movements that startle even some adults.

THE WIZARDING WORLD OF HARRY POTTER—HOGSMEADE

• **FLIGHT OF THE HIPPOGRIFF** Another beginner coaster, comparable to The Barnstormer at the Magic Kingdom. May frighten some preschoolers. Child swap available (see page 187).

• **HAGRID'S MAGICAL CREATURES MOTORBIKE ADVENTURE** A moderately intense outdoor coaster with no loops, but forward and backward launches, dramatic drops, and close encounters with magical creatures may intimidate younger Muggles. Child swap available (see page 187).

• **HARRY POTTER AND THE FORBIDDEN JOURNEY** Extremely intense special effects and macabre visuals with wild simulated movement that may frighten and discombobulate guests of any age. Child swap available (see page 187).

• **HOGWARTS EXPRESS: HOGSMEADE STATION** Not frightening in any respect.

• **OLLIVANDERS** Loud bells and lightning may bother some sensitive kids.

SEUSS LANDING

• **CARO-SEUSS-EL** Not frightening in any respect. Child swap available (see page 187).

• **THE CAT IN THE HAT** Mild spinning motion and modest visual effects may frighten a small percentage of preschoolers. Child swap available (see page 187).

• **THE HIGH IN THE SKY SEUSS TROLLEY TRAIN RIDE!** May scare kids who are afraid of heights; otherwise, not frightening in any respect. Child swap available (see page 187).

• **IF I RAN THE ZOO** Not frightening in any respect.

• **ONE FISH, TWO FISH, RED FISH, BLUE FISH** A tame midway ride that's a great favorite of most young children, though they will likely get wet. Child swap available (see page 187).

EPIC UNIVERSE

CELESTIAL PARK

• **CONSTELLATION CAROUSEL** Not frightening in any respect. Stationary and bench seats available. Child swap available (see page 187).

• *OCULUS NIGHTTIME SPECTACULAR* Loud fireworks may startle small children.

• **STARDUST RACERS** An intense dueling roller coaster featuring high-speed launches, inversions, and near misses with the other train. Child swap available (see page 187).

SUPER NINTENDO WORLD

• **MARIO KART: BOWSER'S CHALLENGE** Slow-moving dark ride with augmented-reality effects simulating high speed and video-game baddies may be too intense for preschoolers. Child swap available (see page 187).

• **MINE-CART MADNESS** A relatively mild family coaster, but the illusion of cars "jumping" off the track may terrify smaller kids. Child swap available (see page 187).

• **YOSHI'S ADVENTURE** May scare kids who are afraid of heights; otherwise, not frightening in any respect. Child swap available (see page 187).

DARK UNIVERSE

• **CURSE OF THE WEREWOLF** Moderately thrilling spinning coaster includes close encounters with a scary werewolf figure. Child swap available (see page 187).

• **MONSTERS UNCHAINED: THE FRANKENSTEIN EXPERIMENT** Visually intimidating inside and out, with extremely intense spooky effects that make this Universal's scariest ride sensory-wise. The ride does some wild maneuvers, but does not have domed simulator screens that sicken some Forbidden Journey riders. Child swap available (see page 187).

THE WIZARDING WORLD OF HARRY POTTER—MINISTRY OF MAGIC

• **HARRY POTTER AND THE BATTLE AT THE MINISTRY** Intense visuals and immersive action with some elevator-style drops. Child swap available (see page 187).

• *LE CIRQUE ARCANUS* Circus stunts and fantastic beasts may frighten sensitive toddlers.

HOW TO TRAIN YOUR DRAGON—ISLE OF BERK

• **DRAGON RACERS RALLY** Spinning, flipping carnival ride that can terrify anyone. Child swap available (see page 187).

• **FYRE DRILL** Not frightening in any respect, but you will get drenched. Child swap available (see page 187).

• **HICCUP'S WING GLIDERS** A moderately thrilling family coaster with launches, but no huge hills or inversions. Child swap available (see page 187).

• *THE UNTRAINABLE DRAGON* Loud drums and battle scenes with huge dragon puppets may startle small children.

• **VIKING TRAINING CAMP** Not frightening in any respect.

VOLCANO BAY

THE VOLCANO

• **VOL'S CAVERNS** Dark pathways may spook sensitive toddlers; otherwise, not frightening.

RAINFOREST VILLAGE

• **KALA & TAI NUI SERPENTINE BODY SLIDES** Even more terrifying than Ko'okiri, with twisting enclosed tubes and extreme g-forces.

• **MAKU ROUND RAFT RIDE** Maku is one of the milder family raft rides in the park, with mostly open troughs and gentle curves. Don't mix it up with Puihi!

• **OHYAH AND OHNO DROP SLIDES** The shortest twisting tube slides in the park, but the final drop of 4–6 feet can knock the wind out of weak swimmers.

• **PUIHI ROUND RAFT RIDE** Puihi is among the scariest family raft rides in the park, with sharp turns that seem to nearly toss you onto the interstate.

• **PUKA ULI LAGOON** Not frightening in any respect.

• **PUNGA RACERS** Enclosed tubes may upset claustrophobes; otherwise, not frightening.

• **TANIWHA TUBES** A moderately fast-moving raft slide with some surprising twists and drops. Each of the four tubes has a different configuration. Accompany smaller kids on a two-seater raft, and ask for a green Tonga slide with more open-air sections if you get claustrophobic.

• **TEAWA THE FEARLESS RIVER** Swift current can swamp smaller swimmers; mandatory life jackets are available in all sizes.

RIVER VILLAGE

• **HONU SLIDE** Honu's hair-raising, highly banked walls will wig out almost anyone. Don't confuse it with its sibling, ika Moana.

• **IKA MOANA SLIDE** Ika Moana is a mild raft ride that most kids can handle.

• **KOPIKO WAI WINDING RIVER** A brief segment floats through a dark, foggy cave; otherwise, not frightening in any respect.

• **KRAKATAU AQUA COASTER** Roller coaster–style dips and brief enclosed tunnels may scare younger kids, but most find it thrilling.

• **RUNAMUKKA REEF** Not frightening in any respect.

• **TOT TIKI REEF** Not frightening in any respect.

WAVE VILLAGE

• **KO'OKIRI BODY PLUNGE** High-speed vertical drop slide that will scare anyone silly.

• **THE REEF** Not frightening in any respect.

• **WATURI BEACH** Larger waves may overwhelm little ones; otherwise, not frightening in any respect.

continued from page 179

6. DARK Many Universal attractions operate indoors in the dark. For some kids, this triggers fear. A child who gets frightened on one dark ride (E.T. Adventure, for example) may be unwilling to try other indoor rides.

7. THE TACTILE EXPERIENCE Some rides are wild enough to cause motion sickness, wrench backs, and discombobulate guests of any age.

As a footnote, be aware that a kid's courage and confidence in regard to riding attractions doesn't necessarily increase as they get older. A ride that delights a child at age 4 may scare them to death at 5; by 6 years old they may be fine again. As a dad from Maryland explains:

> *Just because a child loves a ride at one age doesn't mean that he or she will love it on the next trip.*

A BIT OF PREPARATION

WE RECEIVE MANY TIPS from parents about how they prepared their young children for their theme park experience. A common strategy is to acquaint children with the characters and stories behind the park attractions by reading Universal-related books and watching movies at home.

USF's attractions prominently feature the family-friendly film series *Despicable Me* (*E.T.* should already be on your kids' required viewing list), as well as *Men in Black, Transformers, Fast & Furious,* the Jason Bourne franchise, and *The Mummy* (only bother with the Boris Karloff and Brendan Fraser versions) if they are old enough for PG-13 entertainment. *The Simpsons* is in perpetual reruns, so refreshing your memory of Homer and family shouldn't be hard. For extra credit, screen *Jaws, Ghostbusters,* and the *Back to the Future* movies, and then hunt for hidden tributes to their extinct attractions.

IOA was inspired by literature, so start by reading the classics before bedtime—Dr. Seuss, Stan Lee's superheroes, ancient mythology, and the Sunday funnies. For Jurassic Park, you can cheat and watch the original Spielberg film and 2015's *Jurassic World;* for King Kong (the exception to the literary rule), watch the 2005 Peter Jackson remake, even though the 1933 original is still superior. Of course, you'll want to be well versed in all seven volumes of Harry Potter's academic career (along with the associated films, short stories, and spin-offs) to fully appreciate both Wizarding Worlds; if that's too much work, at a minimum you must watch the first movie before visiting Hogsmeade, and the last one before delving into Diagon Alley.

Epic Universe's central hub is inspired by Greek mythology and astrology, but you needn't be a classical scholar to enjoy the attractions and atmosphere. You will want to rewatch the *How to Train Your Dragon* series before visiting the Isle of Berk, as well as the second *Fantastic Beasts* film (*The Crimes of Grindelwald*) to prepare for 1920s Paris. Exercise your thumbs by brushing up on your Nintendo gaming skills, or simply watch *The Super Mario Bros. Movie* from

2023 (*not* the 1993 version). Be sure to binge the classic black-and-white monster movies—especially *Frankenstein, Bride of Frankenstein, Dracula,* and *The Wolf Man.*

A more direct approach is to watch videos that show the attractions. Online, you'll find good point-of-view videos of most Universal attractions at our **YouTube** channel (youtube.com/theunofficialguide series), as well as Touring Plans, *Attractions Magazine,* Inside Universal, and other bloggers. Videos of dark indoor rides—especially those that use 3-D glasses—never do the attractions justice, but they usually show enough for you to judge whether your child can comfortably handle the real thing. A Lexington, Kentucky, mom reports:

> *My timid 7-year-old daughter and I watched rides and shows on YouTube, and we cut out all the ones that looked too scary.*

ATTRACTIONS THAT EAT ADULTS

YOU MAY SPEND SO MUCH ENERGY worrying about Junior that you forget to take care of yourself. The following attractions can cause motion sickness or other problems for older kids and adults:

POTENTIALLY PROBLEMATIC ATTRACTIONS FOR GROWN-UPS

UNIVERSAL STUDIOS FLORIDA
- **NEW YORK** Hollywood Rip Ride Rockit | Race Through New York Starring Jimmy Fallon | Revenge of the Mummy | Transformers: The Ride–3D
- **SPRINGFIELD: HOME OF THE SIMPSONS** The Simpsons Ride
- **THE WIZARDING WORLD OF HARRY POTTER—DIAGON ALLEY** Harry Potter and the Escape from Gringotts
- **WORLD EXPO** Men in Black Alien Attack

ISLANDS OF ADVENTURE
- **JURASSIC PARK** Jurassic World VelociCoaster
- **MARVEL SUPER HERO ISLAND** The Amazing Adventures of Spider-Man | Doctor Doom's Fearfall | The Incredible Hulk Coaster | Storm Force Accelatron
- **TOON LAGOON** Dudley Do-Right's Ripsaw Falls
- **THE WIZARDING WORLD OF HARRY POTTER—HOGSMEADE** Hagrid's Magical Creatures Motorbike Adventure | Harry Potter and the Forbidden Journey

EPIC UNIVERSE
- **CELESTIAL PARK** Stardust Racers
- **DARK UNIVERSE** Curse of the Werewolf | Monsters Unchained: The Frankenstein Experiment
- **HOW TO TRAIN YOUR DRAGON—ISLE OF BERK** Dragon Racer's Rally | Hiccup's Wing Gliders
- **SUPER NINTENDO WORLD** Mario Kart: Bowser's Challenge | Mine-Cart Madness
- **THE WIZARDING WORLD OF HARRY POTTER—MINISTRY OF MAGIC** Harry Potter and the Battle at the Ministry

VOLCANO BAY
- **RAINFOREST VILLAGE** Kala & Tai Nui Serpentine Body Slides | Ohyah & Ohno Drop Slides | Puihi Round Raft Ride
- **RIVER VILLAGE** Honu Raft Slide • **WAVE VILLAGE** Ko'okiri Body Plunge

A WORD ABOUT HEIGHT REQUIREMENTS

ALL ATTRACTIONS AT UOR require that children be at least 48 inches tall to ride without a supervising companion, also known as an older

ATTRACTION HEIGHT REQUIREMENTS

UNIVERSAL STUDIOS FLORIDA

Despicable Me Minion Mayhem	40" minimum height
E.T. Adventure	34" minimum height
Fast & Furious: Supercharged	40" minimum height
Harry Potter and the Escape from Gringotts	42" minimum height
Hollywood Rip Ride Rockit	51" minimum height; 79" maximum height
Men in Black Alien Attack	42" minimum height
Race Through New York Starring Jimmy Fallon	40" minimum height
Revenge of the Mummy	48" minimum height
The Simpsons Ride	40" minimum height
Transformers: The Ride–3D	40" minimum height
TrollerCoaster	36" minimum height

ISLANDS OF ADVENTURE

The Amazing Adventures of Spider-Man	40" minimum height
The Cat in the Hat	36" minimum height
Doctor Doom's Fearfall	52" minimum height
Dudley Do-Right's Ripsaw Falls	44" minimum height
Flight of the Hippogriff	36" minimum height
Hagrid's Magical Creatures Motorbike Adventure	48" minimum height
Harry Potter and the Forbidden Journey	48" minimum height
The High in the Sky Seuss Trolley Train Ride!	36" minimum height
The Incredible Hulk Coaster	54" minimum height
Jurassic Park River Adventure	42" minimum height
Jurassic World VelociCoaster	51" minimum height
Popeye & Bluto's Bilge-Rat Barges	42" minimum height
Pteranodon Flyers (Guests taller than 56" must be accompanied by a guest 36"–56".)	36" minimum height; 56" maximum height
Skull Island: Reign of Kong	36" minimum height

family member or guardian. Most moving attractions at UOR require children to meet additional minimum height requirements. If you have children too short to ride, instead of skipping the ride or splitting up your group, consider using child swap (see below). For more information, see the table above. Regardless of height requirements, all guests must be able to sit up unassisted on all rides. Handheld infants are welcome in all shows, playgrounds, and walk-through attractions, but the only rides that accommodate handheld infants are **Constellation Carousel** and **Fyre Drill** at Epic Universe; **Caro-Seuss-el** and **One Fish, Two Fish, Red Fish, Blue Fish** in IOA; **Kang & Kodos' Twirl 'n' Hurl** and **Despicable Me Minion Mayhem** (ask for stationary seating) in USF; and **Hogwarts Express.**

Please note that height requirements only relate to the physical needs of a ride's safety restraints and are not a measure of whether an attraction is intellectually or psychologically appropriate for a given child, as this Illinois parent discovered too late:

ATTRACTION HEIGHT REQUIREMENTS *(continued)*

EPIC UNIVERSE

Curse of the Werewolf	40" minimum height
Dragon Racer's Rally	48" minimum height
Harry Potter and the Battle at the Ministry	40" minimum height
Hiccup's Wing Gliders	40" minimum height
Mario Kart: Bowser's Challenge	40" minimum height
Mine-Cart Madness	36" minimum height
Monsters Unchained: The Frankenstein Experiment	48" minimum height
Stardust Racers	48" minimum height
Yoshi's Adventure	34" minimum height

VOLCANO BAY

Honu Raft Slide	48" minimum height
ika Moana Raft Slide	42" minimum height
Kala & Tai Nui Serpentine Body Slides	48" minimum height
Ko'okiri Body Plunge	48" minimum height
Krakatau Aqua Coaster	42" minimum height
Maku Round Raft Ride	42" minimum height
Ohyah and Ohno Drop Slides	48" minimum height
Puihi Round Raft Ride	42" minimum height
Puka Uli Lagoon	under 48" must wear life vest
Punga Racers	42" minimum height
The Reef	under 48" must wear life vest
Taniwha Tubes: Tonga and Raki	42" minimum height
TeAwa the Fearless River	42" minimum height
Waturi Beach	under 48" must wear life vest

It is very important to stress that height requirements are NOT a good indicator for whether a child is ready for a ride. My almost 4-year-old is a big Harry Potter and Transformers fan and met the height requirements for Transformers and Escape from Gringotts, so we let him go on. He went through the entire ride without crying or screaming, but immediately upon the ride stopping in the bay, he turned to me and said, "I am NOT going on that ride again!" In retrospect, it was waaay too intense for a child of that age, whether he met the height requirement or not.

Child Swap (also known as Rider Swap, Baby Swap, or Switching Off)

Most Universal Orlando attractions have minimum height requirements. Some couples with children too small or too young forgo these attractions, while others take turns riding. Missing some of Universal's best rides is an unnecessary sacrifice, and waiting in line twice for the same ride is a tremendous waste of time.

Instead, take advantage of child swap, also known as baby swap, rider swap, or switching off. To child swap, there must be at least two adults. When you reach a team member at the entrance of an attraction, say you want to child swap. Child swap at Universal is similar to Disney's Rider Switch but superior in several respects. Instead of one adult waiting at the exit with the children and returning after through an alternative queue, at Universal the entire family goes through the whole line together before being split into riding and nonriding groups near the loading platform. The nonriding parent and child(ren) wait in a designated room, usually with some sort of entertainment (for example, Harry Potter and the Forbidden Journey at IOA shows the first 20 minutes of *Harry Potter and the Sorcerer's Stone* on a loop), a place to sit down, and sometimes restrooms with changing tables. And nearly every attraction at Universal offers child swap, which can even be used if you don't have children; it works equally well for skittish or infirm adults who don't like thrill rides, or for designated baggage handlers in families who hate to use lockers.

We receive quite a bit of positive feedback from readers who use Universal's child-swap system, such as this mom from Doylestown, Pennsylvania:

> *I was really happy with the child swap setup. It made it possible for us to stay together most of the trip, as we were traveling with a 1-year-old who couldn't ride anything. It also meant my 6-year-old got to see all the cool preshow stuff in Hogwarts Castle, even though he wasn't big enough to ride Forbidden Journey.*

And from a Scarsdale, New York, parent:

> *There wasn't much for our 3-year-old, and what we took her on terrified her, so she started asking to go in "the room" (child swap room) rather than on the ride. Child swap also meant that her sisters got to ride everything twice.*

Attractions where switching off is practiced are oriented to more mature guests. Sometimes it takes a lot of courage for a child just to move through the queue holding a parent's hand, especially in lines like Skull Island with lots of spooky decor. In the boarding area, many children suddenly fear abandonment when one parent leaves to ride. Prepare your children for switching off, or you might have an emotional crisis on your hands. A mom from Edison, New Jersey, writes:

> *Once my son came to understand that the switch off would not leave him abandoned, he did not seem to mind. Practice the switch off on some dry runs at home, so your child isn't concerned that he will be left behind. At the very least, the procedure should be explained in advance so the little ones know what to expect.*

An Ada, Michigan, mother discovered that the child-swap procedure varies among attractions. She says:

> *Parents need to tell the very first attendant they come to that they would like to switch off. Each attraction has a different procedure for this. Tell every other attendant too because they forget quickly.*

As at any theme park, the best tip we can give is to ask the greeter in front of the attraction what you're supposed to do.

UNIVERSAL CHARACTERS

THOUGH OFTEN OVERSHADOWED by the fur-clad cartoon celebrities down the street, Universal Orlando also has a stable of characters to call its own, but the interest in oversize cartoon vermin isn't anywhere near as intense as at Disney World. You'll occasionally see a Minion getting mobbed or a couple dozen families queued to meet SpongeBob, but never anything like the hour-plus waits that Disney's princesses can draw at the Magic Kingdom.

unofficial **TIP**
Don't underestimate your child's excitement at meeting the Universal characters—but also be aware that very small children may find the large costumed characters a little frightening.

PREPARING YOUR CHILDREN TO MEET THE CHARACTERS

ALMOST ALL CHARACTERS ARE quite large, and several, like Shrek, are huge! Small children don't expect this, and preschoolers especially can be intimidated.

Discuss the characters with your children before you go. On first encounter, don't thrust your child at the character. Allow the little one to deal with this big thing from whatever distance feels safe. If two adults are present, one should stay near the youngster while the other approaches the character and demonstrates that it's safe and friendly. Some kids warm to the characters immediately; some never do. Most take a little time and several encounters.

There are two kinds of characters: animated, or those whose costumes include face-covering headpieces (including animal characters and humanlike cartoon characters such as the Simpsons), and celebrities or face characters, those for whom no mask or headpiece is necessary. The latter includes Marilyn Monroe, Doc Brown, and the Knight Bus and Hogwarts Express conductors, among others.

Only face characters speak. Because team members couldn't possibly imitate the animated characters' distinctive cinema voices, Universal has determined that it's more effective to keep such characters silent. Lack of speech notwithstanding, headpiece characters are warm and responsive, and they communicate effectively with gestures. Tell children in advance that these characters don't talk. Exciting exceptions are character encounters such as the Shrek meet and greet with Donkey and the Transformers photo op, where hidden actors or prerecorded audio clips are employed to allow interaction between costumed characters and guests.

Some character costumes are cumbersome and make it hard for the performers to see well. (Eyeholes frequently are in the mouth of the costume or even on the neck or chest.) Children who approach the character from the back or side may not be noticed, even if the child touches

CHARACTER-GREETING LOCATIONS

UNIVERSAL STUDIOS FLORIDA

CELEBRITIES (Face Characters)

- **Beetlejuice** Hollywood
- **Betty Boop** Hollywood
- **Doc Brown from *Back to the Future*** Hollywood; at the DeLorean outside Fast Food Boulevard
- **Knight Bus Conductor and Talking Head** London Waterfront outside Diagon Alley
- **Marilyn Monroe** Hollywood
- **Mummy Stiltwalkers** New York
- **Shaggy, Daphne, Fred, and Velma** Hollywood

ANIMATED (Costumed Characters)

- **Dora the Explorer** Hollywood
- **Death Eaters** Diagon Alley (seasonally)
- ***Despicable Me* Minions** Illumination Theater; exit of Despicable Me Minion Mayhem ride
- **Gabby from *Gabby's Dollhouse*** DreamWorks Land
- **Gru, Agnes, Edith, Margo, and Vector from *Despicable Me*** Illumination Theater
- **Hashtag the Panda** Race Through New York Starring Jimmy Fallon
- **Hello Kitty** Hollywood at her store
- **Homer, Marge, Bart, and Lisa Simpson** Hollywood; Springfield outside Kwik-E-Mart
- **Johnny, Gunter, and Rosita from *Sing*** Illumination Theater in Minion Land
- **Optimus Prime, Bumblebee, and Megatron from *Transformers*** Eighth Avenue near Mel's Drive-In
- **Po from *Kung Fu Panda*** DreamWorks Land
- **Poppy, Branch, and Guy Diamond from *Trolls*** DreamWorks Land
- **Puss in Boots and Kitty Softpaws** DreamWorks Land
- **Scooby-Doo and the Mystery Machine Van** Hollywood
- **Shrek, Donkey, and Princess Fiona** DreamWorks Land
- **Sideshow Bob and Krusty the Clown** Springfield outside Kwik-E-Mart
- **SpongeBob SquarePants, Squidward, and Patrick** SpongeBob StorePants in Hollywood

the character. It's possible in this situation for the character to accidentally step on the child or knock them down. A child should approach a character from the front, but occasionally not even this works. If a character appears to be ignoring your child, the character's handler will get their attention.

Understanding the unpredictability of children, the character will keep their feet still, particularly refraining from moving backward or sideways. Most characters will pose for

CHARACTER-GREETING LOCATIONS

ISLANDS OF ADVENTURE

CELEBRITIES (Face Characters)

- **Captain America** Marvel Super Hero Island
- **Green Goblin and Doctor Doom** Marvel Super Hero Island
- **The Grinch (live-action version) and Whos** Seuss Landing (seasonally)
- **Hogwarts Express conductor** Hogsmeade across from Honeydukes
- **Popeye and Olive Oyl** Toon Lagoon outside Comic Strip Cafe
- **Rogue, Storm, Wolverine, and Cyclops** Marvel Super Hero Island
- **Spider-Man** Marvel Super Hero Island

ANIMATED (Costumed Characters)

- **Blue the velociraptor; baby raptor** Jurassic Park at Raptor Encounter
- **Cat in the Hat, Thing 1, and Thing 2** Seuss Landing at *Oh! The Stories You'll Hear!*
- **The Grinch (cartoon version)** Seuss Landing at *Oh! The Stories You'll Hear!*
- **King Julien from *Madagascar*** Lost Continent
- **The Lorax and Sam-I-Am** Seuss Landing at *Oh! The Stories You'll Hear!*
- **Tigress from *Kung Fu Panda*** Lost Continent

EPIC UNIVERSE

CELEBRITIES (Face Characters)

- **Bride of Frankenstein and Victoria Frankenstein's Monster** Dark Universe
- **Hiccup and Astrid** How to Train Your Dragon—Isle of Berk
- **Monster Hunters and Musicians** Dark Universe
- **Wizards, Aurors, and exchange students** Wizarding World of Harry Potter—Ministry of Magic
- **Ygor and the Invisible Man** Dark Universe

ANIMATED (Costumed Characters)

- **Captain Cacao and Maya** Celestial Park
- **Mario, Luigi, Princess Peach, and Toad** Super Nintendo World
- **Toothless, Stormfly, and Roaming Dragons** How to Train Your Dragon—Isle of Berk

pictures and/or sign autographs. Costumes make it difficult for characters to wield a normal pen, and some characters can't sign autographs at all. If your child collects autographs, carry a pen the width of a Magic Marker.

UNIVERSAL CHARACTER-GREETING LOCATIONS

SOME UNIVERSAL ORLANDO CHARACTERS are confined to a specific location and visit with guests on a schedule. Other characters appear at random times in a few regular areas. Most mornings you'll find a rotating collection of characters near the entrance of the park. Not every character will appear every day; the busier the season, the more likely lesser-known characters will come out.

See the table above for a guide to the places you're likely to see famous friends in Universal's parks. Refer to Universal's smartphone app for appearance times, which can change daily.

CHARACTER DINING

UNIVERSAL ORLANDO OFFERS character meals at its theme parks, but unlike Walt Disney World's rodent royalty, you have a reasonable shot of supping with Spider-Man on short notice.

A Marvel character dinner, featuring favorites from the Avengers and X-Men, is held in IOA every Thursday–Sunday. During the holiday season, the Grinch hosts a breakfast at IOA. For further details, see page 306.

BABYSITTING

IN-ROOM BABYSITTING

CHILDCARE ISN'T AVAILABLE inside the parks, and the kids' clubs that operated in the evenings at the on-site Loews hotels have closed. A couple of companies provide in-room sitting in Universal Orlando and surrounding areas, but **Kid's Nite Out** (☎ 800-696-8105; kidsniteout .com) is the resort's preferred provider, and who the concierge will call if you ask for a babysitter. Kid's Nite Out also serves hotels in the greater Orlando area, including downtown. It provides sitters older than age 18 who are insured, bonded, screened, reference-checked, police-checked, and trained in CPR; bilingual sitters are also available. In addition to caring for your kids in your room, the sitters will, if you direct (and pay), take your children to the theme parks or other venues. Kid's Nite Out cares for children as young as six weeks old and can care for kids with special needs as well. Rates start at $30 per hour for one child, up to $42 per hour for five or more children, plus a $15 transportation fee.

PART 6

UNIVERSAL STUDIOS FLORIDA

LIKE ITS ELDER SIBLING IN HOLLYWOOD, **Universal Studios Florida** (USF) has always offered guests movie- and TV-themed rides and shows, along with limited opportunities to observe actual filming or preview upcoming productions. But if the last time you visited Universal was in the early 2000s, you literally won't recognize the majority of the park. Universal has updated, upgraded, or entirely removed nearly every attraction that debuted during the park's first decade, replacing Kongfrontation with Revenge of the Mummy, Back to the Future with The Simpsons Ride, Jaws with Harry Potter's Diagon Alley, and *Earthquake* (and its descendant *Disaster!*) with Fast & Furious: Supercharged. Each renovation has brought groundbreaking advancements in ride hardware and special effects.

Watching USF's constant evolution has been thrilling, but it can also be disconcerting. USF celebrates its 35th anniversary in 2025, but precious little early history is left intact in the park for longtime visitors who loved long gone opening-day attractions such as *Alfred Hitchcock: The Art of Making Movies,* The Funtastic World of Hanna-Barbera, and *Ghostbusters Spooktacular.* (For a trip down memory lane, visit Universal's retired attraction tributes at theugseries.com/uniretired.)

GETTING ORIENTED *at* UNIVERSAL STUDIOS FLORIDA

USF IS LAID OUT in a P configuration, with the rounded part of the *P* sticking out disproportionately from the stem. Beyond the main entrance plaza (formerly known as the Front Lot), a wide boulevard stretches past several shows and rides to the park's New York area. Branching off this pedestrian thoroughfare to the right are four streets that access other areas of the park and intersect a promenade circling a large, oval

Continued on page 196

Universal Studios Florida

Attractions

1. *Animal Actors on Location!* UX
2. *The Bourne Stuntacular* UX ☑
3. *CineSational: A Symphonic Spectacular* ☑
4. Despicable Me Minion Mayhem UX
5. *DreamWorks Imagination Celebration* UX
6. E.T. Adventure UX
7. Fast & Furious: Supercharged UX
8. Harry Potter and the Escape from Gringotts UX ☑
9. Hogwarts Express: King's Cross Station UX ☑
10. Hollywood Rip Ride Rockit UX
11. Kang & Kodos' Twirl 'n' Hurl UX
12. Men in Black Alien Attack UX ☑
13. Ollivanders

14. Po's Kung Fu Training Camp
15. Race Through New York Starring Jimmy Fallon UX
16. Revenge of the Mummy UX ☑
17. Shrek's Swamp
18. The Simpsons Ride UX
19. Transformers: The Ride–3D UX ☑

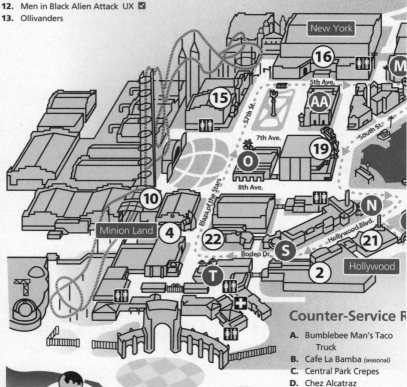

Counter-Service R

A. Bumblebee Man's Taco Truck
B. Cafe La Bamba *(seasonal)*
C. Central Park Crepes
D. Chez Alcatraz
E. Duff Brewery
F. Fast Food Boulevard
G. Florean Fortescue's Ice-Cream Parlour 👍
H. Fountain of Fair Fortune

20. Trolls Trollercoaster UX
21. *Universal Orlando's Horror Make-Up Show* UX ☑
22. Villain-Con Minion Blast UX

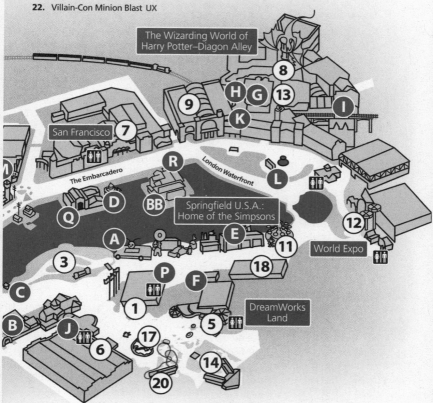

Restaurants

I. The Hopping Pot
J. KidZone Pizza Company *(seasonal)*
K. Leaky Cauldron 👍
L. London Taxi Hut
M. Louie's Italian Restaurant
N. Mel's Drive-In
O. Minion Cafe 👍
P. Moe's Tavern
Q. Richter's Burger Co.
R. San Francisco Pastry Company
S. Schwab's Pharmacy *(seasonal)*
T. Today Cafe 👍

Table-Service Restaurants

AA. Finnegan's Bar & Grill
BB. Lombard's Seafood Grille

UX Attraction Offers Universal Express   ✚ First Aid Station   🚻 Restrooms

👍 Recommended Dining   ☑ Not to Be Missed   ••• Parade Route

continued from page 193

EXTINCT ATTRACTION ARCHAEOLOGY

WHILE FANS OF WALT DISNEY WORLD are used to opening day attractions that are still around 50 years later, Universal Studios Florida has been constantly updated since opening in 1990. Derek Burgan brings us this "Saturday Six" list of small tributes to beloved but replaced rides throughout USF.

6. Back to the Future: The Ride In one of the many new pieces of animation created for The Simpson Ride queue, one segment shows the backstory of how Doc Brown inadvertently lost the rights to the Institute of Future technology (the façade for BTTF: The Ride) to Krusty the Clown.

5. Earthquake/Disaster Fast & Furious: Supercharged currently sits in the area that originally hosted *Earthquake: The Big One* (which was replaced in 2008 by *Disaster!: A Major Motion Picture Ride . . . Starring You!*), and it has references to both previous attractions in its queue. Look for an Earthquake keychain on the wall of pink slips, along with a jacket emblazoned with the Disaster Studios logo and power switches labeled with all three rides' opening dates.

4. Twister . . . Ride it Out! Outside Race Through New York Starring Jimmy Fallon, you'll see an ad for Twister Cola, along with an iconic blue shirt resembling the one worn by Bill Paxton in the preshow of Twister . . . Ride It Out!, the building's previous occupant.

3. Ghostbusters Spooktacular The famous Ghostbusters firehouse facade still remains in the New York section of USF, along with a window dedicated to "co. chief" Michael Morman (who originated the Ghostbuster "Winston" in the opening-day stage show, before eventually leading Universal's entertainment department).

2. Terminator 2: 3D On Hollywood Boulevard, in a window outside *The Bourne Stuntacular,* look for a nod to the attraction Bourne replaced with a Terminator oil can among the automotive decor.

1. Kongfrontation While you'll currently find King Kong at his new home in Islands of Adventure's Skull Island, you'll also see a small statue of the great ape on the left side of Revenge of the Mummy's treasure room. The scarab beetle symbol seen throughout the Mummy's queue and ride also resembles Kong's face.

man-made lake, where the majority of the shows and attractions are located. The area of USF open to visitors is a bit smaller than EPCOT.

Beginning at the park entrance and going clockwise, the first area you'll encounter is **Minion Land on Illumination Avenue,** which includes Despicable Me Minion Mayhem and Villain-Con Minion Blast. At the top of the *P* is the **New York** area, including Race Through New York Starring Jimmy Fallon and Revenge of the Mummy, as well as Hollywood Rip Ride Rockit and Transformers: The Ride–3D (which were absorbed from the previous Production Central area). Next is **San Francisco,** the home of Fast & Furious: Supercharged; **The Wizarding World of Harry Potter—Diagon Alley** with Hogwarts Express–King's Cross Station and Harry Potter and the Escape from Gringotts; **World Expo** with Men in Black Alien Attack; **Springfield: Home of the Simpsons,** featuring, of course, The Simpsons Ride; and **DreamWorks Land,** containing Shrek and Kung Fu Panda play areas. The last themed area, back near the front of the park, is **Hollywood,** featuring *Universal Orlando's Horror Make-Up Show* and *The Bourne Stuntacular,* plus the E.T. Adventure and an animal show.

In most of USF, the line where one themed area begins and another ends is blurry because much of the architecture consists of boring boxlike soundstages barely concealed behind false fronts. No matter; guests orient themselves by the major rides, sets, and landmarks and refer, for instance, to "the waterfront," "over by E.T.," or "by Mel's Drive-In." In diametric contrast, The Wizarding World of Harry Potter—Diagon Alley (and, to a much lesser extent, Minion Land and the Springfield area around The Simpsons Ride) is an immersive themed area whose scope and scale point to the place-making potential of upcoming Universal lands.

Almost all guest services are found just inside the main entrance. Services and amenities include stroller and wheelchair rentals to the left as you enter; lockers, Lost and Found, and First Aid are to the right. You'll also find the **Studio Audience Center,** where you can sign up to be an audience member at any live TV productions that may be recording that day. Past series taped at USF have included game shows, talk shows, cooking shows, Telemundo's *La Voz Kids,* and AEW's *DARK* wrestling. Call ☎ 407-224-6000 to find out what's scheduled during your visit.

A "secret" secondary entrance to USF is tucked under the Hollywood Rip Ride Rockit track, between Despicable Me Minion Mayhem and the Universal Studios Store. Unfortunately, this entrance has been unavailable since the Blue Man Group vacated the adjacent theater. On peak days or during special events, this gate may reopen to provide direct pedestrian access to Seuss Landing in IOA for guests with park-to-park admission, which can be a huge time-saver over taking the Hogwarts Express. During Halloween Horror Nights, this gate may open exclusively for on-site hotel guests.

UNIVERSAL STUDIOS FLORIDA ATTRACTIONS

MINION LAND

AT THE FRONT OF USF, Minion Land on Illumination Avenue occupies most of the area originally known as Production Central and is the first land guests see straight ahead of them upon entering the park. Fortunately, what was once one of the most meh main streets of any theme park got a much-needed glow-up in 2023, with its bland beige buildings brightened up by colorful Minion-themed additions, including an

NOT TO BE MISSED AT UNIVERSAL STUDIOS FLORIDA
NEW YORK • Revenge of the Mummy • Transformers: The Ride-3D
THE WIZARDING WORLD OF HARRY POTTER—DIAGON ALLEY • Harry Potter and the Escape from Gringotts • Hogwarts Express
WORLD EXPO • Men in Black Alien Attack
HOLLYWOOD • *The Bourne Stuntacular* • *Universal Orlando's Horror Make-Up Show* • *CineSational: A Symphonic Celebration*

interactive attraction, several shops and eateries, and **Illumination Theater,** an outdoor meet and greet with rotating characters.

Despicable Me Minion Mayhem *(Universal Express)* ★★★½

APPEAL BY AGE PRESCHOOL ★★★★½ **GRADE SCHOOL** ★★★★½ **TEENS** ★★★★
YOUNG ADULTS ★★★½   **OVER 30** ★★★½   **SENIORS** ★★★½

What it is Motion-simulator ride. **Scope and scale** Major attraction. **When to go** Immediately after park opening or during the hour before closing. **Comments** Child swap available (see page 187). **Duration of ride** 5 minutes. **Loading speed** Moderate–slow.

DESCRIPTION AND COMMENTS Despicable Me Minion Mayhem is a motion-simulator ride similar to Universal's The Simpsons Ride and Star Tours at Disney's Hollywood Studios. You're seated in a ride vehicle that faces a large IMAX-size video screen, onto which the attraction's story is projected. When the story calls for you to drop down the side of a building, your ride vehicle tilts forward as if you were falling; when you need to swerve left or right, your ride vehicle tilts the same way.

The ride's story serves as a mini sequel to the original animated movie *Despicable Me,* starring Gru, the archvillain, along with his adopted daughters and his diminutive yellow Minions. The preshow area is inside Dr. Gru's house, where you see his unique family tree and other artifacts. Our favorite is the mounted lion's head (in the lion's mouth is a dog, in the dog's mouth is a cat, and in the cat's mouth is a mouse). The premise of the ride is that you're being turned into one of Dr. Gru's Minions. Once converted you must navigate the Minion Training Grounds, where your "speed, strength, and ability not to die" are tested. Something soon goes amiss, though, and your training turns into a frenetic rescue operation. The events of this ride take place exactly one year after the original *Despicable Me* film; a subplot of the ride involves Gru's daughters (Edith, Agnes, and Margo) celebrating the anniversary of their adoption.

The ride itself is a fast-paced series of dives, climbs, and tight turns through Gru's Rube Goldberg–esque machines. Like The Simpsons Ride, there are more sight gags and interesting things to see here than anyone possibly could in a single ride. Luckily, it's Universal's least intense motion simulator, so re-rides are less likely to make you lose your lunch. Guests exit the ride into a disco party with interactive video screens and a photo op where they can boogie down with a Minion.

TOURING TIPS Despicable Me Minion Mayhem is unfortunately situated at the very front of the park, within a few yards of the entrance turnstiles, and usually begins operating before the official opening time. As a result, long lines develop as soon as the park opens. If you're among the first to enter and the wait is 20 minutes or less, get in line for Despicable Me, and then ride Hollywood Rip Ride Rockit. However, if the line for Despicable Me exceeds 20 minutes, try late afternoon or the hour before the park closes.

The perspective from simulators on the sides can be skewed, and the vehicles up front are a bit too close. For the best view, you want to be in the middle of one of the center rows. Stationary seating is available for those prone to motion sickness and for children less than 40 inches tall; ask an attendant for directions. On busy days they occasionally open a queue with direct access to stationary seating, which can significantly slash your wait time.

Villain-Con Minion Blast *(Universal Express)* ★★★½

APPEAL BY AGE PRESCHOOL ★★★★½ **GRADE SCHOOL** ★★★½ **TEENS** ★★★½
YOUNG ADULTS ★★★½   **OVER 30** ★★★½   **SENIORS** ★★★½

What it is Stand-up shooting gallery meets moving sidewalk. **Scope and scale** Major attraction. **When to go** After experiencing the park's headliners. **Comments** No minimum height requirement, but children must be able to stand up on their own, and kids under 48" must be accompanied by an adult; child swap available (see page 187). **Duration of ride** Almost 6 minutes. **Loading speed** Fast.

DESCRIPTION AND COMMENTS Universal's second Minion-themed attraction, which opened in the summer of 2023, lets guests attend the annual evildoers' convention—inconspicuously held inside an Orlando theme park—and compete to join the Vicious 6 (as introduced in the second Minions movie) by wreaking havoc with interactive blasters. Televisions tuned to the Villain News Network brief aspiring baddies on the use of their E-Liminator X devices, which riders receive after touring a brief indoor queue of trade show booths bursting with comical sight gags; be sure to get a selfie with the animated alligator in an aquarium.

Unlike Buzz Lightyear or Men in Black, there's no ride vehicle here; rather, guests stand on a moving walkway that can navigate corners, gliding like luggage on an airport conveyor belt past giant video screens surrounded by static physical sets. The wireless guns have two triggers—one for unlimited single shots and a second for launching big blasts, which must be reloaded by hitting marked ammo crates—and each sports a tiny circular screen displaying your score and ammo. Competitors battle the Vicious 6's five current members (voiced by the original actors) through an art gallery, a futuristic sports stadium, and a seizure-inducing discotheque, before arriving at a final showdown against Scarlet Overkill and other rivals above Universal's CityWalk.

TIP: Hit the large glowing cubes to upgrade your primary pew-pew, then target the villain until a special ammo crate appears, and use it to launch their own weapon against them for massive points.

Villain-Con Minion Blast's massive screens are impressively sharp and colorful, and there are more Minions than you can shake a banana at, although their humor is largely lost amid the ceaseless explosions. Crucially, the attraction's gameplay is disappointingly unsatisfying in comparison to its aforementioned predecessors. The on-screen action is often overwhelmingly chaotic, making it difficult to discern which of the tiny targeting reticules belongs to you (your gun will display your color and symbol briefly before you board the belt). Although the blasters buzz with every shot, there's little haptic feedback or sense of accomplishment when you connect, making the whole experience feel like a succession of video game boss battles that you can never win. It's worth a try (or two) if the line isn't long, but it lacks the long-term replay value of similar interactive attractions. Passholding regulars may become hooked on climbing the leaderboard—which displays daily, seasonal, and all-time top competitors—but for most vacationers Minion Blast will be a one-and-done experience. This reaction from a St. Louis, Missouri, family is typical:

> In comparison to Midway Mania, it was very difficult to discern your target and what you were trying to shoot . . . it felt like just standing, moving along a conveyor belt, pulling the trigger but not knowing what to shoot at, and getting a score at the end.

TOURING TIPS Like its Minion Mayhem sibling across the street, Villain-Con's location near the park's entrance dooms it to draw crowds all morning; luckily, the conveyor system (which is capable of carrying a guest every 2.5 seconds) should keep the queue moving consistently. We think Villain-Con is worth about a 30-minute wait at most; if the standby queue fills the barely shaded overflow lot, skip it and try again later.

Use the Universal mobile app to track your scores and virtual trophies by tapping your phone against your blaster between pickup and stepping on the belt. After your first ride, you'll begin completing challenges that unlock permanent upgrades for your blaster, which can be activated in the app before your next attempt. Once aboard, stay put atop your designated dot, or your weapon will stop working; if your gun reports network errors throughout your ride, ask at the exit for another try.

Wheelchair users can roll right onto the belt, but ECV drivers must transfer to a standard chair. The two-handed blasters weigh nearly 4 pounds, and the triggers have a heavy pull with no repeating auto-fire, which may tire out adults (not to mention kids or disabled guests) by the end of the surprisingly lengthy attraction. Lightweight noninteractive toy E-Liminators are offered for li'l villains, and are not-so-coincidentally sold in the exit gift shop. Now that's truly evil!

NEW YORK

THE CITY STREETS OF THE BIG APPLE are re-created in this section of USF. Along with London and Hollywood, New York represents some of the best theming found in the park. Make sure to explore the crooked alleyways behind *The Blues Brothers* stage for some authentic-looking urban backdrops.

In 2023, the remnants of Production Central that weren't transformed into Minion Land were reassigned to New York, including **Music Plaza Stage,** a Hollywood Bowl–inspired amphitheater with an artificial turf viewing lawn (where you'll often find unconscious tourists sprawled on sunny days) that's used during Mardi Gras concerts and similar special events. There's also access (when applicable) from here to the soundstages used for TV production and Halloween haunted houses.

New York has four attractions, one sit-down restaurant, one counter-service restaurant, an arcade, and a Starbucks café. *The Blues Brothers Show* and other musical acts (see page 224) also perform here. First Aid is located in the alley behind Louie's Italian Restaurant.

Hollywood Rip Ride Rockit (Universal Express)   ★★★½

APPEAL BY AGE	PRESCHOOL ★½	GRADE SCHOOL ★★★★	TEENS ★★★★½
YOUNG ADULTS ★★★★		OVER 30 ★★★★	SENIORS ★★★

What it is High-tech roller coaster. **Scope and scale** Headliner. **When to go** The first hour after park opening or late afternoon. **Comments** 51" minimum height requirement; child swap available (see page 187); single-rider line available. **Duration of ride** 2½ minutes. **Loading speed** Moderate.

DESCRIPTION AND COMMENTS Let's start with the basics: Rip Ride Rockit is a sit-down X-Car coaster that runs on a 3,800-foot steel track, with a maximum height of 167 feet and a top speed of 65 mph. Manufactured by German coaster maker Maurer AG, X-Car vehicles are more maneuverable than most other kinds and use less restrictive restraints, making for an exhilarating ride.

You ascend—vertically—at 11 feet per second to crest the 17-story-tall first hill, one of the highest points reached by any roller coaster in Orlando. The drop is almost vertical, too, launching you into Double Take, a 136-foot-tall loop inversion in which you begin on the inside of the loop, twist to the outside at the top (so you're upright), and then twist back inside the loop for the descent. Other innovative track elements include a treble clef–shaped twist and a spiraling negative-g Jump Cut maneuver.

The ride starts behind Minion Land; weaves into the New York area near Race Through New York Starring Jimmy Fallon, popping out over the heads of guests in the square below; and then storms out toward the lagoon separating USF from CityWalk.

Each train consists of two cars, with riders arranged two across in three rows per car. Each row is outfitted with color-changing LEDs and high-end audio and video technology for each seat. Like Rock 'n' Roller Coaster at Disney's Hollywood Studios, the "Triple R" features a musical soundtrack, but in this case you can choose the genre of music you want to hear as you ride: rock, disco, country, hip-hop, or electronica. The ride has dozens of hidden songs in its catalog. Press the Rip Ride Rockit logo on the number pad for 10 seconds, then enter 113 to hear Led Zeppelin's "Immigrant Song." Press 902 to hear The Muppets sing "The Rainbow Connection," or enter 130 to hear The Who's "Won't Get Fooled Again." For the complete list, see theugseries.com/rockitsongs.

When it's over, Universal sells both still photos and a digital video of your ride, which intercuts stock footage of the coaster with clips of you screaming, as recorded by your seat-mounted camera. The video costs $37, or $43 with a 5-by-7-inch print and digital copy; My Universal Photos members pay $21 for just the video.

While perfectly safe, Rip Ride Rockit subjects you to a lot of side-to-side jarring. To crib a phrase from Tina Turner, some folks like it easy . . . and some folks like it *rough*. This reader from Armonk, New York, definitely falls in the former category:

> *Despite the fact that I love roller coasters and am in good physical shape with no issues, Hollywood Rip Ride Rockit hurt my back. My 17-year-old daughter who also loves all rides didn't love it either.*

A Seattle visitor volunteers this visceral warning:

> *Tell older people not to go on Rip Ride Rockit. I don't know how anyone stands it. I call it the Punisher because it was a minute of sheer pain. It is so incredibly bumpy that I felt like I was being hit on the back of the head with a foam baseball bat for a full minute.*

And from another reader in Belgium, Wisconsin:

> *I've ridden many roller coasters in my 35 years, including some that were over 400 feet tall and with speeds in excess of 120 mph, yet I've never ridden one that was as painful and rough as Rip Ride Rockit. With the beating my head and neck took, I'll never ride that one again.*

On the other hand, this family from Lancaster, Pennsylvania, thinks Rockit is worth riding:

> *Our 10-year-old son rode Rip Ride Rockit four times with almost no waiting. This was a ride we hadn't even included in our plan because we thought it would be too scary and the lines not worth the wait. It ended up being a favorite experience of the trip.*

STELLA SAYS

RIP TO THE RIP RIDE ROCKIT? Rumors and speculation for the imminent closure of Hollywood Rip Ride Rockit have been swirling around for a couple of years, but some believe its time may actually be up. The strongest theory for what could replace this aging coaster is for an East Coast version of Universal Studios Hollywood's upcoming *Fast & Furious*–themed drifting coaster to take its spot here in Florida. If Rockit is still around during your next visit, you may want to have one last ride . . . just in case.

This Whalton, England, mom sums up the ride's generational divide:

A fabulous, gut-wrenching coaster that thrilled the socks off my 8- and 9-year-olds. (Mum found it a bit too brutal to repeat.)

TOURING TIPS Because the ride is so close to the USF entrance, it's a crowd magnet, creating bottlenecks from park opening on. Your best chance to ride without a long wait is to be one of the first to enter the queue when it opens (typically 15 minutes after park opening), or use the single-rider entrance. You'll have to empty your pockets into a free locker and pass through a metal detector before queuing.

Race Through New York Starring Jimmy Fallon
(Universal Express) ★★★½

**APPEAL BY AGE   PRESCHOOL ★★★½   GRADE SCHOOL ★★★★   TEENS ★★★½
YOUNG ADULTS ★★★½   OVER 30 ★★★½   SENIORS ★★★★**

What it is Comedic 3-D simulator ride. **Scope and scale** Headliner. **When to go** Before noon or after 4 p.m. **Comments** 40" minimum height requirement; child swap available (see page 187). **Duration of ride** 4 minutes. **Loading speed** Moderate.

Motion Sickness

DESCRIPTION AND COMMENTS Housed in a replica of NBC's historic 30 Rock offices in Manhattan, Race Through New York begins in the NBC offices lobby with a museum paying tribute to the previous hosts of *The Tonight Show:* Steve Allen (1954–1956), Jack Paar (1957–1962), Johnny Carson (1962–1992), Jay Leno (1992–2009 and 2010–2014), and Conan O'Brien (2009–2010).

Once you ascend to the second floor, you await your ride in a fancy lounge out-fitted with couches and touch screen tables with video games inspired by *The Tonight Show Starring Jimmy Fallon.* The main attraction, however, is live appear-ances by *Tonight Show* mascot Hashtag the Panda (a dancing fur character—celeb-rity guests who have worn the costume range from Chris Rock to Miley Cyrus).

Now it's time to make your way to Jimmy Fallon's studio. The Roots, Fallon's house band, rap the safety instructions before you enter a 72-seat theater with a large screen. Next, you'll don 3-D glasses and race against Fallon in his souped-up Tonight Rider roadster. Starting at the *Tonight Show* studio, the competition sends you careening through the streets and subways of New York and eventually to, yes, the moon. Fans create wind effects, and there are the obligatory water sprays. (Hey, it's Universal!)

The preshow areas get a lot of points, and the ride itself has some of the sharpest visuals and smoothest movement in the Universal repertoire. But it breaks no new tech-nical ground for the genre, and it relies on recognition of Fallon's stable of characters (like Ew! Girl and Tight Pants Man) for its jokes, which grow stale after several view-ings. And although Jimmy's simulator doesn't jostle as violently as some, numerous riders report that it nauseated them. Race Through New York gets mixed reviews from our readers; this visitor from Crystal Lake, Illinois, represents the majority opinion:

I was surprised with how unimpressed I was with Race Through New York with Jimmy Fallon. Universal has raised the bar so much and has done such an amazing job with everything that I had big hopes for this ride. In the end, it was OK, but not as good as I expected.

But others agree with this family from Vadnais Heights, Minnesota:

We went on it twice, and all the kids loved it. The kids really liked the games they could play before they went on the ride, and they had fun with Hashtag the Panda.

TOURING TIPS Race Through New York originally operated with a mandatory Virtual Line system, but walk-ins are now accepted throughout the day. The wonderful

Ragtime Gals male vocal quintet sadly only performs their tongue-in-cheek barbershop interpretations of pop hits during peak season (if then). Request a free **studio tour** for a guided glimpse backstage, including a peek into the ride's control room, a visit to the private VIP balcony, and possibly a private audience with Hashtag. Tours are subject to staff availability; try asking at the attraction entrance around 10 a.m. or 4 p.m.

Revenge of the Mummy *(Universal Express)*   ★★★★½

| APPEAL BY AGE | PRESCHOOL ★½ | GRADE SCHOOL ★★★★ | TEENS ★★★★½ |
| YOUNG ADULTS ★★★★½ | | OVER 30 ★★★★½ | SENIORS ★★★★ |

What it is Combination dark ride and roller coaster. **Scope and scale** Headliner. **When to go** The first 2 hours the park is open or after 4 p.m. **Comments** 48" minimum height requirement; child swap available (see page 187); single-rider line available. Not to be missed. **Duration of ride** 3 minutes. **Loading speed** Moderate–fast.

Motion Sickness

DESCRIPTION AND COMMENTS Revenge of the Mummy is a high-tech hybrid indoor roller coaster/dark ride based on the *Mummy* flicks starring Brendan Fraser (with no references to the Tom Cruise reboot). The ride's premise is that a movie production crew has taken over New York's Museum of Antiquities to film a sequel titled *Revenge of the Mummy*. The queuing area serves to establish the story line: you're in a group touring a set from the *Mummy* films when you enter a tomb where the fantasy world of film gives way to the real thing. You'll notice lots of interactive details built into the queue, including hints that the movie filming isn't going according to plan. By the time you board your clunky, jeeplike ride vehicle, you've learned that the movie's villain, Imhotep, is trying to use the film crew's souls to become immortal. Only the mystical Medjai symbol can save you from certain doom (cue dramatic music).

The ride begins as a slow, very elaborate dark ride, passing through various chambers, including one where flesh-eating scarab beetles descend on you. Suddenly your vehicle stops and then drops backward and rotates. Here's where you're shot at high speed up the first hill of the roller-coaster part of the ride. We won't give away any of Mummy's secrets, but here's what you need to know: It's mostly in the dark and there are no loops, inversions, or any kind of upside-downness; there are plenty of tight turns and high-speed drops and a maximum speed of around 45 mph. Though it's a wild ride by anyone's definition, the emphasis remains as much on the visuals, robotics, and special effects as on the ride itself. The track and special effects were given a thorough overhaul in 2022 and look as good as ever: video effects, animatronics, lighting, and enough fire-spewing gas vents to rotisserie a chicken. The endings (yes, plural) are pretty clever.

TOURING TIPS Try to ride during the first 2 hours the park is open. If lines are long, one fallback is to use the singles line, which can cut your wait to a third of the posted wait time and is sometimes more expedient than Universal Express. If you must wait on a hot day, the consolation is that Mummy's air-conditioning system is one of the best in the park.

STELLA SAYS

REVENGE OF THE MUMMY As you enter the building, you can spot two large, ancient-looking doors leaning against the wall on the left of the "Hot Set"–themed first room. These hieroglyphic-filled slabs of wood were used in the actual filming for *The Mummy* starring Brendan Fraser, serving as the doors to the Museum of Antiquities!

The front left seat gets the best view of the animatronic effects, while the back corner seats offer the most air time in the coaster sections. Request row three for extra legroom if you found the test seat outside the attraction entrance to be a tight fit. Concerning motion sickness, if you can ride Space Mountain without ill effect, you should be fine on Revenge of the Mummy. Finally, note that the Mummy's queue contains enough scary stuff to frighten little kids all on its own. While most grade-schoolers we surveyed who were plucky enough to ride the Mummy gave it high marks, one father feels the rating for that age group is inappropriate:

> This ride should NOT be recommended for grade-schoolers. My second-grader (who wasn't scared at all on Space Mountain) was terrified during this ride and cried afterward. I'm really upset I encouraged her to ride it and worried she'll have nightmares. Even I thought it was quite scary, and other adults on our ride echoed the same. You should really consider a warning about the VERY frightening aspects of this ride.

However, this reader thinks we've oversold the Mummy's fright factor:

> We disagree with you about Revenge of the Mummy. We read your description and were anticipating being scared. While the coaster aspect is a fun ride, otherwise it wasn't scary in the slightest.

Ask the greeter out front for a free **production tour;** if it isn't too busy, they may escort you into the maintenance area, where you can watch the coaster cars fly overhead.

Transformers: The Ride–3D *(Universal Express)* ★★★★

APPEAL BY AGE PRESCHOOL ★★★ GRADE SCHOOL ★★★★ TEENS ★★★★
YOUNG ADULTS ★★★★   OVER 30 ★★★★   SENIORS ★★★★

What it is Multisensory 3-D dark ride. **Scope and scale** Super-headliner. **When to go** First hour the park is open or after 4 p.m. **Comments** 40" minimum height requirement; child swap available (see page 187); single-rider line available. Not to be missed. **Duration of ride** 4½ minutes. **Loading speed** Moderate-fast.

DESCRIPTION AND COMMENTS Transformers—those toy robots from the 1980s that you turned and twisted into trucks and planes—have been around long enough to go from commercial to kitsch to cool and back again. Thanks to director-producer Michael Bay's movie series, most recently represented by 2023's *Rise of the Beasts,* "Robots in Disguise" are again a blockbuster global franchise. In 2013 Transformers fans finally received a USF attraction (cloned from earlier rides in Singapore and Hollywood) befitting their pop-culture idols. Recruits to this cybertronic war enlist by entering the N.E.S.T. Base—headquarters of the heroic Autobots and their human allies—beneath a 28-foot-tall statue of Optimus Prime. Inside an extensive, elaborately detailed queue, video monitors catch you up on the backstory. Basically, the Decepticon baddies are after the All-Spark, the source of cybernetic sentience. We're supposed to safeguard the shard by hitching a ride aboard our friendly Autobot ride vehicle EVAC, presumably without getting smooshed like a Lincoln in a souvenir penny press every time he shifts into android form. Needless to say, Megatron and his pals Starscream and Devastator won't make things easy, but you'll have Sideswipe and Bumblebee (in his modern Camaro form; look for an old-school Volkswagen Beetle in the final scene) backing you up. For the ride's 4½ minutes, you play human Ping-Pong ball in an epic battle between these Made in Japan behemoths.

To do justice to this Bay-splosion-packed war of good versus evil, Transformers harnesses the same traveling simulator system behind Islands of Adventure's

STELLA SAYS

AT TRANSFORMERS: THE RIDE–3D, a secret signature can be found just to the right of the ride entrance. "Gr39-0430" is written on the rolling garage door. Gr39 stands for Gregory Hall, an art director for the ride, and 0430 is his birthday, April 30. You may spot his unique signature hidden around other attractions as well.

Amazing Adventures of Spider-Man ride, and it ups the ante with photo-realistic high-definition imagery, boosted by dichroic 3-D glasses that produce remarkably sharp, vivid visuals. The plot amounts to little more than a giant game of keep-away, and the uninitiated will likely be unable to tell one meteoric mass of metal from another, but you'll be too dazzled by the debris whizzing by to notice. Fanboys will squeal with delight at hearing original cartoon actors Peter Cullen and Frank Welker voicing the pugilistic protagonists, and then they'll spill into the postride gift shop to purchase armloads of exclusive merchandise, while the rest of us might need a bench on which to take a breather afterward. We'll admit slight disappointment at not getting to see an actual four-story-tall animatronic transform, but the ride's mix of detailed (though largely static) set pieces and video projections was likely a much more maintenance-friendly solution for bringing these colossi to life. Either way, this is one of the most intense, immersive thrill rides found in any theme park. However, Transformers doesn't hold up as well after repeated rides as The Amazing Adventures of Spider-Man, as it lacks the humor, heart, and moving props of its predecessor. Two millennials had, shall we say, a visceral take on Transformers:

The illusion of being smashed through an office building is pretty convincing. If you've ever wondered what it would be like to be eaten, digested, and pooped out of a giant robot, this is the ride for you.

Hopefully, it's also a ride for those who don't exactly see Transformers as a trip down the alimentary canal. Robots poop? Who knew?

TOURING TIPS This ride draws crowds. Your only solace is that The Wizarding World of Harry Potter—Diagon Alley draws even larger throngs. The single-rider line will get you on board faster, but it may be closed off if it becomes backed up. Finally, it's hard to focus on the fast-moving imagery from the front row; center seats in the second and third rows provide the best perspective.

SAN FRANCISCO

UNIVERSAL'S TRIBUTE TO Baghdad by the Bay is a bit too abbreviated to leave your heart in, but the designers did manage to squeeze in an attraction, along with a number of eateries and shops, into only a couple of blocks of brick and boardwalk. Be on the lookout for Bruce the shark; this trophy formerly stood in front of the Jaws ride and was transplanted to the Frisco wharf once that attraction sailed away.

Fast & Furious: Supercharged *(Universal Express)* ★★½

APPEAL BY AGE	PRESCHOOL ★★	GRADE SCHOOL ★★★	TEENS ★★½
YOUNG ADULTS ★★½		OVER 30 ★★½	SENIORS ★★½

What it is Car chase motion simulator. **Scope and scale** Headliner. **When to go** After experiencing the other headliners. **Comment** 40" minimum height requirement; child swap available (see page 187); single-rider line available. **Duration of ride** 5 minutes. **Loading speed** Fast.

STELLA SAYS

A FAST & FURIOUSLY SLOW DEATH Fast & Furious: Supercharged is now operating on a seasonal basis, which has led many to ponder if it's time to start carving its headstone. While it may be convenient to temporarily close Supercharged during the Halloween Horror Nights months (since a section of its queue is used for a haunted house), that doesn't necessarily mean it's on its way out. However, if Hollywood Rip Ride Rockit is in fact replaced by a new *Fast & Furious*–themed drifting coaster, as some believe, that could be the answer to Dom's "Ride or die" quote.

DESCRIPTION AND COMMENTS Based on the $5.9 billion box office behemoth, the Fast & Furious experience starts in the elaborate industrial queue (inspired by San Francisco's historic Oriental Warehouse) where you can check out some of the high-performance automobiles seen in the films. Gearheads will weep with envy, while anyone who isn't into exotic cars may feel like they're stuck in their local garage waiting for a lube job. The latter can amuse themselves by hunting for hidden references in the queue to the *Beetlejuice* and *Disaster!* attractions that previously occupied the area.

Next, two preshows, featuring live hosts awkwardly interacting with prerecorded clips of Jordana Brewster (Mia Toretto) and Chris "Ludacris" Bridges (Tej), establish the backstory for anyone who hasn't yet seen all—or any—of the 11 (and counting) *Furious* films.

After boarding specially designed 48-passenger tramlike "party buses," you're taken to an underground club, where a postrace rave party is in full swing until the feds crash the party, searching for a crucial crime witness hiding among the guests. Series stars Vin Diesel (Dominic "Dom" Toretto), Dwayne Johnson (Luke Hobbs), Michelle Rodriguez (Letty Ortiz), and Tyrese Gibson (Roman Pearce) appear in holographic form to rescue you from Luke Evans (Owen Shaw), the bad guy from *Fast & Furious 6*. In the attraction's climax, a 360-degree projection tunnel—filled with hydraulic platforms, 400-foot-long screens, and excessive sprays of smoke and water—make it appear as if your ride vehicle is in the midst of a high-stakes car chase, speeding at 100-plus mph through a West Coast urban jungle.

Fast & Furious: Supercharged is similar to Skull Island: Reign of Kong in Islands of Adventure, but without the immersive scenery or impressive animatronics. The dialogue and visual effects are shockingly cheesy even by theme park standards (some consider this part of the appeal). It all goes by in such a nitro-fueled blur that it may not matter to fans of the flicks, but this reader from Nebraska City agrees with our negative assessment:

> *You warned us that the Fast & Furious ride was bad, but we had to try it once. You were right; it is stunningly, laughably bad. So bad! Plus it was hard to see the screens, so we missed what little did happen.*

TOURING TIPS This ride is only open from 10 a.m. to 6 p.m., and closes from late August until November. Standard standby, Universal Express, and single-rider lines are available; as a bonus, single riders bypass the embarrassing preshows.

The best views are from the center/right seats in the first bus; stay to the left if the queue splits before the loading dock. Though less scary than the King Kong ride, Supercharged has a slightly higher height requirement. Luckily, the custom slot car racing game in the child swap room may be more fun than the actual attraction. Ask for a **garage tour** when staff is available for an up-close look at the exotic cars and Easter eggs in the queue.

THE WIZARDING WORLD OF HARRY POTTER—DIAGON ALLEY

BUILT IN THE WAKE of the success of IOA's original Harry Potter land, USF's Wizarding World is a 7-acre self-contained area featuring two London sites that figure prominently in the Potter saga: Diagon Alley, a secret part of London that is a sort of sorcerers' shopping mall, and the King's Cross railroad station, where wizarding students embark for the train trip to Hogwarts. Detailed waterfront facades, anchored by the **King's Cross railroad station** on the left and including **Grimmauld Place** and **Wyndham's Theatre,** recall West London scenes from the books and movies. **Diagon Alley,** secreted behind the London street scene, is accessed through a secluded entrance in the middle of the facade.

Once you're in the London area, take a moment to spot Kreacher (the house elf regularly peers from a second-story window above 12 Grimmauld Place); dial MAGIC (62442) in the red phone booth for a message from the Ministry of Magic; poke your head in the back door of the triple-decker purple Knight Bus; and chat with the Knight Bus conductor and his Caribbean-accented shrunken head. For some Easter eggs from the attraction designers—including the first of several tributes to Jaws, the original occupant of this area—inspect the record albums in the music store window. You'll also find a couple of cabmen's shelters selling snacks (jacket potatoes, British crisps, and hot dogs in cylindrical buns) and London souvenirs, along with an exacting replica of the towering Shaftesbury Memorial Fountain from Piccadilly Circus.

Now enter Diagon Alley next to the Leicester Square marquee in the approximate center of the building facades. As in the books and films, the unmarked portal is concealed within a magical brick wall ordinarily reserved for wizards and the like. (Unfortunately, the wall doesn't actually move, due to safety concerns.) The endless parade of Muggles (also known as plain old humans) in shorts and flip-flops will leave little doubt where that entryway is.

Once admitted, look down the alley to the rounded facade of **Gringotts Wizarding Bank,** where a 40-foot fire-breathing Ukrainian Ironbelly dragon (as seen in *Harry Potter and the Deathly Hallows: Part 2*) perches atop the dome. The dragon doesn't move, but about every 10 minutes (weather permitting), he unleashes a jet of flame; get your camera ready when you hear him growl. To your left is the **Leaky Cauldron,** the area's flagship restaurant, serving authentically hearty British pub fare.

Intersecting Diagon Alley near the Leaky Cauldron is **Knockturn Alley,** a labyrinth of twisting passageways where the Harry Potter bad guys hang out. A covered walk-through area with a projected sky creating perpetual night, it features spooky special effects in the faux shop windows—don't miss the creeping tattoos and crawling spiders! Finally, to the right of Gringotts is **Carkitt Market,** a canopy-covered plaza where short live shows are staged every half hour or so. All the sections of Diagon Alley are crammed with elaborate signage, animated window displays, and seemingly endless hidden details to discover.

Diagon Alley Attractions
Harry Potter and the Escape from Gringotts
(Universal Express) ★★★★½

Motion Sickness

APPEAL BY AGE   PRESCHOOL ★★½   GRADE SCHOOL ★★★★½   TEENS ★★★★½
YOUNG ADULTS ★★★★½   OVER 30 ★★★★½   SENIORS ★★★★

What it is Super-high-tech 3-D dark ride with roller-coaster elements. **Scope and scale** Super-headliner. **When to go** First thing during early entry or in the late afternoon. **Comments** 42″ minimum height requirement; child swap available (see page 187); single-rider line available. Not to be missed. **Duration of ride** 4½ minutes. **Loading speed** Moderate-fast.

DESCRIPTION AND COMMENTS Owned and operated by goblins, Gringotts is the Federal Reserve of the wizarding economy, as well as the scene of memorable sequences from the first and final Potter installments. Harry Potter and the Escape from Gringotts incorporates a substantial part of the overall experience into its elaborate queue, which even nonriders should experience. As Muggles opening new accounts, you enter through the bank's chandelier-adorned lobby, where you're critically appraised by glowering animatronic goblins. Your path takes you to a "security checkpoint," where a souvenir photo may be snapped, and past animated newspapers and office windows, before you experience two full preshows where the scenario is set up. In the first, goblin banker Blordak and Bill Weasley (Ron's curse-breaking big brother, played by Domhnall Gleeson) prepare you for an introductory tour of the underground vaults. Then you're off for a convincing simulated 9-mile plunge into the earth aboard an "elevator" with a bouncing floor and ceiling projections. All this is before you pick up your 3-D glasses and ascend a spiral staircase into the stalactite-festooned boarding cave where your vault cart awaits.

Gringotts's ornately industrial ride vehicles consist of two-car trains, each holding 24 people in rows of four. The ride merges Revenge of the Mummy's indoor coaster aspects with The Amazing Adventures of Spider-Man's seamless integration of high-resolution 3-D film (the finale dome completely surrounds your cart) and massive sculptural sets (some of the rockwork inside is six stories tall), while adding a few new tricks, such as independently rotating carts and motion-simulator bases built into the track. There are no animatronic figures or pyrotechnics along the ride, but you will get spritzed with water, blasted with warm air, and sprayed with fog—this is Universal, after all.

Visitors enter the bank at the exact moment Harry, Ron, Hermione, and Griphook have arrived to liberate Helga Hufflepuff's Cup Horcrux from Bellatrix Lestrange's vault, as seen in *Harry Potter and the Deathly Hallows: Part 2*. Familiar film moments, featuring the vaults' guardian dragon, play out in the ride's background as Bellatrix and Lord Voldemort (Helena Bonham Carter and Ralph Fiennes, reprising their screen roles) appear to menace you with snakes and sinister spells, whereupon the heroic trio pauses its quest to save your hapless posteriors. The storytelling is much more coherent than Forbidden Journey's hodgepodge approach, cleverly allowing fans to relive a favorite adventure without merely rehashing the plot.

The result is a ride that combines favorite innovations from its predecessors in an exhilarating way, making it (despite some murky visuals and muddled dialogue) one of Universal's most iconic themed thrill attractions. These New England honeymooners speak for most of our readers:

> *Gringotts is a terrific ride! Less intense than the Forbidden Journey but still full of surprises.*

TOURING TIPS If you're a Universal resort guest and you qualify for early entry, use it; Express Passes aren't valid during early entry, so the line moves swiftly.

Otherwise, try the attraction around lunchtime or in the late afternoon; wait times usually peak after opening but become reasonable later in the day.

As far as physical thrills go, Gringotts falls somewhere between Disney's Seven Dwarfs Mine Train and Space Mountain, with only one short (albeit unique) drop and no upside-down flips. It was designed to be less intense (read: less nauseating) than Forbidden Journey. The restraints are similar to Revenge of the Mummy's, with bars across your lap and shins, but slightly more restrictive. Use the test seat to the left of the front entrance if you're unsure, and request the third or sixth row for additional legroom.

The front row is closest to the action and has the scariest view of the drop; 3-D effects look better farther back. The sixth row gets the most coaster action, especially from the initial fall, but the screens are slightly distorted. The far right seat in row four is the sweet spot.

You must leave your bags in a free locker. The only part of the preshow experience that Universal Express guests miss is the boring outdoor queue. The singles line will cut your wait to about a third of the posted standby time, but you'll skip all the preshows past the lobby; we don't advise this option until after your first ride. Ask for a **bank tour** to explore the queue's details without riding (when staff is available).

Hogwarts Express *(Universal Express)* ★★★★½

What it is Transportation attraction. **Scope and scale** Headliner. **When to go** Late morning or just before park closing. **Comments** Requires a park-to-park ticket. Not to be missed. **Duration of ride** 4 minutes. **Loading speed** Moderate.

DESCRIPTION AND COMMENTS Part of the genius of creating Diagon Alley at USF is that it's connected to Hogsmeade at IOA (see Part Seven) by Hogwarts Express, just as in the novels and films. The counterpart to Hogsmeade Station in IOA is USF's King's Cross Station, a landmark London train depot that has been re-created a few doors down from Diagon Alley's hidden entrance. (Note that King's Cross has a separate entrance and exit from Diagon Alley; you can't go directly between them without crossing through the London Waterfront.)

The passage to Platform 9¾, from which Hogwarts students depart on their way to school, is concealed from Muggles by a seemingly solid brick wall, through which you'll witness guests ahead of you dematerializing. (Spoiler: The Pepper's Ghost effect creates a clever but congestion-prone photo op, but you experience only a dark corridor with whooshing sound effects when crossing over yourself.)

Once on the platform, you'll pass an animatronic Hedwig owl perching atop a pile of luggage before being assigned to one of the three train cars' seven compartments. The train itself looks exactly authentic to the *n*th degree, from the billowing steam to the brass fixtures and upholstery in your eight-passenger private cabin. Along your one-way Hogwarts Express journey, you'll see moving images projected beyond the windows of the car rather than the park's backstage areas, with the streets of London and the Scottish countryside rolling past outside your window. The screen isn't 3-D, but it's slightly curved to conceal the edges and create a convincing illusion of depth. Even more impressive are the frosted-glass doors you enter through, which turn out to be amazing screens that make it seem as if someone is standing on the other side. You experience a different presentation coming and going, and in addition to pastoral scenery, there are surprise appearances by secondary characters (Fred and George Weasley, Hagrid) and threats en route (bone-chilling Dementors, licorice spiders), augmented by vibration and sound effects in the cars.

Hogwarts Express isn't an adrenaline rush in the same way that Escape from Gringotts is, but for those invested in Potter lore, it may be even more emotionally thrilling. And unlike most Potter attractions, it can be experienced by the whole family, regardless of size.

TOURING TIPS Because taking the train involves park-hopping, passengers need a valid park-to-park ticket. Disembarking passengers must enter the second park and, if desired, queue again for their return trip. You'll be allowed to upgrade your one-park Base Ticket at the station entrance.

Lines rarely exceed 15 minutes in the morning, though the queue may swell to an hour in midafternoon, or in the evening when one park closes before the other. At these times, the wait for Express may be as long as one-third of the posted standby estimate. The walk from one train station to the other is just under a mile and takes 20 minutes at a moderate pace. If the posted wait is more than 15 minutes, it's typically quicker to walk to the other Wizarding World than to take the train.

Guests exiting in Hogsmeade have a chance to take a photo with the locomotive before it backs out for its next run. Guests departing from Hogsmeade should pose with the static train outside the station before they queue up.

Ollivanders ★★★★

APPEAL BY AGE PRESCHOOL ★★★★ GRADE SCHOOL ★★★★½ TEENS ★★★★
YOUNG ADULTS ★★★★   OVER 30 ★★★★   SENIORS ★★★★

What it is Combination wizarding demonstration and shopping op. **Scope and scale** Minor attraction. **When to go** First thing in the morning or after 4 p.m. **Comments** Audience stands. **Duration of presentation** 6 minutes.

DESCRIPTION AND COMMENTS Ollivanders, which is located in Diagon Alley in the books and films, is represented by both a small branch in IOA (see page 264) and this much larger location in USF. While the original Hogsmeade outpost is a horrendous bottleneck, where guests roast in an unshaded queue, the Diagon Alley version has multiple cleverly concealed choosing chambers, changing it from a popular curiosity into an actual attraction. The experience inside both shops is identical in script and special effects.

Every few minutes, following a scene from the Harry Potter books, a wand-selection show takes place, where a random customer (often a child dressed in Potter regalia) is selected to take part in a wand-choosing ceremony. Usually just one person in each group gets to be chosen by a wand, though occasionally siblings are selected together. This is one of the most truly imaginative elements of The Wizarding World: A Wandkeeper sizes you up and presents a wand, inviting you to try it out; your attempted spells produce unintended, unwanted, and highly amusing consequences. Ultimately, a wand chooses you, with all the attendant special effects. After the presentation, guests exit into a greatly enlarged gift shop, where interactive wands are available for purchase.

STELLA SAYS

NEW WAVE WANDS A new generation of wands—which connect with your smartphone app to earn "house points" and compete against fellow wizards—should become available before Epic Universe opens. Old wands will continue to work at current spellcasting locations in Diagon Alley and Hogsmeade, but updated wands may be required to take full advantage of the enhanced interactive experiences around the Ministry of Magic, as well as unlock a few brand-new effects hiding around the original Wizarding Worlds.

TOURING TIPS Ollivanders may distribute free return time reservations when the standby wait becomes excessive, which can all be claimed by midmorning on busy days. Ask an employee at the attraction entrance for details. Check out the self-sweeping broom (shades of *Fantasia*?) while waiting for the show. To increase your odds of being picked, be a cute kid, stand up front, and make eye contact. If your young 'un is selected to test-drive a wand, be forewarned that you'll have to buy it if you want to take it home.

Interactive Wands and Spell-Casting Locations in Diagon Alley

Interactive wands ($69) are available in 13 Ollivanders Original styles, including one exclusive to Universal Orlando; each comes with an explanation of the wand's lore. Interactive wands modeled after those wielded by a variety of characters (including Harry, Hermione, Dumbledore, Sirius Black, and Luna Lovegood) are also available at both **Ollivanders** outposts and in the smaller selection at **Wands by Gregorovitch** in Diagon Alley. The widest selection of wands is found in the two Ollivanders shops. Outside The Wizarding Worlds, stores at the entrance of each park, as well as at Universal Studios Stores in CityWalk and resort hotels, carry a limited variety of interactive wands, as well as toy "learner" wands ($32) for li'l wizards. Wands can also be ordered from Universal Orlando's merchandise website. *Note:* Noninteractive wands have been phased out at Universal Orlando; all wands currently for sale at the resort are interactive.

Medallions embedded in the ground designate a couple dozen locations split between the two Wizarding Worlds, where hidden cameras in storefront windows can detect the waving of these special wands and respond to the correct motions with special effects both projected and practical. You might use the swish and flick of Wingardium Leviosa to levitate an object or the figure-four Locomotor spell to animate another.

It can take some practice to get the hang of spell casting. Wizards wander around the area to assist novices and demonstrate spells (though they can't loan their wands), but queues to trigger certain effects can grow to a dozen deep at peak times. A map provided with each wand purchase details the location and movement for most effects, but there are some secret ones to uncover on your own. (Hint: One is in Scribbulus's window, and another is in the Slug & Jiggers storefront.) Look at your map under the ultraviolet lights in Knockturn Alley for another surprise.

Note that the price of the interactive wands includes unlimited activations of the hidden effects; you don't have to pay to recharge your wand on subsequent visits, or even replace a battery. Damaged wands are cheerfully repaired for free (even without the original box or receipt) at any Ollivanders, and globe-trotting wizards will be happy to know that their wands will also function at The Wizarding Worlds in Hollywood and Japan. If you encounter a spell-casting location with a sign saying CURRENTLY HAS AN ANTI-JINX IN PLACE, just move along to the next one; that's Potter-speak for "it's broken."

We've mostly received positive feedback on the interactive wands, like this praise from a New York family:

We took our interactive wand and explored all the many surprises for well over an hour and had a fantastic time. An interactive wand is highly recommended. Our girls are 12 and 14, and they had a blast making the wand motions and watching the windows come to life.

This Saint Paul, Minnesota, reader says Potter-loving visitors should set aside significant time for the interactive experiences:

I didn't realize how much of the Universal parks were the "experience" of the Harry Potter areas. Wandering around, sightseeing, and using the interactive wands in these areas were as important (maybe more so, for our family) as hitting the rides. I advise devoting prime time for this, especially early mornings before the lines for each interactive wand area get too long.

On the other hand, a cost-conscious dad from Rigby, Idaho, sends this advice:

If you don't want massive pressure from your kid to buy one of Universal's EXPENSIVE wands, don't do the wand ceremony. If you do it anyway, speak to an attendant prior to entering the ceremony room, and advise him or her that your kids ARE NOT to be wanded! Not getting your kid one of Universal's expensive wands will not ruin their lives—honest. And from what we saw, about half of the users couldn't get their wands to work reliably. The kids get very frustrated when the 5-year-old in front of them can make things appear, move, talk, or whatever, but they can't!

Entertainment in Diagon Alley

An elevated area in **Carkitt Market,** between The Hopping Pot and the Gringotts Money Exchange, comes to life with short shows inspired by the Potter stories. Though modest in scope, these are some of the best performances found at Universal, and well worth working into your touring plan if you have more than one day at the resort. Showtimes are listed in the smartphone app; performances usually start every 30 minutes on the hour and half hour.

Celestina Warbeck and the Banshees (★★★½) is a live musical showcasing the Ella Fitzgerald–esque Singing Sorceress with her comely backup crew, swinging to jazzy tunes with a 1940s big band feel. With swinging tunes such as "You Stole My Cauldron But You Can't Have My Heart," "A Cauldron Full of Hot Strong Love," and "You Charmed the Heart Right Out of Me," Celestina and her three Banshees perform a lively show. While the songs contain a plethora of references to the Potter books and movies that fans will love, guests who don't know (or care) about the Harry Potter universe will still enjoy the elaborate choreography, fantastic singing, and witty music and lyrics courtesy of Michael Weiner and Alan Zachary, the duo behind Disney Cruise Line's *Twice Charmed: An Original Twist on the Cinderella Story* and *Once Upon a Time*'s musical episode. During the holiday season, a special Christmas version is performed with different songs and costumes. The show runs about 12–13 minutes.

Tales of Beedle the Bard (★★★½) recounts the wizard fable "The Three Brothers" from *Harry Potter and the Deathly Hallows* using puppets crafted by Michael Curry (Broadway's *The Lion King* and *Finding Nemo—The Musical*). The puppets are gorgeous in a creepy kind of way, and the way the actors perform while maneuvering them is quite clever, though some of the dialogue can be difficult to understand. Some preschoolers may be scared of the large Death puppet. The show runs 8 minutes.

During September and October, **Lord Voldemort's masked Death Eaters** may be spotted roaming around Diagon Alley, lurking along the London waterfront, and stalking Knockturn's dark alleyways. They emerge during Halloween Horror Nights season, about an hour before the regular park closing time, and continue haunting the area throughout the evening event (see page 230).

Shopping in Diagon Alley

Shopping is a major component of Diagon Alley in Potter lore; while Hogsmeade visitors went wild for the few wizardly shops there, Diagon Alley is the planet's wackiest mall, with a vastly expanded array of enchanted tchotchkes to declare bankruptcy over. Shops include:

BORGIN AND BURKES in Knockturn Alley stocks objects from the dark side of magic (watch out for the mummified hand!).

GLOBUS MUNDI *(seasonal)* is a small travel agency–inspired shop in Carkitt Market that carries luggage tags, key chains, pins, and the like.

MADAM MALKIN'S ROBES FOR ALL OCCASIONS stocks school uniforms, Scottish wool sweaters, and dress robes for wizards and witches.

MAGICAL MENAGERIE is the place to adopt a plush cat, owl, or hippogriff; the adorable animatronic Kneazle is unfortunately not for sale.

OWL POST *(seasonal)* offers themed package wrapping, free postmarks, and shipping services from a small window near the Diagon Alley exit.

QUALITY QUIDDITCH SUPPLIES sells golden snitches and jerseys for your favorite Hogwarts house teams.

SCRIBBULUS carries quills, notebooks, and similar school supplies.

SHUTTERBUTTON'S will film your family in front of a green screen and insert you into a DVD of Potter scenes ($85 in a souvenir case) or a selection of still shots ($43 each, $133 for five; $32 each, $106 for five with My Universal Photos package). Loaner Gryffindor robes are available to pose in, but you'll have to bring your own wardrobe to represent a different Hogwarts house. Be warned that Slytherin-wear can interfere with the green screen effects.

SUGARPLUM'S SWEET SHOP tempts guests with fudge (including an unbearably sweet Butterbeer variety), pastries, no-melt ice cream (also known as a cup of icing), and Potter-themed candies.

WEASLEYS' WIZARD WHEEZES is a joke shop with toys and gags such as Skiving Snackboxes and Decoy Detonators. Look up through the three-story shop's glass ceiling for fireworks.

WISEACRE'S WIZARDING EQUIPMENT, located at the exit of Harry Potter and the Escape from Gringotts, sells crystal balls, compasses, and hourglasses.

You can pay for all this loot in **Gringotts bank notes,** which you can purchase inside the **Gringotts Money Exchange** overseen by an imperious interactive animatronic goblin, and then spend it anywhere within Universal Orlando; see page 140 for details. Even if you don't want to exchange any of your Muggle money, take a moment to query the proprietor about his age, the current exchange rate, or almost anything you've ever wanted to learn from a goblin (but were afraid to ask).

WORLD EXPO

THIS AREA STRETCHES around USF's central lagoon from Diagon Alley to The Simpsons Ride and somewhat clumsily incorporates several competing aesthetics. The World Expo name, as well as the theming of Men in Black Alien Attack in the area's center, is derived from the New York State Pavilion in the 1964 World's Fair. Though not exactly an attraction, the space-age Coca-Cola kiosk near Men in Black lets you type your name on a digital soda bottle and refill your Freestyle cup. *Note:* World Expo doesn't open to guests until 10 a.m.

Men in Black Alien Attack *(Universal Express)* ★★★★

APPEAL BY AGE	PRESCHOOL ★★★½	GRADE SCHOOL ★★★★	TEENS ★★★★
YOUNG ADULTS ★★★★	OVER 30 ★★★★		SENIORS ★★★★

What it is Interactive dark thrill ride. **Scope and scale** Headliner. **When to go** During the first hour the ride is open or after 4 p.m. **Comments** 42" minimum height requirement; child swap available (see page 187); single-rider line available. Not to be missed. **Duration of ride** 4½ minutes. **Loading speed** Moderate–fast.

Motion Sickness

DESCRIPTION AND COMMENTS Men in Black Alien Attack brings together Will Smith and Rip Torn (as Agent J and Men in Black [MIB] director Zed) for an interactive sequel to the hit sci-fi franchise. You'll notice that the ride's building pays homage to the architecture from the 1964 World's Fair, including the observation towers from the New York State Pavilion that featured in the 1997 film's finale. That theme is carried over to the attraction's preshow, which perfectly parodies the style of *Walt Disney's Carousel of Progress* before taking a surprise turn. In the story line, you've been recruited as an MIB trainee. After an introduction warning that aliens "live among us" and articulating MIB's mission to round them up, Zed expounds on the finer points of alien spotting and familiarizes you with your training vehicle and your weapon, an alien zapper.

You then load up in a six-passenger spinning ride vehicle and are dispatched into an innocuous training room, which is a shooting gallery full of plywood targets shaped like aliens. Your training is cut short when it's revealed that a real alien spaceship has landed in New York and you must save the city. The meat of the ride consists of careening around Manhattan in your MIB vehicle and shooting aliens. There are more targets than anyone could possibly shoot, and they're presented at a fast pace. Each ride vehicle is paired with another ride vehicle running on a parallel track, and both vehicles compete to see who can shoot the most aliens. At a certain point during the ride, you'll be able to shoot at the "fusion exhaust port" of the opposing ride vehicle, causing it to spin momentarily. This disorients the

STELLA SAYS

MEN IN BLACK ALIEN ATTACK Across the hall from the worm guys chatting it up in the break room area of the queue, you'll pass by two doors marked "Oxygen Free Zone" and "Fingerprint Removal." Give the door handles a good wiggle for some fun surprises.

other riders and causes them to lose precious time splatting the aliens. Of course, the other riders (and some of the aliens!) can shoot at you too.

Men in Black is interactive in that your marksmanship and ability to blast yourself out of some tricky situations will determine how the story ends, from about three dozen possible outcomes. You're awarded both a personal score and a score for your car, but regardless of your score, all recruits' memories of the game are wiped at the end of the ride.

TOURING TIPS Each of the 120-odd aliens has sensors that activate special effects and respond to your zapper. Aim for the eyes and keep shooting because you can score repeatedly on the same target. Your gun has auto-fire and unlimited ammo, so just keep the trigger depressed the whole ride; you'll even get a small number of points for missed shots. Targets above you score the most points: look for aliens behind second-story windows. At the ride's climax, listen carefully for Zed to instruct you to "push the red button," and hold it down when he says "button" to score a bonus 100,000 points. If you're good enough, you can max out with 999,999 points—trust us, it can be done.

The ride is packed with Universal in-jokes. Keep a sharp eye out for an alien seated on a park bench, hiding behind a newspaper. The head on a stick that the alien uses as a disguise bears an uncanny resemblance to Steven Spielberg, executive producer of the *Men in Black* films.

Visitors who are susceptible to motion sickness should heed this warning from a Missouri City, Texas, reader:

This ride was WAY TOO MUCH fast spinning for me. I definitely got dizzy on that one.

Avoid a long wait and ride during the first hour the ride is open, or try the single-rider line if you don't mind splitting your group. However, the singles and Express queues skip the preshow, which is worth seeing at least once. You can re-ride by following the signs for the child swap at the top of the exit stairs.

If it isn't too busy, ask the attendant where you unload for a free **immigration tour.** If you're lucky, they'll take you into the large preshow room below the queue, where you can take selfies sitting at an agent's desk and get a close-up look at the animatronic alien twins. (This tour is only offered intermittently when staff is available.)

SPRINGFIELD: HOME OF THE SIMPSONS

BUTTING UP AGAINST Men in Black's modernist architecture is Springfield: Home of the Simpsons, the setting of the long-running animated sitcom *The Simpsons*. What started as just The Simpsons Ride and Kwik-E-Mart store was hugely expanded in 2013, with a fabulous re-creation of Moe's Tavern, the Jebediah Springfield statue (emblazoned with A NOBLE SPIRIT EMBIGGENS THE SMALLEST MAN), and other cartoon landmarks. *Note:* Springfield doesn't open to guests until 10 a.m.

If you enjoy playing the custom carnival games around The Simpsons Ride, or any of the other skill games found in Islands of Adventure's

STELLA SAYS

BYE BYE, SPRINGFIELD? Many folks believe that The Simpsons Ride, as well as the surrounding Springfield area, could be closed down for something new by 2028 at the latest. Rumors stem from Disney purchasing Fox Studios, insinuating that Universal and Disney may not want to extend the yellow family's licensing contract when up for renewal. Theories for its replacement revolve around Pokemon taking over with a new land and an all-new ride, not just a retheme like Simpsons was after Back to the Future.

Toon Lagoon or Jurassic Park, invest in a **Game Play** card for $30, which saves you $4 per game on five plays; $60 cards come with 10 games and a free gift. Some prizes can also be purchased outright, if you'd rather not wreck your rotator cuff trying to knock down milk cans.

Kang & Kodos' Twirl 'n' Hurl *(Universal Express)* ★★½

**APPEAL BY AGE   PRESCHOOL ★★★★★   GRADE SCHOOL ★★★★   TEENS ★★★
YOUNG ADULTS ★★★½   OVER 30 ★★★   SENIORS ★★★**

What it is Spinning ride. **Scope and scale** Minor attraction. **When to go** Afternoon until closing. **Comments** Child swap available (see page 187). Rarely has a long wait. **Duration of ride** 1½ minutes. **Loading speed** Slow.

DESCRIPTION AND COMMENTS The Twirl 'n' Hurl is primarily eye candy for Springfield. Think of it as Dumbo with Bart's sense of humor: guests ride around in little flying saucers while the alien narrators, Kang and Kodos, hold pictures of *Simpsons* characters. Make the characters speak and spin by steering your craft to the proper altitude. All the while, Kang exhorts you (loudly) to destroy Springfield and makes insulting comments about humans. Preschoolers enjoy the ride, while older kids and *Simpsons* fans crack up over the gags.

TOURING TIPS Twirl 'n' Hurl may not open until noon and rarely attracts long lines, but (like all rides in this style) it can be very slow loading. If you want to enjoy the jokes without the wait, you can easily hear them all from the sidelines. If you have folks who are hot to ride, get them on whenever there are 50 or fewer guests in line.

Twirl 'n' Hurl stops running early on nights when the *CineSational* lagoon spectacular is scheduled, so as not to distract from the show.

The Simpsons Ride *(Universal Express)* ★★★½

**APPEAL BY AGE   PRESCHOOL ★★★   GRADE SCHOOL ★★★★   TEENS ★★★½
YOUNG ADULTS ★★★½   OVER 30 ★★★½   SENIORS ★★★½**

Motion Sickness

What it is Mega-simulator ride. **Scope and scale** Headliner. **When to go** During the first 2 hours the ride is open or after 4 p.m. **Comments** 40″ minimum height requirement; not recommended for pregnant women or people prone to motion sickness; child swap available (see page 187). **Duration of ride** 4⅓ minutes, plus preshow. **Loading speed** Moderate.

DESCRIPTION AND COMMENTS Another animated film coupled to a motion simulator, The Simpsons Ride is as much a satire of theme parks as it is a high-speed thrill ride through the Fox animated series that is TV's longest-running sitcom. Featuring the voices of Dan Castellaneta (Homer), Julie Kavner (Marge), Nancy Cartwright (Bart), Yeardley Smith (Lisa), and other cast members, the attraction uses a visit to Krustyland—the absurdly unsafe amusement park owned by the show's cantankerous Krusty the Clown—as an excuse to skewer Disney, SeaWorld, and even Universal itself.

The queue area and preshows involve *Simpsons* video clips (both classic and newly created) that help define the characters for guests who are unfamiliar with the TV show and that mock virtually every classic Disney attraction from The Haunted Mansion (here as the Haunted Condo, with "999 unhappy teen employees") to *Hall of Presidents* (redone as *Hall of the Secretaries of the Interior*—wait time 0 minutes). Not even ride-safety videos are spared; The Simpsons's version is an outrageous gore-fest starring Itchy and Scratchy demonstrating how *not* to behave.

The attraction itself recycled the foundations of Universal's former Back to the Future ride; watch the queue video for a time-traveling cameo by Doc Brown. The simulator is similar to Star Tours at Disney's Hollywood Studios and Universal's Despicable Me Minion Mayhem, but with a larger curved screen more like that of Soarin' at EPCOT. The ride vehicles hold eight guests in two rows of four.

The story line has the conniving Sideshow Bob secretly arriving at Krustyland and plotting his revenge on Krusty and Bart for sending him to jail. Sideshow Bob gets even by making things go wrong with the attractions that the Simpsons (and you) are riding. While there are dozens of dips, turns, climbs, and drops during the ride, there are probably hundreds of one-liners and visual puns. Like the show on which it's based, The Simpsons Ride definitely has an edge and operates on several levels. There will be jokes and visuals that you'll get but will fly over your children's heads—and most assuredly vice versa.

TOURING TIPS Because the screen you sit in front of is a giant curved dome, anyone sitting outside the central sweet spot gets a distorted view, which may aggravate motion sickness. For the best experience, ask the attendant at the bottom of the ramps for Level 2, and then ask the next attendant you see for Room 6. Taller guests (6 feet or over) should sit in the front row to avoid bumping their heads.

As far as motion simulators go, The Simpsons Ride isn't as sickness-inducing as many. The wider screen seems to help, as this mom from Huntington, New York, said:

> I'm not a fan of wild motion simulators, but I was fine on this ride. The field of vision makes it very engrossing, like Soarin'. However, our family still rates Star Tours higher than The Simpsons Ride, as it was most like actually being a character in the original movie!

Though not as rough and jerky as its predecessor, The Simpsons Ride is a long way from being tame. Skip it if you're an expectant mom or prone to motion sickness. Some parents may find the humor too coarse for younger kids.

DREAMWORKS LAND

PREVIOUSLY WOODY WOODPECKER'S KIDZONE, this cul-de-sac between Hollywood and World Expo was rebuilt and rebranded to feature the DreamWorks Animation franchises *Shrek, Kung Fu Panda,* and *Trolls,* among others. DreamWorks Land holds most of the park's child-themed attractions, including a pint-size roller coaster, an indoor stage show, and several elaborate playgrounds. Near the land's entrance, you'll find a backdrop for meet and greets with Gabby from *Gabby's Dollhouse,* and additional characters roam the area. Lack of shade is a major shortcoming of the entire land, so be aware that the playgrounds can become scorching during the heat of the day. Just outside the DreamWorks area, you'll still find longtime family favorites SpongeBob StorePants, the *Animal Actors* stage, and E.T. Adventure, which were reclassified as part of Hollywood.

DREAMWORKS LAND SURPRISES

UNIVERSAL ORLANDO FILLED DreamWorks Land with many unexpected surprises and delightful hidden details. Derek Burgan brings us this "Saturday Six" list of his favorites.

6. Year-round Beignets A staple of Universal's Mardi Gras celebration, beignets were absent from the parks during the rest of the year until DreamWorks Imagination Café put them on the menu full-time.

5. The Caterbus Other roller coasters have had faces on the front of their ride vehicle, but we're pretty sure the Trollercoaster is the first one to have a butt on the back.

4. The Allure of Alliteration Alliterative attraction names like the Pond of Perpetual Wetness and the Gong of Resounding Resonance bring a big smile to our face.

3. Credit Where Credit is Due The gorgeous mural at the *Imagination Celebration*, featuring many DreamWorks characters drawn in the form of clouds, has something most artwork in Universal does not: the signature of the artist who created it, Pat Vogtli.

2. Safety Signage Fun In Shrek's Swamp for Little Ogres, many of the signs are themed to have been originally used by Shrek to scare people away, but now have been "repurposed" to be safety warnings to kids.

1. Woody Woodpecker We love nods to former attractions, and among the cat portraits lining the walls of Mama Luna's Feline Fiesta, you'll spot one with a tiny red woodpecker on their shoulder.

DreamWorks Imagination Celebration
(Universal Express) ★★★★

APPEAL BY AGE PRESCHOOL ★★★★★ GRADE SCHOOL ★★★★★ TEENS ★★★★
YOUNG ADULTS ★★★★ OVER 30 ★★★★½ SENIORS ★★★★★

What it is Indoor show with DreamWorks characters. **Scope and scale** Major attraction. **When to go** Late morning to midafternoon, according to the show schedule. **Duration of show** 20 minutes.

DESCRIPTION AND COMMENTS This original stage musical features talented live singers and dancers, life-size puppets, and wraparound video screens—along with favorite friends from the *Shrek, Kung Fu Panda,* and *Trolls* films—together in an energetic all-ages production that's enjoyable even if you aren't accompanied by young ones. Staged in the round with immersive special effects, the show surrounds audiences in iconic scenes from the franchises, as a young woman tries to reignite her downhearted friend's imagination with tales of their childhood heroes. The high-decibel soundtrack includes bangers by Justin Timberlake and Rachel Platten, plus a touching rendition of "True Colors," and concludes with a dance party that gets the crowd on their feet. A more-than-worthy successor to Barney the Dinosaur (who was original occupant of the theater), this is the best kids' entertainment in Universal's repertoire, and much more enjoyable for adults than the similar *Disney Junior* show at Hollywood Studios.

TOURING TIPS Check the app for showtimes. There are only a handful of performances each day, so arrive a few minutes early. The queuing area is covered with screens displaying a short video preshow, and the theater itself is blissfully air-conditioned. Guests sit on hard backless benches during the show; there aren't any bad seats, but the rear rows provide a wider view of the stage and screens.

Po's Kung Fu Training Camp, featuring *Po Live!* ★★★½

APPEAL BY AGE PRESCHOOL ★★★★ GRADE SCHOOL ★★★★½ TEENS ★★★★½
YOUNG ADULTS ★★★½ OVER 30 ★★★★ SENIORS ★★★½

What it is Wet and dry outdoor playground with indoor interactive show. **Scope and scale** Minor attraction. **When to go** Anytime.

DESCRIPTION AND COMMENTS In the rear corner of DreamWorks Land, you'll find a *Kung Fu Panda*–inspired interactive playground that exemplifies the Universal obsession with wet stuff. Although not quite as unrelentingly drenching as the former Curious George playground—whose structure was retained and redecorated with wooden pagoda-style details—the right half still holds innumerable spigots, pipes, and spray guns, along with a giant roof-mounted bucket that periodically dumps hundreds of gallons of water. Kids who want to stay dry can try ringing the gong in the center courtyard and playing on the hanging noodles and spinning dishes on the left side of the camp, just past the Pond of Perpetual Wetness splash pad.

Panda Village's central building, where the foam-ball playground once was, now hosts *Po Live!,* a 12-minute-long interactive show starring computer-animated characters similar to *Turtle Talk with Crush* at EPCOT. Full-body motion capture and real-time rendering transform an off-stage Jack Black sound-alike into Po, who appears life-size on a large video display disguised as a sliding paper screen. Guests stand and follow Po's instructions in a brief lesson on focusing their inner chi, and are called upon to wave their arms in order to defeat a foe from the Spirit Realm. The actors do a great job channeling the character, and the CGI is impressively detailed. Shows start every 30 minutes, and there's enough variety to merit a repeat viewing; it's just a shame it's under shade but not air-conditioned.

TOURING TIPS If you're letting your kids loose on the wet playgrounds here, be sure to do it early enough in the day to dry off, or bring along a change of clothes.

Shrek's Swamp   ★★★

APPEAL BY AGE	PRESCHOOL ★★★★★	GRADE SCHOOL ★★★★½	TEENS ★★★★
YOUNG ADULTS ★★		OVER 30 ★★★½	SENIORS ★★★

What it is Interactive playground and meet and greet. **Scope and scale** Minor attraction. **When to go** Anytime. **Comment** Children under 48″ must be accompanied by a supervising companion.

DESCRIPTION AND COMMENTS Universal's long-in-the-tooth KidZone playground themed to Fievel was flattened and replaced with more-modern playscapes based on *Shrek.* Where imaginative oversize cowboy props and a waterslide once towered, you'll now find **Shrek's Swamp for Little Ogres,** a two-story set of wooden bridges and net climbs adorned with faux moss. The entrance is overseen by Pinocchio, whose nose extends when you press a button, and the signature outhouse slide makes farting noises during descent. Across from the playground entrance is **King Harold's Swamp Symphony,** where you can make frogs croak tunes (including a classic beer jingle) by stepping on lily pads, as well as **Mama Luna's Feline Fiesta,** whose on-screen kitties cavort when control buttons are pressed. This section's best attraction is a permanent **meet and greet** with Shrek and Donkey, whose hilarious banter with guests makes the unshaded wait outside the ogre's swampy house (which you can't go inside) worthwhile.

TOURING TIPS Visit after you've experienced all the major attractions. The playground is designed for small kids, and adults attempting to make it down the slide may find themselves uncomfortably stuck.

Trolls Trollercoaster *(Universal Express)*   ★★½

APPEAL BY AGE	PRESCHOOL ★★★½	GRADE SCHOOL ★★★★½	TEENS ★★★½
YOUNG ADULTS ★★★		OVER 30 ★★★½	SENIORS ★★★½

What it is Kids' roller coaster. **Scope and scale** Minor attraction. **When to go** Anytime. **Comment** 36" minimum height requirement; children 36"–48" must be accompanied by a supervising companion; child swap available (see page 187). **Loading speed** Slooow.

DESCRIPTION AND COMMENTS Originally themed to Woody Woodpecker, this short, relatively low roller coaster was retained and renamed after DreamWorks's Trolls, receiving colorful new "Caterbus" caterpillar-themed ride vehicles, and spider webs for them to gently swoop through. Virtually identical to Magic Kingdom's Barnstormer, it is small enough for kids to enjoy but sturdy enough for adults, though its moderate speed might unnerve some smaller children (the minimum height to ride is 36 inches). The entire ride lasts about a minute, and at least 20 of those 60 seconds is spent cranking the train up the first (and only) lift hill. There are several tight turns, but the ride doesn't go upside down or even come close.

TOURING TIPS Visit after you've experienced all the major attractions. If your young child has never before experienced a roller coaster, this would be an appropriate first attempt. For those too little to ride, the toddler-size **Poppy's Playground** is across from the coaster's entrance.

HOLLYWOOD

THE HOLLYWOOD AREA RE-CREATES the glamour and energy of Southern California from the 1930s through the 1950s. Several areas surrounding Hollywood, including Beverly Hills and the Hollywood Hills, are represented. The faux Garden of Allah Villas (famed home of F. Scott Fitzgerald, Marlene Dietrich, and other Hollywood golden age legends) contain the **NBC Media Center** (see page 363).

Animal Actors on Location! (Universal Express)   ★★★½

APPEAL BY AGE PRESCHOOL ★★★★½ **GRADE SCHOOL** ★★★★½ **TEENS** ★★★★
YOUNG ADULTS ★★★★   **OVER 30** ★★★★   **SENIORS** ★★★★½

What it is Animal tricks and comedy show. **Scope and scale** Major attraction. **When to go** Scheduled showtimes; after you've experienced all rides. **Duration of show** 25 minutes.

DESCRIPTION AND COMMENTS *Animal Actors on Location!* is a live show featuring performing dogs, birds, pigs, and a menagerie of other animals in a covered outdoor stadium. This show integrates video segments with live sketches, jokes, and animal tricks performed onstage. A human trainer acts as the host, explaining how the animals are conditioned to execute the tricks. Several of the animal thespians are veterans of TV and movies; many were rescued from shelters. The demonstration usually makes use of audience volunteers (mostly children) in a couple of segments. Sit in the center of the stadium about halfway up for the best chance to be selected.

If you've seen the bird show at Disney's Animal Kingdom, you'll recognize many of the bird routines in *Animal Actors*. What sets *Animal Actors* apart is the use of varied and unusual kinds of animals, as well as the opportunity to see the animals being trained onstage. The animals are trained using only positive reinforcement—that is, rewarding the animal when it performs the correct behavior—and no negative reinforcement (punishing for incorrect behavior).

TOURING TIPS Check the app for showtimes. You shouldn't have any trouble getting into the next performance. The stadium is covered but not enclosed, meaning that it's still hot during summer and cold during winter. Come to the front of the stage at the conclusion to snap a photo with some of the furry stars, and keep an eye out for training sessions with new performers in nearby Central Park.

The Bourne Stuntacular *(Universal Express)* ★★★★½

| APPEAL BY AGE | PRESCHOOL ★★★ | GRADE SCHOOL ★★★★ | TEENS ★★★★½ |
| YOUNG ADULTS ★★★★½ | | OVER 30 ★★★★½ | SENIORS ★★★★½ |

What it is Live-action stunt show. **Scope and scale** Headliner. **When to go** Scheduled showtimes; after you've experienced all rides. **Comments** Not to be missed. May frighten young children. **Duration of show** 25 minutes.

DESCRIPTION AND COMMENTS This fast-paced replacement for the revered *Terminator 2: 3-D* show (which closed in 2017) blurs the boundary between stage and screen to spectacular effect, making it easily the best stunt show in Orlando. Housed within the facade of an Art Deco office building, the *Stuntacular* starts in a polished concrete and stainless steel queue featuring static displays that document Jason Bourne's cinematic career, which launched with the 2002 hit *Bourne Identity.*

Viewers are welcomed into a standing-room-only preshow, where Julia Stiles's plucky undercover operative Nicky Parsons (presumably murdered in the 2016 reboot, but looking healthy here) provides a 6-minute video briefing on Bourne's backstory. Basically, our hoodie-wearing hero is a brainwashed assassin with a heart of gold, who is bent on exposing corrupt government conspiracies.

Audiences become "situation analysts," tasked with observing Bourne's activities via a unique "virtual surveillance observation room," which looks suspiciously like a 700-seat theater. Bourne's action sprints from the rooftops of Tangier to the suburban streets of Washington, D.C., and finally climaxes in midair amid Dubai's skyscrapers, with mercifully brief expository interludes from CIA headquarters bridging the locations.

The stunts themselves range from bare-knuckle fisticuffs and gun battles using authentically ear-popping automatic weapons, to aerial acrobatics high above the ground, including a couple of heart-stopping 22-foot free-falls into pits in the stage.

It's the merging of old-fashioned stunts with next-generation video technology that makes *The Bourne Stuntacular* more than a mere stunt show. *Bourne*'s mammoth 3,640-square-foot LED screen is so sharp and vivid that it defies the eye's ability to determine where the digital world ends and reality begins, without needing 3-D glasses. For example, unless you're sitting in the front row, it's almost impossible to tell that only a handful of the people in the opening scene's cheering crowd are actually there onstage. Paired with robotic set pieces that slide seamlessly in sync with the video, the 130-foot-wide display transforms the entire theater into a roving movie camera, spiraling skyward around a telescoping tower as Bourne climbs to safety, or swooping alongside a high-speed chase while he clings to the roof of a full-size car. Add in bursts of flame, water, wind, and fog, and you have an experience that sometimes feels more like a simulator ride than a stage show, even without any moving seats.

TOURING TIPS Shows start about every 45 minutes according to the performance schedule available in Universal's app, but the theater may fill up on busier days, so arrive at least 5–10 minutes prior to the performance you wish to attend. Seats in the front row are great for fight choreography aficionados, but we prefer the view of the screen from the rear. The *Stuntacular* features loud gunfire and brutal violence (including choke holds) but no blood or guts.

E.T. Adventure *(Universal Express)* ★★★★

| APPEAL BY AGE | PRESCHOOL ★★★★ | GRADE SCHOOL ★★★★ | TEENS ★★★½ |
| YOUNG ADULTS ★★★½ | | OVER 30 ★★★★ | SENIORS ★★★★ |

What it is Indoor adventure ride based on the beloved movie. **Scope and scale** Major attraction. **When to go** Within 30 minutes of ride opening or late afternoon. **Comments**

STELLA SAYS

E.T. ADVENTURE The forest queue not only offers immaculate vibes and an intoxicating fresh pine scent, but it can also serve as a sort of scavenger hunt. See if your "search party" can spot the two rabbits and two owls hiding among the trees and rocks!

34" minimum height requirement; child swap available (see page 187). **Duration of ride** 4½ minutes. **Loading speed** Moderate.

DESCRIPTION AND COMMENTS Inspired by Steven Spielberg's classic 1982 film (and the not-so-classic 1985 sequel novel *Book of the Green Planet*), this is the only ride at Universal that's remained essentially unchanged since opening day. Guests board bicycle-like ride vehicles (suspended from the ceiling) on an adventure to return everyone's favorite extra-terrestrial to his dying home planet.

After a brief video introduction from Spielberg himself, guests provide their first name to an attendant and receive a credit card–size interplanetary passport (more on this later) before wending their way through a dark forest of tall pine trees; this is one of the most evocative indoor ride queues in any park. As the ride itself starts, you're weaving through the woods, evading the moon-suited scientists and earthly law enforcement officials trying to capture E.T. As in the film, you're airborne soon enough, flying over Los Angeles (a lovely tableau) and into a warp tunnel to E.T.'s home planet. You arrive just in time to allow E.T.'s healing touch to save everything, and the ride ends in a mash-up of colorful flowers, lighting, and aliens. Concerning the latter, where E.T. is reunited with family and friends, Len Testa likens it to *The Wizard of Oz*'s Technicolor transition, only restaged with a cave full of naked mole rats. (C'mon, Len, where's the love?)

Before you return home, E.T. bids each rider farewell by name, thanks to those passports you received earlier. E.T. can say more than 20,000 names, though he misidentifies riders more often than not. A Baton, North Carolina, reader with perhaps too much time on his hands got to wondering:

> *Why do the inhabitants of E.T.'s home planet, who presumably have never visited Earth, speak better English than he does?*

While the attraction had lost some luster over its 35-year run, it received long-overdue updates ahead of DreamWorks Land's opening. The human animatronics in the first half still look laughably like dime-store dummies, but the animatronics of E.T. and his pals in the acid-soaked second act are no longer disturbingly out of synch. Since E.T. is one of Universal's only family-friendly dark rides that relies on sets and robotics instead of screens—a type of attraction the resort could use more of—we're glad it got some TLC, and hope it sticks around for a long time to come.

TOURING TIPS Most preschoolers and grade-school children love E.T. We think it's worth a 20- to 30-minute wait, but no longer than that. The ride often doesn't open until 10 a.m., and lines build quickly within 30 minutes of opening; waits can reach 2 hours on busy days. Ride in the morning or late afternoon. On peak days, a time-saving single-rider line is occasionally opened.

A mother from Columbus, Ohio, writes about horrendous lines at E.T.:

> *The line for E.T. took 2 hours! The rest of the family waiting outside thought we had really gone to E.T.'s planet.*

Universal Orlando's Horror Make-Up Show
(Universal Express) ★★★★½

What it is Theater presentation on the art of makeup. **Scope and scale** Major attraction. **When to go** Scheduled showtimes; after you've experienced all rides. **Comments** May frighten young children. Not to be missed. **Duration of show** 25 minutes.

DESCRIPTION AND COMMENTS The *Horror Make-Up Show* is a brief but humorous look at how basic monster-movie special effects are done. The show includes onstage demonstrations of effects, such as blood-spurting fake knives and rubber limbs, plus how mechanical effects are combined with latex masks to transform human heads into wolf-shaped skulls. The hosts pay tribute to Universal makeup pioneers such as Lon Chaney, Jack Pierce, Tom Savini, and Rick Baker, while also poking fun at some of the studio's less successful spooks. Film clips are interspersed throughout, showing how computer-generated special effects are blended into live-action films like Tom Cruise's 2017 reboot of *The Mummy*. The finale involves an audience volunteer and a remote-controlled creature that isn't all that he appears.

This may be Universal's most entertaining live show. While there's plenty of fake blood thrown around, the script is much more funny than scary. The hosts keep everything moving along at a fast pace (except when they start to improv and crack each other up like the old Carol Burnett show), and their running commentary about horror-filmmaking is interspersed with plenty of pop-culture jokes for the kids, along with some surprisingly subversive stabs at the hand that feeds them; after offering a dry towel to a damp volunteer, they'll demand cash, smiling, "Welcome to Orlando!"

TOURING TIPS The *Horror Make-Up Show* is the sleeper attraction at Universal, and one of the only theme park comedy shows we can watch over and over again. Its humor and tongue-in-cheek style transcend the gruesome effects, and most folks (including preschoolers) take the blood and guts in stride. But it's the exception that proves the rule, as this reader relates:

> My 7- and 9-year-olds were scared by the Horror Make-Up Show (despite me telling them that the guy wasn't really cutting anyone's arm off!). We ended up leaving before the show was over.

And from a New Orleans family:

> My husband and I really enjoyed the humor; it was just corny enough. The special effects with the audience member were pretty cool, and we thought the whole thing was fun. My kids were not quite as taken with this show. My son (5) hid his face against my arm most of the time, and my daughter (10) had her hands over her eyes a lot. The video montage of horror clips was especially upsetting to them. As we were leaving the theater, they both commented that the show was really scary, and they didn't like it.

A good test is to take your child into the theater lobby between shows, where display cases filled with bloody props and monster masks act as a mini-museum of Universal horror history from *The Hunchback of Notre Dame* to Halloween Horror Nights. If the static severed heads here send your kid into hysterics, the show itself may have you paying therapy bills for decades to come.

Look for the second-story windows to the left of the theater marquee for a touching tribute to victims of the 2016 Pulse nightclub tragedy.

LIVE ENTERTAINMENT *at* UNIVERSAL STUDIOS FLORIDA

IN ADDITION TO THE SHOWS profiled previously, USF offers a daytime parade and a nighttime spectacular, along with a wide range of smaller street performances.

Costumed comic book and cartoon characters (Shrek and Donkey, SpongeBob SquarePants, Transformers) pose for guests at organized meet and greets marked on the park maps. Others, like Scooby-Doo, along with look-alikes of movie stars (both living and deceased), roam the Hollywood area for photo ops. See pages 189–192 for more character information.

In New York, Hollywood, and San Francisco, several small-scale shows entertain the crowds. **The Blues Brothers Show** (★★★½) is a 12-minute rhythm and blues concert. Held on the corner of the New York area, across from the lagoon, *The Blues Brothers Show* features Jake and Elwood performing a few of the hit songs from the classic 1980 movie musical, including "Soul Man" and "Shake a Tail Feather." The brothers are joined onstage by Jazz the saxophone player and Mabel the waitress, who belts an Aretha Franklin cover to start the show. *Blues Brothers* is one of the better musical performances in the Studios. The singers have captured many of the movie's dance moves and vocal styles, and the music's tempo keeps everyone's toes tapping. The concert is a great pick-me-up, and the short running time keeps the energy high. During the holiday season, a special *Blues Brothers Holiday Show* is performed, featuring songs such as "Blue Christmas" and "Run Rudolph Run," sung around a festive tree festooned with beer cans and cigarette packs. It's even better than the regular show.

Marilyn Monroe and the Diamond Bellas (★★½) perform a 4-minute song-and-dance routine (anachronistically lip-synched to the *Moulin Rouge* cover of her signature song) in Hollywood in front of Mel's Drive-In, followed by a photo op; during the holiday season, "Santa Baby" joins the set list. The **Beat Builders** (★★★) are a quartet of beefy guys who hang out on the scaffolding outside Louie's Italian Restaurant and turn their construction equipment into percussion instruments, in the tradition of *Stomp*. *¡Vamos!—Báilalo* (★★★½), a 15-minute high-energy Latin dance show inspired by *West Side Story* and *In the Heights,* takes over the intersection outside Louie's with a dozen colorful choreographed performers who coax audience members into partying along to tunes by Jennifer Lopez, Celia Cruz, and Marc Anthony.

All of these shows have performance times listed in the app's show schedule, and only a few are worth going out of your way for. If you aren't on a tight touring plan and see one starting as you walk by, stop and watch until you get bored.

CineSational: A Symphonic Spectacular ★★★★½

APPEAL BY AGE PRESCHOOL ★★ GRADE SCHOOL ★★★★★ TEENS ★★★★½
YOUNG ADULTS ★★★★½   OVER 30 ★★★★★   SENIORS ★★★★★

What it is Fountain show with fireworks and drones. **Scope and scale** Headliner. **When to go** At park closing on select nights; see app for show schedule. **Comments** Presented seasonally, when the park is open after dark; not to be missed. **Duration of show** 22 minutes.

DESCRIPTION AND COMMENTS *CineSational: A Symphonic Spectacular,* the night-time lagoon show that debuted in summer 2024, celebrates musical scores and scenes from blockbuster films that inspired Universal Orlando attractions of yesterday and today, including the Wizarding World series, *Jurassic World, Jaws, Shrek, Ghostbusters, Trolls, Back to the Future,* Universal's Classic Monsters, *Transformers, How to Train Your Dragon, E.T., Fast & Furious, The Super Mario Bros. Movie, Minions, The Mummy,* and *King Kong.*

The 22-minute production projects iconic movie scenes onto multiple enormous mist screens, which are made using 228 fountains with 16,000 individual nozzles, capable of launching water over 130 feet in the air. 4K projection mapping brings the buildings in the background to life, and judicious use of fireworks (deployed sparingly, in deference to the residential neighborhood across the street) adds spark and sizzle to key moments. But the stars of this show are the fleet of 660 remote-controlled aerial drones, which form glowing constellations of favorite characters that magically appear hovering in midair. (The drones might not fly if there is rain shortly before or during the performance, but the rest of the show is still well worth watching without them.)

With a custom-orchestrated score that seamlessly integrates dozens of beloved musical themes, and tightly paced transitions that smoothly shift from action and horror to comedy and romance, *CineSational* is easily the most satisfying nighttime spectacular Universal Orlando has ever created. It stands shoulder-to-shoulder with Disney's best shows; we even like it a bit better than the similar *World of Color* at Disney California Adventure.

TOURING TIPS The terraced Central Park across the lagoon from San Francisco is the primary viewing location for this show, with additional viewing between Mel's Drive-In and Transformers, and near Duff Brewery. No reservations are required, and you should be able to get a good view by arriving at least 15–20 minutes before showtime. The grassy field in the rear of Central Park provides the best perspective on the wide-screen presentation, but it's sometimes reserved for VIPs or Universal Rewards Visa cardholders.

Universal Mega Movie Parade ★★★★

APPEAL BY AGE   PRESCHOOL   GRADE SCHOOL ★★★★   TEENS ★★★½
YOUNG ADULTS ★★★★★   OVER 30 ★★★★   SENIORS ★★★★★

What it is Daytime character parade. **Scope and scale** Major attraction. **When to go** Select afternoons; see app for show schedule. **Comments** Usually presented daily, except during the holiday season. **Duration of show** 15 minutes.

DESCRIPTION AND COMMENTS After a few years with no regular afternoon parade, in summer 2024 Universal Studios Florida introduced their biggest daytime processional ever in the Universal Mega Movie Parade. It features nearly 100 performers and 13 floats celebrating iconic Universal Studios films like *E.T.* and *Back to the Future,* along with Illumination's *Minions* and *Sing,* and DreamWorks Animation's *Trolls* and *Kung Fu Panda.* 1990s nostalgia will give GenX-ers the feels, while their offspring should perk up for Po and Poppy. Highlights include a 16-foot-tall Stay-Puft Marshmallow Man atop the *Ghostbusters* float, a marching band drumline playing the *Jaws* theme, and a Jurassic finale featuring a giant Tyrannosaurus rex puppet.

With a throwback soundtrack that includes "Back In Time" and "We Are Family," plus highly interactive characters who roller skate, ride BMX bikes, and twirl batons, this is certainly Universal Orlando's most ambitious attempt yet at a Disney-style parade. The floats are impressively large and detailed, with clever cinematic Easter eggs—search for Slimer, E.T.'s Speak & Spell, and an "OUTATIME" license plate—but (aside from the dinosaur) they are disappointingly static, lacking many kinetic lighting or animated effects.

The new parade runs once daily, typically at 6 p.m. when the park stays open late, or at 2 p.m. when it closes early (like during Halloween Horror Nights). The procession lasts around 45 minutes total, and it takes about 15 minutes to pass by any particular point, traveling clockwise around the park in the same direction as the holiday parade (but opposite the old daytime parade). The route begins at the Esoteric Pictures gate in Hollywood between Universal Orlando's Horror Make-Up Show and Cafe La Bamba. It turns left onto Hollywood Boulevard, then makes a hard right near the park entrance into Minion Land on Illumination Avenue, and heads toward New York. From there, it turns right and proceeds along Fifth Avenue past Revenge of the Mummy, then takes a right at Louie's Italian Restaurant and follows the waterfront past Transformers: The Ride-3D and Mel's Drive-In, before disappearing backstage through the gate where it entered.

TOURING TIPS The best viewing spots are along Fifth Avenue, on the front steps of faux buildings in New York, and along Hollywood Boulevard. The wheelchair viewing area is in front of the Macy's facade; a section is reserved for Universal Visa cardholders across from *The Bourne Stuntacular;* and annual passholders sometimes get exclusive access to the corner in front of Mel's Drive-In, where you can watch the show twice. If you plan to leave the park after seeing the parade, you can watch it step off in Hollywood, then follow it down the street and slip out the park exit before it loops back around. The interactive bubble wands sold in DreamWorks Land also react to select parade floats. Be warned that this parade is frequently delayed or canceled due to afternoon thunderstorms.

SPECIAL EVENTS *at* UNIVERSAL STUDIOS FLORIDA

BEYOND ITS YEAR-ROUND OFFERINGS, USF also hosts some of the best seasonal events in the theme park industry, and most of them are included with any regular admission (including annual passes). For those events that aren't—Rock the Universe and Halloween Horror Nights—you'll need to purchase a separate ticket, and daytime Universal Express Passes (including those offered with hotel rooms) won't be honored.

ROCK THE UNIVERSE *(late January)*

UNIVERSAL ORLANDO BILLS Rock the Universe, its annual weekend of fist-pumping praise-rock and roller coasters, as "Florida's biggest Christian music festival." This hard-ticket after-hours event attracts hordes of church youth groups, who get access to the parks starting at

4 p.m. and keep boogying for the Lord until 1 a.m. It is scheduled to return January 24–25, 2025.

Concerts take place across three stages inside USF and start after the park closes to day guests at 6 p.m. Past acts have included Zach Williams, Switchfoot, Newsboys, For King and Country, TobyMac, Skillet, Crowder, LECRAE, Matthew West, We the Kingdom, and Casting Crowns. The headliners perform on the Music Plaza stage, drawing a large percentage of the event's attendees to their hour-plus-long sets. The audiences for these shows rival those at Mardi Gras concerts in size and enthusiasm (if not inebriation), so be sure to show up early if you want a close-up view of your favorite band. Coca-Cola sponsors a Fanzone that features autograph sessions, where attendees can meet and greet all of the headlining artists on a first-come, first-serve basis. Most of the park's thrill rides operate during Rock the Universe, including Gringotts in Diagon Alley. There's also a Saturday night candle-lighting ceremony just before midnight and a Sunday morning worship service.

Single-night tickets start around $90, while two-night tickets cost about $133; annual passholders can attend for as little as $30. Attendees can buy discounted Rock Your Weekend tickets that combine both event nights with daytime park tickets. Three-park access Friday–Sunday goes for about $161 ($209 for park-to-park). Universal Express Passes run an additional $32 per night for one-time use per ride, or $43 for unlimited use. Youth group leaders get a free ticket for every 10 their charges purchase, plus free access to Universal Express ride queues and lounges with free snacks. Learn more at rocktheuniverse.com.

MARDI GRAS *(early February–late March)*

YOU ARE NO DOUBT FAMILIAR with the gigantic Mardi Gras celebration in New Orleans, or at least the idea of it. Well, USF has a yearly festival as well that celebrates its 30th anniversary in 2025. Sure, it's not quite as bawdy as its French Quarter compatriot, but it is exceedingly fun and probably a better event to bring the kids along.

Mardi Gras originated in the religious observation of Fat Tuesday (the literal translation of the name), which is the day before Ash Wednesday on the Catholic calendar and the start of Lent's 40 days of dietary restrictions. People bid "farewell to flesh" with a carnival where they indulge in the meat and drink they're about to forswear. Mardi Gras is the New Orleans variation on this tradition—which is echoed in other cities from Venice to Rio de Janeiro.

Over the centuries, the religious significance has been stripped away, and most Mardi Gras revelers attend for strictly secular reasons—namely, epic quantities of booze, beads, and bare breasts. Universal took a look at the festivities and said, "This will make a fine family-friendly event"—minus the bare breasts, of course—and amazingly, it is. But that doesn't mean it's inauthentic. Universal engages Kern Studios, the same company that's been building floats for the real deal since 1932, to create the park's parade platforms. And music and recipes imported from the Big Easy add to the French Quarter feel. Of course, the real Bourbon Street doesn't have concerts from big-name recording artists after the parade (on select nights), much less a high-speed roller coaster cruising by in the background.

In addition to the parade and headliner concerts, Universal carves a miniature Bourbon Street out of its New York back lot. Chef Steven Jayson and his culinary team pride themselves on the authentic N'awlins flavors they bring to the temporary food and beverage booths that operate each Mardi Gras event night. The jambalaya, andouille sausage, and beignets are all pretty good. In recent years, the event's culinary offering expanded into a park-wide international food and drink festival, with booths serving tastes of Carnival-celebrating cultures around the world, along with festive foods from India and Asia (including several plant-based options). Guests can save money on bites and beers by buying a discounted nonexpiring card valid for food and beverage from the Mardi Gras event booths, as well as select locations throughout the theme parks and CityWalk. Tasting cards cost $65 for $75 worth of credit; annual passholders pay $120 for $150, and their regular discounts still apply.

Viewing of the parade and concerts are included with any valid admission, and all annual passholders are admitted in the evening, except Seasonal passholders who are blocked out on concert nights. For more information, visit theugseries.com/unimardigras.

Mardi Gras Parade

Universal's version of a Mardi Gras parade includes the crazy characters of the New Orleans version but is much more compact. Floats are updated every year with new themes—2024 featured an "Elements" theme, with six updated floats featuring earth, wind, fire, water, and the sun and moon—but you can always count on the massive King Gator float and multistory Riverboat to roll down Universal's boulevards. The floats are each accompanied by dozens of strolling performers and stilt walkers, while costumed revelers ride upon them and toss colorful plastic beads to the crowds below.

The parade begins at the Esoteric Pictures gate in Hollywood between the *Horror Make-Up Show* and Cafe La Bamba. It turns left onto Hollywood Boulevard, then makes a hard right near the park entrance into Minion Land on Illumination Avenue, and heads toward New York. From here, it turns right and proceeds along 5th Avenue past Revenge of the Mummy, then takes a right at Louie's Italian Restaurant and follows the waterfront past Transformers: The Ride–3D and Mel's Drive-In, before disappearing backstage through the gate where it entered.

Viewing Tips: The parade takes about 15 minutes to pass by any one spot, and it lasts around 45 minutes. The parade generally begins at 7:30 or 7:45 p.m., but it may step off as early as 5:15 p.m. on certain nights. Times may vary with operating hours, so check the smartphone app for details. You can find good viewing anywhere along the parade route, and unless you insist on standing right up front, there's no need to save your spot more than 10 or 15 minutes in advance. In front of the *Bourne Stuntacular* is an excellent viewing spot to watch from, if you want to exit the park immediately after the procession.

Special reserved viewing areas are also available for annual passholders (near Mel's Drive-In), guests with disabilities (near Macy's in New York), and young Little Jesters and their families (in front of the Brown Derby).

If you really want to get in on the action, it's possible to volunteer as a bead-tossing float rider. Annual passholders can sign up for themselves and a guest online; you must RSVP as soon as availability is announced because reservations sold out within an hour in 2024. Slots are also saved for on-site resort guests; watch Universal's website for preregistration or inquire at your hotel's Vacation Planning Center.

Guests can purchase a $91 dining package that includes a sit-down meal at a select restaurant in CityWalk or USF and a float-rider spot in that evening's Mardi Gras parade. If you purchase a Dine and Ride package, be sure to check in at *Animal Actors* at least an hour before the parade begins or you may lose your spot.

A limited number of free Mardi Gras float-riding spots are available through Universal's app. There is no physical standby line for free same-day float-riding spots, but they may be distributed sporadically during the day through the app's Virtual Line feature. Unclaimed float-riding reservations are released about 45 minutes prior to stepoff through the Virtual Line system, and must be redeemed within a few minutes; hang around the *Animal Actors* check-in area to hear when availability is announced.

Riding the float as you fling beads is a blast but takes 2–3 hours, and you'll probably miss the beginning of the concert if you participate. All riders must be at least 18 years old (or accompanied by an adult) and 48 inches tall. Also be aware that you'll have no restroom access for about an hour when riding the floats. Be sure to visit the photo center before exiting the park and tell them which float you were on to purchase pictures of yourself in the parade.

Mardi Gras Live Concerts

Every Saturday night (and select Sundays) during the Mardi Gras event, after the parade concludes (approximately 45 minutes after it begins), a big-name concert kicks off on Music Plaza Stage underneath Hollywood Rip Ride Rockit. The concerts are a definite highlight of Universal's Mardi Gras celebration. With dozens of great musical acts entertaining the crowd at no extra cost, there is really no downside to these fantastic concerts, other than the extraordinary crowds that popular artists can draw. To get an idea of the quality of the acts, performers in recent years have included heavyweights from the past—KC and The Sunshine Band; Earth, Wind & Fire; Patti LaBelle; Queen Latifah; the Steve Miller Band; REO Speedwagon; 3 Doors Down; Goo Goo Dolls; Barenaked Ladies;

and Styx—and present, such as Luis Fonsi, Zedd, JVKE, Macklemore, WILLOW, Karol G, Lauren Daigle, and Marshmello.

Viewing Tips: There is no additional charge for Mardi Gras concerts; they are included with park admission. All concerts are standing-room only and first come, first served. Crowds can be enormous, and folks sometimes start lining up shortly after park opening for the hottest acts. There is no extra-cost VIP area available, but there is an ADA-accessible viewing section near the Race Through New York restrooms. Large video screens broadcast the stage to those standing in the far back, so consider watching from the New York Battery Park area if you aren't an überfan of the artist.

HALLOWEEN HORROR NIGHTS
(late August–early November)

THE GODFATHER (or is that gorefather?) of all Universal Orlando seasonal events, Halloween Horror Nights (or HHN, as it's known to its legions of bloodthirsty fans) is recognized as the nation's most popular and industry-awarded haunted theme park event. Originally a locals-friendly filler during a normally slow season, USF's Halloween celebration started in 1991 as a single weekend of Fright Nights, and marked its 30th anniversary in 2021. In fact, HHN has grown so famous that the eight-week-long scare-abration can provide a significant percentage of USF's annual attendance statistics. Much like visiting any of Orlando's theme parks during a peak holiday season, an evening at HHN can be tremendous fun if you go in with a solid plan and sane expectations. Without those things . . . well, you might be better off eaten by zombies! This reader, who traveled all the way from Belgium to attend the event, summarizes the sentiments of many haunt fans:

> Halloween Horror Nights is truly the world's premier Halloween event. I recommend it to any adult or teen who is a Halloween fan. I've been twice and will certainly do it again; it's worth the money!

We've been attending HHN every year since 1996, and it has become one of our favorite after-dark activities in any park, but it isn't for everybody. Before attending, make sure that Universal's brand of Halloween is right for you; this ain't Mickey's Not-So-Scary Halloween Party. HHN is a gory, gruesome bacchanalia of simulated violence and tasteless satire, marinated with a liberal dose of alcohol and rock 'n' roll. In other words, it's a heck of a party as long as you know what you're getting into. If the idea of copious blood, guts, and booze doesn't appeal to you, we advise staying far, far away. Needless to say, it's not appropriate for young children, though you will likely see many there.

The three basic elements of each year's event are haunted houses (or mazes), outdoor scare zones, and theater shows. Universal also makes many of its regular rides available during HHN, including Harry Potter and the Escape from Gringotts (though not the Hogwarts Express) in The Wizarding World of Harry Potter—Diagon Alley.

Planning for Halloween Horror Nights

Even more so than daytime touring, a successful HHN visit requires a careful date selection. In 2024, HHN ran from August 30–November 3; visit orlando.halloweenhorrornights.com for the calendar. In short, you want to avoid all Saturdays (especially the final three Saturdays leading up to Halloween) like the plague. Fridays in October—particularly the last two Fridays before Halloween—aren't much better. Wednesdays are usually the least crowded, followed by Thursdays (especially the first two) and Sundays (especially the first, but excluding the last). Opening weekend brings out all the local fans, so your best bets are the last three weeks of September or the first week of October. Halloween night itself and any nights after it are often extremely quiet. The price of Express Passes on a given night (as listed at theugseries.com/UOHHNExpress) is your best guide to how busy it will be: the larger the cost, the larger the crowds.

If you walk up to the box office on the night of the event, you'll pay over $150—a frightening sum for as little as 7½ hours in the park—and likely wait in a ridiculously long line for the privilege. Instead, study the myriad online ticket options in advance and purchase before you leave home.

Deep discounts are offered on advance purchases of date-specific tickets. You need to know what night you want to attend when purchasing online because prices range from $88 for a Wednesday in September up to $131 on October's busiest Saturday. If you already have daytime admission to a Universal park, you can purchase an add-on ticket at the park that allows you to remain through the evening's event for a discounted price, depending on the night.

Finally, if you are a hard-core haunt fan and are spending more than a night in the area, you'll want a Frequent Fear (valid every Sunday–Thursday event night plus opening weekend, with Fridays and the final Saturday also included in the Plus version for an extra fee) or Rush of Fear (valid every event night through the first four weekends) multiday pass. Universal also offers an Ultimate Frequent Fear Pass valid every event night, in case you feel like spending more than the cost of an annual pass for a few weeks of scares. Multiday passes range from $192 to $426, and are only available online, but you must select a starting date for the pass at time of purchase. If you come for an evening and like what you see, any single-night ticket (except the free one included with Premier Annual Passes) can be upgraded to a seasonal pass before you depart.

unofficial **TIP** You can buy a Rush of Fear ticket and upgrade it to an Ultimate Frequent Fear ticket on or before its expiration date.

Universal Orlando's paid line-skipping service is a welcome luxury during the day but an absolute lifesaver at night. On peak event nights, queues for the haunted houses will approach 3 hours, and even on the slowest nights, they'll hit 60 minutes. HHN Express Passes reduce that wait to 25%–50% of what it would otherwise be, which can make the difference between experiencing two or three houses in a night to visiting seven or more. The only catch is that Express starts at $160 per person and goes up to $256 depending on the night. Express is also available as an add-on for Rush of Fear or Frequent Fear multinight passes for an additional $458–$586. Express Passes often sell out and may be more expensive or unavailable inside the park, so if you do want them, buy in advance. On off-peak nights it's possible to experience all the haunted houses and at least one show without Express, if you arrive early and stay until closing. On peak nights it's virtually impossible to do the same without Express Passes, and it can be challenging even with them.

If you're feeling particularly flush and are fed up with any kind of queue, the **RIP guided tour** will whisk you to the head of every line for $394–$501 depending on the night, admission not included; half-night tours may be available for half price. A private RIP tour for you and nine of your friends starts at around $4,000 and goes up to almost $10,000, with the ability to add up to two more guests at an additional cost (again, admission not included, but annual pass discounts apply). When money is no object, the RIP tours are highly recommended. Call ☎ 866-346-9350 or email vipexperience@universalorlando .com for pricing and reservations.

For the superfans with extra spending money, Universal offers a choice of in-depth HHN experiences. Join one of Universal's designers on daytime lights-on trips through three or six houses on an **Unmasking the Horror** behind-the-scenes tour ($106–$170 for three-house tour, $192–$224 for six; no admission required). A **Premium Scream Night** event is held the evening before HHN officially opens, with limited attendance and staggered entry for the haunted houses, plus unlimited food and nonalcoholic drinks. Tickets cost $373 plus tax ($346 for passholders). These upgrades can be booked online at theugseries.com/UOHHNExtras.

To arm yourself with knowledge before braving HHN, visit the official website (orlando.halloweenhorrornights.com), along with the fan-run websites horrornightnightmares.com and hhnunofficial.com. If you can't wait for formal announcements of the event's attractions, follow @HNNightmares on social media for "speculation maps" with rumored haunted houses and attractions. Finally, while our standard advice on what to bring (or not bring) to the parks still applies, when preparing for Halloween Horror Nights be especially sure to pack raingear (bad weather is an HHN tradition), comfy shoes, and a refillable cup or bottle.

Halloween Horror Nights Touring Tips

The event officially begins each evening at 6:30 p.m., but the front gates typically open as early as 6 p.m. If you have an HHN ticket but not daytime admission, you'll want to be outside the park gates, ticket in hand, by 5:45 p.m. at the latest on slow nights, and as early as 5 p.m. on peak nights. Be sure to leave ample time for I-4 traffic and parking, which is full price until midnight. Valet parking is available, but remember that the usual annual pass discounts on valet parking don't apply on event nights.

After navigating the security screening in the parking hub, your goal is to secure a spot as close to the USF turnstiles as possible. On-site hotel guests also get their own exclusive entrance near the Hard Rock Cafe. (Note that the Express Unlimited access included with some resort rooms is not valid during HHN.) Early arrivals may also get a view of a gate-opening performance, which usually occurs just inside the main entrance. Don't worry if you miss this minor event; it's a nice touch but not essential.

Better yet, get a jump on the general public outside the gates by being inside the park before they open. The park closes to daytime guests at 5 p.m. on event nights, but anyone holding a ticket for that night's HHN is allowed to remain inside the park in designated holding areas. Anyone can access this opportunity if they have any valid daytime park ticket, including annual passholders, or you can add a $59 Scream Early option onto your HHN ticket to enter the park between 3 and 5 p.m.

Note that the park is officially open for regular operations until 5 p.m., but you'll want to enter before 4:30 p.m. to avoid dealing with the arrival of the evening crowds. Don't cut your arrival too close, especially if utilizing the HHN ticket included with Premier annual passes; Universal's computers make you wait 5–10 minutes between scanning your admission at the park turnstiles and entering a Stay & Scream zone. Between the park's closing and reopening, guests remaining in the park are confined to one of the following locations:

- **World Expo** and the adjoining **Springfield** section offer priority access to the haunted houses behind MEN IN BLACK and The Simpsons Ride. Stay & Scream guests can check in near Lombard's at 4 p.m. and should be released into the first two houses by 5:45 p.m., with the remainder of the mazes opening around 6 p.m.; you can enjoy a selection of food and drinks for purchase while waiting for daytime guests to exit. By using this Stay & Scream location, you should be able to enjoy four or five haunted houses before 8 p.m.

- The **New York** holding area includes Finnegan's Bar and Grill, which offers a full bar and table-service food, though reservations aren't accepted and tables are virtually impossible to secure on event afternoons. Guests can check in across from Minion Cafe by 4 p.m. and are released around 5:15 p.m., giving them first crack at the most popular soundstage houses.

- A **San Francisco** holding area may be located at Richter's, where you can get a burger while waiting for first access to the house inside the Fast & Furious: Supercharged queue. (This area may not be available.)

- A small overflow holding area is located in **Hollywood** near the Today Cafe, where food and beverages are available. From here, you may get early access to the maze closest to the park entrance. Another small pen across the street is dedicated to hotel guests using their exclusive entrance, but it doesn't offer early access to the houses.

• Finally, **Diagon Alley** is **not** a holding area for HHN, and the Hogwarts Express train stops running in both directions as soon as USF's closing time arrives.

The 10 haunted houses are the signature attractions at HHN and quickly develop wait times ranging from moderate to absolutely ridiculous. Five haunted mazes are housed in the huge production soundstages behind Hollywood Rip Ride Rockit; four are located in large sprung tents erected backstage behind Springfield and World Expo; and one takes over the queue of Fast & Furious: Supercharged. (There is also empty space inside the Villain-Con building that could hold a haunted house.) Each year, due to theme or location, some houses seem to attract longer queues than others. Typically, the houses near the front entrance and those based on familiar intellectual properties (such as *A Quiet Place, Ghostbusters,* and the Universal Classic Monsters) have been the most popular, while the original-concept mazes in the rear of the park draw shorter lines than average. Keep this in mind when deciding whether to bite the bullet and queue up for a particular maze.

unofficial **TIP**
Houses that don't open before 6 p.m. will accumulate a large backlog of guests before early entry ends, so save them for later in the night. Instead, spend Stay & Scream enjoying mazes that are operating.

Even the least popular houses, however, will have peak waits of 30 minutes or more, even on less busy nights. Your first hour at the event is therefore essential to making the most of the evening, and your initial plan of attack is determined by which location you start your night from:

• **WORLD EXPO/SPRINGFIELD HOLDING AREA:** If you're among the first inside the World Expo holding area, queue up for the house with the biggest buzz. If one of the houses already has a long line by the time you get there, grab a snack and wait in the shorter queue instead. After experiencing your first house, get in line for the other World Expo haunts if the wait is less than 25 minutes; otherwise, save them for the end of the night. Next, move on to the house entrances near The Simpsons Ride and Fast & Furious.

• **FINNEGAN'S BAR AND GRILL HOLDING AREA:** Enter the New York holding area between 3:45 and 4 p.m. (the earlier the better, especially if you want to get food or drink), and relax in the holding pen for your pick of the designated early-entry mazes. You'll be walked to the soundstage queues around 5 p.m., with the scares starting up around 5:15 p.m. Once the general public is admitted through the front gates (as early as 6 p.m.), queues at the soundstage houses will swiftly build. See as many as you can until waits exceed 30 minutes, and then proceed to the houses in the back of the park.

• **RICHTER'S HOLDING AREA:** Enter the San Francisco holding area between 4 p.m. and 5 p.m., grab some food or a cocktail from Chez Alcatraz, and wait to be released toward Fast & Furious: Supercharged. Once you're through the house found in that attraction's queue, head toward the back of the park and hit the ones in World Expo before crowds build. (This area may not be available.)

• **HOLLYWOOD HOLDING AREA:** Check into the holding area outside the Today Cafe before park closing, then work your way through the plaza as close to Despicable Me Minion Mayhem as possible. Guests will be released shortly before the front gates open, when they can make a mad dash to the nearest maze entrance. By the time the first holding area guests exit the haunted house, the line behind them may be an hour or more, so you should head toward World Expo immediately afterward.

- **GENERAL ADMISSION:** If you're among the first folks through the gates when they open around 6 p.m., head straight to the open soundstage houses and jump in line if the wait is still 15 minutes or less. Otherwise, the majority of guests will mob the houses in the soundstages near the front of the park. You should avoid the horde by heading in the opposite direction, toward Springfield, which should have processed the majority of guests who were already in the park by now. You can also continue through Springfield to the houses in World Expo or San Francisco.

This reader from Highlands Ranch, Colorado, followed our Halloween touring advice with great success:

Being a day guest at the park gave us a tremendous head start on Halloween Horror Nights. Using the recommendations in the guide, we waited in the Springfield holding area, which gave us access to several of the houses that opened before the official start. We were thus able to see four houses in roughly an hour and still catch the first show.

Likewise, our tips led this couple from Rochester, New York, to an enjoyable HHN experience:

We attended the Halloween Horror Nights and were able to get through all 10 of the haunted houses without an Express pass. We would not have been able to do this without following the guidelines in the Unofficial Guide. Getting into the park before the event and getting in line for the [most popular] haunted house was the key to our success.

After the haunted houses, the live pyrotechnics-packed *Halloween Nightmare Fuel* dance show, held inside the former *Fear Factor Live* stadium, is the top draw. The scantily clad performers are all dynamic dancers, and their crowd-enflaming gyrations are accompanied by daring acrobatics, explosive fire-juggling, and electronic music loud enough to wake the dead. The first and last performances of the night are always the least crowded, but you shouldn't have trouble finding a seat if you arrive at least 30 minutes in advance of any showing.

After the sun sets (around 7:30 p.m.) and the waits for the houses become unbearable, begin exploring the scare zones, which have evolved from open-air haunted mazes (minus the conga line queues) into social media–friendly selfie opportunities. Just as much fun as getting scared yourself is finding a vantage point to stand still and see others getting spooked; this is some of the best people-watching you'll ever find. Be on the lookout for staged scenes, in which actors attack planted "victims" within the crowd.

By the midpoint of the evening, standby waits for all the houses will be substantial, and lines for the rides will be astronomical on

Saturdays, but experiencing several top attractions should still be manageable using single-rider queues. Men in Black Alien Attack, Revenge of the Mummy, Harry Potter and the Escape from Gringotts, and Transformers: The Ride–3D all have fairly efficient single-rider operations. Hollywood Rip Ride Rockit has a single-rider line, but it's often as long as the standby queue. On off-peak nights, you may find ride queues shockingly short; just be aware that some rides (including Gringotts) shut down at 11 p.m.

Another HHN must-see is the seasonal lagoon show, which features footage of your favorite film fiends projected on massive water fountains. The 10-minute show, which is repeated hourly starting at 9 p.m., lacks pyrotechnics, but the pulsating lasers and pumping soundtrack make it pretty impressive. You should be able to walk up shortly before the second or third performance; see the lagoon show profile under Live Entertainment on page 225 for viewing tips. (The lagoon show was not performed in 2023 and 2024, but it may return in 2025.)

Even on a slow night, Horror Nights crowds can drive you to drink, and many of your fellow guests will doubtlessly be imbibing. Temporary bars serve beer and overpriced premixed cocktails on seemingly every spare square foot of sidewalk, but for serious in-park boozing, we prefer Finnegan's Bar in New York or Duff Brewery in Springfield. Better yet, get out of Dodge for an hour or so and retreat to CityWalk, where you can grab a drink at the Red Coconut Club (which gets a monstrous makeover into the Dead Coconut Club).

Listening to complaints from HHN guests that alcohol was easily obtainable but actual edibles could be harder to find, Universal offers food festival–style booths around the park, serving exclusive gut busters like twisted taters, pizza fries, and cannibal-themed barbecue. The Halloween Tribute Store (located either in Hollywood across from the Horror Make-Up Show or in New York next to Revenge of the Mummy) is open to both daytime and event guests throughout the fall, and it doubles as both a haunted shopping opportunity and seasonal confectionery, serving up ghoulish treats like beating gelatin hearts.

As the evening's event approaches its final hour, wait times at the haunted mazes drop dramatically. If you're interested in the headliner show and didn't catch an earlier showing, arrive 20–30 minutes before the last performance on peak nights (or 15–20 minutes before showtime off-peak). Otherwise, use the final hours to catch up on the houses you missed earlier. The last 30–60 minutes before park closing is the best time to hit the most popular houses. If you didn't see the popular mazes at the start of the night, step into line for one of them a few minutes before closing; you should be allowed to stay in the queue until you're through, barring technical difficulties.

Unless you leave significantly before closing time, you're best off dawdling in the park or CityWalk on the way out. The parking garage exits will be at a standstill, so you might as well grab a seat outside and relax rather than breathing fumes in a traffic jam.

HOLIDAYS AT UNIVERSAL STUDIOS
(mid-November–early January)

UNIVERSAL ORLANDO celebrates the holiday season every year from two weeks before Thanksgiving through New Year's weekend. Universal Orlando holidays might not have quite the nostalgic lure of Mickey's merrymaking, but its options are every bit as expertly produced and have the benefit of all being included with regular park admission (unlike the extra-cost hard-ticket nighttime parties at the Magic Kingdom).

USF's holiday festivities feature seasonal decorations on the front archway and throughout the park, holiday songs broadcasting from speakers in the streets, and a giant tree that is ceremoniously lit every evening at sunset. Several park attractions, such as *The Blues Brothers Show,* get into the spirit with special versions tied to the season. Universal also celebrates the holidays Harry Potter style with **Christmas in The Wizarding World.** Holiday decor adorns Diagon Alley's streets and shops, and the Leaky Cauldron serves seasonal snacks. But the star of the holidays at Universal Studios is undoubtedly **Universal's Holiday Parade Featuring Macy's.**

USF has been bringing elements of Macy's famous New York parade down to Orlando for a post-Thanksgiving encore every December for over two decades. Today's procession includes elaborate floats showcasing characters from *Shrek, Madagascar,* and *Despicable Me.* Macy's balloons are still a big part of the fun: while the largest balloons you've seen sailing through Manhattan on TV can't make it down the narrower streets of USF, several of the smaller ones are paraded through both productions.

Universal's Holiday Parade begins each evening around 5 p.m. (subject to change; check the show schedule in the smartphone app) near the *Horror Make-Up Show,* continues down Hollywood Boulevard toward the park entrance, travels past Despicable Me Minion Mayhem and Music Plaza toward New York, and then turns near Revenge of the Mummy and again past Transformers, exiting through the gate it originally entered.

You can get a good view of the parade from anywhere along the route, but ideal viewing spots are near Mel's Drive-In at the beginning of the route and near the large tree in New York toward the end. Reserved viewing areas are available for guests with disabilities (in front of Macy's in New York), for annual passholders (near Mel's Drive-In), and for young Little Stars and their families (near Hollywood's Brown Derby).

If you've always fantasized about guiding a giant inflatable animal down Fifth Avenue, you can volunteer to participate in the parade as a balloon handler for free. Volunteers must be 18 years or older, at least 48 inches tall and 125 pounds, English speaking, and able to walk the mile-long route for up to an hour. Sign-up is held daily 2 hours before the parade starts near Animal Actors. A limited number of spots are available for guests each day, and you'll have to sign a waiver to participate.

After the parade on select nights, USF's Music Plaza Stage hosts live concerts by **Mannheim Steamroller**. The electrified orchestra usually performs its amped-up holiday classics on the first two Saturdays and Sundays in December. These shows can be popular, so arrive at least 45 minutes early if you want a close-up view.

UNIVERSAL STUDIOS FLORIDA TOURING PLANS

OUR STEP-BY-STEP touring plans are field-tested for seeing *as much as possible* in one day with a minimum amount of time wasted in lines. They're designed to help you avoid crowds and bottlenecks on days of moderate to heavy attendance. Understand, however, that there's more to see at USF than can be experienced in one day during peak season. If you're visiting on days of lighter attendance (see "Trying to Reason with the Tourist Season," page 25) or using Universal Express (see page 57), our plans will save you time but won't be as critical to successful touring as on busier days.

In general, most visitors find that they can be far more flexible with their touring plans at Universal than at Disney and still see everything they want to see. But if you're at the parks on a busy day, you'll want to stick to the script, at least until you get the most popular attractions out of the way. Afternoon touring at USF is largely dependent on the park's ever-shifting show schedule, so check showtimes in the smartphone app as soon as you arrive and shuffle the steps accordingly.

Before using any of our Universal Orlando touring plans, first become familiar with Universal's park-opening procedures, as described on page 51. Purchase your admission ahead of time, and call ☎ 407-363-8000 or check universalorlando.com the day before you go to verify official operating hours. If you're eligible for Early Park Admission (see page 53), arrive at USF 90–120 minutes before the official park opening time. If you're not eligible for early entry, arrive at the park 30–45 minutes prior to opening time.

If you're using TouringPlans' Lines smartphone app, you can select any of the following premium touring plans, copy it to your list of personalized plans, and optimize the plan steps to your preferences. Once you arrive at the park, select the appropriate plan in the app to make it active, and track your progress during the day by marking each attraction as complete after exiting. Optimize the plan repeatedly during the day to refine it with the latest wait-time information. If you're following a two-park plan, a link to part two will appear at the top of the plan; switch to the second part when moving to the second park, and then return to part one when you return to the original park.

Once you're admitted into the park, move quickly from attraction to attraction, following your chosen touring plan. If you're not interested in an attraction it lists, simply skip that attraction and proceed to the next. When you encounter a very long line at an attraction that the touring plan calls for, skip the attraction in question and go to the next step, returning later to retry. Don't worry that other people will be following the plans and render them useless. Fewer than 2 in every 100 people in the park will have been exposed to this information.

CHOOSING THE APPROPRIATE TOURING PLAN

WE PRESENT FOUR USF touring plans:

- One-Day Touring Plan for Adults
- One-Day Touring Plan for Families with Small Children
- One-Day Touring Plan for Families with Tweens
- One-Day Touring Plan for Seniors

In addition, we have four Universal Orlando touring plans that combine both USF and IOA, for guests with park-to-park admission:

- Universal Orlando Highlights One-Day/Two-Park Touring Plan (Two Versions)
- Wizarding World One-Day/Two-Park Touring Plan
- Universal Orlando Comprehensive Two-Day/Two-Park Touring Plan

If you have two days at Universal Orlando, the Comprehensive Two-Day/Two-Park Touring Plan is by far the most relaxed. The two-day plan takes advantage of early morning, when lines are short and the park hasn't filled with guests. This plan works well year-round and eliminates much of the extra walking required by the one-day plans. No matter when the park closes, our two-day plan guarantees the most efficient touring and the least time in lines. The plan is perfect for guests who wish to explore the attractions and the atmosphere of USF and IOA, with an emphasis on both Wizarding Worlds.

If you have only one day to visit USF and don't have park-to-park tickets, then use the One-Day Touring Plan for Adults. It's exhausting, but it packs in the maximum. If you have one-day park-to-park passes, a Universal Orlando Highlights Touring Plan will help you pack in all of the best thrill rides at USF and IOA, including The Wizarding World ones, at the expense of most shows and a lot of shoe leather. We offer one version that starts and finishes in Universal Studios Florida and another that begins and ends in Islands of Adventure; both highlight the resort's top headliners, but they include alternate second-tier attractions in the afternoon. Alternatively, Harry Potter superfans who have one-day park-to-park passes and zero interest in anything at Universal outside Hogsmeade and Diagon Alley (a mistake in our estimation, but it's your money) can follow the Wizarding World One-Day/Two-Park Touring Plan to maximize their magical immersion.

If you have young ones in tow, adopt the One-Day Touring Plan for Families with Small Children. It's a compromise, blending the preferences of younger children with those of older siblings and adults. The plan includes many children's rides but omits roller coasters and other attractions that frighten young children or are off-limits because of height requirements greater than 40 inches. The plan for Families with Tweens includes some moderate roller coasters and thrill rides with height requirements up to 52 inches (the height of an average 9-year-old), with warnings on anything over a 48-inch requirement. Or use the One-Day Touring Plan for Adults and take advantage of child swap, a technique whereby children accompany adults to the loading area of a ride with age and height requirements but don't board (see page 187).

If you have three days at Universal Orlando, use the Comprehensive Two-Day/Two-Park Touring Plan on the first two days, and use a Universal Orlando Highlights One-Day/Two-Park Touring Plan or Wizarding World Touring Plan on your last day. With four or more days, you can pretty much explore the parks at your leisure, using any of the plans as a general guideline.

After Epic Universe opens, to experience all three theme parks combine one of our One-Day plans for the new park (see pages 288–289) with your choice of the following Two-Park plans for USF and IOA. You'll need a bare minimum of two full days, and we strongly recommend spreading your visit out over three or four.

ONE-DAY TOURING PLAN FOR ADULTS *(page 395)*

THIS PLAN IS FOR GUESTS without park-to-park tickets and includes every recommended attraction at USF. If a ride or show is listed that you don't want to experience, skip that step and proceed to the next. Move quickly from attraction to attraction, and, if possible, hold off on lunch until after experiencing at least six rides.

ONE-DAY TOURING PLAN FOR FAMILIES WITH SMALL CHILDREN *(page 396)*

THIS PLAN IS FOR GUESTS without park-to-park tickets and eliminates all rides with a minimum height requirement greater than 40 inches. The plan includes a midday break of at least 2 hours back at your hotel.

ONE-DAY TOURING PLAN FOR FAMILIES WITH TWEENS *(page 397)*

THIS PLAN IS FOR GUESTS without park-to-park tickets and eliminates all rides with a minimum height requirement greater than 52 inches; rides with height requirements over 48 inches include warnings.

ONE-DAY TOURING PLAN FOR SENIORS
(page 398)

THIS PLAN IS FOR GUESTS without park-to-park tickets and is specifically designed for seniors and grandparents, taking walking distances and attraction ratings from this group into account. This plan focuses on shows and family-friendly attractions and avoids thrill rides.

UNIVERSAL ORLANDO HIGHLIGHTS ONE-DAY/ TWO-PARK TOURING PLANS *(Two Versions, pages 403–406)*

THESE PLANS ARE FOR GUESTS with park-to-park tickets who wish to see the highlights of USF and IOA in a single day. If your primary focus is on Diagon Alley, pick the version that starts in USF; visitors prioritizing VelociCoaster or Hagrid's should select the one starting in IOA. The plans use Hogwarts Express to get from one park to the other and back again; you can walk back for the return leg if the line is too long. Both plans include lunch and dinner. During holiday periods, you may need to substitute a quick-service snack for one or both meals to fit in all of the plan's attractions.

WIZARDING WORLD ONE-DAY/TWO-PARK TOURING PLAN *(pages 407–408)*

THIS PLAN IS FOR GUESTS with one-day park-to-park tickets who wish to experience The Wizarding Worlds of Harry Potter to the exclusion of everything else Universal has to offer. The plan uses Hogwarts Express to get from one park to the other and then back again; you can walk back to the first park for the return leg if the line is too long. The plan includes lunch at Three Broomsticks and dinner at the Leaky Cauldron. During holiday periods, you may need to substitute a quick-service snack for one or both meals to fit in all of the plan's attractions.

UNIVERSAL ORLANDO COMPREHENSIVE TWO-DAY/ TWO-PARK TOURING PLAN *(pages 409–412)*

THIS PLAN IS FOR GUESTS with multiday park-to-park tickets who wish to explore USF and IOA in-depth over two days. The plan includes one Hogwarts Express trip between parks per day. Incidentally, all the water rides are concentrated in the morning of the first day, so if bad weather is in the forecast, consider flipping the plan days.

PART 7

UNIVERSAL ISLANDS *of* ADVENTURE

UNIVERSAL STUDIOS FLORIDA HAD BARELY opened before planning began on Project X, the second theme park that would provide Universal with enough critical mass to actually compete with Disney. Originally envisioned as Cartoon World, with areas devoted to DC Comics superheroes and Looney Tunes characters, the concept evolved into **Islands of Adventure** (IOA), a fully themed fantasy park inspired by family-friendly literature.

Designed from its very inception to directly compete with Disney's Magic Kingdom, IOA has kid-friendly rides and cartoon characters (like Fantasyland), thrill rides in a sci-fi city (like Tomorrowland), and a jungle river with robot creatures (like Adventureland).

IOA debuted in 1999 as a state-of-the-art park competing with a Disney park decades older, but it didn't initially do gangbuster business, thanks partly to a botched marketing rollout and Universal's failure to add any major attractions during IOA's first decade. That all changed in 2010, when Universal opened the first Harry Potter–themed area within the park. Universal went all out to create a setting and attractions designed to be the envy of the industry.

BEWARE OF THE WET AND WILD

THOUGH WE'VE DESCRIBED IOA as a direct competitor to the Magic Kingdom, know this: whereas most Disney attractions are designed to be enjoyed by guests of any age, the roller coasters at Universal are serious with a capital *S,* making Space Mountain and Big Thunder Mountain Railroad look about as frightening as Dumbo. In fact, eight of the top ten attractions at IOA are thrill rides; of these, three will not only scare the crap out of you but will also drench you with water. And about that water: It ain't exactly Evian, as a reader from New York learned the hard way:

The amount of water dumped on us at Popeye & Bluto's Bilge-Rat Barges was incredible, and the chlorine was so bad that one of us couldn't see.

After your chemical baptism, you may be tempted by the heated full-body drying booths strategically positioned near the exit of each drenching attraction, but this Pennsylvania reader has a warning:

The People Dryers are a waste of $7. We used one and were no drier than before, just poorer.

If you get soaked, you're better off just walking off the wetness in warm weather, or packing a change of clothes if it's cool.

For families, there are three interactive playgrounds as well as six rides or shows without height restrictions that young children can enjoy. Of the thrill rides, only The Amazing Adventures of Spider-Man, Skull Island, and the two in Toon Lagoon (described later) are marginally appropriate for little kids, and even on these rides, your child needs to be fairly hardy.

GETTING ORIENTED *at* UNIVERSAL ISLANDS *of* ADVENTURE

LAID OUT MUCH LIKE EPCOT's World Showcase—with a central entry corridor leading to a ring of connected lands surrounding a large lagoon—IOA evinces the same thematic continuity present in the Magic Kingdom. Each "island" (actually peninsula) is self-contained and visually consistent in its theme, separated from its neighbors by bridge-covered estuaries.

You first encounter **Port of Entry,** a mélange of Middle Eastern and Asian architecture, where you'll find Guest Services, lockers, stroller and wheelchair rentals, ATM banking, Lost and Found, and shopping. From the Port of Entry, moving clockwise around the lagoon, you access **Marvel Super Hero Island, Toon Lagoon, Skull Island, Jurassic Park, The Wizarding World of Harry Potter—Hogsmeade, The Lost Continent,** and **Seuss Landing.** There is no in-park transportation to move you between lands.

As you enter IOA, lockers and rentals are to your left, and First Aid and Guest Services are to your right. Before bolting through Port of Entry to your first adventure—or at least on your way out before leaving—take a few moments to appreciate the details that Universal lavished on this area, from the fountain made of giant leaves, to the sounds of gamblers from an upstairs casino, to the jail that's been broken and the fire station that burned down. Also listen for the original background music, which is synchronized throughout the park and changes as you move from island to island. While passing through, you may encounter interactive adventurers or a band of storytelling pirates who retell the lost legend of Sindbad's eighth voyage. Port of Entry doesn't have any attractions, but it does have dining (including a Starbucks) and shopping options.

NOT TO BE MISSED AT ISLANDS OF ADVENTURE

MARVEL SUPER HERO ISLAND
- The Amazing Adventures of Spider-Man   • The Incredible Hulk Coaster

TOON LAGOON   • Popeye & Bluto's Bilge-Rat Barges

JURASSIC PARK   • Jurassic Park River Adventure   • Jurassic World VelociCoaster

THE WIZARDING WORLD OF HARRY POTTER—HOGSMEADE
- Hagrid's Magical Creatures Motorbike Adventure
- Harry Potter and the Forbidden Journey   • Hogwarts Express

UNIVERSAL ISLANDS *of* ADVENTURE ATTRACTIONS

MARVEL SUPER HERO ISLAND

THIS ISLAND, WITH ITS FUTURISTIC and retro-future design and comic book signage, offers shopping, dining, and two of Orlando's best thrill rides, all based on Marvel Comics characters. The architecture, which some fault as flat, seeks to re-create the Pop Art look of comic book backgrounds; some buildings have Chrome Illusion paint that changes colors depending on the angle of sunlight. Look for the meteor impact sculpture covered in hundreds of Marvel characters, as well as communication booths delivering messages from S.H.I.E.L.D.

Several times a day on a published schedule, Marvel heroes parade in and take over the streets greeting guests; the activity can make it tough to navigate through the area. Between the roar of The Incredible Hulk Coaster and the bass beats surrounding The Amazing Adventures of Spider-Man building, Super Hero Island is also one of the loudest sections of the park; seek refuge along the water behind Captain America Diner.

In case you were curious: Yes, Disney now owns Marvel Comics, but Universal locked up the theme park rights to certain character groups—the Avengers, Spider-Man, the Fantastic Four, and X-Men—in perpetuity on the East Coast. You may see Black Panther, Iron Man, and Captain America in Disneyland or in Mickey's international parks, but they are exclusive to IOA in Orlando for the indefinite future. The Guardians of the Galaxy, who have their own roller coaster at EPCOT, are an exception to this restriction.

STELLA SAYS

MARVEL SUPER HERO ISLAND Comic book illustrator Adam Kubert was tasked with creating the art for the larger-than-life murals throughout the area, and he hid his signature in nearly every one. Search for at least 22 "ADAM" signatures hiding in each of the character cutouts, often found lurking in character shading, wrinkles of clothing, and even Wolverine's arm hair!

The Amazing Adventures of Spider-Man *(Universal Express)*
★★★★★

What it is Indoor adventure 3-D simulator ride. **Scope and scale** Super-headliner. **When to go** During the first 40 minutes the park is open. **Comments** 40″ minimum height requirement; child swap available (see page 187); single-rider line available; not to be missed. **Duration of ride** 4½ minutes. **Loading speed** Moderate-fast.

Motion Sickness

DESCRIPTION AND COMMENTS Widely regarded as one of the best theme park attractions anywhere in the world, The Amazing Adventures of Spider-Man moves a spinning, tilting ride vehicle through 13 scenes (covering 1.5 acres) of mayhem, seamlessly fusing 4K 3-D digital projections with physical sets and special effects, including fog, water, and fire. The total package is astonishing—frenetic yet fluid, wild yet smooth, and visually rich. Though the attraction opened more than 20 years ago, Spider-Man is still technologically ahead of almost everything at Walt Disney World outside Pandora: The World of Avatar or Star Wars: Galaxy's Edge—which is to say that it will leave you in awe.

The story line is that you're visiting the *Daily Bugle* newspaper (where Peter Parker, also known as Spider-Man, works as a mild-mannered photographer) when it's discovered that Sinister Syndicate—consisting of Spidey's archenemies Doctor Octopus, Hobgoblin, Electro, Hydro-Man, and Scream—has used an antigravity gun to steal (we promise we're not making this up) the Statue of Liberty. You're drafted on the spot by cantankerous editor J. Jonah Jameson to get the story. You board a 12-passenger SCOOP vehicle—a mobile open-top motion simulator identical to the cars used in Universal Studios Florida's (USF's) Transformers—and follow the "Spider Signal" straight into an epic battle between the web-slinger and his foes. After speeding around the city, you experience a 400-foot "sensory drop" from a skyscraper roof all the way to the pavement, a remarkably convincing effect.

Spidey is less frantic than the similar Transformers ride next door and features more dialogue and humor. And despite using similar systems, some folks who get motion sick on Transformers find that they can tolerate this ride better.

The late Marvel Comics founder Stan Lee made cameo appearances in nearly every film featuring the characters he helped create, and The Amazing Adventures of Spider-Man ride is no exception. Lee appears as the truck driver who swerves to miss your SCOOP vehicle early in the ride, outside the theater as Spidey and Doc Ock duke it out, in the street after your vehicle falls to the ground, and finally with the cops as the stolen Statue of Liberty is being flown back into place. He is also the voice who bids you farewell before disembarking.

TOURING TIPS If you were on hand for Early Park Admission, ride after experiencing The Wizarding World and Skull Island: Reign of Kong. If you elect to bypass The Wizarding World congestion, ride after Hulk.

Seats in the first row are the most immersive, but we find that the 3-D effects focus better from a row or two back. The rear corners get the most movement, while the center of the second row is the most stable. There is an on-ride photo, but the camera is in an odd position, so everyone usually comes out facing the wrong way.

The standby and Express queues both wind through portions of the *Daily Bugle* newsroom; Express cuts through Peter Parker's darkroom (look for Spidey's glowing handprints on the ceiling), while standby passes by J. J.'s trophy case, with hidden tributes to the designers. The single-rider option, when available, bypasses

continued on page 248

Universal Islands of Adventure

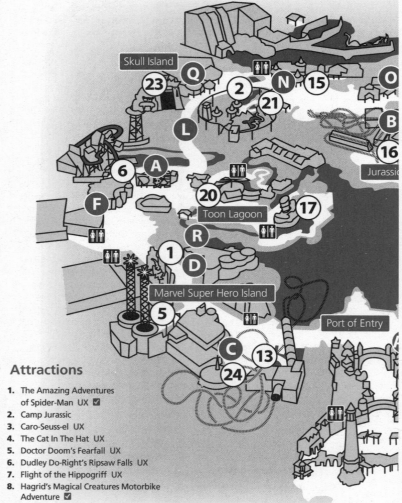

Attractions

1. The Amazing Adventures of Spider-Man UX ☑
2. Camp Jurassic
3. Caro-Seuss-el UX
4. The Cat In The Hat UX
5. Doctor Doom's Fearfall UX
6. Dudley Do-Right's Ripsaw Falls UX
7. Flight of the Hippogriff UX
8. Hagrid's Magical Creatures Motorbike Adventure ☑
9. Harry Potter and the Forbidden Journey UX ☑
10. The High in the Sky Seuss Trolley Train Ride! UX
11. Hogwarts Express: Hogsmeade Station UX ☑
12. If I Ran The Zoo
13. The Incredible Hulk Coaster UX ☑
14. Jurassic Park Discovery Center

15. Jurassic Park River Adventure UX ☑
16. Jurassic World VelociCoaster UX ☑
17. Me Ship, *The Olive*
18. Ollivanders
19. One Fish, Two Fish, Red Fish, Blue Fish UX
20. Popeye & Bluto's Bilge-Rat Barges UX ☑

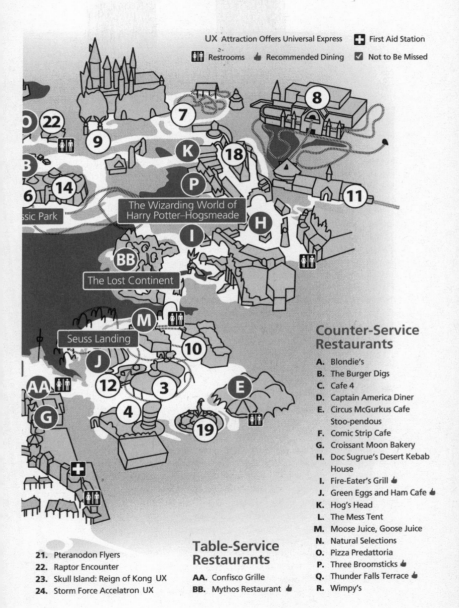

UX Attraction Offers Universal Express   ✚ First Aid Station

🚻 Restrooms   👍 Recommended Dining   ☑ Not to Be Missed

The Wizarding World of Harry Potter–Hogsmeade

The Lost Continent

Seuss Landing

ssic Park

Counter-Service Restaurants

A. Blondie's
B. The Burger Digs
C. Cafe 4
D. Captain America Diner
E. Circus McGurkus Cafe Stoo-pendous
F. Comic Strip Cafe
G. Croissant Moon Bakery
H. Doc Sugrue's Desert Kebab House
I. Fire-Eater's Grill 👍
J. Green Eggs and Ham Cafe 👍
K. Hog's Head
L. The Mess Tent
M. Moose Juice, Goose Juice
N. Natural Selections
O. Pizza Predattoria
P. Three Broomsticks 👍
Q. Thunder Falls Terrace 👍
R. Wimpy's

Table-Service Restaurants

AA. Confisco Grille
BB. Mythos Restaurant 👍

21. Pteranodon Flyers
22. Raptor Encounter
23. Skull Island: Reign of Kong UX
24. Storm Force Accelatron UX

continued from page 245

most of the buildup but can greatly cut your wait as long as the line doesn't reach the stroller parking area.

Doctor Doom's Fearfall *(Universal Express)* ★★★

APPEAL BY AGE	PRESCHOOL ★	GRADE SCHOOL ★★★½	TEENS ★★★★
YOUNG ADULTS ★★★★		OVER 30 ★★★½	SENIORS ★★★

What it is Tower launch and free fall. **Scope and scale** Major attraction. **When to go** During the first hour the park is open or after 3 p.m. **Comments** 52" minimum height requirement; child swap available (see page 187); single-rider line available. **Duration of ride** 40 seconds. **Loading speed** Slow.

DESCRIPTION AND COMMENTS Here you are (again), strapped into a seat with your feet dangling, blasted 200 feet up in the air, and then allowed to partially free-fall back down. Imagine the midway game where a macho guy swings a sledgehammer, propelling a metal sphere up a vertical shaft to ring a bell—on this ride, you're the metal sphere.

That prospect sounds worse than it actually is. The scariest part of the ride is the apprehension that builds as you sit, strapped in, waiting for the ride to launch. Blasting up and falling down are actually pleasant, with one exhilarating, fleeting moment of negative-gravity air time at the top. Riders in chambers three and four get a great view of the park, while those in one and two look out over I-4 and International Drive.

TOURING TIPS We've seen glaciers that move faster than the line for Doctor Doom's Fearfall, though the ominous queue and satirical propaganda films compensate slightly; ask for a **villains tour** to learn some of the line's sinister secrets. If you want to ride without investing half an hour, be one of the first to ride. If you're on hand at opening time, being among the first isn't too difficult (mainly because The Wizarding World, Hulk, and Spider-Man attractions are bigger draws). Alternatively, the ride often has no wait near the end of the operating day, and the view is especially nice at night.

Fortunately, Doctor Doom also has a singles line (when available); look for the stairwell to the left of the ride's entrance.

The Incredible Hulk Coaster *(Universal Express)* ★★★★

APPEAL BY AGE	PRESCHOOL ★½	GRADE SCHOOL ★★★★	TEENS ★★★★½
YOUNG ADULTS ★★★★½		OVER 30 ★★★★	SENIORS ★★★

What it is Roller coaster. **Scope and scale** Super-headliner. **When to go** During the first 40 minutes the park is open or after 3 p.m. **Comments** 54" minimum height requirement; child swap available (see page 187); single-rider line available; not to be missed. **Duration of ride** 2¼ minutes. **Loading speed** Moderate–fast.

Motion Sickness

DESCRIPTION AND COMMENTS The Incredible Hulk's towering loops are some of the most iconic elements of the IOA skyline, and the big green guy's ride remains one of the most powerful coasters in Florida, providing a ride comparable to that of Kumba (Busch Gardens) or Kraken (Sea-World) with the added thrill of an accelerated launch. The story line set up by videos and props in the queue sees guests volunteering for General Thaddeus "Thunderbolt" Ross's experimental attempt to create super-soldiers via gamma ray bombardment. (Ask a team member for a **gamma tour** to examine the Marvel Comics Easter eggs hidden along the line.)

What you need to know about this attraction is simple. You'll be shot like a carrier-launched jet from 0 to 40 mph in 2 seconds, flung upside down into a zero gravity barrel roll 100 feet off the ground (which will, of course, induce weightlessness), and then thrown immediately into a pair of cobra rolls and a vertical loop of more than 100 feet, into a belowground tunnel, no less! Two more rolls and another loop follow, for a total of seven upside-down experiences in a ride of a little more than 2 minutes. At the end of the ride, you may be just as green as the Hulk.

While still a far cry from the side-to-side shaking of Hollywood Rip Ride Rockit next door, Hulk has developed a tendency toward head-banging, so be mindful of the horse-collar shoulder restraints.

TOURING TIPS If you don't have early entry, our advice is to skip The Wizarding World attractions in the early morning and ride The Incredible Hulk Coaster first thing. Alternatively, if you insist on going to Hogsmeade at rope drop (or if you're eligible for Early Park Admission), you should ride Hulk immediately after you've enjoyed the Harry Potter attractions or save it for late in the day.

Universal provides electronic lockers near the entrance of The Incredible Hulk Coaster to deposit any items that might depart your person during the ride. Use the mandatory free lockers for anything—and we mean anything—that could be dislodged during your ride: hats, glasses, cell phones, camera bags, and toupees. The only thing you have to hold on to is your park ticket (in your pocket or on a lanyard) in order to reopen your locker afterward. Be prepared to pat down your pockets for loose change, or you'll be pulled aside for a TSA-style wanding after triggering the metal detectors. Single riders must wait in the same security queue as standby guests, but then get to skip straight to the boarding area.

If the line is short enough, opt for the special front-row queue near the boarding area. It's worth waiting an extra 5–10 minutes to get a spectacular, brief view of the park. The back left seat gets the best zero gravity effect from the opening inversion.

Storm Force Accelatron (*Universal Express*) ★★½

APPEAL BY AGE PRESCHOOL ★★★★ **GRADE SCHOOL** ★★★★ **TEENS** ★★★½
YOUNG ADULTS ★★★½   **OVER 30** ★★★   **SENIORS** ★★★

What it is Covered spinning ride. **Scope and scale** Minor attraction. **When to go** Anytime. **Comments** Child swap available (see page 187). **Duration of ride** 1½ minutes. **Loading speed** Slow.

Motion Sickness

DESCRIPTION AND COMMENTS Storm Force Accelatron is a spiffed-up version of Disney's nausea-inducing Mad Tea Party. In Storm Force Accelatron, up to five people are seated in a round plastic ride vehicle that has a metal wheel mounted in the center. Turning the metal wheel causes the ride vehicle to spin on its central axis. While that's happening, each ride vehicle is part of a group of three similar vehicles, also spinning around a common axis. And the entire group of 12 ride vehicles is simultaneously spinning around the Accelatron's center.

In Universal's take on this carnival classic, you spin to the accompaniment of a simulated thunderstorm. Flashing lights and loud music either really enhance the experience or make it much, much worse, depending on your stomach. A story line involving the X-Men heroine Storm loosely ties this midway-type ride to the Marvel Super Hero Island area, but it's largely irrelevant and offers no advice on keeping your lunch down.

Young children, teens, and masochists like to lure the unsuspecting onto the ride, and then turn the wheel like maniacs. The ride is effective for determining if you've recently developed any kind of inner-ear disorder.

TOURING TIPS Storm Force is hidden behind Hulk's locker banks and is largely overlooked by the crowds. The ride doesn't open until 10 a.m. and is typically a walk-on; even on the busiest days, the wait rarely tops 20 minutes. If you're prone to motion sickness, keep your distance.

TOON LAGOON

WHIMSICAL AND GAILY COLORED, with rounded and exaggerated lines, Toon Lagoon translates cartoon art into real buildings and settings. King's Row and Comic Strip Lane, the main drags of Toon Lagoon, are the domains of such vintage Sunday-funnies favorites as *Beetle Bailey, The Family Circus,* and *Blondie*—in other words, intellectual property that Universal could get for cheap. Across a bridge lies Sweethaven, home to Popeye and Olive Oyl, and a mountain dedicated to Dudley Do-Right looms around the corner.

The island's King Features Syndicate and Jay Ward comic characters, though classic, are probably unrecognizable to anyone born after 1980, but that doesn't stop kids from enjoying the resort's two wettest water rides, both of which are found here. Entering Toon Lagoon from Marvel Super Hero Island, you'll have to pass a midway of barely themed carnival games and an enormous amphitheater that has sat empty for ages, making this transition the biggest eyesore in an otherwise exquisite park. There are some great photo ops here, especially the sideways sign where you can snap a gravity-defying shot with Marmaduke the Great Dane.

If your kids want to get wet but are too small for the water rides (or you don't want to wait in line), send them to the splash pads at either entrance to Toon Lagoon. A few minutes frolicking in fountains of sulfurous water should satisfy them.

Dudley Do-Right's Ripsaw Falls *(Universal Express)* ★★★½

APPEAL BY AGE	PRESCHOOL ★★★½	GRADE SCHOOL ★★★★½	TEENS ★★★★
YOUNG ADULTS ★★★★		OVER 30 ★★★★	SENIORS ★★★

What it is Flume ride. **Scope and scale** Headliner. **When to go** Before 11 a.m. **Comments** 44" minimum height requirement; child swap available (see page 187). **Duration of ride** 5 minutes. **Loading speed** Moderate.

DESCRIPTION AND COMMENTS Dudley Do-Right's Ripsaw Falls features characters spun off from the old Rocky and Bullwinkle TV show. Dudley is a cheerfully incompetent Canadian Mountie who pursues Snidely Whiplash, his nemesis, throughout the Great White North. Snidely inevitably tries to kidnap Nell, the girl of Dudley's dreams, and Dudley (with trusted horse, Horse) rescues her, usually in spite of himself. The original cartoons parodied everything from the implausible plots of early silent movie melodramas to the "friendly Canadian" trope, complete with really bad Quebecois accents. We think this attraction may have been inspired by Dudley's "Saw Mill" cartoon circa 1962.

Story line aside, IOA's tribute to the cartoon is a flume ride similar to Tiana's Bayou Adventure at the Magic Kingdom (formerly Splash Mountain). Riders sit single file in loglike boats and bob along a man-made river, floating past mostly static scenes telling the story of Snidely kidnapping Nell, with Dudley's eventual rescuing.

As far as log flume rides go, Ripsaw Falls is pretty good. There are several medium-size drops during the 5-minute ride, and a heart-stopping 75-foot one near the end. Universal claims this is the first flume ride to "send riders plummeting 15 feet below the surface of the water"; you're just plummeting into a tunnel, but it's a nifty effect. The ride queue and loading area have some visual gags that would make the original show's writers proud, and the on-board ride audio is also good.

That being said, the theming and visuals of Ripsaw Falls aren't in the same league as Disney's attraction, to which everyone inevitably compares it. Most of Ripsaw Falls's effects are nonmoving statues, whereas Disney's flume ride is loaded with moving animatronics, water effects, and gorgeous scenery. Dudley's defects are partly intentional, in keeping with the cartoon's satirical spirit, like an exposed view of backstage following the "scenic overlook" that's cheekily labeled "overlooked scenery." But the flaws are mostly due to the ride's rushed completion (it opened a year earlier than originally scheduled), resulting in a potential classic that was never properly finished.

TOURING TIPS This ride will get you wet, but on average not as soaked as on Popeye & Bluto's Bilge-Rat Barges. If you want to stay dry, arrive prepared with a poncho; however, no poncho can protect your feet, as this Seattle reader observed:

> It's a conundrum that you have to wear shoes on all rides, but your feet get soaked on Ripsaw Falls. I saw one mother putting small plastic bags over her kids' shoes—it looked funny but perhaps it worked.

If you're going to ride both Ripsaw Falls and Bilge-Rat Barges, see them one after another during the morning (if it's sunny enough to dry you off) or at the end of the day before slogging back to your hotel. After riding, take a moment to gauge the timing of the water cannons that go off along the exit walk. This is where you can really get drenched. Ride this after experiencing all the Marvel Super Hero rides.

This is one of the few single-file log flumes that uses lap bar restraints, and it makes for a mighty tight fit. Make sure you try the test seat outside the queue before waiting in line. If you don't want to ride, you can pump money into the water sprayers along the bridge leading to Skull Island and amuse yourself by dousing guests who just survived the big drop.

Me Ship, *The Olive* ★★★

APPEAL BY AGE	PRESCHOOL ★★★½	GRADE SCHOOL ★★★★	TEENS ★★★½
YOUNG ADULTS ★★★		OVER 30 ★★★	SENIORS ★★★½

What it is Interactive playground. **Scope and scale** Minor attraction. **When to go** Anytime.

DESCRIPTION AND COMMENTS *The Olive* is Popeye's beloved boat coming to life as a three-floor interactive playground. *The Olive* offers a chance for kids to run around and expend some of the energy they've pent up while waiting in lines. Besides slides, stairs, and climbing platforms, kids can play with props, including the ship's wheel, bell, and throttle. Those who climb to the second floor will find water cannons that can reach riders on the nearby Bilge-Rat Barges. A separate play area, called Swee'Pea's Playpen, is available for smaller children.

TOURING TIPS Usually opens an hour after the park opens and shuts down an hour before park closing. If you're into the big rides, save this for later in the day. Also, take a few minutes to explore the shoreline pathways behind the ship; you'll find some punny Popeye props and a little peace and quiet.

Popeye & Bluto's Bilge-Rat Barges (*Universal Express*)
★★★★

APPEAL BY AGE	PRESCHOOL ★★★★	GRADE SCHOOL ★★★★	TEENS ★★★★
YOUNG ADULTS ★★★★½		OVER 30 ★★★★	SENIORS ★★★½

STELLA SAYS

POPEYE & BLUTO'S BILGE-RAT BARGES When in line, keep an eye out for a little office that looks like it belongs to Bluto. Seems like his cannon has blasted a hole right through the wall . . . and the next wall . . . and even the next wall too! By the time you're outside you'll be able to spot the cannonball itself, stuck in a pole.

What it is Whitewater rapids raft ride. **Scope and scale** Headliner. **When to go** Before 11 a.m. **Comments** 42" minimum height requirement; child swap available (see page 187); not to be missed. **Duration of ride** 4½ minutes. **Loading speed** Moderate–fast.

DESCRIPTION AND COMMENTS Hands down our favorite whitewater raft ride on the East Coast, Bilge-Rat Barges is only bested in its genre by Grizzly River Run at Disney California Adventure. Bilge-Rat Barges seats 10 riders at a time on a circular raft down a man-made canyon of gushing rapids, waterfalls, twists, turns, and dips. Some of the scenery is visually interesting, such as the 18-foot octopus crammed into a cave two sizes too small, but the minimally moving props along the side don't quite make for an immersive story line.

TOURING TIPS If you didn't drown on Dudley Do-Right, here's a second chance. You'll get a lot wetter from the knees down on this ride, so use your poncho or garbage bag and ride barefoot with your britches rolled up. Each raft has a covered center console into which you can place backpacks, socks, and shoes; lockers or zip-top bags are strongly suggested for anything electronic. If you don't believe us, listen to this reader from Kinross, Scotland:

> I had seen people coming off the ride soaked but had no clue that every rider gets saturated to the skin!

This ride usually opens an hour later than the rest of the park and may close an hour earlier. Experience the barges in the morning after the Marvel Super Hero attractions and Dudley Do-Right. Some people ride Bilge-Rat Barges and Ripsaw Falls consecutively, right before leaving the park, to avoid sloshing around in wet clothes most of the day.

Some children may be frightened more by the way the rapids look, and by the screams coming from the ride as it passes through Toon Lagoon, than by the roughness of the ride itself. These are screams of laughter. If your child is apprehensive about riding, take them to any of the platforms overlooking the ride to see how much fun everyone is having.

SKULL ISLAND

WE'RE NOT ENTIRELY SURE how Skull Island qualifies as its own land on IOA's map when it consists of a single attraction and a couple of kiosks crammed in between Toon Lagoon and Thunder Falls Terrace, but that's a question for Universal's crack cartographers. While it's the smallest stand-alone section of this (or perhaps any) park, Skull Island makes a big visual impact on guests passing through to Jurassic Park, with which it shares an aesthetic kinship.

Skull Island: Reign of Kong *(Universal Express)*   ★★★½

APPEAL BY AGE   PRESCHOOL ★★★   **GRADE SCHOOL** ★★★½   **TEENS** ★★★½
YOUNG ADULTS ★★★★   **OVER 30** ★★★★   **SENIORS** ★★★★

What it is Indoor–outdoor truck safari with motion simulation. **Scope and scale** Headliner. **When to go** Immediately after attraction opening or after 4 p.m. **Comments** 36″ minimum height requirement; child swap available (see page 187); single-rider line available. Too dark and scary for small children. **Duration of ride** About 6 minutes; 4 minutes when exterior is bypassed. **Loading speed** Fast.

DESCRIPTION AND COMMENTS Skull Island: Reign of Kong is an original adventure set in the 1930s, casting guests as explorers with the Eighth Wonder Expedition Company, which has set up its jungle base camp in an ancient temple inhabited by a hostile Kong-worshipping Indigenous tribe.

The winding, skeleton-strewn queue, featuring lifelike animatronics and projection effects that startle unwitting guests, eventually leads to your transportation: an oversize "expedition vehicle" that superficially resembles Disney's Animal Kingdom's Kilimanjaro Safaris trucks. It's helmed by one of five different animatronic tour guides, each with their own personality and backstory, which helps make each ride experience unique. Your ride begins with a short loop outside through the jungle (which may be bypassed due to maintenance issues or inclement weather, abbreviating the experience by almost 2 minutes), ending at the massive torch-framed doors in the center of Skull Island's imposing stony facade. The doors open, allowing you passage into a maze of caves, where you're swiftly assaulted by all manner of icky prehistoric bats, bugs, and beasties, brought to gruesome life through a mix of detailed physical effects and razor-sharp video screens. After barely surviving a preliminary series of multisensory near misses, you're thrust into the center of a raging battle between vicious *V. Rex* dinosaurs and the big ape himself. Finally, just when you think it's all over, you'll have one last face-to-face encounter with the "eighth wonder of the world," only this time in the fur-covered flesh.

Although it's still among the top 10 rides in IOA's impressive lineup, some creative missteps made Kong's long-awaited return fall somewhat short. The atmospheric queue's muffled radio reports do an inadequate job of establishing the plot before boarding, and the initial scenes introduce characters that are completely abandoned mid-ride. The centerpiece simulator tunnel, while noticeably upgraded since its original incarnation as the *King Kong 360* 3-D segment of Universal Studios Hollywood's tram tour, doesn't coherently connect to the opening, and the coda's animatronic Kong is stunningly fluid but anticlimactically passive. Most importantly, the ride's original 3-D effects were removed, and the outdoor portions indefinitely disabled, diminishing the experience's intended immersiveness and epic scope.

TOURING TIPS Reign of Kong may start running 30 minutes after park opening, so you can hit Skull Island first thing in the morning after the Marvel rides, or immediately following the Hogsmeade attractions if you're using Early Park Admission, and still be among the first in line. A single-rider queue can help cut your wait, but it misses all the preshow elements and closes intermittently.

Kong's minimum height requirement is just 36 inches—one of the lowest in the resort—and the ride is designed to be physically accessible to most people. However, on a sensory and psychological level, it's extremely intense; the standby queue alone is enough to reduce fearful kids to tears, though the Express line bypasses most of the scares. If you or your little one has a fear of darkness, insects, or man-eating monsters, you may want to forgo this ride. A child swap room (with benches and a TV showing clips of the 2005 film) is available, but you're directed to navigate the scary standby queue to reach it. If needed, ask a team member if you can access it via the accommodation line instead. And you don't have to be a small fry for Skull Island to leave you shaken, as this honest reader admitted:

Being the grown-up I am, I wasn't expecting to be scared by any rides. However, Reign of Kong was absolutely terrifying. When you're sitting on the very edge and a dinosaur looks like it's going to eat you, you lose all the bravery you never had.

For those brave enough to board, the experience is far better in the back half of the truck (ideally, rows seven, eight, or nine), with guests on the right side getting the best view of the finale. Sitting at either end of a row reveals the edges of the screens.

Ask at the entrance for a **temple tour** to learn technical details about the ride's self-driving trucks, hear about tributes hidden in the queue, and (if you're lucky) skip the standby line.

JURASSIC PARK

JURASSIC PARK, and its *Jurassic World* follow-up trilogy, is a Steven Spielberg film franchise about a fictitious theme park with real dinosaurs. Jurassic Park at IOA is a real theme park (or at least a section of one) with fictitious dinosaurs. The iconic visitor center from the original film is one of the first things guests will see across the lagoon after walking through Port of Entry. The amount of space within Jurassic Park is deceptively large, and the entire area is completely immersive as you walk through it (except where Harry Potter's Hogwarts intrusively pokes above the trees).

There are two main entrances to this island, one from Toon Lagoon via Skull Island and another from The Wizarding World of Harry Potter. A third way in is the bridge between Lost Continent and Jurassic Park, which allows guests to bypass Hogsmeade on busy days and head directly to the Jurassic World VelociCoaster.

Camp Jurassic ★★★½

What it is Interactive play area. **Scope and scale** Minor attraction. **When to go** Anytime. **Comments** Closes at 8 p.m.

DESCRIPTION AND COMMENTS Camp Jurassic is the most elaborate kid's play area at Universal, and one of the best theme park playgrounds you'll find anywhere. A sort of dinosaur-themed Tom Sawyer Island (minus the rafts), it allows kids to explore lava pits, caves, mines, and a rainforest. Explore and you'll find an echo cavern, bat caves, amber-bound bugs, and dilophosaurus heads that double as water blasters. The playground is big enough for many kids to spend a solid hour just running around. You may end up having to go into Camp Jurassic just to get the little nippers out, if you can find them. A parent from Rugby, Indiana, wrote in praise of the playground:

For kids up to age 11 (depending on size and maturity), Camp Jurassic is an absolutely WONDERFUL experience! It was hilarious to see the 4-year-old enjoying shooting BIG water cannons at people, and his utter incredulity when they started shooting back! The (very!) high rope bridges were adventurous yet safe for all ages. The caves, hidden places, and twisting paths added mystery to the experience. If you have kids 10 and under, this is the place to let them go crazy, as they can safely experience everything.

Most of CJ is accessible to wheelchairs, excepting the ropes and higher platforms. Even the cave paths were navigable for a powered scooter. There are very few sitting spots inside CJ, so adults may want to wait outside in the nice, mostly shaded sitting area at CJ's front entrance. However, there are a couple of hard-to-find-but-there ways in and out, and if your child is easily disoriented, younger, or prone to panic if they lose their adults, they may need an adult to stay with them.

TOURING TIPS Camp Jurassic will fire the imaginations of the under-13 set. If you don't impose a time limit on the exploration, you could be here awhile. The layout of the play area is confusing and intersects the queuing area for Pteranodon Flyers. It's easy for kids and parents to get disoriented. If you think your children may get lost, you may end up having to climb, crawl, and slide along with them. Your chiropractor will thank you.

Jurassic Park Discovery Center ★★½

APPEAL BY AGE PRESCHOOL ★★★★½ GRADE SCHOOL ★★★★ TEENS ★★★½
YOUNG ADULTS ★★★   OVER 30 ★★★½   SENIORS ★★★

What it is Interactive natural history exhibit. **Scope and scale** Minor attraction. **When to go** Anytime.

DESCRIPTION AND COMMENTS This interactive educational exhibit mixes fiction from the *Jurassic Park* movies, such as using fossil DNA to bring dinosaurs to life, with skeletal remains and other paleontological displays. The best exhibit here lets guests watch an animatronic raptor being hatched, with a young witness getting to name the newborn. They generally emerge every hour on the half hour, so ask an attendant if you should stick around. Other exhibits allow you to digitally "fuse" your DNA with a dinosaur's to see what the resultant creature would look like, play a cheesy game show with dino trivia, or scan the nursery's eggs to reveal which species are gestating inside.

TOURING TIPS The lower level of the Discovery Center also doubles as a postride gift shop and oversize locker area for the VelociCoaster, but all of the exhibits are still accessible. Cycle back after experiencing all the rides or on a second day. Most folks can digest this exhibit in 10–15 minutes. If it isn't busy, ask a lab assistant for a **nursery tour** to go inside the raptor hatchery and get an up-close look at props that were used in the films.

Jurassic Park River Adventure *(Universal Express)* ★★★★

APPEAL BY AGE PRESCHOOL ★★★½ GRADE SCHOOL ★★★★ TEENS ★★★★
YOUNG ADULTS ★★★★½   OVER 30 ★★★★   SENIORS ★★★½

What it is Indoor-outdoor river-raft adventure ride. **Scope and scale** Headliner. **When to go** Before 11 a.m. **Comments** 42" minimum height requirement; child swap available (see page 187); single-rider line available; not to be missed. **Duration of ride** 6½ minutes. **Loading speed** Fast.

DESCRIPTION AND COMMENTS One of IOA's original headliner attractions, Jurassic Park River Adventure is inspired by a scene in author Michael Crichton's original *Jurassic Park* novel. Guests board tour boats for an aquatic ride through the grounds of Jurassic Park. Everything is tranquil as the tour begins, as the boat floats among large herbivorous dinosaurs such as ultrasaurus and stegosaurus, along with prehistoric-looking plants and the occasional geyser.

To no one's surprise, something goes horribly wrong, and your tour boat is nudged off course by a dinosaur at exactly the most inopportune time: just as you're floating past the vicious raptor enclosure, whose gates have been mysteriously unlocked and left open. Before you have time to ask what OSHA's inspectors really do during the day, your boat is climbing through the inside of the raptor facility amid the destruction and carnage wrought by the escaped animals. Your first face-to-face encounter with a *T. Rex* is also your last, as you find rescue by plunging 85 feet (the tallest water descent in the world when it was built) into the river below.

The drop is a doozy; the scenery, background music, and ride narration are all done well; and Jurassic Park River Adventure is overall one of the more immersive attractions in the entire resort. But the dinosaurs look increasingly arthritic, especially in comparison to this ride's California cousin, which was rethemed to the *Jurassic World* franchise in 2019.

TOURING TIPS Riders don't get as wet on River Adventure as they do on Bilge-Rat Barges or Ripsaw Falls. Though the boats make a huge splash at the bottom of the 85-foot drop, you can stay relatively dry if you're sitting in an interior seat; sitting behind a larger person and keeping your arms down can also help. Still, bring a poncho or plastic bag if you want to keep as dry as possible. Paid lockers are located inside the queue. There's a viewing area to the left of the ride's final, big drop, where you can see how wet riders are getting before you decide to ride.

A Honolulu reader thinks Jurassic Park doesn't pass the smell test:

> *The Jurassic Park ride is a lot of fun—so fun, in fact, that you won't realize how truly HEINOUS the water that drenches you during the climactic splashdown is until much later. We sat in the front row for the ride and got soaked. Three hours later, my girlfriend and I realized that we reeked.*

Young children must endure a double whammy on this ride. First, they're stalked by giant, salivating (sometimes spitting) reptiles, and then sent catapulting over the falls. Unless your children are fairly hardy, wait a year or two before you spring the River Adventure on them.

Because the Jurassic Park section of IOA is situated between The Wizarding World of Harry Potter—Hogsmeade and Skull Island: Reign of Kong, the boat ride may experience heavy crowds earlier in the day. Try to ride before 11 a.m., or use the single-rider queue, which (when available) often has little to no wait.

Jurassic World VelociCoaster *(Universal Express)* ★★★★★

APPEAL BY AGE	PRESCHOOL ★	GRADE SCHOOL ★★★★½	TEENS ★★★★★
YOUNG ADULTS ★★★★★		OVER 30 ★★★★★	SENIORS ★★★

What it is Roller coaster. **Scope and scale** Super-headliner. **When to go** Immediately after Hagrid's during early entry, late morning, or just before closing. **Comments** 51" minimum height requirement; child swap available (see page 187); single-rider line available; not to be missed. **Duration of ride** About 2 minutes. **Loading speed** Medium-fast.

DESCRIPTION AND COMMENTS Universal Orlando's most extreme roller coaster to date blurs the line between the original film franchise and its *Jurassic World* follow-ups with queue cameos from Chris Pratt (Owen Grady), Bryce Dallas Howard (Claire Dearing), and BD Wong (Dr. Henry Wu), who are offering guests scenic tours of the maximum-security paddocks where Blue and her carnivorous pals camp out. What could possibly go wrong?

Raptor statues loom over the waterfront entrance plaza behind the Jurassic Park Discovery Center, and coaster trains scream past the lagoon along an intimidating pretzel of Intamin-built tracks. En route to your ride, you'll see coasters speeding by, followed by a pack of rampaging raptors—a remarkable effect accomplished with translucent screens that double as windows—before encountering animatronic raptors in the grooming room that breathe, blink, and rattle their harnesses. Ask for a **facilities tour** (when staffing is available) to learn about the queue's hidden details without riding.

Riders board 24-passenger trains to experience two high-speed launches, an 80-degree dive down a towering 155-foot-tall "top hat," and close encounters with realistic rockwork and sculpted dinosaurs. With a top speed of 70 mph and an astounding 12 moments of out-of-your-seat air time (including a first-of-its-kind zero-g inverted stall), VelociCoaster is one of the most intense scream machines in town, if not on Earth.

From the first burst of acceleration until you hit the final brake run, VelociCoaster delivers nonstop adrenaline. The first half is full of tight, surprising turns and head-chopping overhangs, while the second supplies face-peeling g-forces that make you feel like a Barbie in the hands of an angry toddler. Thankfully, the lap restraints rest comfortably across your hips and upper thighs, holding you securely, even as you're flung helplessly through the finale's heart-stopping "Mosasaurus roll" above the lagoon. (Loose-fitting eyeglasses may not be so lucky.) Other roller coasters may have a taller drop or greater maximum velocity, but nothing else strings together so many exhilarating elements into 4,700 feet of relentlessly paced track.

TOURING TIPS VelociCoaster quickly overtook The Incredible Hulk Coaster as the hard-core thrill junkies' favorite ride, but Hagrid's continues to attract bigger crowds because it's accessible to a wider range of guests. If you can fight the urge to be among the first riders of the day, try to hit VelociCoaster in late morning after experiencing the other top attractions. Otherwise, make it your last ride of the night; it's even scarier in the dark.

Double-sided lockers allow guests here to hold onto their cell phones, wallets, and other loose items until just before boarding, where they pass through a mandatory metal detector, then retrieve them immediately after disembarking. (If you want to wear your glasses, a safety strap is strongly advised.) The locker area even features sinks to empty and rinse out your souvenir drink cups. The small lockers inside the queue should be sufficient for most smaller bags. Larger lockers are available for a fee in the lowest level of the Discovery Center. Be sure to stow your oversize baggage before getting in line for the ride.

VelociCoaster features a single-rider entrance (which temporarily closes when it reaches a 30–45-minute wait) and a Universal Express queue. The Express line experiences most of the theming seen in the standby queue; single riders skip all the setup but have their own locker area in the exit hallway.

The boarding station features a separate line for guests wishing to wait for the front row; the unobstructed view is spectacular and worth an extra 15 minutes in line, but ride designer Shelby Honea recommends the left seat in the third row. While the experience is intense in any seat, be warned that the back row packs some serious bite!

The entrance is on the lower level behind the Discovery Center and is not directly accessible from Jurassic Park's main pathway; take the bridge from Lost Continent for the most direct route from the park entrance, or take the pathway in Jurassic Park near the Watering Hole. You can get a preview of the ride's launch by peeking through the wall across from the Raptor Encounter entrance. Even if you aren't brave enough to ride, the illuminated trains make for a beautiful sight after sunset.

STELLA SAYS

THE VELOCICOASTER QUEUE offers a plethora of Easter eggs for fans of the franchise, but a hard-to-spot one is sitting by a speed-radar gun on the windowsill where the trains (and animated raptors) roar past. See if you can spot the permanent ripples in the cup of water, a nod to the original *Jurassic Park* film.

Pteranodon Flyers ★★★

APPEAL BY AGE   PRESCHOOL ★★★★½   GRADE SCHOOL ★★★★   TEENS ★★★
YOUNG ADULTS ★★★   OVER 30 ★★★   SENIORS ★★★½

What it is Kiddie suspended coaster. **Scope and scale** Minor attraction. **When to go** In the first or last 30 minutes of the day. **Comments** 36" minimum height requirement; adults and older children must be accompanied by a child 36"–56" tall. **Duration of ride** 1¼ minutes. **Loading speed** Slower than a hog in quicksand.

DESCRIPTION AND COMMENTS This two-seater kiddie coaster dangles you on a swing below a track that passes over a small part of Jurassic Park. The queue moves at a glacial pace, and the ride itself lasts barely 75 seconds, but you get a gorgeous view of the island's greenery, and the swinging cars deliver a surprisingly satisfying snap as they negotiate the track's curves.

TOURING TIPS This attraction is designed for children 36–56 inches in height. An adult or older child over 56 inches in height must accompany a child meeting the 36- to 56-inch height requirement.

For years, we suggested skipping Pteranodon Flyers due to its low capacity and paltry length. But recent re-rides, and letters like this one from a Baltimore, Maryland, mom, made us reconsider:

> *Even my thrill-riding, 55-inch-tall 10-year-old loved this one! I feel bad for the ride operators who spend the entire day turning people away who don't have a child in the right height range to go. Greatly underrated ride, but you were spot on with the lines by midday.*

We still don't think Pteranodon Flyers is worth a long wait, and Universal Express isn't valid on the attraction. If your children insist on riding and abject bribery fails, get in line as quickly as possible after opening. *Note:* At press time, this ride was closed indefinitely.

Raptor Encounter ★★★½

APPEAL BY AGE   PRESCHOOL ★★★½   GRADE SCHOOL ★★★★   TEENS ★★★★
YOUNG ADULTS ★★★★½   OVER 30 ★★★★½   SENIORS ★★★★

What it is Photo op with lifelike dinosaur. **Scope and scale** Minor attraction. **When to go** Before noon. **Comments** Sure to scare the spit out of small kids. **Duration of encounter** About a minute. **Queue speed** Slow.

DESCRIPTION AND COMMENTS Just when everyone thinks Disney has a lock on the meet and greet market, Universal does the impossible—breeds a live velociraptor and makes it pose for pictures! OK, it isn't actually a real dinosaur on display. In fact, it's an amazingly realistic puppet, created by Michael Curry (who created designs for Disney's *Lion King* and *Finding Nemo* musicals, as well as Diagon Alley's *Tales of Beedle the Bard* show) and brought to life by talented performers.

Blue, *Jurassic World*'s semi-tame saurian star, makes regular appearances in her paddock next to the River Adventure. A game warden briefs one family at a time regarding proper safety procedures (convey calm assurance, move in slowly, and try not to smell like meat) before they step up for a photo. Don't peer too closely over the edge of the raptor enclosure; you'll spot the cleverly camouflaged legs of the puppeteer inside and spoil the illusion. A Universal photographer will take your picture with their camera (included with My Universal Photos packages), and selfies are also encouraged—just don't be surprised if the dino snaps when you say, "Smile!"

Raptor Encounter isn't among IOA's major attractions, and the queue can move at a crawl, but this crew from Calgary, Canada, says you shouldn't overlook it:

I was really intrigued by the Raptor Encounter. We probably would have missed it if it hadn't been for the guide. It was one of the highlights of our day!

TOURING TIPS The Raptor Encounter has become quite popular, so ask a team member stationed outside the paddock entrance approximately how long your wait will be before queuing. Don't try to touch the raptor, or you may come home minus a hand; surreptitiously feeding your offspring to the dinosaurs is also discouraged by management. When the full-grown Blue needs a break, an adorable (but equally deadly) handheld baby velociraptor may take her place.

THE WIZARDING WORLD OF HARRY POTTER— HOGSMEADE

THE ORIGINAL WIZARDING WORLD of Harry Potter is an amalgamation of landmarks, creatures, and themes that are faithful to the first five films and books. You access the area from The Lost Continent through an imposing stone archway that opens onto **Hogsmeade,** depicted in winter and covered in snow.

The village setting is rendered in exquisite detail: stone cottages and shops have steeply pitched slate roofs, bowed multipaned windows, gables, and tall, crooked chimneys. The **Hogwarts Express** locomotive sits belching steam on your right.

Set back from the main street is **Three Broomsticks,** a rustic tavern serving English staples. To the rear of the tavern is the **Hog's Head pub,** which serves a nice selection of beer as well as The Wizarding World's signature nonalcoholic brew, Butterbeer (see page 310). Beside the pub is **Honeydukes,** specializing in Potter-themed candy such as Acid Pops, Tooth Splintering Strong Mints, and Fizzing Whizbees. Avoid the prepackaged Cauldron Cakes, which look much better than they taste. Chocolate Frogs, available in dark, white, and milk varieties, are dense and waxy, but the packaging looks as if it came straight from a *Harry Potter* film, complete with a random lenticular wizard trading card; buy one in a collectible tin to get a full set of cards.

Roughly across the street from the pub is the entrance to **Hagrid's Magical Creatures Motorbike Adventure** roller coaster, as well as benches in the shade at the **Owlery,** where animatronic owls (complete with lifelike poop) ruffle and hoot from the rafters. Next to the Owlery is the **Owl Post,** which sells stationery, toy owls, and magic wands. Owl Post interconnects with both the wand-choosing demonstration at **Ollivanders** (see page 264) and **Dervish and Banges,** a magic-supplies shop.

At the far end of the village, the massive **Hogwarts Castle** comes into view, set atop a rock face and towering over Hogsmeade and the entire Wizarding World. Universal went all out on the castle, with the intention of creating an icon even more beloved and powerful than Cinderella Castle at Disney's Magic Kingdom, and very nearly succeeded—if only they'd added a bit more brick and rockwork to conceal the big honking soundstage that holds the land's groundbreaking ride, **Harry Potter and the Forbidden Journey.** Below the castle and to the right, at the base of the cliff, are the **Forbidden Forest, Hagrid's Hut,** and the **Flight of the Hippogriff** children's roller coaster. Also beneath Hogwarts, at Forbidden Journey's exit, is **Filch's Emporium of Confiscated Goods,** which offers all manner of Potter-themed gear, including Quidditch clothing, magical-creature toys, film-inspired chess sets, and, of course, Death Eater masks (breath mints extra).

In keeping with the stores depicted in the Potter films, the shopping venues in Hogsmeade are small and intimate—so intimate, in fact, that they feel congested when they're serving only 12–20 shoppers. Because the stores are so jammed, IOA sells some Potter merchandise, including wands, through street vendors and in Port of Entry shops.

At the end of the village and to the left is the bridge to **Jurassic Park,** the themed area contiguous to The Wizarding World. This is the best vantage point to get your photo with Hogwarts Castle in the background, as the hordes of people posing in the middle of the walkway will attest.

Flight of the Hippogriff *(Universal Express)* ★★★

APPEAL BY AGE	PRESCHOOL ★★★★½	GRADE SCHOOL ★★★★	TEENS ★★★½
YOUNG ADULTS ★★★½	OVER 30 ★★★½		SENIORS ★★★½

What it is Kiddie roller coaster. **Scope and scale** Minor attraction. **When to go** First 90 minutes the park is open or after 4 p.m. **Comments** 36" minimum height requirement; child swap available (see page 187). **Duration of ride** 1 minute. **Average wait in line per 100 people ahead of you** 6½ minutes. **Loading speed** Slow.

DESCRIPTION AND COMMENTS Below and to the right of Hogwarts Castle, next to Hagrid's Hut, the Hippogriff is short and sweet but not worth much of a wait. An outdoor, elevated coaster designed for children old enough to know about Harry Potter but not yet tall enough to ride Forbidden Journey, the ride affords excellent views of the area within Wizarding World and of Hogwarts. The theming is also very good, considering that this isn't a major attraction. As a children's coaster only slightly taller and longer than the Magic Kingdom's Barnstormer, it has no loops, inversions, or rolls. It's just one big hill and some mild turns, and almost half of the 1-minute ride time is spent going up the lift hill. Unfortunately, Orlando's Hippogriff has become increasingly rough over the years, and it's not as pleasant to ride as the identically named coaster at Universal Studios Hollywood.

For fans of Harry Potter, there are two gorgeous items in this attraction that you'll want to see. The first is a faithful re-creation of Hagrid's Hut in the queue (complete with the sound of Fang howling), while the second is an incredible animatronic of Buckbeak that you pass by while on the ride. Remember that when Muggles encounter hippogriffs such as Buckbeak, proper etiquette must be maintained to avoid any danger. Hippogriffs are extremely proud creatures; show them the proper respect by bowing to them and waiting for them to bow in return.

TOURING TIPS Have your kids ride soon after the park opens while older siblings enjoy the roller coasters or Forbidden Journey.

Hagrid's Magical Creatures Motorbike Adventure ★★★★★

APPEAL BY AGE	PRESCHOOL ★★½	GRADE SCHOOL ★★★★★	TEENS ★★★★★
YOUNG ADULTS ★★★★★	OVER 30 ★★★★★		SENIORS ★★★★½

What it is Indoor-outdoor roller coaster. **Scope and scale** Super-headliner. **When to go** First thing during early entry, around midday, or after sunset. **Comments** 48" minimum height requirement; child swap available (see page 187); single-rider line available; not to be missed. **Duration of ride** About 3 minutes. **Loading speed** Moderate.

Motion Sickness

DESCRIPTION AND COMMENTS This family-friendly thrill ride featuring everyone's favorite half-giant groundskeeper is a highly themed roller coaster without huge hills or upside-down loops. Instead, it focuses on multiple high-speed launches through the heavily forested terrain during outdoor segments, as well as close encounters with animatronic beasties inside and between the ride's indoor show buildings.

Riders begin with a walking tour of the gardens behind Hagrid's Hut (whose front side is seen from Flight of the Hippogriff's queue) before entering the moss-covered ruins on the fringe of the Forbidden Forest, where Hagrid holds his Care of Magical Creatures classes. A projected preshow similar to the one in Harry Potter and the Escape from Gringotts succinctly establishes the premise: Arthur Weasley has cloned a Muggle motorcycle, so your class can take a field trip to see Hagrid's latest pet, the never-before-seen fire crab. The preshow (which is often bypassed) isn't as essential as the setups in the other Potter headliners, and the meandering queue that follows, although decorated with Easter eggs referencing the books and films, mostly consists of monotonous stone walls.

At nearly a mile long, the coaster's track is among the longest found in Florida, and a record-setting multiplicity of magnetic launches propels riders along its curvy course in 14-passenger trains from Intamin that resemble Hagrid's vintage motorbike, complete with low-slung sidecars. Highlights of the adventure include a vertical spike that leads into a backward helix, followed by a dropping track in the darkness. Fantastic beasts and familiar figures from the Potter world, including the flying Ford Anglia, Fluffy the three-headed dog, and old Hagrid himself (an impressively lifelike animatronic), make appearances during your experience.

Bucking Universal's dependence on video screens and simulated movement, Hagrid has richly detailed scenery, spectacular practical effects, and accelerated air time that's exhilarating but not too extreme for tweens and parents to enjoy together. While the coaster's 50-mph top speed might not sound terribly swift, it feels far faster when you're navigating ground-hugging twists and turns through a grove of 1,200 real trees. Hagrid's is the best "story coaster" in Orlando, and a strong contender for the best ride at Universal Orlando.

TOURING TIPS The word is out about how good Hagrid's is, and the ride receives a huge rush of guests every morning at rope drop. If you're swift enough to be among the very first guests in line, your wait should be brief, assuming the ride begins running on time. However, if you're even a few hundred people behind the leading wave, you'll find yourself slowly snaking through a seemingly endless queue.

Exacerbating the attraction's limited carrying capacity is its tendency to frequently shut down due to bad weather or mechanical issues, which can sometimes take hours to resolve. Your best options are to check the queue in early afternoon (wait

STELLA SAYS

HAGRID'S MAGICAL CREATURES MOTORBIKE ADVENTURE As soon as you enter the interior queue, look for a tribute to the Dueling Dragons roller coaster that originally sat in this spot. On the wall, a faded mural for the "Dueling Club" features a blue dragon on the left and a red dragon on the right. Locked in battle, the poses of these two eternal enemies mimic the original ride entrance for the former coaster.

times tend to dip briefly around lunchtime) or in early evening, especially after a late-afternoon rainstorm has passed; the effects are especially magical after sunset.

Hagrid's does not currently offer Universal Express access, but it may in the future. A single-rider queue is intermittently available, but it isn't very efficient; the singles line is at least a 30-minute wait if it extends outside the castle.

Each of the coaster's two seating options provides a slightly different experience. The sidecar sits lower but closer to the effects, so every rider gets a good view. Larger guests (over 40-inch waists) should test the sample seats before lining up and request the motorbike seat to enjoy a little more breathing room than the cramped sidecar.

Harry Potter and the Forbidden Journey
(Universal Express) ★★★★★

What it is Motion-simulator dark ride. **Scope and scale** Super-headliner. **When to go** At the end of early-entry hour or in the last hours before closing. **Comments** 48″ minimum height requirement; child swap available (see page 187); single-rider line available; not to be missed. **Duration of ride** 4¼ minutes. **Loading speed** Fast.

DESCRIPTION AND COMMENTS More than a decade after its debut, the thrilling dark ride inside Hogwarts Castle remains one of Universal's most impressive attractions, as well as the only place for fans to encounter Harry, Ron, Hermione, and Dumbledore as portrayed by the original actors. From Hogsmeade, guests approach the castle's imposing Winged Boar gates and walk through a dungeon festooned with various prop replicas from the Potter flicks, including the Mirror of Erised from *Harry Potter and the Sorcerer's Stone,* before touring the Hogwarts greenhouses, which compose the larger part of the Forbidden Journey's standby queuing area.

Upon entering the castle's passageways, after passing towering statues and tapestries, you'll meet the moving portraits of the four founders of Hogwarts, who argue about Dumbledore's controversial decision to host an open house at Hogwarts for Muggles (garden-variety mortals). Next, the wizard headmaster himself welcomes you to his office (as a Musion EyeLiner high-definition "hologram") and dispatches you to the Defense Against the Dark Arts classroom, where Harry, Ron, and Hermione pop out from beneath an invisibility cloak, inviting you to join them for a Quidditch match. The safety briefing and instructions—presented inside the Gryffindor Common Room by animated portraits and an animatronic Sorting Hat—lead to the Room of Requirement, where hundreds of candles float overhead as you board the ride vehicle: a four-seat flying bench mounted on the end of a Kuka robotic arm similar to the kind used in heavy manufacturing.

Your mind-blowing 4¼-minute adventure is a headlong sprint through the most action-packed moments from the first few Potter books: you'll soar over Hogwarts Castle, narrowly evade an attacking dragon, spar with the Whomping Willow, get tossed into a Quidditch match, and fight off Dementors inside the Chamber of Secrets. Scenes alternate between enormous physical sets (complete with animatronic creatures) and high-frame-rate 4K video-projection domes that surround your field of view, similar to Disney's Soarin' or The Simpsons Ride. Those Kuka-powered benches "levitate" in a manner that feels remarkably like free flight, and while you don't go upside down, the sensation of floating on your back or being slung from side to side is certainly unique. The greatest-hits montage plotline may be a bit muddled, but the ride is enormously effective at leaving you feeling as though you just survived the scariest scrapes from the early educational career of The Boy Who Lived.

TOURING TIPS Free lockers, which are required for bags and wands, are located outside the castle. This ride makes a couple of moves that will empty your trousers faster than a master pickpocket—ditto and worse for shirt pockets.

The single-rider line, located to the left upon entering the castle, is not clearly marked and bypasses most of the preshows, so relatively few guests use it; as a result, it is usually under a 20-minute wait, and can be as little as one-tenth of the wait in the standby line. Because the individual seating separates you from the other riders whether your party stays together or not, the singles line (when available) is a great option, as this woman from Edinburgh, Scotland, discovered:

> *Trust me—sitting next to hubby on Forbidden Journey, romantic though it may be, is not as awesome as having to wait only 15 minutes as a single rider.*

> **unofficial TIP**
> Even if your child meets the height requirement, consider carefully whether Forbidden Journey is an experience they can handle. Because the seats on the benches are compartmentalized, kids can't see or touch Mom or Dad if they get frightened.

To understand the story line and get the most out of the attraction, watch a full run-through of each preshow, which takes 20–25 minutes. Try to find a place to stop where you can let those behind you pass; as long as you're not creating a logjam, the team members should leave you alone. Universal Express users get to see all the important preshow elements, only bypassing the greenhouses and some minor scenery. Ask for a **castle tour** (when staffing is available) to explore the castle queue without riding.

Forbidden Journey is one of our favorite rides in the world, and it's a big hit with our readers, like this mother of three from Crystal Lake, Illinois:

> *I was in awe from the minute I stepped into line, [and] from the minute I began "flying," I was like a little kid. The integration of movement, video screens, and real scenery was so seamless that I truly felt like I was part of the movie. Here I was, a 40-year-old woman, and I literally walked off the ride with tears in my eyes and happiness in my heart. It was the most amazing ride I'd ever been on, and I believe any ride would be hard-pressed to bring about the same feeling of joy!*

But much as we enjoy Forbidden Journey, it behooves us to pass along this warning from a mom in St. Louis:

> *A security person at Universal told me that Harry Potter and the Forbidden Journey is THE most motion sickness–inducing ride in the two Universal parks. My husband and daughter went on the ride, and then somehow convinced me to try it. I should have listened to the security person!*

As well as this, from a reader in Ann Arbor, Michigan:

> *The Forbidden Journey ride scared me a lot, and I am not a wimp. I loved Gringotts and Hagrid's Motorbike, loved Spider-Man, but Forbidden Journey was just too much.*

If you start getting queasy, fix your gaze on your feet and try to exclude as much from your peripheral vision as possible.

The end seats on each flying bench are designed to accommodate a wider variety of body shapes and sizes, but some larger guests are still denied rides. Before getting in line, sit in the test seat outside the queue, and pull down on the safety harness as far as you can. A green light indicates that you can fit into any seat, a yellow light means that you should ask for one of the modified seats on the outside of the bench, and a red light means that the harness can't engage enough for you to ride safely. Team members also test guests "at random" right before boarding. For you to be cleared to ride, the overhead restraint has to click three times; it's body shape rather than weight that's key.

Hogwarts Express *(Universal Express)* ★★★★½

APPEAL BY AGE PRESCHOOL ★★★★½ GRADE SCHOOL ★★★★½ TEENS ★★★★½
YOUNG ADULTS ★★★★½   OVER 30 ★★★★½   SENIORS ★★★★½

What it is Transportation attraction with special effects. **Scope and scale** Headliner. **When to go** Immediately after park opening until midafternoon. **Comments** Requires park-to-park admission; not to be missed. **Duration of ride** 4 minutes. **Loading speed** Moderate.

DESCRIPTION AND COMMENTS The counterpart to USF's King's Cross is Hogsmeade Station, which sits on the border between IOA's Hogsmeade and Lost Continent. See Part Six, page 209, for a full review of the Hogwarts Express experience.

TOURING TIPS Because the Hogsmeade Station doesn't include the cool Platform 9¾ effect found at the King's Cross end, you'd expect waits for the one-way trip to be shorter here. Surprisingly, lines can be longer here than at USF on slower days, though King's Cross is the busier end during peak periods. Lines are usually less than 20 minutes through the morning but can build later in the day. Hogsmeade Station also lacks other King's Cross amenities, such as air-conditioning and an in-queue snack stand.

If you wish to experience the train, do so before the queue builds in midafternoon.

Ollivanders ★★★★

APPEAL BY AGE PRESCHOOL ★★★★ GRADE SCHOOL ★★★★½ TEENS ★★★★
YOUNG ADULTS ★★★★½   OVER 30 ★★★★   SENIORS ★★★★½

What it is Combination wizarding demonstration and shopping op. **Scope and scale** Minor attraction. **When to go** In the first or last hours of the day. **Comments** Audience stands; identical to USF version but with a much slower line. **Duration of presentation** 6 minutes.

DESCRIPTION AND COMMENTS Next to the Owl Post is Ollivanders, a musty little shop stacked to the ceiling with boxes of magic wands. Inside you'll find the same intimate wand-choosing ceremony found in the Diagon Alley attraction of the same name (see page 210). It's great fun, but the tiny shop can accommodate at most only about 25 guests at a time. After the show, the whole group is dispatched to the Owl Post and Dervish and Banges to make purchases.

The wand experience is almost as popular as the Potter rides. Lines build quickly after opening, and there's little to no shade. If you're just looking to buy a wand without seeing the ceremony, a cart is set up near the *Frog Choir* stage, usually with little to no wait.

TOURING TIPS Due to its very low capacity (fewer than 150 guests per hour), long waits for the show at Ollivanders can form. If you need to see this show, and you can't go to the USF branch, go first thing in the morning or as late as possible.

You don't need to see the wand-selection show to purchase a wand at Ollivanders—just enter the store directly rather than waiting in the long outdoor queue. Interactive wands and other Harry Potter merchandise are also available online and at an outdoor cart near the *Frog Choir* stage, as well as at Islands of Adventure Trading Company.

Interactive Wands and Spell-Casting Locations in Hogsmeade

Interactive wands sold in either park come with a map that shows Diagon Alley spell-casting locations on one side and Hogsmeade locations on the other. All of the spells in Hogsmeade are found in the central village, not near Hogwarts Castle or the Hogwarts Express. Effects aren't as numerous or as elaborate in Hogsmeade as they are in Diagon Alley, and several are adaptations of older effects that previously ran automatically. There are also no hidden effects in Hogsmeade (as far as we know). On the other hand, there usually aren't quite as many kids trying to trigger effects here. If you're only visiting IOA, it probably isn't worthwhile to buy an interactive wand, but if you're visiting both parks, make sure to test out your purchase from USF's Ollivanders here.

Entertainment in Hogsmeade

Two brief street entertainments are staged in a raised outdoor alcove at the Forbidden Journey end of Hogsmeade. Showtimes are listed in the smartphone app; performances alternate, usually starting every 30 minutes on the hour and half hour.

The **Frog Choir** (★★★) is composed of four singers, two of whom are holding large amphibian puppets sitting on pillows. Inspired by a brief scene in *Harry Potter and the Prisoner of Azkaban,* the group sings a cappella three or four wizard-related songs, including "Hedwig's Theme" and "Something Wicked This Way Comes." The 10-minute show is followed by a photo op. Though cute, the Frog Choir isn't much more than filler for IOA's attraction list and probably isn't worth going out of your way for. A special set of Yuletide tunes is performed during the annual Christmas in The Wizarding World celebration.

The **Triwizard Spirit Rally** (★★★) showcases a group of three men, who perform martial arts–type moves including jumps, kicks, and simulated battle with sticks; and a group of four women, who perform simple rhythmic gymnastic moves with ribbons. After each 6-minute show, the students of Beauxbatons Academy of Magic and the Durmstrang Institute are available for group photos. Though marginally more exciting than the Frog Choir, this is only a must-do for major Potter fans.

On select evenings throughout the year, **Hogwarts Always** (★★★½) brings the Forbidden Journey facade to life with colorful spells and magical creatures cavorting to John Williams's stirring film score, all thanks to the Muggle miracle of digital projection mapping. Powerful video projectors (some cleverly disguised as owl roosts) are hidden around Hogsmeade, all pointing at Hogwarts and the mountain on which it sits, and twinkle lights in the trees change colors to complement the castle. The images evoke iconic milestones from a year in the life of a Hogwarts student, from shopping for school supplies in Diagon Alley, to celebrating the winner of the House Cup; with four different rotating endings, each house gets its chance to shine. The

7-minute celebration, which also features vocal cameos from Dumbledore and Hagrid, is capped with a quick burst of pyrotechnics.

The Dark Arts at Hogwarts Castle show sometimes runs during the Halloween season. Using the same projection technology as *Hogwarts Always*, this 8-minute show features all of The Wizarding World's wickedest characters, from Aragog to Dementors to Trolls, and finally Lord Voldemort himself. Fortunately, just when all seems lost, a familiar Patronus gallops in to put things right. With clouds of spooky fog and surprising bursts of flame, this version of the castle light show is more frightening for young children and more exciting for older ones. Watch out for a pack of Death Eaters, who may stalk Hogsmeade Village starting 30 minutes before the first show.

During the holiday season's Christmas in The Wizarding World event, a special **Magic of Christmas at Hogwarts** version of the projection show is presented. About 7 minutes long, it features additional fan-favorite characters like the Weasley twins, who transform the castle's turret into a big Boggart Banger. It's well worth seeing even if you've already experienced the other versions.

The best viewing area for the castle shows is in front of the *Frog Choir* stage or on the bridge to Jurassic Park. The show is repeated every 15–20 minutes from sunset to park closing. The first couple of showings are the most crowded, and the last is the least attended. Prior to showtime, the bridge to Jurassic Park is restricted to exiting traffic only, and guests entering Hogsmeade through The Lost Continent are held in front of Ollivanders (where there is no view of the show) once the courtyard around the castle is full. Our recommendation is to make your way into Hogsmeade shortly before the first performance, and enjoy Forbidden Journey and Flight of the Hippogriff during the first couple of showings. You'll be able to access the rides via designated walkways, and lines should be nonexistent. Then wait for the crowd to begin exiting after a show, and grab a good spot for one of the later runs.

THE LOST CONTINENT

ONCE AMONG IOA'S LARGEST AREAS, The Lost Continent surrendered its medieval Merlinwood section to be turned into The Wizarding World of Harry Potter—Hogsmeade, leaving only the Arabian and Ancient Greek portions intact. What's left of Lost Continent is extremely

STELLA SAYS

LOST CONTINENT LOST TO ZELDA? The Lost Continent has been lost to time, with both its *Eighth Voyage of Sindbad* stunt show and *Poseidon's Fury* walkthrough attraction now sitting shuttered. Strong rumors suggest what's left of Lost Continent could be transformed into a new land based on Nintendo's The Legend of Zelda game series in the coming years. While no one is certain what types of attractions this possible new land could bring, rumor is the popular Mythos restaurant could be the only element of the land to be retained, but with a new theme.

well themed and features the park's only environments that aren't tied to a licensed intellectual property. Lost Continent can be reached directly from Hogsmeade or Seuss Landing, or via a bypass bridge to Jurassic Park.

The best—and only—attraction in Lost Continent at the moment is **Mystic Fountain,** an interactive talking fountain. A team member behind the scenes controls the fountain and is able to talk to and hear from anyone who approaches. Many kids seem mesmerized by it. Parents can grab a quick snack or drink while the little ones are entertained by the fountain mere steps away. The park's second First Aid station is also located here, behind the kebab house.

SEUSS LANDING

THIS 10-ACRE THEMED AREA is based on Dr. Seuss's famous children's books. Buildings and attractions replicate a whimsical, brightly colored cartoon style with exaggerated features and rounded lines. The odd-shaped facades were carved from Styrofoam and sprayed with concrete, and the impossibly bent palm trees were salvaged from Hurricane Andrew, resulting in a land without a single straight line or right angle.

Featuring many of Dr. Seuss's most beloved characters (including the Lorax, the Grinch, Thing 1 and Thing 2, Sam-I-Am, and the Cat in the Hat), *Oh! The Stories You'll Hear!* (★★★) is a fun singing and dancing show staged in an outdoor area between Circus McGurkus Cafe Stoo-pendous and All the Books You Can Read. After each 9-minute show, the characters separate for individual meet and greets and autographs. Showtimes are listed in the Universal app. During inclement weather, the show may relocate within the Circus McGurkus Cafe Stoo-pendous restaurant nearby.

Caro-Seuss-el *(Universal Express)*   ★★★

APPEAL BY AGE PRESCHOOL ★★★★½ **GRADE SCHOOL** ★★★★ **TEENS** ★★★
YOUNG ADULTS ★★★   **OVER 30** ★★★½   **SENIORS** ★★★★

What it is Merry-go-round. **Scope and scale** Minor attraction. **When to go** Anytime. **Comments** Child swap available (see page 187). **Duration of ride** 2 minutes. **Loading speed** Slow.

DESCRIPTION AND COMMENTS Totally outrageous, this full-scale, 56-mount merry-go-round is made up entirely of Dr. Seuss characters, each of which has an interactive effect (wagging tongues, blinking eyes) that the rider can control. While you turn, a Seussian orchestra of ridiculous instruments plays like a cacophonous calliope.

TOURING TIPS A gentle ride, even for the smallest children. If you are too old or don't want to ride, Caro-Seuss-el is still worth an inspection. If you do want to ride, waits are usually not too long, even in the middle of the day.

The Cat in the Hat *(Universal Express)*   ★★★

APPEAL BY AGE PRESCHOOL ★★★★½ **GRADE SCHOOL** ★★★½ **TEENS** ★★★
YOUNG ADULTS ★★★   **OVER 30** ★★★½   **SENIORS** ★★★★

What it is Indoor cartoon dark ride. **Scope and scale** Major attraction. **When to go** Before 11:30 a.m. or after 4 p.m. **Comments** 36" minimum height requirement; child swap available (see page 187). **Duration of ride** 3¾ minutes. **Loading speed** Moderate.

STELLA SAYS

IN SEUSS LANDING, look for a photo op with top-hatted dignitaries outside the Mulberry Street Store; the figure with the beard and glasses is Dr. Theodor "Seuss" Geisel himself.

DESCRIPTION AND COMMENTS Universal's answer to Disney's vintage Fantasyland dark rides, this indoor, sit-down attraction recounts the entire *Cat in the Hat* story from beginning to end in a little less than 4 minutes. Guests ride on "couches" through 18 different sets inhabited by animatronic Seuss characters. Of course, mayhem ensues when Cat brings Thing 1 and Thing 2 over to play, as the beleaguered goldfish tries to maintain order in the midst of bedlam, but the entire mess is cleaned up just before Mom gets home.

The audio narration is clear, and each scene is crammed with the kind of crazy furniture and bizarre housewares found in the book. The ride is straightforward enough, but we wish it had more sophisticated animatronics and better effects.

TOURING TIPS This is fun for all ages. Try to ride early, or ride late in the day after families with young children have started to depart.

We think there's almost nothing here to frighten small children beyond some loud noises. A father of three from Natick, Massachusetts, disagrees:

> The Cat in the Hat ride has quite the fright potential. My wife took my fairly advanced 3½-year-old daughter on the ride, and she was screaming her head off. Nearly two years later, she still reminds me of the scary Cat in the Hat ride (it hasn't affected her love for the books, though!).

The High in the Sky Seuss Trolley Train Ride!
(Universal Express) ★★★½

APPEAL BY AGE	PRESCHOOL ★★★★½	GRADE SCHOOL ★★★★	TEENS ★★★
YOUNG ADULTS ★★★½	OVER 30 ★★★½	SENIORS ★★★★	

What it is Elevated train. **Scope and scale** Major attraction. **When to go** Before 11:30 a.m. or just before closing. **Comments** 36" minimum height requirement; child swap available (see page 187). **Duration of ride** 3½ minutes. **Loading speed** Molasses.

DESCRIPTION AND COMMENTS An elevated train ride through and around the buildings in Seuss Landing, the Trolley Train putters along elevated tracks while a voice reads a Dr. Seuss story over the train's speakers. As each train makes its way through Seuss Landing, it passes a series of simple animatronic characters in scenes that are part of the story being told. The slow ride around Seuss Landing is pleasant and affords great views of most of the park. Little tunnels and a few mild turns make this a charming attraction, but a 36" minimum height requirement means that many in the trolley's target demographic are banned from riding.

Note that you can choose from two different train tracks at the boarding station. As you face the platform, to your left is the Beech track, which is aquamarine; to your right is the Star track, which is purple. If you're riding with a large group, keep your group together if you all want the same experience because the track on each side offers different visuals and two randomly selected ride soundtracks.

TOURING TIPS The line for this ride is much less charming than the attraction. The trains are small, fitting about 20 people, and the loading speed is glacial. Save High in the Sky for the end of the day or ride first thing in the morning. There is no on-ride photo, but a photo op is sometimes available in the standby queue.

If I Ran the Zoo   ★★★

APPEAL BY AGE	PRESCHOOL ★★★★★	GRADE SCHOOL ★★★½	TEENS ★★★
YOUNG ADULTS ★★★		OVER 30 ★★★	SENIORS ★★★½

What it is Play area. **Scope and scale** Diversion. **When to go** Anytime. **Comments** Kids may get wet.

DESCRIPTION AND COMMENTS This interactive play area and outdoor maze, themed to Dr. Seuss rhymes, is filled with fantastic animals and gizmos from the stories. It's great for kids even if they don't know the book it's based on, and it provides a nice break for parents.

TOURING TIPS Tour anytime. Note that much of the play area is unshaded. Bring a drink and hat for the little ones.

One Fish, Two Fish, Red Fish, Blue Fish
(Universal Express) ★★★

APPEAL BY AGE	PRESCHOOL ★★★★★	GRADE SCHOOL ★★★★	TEENS ★★★
YOUNG ADULTS ★★½		OVER 30 ★★★½	SENIORS ★★★★

What it is Wet version of Dumbo the Flying Elephant. **Scope and scale** Minor attraction. **When to go** Before 11:30 a.m. **Comments** Child swap available (see page 187). Plan on getting wet. **Duration of ride** 2 minutes. **Loading speed** Slow.

DESCRIPTION AND COMMENTS Imagine a mild spinning ride similar to Disney's Magic Carpets of Aladdin, TriceraTop Spin, and Dumbo rides, only with Seuss-style fish for ride vehicles, and you have half the story. The other half involves yet another opportunity to get soaked.

Guests board a fish-shaped ride vehicle mounted to an arm attached to a central axis, around which the vehicles spin. Guests can raise and lower their fish 15 feet in the air while traveling in circles and trying to avoid streams of water sprayed by other fish mounted to squirt posts around the ride's perimeter.

You can avoid most of the spray by going up or down at the right time. If you pay attention to the color of your vehicle and listen to the song played in the background, you can (eventually) figure out when to move your fish.

TOURING TIPS We don't know what it is about this theme park and water, but you'll get wetter than at a full-immersion baptism. Lines can build in the afternoon, so ride early while you'll still have time to dry off.

SPECIAL EVENTS *at* UNIVERSAL ISLANDS *of* ADVENTURE

IOA DOESN'T HOST NEARLY AS MANY special events throughout the year as USF, but the one it has is first-rate and included with standard admission.

HOLIDAYS *(mid-November–early January)*

YOU'LL FIND CHRISTMAS DECOR throughout IOA's Port of Entry, and Hogsmeade celebrates **Christmas in The Wizarding World** with festive ornamentation, holiday treats, and a spectacular light show on Hogwarts Castle (see page 266). But the epicenter of the holiday at IOA is obviously Seuss Landing. The star, naturally, is the Grinch, the iconic icky-green grump who famously stole Christmas from the Whos, only to return it when his undersized heart finally grew.

The Grinch is normally represented in the park by a masked representation of the cartoon character, but during Grinchmas, a speaking actor wearing professional prosthetic makeup impersonates Jim Carrey's live-action film incarnation. The Grinch meets and greets guests during the day inside a Seuss Landing store; he takes time to interact before each photograph, usually to hilarious effect, which results in a very slow-moving line. The Grinchmas meet and greet attracts a standby queue that often exceeds 3 hours. If meeting the Grinch is a priority, get in line as soon as the park opens. You can also secure face time with the Mean One and his dog Max by purchasing a holiday tour ($85), which also includes a meeting with Santa, reserved viewing for the holiday entertainment, and a buffet of treats. Of course, you don't need to line up or pay extra to interact with the friendly citizens of Whoville, who may be found roaming Seuss Landing throughout the day.

In addition to greeting guests, the Grinch stars in his own *Grinchmas Who-liday Spectacular* (★★★★½), a 30-minute musical performed six to eight times each day inside the former Blue Man Group theater between IOA and USF. Access to the venue is via a pathway behind Circus McGurkus. The large theater provides ample comfortable seating with good sightlines, but arrive early if you want to sit up front.

The show, which blends the original book and cartoon with elements from the 2000 live-action flick and musical accompaniment arranged by Chip Davis of Mannheim Steamroller, is a must-see for

DEREK'S GRINCHMAS "SATURDAY SIX"

DEREK BURGAN'S HEART grows three sizes every Grinchmas season, and here's his "Saturday Six" list of top reasons why he loves IOA's annual Seussian celebration.

6. Snacks Seuss Landing is filled with incredible snack options the whole year round, but for the holiday season their spotlight focuses on the Grinch. Several annual treat options return for Grinchmas, including a *How the Grinch Stole Christmas* "book" cupcake, sugar cookies, and hot chocolate.

5. Merchandise If you are a fan of the Grinch character, the merchandise selection is truly amazing. It's really stupendous, fantastic, bombastic, and downright tremendous!

4. The Whos Whoville's citizens come out to walk the streets as part of the Whoville Decorating Committee. They'll often be working in teams to help further decorate the park . . . and even guests! And they're always ready to have silly photo ops.

3. Decor Seuss Landing is already the most whimsically designed land in IOA, but over-the-top holiday decorations take everything to the next level. Look for McElligot's Pool near the land's entrance; all coins thrown into this water feature are donated to Give Kids the World Village.

2. *Grinchmas Who-liday Spectacular* This must-see stage show presentation of *How the Grinch Stole Christmas* combines elements of both the beloved animated version along with the Jim Carrey live-action film.

1. Breakfast with The Grinch & Friends Tons of food options, lots of character interactions, and digital photos from an official photographer that are included with the meal—can't beat that! The bad news is that it sells out fast, but a limited number of walk-ups are accepted.

Grinch fans. It features a first-rate cast (some of whom have appeared on Broadway), an expansive set, and even an appearance by a live canine as the Grinch's faithful pet, Max.

Showtimes are listed in the Universal app and typically begin between 10:45 a.m. and noon and continue until around 6 p.m. Line up near the One Fish, Two Fish ride a minimum of 30–45 minutes before showtime, as performances fill to capacity early on busy days. You will be directed to a seat once inside, but the venue is shallow enough that even the back row has an acceptable view.

The **Grinch character breakfast** is held in Circus McGurkus Cafe Stoo-pendous or Confisco Grille on select mornings during November and December. It costs $63 (plus gratuity) for adults and $35 for kids age 9 and under. Theme park admission is required; see "Character Meals" on page 306 for more information.

UNIVERSAL ISLANDS *of* ADVENTURE TOURING PLANS

DECISIONS, DECISIONS

WHEN IT COMES TO TOURING IOA efficiently in a single day, you have two basic choices, and as you might expect, there are trade-offs. The Wizarding World of Harry Potter—Hogsmeade sucks up guests like a Hoover vacuum and is quickly overrun by crowds on days of moderately heavy attendance. Even on slow days, Hagrid's Magical Creatures Motorbike Adventure can attract an hour-plus wait within minutes after early park admission begins.

If you're intent on experiencing **Hagrid's Magical Creatures Motorbike Adventure** first thing during early park admission, be at the turnstiles waiting to be admitted at least 30–60 minutes before the park opens. The park's gates will open 5–15 minutes before the appointed hour, with Potter-bound guests racing counterclockwise from Port of Entry through Seuss Landing. Once you're permitted, move as swiftly as possible to The Wizarding World and then ride Hagrid's Magical Creatures, followed by Jurassic World VelociCoaster or Flight of the Hippogriff, depending on your thrill tolerance. Then get in line for Forbidden Journey (if time remains before official opening) or journey through Jurassic Park toward Skull Island.

If the rides operate as designed, you're golden. You can get Hogsmeade out of the way during the early-entry hour, and be off to other must-see attractions before the park gets crowded. Then come back to The Wizarding World late in the day to explore Hogsmeade and the shops. If, on the other hand, the rides suffer technical difficulties, you may be stuck in line a long while, during which time the crowds will have spread to other areas of IOA. By the time you exit, there will be long lines for all of the park's other popular attractions.

Even if you do take advantage of Early Park Admission (EPA), Forbidden Journey frustratingly doesn't open for the first half of the hour, and then runs only a small fraction of its available benches during the second half, often making what should be a nominal wait stretch to 30 minutes or more. As a consequence, Forbidden Journey's wait is sometimes longer during EPA than it will be later that same afternoon. If the queue is backed up beyond the talking portraits, save Forbidden Journey until after it has been brought up to full speed. Otherwise, you'll waste your entire early-entry hour standing in the Gryffindor Common Room and risk missing the opening rush toward Jurassic Park and Skull Island.

If you don't have EPA privileges at IOA, a much better choice (and the path we follow in our recommended touring plans) is to skip Potterville first thing. Instead, enjoy other attractions in IOA, starting at Marvel Super Hero Island and Skull Island. The good news is that The Wizarding World usually clears out in the afternoon, and its queues are often empty in the last hour, even on busy days. You can usually ride Forbidden Journey with a minimal wait if you step in the queue shortly before closing time.

ONE-DAY TOURING PLAN FOR ADULTS *(page 399)*

THIS TOURING PLAN IS FOR GUESTS without park-to-park tickets and is appropriate for groups of all sizes and ages. It includes thrill rides that may induce motion sickness or get you wet. If the plan calls for you to experience an attraction that doesn't interest you, simply skip it and go to the next step. Be aware that the plan calls for some backtracking. If you have young children in your party, customize the plan to fit their needs and take advantage of child swap at thrill rides.

ONE-DAY TOURING PLAN FOR
FAMILIES WITH SMALL CHILDREN *(page 400)*

THIS PLAN IS FOR GUESTS without park-to-park tickets and eliminates all rides with a minimum height requirement greater than 40 inches. The plan includes a midday break of at least 2 hours back at your hotel.

ONE-DAY TOURING PLAN FOR
FAMILIES WITH TWEENS *(page 401)*

THIS PLAN IS FOR GUESTS without park-to-park tickets and eliminates all rides with a minimum height requirement greater than 52 inches; rides with height requirements over 48 inches include warnings.

ONE-DAY TOURING PLAN FOR SENIORS *(page 402)*

THIS PLAN IS FOR GUESTS without park-to-park tickets and is specifically designed for seniors and grandparents, taking walking distances and attraction ratings from this group into account. This plan focuses on shows and family-friendly attractions and avoids thrill rides.

Also see page 241 in Part Six for descriptions of our multiday and multipark touring plans.

PART 8

UNIVERSAL EPIC UNIVERSE

ON AUGUST 1, 2019, Universal officially announced plans for its second resort campus, called **Universal Epic Universe.** Since then, we've seen years of construction activity on the more than 750 acres acquired by Universal near the Orange County Convention Center (about 2 miles south of the current resort), as well as an extension of Kirkman Road that will directly connect the two properties.

The new park is built around a central hub with fountain-filled lagoons and surrounded by three hotels—the luxury 500-room **Helios Grand** attached to the rear of the hub, as well as two moderately priced 750-room hotels (named **Terra Luna** and **Stella Nova**) across the street—multiple restaurants, and four highly themed lands. You may not even need a physical ticket to traverse the new resort because Universal has patented facial recognition technology to replace traditional turnstiles. (Of course, all of these plans are speculative and subject to change.)

Originally anticipated to open in 2023, Epic Universe was delayed when the pandemic began, but construction resumed as of March 3, 2021; an exact opening date has not been officially announced, but the theme park is on track to be operational by summer 2025.

GETTING ORIENTED *at* UNIVERSAL EPIC UNIVERSE

EPIC UNIVERSE IS LAID OUT IN a hub-and-spoke configuration, but, unlike theme parks like Magic Kingdom, each land has only one entrance in and one exit back to the hub. This center area of Epic Universe is also much larger than Magic Kingdom's hub, acting as the park's fifth land.

Beginning at the park entrance and going clockwise, you'll encounter entry portals into **Super Nintendo World, Dark Universe, The Wizarding World of Harry Potter—Ministry of Magic,** and **How to Train Your Dragon—Isle of Berk.**

Continued on page 276

Universal Epic Universe

Attractions

1. Constellation Carousel UX
2. Curse of the Werewolf UX
3. Dragon Racer's Rally ˙UX
4. Fyre Drill UX
5. Harry Potter and the Battle
   at the Ministry UX ☑
6. Hiccup's Wing Gliders UX ☑
7. *Le Cirque Arcanus* UX ☑
8. Mario Kart: Bowser's Challenge UX ☑
9. Mine-Cart Madness UX ☑
10. Monsters Unchained:
    The Frankenstein Experiment UX ☑
11. *Oculus Nighttime Spectacular* ☑
12. Stardust Racers UX ☑
13. *The Untrainable Dragon* UX ☑
14. Viking Training Camp UX
15. Yoshi's Adventure

Counter-Service Restaurants

A. The Bubbly Barrel
B. Burning Blade Tavern
C. Cafe L'air la Sirene
D. Das Stakehaus
E. De Lacey's Cottage
F. Hooligan's Grog & Gruel
G. Le Gobelet Noir
H. Mead Hall
I. Meteor Astropub
J. The Oak and Star Tavern
K. Pizza Moon
L. Spit Fyre Grill

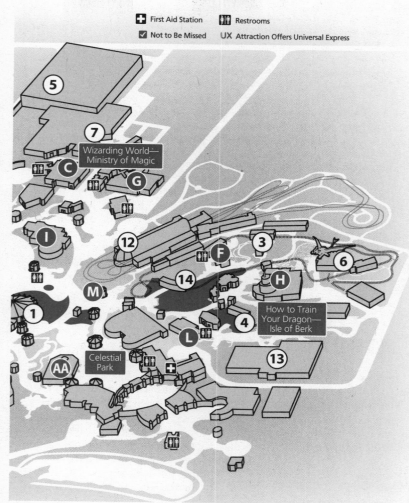

First Aid Station   Restrooms

Not to Be Missed   UX Attraction Offers Universal Express

5

7
Wizarding World—
Ministry of Magic

C

G

I

12

F

3

6

14

M

H

1

4
How to Train
Your Dragon—
Isle of Berk

L

AA
Celestial
Park

13

Table-Service Restaurants

M. Star Sui Bao
N. Toadstool Cafe
O. Turbo Boost Treats
P. Yoshi's Snack Island

AA. Atlantic
BB. Blue Dragon
      Pan-Asian Restaurant

Continued from page 273

NOT TO BE MISSED AT UNIVERSAL EPIC UNIVERSE
CELESTIAL PARK • Stardust Racers • *Oculus Nighttime Spectacular*
SUPER NINTENDO WORLD • Mario Kart: Bowser's Challenge • Mine-Cart Madness
DARK UNIVERSE • Monsters Unchained: The Frankenstein Experiment
THE WIZARDING WORLD OF HARRY POTTER—MINISTRY OF MAGIC • Harry Potter and the Battle at the Ministry
HOW TO TRAIN YOUR DRAGON—ISLE OF BERK • Hiccup's Wing Gliders • *The Untrainable Dragon*

As you enter Epic Universe, lockers and wheelchair and stroller rentals are to your left, and First Aid and Guest Services are to your right. Like the rest of the park's massive central hub, this entry area is a part of **Celestial Park,** Epic Universe's fifth world. The entry area also contains the usual Starbucks, the park's largest gift shop, a candy store named Moonship Chocolates & Celestial Sweets, and a photo pick-up location. Before deciding whether to go left or right to head to your first themed land, take a moment to look forward at the **Luna Overlook.** Here, you can get a view straight through to the back of the park with a large statue, cascading waterfalls flowing toward central lagoons, and acres of rolling gardens visible ahead.

UNIVERSAL EPIC UNIVERSE ATTRACTIONS

CELESTIAL PARK

AT THE HEART OF EPIC UNIVERSE, the park's expansive hub itself is home to a couple of rides of its own, as well as dining, shopping, entertainment, and a few other surprises. Even after the lands close, guests can enjoy the amenities of this *central park* for several hours before capping off the day with a nightly fireworks and fountain show.

Acting somewhat like a second CityWalk location, as well as a central hub, Celestial Park has multiple full-service dining locations, including the undersea-themed upscale **Atlantic** and **The Blue Dragon Pan-Asian Restaurant,** as well as indoor and outdoor bars, unique shopping, and even live entertainment.

Mimicking the action of the massive show fountains nearby, the **Astronomica** splash pad allows kids to run and play through spraying water, while acting as the park's compass rose within the center of Epic Universe.

Due to the unique layout of Epic Universe, you will be passing through the central areas of Celestial Park between your visits to any of the four main worlds of the park. Each world can only be entered via their portals, and all have a tall spire on top for easy wayfinding within the center of park. Each world has only one exit as well, which takes you back into Celestial Park.

Constellation Carousel *(Universal Express)*

What it is Astronomy-inspired merry-go-round. **Scope and scale** Minor attraction. **When to go** After experiencing the other major attractions. **Comments** No height requirement. **Duration of ride** Around 2 minutes. **Loading speed** Moderate.

DESCRIPTION AND COMMENTS Constellation Carousel sits atop the park's central lagoon and is covered by an exquisitely decorated canopy. Kids and kids-at-heart can ride on animals inspired by real constellations in the sky on this fanciful carousel. Guest seating options include celestial lions, dragons, peacocks, and more. Above the ride, the Star Tracker ceiling installation features celestial star patterns with a center Mesmerizer that creates a ribbon cone effect.

Unlike conventional carousels, Constellation Carousel features animal seating situated on inner rotating circles moving 360 degrees themselves while also traveling around the main rotating base, giving this ride an extra dimension of movement.

TOURING TIPS Nonrotating seating and benches, located on the outside ring of the carousel, are available upon request for less motion. This attraction has no height requirement, but children must be able to sit up on their own to ride.

Stardust Racers *(Universal Express)*

What it is High-speed dueling roller coasters. **Scope and scale** Super-headliner. **When to go** During the first or last hour of the day. **Comments** 48″ minimum height requirement; child swap available (see page 187); single-rider line available; not to be missed. **Duration of ride** About 90 seconds. **Loading speed** Moderate.

Motion Sickness

DESCRIPTION AND COMMENTS Epic Universe's fastest and most thrilling attraction, Stardust Racers allows guests to engage in comet racing, the favorite pastime of Celestians (as Celestial Park's citizens are known). This dual track–launched steel coaster from Mack Rides boasts two separate circuits weaving around and racing against each other, with some extreme airtime moments that are sure to satisfy both coaster junkies and casual thrill-seekers alike.

Enjoy on-board ethereal music as you reach speeds up to 62 miles per hour and heights up to 133 feet, hurtling like a comet along 5,000 feet of track. At night, the track features no lighting, so the fully illuminated ride vehicles appear to streak across the sky like shooting stars. The signature maneuver for Stardust Racers is called the "Celestial Spin," where both trains barrel roll around each other, in a synchronized ballet of crisscrossing inversions.

TOURING TIPS Both tracks offer a near identical ride experience, with only one notable difference near the start of the ride as they cross over the station, before passing each other head on. The rest of the ride is spent with the two trains racing side by side.

Double-sided lockers are available within the queue, before the station, and all riders are required to empty their pockets before passing through metal detectors.

SUPER NINTENDO WORLD

THE MULTILEVEL AND HIGHLY INTERACTIVE Super Nintendo World is based on settings and characters from Super Mario Bros. and its spin-offs, which have been best-selling video games since the 1980s.

Guests enter the vibrant and lively land through an iconic green warp pipe, ascend an escalator, and emerge through a swirl of colored lights and 8-bit sound effects into a Mushroom Kingdom–inspired courtyard flanked by **Princess Peach's Castle** on one side and **Bowser's Fortress** on the other. Flag-topped Mount Beanpole and a range of terraced hills screen out the surrounding park, and everywhere you turn there's another moving animatronic—marching Koopas, waddling Goombas, and spinning coins—enlivening the area with infectious kinetic energy. Beyond this colorful Super Mario Land is also a **Donkey Kong Country** mini-land, which is accessed via another warp pipe within the world.

Featuring more than its three standout rides, the Super Nintendo World area also contains multiple opportunities to meet iconic Nintendo characters, including Mario, Luigi, Princess Peach, Toad, and more. Go beyond the attractions with the purchasable **Power-Up Bands** (see below), and unlock additional areas to explore. Shop for exclusive Super Nintendo World merchandise at the **1-UP Factory** store, and indulge in 8-bit-inspired meals at **Toadstool Cafe** or kawaii-style eats at several snack locations.

On days when Super Nintendo World may temporarily reach capacity, especially in the mornings, you may need a Virtual Line reservation to enter the land. These reservations are not always required, but you may want to check the official app on the day of your visit just in case.

Mario Kart: Bowser's Challenge *(Universal Express)*

What it is Augmented-reality dark ride. **Scope and scale** Super-headliner. **When to go** As soon as the park opens, just before closing, or whenever possible using single-rider. **Comments** 40″ minimum height requirement; child swap available (see page 187); single-rider line available; not to be missed. **Duration of ride** About 5 minutes. **Average wait time per 100 people ahead of you** 4 minutes. **Loading speed** Moderate.

Motion Sickness

DESCRIPTION AND COMMENTS Based on the long-running series of racing games, Mario Kart combines traditional dark ride elements with cutting-edge augmented reality technology that blurs the line between the real and virtual worlds. The storyline sees Bowser, the villainous King of the Koopas, challenging Mario and his pals to a kart race through flaming lava fields, floating clouds, and other iconic tracks from the best-selling Mario Kart games. Prospective competitors enter Bowser's castle, touring its bowels where his anthropomorphic bomb minions are built, before being handed special visors styled after Mario's distinctive red cap. Once riders strap into the four-seater vehicles, a video display with angled transparent lenses snaps onto the visor, creating Pepper's Ghost–style digital holograms that appear to float in front of you among the physical sets.

During the ride, racers cooperate to claim the coveted Universal Cup by aiming at their virtual opponents with their heads, then pressing buttons on their steering wheels to shoot shells, as well as by turning the wheels in response to flashing arrows. Everyone on your team will need to collect at least 100 coins in order to beat Bowser to the finish line, and ammunition is limited, so look down along the track for crystal blocks to reload. **TIP:** Press both buttons during the starting countdown on "2" for a bonus, and look behind you for hidden coin blocks.

STELLA SAYS

SUPER SUPER NINTENDO WORLD? Even though Epic Universe is opening this year, that doesn't mean Universal is done building it! Some dining locations within Celestial Park may not be ready for the park's opening but should come online soon after. More interestingly, there are rumors that an expansion to Super Nintendo World may already be in development to be ready as early as a year or two after the park opens. The top rumor is for a spooky Luigi's Mansion mini-land, featuring an interactive ride where you seek out ghosts on an omnimover ride system.

The ride spins quite a bit but doesn't actually move particularly fast; however, the combination of game-play elements and projection effects creates a chaotic sense of speed, especially during the climactic Rainbow Road sequence.

TOURING TIPS Mario Kart develops a multihour wait as soon as the land opens in the morning, and lines don't drop until closing time. Although the best time to ride Mario Kart is at rope drop, be warned that the attraction may open late or close early due to maintenance. The easily overlooked single-rider entrance (on the right immediately inside the queue) can be a lifesaver, although it bypasses the Easter egg–filled queue and the cartoon preshows instructing players on how to score. Universal advises guests with waist sizes over 40 inches to test the vehicle restraints outside the attraction before entering the queue, but the lap bars are actually less restrictive than those on some other rides in the resort, such as Revenge of the Mummy or Gringotts.

Mine-Cart Madness *(Universal Express)*

What it is Family-friendly "leaping" roller coaster. **Scope and scale** Headliner. **When to go** Immediately upon opening. **Comments** 36" minimum height requirement; child swap available (see page 187); single-rider line available; not to be missed. **Duration of ride** 2 minutes. **Loading speed** Fast.

DESCRIPTION AND COMMENTS Mine-Cart Madness is a new type of roller-coaster attraction, with both outdoor and indoor scenes, that can make it appear that your out-of-control cart is jumping over gaps in the track. Encounter characters from the Donkey Kong games, such as Donkey Kong, Diddy Kong, Cranky Kong, and more, on the ride and in the queue, and come face to face with the floating antagonist, Tiki Tong.

Without the extreme speeds of more intense roller coasters, and because it never goes upside down, Mine-Cart Madness is a good in-between coaster that most of the family can enjoy together. But what it lacks in speed, it makes up for in its wildly unpredictable maneuvers and death-defying "jumps" over apparent gaps in the track. Despite the fast action, this attraction features physical sets and animatronics, without a reliance on screen-based media, so it can offer a refreshing counterbalance to the area's other headlining attraction, Mario Kart: Bowser's Challenge.

TOURING TIPS Although the four-passenger mine cars load continuously using a conveyor belt, capacity for this unique roller-coaster attraction is not as great as the other coasters at the park, so the line may back up in the middle of the day. If members of your group are fans of the Donkey Kong games or are in the mood for a more visceral attraction within Super Nintendo World, you may want to prioritize this ride over Mario Kart first. The ride does offer a single-rider line (when available), but it may not save you as much time waiting as other single-rider lines due to the limited seating per ride vehicle and tendency for older thrill-seekers to be comfortable riding alone, which can clog the queue.

Yoshi's Adventure

What it is Slow-moving indoor/outdoor dark ride. **Scope and scale** Major attraction. **When to go** After experiencing the other major attractions. **Comments** 34" minimum height requirement; child swap available (see page 187). **Duration of ride** 4½ minutes. **Loading speed** Moderate.

DESCRIPTION AND COMMENTS Take a ride with Yoshi over the Mushroom Kingdom, with incredible views you can only achieve from this family-friendly attraction. Fans of games like Yoshi's Island or Crafted World will recognize many of the characters from this kid-centric, slow-moving, omnimover-type attraction, including Kamek, Baby Mario, Baby Peach, Poochy, and more.

Geared toward families with children, Yoshi's Adventure offers an interactive experience for a smaller audience that's easier to understand than the more involved Mario Kart ride. See Toadette in the queue for a list of instructions on your way to the colorful Yoshi-shaped ride vehicles. Each ride vehicle is equipped with three egg-shaped buttons for each of its two seats. When a rider sees each of the red, blue, and green eggs on the ride, which are quite easy to spot, they press the corresponding egg button on the car. An animatronic Captain Toad will let you know if you were successful or not at the ride's conclusion.

TOURING TIPS Older kids and teens may rather spend time waiting for the Mario Kart or Donkey Kong rides, so this can be skipped if the line is too long, but with a limited number of small-kid-friendly attractions overall, this may be a must-do for families with young ones. While the ride moves extremely slow, it still requires children to be at least 34" tall to ride, or at least 48" tall to ride alone.

Interactive Power-Up Bands and Key Challenges

To keep track of your Mario Kart score, as well as fully participate in the interactive elements around the land, we strongly suggest that you install the smartphone app and purchase a colorful character-themed Power-Up Band ($40), which allows you to "punch" blocks and participate in activities throughout the multilevel complex. Even though these basic bands don't need batteries or charging, their level of interactivity is far more sophisticated than Hogsmeade's magic windows, reacting readily to the scores of sensors secreted around the land.

Tip: To save time on the day of your visit to Epic Universe, you can purchase your Power-Up Band from the Super Nintendo World store in CityWalk and link it to your phone ahead of time.

Beyond simply discovering all the sound and light effects that you can activate—thereby adding digital badges to your app's bragging board—you can participate in several physical challenges, each with multiple difficulty levels to keep veterans on their toes. Once you've conquered at least three of the key activities (see full list below), you and one companion are allowed inside **Bowser Jr.'s lair** for an arm-waving interactive "boss battle" that's a fantastic full-body workout. After you've beaten Bowser Jr., head upstairs to the **Frosted Glacier** overlook and use the augmented reality binoculars to find the final hidden key on the hovering airship.

Use your Power-Up Band to play the following challenges to collect keys:

- **Bob-omb Kaboom Room**, located inside the caves, has you scrambling to locate and assemble the key fragments before the Bob-omb goes kaboom.
- **Goomba Crazy Crank** has you working fast to spin a crank until you knock down a running Goomba.
- **Koopa Troopa POWer Punch** is where you punch a POW block at just the right time to knock down the Koopa Troopa with a spinning shell. On easy mode, hit the block as the shell enters the green pipe; on hard mode, punch just after it bounces off the wall.
- **Piranha Plant Nap Mishap** has you working as a team to smack buzzing alarm clocks before waking the sleeping plant.
- **Thwomp Panel Panic**, also indoors, has your group touching every tile on the wall until they're the same color. This game is much easier with two players.

DARK UNIVERSE

THE LEGENDARY FIENDS from Universal's vintage black-and-white fright flicks finally get their due with the first-ever theme park land inspired by the classic monsters first made famous by Karloff, Chaney, Lugosi, and Lanchester. Step into the rustic European village of **Darkmoor,** a land where monsters still roam, and danger could be lurking around every corner. In this dark universe, those iconic films were actually documentaries; now it's your turn to face off with a new generation of nightmares in your very own creature feature.

Between riding two hair-raising attractions and meeting the monsters in person, guests can enjoy a frightfully good dinner at **Das Stakehaus** or grab a drink from **The Burning Blade Tavern,** inspired by the windmill from Frankenstein, which bursts into flames every 20 minutes. And to complete the eerie atmosphere, an original musical score by *Beetlejuice* and *The Nightmare Before Christmas* composer Danny Elfman echoes throughout the land.

Dark Universe is split into multiple areas, with the village street beckoning you in first. Pass by decaying stone walls and long-neglected crumbling towers as you make your way deeper into the foggy town square. Here you can find unique wares for sale at **Pretorius' Scientific Oddities** shop, or pop into the **Darkmoor Monster Makeup Experience** for a macabre makeover.

Deeper into Darkmoor, you'll approach **Frankenstein Manor,** which stands looming over the village in the distance. This is the home to the land's main attraction, and one of Epic Universe's crowning jewels, **Monsters Unchained: The Frankenstein Experiment,** an exciting indoor ride.

The final area to explore, hidden behind the village, contains a traveling caravan of colorful fortune teller tents and wagons, which have set up shop deep in the forest. This is home to the land's outdoor spinning roller coaster, **Curse of the Werewolf.**

Curse of the Werewolf *(Universal Express)*

What it is Family launched spinning roller coaster. **Scope and scale** Headliner. **When to go** The first 2 hours the park is open or after 4 p.m. **Comments** 40″ minimum height requirement; child swap available (see page 187); single-rider line available. **Duration of ride** About 2 minutes. **Loading speed** Moderate.

DESCRIPTION AND COMMENTS Curse of the Werewolf is a Mack spinning roller coaster starring Maleva, the fortune teller who has set up camp at the edge of the village. After becoming afflicted with the curse yourself, your coaster train car spins out of control on this outdoor swing-launched family coaster, where no matter what time it is, it's always a full moon.

Motion Sickness

While this coaster features a fairly short track layout, the middle of the ride does include a swing launch where we pass through the same spot, back and forth, multiple times, extending the ride time.

TOURING TIPS With a top speed of only 37 mph, the thrill level for the ride's layout itself may not be too intense, but some may find the free-spinning nature of the attraction nauseating. Also, despite being a family-friendly roller coaster, be warned that children may find the Wolf Man animatronics hiding in the barn scene a bit frightening.

Monsters Unchained: The Frankenstein Experiment
(Universal Express)

What it is High-tech indoor dark ride. **Scope and scale** Super-headliner. **When to go** The first 2 hours the park is open or after 4 p.m. **Comments** 48" minimum height requirement; child swap available (see page 187); single-rider line available; not to be missed. **Duration of ride** 4½ minutes. **Loading speed** Fast.

DESCRIPTION AND COMMENTS Monsters Unchained: The Frankenstein Experiment sees us entering a Gothic manor at the back of the village. Dr. Victoria Frankenstein, the great-great-granddaughter of the original mad scientist, invites us to witness her newest experiment, in which she attempts to control the world's most dangerous monsters. Her new technology has already worked on a new incarnation of her ancestor's greatest experiment, Frankenstein's Monster himself, who is now as friendly as her loyal assistant, Ygor. Brave guests are strapped onto KUKA robotic arms within Dr. Frankenstein's laboratory, where Victoria's attempt to tame the formidable Count Dracula doesn't go quite as planned, unleashing all the Universal classic monsters, including iconic boogeymen like the Mummy, the Phantom of the Opera, the Creature from the Black Lagoon, and more. Before you know it, you're on a wild ride through the dark catacombs beneath Frankenstein Manor, attempting to escape from the revitalized villains.

This attraction utilizes state-of-the-art uber-aggressive animatronics and intricate set pieces enhanced by large high-tech screens, all woven together to create a sense of a pure chaotic madness, especially when combined with the unwieldy motion profile of robot arm-mounted ride vehicles. While Harry Potter and the Forbidden Journey alternates between screen moments and physical sets, this ride attempts to blur the line between the two so you're never quite sure what's real and what's not.

TOURING TIPS Universal bills this as the scariest ride they've ever built, but the frights come more from the spooky sights and sensations (such as breath on the back of your neck or beating bat wings) rather than extreme physical movements. Those susceptible to motion sickness from Forbidden Journey's simulator domes should find Monsters Unchained much less nauseating. Lockers are required for loose articles, but they are located deep within the queue, so you can carry your belongings with you while you wait. You will want to store all your belongings, including phones, so they do not slip out of your pockets during this turbulent ride.

Interactive Experiences in Dark Universe

You can encounter some of your favorite Universal Monsters in the flesh, including the Bride of Frankenstein and her boo, at the **Meet the Monsters** meet and greet; then bump into the Invisible Man or a strolling musician on the street. Become a monster hunter while exploring the village in a land-wide interactive game and get a realistic temporary tattoo or ghoulish face paint at the **Darkmoor Monster Makeup Experience** inside Dr. Pretorius' old laboratory.

THE WIZARDING WORLD OF HARRY POTTER— MINISTRY OF MAGIC

UNIVERSAL'S THIRD—and presumably final—Wizarding World re-creates the streets of Paris from the *Fantastic Beasts* spin-off series, as well as the Ministry of Magic in London, as seen in the original Potter films. Guests will travel through time and space between 1920s Paris and late-1990s London via Métro-Floo, emerging from magical green fireplaces into the Ministry's grand atrium.

The **Place Cachée** part of the land features full-scale Parisian buildings (like a beefed-up EPCOT pavilion) filled with magical creatures around every corner. Of course, it wouldn't be a Wizarding World without a cart that serves Butterbeer (known here as Bièraubeurre), uniquely themed foods, merchandise—including clothing, robes, and wands—as well as a whole new land's worth of interactive wand displays to cast a spell on. This land includes two large quick-service dining locations, including one tucked away in a hidden alley on the right side of the area.

The standout draw for this Wizarding World is its main attraction, a state-of-the-art new dark ride set within the **Ministry of Magic,** featuring an entirely new type of simulator-base ride vehicle. A live stage show featuring Newt and his Fantastic Beasts rounds out the land's attractions.

Harry Potter and the Battle at the Ministry *(Universal Express)*

What it is High-tech indoor dark ride. **Scope and scale** Super-headliner. **When to go** The first or last hour the park is open. **Comments** 40" minimum height requirement; child swap available (see page 187); single-rider line available; not to be missed. **Duration of ride** 4½ minutes. **Loading speed** Moderate-fast.

Motion Sickness

DESCRIPTION AND COMMENTS Harry Potter and the Battle at the Ministry takes us beyond the Harry Potter stories, as we go on a new adventure to defeat the diabolical Dolores Umbridge (Oscar nominee Imelda Staunton), aboard enchanted elevators that can travel in any direction. This high-tech dark ride combines animatronics, moving set pieces, and projection mapping, along with a new type of tracked motion base ride system, to create another level of immersive experience.

Featuring new settings not seen in the films, magical creatures that were first seen in the Fantastic Beasts series, and new characters developed specifically for this ride, Battle at the Ministry extends the Harry Potter story, taking place after the events of the initial series.

Similar to the impressive experiences of walking the halls of Hogwarts Castle and entering the lobby of Gringotts Bank, the queue for this attraction is not to be missed. Travel magically from Paris to London to find yourself in the massive atrium of the British Ministry of Magic, where Dumbledore and Voldemort once battled, with office windows reaching five-stories up and wizarding statues towering 40 feet tall.

After touring some of the Ministry's more recognizable workspaces, including Umbridge's feline-filled office, guests are invited to attend the trial of the infamous ex-headmaster, alongside Wizarding World luminaries like Harry, Ron, and Hermione. But before the abusive educator can face justice, she's jailbroken by a band of fellow Death Eaters; now, you must help the heroic trio and Higgledy (Umbridge's long-suffering house elf) to recapture her, before she can repair a broken Time-Turner and revive Voldemort's reign.

TOURING TIPS While you do load into elevator-style seating, rest assured that this ride is not a drop-tower attraction like the Tower of Terror. It does simulate the motion of rising and falling between the larger-scope show scenes, but without the extreme thrill. Visitors who have trouble with rides like The Amazing Adventures of Spider-Man or Transformers: The Ride—3D may still have issues with motion sickness, despite this attraction opting not to utilize 3D glasses.

Le Cirque Arcanus (Universal Express)

What it is Indoor show with special effects. Scope and scale Major attraction. When to go After experiencing the other major attractions. Comments Not to be missed by Wizarding World fans; may frighten or bore small children. Duration of show Around 20 minutes.

DESCRIPTION AND COMMENTS Join Newt Scamander and Gwenlyn (a squib circus assistant), as they try to rescue his famous suitcase full of fantastic beasts from Skender, an unscrupulous ringmaster who plans to use its inhabitants to revive his once-fashionable show's fading fortunes. This all-new live production brings magical creatures—like a Demiguise, Zouwu, Kelpie, and Mooncalves—to life right before audiences' eyes, using uniquely integrated media, high-tech puppetry, aerial acrobatics, and special theatrical effects. Enter the circus tent in the center of Paris, based on the one seen in *Fantastic Beasts: The Crimes of Grindelwald,* and you'll find yourself in a space that is much larger inside than it appeared outside.

TOURING TIPS Shows may be continuous throughout the day, but if the line is extending beyond the tent, you may want to come back later to experience this attraction. There is still a queue inside, followed by a holding room that can fit a full theater's worth of guests after passing through the tent outside.

Interactive Wands and Spell-Casting Locations in the Wizarding World

The Wizarding World of Harry Potter—Ministry of Magic takes interactive wands to the next level. Not only can you create magic by casting spells in front of a whole slew of new windows here—including adorable animatronic Nifflers and Bowtruckles, and enchanted portraits that converse using customized quips—but you can also unlock secret areas by completing tasks.

With the help of the official app (like the way Power-Up Bands work in Super Nintendo World), this Wizarding World was built with a new level of interactivity in mind—and some areas you may recognize from *Fantastic Beasts* can only be entered with an interactive wand after completing special challenges.

Shopping in the Wizarding World

Just as it has been within the existing Hogsmeade and Diagon Alley areas, this new Wizarding World features a whole new array of shopping opportunities. Leaning into Parisian theming, you can find certain spots with all-new French-inspired treats and wares, as well as classic Wizarding staples like house robes, wands, and even Butterbeer. Shops include:

- **Bar Moonshine** is an American-style walk-up bar that not only features alcoholic spirits, but also nonalcoholic drinks like Butterbeer, Pumpkin Juice, and more.

- **Cosme Acajor Baguettes Magique** The Parisian counterpart to Ollivanders doesn't offer the selection experience found there, but it does sell an exclusive range of new interactive wand designs, which come wrapped in unique colorful triangle boxes, along with a selection of English imports.

- **K. Ramelle** is a sweet shop near the front of the land featuring freshly made desserts in addition to classic packaged treats and snacks.

- **Les Galeries Mirifiques** is a Parisian department store located within the center of the land.

- **Mademoiselle Malkins** is a robe shop, for all your school uniform needs.

- **Patisserie Matagot** is a bakery window at the back of the land. (*Note:* This location may not be open yet when the park debuts.)

- **Tour en Floo** is a travel agency–themed gift shop at the exit of the Battle at the Ministry ride.

HOW TO TRAIN YOUR DRAGON—ISLE OF BERK

DREAMWORKS'S ISLE OF BERK IS the most densely packed land in Epic Universe, with multiple attractions and eateries woven around a whimsical waterfront filled with the kinetic motion of roller coaster trains, water-spraying boats, flying dragons, and fire-breathing statues.

Bringing the colorful world of the *How to Train Your Dragon* films to life, the Isle of Berk is populated by dragons perched atop every building, as this Viking village is where humans and dragons live in harmony. Keep an eye on the sky because you may even spot dragon-shaped drones soaring overhead! In addition to spotting various dragons around the land—and in the impressive live stage show—kids of all ages will love meeting Toothless in the flesh, brought to life through innovative puppet-animatronic hybrid technology.

After experiencing the land's major attractions, let the kids burn off excess energy in the play area and enjoy a relaxing meal at the indoor **Mead Hall** or grab a quick bite at the outdoor **Spit Fyre Grill,** where fire-breathing dragons cook your food.

Dragon Racer's Rally *(Universal Express)*

What it is Spinning carnival-style ride. **Scope and scale** Minor attraction. **When to go** Before 11 a.m. or after 3 p.m. **Comments** 48″ minimum height requirement; child swap available (see page 187). **Duration of ride** 2 minutes. **Loading speed** Slow.

DESCRIPTION AND COMMENTS Dragon Racer's Rally features two stand-alone passenger-controlled spinning rides (like Dumbo the Flying Elephant, except the lever allows them to do barrel roll flips). Mounted dragon figures on the end of the spinning ride's post make it appear as though they're powering the attraction, which gives it a homemade, almost Flintstones feel.

A bit of a one-trick pony, this spinning flat ride just goes around and around, and while the ability to do flips is novel, it's not as easy as it looks, requiring a bit of strength and perseverance to pull off. Daredevils who are up to the challenge (and have the stomach for it) may have a fun time, but this low-capacity attraction may not be for everyone.

TOURING TIPS Despite having two of these rides side by side, this attraction still suffers from low capacity, so the line may move at a crawl at peak times of day.

Fyre Drill *(Universal Express)*

What it is Slow-moving interactive boat ride. **Scope and scale** Major attraction. **When to go** Before 11 a.m. or after 3 p.m. **Comments** No height requirement; child swap available (see page 187). **Duration of ride** 4 minutes. **Loading speed** Slow.

DESCRIPTION AND COMMENTS Fyre Drill is an extremely slow-moving interactive boat ride where riders of all ages get to control on-board water cannons at targets throughout the course. The story for this ride has your boat working together to spray "handmade" targets to put out fires and save a miniature version of Berk from going up in make-believe flames.

TOURING TIPS Prepare to get wet. If the geysers and sprayers on the ride don't get you, the landlubbers outside the ride firing their own water cannons at unsuspecting riders will.

This attraction does not have a height requirement, so anyone who can stand or sit on their own is allowed to ride, but hand-held infants are not permitted. Parents can help smaller children with the crank-style water cannons, so their little ones can focus on aiming.

Hiccup's Wing Gliders *(Universal Express)*

What it is Family-friendly launched roller coaster. **Scope and scale** Headliner. **When to go** The first or last hour the park is open. **Comments** 40" minimum height requirement; child swap available (see page 187); not to be missed. **Duration of ride** 2½ minutes. **Loading speed** Moderate.

DESCRIPTION AND COMMENTS Hiccup's Wing Gliders is an Intamin launched steel roller coaster (think of a tamer version of VelociCoaster) that encircles much of the land, zooming over pathways and under bridges, creating the sensation of flying with a dragon. The ride features two launches that act as small show scenes, featuring Hiccup and Toothless, who are working to help power this Viking-made coaster experience, as well as some Gronckle dragons, who've recently hatched from their eggs. While the launches are a bit punchy and the curves heavily banked, this ride does not go upside down, making it a good in-between coaster for younger riders ready to graduate from kiddie coasters to something a bit more adventurous.

Fans of the films will enjoy being able to walk through Hiccup's home as they enter the attraction, as well as see his various inventions scattered about the queue, coaster station, and exit shop. This includes a real-life version of his wingsuit, which is the inspiration for the ride vehicle's design.

TOURING TIPS If pressed for time, the younger members of your family may enjoy this attraction while their older teen siblings wait in line for Stardust Racers located next door, just outside of the How to Train Your Dragon entry portal.

The Untrainable Dragon *(Universal Express)*

What it is Indoor show with large puppets. **Scope and scale** Headliner. **When to go** After experiencing the other major attractions or during inclement weather. **Comments** Not to be missed. **Duration of show** 20 minutes.

DESCRIPTION AND COMMENTS Experience an all-new story from the world of *How to Train Your Dragon* via the massive indoor stage show, *The Untrainable Dragon*, and then meet Hiccup, Toothless, and their friends afterward. Featuring characters and locations from the film series, this impressive stage show chooses to tell an original story, rather than simply re-telling any of the stories from the films. Featuring large dragon puppets, special effects, and original music, this show is impressive enough for those who may be uninitiated on the films, while expanding the canon for die-hard fans.

TOURING TIPS Plan to see the show in the middle of the day, while the lines for many of the park's rides are at their longest.

Viking Training Camp

What it is Interactive play area. **Scope and scale** Minor attraction. **When to go** Anytime.

DESCRIPTION AND COMMENTS Viking Training Camp is a large play area where kids can explore elevated walkways, climb towers, and slide, all while encountering dragon-themed obstacles. The area is flanked by beautiful rockwork, continuing the scenery from the nearby roller coaster attraction.

TOURING TIPS Conveniently located family restrooms can be found at the back of this play area, making it a good spot for a pit stop.

Interactive Experiences and Entertainment in Isle of Berk

If you're up to the challenge of training your own dragon, you can "adopt" one and unlock additional interactive elements throughout the land. These adorable electronic dragon toys are available for purchase at retail locations like **Toothless' Treasure** near the land's theater. Each interactive dragon comes with its own carrying sack, which it sleeps in (recharges), and can be trained to do tricks, be fed, and interact with some of the larger dragons around the land. Visit the **Haddock Paddock** meet and greet, also located near the theater, to encounter stables filled with full-scale dragons like Toothless, and enjoy a moment with Hiccup and his best friend.

LIVE ENTERTAINMENT *at* UNIVERSAL EPIC UNIVERSE

IN ADDITION TO THE SHOWS profiled previously, Epic Universe offers one major outdoor nighttime spectacular, along with a wide range of smaller street performances. Catch small street-side shows throughout the day at the **Hemisphere Stage**, located near the

Starbucks on the left side of The Oculus large fountain at the back of Celestial Park, and find random entertainers located within **Luna Overlook** near the park's entrance.

While most of the costumed characters for Epic Universe can be found within the individual lands—Mario and friends in Super Nintendo World, Toothless and Hiccup in the Isle of Berk, and so on—you can meet some new characters created specifically for Celestial Park. At **Moonship Chocolates & Celestial Sweets,** you may be able to find Maya, a chocolatier and world traveler, along with her teddy bear ship captain, Cacao. See pages 189–191 for more character information.

Oculus Nighttime Spectacular

What it is Vegas-style outdoor fountain show. **Scope and scale** Headliner. **When to go** When scheduled at the end of the evening. **Comments** Not to be missed. **Duration of show** TBD.

DESCRIPTION AND COMMENTS At the northern end of the hub, a large fountain outside the Helios Grand Hotel, called The Oculus, offers Bellagio-style water shows all day, as well as a performance synchronized with fireworks and lighting effects during the nighttime spectacular.

TOURING TIPS Guests staying at the Helios Grand Hotel can get a bird's-eye view of the show from the rooftop viewing area. Regular park guests will be able to see the show on the ground, within the tiered viewing rings surrounding the large fountain, or anywhere in the northern section of Celestial Park. The show is not viewable from within the other lands of Epic Universe.

UNIVERSAL EPIC UNIVERSE TOURING PLANS

TOURING EPIC UNIVERSE is certain to require plenty of planning and patience, particularly during its opening year. All of our earlier advice for USF or IOA about arriving early and quickly hitting the top headliners goes double at EU. Efficient touring of EU is complicated by the hub-and-spoke design, which requires returning to Celestial Park rather than directly hopping from land to land. Although the park has fewer rides than either IOA or USF, its expansive size, interactive experiences, and expected popularity means you'll want to devote at least a full day to exploring it.

Bear in mind that all of the Epic Universe plans in this book are preliminary and based on pre-opening information; watch touringplans .com for updated itineraries after the park debuts.

ONE-DAY TOURING PLAN FOR ADULTS *(page 413)*

THIS TOURING PLAN IS appropriate for groups of all sizes and ages. It includes thrill rides that may induce motion sickness or get you wet. If the plan calls for you to experience an attraction that doesn't interest you, simply skip it and go to the next step. Be aware that the plan calls for some backtracking. If you have young children in your party, customize the plan to fit their needs and take advantage of child swap at thrill rides. Consider using some single-rider queues if you don't mind splitting your party up, especially if doing all the big rides in one day is important.

ONE-DAY TOURING PLAN FOR FAMILIES WITH SMALL CHILDREN *(page 414)*

THIS PLAN eliminates all rides with a minimum height requirement greater than 40 inches. The plan includes a midday break of at least 2 hours back at your hotel.

ONE-DAY TOURING PLAN FOR FAMILIES WITH TWEENS *(page 415)*

THIS PLAN features attractions that appeal to children ages 8–12, all with a minimum height requirement of 48 inches or under.

ONE-DAY TOURING PLAN FOR SENIORS *(page 416)*

THIS PLAN IS specifically designed for seniors and grandparents, taking walking distances and attraction ratings from this group into account. This plan focuses on shows and family-friendly attractions and avoids thrill rides.

PART 9

UNIVERSAL VOLCANO BAY

UNIVERSAL ORLANDO DESCRIBES **Volcano Bay**'s 28 acres as "a lush, tropical oasis that unfolds before you, instantly transporting you to a little-known Pacific isle." Unlike the former Wet 'n Wild, whose only themes appeared to be concrete and plastic, Volcano Bay showcases a scenic, man-made mountain and a colorful atmosphere that goes toe to toe with those of Disney's water parks.

The park looks like an upscale resort in the South Pacific, with lush palm trees, thatched roofs, and tiki carvings created by some of the same craftsmen behind Trader Sam's bar at Disney. As long as you're at ground level, you'll hardly guess that there's a busy interstate only yards away.

Volcano Bay has an elaborate backstory (detailed at theugseries .com/waturi) based on the fictional Waturi tribe, an ancient Polynesian people who set out on their outrigger canoes to find a new home with the mantra "Water Is Life. Life Is Joy." The Waturi visited many islands, drawing elements from each culture, until they caught sight of the legendary fish Kunuku playing in the waves of Volcano Bay and settled there. The Waturi legend also influenced the unpronounceable names of most of the attractions, but that's about as far as the theming goes on the slides—don't expect any animatronics or elaborate effects.

If you're staying on-site (or if you temper your attraction-riding expectations) and can relax into the park's immersive atmosphere, Volcano Bay may just be your slice of paradise alongside I-4. A Seattle family wrote to us comparing Volcano Bay with Disney's aquatic offerings:

> *Typhoon Lagoon really suffered in comparison to Volcano Bay. Slides at VB were faster, longer, and more fun overall, and I cannot overstate the convenience of not having to carry your own tubes up the stairs.*

A family from Grafton, Massachusetts, shared their feelings:

> *We all agreed it's the best water park we've ever been to. The variety of activities, the park layout, the food—everything was wonderful. The*

Universal Volcano Bay

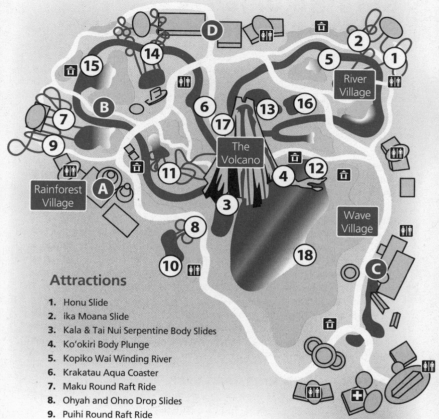

Attractions

1. Honu Slide
2. ika Moana Slide
3. Kala & Tai Nui Serpentine Body Slides
4. Ko'okiri Body Plunge
5. Kopiko Wai Winding River
6. Krakatau Aqua Coaster
7. Maku Round Raft Ride
8. Ohyah and Ohno Drop Slides
9. Puihi Round Raft Ride
10. Puka Uli Lagoon
11. Punga Racers
12. The Reef
13. Runamukka Reef
14. Taniwha Tubes: Tonga & Raki
15. TeAwa the Fearless River
16. Tot Tiki Reef
17. Vol's Caverns
18. Waturi Beach

Restaurants

A. Bambu
B. The Feasting Frog
C. Kohola Reef Restaurant & Social Club
D. Whakawaiwai Eats

 First Aid Station Restrooms ☐ Cabanas

early issues with TapuTapu seem to have been ironed out; the system worked great both days we were there.

GETTING ORIENTED *at* UNIVERSAL VOLCANO BAY

ONCE DROPPED OFF at Volcano Bay's bus plaza, guests are ushered through an ornate underground tunnel (seemingly hewn from stone) before ascending an escalator into the park. At the entryway, fountains burble beside an Easter Island–style statue that occasionally speaks; you'll also find more prosaic objects like an ATM, lockers, and Guest Services window outside the park's turnstiles.

Volcano Bay is divided into four primary areas (also known as lands), each with a unique theme, but because all of the areas sport the same lush South Seas scenery, it's impossible to tell where one section ends and another begins without a map. Guests enter the park at **Wave Village,** which is dominated by the **Waturi Beach** multidirectional wave pool and **The Reef** leisure pool. Paths from there lead clockwise to **Rainforest Village,** home to the park's densest collection of thrill rides, including **TeAwa the Fearless River,** and counterclockwise to **River Village,** which has family-friendly attractions like the signature **Krakatau Aqua Coaster** and **Kopiko Wai** lazy river. The heart of the park puts **The Volcano** in Volcano Bay: 200-foot-tall **Krakatau,** home to hidden caverns with cascading waterfalls and special effects triggered by your TapuTapu band (see next section).

While there are signposts throughout the park, the winding walkways can make it confusing to find your way. Blissfully, many of the cement sidewalks are cooled by sprinklers, so at least you won't burn your bare feet while wandering in circles.

TAPUTAPU AND VIRTUAL LINES

UNIVERSAL BOASTS THAT IT HAS eliminated the biggest hassles at water parks—standing in long lines for slides—by replacing queues with a Virtual Line mandatory reservation system. Where it differs from Universal Express is that there is no standby line at all; all guests save their places in line with their TapuTapu wearables, allowing them to do other things as they await their turns.

Every visitor is issued a waterproof TapuTapu wristband (think a slightly bulkier Apple Watch with a rubber wristband) that you use to claim your place in the Virtual Lines, as well as reserve and open lockers, and make payments throughout the park. The TapuTapu bands also trigger special effects throughout Volcano Bay, such as controlling streams of water in Tot Tiki Reef or shooting water cannons at other guests who are enjoying the Kopiko Wai Winding River.

To enter Volcano Bay, you must first register a ticket with an online account and assign it to your name; setting up a credit card charge account (with a secure PIN and custom spending limits for each family member) is optional. Attendants will assist you with this at the turnstiles, but your entry will be far smoother if you set everything up ahead of time through universalorlando.com or the official Universal mobile app when purchasing your tickets in advance.

Every attraction that uses Virtual Lines has a tiki totem outside its entrance with a digital display. For the first hour or so after opening, most slides will show "Ride Now," indicating that there is little to no wait to ride. Once its queue begins to build, each attraction activates its Virtual Line, and the totem displays a wait time; by 11 a.m., most slides will report at least an hour virtual wait.

Tap your TapuTapu band against the glowing symbol below any of the touch screens surrounding the tiki, and you'll be assigned an approximate time when you can return. Your actual return time may be earlier than expected if other guests skip their return times, or later if the attraction temporarily closes due to weather or technical problems; TapuTapu will notify you of any changes. You can hold a reservation for only one ride at a time, and TapuTapu will alert you when it's time to return with a minimal wait—typically 5–15 minutes, but we've experienced waits of more than 30 minutes during technical difficulties.

Reservations don't expire once they become active, so you don't have to rush to ride, but you can't get in another Virtual Line until you use or cancel your first ride. You may, however, jump into any queue displaying "Ride Now" without losing your place in a Virtual Line. Conversely, if a tiki says "Ride Full," all the day's reservations are claimed, but don't lose hope; closed Virtual Lines often reopen in the hours before closing as other guests exit, abandoning their spots.

In theory, Volcano Bay's Virtual Line system should allow guests to enjoy wait-free attractions like the wave pool and lazy river instead of standing in hot queues. In *reality,* guests who don't enter early spend a lot of time baking on the beach and may get to ride only four or five slides on a busy day. We love the idea of the Virtual Line and being able to relax while waiting our turn. TapuTapu's implementation has made great strides since opening day, and we were able to experience everything we wanted to during recent visits. That said, the system still doesn't feel completely seamless, so we recommend visiting with measured expectations of how many slides you'll ride in a day.

One final hitch: though the TapuTapu wristband has two snaps and a rubber ring to hold it more securely, it has a habit of coming loose, especially in TeAwa the Fearless River. If your TapuTapu takes a swim, swing by Guest Services for a free (though time-consuming) replacement.

Volcano Bay Universal Express Passes, which bypass the Virtual Lines and provide immediate access to the slides' boarding queues, are sold in advance online and inside the park at the concierge huts; quantities are limited and sell out on busy days. Express at Volcano Bay is not free for anyone—even those staying in Signature Collection on-site hotels—and it's available only for one-time use, not unlimited.

However, it's cheaper than purchasing Express at the theme parks, especially if you go for the version valid only on select slides. See page 60 for details.

CABANAS AND PREMIUM SEATING

YOU CAN UPGRADE YOUR VISIT with reserved padded loungers (about $150 and up per pair), 6-person cabanas ($750 and up), or 16-person Family Suite cabanas ($1,600 and up); prices, which are not published and vary daily, do not include park admission, and there are no refunds for midday weather closures. While they're not a necessity, we recommend the private loungers for their included shade canopy, locking storage box, and attendant to deliver Mobile Orders of food and drink, including upscale appetizers (such as conch fritters and pork belly flatbread) that aren't offered on the regular menus. The locker's mechanism can only be activated by one TapuTapu at a time and is frustratingly finicky; carefully align your wristband with the sensor, and firmly push down until you hear it click.

The cabanas get all the same perks, plus towel service, fruit and bottled water, and a private kiosk for making TapuTapu reservations. Note, however, that many cabanas don't offer much privacy, and the attendants get mixed reviews on their attentiveness, making them a dubious value.

The private loungers and cabanas are yours to use all day, even if you exit and return to the park, but they sell out early. Call ☎ 877-489-8068 (for loungers) or 877-801-9720 (for cabanas) up to 60 days in advance for reservations, and bring a printout of your confirmation to the park. When selecting a seat location, keep in mind that Wave Village is nearest to the entrance and gets the most morning sun; River Village is closest to the kids' playgrounds; and Rainforest Village is right up against the interstate. Upon arriving, head to a concierge hut to be checked in and walked to your reserved area; most guests make a beeline to the concierge closest to the entrance, while there's rarely a wait at the one in River Village. If you've booked upgraded seating, it's still best to arrive at the park as early as possible and link your tickets in the app ahead of time, or else you'll loose valuable time in the morning like this Phoenix, Arizona, family:

> We had a very bad experience using Concierge at Volcano Bay. It took over 90 minutes from arrival at the gates until we were assigned our premium seating and able to experience our first attraction. Most of the waiting was at Concierge, including the painstaking process of linking our tickets/wristbands.

LOCKERS AND TOWELS

RESTROOM AND CHANGING FACILITIES with large banks of lockers are located around the park; the ones in Wave Village closest to the park entrance are always the most crowded, while the ones at the back of the park in River Village are rarely busy. Lockers come in three sizes and cost between $14 and $25. (Note that you'll need a credit card—either in hand or linked to your TapuTapu account—to rent directly at the locker; see an attendant to pay with cash or a hotel key.) Lockers are yours for the full day and are opened and closed with your TapuTapu. Up to four other members of your party can also be assigned access to your locker; follow the prompts on the locker kiosk's touch screen to add additional authorized users.

A bank of all-day lockers ($20–$25) is located immediately outside the park, but we don't recommend using them because you must return your TapuTapu and forfeit any Virtual Line reservations each time you exit.

Towels are not provided free (as they are at some other water parks), but you can rent one for about $7 at any concierge hut. You'll have to dry it in the sun between swims because that fee doesn't include swapping out wet towels (unless you luck into a sympathetic employee). Souvenir towels are also sold for around $30.

UNIVERSAL VOLCANO BAY ATTRACTIONS

THE BULK OF VOLCANO BAY'S SLIDES are hidden from the view of guests as they enter behind the mountain's blown-out back side. Attractions range from mild family-friendly raft rides (all with convenient conveyor belts that carry your raft uphill for you) to heart-seizing drop slides from the caldera's summit. Read the posted warnings carefully before you climb 20 stories to the top, and be prepared for a discreet weigh-in before most slides to ensure your safety.

THE VOLCANO

THE 200-FOOT VOLCANO **Krakatau** lies at the center of the park. Inside, guests can explore hidden caverns with cascading waterfalls.

Vol's Caverns ★★★

APPEAL BY AGE PRESCHOOL ★★★ GRADE SCHOOL ★★★★½ TEENS ★★★★
YOUNG ADULTS ★★★★½   OVER 30 ★★★★½   SENIORS ★★★

What it is Interactive walk-through. **Scope and scale** Diversion.

The volcano contains a network of caverns concealed behind waterfalls and curtains of steam; look for entrances near the queues for Krakatau Aqua Coaster, Ko'okiri Body Plunge, and Kala & Tai Nui Serpentine Body Slides. Once inside, you'll find colorful fountains surrounding Vol, the spirit of the mountain who converses with guests through a digital projection, similar to the Mystic Fountain in Islands of Adventure. Ask Vol to tell you the legend of Volcano Bay's discovery, and make sure you trigger the light display depicting Kunuku, the mythical fish, on the cave wall.

RAINFOREST VILLAGE

THIS VILLAGE HOUSES the park's densest collection of thrill rides. Note that most of this area's attractions—including Maku and Puihi,

Punga Racers, Taniwha Tubes, and TeAwa the Fearless River—as well as the bridge connecting this area with River Village, will not open in the mornings until the end of the Early Park Admission hour.

Kala & Tai Nui Serpentine Body Slides
★★★★½

| APPEAL BY AGE | PRESCHOOL ★★½ | GRADE SCHOOL ★★★½ | TEENS ★★★★ |
| YOUNG ADULTS ★★★★ | | OVER 30 ★★★★ | SENIORS ★★★½ |

What it is Two extreme twisting body slides. **Scope and scale** Headliner. **Comments** 48" minimum height requirement; 300-pound maximum weight requirement per rider. **Duration of ride** About 25–30 seconds.

After falling through a drop door, two riders go down 124-foot body slides simultaneously. Their paths cross several times as they hurtle down translucent intertwining tubes. The blue Kala slide is intense enough, but the green Tai Nui side is like the VelociCoaster of slides: it starts fast and gets even faster as it goes. These slides are sometimes "Ride Now" even when other attractions have long virtual waits, perhaps because they are so intimidating. Note that you must climb more than 200 steps to reach the top of these slides.

Maku Round Raft Ride   ★★★

| APPEAL BY AGE | PRESCHOOL ★★★½ | GRADE SCHOOL ★★★★ | TEENS ★★★★ |
| YOUNG ADULTS ★★★★ | | OVER 30 ★★★★ | SENIORS ★★★★½ |

What it is Mild family raft ride. **Scope and scale** Major attraction. **Comments** 42" minimum height requirement; 48" minimum height requirement if riding alone; 1,050-pound maximum weight requirement per raft. **Duration of ride** About 30–40 seconds.

Maku and Puihi mean "wet" and "wild," respectively, in the fictional Waturi language, making this pair of group raft slides a subtle tribute to Volcano Bay's predecessor. North America's first "saucer ride," the six-person Maku round raft plunges riders through bowl-like formations that are surrounded by erupting geysers before ending in a pool. Unfortunately, the advertised fountains usually fail to deliver on the slide's name, making it one of the park's bigger busts. On the plus side, there's rarely a long wait for Maku, and the tower it shares with Puihi has one of the park's only elevators, for those unable to climb stairs.

Ohyah and Ohno Drop Slides   ★★★½

| APPEAL BY AGE | PRESCHOOL ★★ | GRADE SCHOOL ★★★★ | TEENS ★★★★½ |
| YOUNG ADULTS ★★★★★ | | OVER 30 ★★★★½ | SENIORS ★★★★ |

What it is Two twisting body slides with drop endings. **Scope and scale** Minor attraction. **Comments** 48" minimum height requirement. **Duration of ride** About 15 seconds.

Two short but intense twisting slides launch guests 4 and 6 feet above the water at the end, guaranteeing that splashdown sends water straight up your sinuses. Ohno is the taller of the two and typically has a longer wait; the extra 2 feet of free fall isn't worth an additional 20 minutes.

Puihi Round Raft Ride   ★★★★½

| APPEAL BY AGE | PRESCHOOL ★★★ | GRADE SCHOOL ★★★★ | TEENS ★★★★ |
| YOUNG ADULTS ★★★★ | | OVER 30 ★★★★ | SENIORS ★★★★½ |

What it is Thrilling family raft ride. **Scope and scale** Major attraction. **Comments** 42" minimum height requirement; 48" minimum height requirement if riding alone; 850-pound maximum weight requirement per raft. **Duration of ride** About 45 seconds.

Maku's mate, Puihi, is the far more frightening slide of the pair: a six-person raft launches down a dark, winding tunnel before shooting up a banked curve; riders glimpse the highway below and momentarily experience zero gravity prior to sliding back down. Among the park's family raft slides, this is second only to Honu for making riders scream in terror.

Puka Uli Lagoon ★★½

**APPEAL BY AGE PRESCHOOL ★★★★   GRADE SCHOOL ★★★★   TEENS ★★½
YOUNG ADULTS ★★★★   OVER 30 ★★★★   SENIORS ★★★**

What it is Kiddie pool with fountains. **Scope and scale** Diversion.

This shallow pool near the Ohyah and Ohno Drop Slides is framed by towering tikis and windmill-like contraptions that spray water when TapuTapu sensors are activated. The area around Puka Uli is a great spot to set up camp if you're keeping an eye on young kids, but not so much if you're looking for peace and quiet.

Punga Racers ★★★½

**APPEAL BY AGE PRESCHOOL ★★★   GRADE SCHOOL ★★★½   TEENS ★★★½
YOUNG ADULTS ★★★★   OVER 30 ★★★½   SENIORS ★★★★**

What it is Side-by-side body slides. **Scope and scale** Minor attraction. **Comments** 42" minimum height requirement; 48" minimum height requirement if riding alone; 300-pound maximum weight requirement per rider. **Duration of ride** About 20 seconds.

Guests go feet first down enclosed body slides across four lanes and through "underwater sea caves" (that is, plastic tubes). The orange slide in the center feels the fastest, while the two outside tubes are twistier; tuck your elbows in on the turns or you may be bruised. Punga Racers originally featured racing mats that guests rode while facing forward, but after several guest injuries, the ride was redesigned without mats and with a safer splashdown landing.

Taniwha Tubes: Tonga & Raki ★★★★

**APPEAL BY AGE PRESCHOOL ★★★   GRADE SCHOOL ★★★★   TEENS ★★★★½
YOUNG ADULTS ★★★★½   OVER 30 ★★★★   SENIORS ★★★★**

What it is Four intertwined two-passenger raft slides. **Scope and scale** Major attraction. **Comments** 42" minimum height requirement; 48" minimum height requirement if riding alone; 300-pound maximum weight requirement per rider; 450-pound maximum weight requirement per raft. **Duration of ride** About 25–30 seconds.

One tower sports four Easter Island–inspired waterslides with rafts for single or double riders, who sit single file bobsled-style. The slides are similar but not identical—bear left to Tonga (the green slides) with more open-air sections if you get claustrophobic, or go right to Raki (the blue ones) if you like enclosed slides with lots of twists. The best thing about Taniwha Tubes is that they're almost always "Ride Now," and you'll rarely wait more than a few minutes for your turn, so you can try out all four slides to find your favorite. This attraction may open 1 hour after the rest of the park.

TeAwa the Fearless River ★★★★½

**APPEAL BY AGE PRESCHOOL ★★½ GRADE SCHOOL ★★★★½ TEENS ★★★★½
YOUNG ADULTS ★★★★½   OVER 30 ★★★★★   SENIORS ★★★★★**

What it is Rapids river. **Scope and scale** Headliner. **Comments** 42" minimum height requirement; 48" minimum height requirement if riding alone; every rider must wear an approved life vest.

On this racing-torrent river, guests hang ten in their mandatory life vests amid roaring whitewater rapids as they surf beneath the slides inside Krakatau. This is the best attraction of its kind that we've experienced outside of the Atlantis resort in the Bahamas, but if you're looking for a lazy river, this ain't it! A tip for hopeful surfers: paddle upstream as you exit from under the volcano long enough to catch a curl from the wave generator.

RIVER VILLAGE

NAMED AFTER THE WATERWAY that winds through it, River Village features family-friendly attractions.

Honu Slide ★★★★★

APPEAL BY AGE PRESCHOOL ★★★½ GRADE SCHOOL ★★★★½ TEENS ★★★★½
YOUNG ADULTS ★★★★½   OVER 30 ★★★★½   SENIORS ★★★★★

What it is Extreme family raft ride. **Scope and scale** Headliner. **Comments** 42″ minimum height requirement; 49″ minimum height requirement if riding alone; 700-pound maximum weight requirement per raft. **Duration of ride** About 35–40 seconds.

Honu and ika Moana are two separate slides attached to the same tower, where guests board multiperson animal-themed rafts (a sea turtle and a whale, respectively) before speeding down into a pool. Honu is a blue raft slide that sends two to five riders vertically up two giant sloped walls before sliding back down, giving a terrifying taste of what skateboarders call hang time at the top. It's the scariest group raft ride in the park, and our pick as the best. It's also the most popular, along with Krakatau Aqua Coaster, so make it one of your top priorities on arrival.

ika Moana Slide ★★★½

APPEAL BY AGE PRESCHOOL — GRADE SCHOOL ★★★★ TEENS ★★★★
YOUNG ADULTS ★★★★½   OVER 30 ★★★★½   SENIORS ★★★★

What it is Moderate family raft ride. **Scope and scale** Major attraction. **Comments** 42″ minimum height requirement; 48″ minimum height requirement if riding alone; 750-pound maximum weight requirement per raft. **Duration of ride** About 45 seconds.

Though both are boarded from the same platform, don't confuse ika Moana with its neighbor, Honu. Ika Moana (no relation to the Disney princess) is a much gentler journey in and out of twisting green tunnels, on a raft that's supposed to spray water from its center. Much like Maku and Puihi, ika Moana isn't necessarily a bad ride, and riders in a full boat will enjoy some snappy spinning around the sharper turns; it's simply upstaged by its sibling.

Kopiko Wai Winding River ★★★★

APPEAL BY AGE PRESCHOOL ★★★½ GRADE SCHOOL ★★★★ TEENS ★★★★
YOUNG ADULTS ★★★★½   OVER 30 ★★★★   SENIORS ★★★★

What it is Lazy river. **Scope and scale** Headliner. **Comments** Children under 48″ must wear an approved life vest and be accompanied by a supervising companion.

This gentle lazy river passes through the water park's landscape and into the volcano's hidden caves. The highlight of the ride is Stargazer Cavern, a mist-filled grotto with constellations of pinpoint lights blanketing the rocky ceiling. Beware of spots where guests on dry land can soak you by triggering TapuTapu-activated fountains. You're allowed to swim along without an inner tube, but snag one anyway for maximum relaxation.

Krakatau Aqua Coaster ★★★★★

APPEAL BY AGE PRESCHOOL ★★★½ GRADE SCHOOL ★★★★½ TEENS ★★★★½
YOUNG ADULTS ★★★★★   OVER 30 ★★★★½   SENIORS ★★★★★

What it is Roller coaster–style family raft ride. **Scope and scale** Super-headliner. **Comments** 42″ minimum height requirement; 48″ minimum height requirement if riding alone; 700-pound maximum weight requirement per raft. **Duration of ride** 1⅓ minutes.

Guests board a specially designed canoe that seats up to four. The ride uses linear induction motor technology, which launches the canoe uphill as well as downhill as you twist and turn around the volcano's blown-out interior. It's similar to Crush 'n' Gusher at Disney's Typhoon Lagoon but far longer and more thrilling, delivering delightful moments of air time like a real coaster. It's a shame that Universal didn't make Krakatau a full-blown dark ride by including indoor scenes or special effects, but this is still the best waterslide we've ever been on. Krakatau is the park's starring headliner and can only service about 700 guests per hour, so either take advantage of "Ride Now" at rope drop or get your Virtual Line reservation as early as possible.

Runamukka Reef ★★★½

APPEAL BY AGE PRESCHOOL ★★★★ GRADE SCHOOL ★★★★ TEENS ★★★½
YOUNG ADULTS ★★★   OVER 30 ★★★½   SENIORS ★★★½

What it is Wet playground. **Scope and scale** Minor attraction. **Comments** 48″ maximum height requirement for slides.

This three-story water playground for older children inspired by a coral reef includes twisting slides, sprinklers, and more. Even though it's intended for kids, parents will want to clamber around the structure too.

Tot Tiki Reef ★★½

APPEAL BY AGE PRESCHOOL ★★★★★ GRADE SCHOOL ★★★★ TEENS ★½
YOUNG ADULTS ★★★   OVER 30 ★★★½   SENIORS ★★★½

What it is Infant splash area. **Scope and scale** Diversion. **Comments** 48″ maximum height requirement for slides.

This small toddler play area has spraying Maori fountains, slides, and a kid-size volcano. Visually imaginative but hardly expansive, this is little more than a glorified splash pad, but it's entertaining enough for the swim-diaper set. Speaking of which, swim diapers are mandatory for all babies and may be bought at Whakawaiwai Eats.

WAVE VILLAGE

LOCATED AT THE BASE of Krakatau, Wave Village contains wave and leisure pools, as well as the park's largest beach.

Ko'okiri Body Plunge ★★★★½

APPEAL BY AGE PRESCHOOL ★★½ GRADE SCHOOL ★★ TEENS ★★★★½
YOUNG ADULTS ★★★★★   OVER 30 ★★★★½   SENIORS ★★★

What it is High-speed vertical drop slide. **Scope and scale** Headliner. **Comments** 48″ minimum height requirement; 300-pound maximum weight requirement per rider. **Duration of ride** About 20 seconds.

Hop on this 125-foot slide, featuring a drop door with a 70-degree-angle descent, straight through the heart of the mountain. Drumbeats building up to the drop get your heart pounding, but the plunge itself is over before you have time to scream. You won't be able to see much with all the water in your face, but other guests can watch your splashdown through a clear tube located between Waturi Beach's wave pool and The Reef pool. As with all body slides, cross your ankles, fold your arms across your chest, and arch your back for the best ride. Ko'okiri's queue moves the slowest of the extreme body slides, so daredevils should make it one of their first stops. Note that you must climb more than 200 steps to reach the top of this slide.

The Reef ★★★

APPEAL BY AGE PRESCHOOL ★★★★ GRADE SCHOOL ★★★½ TEENS ★★★★
YOUNG ADULTS ★★★ OVER 30 ★★★★ SENIORS ★★★★

What it is Calm pool with a view. **Scope and scale** Minor attraction. **Comments** Children under 48″ must wear an approved life vest.

Relax in this leisure pool with calm waters and its own waterfall, and watch braver souls shoot down the Ko'okiri Body Plunge through a clear tunnel where the pool meets Waturi Beach.

Waturi Beach ★★★★

APPEAL BY AGE PRESCHOOL ★★★★ GRADE SCHOOL ★★★½ TEENS ★★★★
YOUNG ADULTS ★★★★ OVER 30 ★★★★ SENIORS ★★★★½

What it is Wave pool. **Scope and scale** Super-headliner. **Comments** Children under 48″ must wear an approved life vest.

The central swimming lagoon at Volcano Bay, situated at the foot of Krakatau Lagoon and fed by waterfalls cascading off the volcano's peak, contains a cutting-edge wave pool capable of cycling through different types of surf. A musical fanfare sounds every 10 minutes as the sign above the pool rotates, indicating a shift in the seas: from calm waters, to moderate multidirectional chop, to powerful unified breakers.

UNIVERSAL VOLCANO BAY TOURING STRATEGY

DUE TO THE NATURE of the Virtual Line system, it's impossible for us to provide a precise touring plan for Volcano Bay as we do for other parks. We can, however, share basic strategies to maximize the number of attractions you can experience during your visit, which worked out well for these readers from Lee's Summit, Missouri:

> We followed the touring advice exactly. The park closed due to capacity, but we did everything and didn't feel like it was too hard to ride things. We were done and chilling out when it got busy.

Just remember that your enjoyment of Volcano Bay isn't dictated by the quantity of slides you ride. Simply vegetating in a lounge chair or lazy river all day is perfectly valid:

1. Purchase your admission in advance, and create an online account at universalorlando.com or through the Universal Orlando mobile app to register your tickets and members of your party. You can also set up a credit card for charging purposes if you wish.

2. Arrive at Volcano Bay's turnstiles at least 15–30 minutes before early-park admission begins, if eligible; otherwise, be parked and ready to board the bus 15–30 minutes prior to official park opening.

3. Upon entering, secure seats and a locker, if needed. The loungers on Waturi Beach are the first to be claimed, but you'll find plenty of options around the rear side of the volcano until midmorning. Families with toddlers should claim chairs near Tot Tiki Reef.

4. Tackle the most popular slides while the queues are in "Ride Now" mode, starting with Krakatau Aqua Coaster, Honu, and Ko'okiri Body Plunge (for thrill seekers only), in that order.

5. Circle counterclockwise from River Village to Punga Racers; ride a couple of times if there's no line, then tackle Puihi in Rainforest Village.

6. By now you've experienced the majority of the popular slides, and the Virtual Line system has probably been activated. Get a return time for Ohyah or Ohno (whichever is sooner). While waiting, ride Kala & Tai Nui (if you're brave and they still show "Ride Now") or relax in the Puka Uli Lagoon.

7. After using your Ohyah or Ohno return time, backtrack clockwise to experience Maku, which should still say "Ride Now."

8. Cross the park back to River Village and ride ika Moana. Check one of the park's wait time boards while walking there; if ika Moana is "Ride Now," you can use TapuTapu to get a return time for your second ride on Krakatau Aqua Coaster, Ko'okiri Body Plunge, or Honu along the way.

9. You've now conquered all of the park's slides save for Taniwha Tubes, which you can experience at any time. Virtual Line waits may be in the triple digits by now, so enjoy the wave pool, Fearless and Winding Rivers, and any other slides still showing "Ride Now" while waiting for your next return time. Also take time to explore the volcano's caverns and search for interactive TapuTapu effects.

10. Lines for food at Volcano Bay build early and move slowly. Order an early lunch before 11 a.m. or wait until after 3 p.m. It's important to stay hydrated, so feel free to visit the bars early and often. Restaurants begin to shutter 2 hours prior to park closing; Kohola Reef and Dancing Dragons typically stay open the latest.

11. During the summer, you can count on a thunderstorm sweeping through in midafternoon. Everyone is ushered out of the water as soon as lightning strikes within 5 miles, and many guests flee for the parking buses once a downpour starts. Sit tight; Orlando showers are usually short-lived, and you'll have the slides to yourself once the all clear is given.

12. As closing time approaches, Virtual Line waits begin to drop, and some queues that were formerly full may reopen, so secure your last re-rides on any favorites.

13. Try to stay in the park past sunset to see the volcano erupt with crimson water. Don't forget to return your TapuTapu wristbands on your way out.

PART 10

DINING *and* SHOPPING *at* UNIVERSAL ORLANDO

WHEN FOODIES ARE ASKED TO NAME great gourmet vacation spots around the world—New York, Paris, Singapore—Orlando probably doesn't immediately pop to the top of their wish lists. But believe it or not, Central Florida has developed a substantial culinary culture, from the prototype concepts tested by major chains along Sand Lake Road's Restaurant Row and the lauded gastropubs that have sprouted around downtown, to the thriving local community of upscale food trucks.

Even so, while adventurous eaters have always known that there's plenty to explore in the greater Orlando area, and even tourist-phobic locals have long been lured to Walt Disney World (WDW) property by its lengthy list of restaurants, Universal has often been left out of the conversation. Thanks to the uniform mediocrity of Universal Studios Florida's (USF's) counter-service food during the resort's formative years, the conventional wisdom was that Universal Orlando's food options simply weren't as delicious or as diverse as those at Disney.

The good news is that, while Universal's counter-service food still lags behind Disney's in quality and value, the opposite is true of the table-service restaurants in Universal, which are almost always on par with, or a step ahead of, what you can find at WDW and other parks. Thanks largely to the efforts of the resort's award-winning executive chef, Steven Jayson, more variety, better preparations, and more current trends are generally the rule at Universal. And best of all, a first-class meal at Universal will almost always leave less of a dent in your credit card than the equivalent repast would at Mickey's table.

Note that portion sizes have decreased while prices have increased across the resort since the pandemic, as they have throughout the entire economy. However, the "shrinkflation" has been less egregious at Universal Orlando than at many chain restaurants or your local grocery store.

Quick-service (or counter-service, as it is sometimes called) offerings inside USF and Islands of Adventure (IOA) are largely lackluster, but Harry Potter's **Leaky Cauldron** and **Three Broomsticks,** The Simpsons' **Fast Food Boulevard**, and Minion Land's **Minion Cafe** set a new bar for theme park fast food, and the fare at Volcano Bay is far fresher and more diverse than you'd expect from a water park.

USF's two full-service restaurants are **Finnegan's Bar and Grill** in New York and **Lombard's Seafood Grille** in San Francisco. Finnegan's serves typical bar food—burgers and wings—as well as fresh fish and chips and other takes on Irish cuisine. Lombard's is the better restaurant, but it's not in the same stratosphere as Disney's Hollywood Brown Derby (in quality or price).

IOA has two sit-down restaurants: **Confisco Grille** in Port of Entry and **Mythos Restaurant** in The Lost Continent. Confisco is fine for appetizers and drinks. Despite its Hellenic-sounding name, Mythos isn't strictly a Greek restaurant; rather it serves something-for-everyone fusion fare with Mediterranean flair, including Italian risotto, Asian noodles, and Spanish octopus, plus steaks and burgers.

While most restaurants at Epic Universe use modified quick-service with mobile app ordering and table delivery, there are two full-service restaurants—**Atlantic,** an upscale seafood eatery inside an aquarium, and **Blue Dragon Pan-Asian Restaurant,** offering Japanese and Thai dishes—with more options inside the adjoining **Helios Grand Hotel.**

For even better eating options, exit the parks into **CityWalk,** Universal's dining, shopping, and entertainment district. CityWalk has seen welcome upgrades to its restaurant lineup in recent years with the addition of **Bigfire, Vivo Italian Kitchen, Toothsome Chocolate Emporium,** and **Antojitos Authentic Mexican Food,** along with **NBC Sports Grill & Brew** and **The Cowfish**'s much-better-than-it-sounds burger/sushi bar. We also like **Bob Marley** and **Pat O'Brien's** for drinks and music.

Many of the older CityWalk restaurants' menus are similar to Applebee's or Chili's. Given the average entrée from **Hard Rock Cafe** or **Jimmy Buffett's Margaritaville,** a blindfolded diner would find it difficult to be certain from which restaurant it came. That blindfolded diner would probably guess that any plate with shrimp on it had a decent chance of coming from the **Bubba Gump Shrimp Co.,** but there's little else of note on its menu.

Virtually all of Universal's quick-service and table-service restaurants offer outdoor seating (weather permitting). If you feel more comfortable eating outside, make that known when booking your reservation or upon arriving at the restaurant.

Some of Universal's best sit-down restaurants are found at the resort hotels, where the **Flavor by Loews** program features locally produced ingredients such as bread, honey, and beer. **The Palm Restaurant,** an upscale steakhouse in the Hard Rock Hotel, serves grade-A meat at prices to match. If you're in the mood for Italian, try **Bice** (expensive) or **Mama Della's Ristorante** (moderate), both at Portofino Bay. Asian food is the specialty at Royal Pacific, where **Islands Dining Room** is the primary sit-down destination. **Amatista Cookhouse,** the table-service restaurant at Sapphire Falls, leans toward Caribbean comfort food, but the tapas and rum at **Strong Water Tavern** upstairs are top-shelf, as are the small plates and craft cocktails at **Bar 17 Bistro,** on the roof of the neighboring Aventura Hotel.

Probably because they handle a lot of convention traffic, menu prices at Universal's Signature Collection resorts tend to be higher than you might expect, though they're still easier to swallow than the bill at Disney's top tables.

RESERVATIONS

ONE OF THE BIGGEST DIFFERENCES between WDW and Universal Orlando is the ease with which you can secure dining reservations at the latter resort. If you're used to frantically booking your Disney Advance Dining Reservations months before your vacation, you can relax. During slower times of the year, you can walk up and get a table at many Universal Orlando eateries with only a modest wait; guests staying at select on-site Signature Collection hotels can flash their key card to get seated even sooner.

While reservations are often not needed at Universal, we nonetheless recommend making them to ensure an air-conditioned break in

unofficial **TIP**
If you're visiting Universal at a peak time of the year (such as during the summer, spring break, or a holiday) or during a major convention, we suggest making table-service reservations a couple of weeks to a month in advance.

your day. You can use the Resy app or website (resy.com) to search for a seating at most of the sit-down hotel restaurants; a few independently owned hotel restaurants (like Bice, Hard Rock Cafe, and The Palm) use OpenTable.com. City-Walk locations and in-park table-service restaurants use Universal Orlando's own reservation system, which is available through its website and smartphone app; you'll need to log in with an email and password to book a table. If you're not sure which reservation system to use, visit

theugseries.com/uniresdining, and click the RESERVE NOW button next to the restaurant where you wish to dine to see availability and make special requests. Alternatively, you can call ☎ 407-224-FOOD (3663) for in-park and CityWalk dining reservations and ☎ 407-503-DINE (3463) for hotel restaurants.

No deposit is necessary to book a Universal restaurant reservation, so there's no penalty when your dinner plans inevitably change. If you book through Universal's app, check your inbox for an email confirmation with links to cancel or modify your reservation, or tap "Dining Reservations" under the app's Profile tab. Most of the Universal Orlando restaurants accept reservations 180 days out, and The Palm will let you reserve for next year.

DRESS

DRESS IS INFORMAL at all park restaurants and in CityWalk's restaurants. At upscale resort restaurants such as Hard Rock's Palm Restaurant or Portofino Bay's Bice, men are not permitted to wear sleeveless shirts, and resort casual wear is appropriate (but not required) for dinner: khakis, dress slacks, jeans, or dress shorts with a collared shirt for men and Capris, skirts, dresses, jeans, or dress shorts for women.

PLANT-BASED DINING AT UNIVERSAL

WITH AN EVER-INCREASING NUMBER OF PATRONS picking plant-based diets for heath or ethical reasons, Universal has improved their flesh-free dining options across the resort. So while we once warned vegans and vegetarians with doubts about menu descriptions to default to the simplest, most-likely-to-be-acceptable item, every sit-down and quick-service restaurant at Universal now offers at least one plant-based meal (often using mock meats like Beyond Burger or Gardein Chick'n), and many more can be modified to omit animal products. Here are some more exciting plant-forward meals and snacks found around Universal Orlando that are enthusiastically recommended by Shelby Castle, who maintains the helpful website universalorlandovegans.com.

UNIVERSAL STUDIOS FLORIDA

• Avocado toast, I Heart Vegan Sandwich, and overnight oats *(TODAY Cafe)* • Bavarian pretzel w/out cheese *(Duff Gardens)* • Carl's Crispy Cauliflower *(Minion Cafe)* • Cinnamon sugar donut stick *(San Francisco Trolley Snacks)* • Dole Whip pineapple sorbet *(Schwab's Pharmacy)* • Double chocolate chunk brownie, tofu noodle salad *(San Francisco Pastry Co.)* • Field roast chili dog *(Mel's Drive-In)* • Homemade hummus with pita and veggies *(Fast Food Boulevard)* • Jacket potato (no butter) with broccoli and/ or beans *(London Taxi Hut)* • Roasted garlic edamame *(Lombard's Seafood Grille)* • Seasonal vegan crepe *(Central Park Crepes)* • Shrek & Donkey ice pops *(Swamp Snacks)* • Vegan sausage and peppers, vegan garlic knots *(Louie's; off menu)* • Vegetable curry, shepherd's pasty, cold or frozen Butterbeer *(Leaky Cauldron)* • Vegan shepherd's pie, apple beet salad (off menu) *(Finnegan's Bar & Grill)*

ISLANDS OF ADVENTURE

• Bavarian pretzel w/out cheese *(Kong Mess Tent)* • Double chocolate chunk brownie, elderberry or chocolate praline croissant *(Croissant Moon)* • Fettuccine Alfredo, breadsticks *(Cafe 4)* • Falafel gyro w/out tzatziki *(Fire Eater's Grill)* • Herbivore burger platter *(Burger Digs)* • Mushroom pie platter, cold or frozen Butterbeer *(Three Broomsticks)* • Pad Thai with crispy tofu, couscous bowl w/out feta & sauce *(Mythos)* • Pina colada sundae *(Marvel Ice Cream)* • Rice bowl with meatless chorizo w/out cheese *(Thunder Falls Terrace)* • Vegan crab cake, superfood salad, pad Thai *(Confisco Grille)* • Vegan magician meatball cone, tamed dragon salad *(Circus McGurkus)* • Vegan meatball kebab, hummus *(Doc Sugrue's)* • Vegan pizza tots *(Green Eggs & Ham Cafe)* • Vegan supreme cheeseburger, Dole Whip *(Wimpy's)*

VOLCANO BAY

• Hummus and carrot sticks, tropical fruit salad *(Whakawaiwai Eats)* • Tropical baby greens, sushi vegetable roll, and veggie wrap *(Kohola Reef)* • Vegan chorizo bowl *(The Feasting Frog)*

CITYWALK

• Cauliflower steak, vegan sausage cassoulet *(BigFire)* • Dole Whip fruit sorbet *(Menchie's)* • Fajitas Vegetal and Enchiladas Vegetarianas *(Antojitos)* • Vegan field dog *(Hot Dog Hall of Fame)* • Hot Vegan Sandwich *(Bread Box)* • Impossible Whopper w/out mayo *(BK Whopper Bar)* • Ital Eats stuffed peppers, jerk cauliflower bites *(Bob Marley's)* • Minestrone soup and vegan sausage pasta *(Vivo Italian Kitchen)* • Noodle bowl w/out salmon *(Hard Rock Cafe)* • Right Side Up Shake *(Toothsome Chocolate Emporium)* • Tree Hugger Roll *(The Cowfish)* • Vegan Portland Creme *(Voodoo Doughnut)* • Vegan jambalaya *(Pat O'Brien's)*

RESORT HOTELS

• Great Beyond burger, tofu wok bowl *(Urban Pantry at Aventura)* • Mindful Chik'n stir fry *(Bayliner at Cabana Bay)* • Penne all'Arrabbiata *(Bice at Portofino)* • Vegan bolognaise, strawberry shortcake trifle *(The Kitchen at Hard Rock)* • Vegan hot pot *(Strong Water Tavern at Sapphire Falls)* • Vegan sweet chipotle arepa and masala curry chik'n *(Amatista Cookhouse at Sapphire Falls)* • Wok experience, dark chocolate mousse cake *(Islands Dining Room at Royal Pacific)*

FOOD ALLERGIES AND SPECIAL REQUESTS

FOR SIT-DOWN MEALS, if you have food allergies or observe a specific diet, such as eating kosher or gluten-free, make your needs known when you make your dining reservation and again when your waiter greets your table. The waitstaff or chef will be able to tell you the kinds of accommodations the kitchen is prepared to make for your meal.

Accommodating dietary needs is more difficult at fast-food places because staff may not be as familiar with the menu's ingredients or preparation. Ask to see the allergen information book, which should be behind the counter at every quick-service location; it lists the menu items that can be made or modified for various diets. See page 160 for additional dietary details.

█ CHARACTER MEALS

UNIVERSAL OFFERS ONE YEAR-ROUND in-park character dinner, held every Thursday–Sunday starting at 5 p.m. at **Cafe 4** inside IOA. At the **Marvel Character Dinner,** guests dine with characters from the X-Men like Wolverine and Storm, plus Spider-Man and Captain America from the Avengers. The cost is $61 for adults and $34 for kids; park admission is required and not included, nor is gratuity. A buffet meal with your choice of salads, pastas, pizzas, and entrées, along with soft drinks and dessert, is served. The food is a notch above Cafe 4's standard fare, with pork pernil, carved beef loin, and roasted chicken on the menu. Attendees also get a digital photo card documenting their Marvel-ous meal. The half-dozen heroes circulate among the tables separately, and all excel at interacting with fans of every age. Days and times are subject to change. You can book online at theugseries.com/marveldinner, but you *must* call ☎ 407-224-3663 at least 24 hours before your meal to reserve your table.

During the holiday season, Universal offers a breakfast in IOA with the Grinch, played by an extremely interactive actor in film-quality prosthetic makeup. This meal—which may include green eggs and ham, if you wish—is held only on select mornings in November and December, 7–9:30 a.m. Pricing is $63 (plus gratuity) for adults and

Hello, Casting? There's been a mistake. We were supposed to get the Assorted Character Package with one SpongeBob, one Minion, one Gru . . .

$35 for kids age 9 and under, and theme park admission is required; visit theugseries.com/uogrinchbkft for booking details.

FAST FOOD *in* UNIVERSAL ORLANDO'S PARKS

FAST FOOD IS AVAILABLE THROUGHOUT USF, IOA, Volcano Bay, and CityWalk. The food compares in quality to McDonald's, Arby's, or Taco Bell but is more expensive, though often served in larger portions. Quick-service prices are fairly consistent from park to park. *Note:* The following menu prices include sales tax, unless otherwise noted.

QUICK-SERVICE RECOMMENDATIONS AT UNIVERSAL STUDIOS FLORIDA

MUCH OF THE QUICK SERVICE at USF is utterly unremarkable: burgers, pizza, pasta, chicken fingers, sandwiches, and salads. The mediocre food is matched by the predictable theming in the park's original fast-food joints: American diner? Check. New York Italian? Got it. However, the more creative menus at **Today Cafe** and **Minion Cafe** prove Universal's quick-service eateries are capable of delivering delicious, memorable meals.

The best quick-service food in USF can currently be found at the **Leaky Cauldron.** Diagon Alley's flagship restaurant serves authentically hearty British pub fare such as bangers and mash, cottage pie, toad-in-the-hole, Guinness stew, and a ploughman's platter for two of Scotch eggs and imported cheeses. When you're done, head over to **Florean Fortescue's Ice-Cream Parlour** for some delicious Butterbeer ice cream.

QUICK-SERVICE RECOMMENDATIONS AT ISLANDS OF ADVENTURE

OF IOA'S QUICK-SERVICE OFFERINGS, we like **Three Broomsticks,** the counter-service restaurant in The Wizarding World of Harry Potter–Hogsmeade, which serves rotisserie chicken, plus fish and chips, shepherd's pie, and barbecue ribs. The **Hog's Head** pub, attached to Three Broomsticks, serves beer, wine, mixed drinks, and the obligatory Butterbeer (see page 310).

We're also fond of the gyros at **Fire-Eater's Grill,** the smothered tots at **Green Eggs and Ham,** and the rice bowls and roasted corn at **Thunder Falls Terrace.** Almost all of the other IOA counter-service places serve some variation of burgers, chicken, pizza, or pasta, and while your superhero-loving kids are going to be drawn toward Marvel Island's **Cafe 4** and **Captain America Diner** as if the Pied Piper himself was leading them there, avoid both, as there are much better places to eat.

QUICK-SERVICE RECOMMENDATIONS AT EPIC UNIVERSE

QUICK-SERVICE OFFERINGS AT Epic Universe, like the park's attractions, aim to elevate the theme park experience to a new level. **Toadstool Cafe** has proved a huge hit at Universal Studios Hollywood's Super Nintendo World, so expect a long wait for food that's almost too kawaii to eat. Carnivores will find plenty to sink their teeth into at Dark Universe's **Das Stakehaus** or the Isle of Berk's **Meade Hall.** But you'll probably find us in the Wizarding World outside **Cafe L'air la Sirene,** enjoying French pastries and coffee on the sidewalk.

QUICK-SERVICE RECOMMENDATIONS AT VOLCANO BAY

VOLCANO BAY OFFERS exotic, island-inspired fare that far exceeds standard water park counter-service snacks. At **Bambu** in Rainforest Village, we enjoy the creamy coconut chicken salad, the quinoa-edamame burger (topped with roasted shiitake mushrooms and sriracha mayo), and the chocolate pineapple upside-down cake. Also at Rainforest Village is **The Feasting Frog;** try the ahi tuna poké with plantain chips. At River Village, **Whakawaiwai Eats** is home to Hawaiian pizza (with caramelized pineapple, diced ham, and jalapeños) and mac and cheese with jerk shrimp. At **Kohola Reef Restaurant & Social Club** in Wave Village, we love the slow-smoked ribs and the coconut curry chicken with sweet plantains. For dessert, choose the chocolate lava cake. **Dancing Dragons Boat Bar** (Rainforest Village) and **Kunuku Boat Bar** (Wave Village) serve exotic drinks, but the signature cocktails are far too sugary for our taste. Stick with the locally brewed Volcano Blossom beer instead.

QUICK-SERVICE RECOMMENDATIONS AT CITYWALK AND RESORT HOTELS

DINING OPTIONS AT CITYWALK and the resort hotels are oriented toward sit-down restaurants, but there are some counter-service choices worth considering. The chain franchises on CityWalk's upper floor have a following for their familiarity, but **Hot Dog Hall of Fame** and **Bread Box** serve food that's a step above the drive-thru. **Red Oven Pizza** is a fast-casual cross between quick-service and sit-down, and it's delicious no matter how you slice it. For a snack, **Menchie's Frozen Yogurt** and **Voodoo Doughnut** don't disappoint. The best quick-service hotel food is found at Portofino Bay's **Sal's Market Deli,** whose pies and salads are second only to Red Oven, and at Aventura's **Urban Pantry** food hall; Cabana Bay's **Bayliner Diner** food court has the widest range of selections, while the cafés at Endless Summer offer the best values.

QUICK-SERVICE KIDS' MEALS

KIDS' MEALS ARE AVAILABLE at select indoor fast-food restaurants for $9, and they include a child-friendly entrée—hamburger, chicken fingers, mac and cheese, etc.—with a side of fruit. Unlike at Disney, Universal's kids' meals don't include a beverage, and the meals are not usually listed in the online menus or Mobile Ordering system, so you'll need to seek out a cashier to purchase one. Adults with smaller appetites or finicky palates can order quick-service kids' meals for themselves; Seth loves ordering a kids' fish and chips from the Leaky Cauldron or Three Broomsticks as an afternoon snack.

QUICK-SERVICE COURTESY

GETTING YOUR ACT TOGETHER regarding quick-service restaurants in the parks is more a matter of courtesy than necessity. Rude guests rank high among reader complaints. A mother from Fort Wayne, Indiana, points out that indecision can be as maddening as outright discourtesy, especially when you're hungry:

> Every fast-food restaurant has menu signs the size of billboards, but do you think anybody reads them? People waiting in line spend enough time in front of these signs to memorize them and still don't have a clue what they want when they finally get to the counter. If, by some miracle, they've managed to choose between the hot dog and the hamburger, they then fiddle around another 10 minutes deciding what size Coke to order. Folks, PULEEEZ get your orders together ahead of time!

On that note, it's also courteous to have your form of payment (cash, credit, hotel key, or smartphone) in hand by the time you approach the cashier.

A close second on the frustrating scale are folks without food who monopolize restaurant tables while others balance trays, searching for a place to sit and eat. It's polite to wait until you've received your food before claiming a seat, and employees may enforce this policy on busy days, as one family discovered:

> Many of the indoor counter-service restaurants require you to purchase your meal before they seat you. We were looking for a break

from the sun with our turkey leg and other things bought from a cart. If we had known, we would have bought food from the specific counter-service place with indoor seating.

MOBILE FOOD AND DRINK ORDERING

A GROWING NUMBER of quick-service locations in Universal Orlando offer Mobile Ordering, which allows guests to select and purchase their meals through the smartphone app. Payment must be made by credit card (no gift/dining cards), but users get to bypass the queue for a cashier. Menu prices are the same as if ordering in person, and you can customize some entrées and side items or indicate that you have an allergy concern. Annual passholders can mobile-order exclusive seasonal items and apply their dining discount by scanning the barcode on their pass at checkout.

If you haven't already, you'll first need to download Universal's mobile app to set up your account and link your credit card to the digital wallet, ensuring that your associated billing address is also entered correctly. Click "Mobile Food & Drink Ordering" in the app's main menu to see which dining venues are currently participating (restaurants that usually offer Mobile Ordering are noted in the reviews beginning on page 317). You can browse the menus, make your selections, and pick an available 15-minute pickup window at any time, from anywhere on Universal property you like; your food won't be prepared until you pay and verify that you're ready to eat.

Outdoor eateries with takeaway windows and indoor counter-service restaurants marked as "Pickup" in the app's Mobile Dining menu will have one window marked MOBILE ORDER that app users can make a beeline toward once the app announces that their food has been prepared. At indoor locations designated "Table Delivery," you'll be seated and asked to place your order through the mobile app, then scan your table number to ensure delivery of your food. You may need to manually input the code number on your table if tapping your phone against the RFID tag doesn't work (which is most of the time).

We are generally fans of using Mobile Ordering, which has saved us up to 30 minutes of standing in line for a register, and the addition of pickup time windows has made the system work far more efficiently. Mobile Ordering at Pickup Window locations is usually very efficient, but at Table Delivery restaurants, you may wait 20–30 minutes after scanning in before your food arrives. Mandatory Mobile Ordering may be enforced at select restaurants, like Circus McGurkus and Minion Cafe, but a cashier is usually available if you don't use the app.

THE WIZARDING WORLD OF BEVERAGES: BUTTERBEER AND BEYOND

The Butterbeer Craze

In the fictional Wizarding World, **Butterbeer** is a mildly intoxicating treat favored by Harry Potter and other Hogwarts students. It made its first appearance in the book *Harry Potter and the Prisoner of Azkaban*, and ever since it has made fans' mouths water with dreams of the taste, enticingly described as "a little bit like less-sickly butterscotch."

In the real world, the Butterbeer served at Universal Orlando is a nonalcoholic beverage served from a tap, with a butterscotch-y marshmallow foam head that's added after the drink is poured; it's guaranteed to leave you with a selfie-worthy mustache. Whereas in the books Butterbeer can be bought cold in bottles or hot in "foaming tankards," at Universal there are three liquid varieties, none of which are packaged for taking home, plus several Butterbeer-flavored solid snacks. (Official bottled Butterbeer can be ordered for home delivery in the USA from harrypottershop.com.)

First, there is the basic **cold Butterbeer,** which is a vanilla cream soda–style liquid with the foam topping. There's also a **frozen Butterbeer** that's sort of like a slushy made from the same cream soda base, again topped with foam. Frozen is the only variety that comes with a straw; beware of putting a straw in the cold kind because stirring the liquid can cause an embarrassing eruption. Both are tasty and refreshing, albeit *really* sweet.

Hot Butterbeer was originally served only seasonally during colder months but can now be enjoyed year-round. The hot variety eschews the soda base for a rich, creamy beverage that resembles a vanilla chai latte, light on the chai. The signature foam stays on top, natch.

The cold and frozen versions go for $10 in a 16-ounce plastic cup. The same drink in a Harry Potter souvenir cup sells for $15, but there is no discount on Butterbeer refills. The hot version is sold in a 12-ounce paper cup for $10.

In IOA's **Hogsmeade,** the ambrosial liquid is sold only at **Three Broomsticks,** at the **Hog's Head** pub, and by two street vendors. That can mean long waits, as many guests buy from the outside carts, waiting 30 minutes or more in line to be served. We recommend trying your luck at the Hog's Head; the wait here is generally 10 minutes or less, and often there's nobody in line, even when the outdoor carts have lines 30 people deep only 20 feet away. Once served, you can relax with your drink at a table in the pub or out on the rear patio.

In USF's **Diagon Alley,** Butterbeer flows freely in the **Leaky Cauldron, The Hopping Pot,** and **Fountain of Fair Fortune.** Unfortunately, there's not enough seating to enjoy your drink. Once the picnic tables in Carkitt Market are full, your best bet is to squat on the "stairs to nowhere" next to Harry Potter and the Escape from Gringotts.

If he's forced to choose among the different types of Butterbeer, Seth's hands-down favorite is the frozen version—the ice crystals seem to dull the overpowering sweetness. That is, unless it's cold out or early in the morning, in which case hot Butterbeer is the clear winner. Lastly, while it's officially forbidden to adulterate your Butterbeer, if you want to order a cup of the frozen stuff at the Hog's Head alongside a shot of, say, Irish cream . . . we won't tell if you pour it in while the barkeep's back is turned.

Finally, Diagon Alley introduced the world to **soft-serve Butterbeer ice cream,** which tastes almost exactly like the drinks. You can get it at **Florean Fortescue**'s in a waffle cone ($7) or plastic souvenir sundae glass ($11). If you just want a cup of soft-serve unadorned by toppings, it's also available off-menu at **The Hopping Pot** and **Fountain of Fair Fortune,** where you'll find a shorter wait. **Three Broomsticks** and a cart in Hogsmeade serve **hard-packed Butterbeer ice cream** in prepackaged cups ($7), but it isn't as good as the soft-serve. In Diagon Alley you'll also find **Butterbeer potted cream** (a deliciously light butterscotch mousse) at the **Leaky Cauldron, Butterbeer fudge** (inedibly saccharine, with a candy corn–like crust) at **Sugarplum's,** and refreshing **Butterbeer ice pops,** which are sold seasonally at snack carts.

Beyond Butterbeer

Though Butterbeer gets most of the buzz, Hogsmeade and Diagon Alley serve other signature Harry Potter drinks too. You might as well try one, because you won't find any Coca-Cola products whatsoever inside The Wizarding Worlds.

Foremost at both parks is **Pumpkin Juice** ($6), which has a slightly pulpy texture and tastes like Thanksgiving dessert; a sparkling **Pumpkin Fizz** version ($6) is served only in Hogsmeade. Refreshing nonalcoholic **Cider** ($5) is also on draft in apple or pear flavors. Other exclusive drinks in Diagon Alley include the following:

TONGUE TYING LEMON SQUASH ($7) A tart, refreshing, squeezed-to-order lemonade.

OTTER'S FIZZY ORANGE JUICE ($7) A lightly carbonated orange drink with a lip-smacking crust of cinnamon-sugar on the cup's rim; one of our favorites.

FISHY GREEN ALE ($7) Green cinnamon-mint boba tea with blueberry "fish eggs" that burst blueberry in your mouth when sucked through a straw. A must-try for the novelty factor but not necessarily a must-finish; many find it downright gross.

PEACHTREE FIZZING TEA ($7) Lightly carbonated, sweetened iced tea with peach and ginger flavors.

GILLYWATER ($6) A small plastic bottle of filtered water with a Harry Potter label—seriously. For an extra $5, you can get it paired with a vial of flavored "magical elixir," available in four varieties: **Fire Protection** (watermelon, peach, and strawberry); **Babbling Beverage** (fruit punch); **Draught of Peace** (blueberry, blackberry, and cherry); and **Euphoria** (pineapple and mint). The most magical thing about the elixirs is how much money Universal has made disappear from Muggles' wallets with fancy punch.

Finally, adults who imbibe shouldn't feel left out of the fun; Universal contracted Florida Beer Company to come up with a trio of exclusive beers served only inside The Wizarding Worlds. In **Hogsmeade,** Three Broomsticks and Hog's Head pub serve **Hog's Head Brew,** a hoppy Scottish ale. **Diagon Alley's** Leaky Cauldron, The Hopping Pot, and Fountain of Fair Fortune pour **Wizard's Brew,** a heavy dark porter with chocolate notes. Both lands also offer **Dark Forest Ale,** a traditional brown ale; **Daisyroot Ale,** a Stella-style lighter ale; and **Dragon Scale,** a Viennese-style amber lager. All are served in 20-ounce cups for $14 (or $18 in a stout see-through souvenir stein) and are poured from creative custom-carved taps. Ask your bartender about secret off-menu concoctions, such as the **Triple** (unofficially known as a **Deathly Hallows**), made from layers of Strongbow, Hog's Head Brew, and Guinness.

For an added kick, try **Blishen's Fire Whisky,** a 70-proof cinnamon-flavored liquor distilled exclusively for the parks by TerrePURE Spirits of South Carolina. The flavor is warm but wonderfully smooth—much more drinkable than the superficially similar Fireball Cinnamon Whisky. Fire Whisky is available at the Leaky Cauldron and Hopping Pot in USF and at the Hog's Head in IOA. It's served neat or on the rocks for $13 per shot ($18 for a double) and can be mixed into non-alcoholic apple or pear cider for the same price. A pint of Strongbow cider with a Fire shot ($17) tastes like apple pie. While Fire Whisky can't officially be served in Butterbeer, we can vouch for a shot snuck into a cup of hot Butterbeer as a breakfast eye-opener.

REFILLABLE DRINKS AND POPCORN

ONE SMART WAY TO CUT snacking costs—if not calories—around Universal Orlando is by investing in refillable souvenir containers. Souvenir cups never expire and can be brought back to the park months or years in the future.

Universal sells two different types of refillable soft drink cups. The standard **collectible souvenir cups** can be found around the resort in various styles starting at about $20, including your first fill-up. Souvenir cups can be filled with soft drinks at select quick-service dining locations and snack stands in the parks or CityWalk for $2 per one-time refill, but this offer may not be available at all locations. In that case, you won't receive any discount off the regular menu price on refills, but depending on the cup's size, you may get a few bonus ounces of beverage.

Also, note that the cups can be refilled only with regular fountain flavors—Coke, Diet Coke, Hi-C, root beer, or Sprite—and not with specialty drinks. Pricier character cups (shaped like Transformers or Minions) and specialty souvenir cups (like Butterbeer mugs) can also be refilled with sodas outside the Wizarding World for the regular price, but you only get as much as those sometimes-skimpy cups can contain.

Universal also sells **Coca-Cola Freestyle souvenir cups** at dining locations with Freestyle soda machines. These massive marvels can mix dozens of different drink brands and additional flavorings together to dispense more than 100 soft drink combinations.

The self-service Freestyle fountains can be activated only by the RFID chip on the base of the cup. You can purchase a single-use Free-style cup from select quick-service restaurants for $5, or you can buy a reusable souvenir cup that's valid for unlimited refills (with a 10-minute pause in between pours) for the entire day; they even work until the wee hours during Halloween Horror Nights. Freestyle cups cost $20 for one, $36 for two, or $16 each for three to six, and can be reactivated for an additional $13 per day ($12 for annual passholders)—rinse and repeat for as many days as you like. There's also a larger insulated souvenir cup that can be either refilled à la carte at regular prices or optionally activated for unlimited

unofficial **TIP**
If you opt for a Freestyle souvenir cup, you won't be eligible for free refills inside either of the Wizarding Worlds. You can get your cup filled with lemonade, iced tea, or nonalcoholic cider for the regular menu price, but if you don't want to pay extra, you'll have to trek outside the Potter areas.

Freestyle refills for $13 per day; they cost $32, including the first day of Freestyle activation. Freestyle cups can also be refilled for free with frozen Icee slushies. (Moose Juice and Goose Juice at IOA's Seuss Landing are eligible, but Springfield Squishees, alas, are not.)

Freestyle cups can't be refilled free at regular soda fountains, but Freestyle machines can be found at nearly every quick-service restaurant, with dozens of dispensers in each theme park, plus a handful at Volcano Bay and CityWalk. All Freestyle machines will dispense free filtered water without an activated cup, and any restaurant will give you a cup of free ice water on request, which tastes much better than the sulfurous, lukewarm liquid flowing from the parks' drinking fountains. The major downside of Freestyle is that machines often run out of ice and popular flavors on warmer days. Outdoor dispensers along highly trafficked pathways are usually the first to empty; indoor locations (like Minion Cafe, Circus McGurkus, and the Coke kiosk near Men in Black) are more likely to get restocked.

A related program is the **Souvenir Cup Drink Package**, sold exclusively at **Aventura Hotel, Endless Summer Resort, Cabana Bay Beach Resort, Royal Pacific Resort,** and **Sapphire Falls Resort.** At Signature Collection hotels, this cup costs $11 for one day of use, $18 for three days, or $20 for the entire length of your stay at the resort. At Prime Value hotels and Cabana Bay Beach Resort, you'll pay $20 for up to 3 days, $27 for 4–7 days, or $32 for 8 or more days; prices are slightly cheaper at Endless Summer. A day is considered a calendar day and ends at midnight.

Souvenir mugs can be refilled at the Coke Freestyle soda stations in the **Bayliner Diner, Galaxy Bowl,** and **pool areas** at Cabana Bay; at Aventura's **Urban Pantry;** at Endless Summer Resort's **Beach Cafe** and **Pier 8 Market;** at **Omega Cafe** and **Moonrise Grill** at Terra Luna Resort and

Cosmos Cafe and **Galaxy Grill** at Stella Nova Resort; at Royal Pacific Resort's **Tuk Tuk Market;** and in **New Dutch Trading Co.** and the **pool area** at Sapphire Falls. The cups are compatible only with the Freestyle machines at the hotel they were purchased at and can't be used inside the parks, nor can the parks' Freestyle cups be used at the hotels.

If you're looking for something harder to wet your whistle, all of the hotels' pool bars sell **cocktails in souvenir cups** for about $17 ($1 cheaper at Endless Summer), and bars at the Prime Value and Value Inns and Suites resorts will refill them for just $13. Cabana Bay Beach Resort even sells a special watertight **pool cup** that allows you to drink while drifting on the lazy river, which is normally a no-no. Refillable souvenir cocktail glasses are also available in **CityWalk** at **Fat Tuesday's** and at **Jurassic Park's Watering Hole** in **IOA.** Souvenir beer pilsners are sold inside the parks at select bars (including **Moe's Tavern** and **Chez Alcatraz** in USF) for about $17; refills cost $1 less than a regular drink, and you get a couple of extra ounces for free. Refillable cocktail cups with blinking lights (in case you get blind drunk?) are sold at a similar price during events like Halloween Horror Nights and Mardi Gras.

Lastly, street-cart vendors sell fresh popcorn in either $6 single servings or $13 **souvenir popcorn buckets** that can be refilled as often as your sodium level can stand for only $2. Flavored varieties such as caramel (available at the exit of IOA) or banana (near IOA's Minion Cafe) can be refilled for $4, and (like the soda cups) buckets can be brought back on future trips. Adorable Minion-shaped souvenir popcorn buckets are available for $30–$40, including the first fill-up.

CUTTING YOUR DINING TIME AT THE THEME PARKS

EVEN IF YOU CONFINE YOUR MEALS to vendor and quick-service fast food, you lose a lot of time getting food in the theme parks. Here are some ways to minimize the time you spend hunting and gathering:

1. Eat breakfast before you arrive. Restaurants outside the parks offer some outstanding breakfast specials. Plus, some hotels furnish small refrigerators in their guest rooms, or you can rent a fridge or bring a cooler. If you can get by on cold cereal, pastries, fruit, and juice, this will save a ton of time.

2. After breakfast, buy snacks from vendors in the parks as you tour, or stuff your own snacks in a fanny pack.

3. All theme park restaurants are busiest between 11:30 a.m. and 2:15 p.m. for lunch and 6 and 9 p.m. for dinner. For shorter lines and faster service, don't eat during these hours, especially 12:30–1:30 p.m.

4. Many quick-service restaurants sell cold sandwiches. Buy a cold lunch minus drinks before 11:30 a.m., and carry it in small plastic bags until you're ready to eat (within an hour or so of purchase). Ditto for dinner. Buy drinks at the appropriate time from any convenient vendor.

5. If it's available, use the Universal Orlando app's Mobile Ordering feature (see page 310) to reduce your wait. Make your selections while queuing for your last attraction before mealtime, so you can confirm your order as soon as you arrive at the restaurant.

6. If you need to order in person, most fast-food eateries have more than one service window. Regardless of the time of day, check the lines at all windows before queuing. Sometimes a window that's staffed but out of the way will have a much shorter line or none at all. Note, however, that some windows may offer only certain items.

7. If you're short on time and the park closes early, stay until closing and eat dinner outside the park before returning to your hotel. If the park stays open late, eat dinner about 4 or 4:30 p.m. at the restaurant of your choice. You should sneak in just ahead of the dinner crowd.

8. Be warned that if you wait until after the dinner rush to eat, you'll discover that most restaurants outside The Wizarding World stop serving at least an hour before the parks close, leaving CityWalk's or Celestial Park's eateries as your best option for a late supper.

Beyond Quick-Service: Tips for Saving Money on Food

Though buying food from quick-service restaurants and vendors will save time and money (compared with full-service dining), additional strategies can bolster your budget and maintain your waistline.

Our readers offer the following suggestions for stretching food dollars. A Missouri mom writes:

We stocked our steel cooler with milk and sandwich fixings. I froze a block of ice in a milk bottle, and we replenished the cooler daily with ice from the resort ice machine. I also froze small packages of deli meats for later in the week. We ate cereal, milk, and fruit each morning, with boxed juices. I also brought a hot pot to boil water for instant coffee, oatmeal, and soup. Each child had a belt bag of his own, which he filled from a special box of goodies each day, such as packages of crackers and cheese, peanuts, and raisins or candy and gum. Each child also had a small plastic water bottle that could hang on the belt. We filled these at water fountains before getting into lines. We left the park before noon; ate sandwiches, chips, and soda in the room; and napped. We purchased our evening meal in the park at a quick-service eatery. We budgeted for both morning and evening snacks from a vendor but often didn't need them.

A Whiteland, Indiana, mom suggests:

One must-take item if you're traveling with younger kids is a supply of small paper or plastic cups to split drinks, which are both huge and expensive.

Our top budget-trimming tip is to skip the soft drinks and instead order **free ice water** with every meal. It's far healthier and more hydrating than soda (sugared or artificially sweetened), and at $5 per fountain drink, you'll be shocked at how swiftly the savings add up. The parks' drinking fountains are potable in a pinch, but the filtered water that all counter-service restaurants (excluding vending carts) give away tastes as good as the bottled water they sell, which goes for $4 from outdoor vending carts and $6 at indoor restaurants.

UNIVERSAL ORLANDO QUICK-SERVICE RESTAURANT MINI-PROFILES

TO HELP YOU FIND FLAVORFUL FAST FOOD while staying fleet of foot, we've developed mini-profiles of Universal Orlando's quick-service restaurants. The restaurants are listed alphabetically by location. Detailed profiles of all Universal Orlando full-service restaurants begin on page 339.

The restaurants profiled in the following pages are rated for quality and portion size as well as value. The value rating ranges from A to F as follows:

A Exceptional value; a real bargain		**D** Somewhat overpriced	
B Good value		**F** Extremely overpriced	
C Fair value; you get exactly what you pay for			

In addition to the locations profiled following, you'll also encounter counter-service kiosks and takeout windows from several familiar franchises—including **Auntie Anne's, Cinnabon, Cold Stone Creamery, Fat Tuesday, Häagen-Dazs,** and **Menchie's**—with snack prices only slightly more exorbitant than what you'd pay at your local mall.

UNIVERSAL STUDIOS FLORIDA

Bumblebee Man's Taco Truck

LOCATION Springfield	QUALITY Good	VALUE B−	PORTION Medium
READER-SURVEY RESPONSES	90% 👍	10% 👎	

SELECTIONS Chicken, pork, and beef soft-shell tacos served with tortilla chips. Coca-Cola fountain products; Buzz Cola; Duff, Duff Lite, and Duff Dry beers.

COMMENTS Capitalizing on the popular trend of food trucks, Bumblebee Man's Taco Truck is the first eatery guests encounter walking into Springfield: Home of the Simpsons from the main gates. The truck is adorned with a huge taco on the front bumper and an even bigger Bumblebee Man head coming out of the roof. Each of the selections is well done. The quality is very competitive with the food at Moe's Southwest Grill in CityWalk. Our favorite picks are the carne asada and the pork carnitas. Ask for green salsa, which has more kick than the mild red variety.

Cafe La Bamba *(seasonal; Mobile Ordering)*

LOCATION Hollywood	QUALITY Good	VALUE B+	PORTION Medium–Large
READER-SURVEY RESPONSES	82% 👍	18% 👎	

SELECTIONS Tacos, burritos, and rice bowls with choice of chicken, shrimp, pork, beef, or vegan protein; salads, chips and salsa with guacamole; très leches cake; specialty cocktails, sangria, beer, and wine.

COMMENTS Modeled after the legendary Hollywood Hotel, home to many early 20th-century movie stars, this is a lovely place to dine in, when it's open to the public. VIP tour guests get served breakfast here, and it's often closed in the off-season or during special events. When operating, it serves better-than-average SoCal-style Mexican food. We especially like the vegan chorizo and al pastor mushrooms. Spicy margaritas (also available from a walk-up window) have a bite, and the salsa flight with guac makes an excellent snack, but pass on the prepackaged chicharrones.

Central Park Crepes

LOCATION Hollywood	QUALITY Good–Excellent	VALUE B+	PORTION Medium–Large
READER-SURVEY RESPONSES 90% 👍 10% 👎			

SELECTIONS Fresh crepes with savory or sweet toppings; Freestyle soda.

COMMENTS This tiny booth between Cafe La Bamba and the lagoon attracts long lines with its made-to-order fancy French pancakes, stuffed with savory or sweet fillings. The menu changes often in concert with seasonal events. These crepes are large enough to share, and the quality of ingredients exceeds standard theme park food. Because of the shape of these crepes, get plenty of napkins to avoid a mess. Only soft drinks are served here, except during some seasonal events. Coke Freestyle machines are located on the side of the kiosk, but they are often out of ice on busy days.

Chez Alcatraz

LOCATION San Francisco	QUALITY Fair–Good	VALUE B	PORTION Medium–Large
READER-SURVEY RESPONSES 85% 👍 15% 👎			

SELECTIONS Mixed drinks, beer, soda, and bagged snacks.

COMMENTS With usually little to no wait and plenty of seating, Chez Alcatraz can be a great place to relax and unwind with an adult beverage and a bag of chips. The friendly bartenders shake up signature concoctions like the "Ocean Attack," with Don Q and blue curaçao. And you just happen to be next to one of the best photo ops in USF: Bruce the shark from *Jaws*.

City Snack Stands

LOCATION Various	QUALITY Good	VALUE B	PORTION Medium
READER-SURVEY RESPONSES Too new to rate			

SELECTIONS Savory and sweet snacks representing different cultures; bottled and draft drinks.

COMMENTS Universal Studios sports a handful of upgraded outdoor snack stands that go beyond your typical carts vending turkey legs and popcorn. One in Hollywood near the park entrance has Belgian waffles; the pair around New York's Gramercy Park serve Italian calzones and Latin American arepas; and the stand across from San Francisco's Pastry Co. offers Asian street food and boba beverages.

DreamWorks Imagination Cafe

LOCATION Dreamworks Land	QUALITY Fair–Good	VALUE B-	PORTION Medium
READER-SURVEY RESPONSES Too new to rate			

SELECTIONS Pizza, pastries, fruit bowl.

COMMENTS Located at the front of DreamWorks Land next to SpongeBob Store-Pants, this window (which was formerly Kidzone Pizza Co.) serves unusual "Ogreoni" pizzas with cheese and pepperoni on a fluffy, irregularly shaped crust. For dessert, try the warm beignets or a sprinkle-laden donut. There's no indoor seating, and even the few seats outdoors can fill up quickly during the busier times.

Duff Brewery

LOCATION Springfield	QUALITY Fair–Good	VALUE C	PORTION Medium
READER-SURVEY RESPONSES	85% 👍	15% 👎	

SELECTIONS Corn dogs, pretzels with spicy mustard, and assorted snacks. Beverages include Coca-Cola products, Buzz Cola, frozen Squishees (banana is especially tasty), Duff beer, and other *Simpsons*-related drinks. In *The Simpsons* TV show, Duff, Duff Lite, and Duff Dry are all the exact same beer, but the Duff beers here are completely different from each other. Duff beer is most equivalent to Yuengling, Duff Lite is closer to your standard light beer (like Miller Lite), and Duff Dry is a stout dark beer comparable to Guinness but with a strong coffee taste. Seasonal brews like Dufftoberfest are periodically poured.

COMMENTS Duff Brewery is an outdoor bar area with plenty of seating nearby to relax. It's part of the larger Duff Gardens, which, in *The Simpsons* TV show, is a theme park run by a beer-brewing company. The character of Duffman is available for photo ops, and there are hilarious topiaries of the Seven Duffs (Tipsy, Queasy, Surly, Sleazy, Edgy, Dizzy, and Remorseful), a parody of Disney's Seven Dwarfs and the mascots of Duff Gardens. Duff beers are brewed exclusively for Universal by the Florida Beer Company, which also brews beers for The Wizarding Worlds of Harry Potter. Because Duff Brewery is out in the open and in view of every guest, it can often attract a big crowd, especially on a hot day. The waterfront-viewing terrace is a fine place to enjoy the evening lagoon show if the Central Park viewing area is overcrowded.

Fast Food Boulevard *(Mobile Ordering)*

LOCATION Springfield	QUALITY Good	VALUE B+	PORTION Large
READER-SURVEY RESPONSES	75% 👍	25% 👎	

SELECTIONS Burgers, chicken, pizza, seafood, sandwiches, and salads. Different eateries pulled straight from *The Simpsons* TV series include Krusty Burger, The Frying Dutchman, Flaming Moe's, Cletus' Chicken Shack, Luigi's Pizza, Lard Lad Donuts, and Lisa's Teahouse of Horror.

COMMENTS Besides the hilarious menus themselves (taste-tested by writers of *The Simpsons* TV show), Fast Food Boulevard contains items you can't get anywhere else in the park, including a pulled-pork sandwich and the gloriously messy Clogger Burger. Reader scores for Fast Food Boulevard have dropped significantly in recent surveys, but we still like the tender fried calamari and the chicken-and-waffle sandwich (with extra maple mayo on the side). Note that this is a very popular spot for lunch; a long line can develop, and the TVs broadcast a loop of classic *Simpsons* clips that is maddeningly brief. Cut your wait by using Mobile Ordering to bypass the queue, then grab your food from the Flaming Moe's window at the far left. An Ambler, Pennsylvania, couple sampled the offerings:

> The doughnuts at Lard Lad were fresh, flavorful, and surprisingly delicious. (Mmm . . . doughnuts.) My husband's Krusty Burger was pretty good; my chicken-and-waffle sandwich was excellent.

Florean Fortescue's Ice-Cream Parlour

LOCATION Diagon Alley	QUALITY Excellent	VALUE B	PORTION Medium–Large
READER-SURVEY RESPONSES	97% 👍	3% 👎	

SELECTIONS Ice cream is served in waffle cones and plastic souvenir sundae glasses. A single order can contain two different flavors, and you can add unusual toppings such as shortbread crumbles and meringue pieces for about a dollar.

COMMENTS Readers of the Harry Potter books will remember Florean Fortescue's Ice-Cream Parlour for its prominent appearance in *Harry Potter and the Prisoner of Azkaban.* When Harry spent several weeks staying in a room above the Leaky Cauldron, he would spend time there, and Florean himself gave Harry free ice cream sundaes every half hour. Now Muggles can have their own sundaes in this very establishment, with some very "magical" flavors, including Butterbeer-flavored ice cream. Our favorites are the salted-caramel blondie and chocolate chili—but be warned, the latter has a bite!

Fountain of Fair Fortune

LOCATION Diagon Alley	QUALITY Good–Excellent	VALUE B-	PORTION Medium
READER-SURVEY RESPONSES 96% 👍	4% 👎		

SELECTIONS Potter-themed drinks, both soft and hard.

COMMENTS Named after a short story in *Tales of Beedle the Bard*, this pub sells Fishy Green Ale, Gillywater, Wizard's Brew, and Dragon Scale (see page 312)—and features an exclusive Butterbeer souvenir mug not found in Hogsmeade. You can also get a cup of Butterbeer soft-serve here, usually with a much shorter wait than at the ice cream shop next door.

The Hopping Pot

LOCATION Diagon Alley	QUALITY Good–Excellent	VALUE B-	PORTION Medium
READER-SURVEY RESPONSES 99% 👍	1% 👎		

SELECTIONS Potter-themed drinks, including all four varieties of Butterbeer: cold, frozen, hot, or soft-serve. Beef, chicken, or vegan pasties and bags of potato chips.

COMMENTS Outdoor bar with eight different brews—including Wizard's Brew (a heavy porter) and Dragon Scale (a hoppy amber)—on draft, each with its own customized tap handle, along with the area's most complete selection of signature nonalcoholic drinks. Much better food is available elsewhere in Diagon Alley. Seating is at a limited number of picnic tables, within sight of the Carkitt Market stage.

Leaky Cauldron *(Mobile Ordering)*

LOCATION Diagon Alley	QUALITY Good–Excellent	VALUE A-	PORTION Medium–Large
READER-SURVEY RESPONSES 90% 👍	10% 👎		

SELECTIONS Traditional English breakfast, pancakes, or egg, leek, and mushroom pasty. Lunch and dinner selections include bangers and mash, cottage pie, toad-in-the-hole, vegan curry, Guinness stew, fish and chips, shepherd's pie, and a ploughman's platter.

COMMENTS Leaky Cauldron serves hearty British pub fare and authentically Anglo favorites. Reserve breakfast (served until 10:30 a.m. daily; $20 for adults, $14 for kids) through your travel agent or the Vacation Planning Center at your Universal Resort hotel; walk-ins are also usually available. The breakfast is fair at best (and the scrambled eggs are awful), so if you really want to eat breakfast here, do it as late as possible—early-entry time is better spent exploring Diagon Alley.

The star of the lunch and dinner menu is the ploughman's platter for two, with an array of gloriously stinky imported cheeses; order a Scotch egg (a hardboiled egg coated in sausage and deep-fried) à la carte for a cheap, protein-packed snack. The bangers are also bang-on, whether ordered with mash, in a sandwich, or (best of all) baked into a toad-in-the-hole with Yorkshire pudding. The fisherman's pie is extremely salty, as is the Guinness stew, which comes in a nearly inedible bread bowl. Try chocolate or Butterbeer potted cream or sticky toffee pudding for dessert. Kids' menu items include macaroni and cheese; fish and chips; and, for the budding Sweeney Todd enthusiast, mini meat pies.

Leaky Cauldron uses a modified table service, where food is brought to your table after you order at a counter or via the app, and can be overwhelmed by Diagon Alley crowds. To avoid long waits, eat early or late.

London Taxi Hut

LOCATION Outside Diagon Alley	**QUALITY** Fair–Good	**VALUE** C	**PORTION** Medium
READER-SURVEY RESPONSES 92% 👍 8% 👎			

SELECTIONS You can get a jacket potato (baked potato to Americans) smothered with baked beans and cheese, broccoli and cheese, or the salty stuffing from a shepherd's pie. Bags of crisps (British potato chips), hot dogs, and canned European beers fill out the brief menu.

COMMENTS Outside the gorgeous London Waterfront facade in front of Diagon Alley are two "cabman shelter" kiosks. One sells London-themed merchandise such as T-shirts, and this one sells quick-service food and drink items. The signature item is an extralong hot dog in an odd tubelike bun; shape aside, it tastes about the same.

Louie's Italian Restaurant *(Mobile Ordering)*

LOCATION New York	**QUALITY** Fair–Good	**VALUE** C	**PORTION** Medium
READER-SURVEY RESPONSES 81% 👍 19% 👎			

SELECTIONS Spaghetti with meatballs; vegan sausage and peppers; fettuccine Alfredo; meatball sandwich; cheese, pepperoni, chicken Alfredo, or veggie pizza; Caesar salad; soup; garlic knots; cookies; cake; fruit cups; gelato; Italian ices; Freestyle soda; beer.

COMMENTS One of the largest indoor restaurants in the Studios and a good choice for getting out of the hot sun. The name of the restaurant is an homage to the movie *The Godfather,* which had a very famous scene set at Louie's Restaurant. The food is nothing special, and the whole pies are outrageously expensive, at more than $42–$47 apiece, but it's hard to screw up pizza and pasta. The Coke Freestyle machines here are refreshed frequently. Guido's, a small counter in the corner, offers a limited selection of frozen Italian desserts. *Be warned:* It can be very crowded throughout the afternoon.

Mel's Drive-In *(Mobile Ordering)*

LOCATION Hollywood	**QUALITY** Fair	**VALUE** C	**PORTION** Medium–Large
READER-SURVEY RESPONSES 67% 👍 33% 👎			

SELECTIONS Hamburgers, bacon cheeseburgers, vegan chili dogs, chicken fingers, grilled or crispy chicken sandwiches, Cobb chicken salad, cheese fries, onion rings, pies, and milkshakes.

COMMENTS Based on the drive-in joint from the movie *American Graffiti,* Mel's has several vintage automobiles in the parking lot for photo ops. Check out the license plates for some fun references. During Halloween Horror Nights, the neon lights in the diner's sign are cleverly changed to spell out MEL'S DIE-IN.

Mel's menu received a makeover in 2024, which upgraded the milkshakes and added pies and Buffalo chicken sandwiches, but the burgers are still pretty bland. Other than the excellent vegan chili (which is better than their meaty version), we wouldn't make a special trip here for anything.

Minion Cafe *(Mobile Ordering)*

LOCATION Minion Land	QUALITY Good	VALUE B+	PORTION Medium
READER-SURVEY RESPONSES	91% 👍	9% 👎	

SELECTIONS Soups, salads, and sandwiches, with Asian and Latin twists; photogenic desserts and specialty drinks. Don't worry, few items taste like bananas.

COMMENTS Mischievous Minions run this colorful cafe, and you can dine in their dormitory, kitchen, or break room, all packed with references to the films that fans will love (see the sidebar below). Standout options on the creative menu include Chicken Stuart's Szechuan Surprise (a sizable half bird with stir-fried noodles); the "Cheese Ray" roast beef sandwich with pimento cheddar; the herbaceous grilled cheese sandwich, dipped in tart green tomato soup; and Uncle Dru's messy-but-mouthwatering porchetta on a pretzel bun. Carl's Crispy Cauliflower, which comes tempura fried with sweet chili sauce and coconut blue rice, is among the best vegan entrées on property. Pay to upgrade your sandwich's side from plantain chips to the crispy Minion-shaped tots with mashed-potato filling. For dessert, the peanut butter–and–jelly Pet Rock is as adorbs as it is delish, as is the Minion sweet roll (if you like pineapple and passion fruit).

Between the two signature drinks, we far prefer the yellow banana Antidote over the lemonade purple PX-41 Punch, but both have too much sweet buttercream topping. You can get both, along with banana-flavored popcorn, at the **Pop-A-Nana** stand just outside. Also nearby are **Freeze Ray Pops** (specializing in Nutella Gru and banana Minion popsicles, plus plant-based flavors) and **Bake My Day** (character-shaped cookies and cupcakes).

Guests at Minion Cafe are strongly urged to use Mobile Ordering, with options in the app for pickup or table delivery. Pickups are from an outdoor

---

MINION CAFE DETAILS

AS THE MAIN ANCHOR OF MINION LAND'S EATERIES, Minion Cafe not only has some of the best food offerings in the park but also some of the most fun details, and Derek Burgan brings us this "Saturday Six" list of his favorites.

6. Boxes of Girl Scout Cookies In the first Despicable Me films, Gru's daughters infiltrated the villain's lair by selling Vector cookies. In the Minion Break Room seating area, there is a vending machine with boxes of these very same cookies, including Coconutties, Slam Jams, Loopy Lemons, and Minty Mints.

5. Spaghetti Shoe The restaurant's central display features several Minions working on a Rube Goldberg–esque machine that's making the meals for guests. One plate has a shoe filled with spaghetti. Look above and you'll see a Minion sticking out of the machinery, with one foot missing a shoe!

4. Motivational Posters Look for great motivational posters throughout Minion Cafe for inspiration such as "Communication," "Punctuality," and "Collaboration," each having fun with the idea. My favorite? "Procrastination: Because Great Food Takes Time."

3. Lost Duck/Duck For Sale In a glass-enclosed case a bulletin board is filled with many details. Look for the ad from Minion Dave asking if anyone has seen his lost rubber ducky, and another ad from Minion Carl trying to sell a rubber ducky that looks awfully familiar.

2. Frozen Food The main dining area has a freezer case featuring items you would generally find in a similar case at any restaurant: bags of ice, ice cream sundaes, and cans of whipped cream. This case has something special though: a Minion who got locked inside.

1. How to Take a Break There is artwork all around Minion Cafe, including a series of painted rocks and a wall dedicated to Tim the plush bear, but I think the best is a really fun poster with Minions showing "33 Ways to Take a Minion Break." Some of these ways include traditional avenues such as stretching, reading a book, and cardio. But other options are truly hilarious, including sucking up to the boss, going on strike, getting fired, and—my favorite—working more.

window near Freeze Ray Pops. If you are unable to use Mobile Ordering, you can order with a person at a small counter to the right of the entrance.

Moe's Tavern

LOCATION Springfield	QUALITY Good	VALUE C+	PORTION Medium
READER-SURVEY RESPONSES 82% 👍 18% 👎			

SELECTIONS Duff beer and Flaming Moe.

COMMENTS Grab a Duff beer (regular or Duff Lite on draft or in a bottle; Duff Dry in a bottle only) or a Flaming Moe from this replica of Homer and Barney's haunt from *The Simpsons* TV series. Filled with nods to the TV show, the tavern has a large photo op with Barney, along with a working Love Tester. If you're lucky and sitting by the red phone on the bar top, you may just happen to take a prank phone call. The Flaming Moe is a signature "drink experience," which comes in a souvenir cup that does a good job of hiding dry ice via a separate compartment. The orange soda–tasting drink bubbles up with smoke billowing out, giving a really good representation of being on fire. The nonalcoholic Flaming Moe is sure to be a hit with the younger set when they see it for the first time, as it was with this Austin reader:

> The Flaming Moe tastes like a bubbly orange soda; it really did seem to give me energy! It's only [a few dollars] more than that horrible Fishy Green Ale AND you keep the glass.

Richter's Burger Co. *(Mobile Ordering)*

LOCATION San Francisco	QUALITY Fair	VALUE C	PORTION Medium-Large
READER-SURVEY RESPONSES 71% 👍 29% 👎			

SELECTIONS Burgers, chicken sandwiches, plant-based burgers, chili-cheese fries, salads, and milkshakes.

COMMENTS Near the Fast & Furious attraction, Richter's Burger Co. has a theme tied to the 1906 San Francisco earthquake. All of the menu items have earthquake-related names, and the decor includes photos, hilarious advertisements, and seismologist props from that era, as well as a faithful re-creation of the Louis Agassiz statue that fell off a Stanford University building during the 1906 earthquake; the statue lodged itself firmly into the concrete, head first. The food here is nothing to start quaking over, but they do offer an upgraded Angus patty, topped with mushrooms and truffle aioli, and some unique sides like Parmesan-truffle fries. This indoor spot comes in handy as a hiding place during late-afternoon thunderstorms.

San Francisco Pastry Company *(Mobile Ordering)*

LOCATION San Francisco	QUALITY Fair–Good	VALUE C+	PORTION Medium-Large
READER-SURVEY RESPONSES 74% 👍 26% 👎			

SELECTIONS Egg-and-cheese croissants for breakfast. Soup served in a bread bowl or with grilled cheese; caprese, turkey, or roast beef sandwiches; fruit plates; chilled noodle salads; cookies, cakes, pies, and pastries; espresso, cappuccino, and coffee; beer and wine.

COMMENTS The selection is similar to the Today Cafe at the front of the park but a little less upscale. The pastries and coffee make a good pick-me-up if you're in the area during the afternoon, and the sandwiches are premade but can be served heated. The chilled noodles with seared tuna makes a refreshing light meal, and the clam chowder is the same recipe served next door in Lombard's for double the price.

Schwab's Pharmacy *(seasonal)*

LOCATION Hollywood	QUALITY Good	VALUE C+	PORTION Medium
READER-SURVEY RESPONSES	94% 👍 6% 👎		

SELECTIONS Ice cream sundaes and milkshakes.

COMMENTS Modeled after the legendary Hollywood drugstore counter where a young Lana Turner was supposedly discovered, Schwab's Pharmacy serves frozen treats made with Häagen-Dazs ice cream. You can also get a famous Dole Whip pineapple soft-serve in a cup or cone here cheaper than at Disney's Magic Kingdom. The medicines here are for display only; if you need a nostrum, head to First Aid. Schwab's is open for just a few hours each afternoon, and it often doesn't open at all in the off-season.

Swamp Snacks & Troll Treats

LOCATION DreamWorks Land	QUALITY Fair–Good	VALUE C+	PORTION Small–Medium
READER-SURVEY RESPONSES	Too new to rate		

SELECTIONS Stuffed waffles, ice-cream cones, ice pops, Shrek-shaped pretzel, pizza-wrapped hot dog, soft drinks, and beer.

COMMENTS Located just inside DreamWorks Land across from Shrek's home, Swamp Snacks serves the "Shrekzel," which became a viral star with its moss-green cheese dip despite being bland and flat. The pepperoni-stuffed waffles are underwhelming, but the herb-laden swamp dog is very satisfying, as are the vegan ice pops. The land's best snacks are the pink lemonade and huckleberry soft-serve ice-cream cones at Trolls Treats, the boombox-shaped window at the base of the Trollercoaster. Neither offers shade or seating, so take your snacks inside Po's training camp, or backtrack to the shelter outside Animal Actors.

Today Cafe *(Mobile Ordering)*

LOCATION Hollywood	QUALITY Good–Excellent	VALUE B+	PORTION Medium–Large
READER-SURVEY RESPONSES	85% 👍 15% 👎		

SELECTIONS Hot breakfast sandwiches, overnight oatmeal; fresh deli sandwiches and gourmet salads; cookies, cakes, and pastries; draft beer, wine, and cold-brew coffee.

COMMENTS Inspired by the studio of its namesake, Today Cafe's white-and-orange color scheme captures the up-and-at-'em cheerfulness of NBC's long-running *Today* show. Located near the park's front gates, Today Cafe, complete with Al Roker and the gang watching over your meal from omnipresent TV screens, is a convenient spot to grab coffee and a breakfast pastry, but don't dally here during rope drop if the lines wrap outside. It's usually not as crowded as other restaurants for lunch. We like The Bulls & The Bears (beef brisket and Cheddar) and Carnegie (pastrami and Swiss) sandwiches the best, especially when served hot with tangy potato salad. Portions aren't huge, but the entrées are filling with unexpectedly elevated ingredients. Be sure to save room for a dessert from the tempting pastry trays—the green matcha tea cream puff, deliciously airy and not too sweet, pairs well with an iced nitro coffee.

ISLANDS OF ADVENTURE

Blondie's *(Mobile Ordering)*

LOCATION Toon Lagoon	QUALITY Fair–Good	VALUE C+	PORTION Large
READER-SURVEY RESPONSES	72% 👍 28% 👎		

SELECTIONS Dagwood deli sandwiches; made-to-order roast beef, turkey, tuna, and ham sandwiches; Nathan's hot dogs; "brookies" (brownie–cookie hybrids).

COMMENTS Skip the signature sandwich—the Dagwood—which is premade and refrigerated until ready to serve; it also has more bread than necessary, making it dry. If you're in the mood for a really good sandwich, try one of the made-to-order turkey or ham subs (the roast beef is invariably too dry). Blondie's serves subs on white or multigrain rolls, accompanied by a side of potato salad. If you like hot dogs, Blondie's serves Nathan's chili dogs and Chicago-styles and pairs them with crinkle-cut fries. Mobile ordering is mandatory here; there is no cashier option.

The Burger Digs (Mobile Ordering)

LOCATION Jurassic Park	QUALITY Fair	VALUE C	PORTION Medium–Large
READER-SURVEY RESPONSES	72% 👍	28% 👎	

SELECTIONS Bacon cheeseburger, chicken sandwich, onion rings, portobello mushroom sandwich, and milkshakes.

COMMENTS Burger Digs has indoor and outdoor seating. The burgers and chicken sandwiches are nothing special, though they come on kaiser rolls and a cold toppings bar allows for customization. The Costa Rican–inspired Casado Burger is topped with sweet plantains, avocado, and pork belly. For a lighter meal, try the spring salad with corn, black beans, and pineapple vinaigrette, or the portobello mushroom sandwich with tempeh bacon. If you're looking for better food, try **Thunder Falls Terrace,** a little farther along in Jurassic Park. Balcony seating in the rear provides panoramic views of the VelociCoaster.

Cafe 4 (Mobile Ordering)

LOCATION Marvel Super Hero Island	QUALITY Fair	VALUE C-	PORTION Medium
READER-SURVEY RESPONSES	65% 👍	35% 👎	

SELECTIONS Pizza, pasta, vegan fettuccine Alfredo, meatball or chicken Parmesan sub, Caesar salad, and breadsticks.

COMMENTS The food is generic and mostly flavorless, but it's served rather speedily. However, Doctor Doom seems to think an average price of $19 for a single slice of pizza and side salad (or a jaw-dropping $42–$47 for a whole pie) is reasonable in a theme park setting. This is not EPCOT's Via Napoli by any "stretch" of the imagination (a reference for the Mr. Fantastic fans), but the café does make specialties such as vegetable and three-meat pizza. The exact same salads, meatball subs, and basic pastas and sauces that are served at Louie's in USF round out the not-so-Fantastic menu. At 5 p.m. on select nights, this location turns into a Marvel character buffet (see page 306).

Captain America Diner (Mobile Ordering)

LOCATION Marvel Super Hero Island	QUALITY Fair	VALUE C	PORTION Medium–Large
READER-SURVEY RESPONSES	72% 👍	28% 👎	

SELECTIONS Cheeseburgers, chicken sandwiches, vegan burgers, chicken fingers, chicken salad, milkshakes, and onion rings.

COMMENTS The burger meat is entirely average but comes served on a sesame-seed bun and topped with pulled pork; the specialty chicken sandwich is topped with hot honey and pepper jack. While the name of the restaurant is Captain America Diner, the air-conditioned inside is themed to the Marvel Comics version of The Avengers, including references to C-level characters in the group such as the Black Knight and Wonder Man—even the flooring is themed. Inside seating features a gorgeous look outside into the lagoon (with a great view of Mythos and Hogwarts Castle).

Circus McGurkus Cafe Stoo-pendous *(Mobile Ordering)*

LOCATION Seuss Landing   **QUALITY** Fair–Good   **VALUE** C+   **PORTION** Medium-Large
READER-SURVEY RESPONSES 73% 👍 27% 👎

SELECTIONS Fried chicken tenders or shrimp, pasta, cheeseburgers and meat-loaf sandwiches, tuna poke, fruit and quinoa salad, and cupcakes.

COMMENTS This is certainly one of the more visually interesting counter-service venues—The High in the Sky Seuss Trolley Train Ride! passes through overhead. An all-new menu introduced in 2024 features roast beast sandwiches (meatloaf and rib eye with cheddar and onions on a pretzel bun) and garlic bread cones filled with pasta marinara and meatballs (meat or plant-based), plus Green Eggs and Ham–inspired chocolate cheesecake or caramel popcorn cupcakes. The Red Fish Blue Fish Poke, with ahi tuna and edamame on blue glass noodles, is disappointingly gummy, and the box of fried shrimp on garlic popcorn is bone-dry; chicken tenders with hot honey biscuits are your best bet. This restaurant uses mandatory Mobile Order with table delivery, similar to Minion Cafe. Pickup orders are available from an exterior window to the right of the main entrance, which is the only place to get a spicy sausage and cheese corn dog.

Comic Strip Cafe

LOCATION Toon Lagoon   **QUALITY** Fair   **VALUE** C+   **PORTION** Medium-Large
READER-SURVEY RESPONSES 75% 👍 25% 👎

SELECTIONS Asian noodle and rice bowls, chicken sandwiches, personal pizzas, salads, and bacon cheeseburgers.

COMMENTS Long notorious for serving the worst fast food in IOA, Comic Strip Cafe has expanded and improved its menu by adding Latin dishes like yucca fries and très leches cake. Unfortunately, the burgers and pizza remain below average. Try the char sui ramen with pork belly or beef bulgogi rice bowl; skip the egg rolls, which are still sub-par. Look for a new menu here before long.

Croissant Moon Bakery

LOCATION Port of Entry   **QUALITY** Good   **VALUE** B-   **PORTION** Medium-Large
READER-SURVEY RESPONSES 96% 👍 4% 👎

SELECTIONS Hot breakfast sandwiches, deli sandwiches, cold noodle bowls, freshly baked pastries, and Lavazza coffee.

COMMENTS Tucked into the right side of Port of Entry's main walkway as you enter the park, Croissant Moon Bakery is a good place to get a quick breakfast (its "on the run" Continental combo is a great deal) or a pastry and coffee pick-me-up between meals. Prices for fancy flavored lattes are lower here than at the Starbucks across the street. The cold sandwiches tend to be premade and refrigerated, but you can get them heated up on a panini press. The service is fast and friendly, and there's some shaded seating outdoors, where you can people-watch. This location usually closes for the day by 4 p.m.

Doc Sugrue's Desert Kebab House

LOCATION The Lost Continent   **QUALITY** Fair–Good   **VALUE** C   **PORTION** Small-Medium
READER-SURVEY RESPONSES 81% 👍 19% 👎

SELECTIONS Beef, chicken, and vegan kebabs; hummus; Greek salad; churros; and yogurt.

COMMENTS The stand offers seasoned beef and chicken kebabs. It's also vegetarian and vegan friendly, with meatless meatballs, hummus, fruit cups, Greek yogurt, and pretzels on the menu. The skewers make a nice light meal; however, we have noticed that the quality of meat has dropped at this dining option. The vegan kefta provides good chermoula flavor despite including limited vegetables. This location also has the closest Coke Freestyle machines to Hogsmeade. Between the nearby draws of Potter-themed food in Hogsmeade and the award-winning Mythos, both Doc Sugrue's and Fire-Eater's Grill in Lost Continent can be easily overlooked. A limited number of shaded tables are located around the corner.

Fire-Eater's Grill *(Mobile Ordering)*

LOCATION The Lost Continent	QUALITY Good	VALUE B-	PORTION Medium
READER-SURVEY RESPONSES 82% 👍 18% 👎			

SELECTIONS Gyros, falafel, chicken tenders, hot dogs, chili-cheese fries, and salads.

COMMENTS The lamb gyro with hummus is the best and most popular combo here. Vegetarians can request falafel as a meat substitute, and combo platters include pita with tzatziki, Greek honey puffs, or edible cookie dough. You have to admire Universal's ability to combine various entrées to make more meal options. Take a plain chicken-tenders platter, for instance: Add hot sauce, and it becomes the Chicken Stingers platter. Omit the sauce and add lettuce, and it's the Crispy Chicken Salad.

Green Eggs and Ham Cafe

LOCATION Seuss Landing	QUALITY Good	VALUE B	PORTION Medium-Large
READER-SURVEY RESPONSES 92% 👍 8% 👎			

SELECTIONS Potato barrels with a variety of toppings, soft drinks.

COMMENTS This iconic outdoor eatery serves an indulgent menu revolving around potato barrels, better known as Tater Tots. The elementary-school-cafeteria favorites can be smothered in pepperoni-and-sausage pizza toppings (in regular or vegan varieties); other offerings include buffalo chicken tenders with mozzarella and ranch dressing, or the namesake combo of green eggs (colored with natural herbs) and diced ham. The Carnitas Tots are covered in roast pork and salsa. The menu's artery-clogging star has to be the corned beef Who Hash, served with white cheese sauce and scallions in a souvenir can.

Hog's Head

LOCATION Hogsmeade	QUALITY Good	VALUE B-	PORTION Medium
READER-SURVEY RESPONSES 94% 👍 6% 👎			

SELECTIONS Butterbeer, Pumpkin Juice, beer, wine, and mixed drinks.

COMMENTS Wonderfully themed pub attached to the Three Broomsticks restaurant that offers both alcoholic and alcohol-free drinks. If you want a Butterbeer, the line is often shorter here than at either of the outdoor carts. A full liquor selection is kept behind the bar, but there are no sodas to mix with (only juice), nor are the bartenders allowed to add alcohol to nonalcoholic Potter drinks (which is not to say that you can't mix them yourself). There are also some potent secret cocktails available off-menu, like Hog's Tea (a raspberry Long Island iced tea) and a triple-layered cider-ale-porter potion that (for trademark reasons) you should definitely *not* refer to as a Deathly Hallows. The animatronic hog hanging behind the bar is known to snort and snarl if you slide the barkeep a tip.

The Mess Tent

LOCATION Skull Island	QUALITY Fair-Good	VALUE C+	PORTION Medium-Large
READER-SURVEY RESPONSES 75% 👍 25% 👎			

SELECTIONS Hot dogs, pretzels, pizza skulls, churros, frozen slushies, and beer.

COMMENTS Apparently, all an attraction needs to qualify as an entire island on Universal's map is an adjoining souvenir kiosk and snack stand, which explains the presence of this modest mess tent outside Reign of Kong's entrance. Pizza skulls, a fan favorite from Halloween Horror Nights, can be had here year-round. The appropriately oversize ⅓-pound foot-long hot dog comes topped with cheese sauce and relish on a pretzel roll in a Kong Combo. The banana slushy tastes suspiciously like the banana Squishee served at USF's Duff Brewery, but it's still darn tasty.

Moose Juice, Goose Juice

LOCATION Seuss Landing	QUALITY Good	VALUE C	PORTION Medium
READER-SURVEY RESPONSES 83% 👍 17% 👎			

SELECTIONS Corn dogs, pretzels, cookies, and churros; frozen orange, apple, watermelon, or grape juice.

COMMENTS Cartoon animal rights activists rest easy: no geese nor meese were harmed in the making of these drinks. Moose Juice is actually an orange-flavored frozen slushy with a touch of tangerine, and Goose Juice is a green sour apple–flavored slushy. Both can hit the spot on a hot Florida day. More ordinary Icee flavors are also available.

Natural Selections

LOCATION Jurassic Park	QUALITY Good	VALUE C	PORTION Small-Medium
READER-SURVEY RESPONSES 88% 👍 12% 👎			

SELECTIONS Latin American snacks and pastries, fruit, chips, soft drinks, and beer.

COMMENTS This small stand across from the Jurassic Park River Adventure's entrance serves some of the park's most interesting sweet and savory snacks. Flaky beef empanadas and papa rellenas, fresh pineapple topped with tajin spices, and specialty churros all make welcome alternatives to the typical turkey legs and popcorn.

Pizza Predattoria *(Mobile Ordering)*

LOCATION Jurassic Park	QUALITY Fair	VALUE C-	PORTION Medium
READER-SURVEY RESPONSES 76% 👍 24% 👎			

SELECTIONS Personal pizzas, breadsticks, Caesar salad, and brookies.

COMMENTS The meat-lovers' pizza is decent as far as theme park pizza goes. Stick to that or the salads. The brookie—a cookie-brownie hybrid—is a brilliant development in the history of desserts.

Three Broomsticks *(Mobile Ordering)*

LOCATION Hogsmeade	QUALITY Good-Excellent	VALUE B+	PORTION Medium-Large
READER-SURVEY RESPONSES 87% 👍 31% 👎			

SELECTIONS Traditional English bacon, pancakes with bacon, and porridge with fruit. Lunch and dinner offerings are fish and chips, rotisserie chicken, smoked spareribs, shepherd's pie, mushroom jackfruit pie, Cornish pasty, and nonalcoholic Butterbeer.

COMMENTS Open beams, dark furniture, and the contiguous Hog's Head pub (see page 327) make Three Broomsticks a place to linger and savor. The inn seen in the *Harry Potter and the Half-Blood Prince* film was actually based on this theme park version, and the visual detail is incredible. As the only dining option in Hogsmeade, Three Broomsticks stays busy all day.

Like the Leaky Cauldron, you can reserve breakfast at Three Broomsticks (see page 320 for details), but the food options are even more limited, so there are definitely better uses of your morning touring time. For lunch and dinner, the ribs and chicken, or the tasty fish and chips (made from fresh cod) are your best bests. The Great Feast family platter includes ribs, chicken, corn, potatoes, and veggies for four for $78 ($19 each additional portion); even a large family may have leftovers, so bring along doggie bags.

Thunder Falls Terrace *(Mobile Ordering)*

LOCATION Jurassic Park	QUALITY Good–Excellent	VALUE A-	PORTION Large
READER-SURVEY RESPONSES 87% 👍 13% 👎			

SELECTIONS Rotisserie chicken, chargrilled ribs, pernil (Puerto Rican roast pork), jumbo chicken wings, rice-and-beans bowl, and salads.

COMMENTS A nice change from the usual theme park burgers and pizza served throughout IOA. The ribs and roasted corn on the cob are excellent, as are the seasoned rice and black bean bowls topped with meat or vegan chorizo. Thunder Falls is possibly the best bet for a meal in the park—it's not as busy as Three Broomsticks and serves food almost as good, making this location a winner.

Wimpy's

LOCATION Toon Lagoon	QUALITY Good	VALUE B-	PORTION Medium–Large
READER-SURVEY RESPONSES 86% 👍 14% 👎			

SELECTIONS Cheeseburgers, vegan burgers, chicken fingers, curly fries, Dole Whip, beer.

COMMENTS This outdoor burger stand, themed to Popeye's perpetually indebted pal, features a Wellington Cheeseburger and Vegan Supreme Cheeseburger. Neither is life-changing, but they are among the parks' better quick-service burgers and (better yet) are served with seasoned curly fries. Wimpy's other main attraction is Dole Whip, the iconic pineapple sorbet from Disney World's Adventureland, available in cups or cones for less money than at the Mouse.

EPIC UNIVERSE

The Bubbly Barrel *(Mobile Ordering)*

LOCATION Super Nintendo World	QUALITY TBD	VALUE TBD	PORTION TBD
READER-SURVEY RESPONSES Too new to rate			

SELECTIONS Tropical snacks and drinks.

COMMENTS Quick kiosk for picking up Donkey Kong Country–themed snacks and frozen beverages.

Burning Blade Tavern *(Mobile Ordering)*

LOCATION Dark Universe	QUALITY TBD	VALUE TBD	PORTION TBD
READER-SURVEY RESPONSES Too new to rate			

SELECTIONS Bratwurst, burgers, wings, pretzels, and specialty beverages.

COMMENTS Dine and drink inside the still-smoldering windmill where Frankenstein once met his fate at this small, tucked away watering hole. Look for the "Hounds," a team of storytelling monster hunters who haunt the tavern, and the gruesome trophies they've collected.

Cafe L'air la Sirene *(Mobile Ordering)*

LOCATION Ministry of Magic	**QUALITY** TBD	**VALUE** TBD	**PORTION** TBD
READER-SURVEY RESPONSES Too new to rate			

SELECTIONS French café–style foods, including sandwiches, plats du jour, and unique desserts. Butterbeer and nonalcoholic drinks; beer, cocktails, and French wines.

COMMENTS The largest of two dining locations within this Wizarding World, this indoor spot features multiple bright and cheery Parisian-inspired dining rooms adorned with elaborate art nouveau decor. Sidewalk seating outside is ideal for Muggle-watching. Be sure to check out the colossal croquembouche sculptures composed of nearly 2,000 cream puffs.

Das Stakehaus *(Mobile Ordering)*

LOCATION Dark Universe	**QUALITY** TBD	**VALUE** TBD	**PORTION** TBD
READER-SURVEY RESPONSES Too new to rate			

SELECTIONS Kebabs (aka steaks on stakes), burgers, and large sandwiches.

COMMENTS Sink your teeth into Darkmoor Village's largest restaurant, where vampires' familiars prepare guests for a bloody banquet beneath artifacts and artwork documenting the classic monsters' deeds.

De Lacey's Cottage *(Mobile Ordering)*

LOCATION Dark Universe	**QUALITY** TBD	**VALUE** TBD	**PORTION** TBD
READER-SURVEY RESPONSES Too new to rate			

SELECTIONS Ice cream, cinnamon bread, fried potatoes on a stick.

COMMENTS The cozy hut where a blind hermit once comforted Frankenstein's Monster has been converted into a snack stand. As Mel Brooks fans, we were hopeful hot soup and espresso would be on the menu, but no cigar.

Hooligan's Grog & Gruel *(Mobile Ordering)*

LOCATION Isle of Berk	**QUALITY** TBD	**VALUE** TBD	**PORTION** TBD
READER-SURVEY RESPONSES Too new to rate			

SELECTIONS This ordering window features small snacks, desserts, and self-serve Coke Freestyle machines.

COMMENTS Good for a quick snack, but better dining locations are available within the Isle of Berk if you're looking for a full meal.

Le Gobelet Noir *(Mobile Ordering)*

LOCATION Ministry of Magic	**QUALITY** TBD	**VALUE** TBD	**PORTION** TBD
READER-SURVEY RESPONSES Too new to rate			

SELECTIONS Wizarding-style French cuisine, including soups, salads, entrées, and desserts.

COMMENTS The smaller of two dining locations within this Wizarding World, this indoor restaurant is somewhat hidden, tucked away in an alley where dark witches gather in the shadows.

Mead Hall *(Mobile Ordering)*

LOCATION Isle of Berk	**QUALITY** TBD	**VALUE** TBD	**PORTION** TBD
READER-SURVEY RESPONSES Too new to rate			

SELECTIONS Hearty meals like roasted meats and fish, sandwiches, along with frosty beverages and beer—perfect fare for feeding starving Vikings.

COMMENTS Take a load off and enjoy the large-scale and rustic dining room of this great hall, where the Viking residents of Berk celebrate and dine together.

Meteor Astropub *(Mobile Ordering)*

LOCATION Celestial Park	QUALITY TBD	VALUE TBD	PORTION TBD
READER-SURVEY RESPONSES Too new to rate			

SELECTIONS Pub food and craft beer, plus their specialty, the Meteor Burger.
COMMENTS Dine inside or at outside seating areas at this brick brewpub-style eatery, which also includes a full bar.

The Oak and Star Tavern *(Mobile Ordering)*

LOCATION Celestial Park	QUALITY TBD	VALUE TBD	PORTION TBD
READER-SURVEY RESPONSES Too new to rate			

SELECTIONS Savory barbecue, featuring dishes that have been smoked and cured over time.
COMMENTS Flanked by massive decorative tree trunks inside and roaring fireplaces, this cozy eatery celebrates fire and nature, while offering plenty of inside seating.

Pizza Moon *(Mobile Ordering)*

LOCATION Celestial Park	QUALITY TBD	VALUE TBD	PORTION TBD
READER-SURVEY RESPONSES Too new to rate			

SELECTIONS Variety of pizzas, breadsticks, and salads.
COMMENTS Inspired by imagery from Méliès' *A Trip to the Moon,* dine among the stars and large scenic pieces that flank a stage-themed window into the kitchen so you can see your pizza being made. Indoor air-conditioned seating is available. A good place to dine while waiting for the crowds to die down inside Super Nintendo World.

Spit Fyre Grill *(Mobile Ordering)*

LOCATION Isle of Berk	QUALITY TBD	VALUE TBD	PORTION TBD
READER-SURVEY RESPONSES Too new to rate			

SELECTIONS Fire-grilled meats and more, with self-serve Coke Freestyle machines.
COMMENTS This walk-up dining location features outdoor covered seating overlooking the land's boat ride.

Star Sui Bao *(Mobile Ordering)*

LOCATION Celestial Park	QUALITY TBD	VALUE TBD	PORTION TBD
READER-SURVEY RESPONSES Too new to rate			

SELECTIONS Bao buns and takeout-style foods.
COMMENTS This kiosk is located between Stardust Racers and the Isle of Berk, and it is great for a quick bite while enjoying the garden areas of Celestial Park.

Toadstool Cafe *(Mobile Ordering)*

LOCATION Super Nintendo World	QUALITY TBD	VALUE TBD	PORTION TBD
READER-SURVEY RESPONSES Too new to rate			

SELECTIONS Family-friendly American fare.
COMMENTS Cute Nintendo character theming makes way for a new spin on theme park burgers and chicken, with unique variations on classic American cuisine. Kids meals offer a good amount of food for the price and include a fun surprise Power-Up themed cookie and toy character figure. Everyone will enjoy the adorable desserts, which are just as tasty as they are photo-ready for sharing on social media.

For an extra layer of fun, watch the Toads preparing food in the kitchen through magical windows (screens). Periodically, the restaurant comes under attack from Bowser's baddies in a fun mini-show that can be seen outside the windows, temporarily changing the dining room's mood via darker lighting and music cues!

Turbo Boost Treats *(Mobile Ordering)*

LOCATION Super Nintendo World	QUALITY TBD	VALUE TBD	PORTION TBD
READER-SURVEY RESPONSES Too new to rate			

SELECTIONS Popcorn, pretzels, and quick snacks.

COMMENTS Pickup window near the Mario Kart ride for a fast bite between rides.

Yoshi's Snack Island *(Mobile Ordering)*

LOCATION Super Nintendo World	QUALITY TBD	VALUE TBD	PORTION TBD
READER-SURVEY RESPONSES Too new to rate			

SELECTIONS Cute snacks and drinks.

COMMENTS Quick pickup window near Yoshi's Adventure for stuffed calzones and adorable beverages.

VOLCANO BAY

Bambu *(Mobile Ordering)*

LOCATION Rainforest Village	QUALITY Good– Excellent	VALUE B	PORTION Medium–Large
READER-SURVEY RESPONSES 88% 👍 12% 👎			

SELECTIONS Cheeseburgers, chicken tenders, salads, and chicken, fish, and vegan sandwiches.

COMMENTS Bamboo-shaded patios provide plenty of sheltered seating near the Maku Puihi slides. The coconut chicken salad with grapes and apples is excellent, as are the quinoa-edamame burger and the pineapple upside-down cake.

The Feasting Frog *(Mobile Ordering)*

LOCATION Rainforest Village	QUALITY Fair–Good	VALUE B-	PORTION Medium
READER-SURVEY RESPONSES 69% 👍 31% 👎			

SELECTIONS Tacos, nachos, and tuna poké.

COMMENTS This charming amphibian-shaped hut serves serviceable carne asada and chicken tacos, though the shells seem to go stale swiftly in the Orlando humidity. Our favorite is the poké bowl, with sashimi-quality ahi tuna and crispy plantain chips. You can grab your food and sit at the neighboring **Kunuku Boat Bar,** which serves a refreshing locally brewed Volcano Blossom beer and an array of supersweet signature cocktails.

Kohola Reef Restaurant & Social Club *(Mobile Ordering)*

LOCATION Wave Village	QUALITY Good–Excellent	VALUE B+	PORTION Medium–Large
READER-SURVEY RESPONSES 91% 👍 9% 👎			

SELECTIONS Hawaiian-style ribs, burgers, vegan burgers, jerk fish or pulled-pork sandwiches, chicken, pizzas, salads, and sushi.

COMMENTS As Volcano Bay's largest eatery and the one closest to the park's entrance, this is usually the most crowded restaurant at mealtimes. Breakfast items are served here during peak periods until 10:30 a.m., and this is the park's only eatery that always stays open until closing time. The burgers are served on Hawaiian rolls, but you're better off skipping them and the "longboard" pizzas in favor of more exotic entrées, like the braised chicken in green coconut curry, smoked ribs, or mango barbecue pulled pork. For lighter fare, we like the jerk-seasoned mahi-mahi with cucumber slaw, watermelon and feta salad, and California rolls. Chocolate lava cake is the can't-miss dessert. If you want an adult beverage with your meal, step across the path to the nearby **Dancing Dragons Boat Bar.**

Whakawaiwai Eats *(Mobile Ordering)*

LOCATION River Village	QUALITY Good		VALUE B-	PORTION Medium
READER-SURVEY RESPONSES	83% 👍	17% 👎		

SELECTIONS Pizza, hot dogs, mac and cheese, and salads.

COMMENTS Somewhat isolated in the rear of the park, this is probably your best bet for getting food without a long wait, though the menu isn't particularly innovative. The same "longboard" pizzas served at Kohola Reef are also found here, plus Hawaiian varieties and an island barbecue version (chicken, Gouda, and mango sauce). The hot dogs are served on pretzel buns and topped with bacon and pineapple, and the upscale mac and cheese is stuffed with jerk-seasoned shrimp.

CITYWALK

Bend the Bao *(Mobile Ordering)*

LOCATION Upper Level	QUALITY Good-Excellent		VALUE C-	PORTION Small
READER-SURVEY RESPONSES	88% 👍	12% 👎		

SELECTIONS Slider-size Chinese steamed buns stuffed with meat, seafood, or vegetables; boba tea and soft drinks.

COMMENTS Bend the Bao, which sits above the entrance to CityWalk's cinema, takes Asia's answer to taco shells and stuffs the soft white buns with kimchee fried chicken, braised beef brisket, roasted mushrooms, and other savory treats. We like the caramelized pork belly with scallions, along with the rich confit duck balanced by spicy slaw. Only the prices give us pause: $13 buys you only two small bao ($5 more for a third), which is barely enough for a snack.

BK Whopper Bar

LOCATION Upper Level	QUALITY Fair-Good		VALUE C	PORTION Large
READER-SURVEY RESPONSES	80% 👍	20% 👎		

SELECTIONS A Burger King location with Whoppers of all kinds, plant-based Impossible burger, fried chicken sandwich or strips, salads, fries, onion rings, shakes, and sundae pie.

COMMENTS Because the menu is so familiar, long lines can develop here during lunchtime. Prices are markedly higher than your local drive-thru, and there's no value menu, but you are getting a Whopper with unique toppings (such as blue cheese or angry onions), and the combos include large fries and a drink.

Bread Box Handcrafted Sandwiches *(Mobile Ordering)*

LOCATION Upper Level	QUALITY Good		VALUE C-	PORTION Small-Medium
READER-SURVEY RESPONSES	86% 👍	14% 👎		

SELECTIONS Hot and cold deli sandwiches, grilled cheese, Sichuan potato chips, soups, salads, root beer floats, and beer.

COMMENTS The Bread Box claims that guests will be "transported back to your childhood kitchen or your favorite street corner deli" through its use of high-quality meats, vegetables, fresh bread, and simple preparation. The menu indeed has a wide selection of sandwiches (stuffed with everything from whipped burrata to turkey pastrami to smoked brisket), along with house-made soups and salads made fresh to order. And you can't complain about s'mores or root beer floats for dessert. Everything we've tasted at Bread Box has been yummy, but the sandwich sizes are modest. If you want a high-quality, creative snack and can stomach the price, give the grilled cheese a go, but save some money for another meal later.

Hot Dog Hall of Fame *(Mobile Ordering)*

LOCATION Lower Level	QUALITY Fair-Good	VALUE C	PORTION Medium-Large
READER-SURVEY RESPONSES 67% 👍 33% 👎			

SELECTIONS Vienna Beef, Nathan's, Kayem, Sabrett, and Koegel hot dogs, plus bratwurst, Italian, and vegan sausages, with a variety of toppings; fries and potato chips; beer and soda.

COMMENTS Hot Dog Hall of Fame is a tribute to the iconic baseball-park food, with large-screen TVs and bleacher-type seating (from actual Major League Baseball parks) for those interested in catching a game. The sausages, buns, and toppings are all authentic and perfectly prepared—there's even a mustard bar, curated by Wisconsin's National Mustard Museum—but the value will vary with the variety. A New York Sabrett with sauerkraut costs double what you'd pay in Times Square, but the Kansas City dog (pulled pork and coleslaw) and Milwaukee dog (bratwurst and grilled onions) deliver a good bang for the buck. There's even a 2-foot dog for just under twice the price, if you want to share, along with a vegan field dog topped with roasted corn and chilies. The posted price includes the pup and shoestring fries or chips (subtract $1 for à la carte); roasted peanuts and Cracker Jacks (natch) are extra.

Moe's Southwest Grill

LOCATION Upper Level	QUALITY Fair-Good	VALUE B-	PORTION Large
READER-SURVEY RESPONSES 77% 👍 23% 👎			

SELECTIONS Tacos, bowls, burritos, quesadillas, nachos, and salads made with steak, ground beef, chicken, tofu, or veggies; chips and salsa; cookies; beer.

COMMENTS The Mexican-food equivalent of a Subway sandwich shop. You place your order (for example, steak tacos) at the front of a long assembly line, and then follow your plate down the line as it's passed from worker to worker, each of whom adds whatever garnishes, sides, and sauces you want. We like Moe's quite a bit. You can buy a breakfast burrito here before rope drop, or get guac and queso for a post-park fourth meal.

Panda Express

LOCATION Upper Level	QUALITY Fair	VALUE C	PORTION Medium-Large
READER-SURVEY RESPONSES 87% 👍 13% 👎			

SELECTIONS Chain-restaurant Chinese food, including entrées of orange chicken, kung pao chicken, beef and broccoli, beef with mushrooms and peppers, and honey-walnut shrimp, with sides of green veggies, chow mein, and white or fried rice.

COMMENTS The kung pao chicken has a darker, smokier flavor than most we've tried, and the sauces are heavier than those at our local Chinese takeouts. Still, Panda Express is a hit with the kids in our group, who want to eat here every time they see it. Panda Express usually has the longest line of the three fast-food joints on CityWalk's upper level. Panda Express's mobile app may be used to order food at the CityWalk location, allowing you to bypass the cashier queue (availability may vary).

Red Oven Pizza Bakery

LOCATION Lower Level	QUALITY Good-Excellent	VALUE A	PORTION Medium-Large
READER-SURVEY RESPONSES	87% 👍	13% 👎	

SELECTIONS White and red pizzas with gourmet toppings, salads, and imported beer and wine.

COMMENTS Red Oven Pizza Bakery may be seen as Universal's answer to Via Napoli in EPCOT, which brought high-quality pizza to the theme park world. Only whole pies, not slices, can be ordered at Red Oven. However, with a reasonable price of under $18 per pizza, two people can eat cheaply. The six white and seven red Neapolitan-style artisan pies are made with San Marzano tomatoes, organic extra-virgin olive oil, buffalo mozzarella, fine-ground "00" flour, and filtered water, and then baked in a 900°F oven while you watch. Salads and a limited selection of beer and wine are available, with free refills on soda.

After ordering your food and receiving your drinks, a server will seat you and bring your order once it's ready; a pickup window for mobile orders is also available. Plenty of covered outdoor seating is available, a welcome relief from the Florida sun (and rain). Because of its location in the main hub of CityWalk, Red Oven is a great place to get a bite to eat and people-watch. Red Oven can also be delivered to the freestanding bars along the CityWalk waterfront (when available).

Starbucks

LOCATION Lower Level	QUALITY Good	VALUE C	PORTION Medium
READER-SURVEY RESPONSES	96% 👍	4% 👎	

SELECTIONS Coffees and teas in many blends and flavors; espresso, cappuccino, frozen coffees, and smoothies; pastries; cookies; and sodas.

COMMENTS While the Starbucks in IOA, USF, and Cabana Bay Beach Resort feature the chain's full sandwich menu, this particular Starbucks offers a more limited selection of pastries. However, it does provide a large amount of seating (with free Wi-Fi and accessible power ports) both inside and out. Though this handsomely designed coffee shop has much more barista capacity than the average franchise, its ground-central location leads to long lines around park opening. *Note:* Starbucks loyalty stars can be earned at Universal locations, but rewards can't be redeemed here. Starbucks gift cards and Universal annual pass discounts are both honored here, however.

Voodoo Doughnut *(Mobile Ordering)*

LOCATION Lower Level	QUALITY Good	VALUE B–	PORTION Medium
READER-SURVEY RESPONSES	88% 👍	12% 👎	

SELECTIONS Raised yeast, cake, or vegan doughnuts, topped with everything from fruit cereal or orange powdered-drink mix to bacon, plus coffee to wash them down.

COMMENTS This Portland-based bakery has built a cult following for its outrageously shaped confections. The signature Voodoo Doll (with a pretzel stake through its heart) is Instagram-worthy, and exclusive varieties for annual passholders arrive regularly, but the naughty, anatomically explicit items that Voodoo Doughnut is infamous for aren't sold at a family-friendly theme park. The vegan Portland Cream is so delicious that you'd never guess it contains no actual cream. Expect long lines outside the shop at breakfast and as the parks empty, so use Mobile Ordering when available to avoid the queue; pickups are at a booth across the walkway from the shop entrance. Even if you don't get anything to eat, pose for a photo on the doughnut throne outside.

RESORT HOTELS

Bayliner Diner

LOCATION Cabana Bay Beach	QUALITY Good	VALUE B	PORTION Medium-Large
READER-SURVEY RESPONSES 85% 👍 15% 👎			

SELECTIONS Cheeseburgers, roasted chicken, hot dogs, beef churrasco, stir fry, seafood, pizza, pasta, flatbread, deli sandwiches, wraps, salads, and pastries.

COMMENTS Cabana Bay's Bayliner Diner is a food court–style cafeteria with several different stations offering a wide range of food options. The preparations are a cut above the counter service found inside the parks. The churrasco-style flat iron with creamy chimichurri is surprisingly tender and tasty for counter-service steak, and the seared ahi tuna on seaweed salad could be served in a nice Asian restaurant if you request it cooked rare. For breakfast, the diner serves up all the usual suspects. Get waffles or French toast, or wait for a made-to-order omelet, but avoid the precooked eggs on the combo platter and the croissant sandwich. The seating area, filled with booths and tables, is large. Large screens play retro commercials to evoke a feeling of nostalgia. The diner offers a considerable amount of usable outlets to charge your phones and tablets, including one outside every booth. **Shakes Malt Shoppe** in the rear of Bayliner's dining room serves smoothies, sundaes, and other ice cream treats. If you prefer to dine poolside, the **Hideaway Bar & Grill** by the lazy river slings burgers, fish tacos, and Honolulu-style hot dogs, while **Atomic Tonic** near the waterslide serves *döner* kebabs and falafel wraps.

Beach Break Cafe

LOCATION Surfside Inn	QUALITY Good	VALUE B+	PORTION Medium
READER-SURVEY RESPONSES 89% 👍 11% 👎			

SELECTIONS Rotisserie chicken, blackened fish, quesadillas, hot sandwiches, Cobb and Caesar salads, pizza, pasta, burgers, fried shrimp, and fresh-squeezed juices.

COMMENTS The cafeteria-style food courts at the Endless Summer properties are the humblest eateries at Universal's on-site hotels, but they're better than most of the franchised family restaurants on nearby International Drive and provide better value to boot. For breakfast, try the blueberry pancakes topped with powdered sugar, and healthy blends of fresh-pressed juice. At lunch and dinner, the All Day burger with a fried egg and bacon costs less than a basic cheeseburger inside the parks, and between the vegan banh mi burger, and the seasoned grilled corn on the cob, there's plenty to satisfy non-carnivores. There's ample seating at communal picnic tables, which surround a self-serve Coca-Cola Freestyle dispenser that allows free refills for 2 hours after any soft drink purchase. Our biggest problem with Beach Break Cafe is the speed of service; our food got cold before our entire order could be assembled, and simple requests prompted employees to disappear for long stretches, suggesting that Universal isn't staffing its budget hotels with the best and brightest.

Cosmos Cafe and Market/Omega Cafe and Market

LOCATION Stella Nova/Terra Luna	QUALITY TBD	VALUE TBD	PORTION TBD
READER-SURVEY RESPONSES Too new to rate			

SELECTIONS Panini sandwiches, hamburgers, pasta, fried chicken.

COMMENTS While neither of the two Prime Value properties at Epic Universe offer table-service dining, they both feature airy counter-service dining rooms off their lobbies, serving nearly identical menus for breakfast, lunch, and dinner. Stella Nova and Terra Luna each also has a casual poolside bar and grill (dubbed **Galaxy** and **Moonrise,** respectively) slinging cocktails and quesadillas, as well as a late-night pizza delivery service.

Emack & Bolio's Marketplace

LOCATION Hard Rock Hotel	QUALITY Good	VALUE C	PORTION Medium
READER-SURVEY RESPONSES	76% 👍 24% 👎		

SELECTIONS Ice cream, sorbet, shakes, sundaes, Starbucks coffee, sandwiches, candy, pizza, snacks, soft drinks, cereal, and pastries.

COMMENTS Boston-based Emack & Bolio's has a long history of associating with rock stars (check out the vintage van doors outside) and naming ice cream flavors after their songs—you can have a cone or sundae made from Chocolate Moose, Grasshopper Pie, or S'moreo. It also has a grab-and-go selection of snacks, cold breakfast foods, and Starbucks drinks to speed you through your morning, plus a decent selection of hot and cold snacks, sandwiches, and takeout pizzas (in 10- or 16-inch pies) after noon.

New Dutch Trading Co.

LOCATION Sapphire Falls	QUALITY Good	VALUE C+	PORTION Medium
READER-SURVEY RESPONSES	84% 👍 16% 👎		

SELECTIONS Hot sandwiches, soups, pizzas, salads, coffee, pastries, hand-scooped ice cream, and milkshakes.

COMMENTS This white-tiled quick-service marketplace in the Sapphire Falls Resort lobby is far smaller than the food hall at Aventura next door, but it manages to pack a lot of options—including Cuban and caprese sandwiches, tropical salads, specialty smoothies, and lattes blended with the house brew—into a small space. Warm pretzels, empanadas, and hot pots are served after 3 p.m. The eatery also doubles as a grab-and-go market for snacks and sundries, where you can secure s'mores kits for the pool's fire pit. About the only thing there isn't space for is seating, with only a handful of stools along a bar, so plan on eating on the run or bringing food back to your room. New Dutch Trading Co. opens at 6 a.m. for breakfast and stays open until 11 p.m., so you can refill the Coke Freestyle mugs available here (see page 313).

Pier 8 Market

LOCATION Dockside Inn	QUALITY Good-Excellent	VALUE A-	PORTION Medium
READER-SURVEY RESPONSES	85% 👍 15% 👎		

SELECTIONS Hot breakfast sandwiches, chicken and waffles, deli sandwiches, pizza, pasta, pastries, frozen yogurt, and smoothies.

COMMENTS The sister cafeteria to Surfside Inn's Beachside Cafe has its own unique menu with similarly low prices, as well as a seaport-inspired layout featuring five grab-and-go serving windows that resemble open-air market stalls. Breakfast specialties include upscale items like avocado toast and Baja burritos, while lunchtime entrées include a French onion burger with caramelized onions and a Volcano turkey burger with pepper jack and pineapple. Dinner offerings include 10-inch personal pizzas, baked ziti, and seared snapper with asparagus and polenta. The best news is that you can have excellent fried chicken and waffles in the morning with maple syrup, and again in the evening with hot sauce and mashed potatoes. Desserts include a Reese's brownie and Key lime pie. Dockside Inn also has a full-service Starbucks, an indoor **Sunset Lounge** lobby bar, and a poolside **Oasis Beach Bar** that serves drinks named after former Wet 'n Wild waterslides.

Sal's Market Deli

LOCATION Portofino Bay	QUALITY Good–Excellent	VALUE C+	PORTION Medium–Large
READER-SURVEY RESPONSES 93% 👍 7% 👎			

SELECTIONS Pizza, calzones, deli sandwiches, salads, wine, and beer.

COMMENTS This casual counter-service deli and pizzeria is practically the only affordable option on Portofino Bay property. The pizza is the best in Universal outside of Red Oven and can be made with gluten-free dough. Around the corner, a full-service Starbucks with an attached *gelateria* and bakery serves breakfast and desserts. Food can be packaged and taken back to your room, undercutting the expensive room service.

Tuk Tuk Market

LOCATION Royal Pacific	QUALITY Good	VALUE B-	PORTION Medium
READER-SURVEY RESPONSES 74% 👍 26% 👎			

SELECTIONS Hot and cold sandwiches, stir fry, salads, coffee, pastries, hand-scooped ice cream, and milkshakes. Coke Freestyle soda, beer, wine, and cocktails by the bottle.

COMMENTS This quick-service convenience store at the rear of Royal Pacific's lobby makes it easy for hotel guests to grab a quick meal or snack on their way to and from the parks. The seating area is small but has a lovely view of the luau pavilion. In keeping with the resort's Pacific theme, the standard quick-service menu items—breakfast cereals and pastries, deli sandwiches and salads, pizzas and chicken tenders—are supplemented by stir-fry. If you have a sweet tooth, try the house-made dessert tarts or hand-scooped gelato. Starbucks coffee drinks, along with a selection of wines and liquors, are also served here.

Urban Pantry Food Hall

LOCATION Aventura	QUALITY Good	VALUE B-	PORTION Medium–Large
READER-SURVEY RESPONSES 79% 👍 21% 👎			

SELECTIONS Burgers, pizzas, steak, chicken, Asian dishes, salads, beer, and wine.

COMMENTS In lieu of a full-service restaurant, Aventura Hotel has a fast-casual food court off the main lobby inspired by big-city indoor markets. It features individual feeding stations, each with its own open kitchen and cash register, in a minimalist industrial environment. In the morning, pancakes, scrambled eggs, and other American breakfast standards—along with Belgian waffles and fresh fruit—are served. For lunch and dinner, start at the stir-fry station for a bowl of beef or chicken lo mein, or a tuna-topped rainbow sushi roll. The burger station grills thick patties—Black Angus beef or the vegan Beyond Meat substitute. The roast station serves rotisserie chickens, fried chicken wings, and build-your-own salad wraps; pizzas can be topped with barbecue chicken, sausage and bacon, or roasted veggies. End your meal with a scoop of gelato or a cookie. We've found the food quality here to generally be above average, but we hear complaints from readers about the hall's confusing layout and slow service. Keep an eye out for rolling robots that deliver dishes to diners.

UNIVERSAL ORLANDO FULL-SERVICE RESTAURANT PROFILES

TO HELP YOU MAKE CHOICES for sit-down meals at breakfast, lunch, or dinner, we've provided full profiles of Universal's full-service restaurants, most of which are located in the resort hotels or CityWalk complex. Each profile lets you quickly check the restaurant's cuisine, location, star rating, cost range, quality rating, and value rating. Restaurants are listed by cuisine in the chart on pages 342–343; restaurant profiles are ordered alphabetically.

STAR RATING

THE STAR RATING REPRESENTS the entire dining experience: style, service, and ambience, in addition to taste, presentation, and food quality. Five stars, the highest rating, indicates that the restaurant offers the best of everything. Four-star restaurants are above average, and three-star restaurants offer good, though not necessarily memorable, meals. Two-star restaurants serve mediocre fare, and one-star restaurants are below par. Our star ratings don't correspond to ratings awarded by AAA, *Forbes, Zagat Survey,* or other restaurant reviewers.

COST RANGE

THE NEXT RATING tells how much an adult full-service entrée will cost. Appetizers, sides, desserts, drinks, taxes, and

Inexpensive	under $15/person
Moderate	$15–$35/person
Expensive	over $35/person

tips aren't included; a gratuity of 18%–25% of the total before taxes and discounts is considered standard, and most restaurants impose an automatic 18% tip for parties of six or more. We've rated the cost as **inexpensive, moderate,** or **expensive.** The entrée ranges listed below are also before tax and gratuity, but prices for all buffets and package meals described in the following reviews do include tax, along with any mandatory service charges (where noted).

QUALITY RATING

THE FOOD QUALITY is rated on a scale of one to five stars, five being the best. The quality rating is based on the taste, freshness of ingredients, preparation, presentation, and creativity of food. There is no consideration of price. If you want the best food available and cost is no issue, look no further than the quality ratings.

VALUE RATING

IF, ON THE OTHER HAND, you're looking for both quality *and* a good meal deal, check the value rating, also expressed as stars, as shown at right.

★★★★★	Exceptional value; a real bargain
★★★★	Good value
★★★	Fair value; you get exactly what you pay for
★★	Somewhat overpriced
★	Extremely overpriced

PAYMENT

ALL UNIVERSAL ORLANDO restaurants accept American Express, MasterCard, Visa, Discover, Diners Club, and Universal Orlando Resort hotel-room charges.

Amatista Cookhouse ★★★

CARIBBEAN	MODERATE-EXPENSIVE	QUALITY ★★★	VALUE ★★★
READER-SURVEY RESPONSES	86% 👍 14% 👎		

Sapphire Falls Resort; ☎ 407-503-5200

Customers Hotel guests. **Reservations** Accepted through Resy. **When to go** Breakfast or dinner. **Entrée range** $16–$48. **Service rating** ★★½. **Friendliness rating** ★★★. **Parking** $5 valet or free self-parking at hotel with validation. **Bar** Full service. **Wine selection** Modest. **Dress** Resort casual. **Disabled access** Good. **Hours** Daily, 7–11 a.m., noon–10 p.m.

SETTING AND ATMOSPHERE A large, sunny room on Sapphire Falls Resort's lower level features an exhibition kitchen and indoor–outdoor seating with a view of the hotel's lagoon. Seating is in the open main area or one of the private dining rooms.

HOUSE SPECIALTIES Buffet breakfast with omelets and smoked salmon; rotisserie chicken, flatbreads, and sandwiches for lunch; Caribbean seafood paella, chargrilled steak, and vegan curry for dinner.

SUMMARY AND COMMENTS Bright and clean, though a bit too big to be cozy, Amatista is the main table-service restaurant at Sapphire Falls and caters to families and conventioneers by serving comfort food favorites with an abundance of Caribbean creativity. We love the jerk-seasoned chicken wings, flaky empanadas, and juicy Black Angus burger. Ordering breakfast à la carte quickly adds up, so if you want more than a muffin, spring for the buffet. Service is friendly but inconsistent; at lunch you may have the place all to yourself, but don't count on a quick dinner here if you're on a tight schedule.

Antojitos Authentic Mexican Food ★★★½

MEXICAN	MODERATE	QUALITY ★★★½	VALUE ★★★½
READER-SURVEY RESPONSES	80% 👍 20% 👎		

CityWalk; ☎ 407-224-FOOD (3663)

Customers Locals and tourists. **Reservations** Accepted through Universal. **When to go** Dinner. **Entrée range** $19–$28. **Service rating** ★★★. **Friendliness rating** ★★★★. **Parking** Universal Orlando garage. **Bar** Full service. **Wine selection** Good. **Dress** Casual; *luchador* masks and sombreros optional. **Disabled access** Good. **Hours** Sunday–Thursday, 4–10 p.m.; Friday–Saturday, 3–10 p.m.

SETTING AND ATMOSPHERE This festive postmodern tribute to Mexican street culture features a large open kitchen framed by graffiti graphics and eye-catching neon, with the central bar and surrounding booths fashioned from reclaimed wood and metal. The downstairs can get very noisy, so if you want a quieter meal, ask for one of the private rooms upstairs. Or grab a seat on the patio or balcony to watch the CityWalk crowds go by.

HOUSE SPECIALTIES Roasted-corn casserole (*esquites*), quesadillas, enchiladas, tacos, fajitas, and flan.

ENTERTAINMENT A modern mariachi ensemble plays outside and inside Antojitos on select nights.

SUMMARY AND COMMENTS A Universal Studios concept, the colorful Antojitos offers unique and craveable tapas-style Mexican food, serving handcrafted tortillas, made-while-you-watch guacamole, and fresh sauces for a taste of Mexico City.

For starters, you'll probably want a drink, and Antojitos has Orlando's best tequila selection this side of EPCOT's La Cava del Tequila. Order from the four-sided bar on the ground floor or from the converted Volkswagen bus outside the entrance. If you don't do straight shots, try a specialty margarita.

When it comes to the food, while it's pricier than your local taco joint, Antojitos prepares familiar plates with exceptionally fresh ingredients. The table-side guacamole is a must-have that will convert the most hardened avocado-hater, and the *esquites* (roasted corn with cotija cheese and jalapeño mayo) is almost a meal in itself. The portion sizes of the enchiladas and tacos aren't enormous, but you'll probably be full after the free chips (served hot with house-made salsa) and the excellent rice and beans accompanying most entrées.

Atlantic (and Aquaria Bar)

SEAFOOD	MODERATE-EXPENSIVE	QUALITY TBD	VALUE TBD
READER-SURVEY RESPONSES	Too new to rate		

Epic Universe; ☎ 407-224-FOOD (3663)

Customers Park guests. **Reservations** Accepted through Universal. **When to go** Dinner. **Entrée range** TBA. **Service rating** TBD. **Friendliness rating** TBD. **Parking** EU lot. **Bar** Full service. **Wine selection** Good. **Dress** Casual. **Disabled access** Good. **Hours** TBA.

SETTING AND ATMOSPHERE Set within an octagonal-shaped building designed to act as a large Victorian aquarium, Atlantic features large, illuminated fish hanging from the ceiling to help sell the illusion. The most impressive elements of this upscale dining location are the massive picture windows overlooking the water features and garden areas of Celestial Park outside.

HOUSE SPECIALTIES A wide selection of exceptional seafood and steaks, along with specialty cocktails.

SUMMARY AND COMMENTS The most visible of the two full-service restaurants within Epic Universe, Atlantic could prove busy for dinner, so reservations are suggested. With views overlooking the dancing fountains of the Neptune pool outside, and ornate decor inside, the vibe here is high-class meets relaxing.

Bar 17 Bistro ★★★½

AMERICAN	INEXPENSIVE-MODERATE	QUALITY ★★★½	VALUE ★★★½
READER-SURVEY RESPONSES	79% 👍 21% 👎		

Aventura Hotel; ☎ 407-503-6000

Customers Locals and hotel guests. **Reservations** Not accepted. **When to go** Dinner. **Entrée range** $10–$23. **Service rating** ★★★½. **Friendliness rating** ★★★½. **Parking** Free self-parking at hotel with validation. **Bar** Full service. **Wine selection** Moderate.

continued on page 343

UNIVERSAL ORLANDO RESTAURANTS BY CUISINE

CUISINE	LOCATION	OVERALL RATING	COST	QUALITY RATING	VALUE RATING
AMERICAN					
The Cowfish Sushi Burger Bar	CITYWALK	★★★★	MOD	★★★★	★★★½
The Kitchen	HARD ROCK HOTEL	★★★½	MOD-EXP	★★★★	★★★
Bar 17 Bistro	AVENTURA HOTEL	★★★½	INEXP-MOD	★★★½	★★★½
Bigfire	CITYWALK	★★★½	MOD-EXP	★★★½	★★★½
Orchid Court Lounge & Sushi Bar	ROYAL PACIFIC RESORT	★★★½	MOD-EXP	★★★½	★★★
Toothsome Chocolate Emporium & Savory Feast Kitchen	CITYWALK	★★★½	MOD	★★★½	★★★
Confisco Grille	ISLANDS OF ADVENTURE	★★★	MOD	★★★	★★★
Hard Rock Cafe	CITYWALK	★★★	MOD	★★★	★★★
Jimmy Buffett's Margaritaville	CITYWALK	★★★	MOD	★★★	★★★
Jake's American Bar	ROYAL PACIFIC RESORT	★★★	MOD	★★★	★★½
NBC Sports Grill & Brew	CITYWALK	★★½	MOD	★★½	★★★
Galaxy Bowl	CABANA BAY BEACH RESORT	★★½	INEXP-MOD	★★½	★★½
ASIAN					
Wantilan Luau	ROYAL PACIFIC RESORT	★★★★	EXP	★★★★	★★★
Islands Dining Room	ROYAL PACIFIC RESORT	★★★½	MOD	★★★½	★★★
Orchid Court Lounge & Sushi Bar	ROYAL PACIFIC RESORT	★★★½	MOD-EXP	★★★½	★★★
Blue Dragon Pan-Asian Restaurant	EPIC UNIVERSE	NA	MOD-EXP	NA	NA
BRITISH AND IRISH					
Finnegan's Bar & Grill	UNIVERSAL STUDIOS FLORIDA	★★★	MOD	★★★	★★★
CAJUN/SOUTHERN					
Pat O'Brien's Orlando	CITYWALK	★★★	MOD	★★★½	★★★½
The Bubba Gump Shrimp Co. Restaurant & Market	CITYWALK	★★½	MOD	★★★	★★½
CARIBBEAN/JAMAICAN					
Strong Water Tavern	SAPPHIRE FALLS RESORT	★★★½	INEXP-MOD	★★★★	★★½
Amatista Cookhouse	SAPPHIRE FALLS RESORT	★★★	MOD-EXP	★★★	★★★
Bob Marley—A Tribute to Freedom	CITYWALK	★★★	INEXP-MOD	★★★	★★★
Jimmy Buffett's Margaritaville	CITYWALK	★★★	MOD	★★★	★★★

UNIVERSAL RESTAURANTS BY CUISINE (continued)

CUISINE	LOCATION	OVERALL RATING	COST	QUALITY RATING	VALUE RATING
ITALIAN					
Vivo Italian Kitchen	CITYWALK	★★★★	MOD	★★★★	★★★★½
Mama Della's Ristorante	PORTOFINO BAY HOTEL	★★★★	MOD-EXP	★★★★	★★★★
Bice Ristorante	PORTOFINO BAY HOTEL	★★★★	EXP	★★★★	★★★½
Trattoria del Porto	PORTOFINO BAY HOTEL	★★★	MOD	★★★	★★
MEXICAN					
Antojitos Authentic Mexican food	CITYWALK	★★★½	MOD	★★★½	★★★½
SEAFOOD					
The Cowfish Sushi Burger Bar	CITYWALK	★★★★	MOD	★★★★	★★★½
Mythos Restaurant	ISLANDS OF ADVENTURE	★★★½	MOD	★★★½	★★★★
Orchid Court Lounge & Sushi Bar	ROYAL PACIFIC RESORT	★★★½	MOD-EXP	★★★½	★★★
Lombard's Seafood Grille	UNIVERSAL STUDIOS FLORIDA	★★★	MOD	★★★½	★★★
The Bubba Gump Shrimp Co. Restaurant & Market	CITYWALK	★★½	MOD	★★★	★★½
Atlantic	EPIC UNIVERSE	NA	MOD-EXP	NA	NA
STEAK					
The Palm	HARD ROCK HOTEL	★★★★	V. EXP	★★★★	★★½
Mythos Restaurant	ISLANDS OF ADVENTURE	★★★½	MOD	★★★½	★★★★
Bigfire	CITYWALK	★★★½	MOD-EXP	★★★½	★★★½
NBC Sports Grill & Brew	CITYWALK	★★½	MOD	★★½	★★★

continued from page 341

Dress Casual. **Disabled access** Good. **Hours** Sunday–Thursday, 5 p.m.–midnight; Friday–Saturday, 5 p.m.–1 a.m. Food service ends at 10:30 p.m.

SETTING AND ATMOSPHERE Located on the roof of the Aventura Hotel, Bar 17 Bistro boasts a better view than any watering hole at Walt Disney World, with 360-degree views of both Universal Orlando—including Volcano Bay—and International Drive.

HOUSE SPECIALTIES Burgers, salads, bao sandwiches, noodles and rice dishes, and bar appetizers.

ENTERTAINMENT DJ from 8 p.m. to midnight on Friday and Saturday evenings.

SUMMARY AND COMMENTS Even if you aren't staying at Aventura, you'll want to visit the hotel just to ride the dedicated elevator to the 17th floor and take in the picture-postcard panorama from the roof. But the carefully balanced craft cocktails and savory small plates of exotic flavors are what will make you want to linger at Bar 17 Bistro long past sunset.

The views and atmosphere make Bar 17, but beverage quality also matches any bar on property. Begin by picking one of the signature cocktails or a draft craft beer. Next, order a couple of appetizers—some guests visit just for the Korean-style spicy fried chicken wings with gochujang sauce. Among the short selection of entrées, don't overlook the signature burger with mushrooms and "secret sauce #17."

A word of warning: Bar 17 Bistro's glorious open-air atmosphere includes complimentary exposure to wind and rain. In case of severe storms, the entire establishment may temporarily shut down, so watch the skies.

Bice Ristorante ★★★★

ITALIAN	EXPENSIVE		QUALITY ★★★★	VALUE ★★★½
READER-SURVEY RESPONSES	95% 👍	5% 👎		

Portofino Bay Hotel; ☎ 407-503-1415

Customers Locals and tourists. **Reservations** Recommended, through OpenTable, in person, or over the phone. **When to go** Dinner. **Entrée range** $28–$62. **Service rating** ★★★★. **Friendliness rating** ★★★★. **Parking** $11 valet or free self-parking at hotel with validation. **Bar** Full service. **Wine selection** Very good. **Dress** Resort dressy. **Disabled access** Good. **Hours** Daily, 5:30–10 p.m.

SETTING AND ATMOSPHERE Cedarwood and marble floors, crisp white linens, opulent flower arrangements, and waiters in black suits give Bice (pronounced BEE-chay) the feeling of a formal restaurant, but there is nothing stiff or fussy about the space or the staff. It's immaculately clean, beautifully lit, and relatively quiet even when crowded. Outdoor seating overlooking the bay is lovely on spring and fall evenings.

HOUSE SPECIALTIES The menu changes seasonally. Selections may include prosciutto with burrata and fig preserves, homemade braised beef short rib ravioli in mushroom-Marsala sauce, veal Milanese with an arugula and cherry tomato salad, or risotto of the day.

ENTERTAINMENT Piano in bar.

SUMMARY AND COMMENTS This is part of a chain of very upscale and quite impressive restaurants found in New York, Tokyo, Las Vegas, and other international locales. Be prepared: Even a modest meal will put a dent in your wallet, and even though the food and service are usually worth it, it may be too expensive for many vacationers. If you want to try a variety of things on the menu, split a salad, appetizer, or pasta dish between two people for a starter; portions are large enough for sharing, and the staff is more than happy to accommodate.

Our favorite appetizer is the fresh burrata mozzarella caprese. The other appetizers, mostly salads and antipasti of meats and cheeses, aren't bad, but you've probably had something similar already.

Among the best entrées is the breaded veal, which is pounded so thin that it takes up almost the entire plate. It's served with a small salad on top, and the salad's dressing keeps the veal juicy. The penne *all'arrabbiata* is even spicier than advertised.

We used to rate Bice as the best restaurant in all of Universal Orlando Resort, but we've received numerous reports of a post-pandemic decline in food and service quality. Bice's neighbor Mama Della's and CityWalk's Vivo are both better values for an Italian meal that's almost as upscale, but Bice still compares favorably to any of the similar restaurants at Walt Disney World. Because the Portofino gets a lot of business-convention traffic, it's probably easier to get a reservation at 5:30 p.m. than 7:30 p.m.

Bigfire ★★★½

AMERICAN/STEAK	MODERATE-EXPENSIVE		QUALITY ★★★½	VALUE ★★★
READER-SURVEY RESPONSES	86% 👍	14% 👎		

CityWalk; ☎ 407-224-2074

Customers Locals and tourists. **Reservations** Accepted through Universal. **When to go** Dinner. **Entrée range** $20–$53. **Service rating** ★★★. **Friendliness rating** ★★★★. **Parking** Universal Orlando garage. **Bar** Full service. **Wine selection** Good. **Dress** Casual. **Disabled access** Good. **Hours** Daily, 4–10 p.m.

SETTING AND ATMOSPHERE Bigfire takes its aesthetic cues from tony lakeside summer homes, with blazing fire pits out front, stained shiplap and decorative oars on the walls, and a skeletal boat's hull dramatically suspended from the vaulted ceiling. Hard surfaces can make the downstairs noisy, so request a table on the upper floor overlooking the main dining room. Fortunately, a powerful ventilation system keeps the blazing open kitchen from overheating the hall. You can also eat at the beautiful white marble bar, which boasts its own hand-selected barrel of Woodford Reserve bourbon.

HOUSE SPECIALTIES Fresh baked bread with herb butter, charred Brussels sprouts, and roasted mussels to start off. Flame-grilled meats cooked over a custom blend of oak and cherrywood is the menu's main focus. In addition to beef and pork, options include lamb, seafood, and vegetarian, as well as conventionally cooked entrées such as roasted chicken, burgers, and salads.

ENTERTAINMENT Prerecorded playlist of baby boomer soft-rock classics from the 1960s and '70s.

SUMMARY AND COMMENTS Bigfire's "American Fare" subtitle suggests even picky eaters will find something familiar on the menu, though the ingredients and preparations are a step above a T.G.I. Friday's–style chain restaurant. For beef eaters, the Florida-raised boneless rib eye is nearly as tender as the steaks served at The Palm but costs about 25% less and includes two sides (normally grilled asparagus and mashed potatoes, but you can upgrade to mac and cheese with bits of pork belly). But don't have a cow if you don't eat cow; the grilled cauliflower steak and vegan sausage cassoulet with black-eyed peas are both excellent, as are the beer-glazed jumbo scallops. For dessert, the tabletop s'mores for two are overpriced considering the vending machine components but are almost worth the entertainment value from flambéing marshmallows over a miniature campfire. Service is pleasant if unevenly paced, and readers have reported inconsistent food quality since this restaurant's debut. However, the current executive chef is making creative seasonal additions to the menu—like watermelon salad and elk sloppy joe—that help Bigfire maintain a balance between fine and family dining.

Blue Dragon Pan-Asian Restaurant (and Tiger Bar)

ASIAN	MODERATE-EXPENSIVE	QUALITY TBD	VALUE TBD
READER-SURVEY RESPONSES	Too new to rate		

Epic Universe; ☎ 407-224-FOOD (3663)

Customers Park guests. **Reservations** Accepted through Universal. **When to go** Dinner. **Entrée range** TBA. **Service rating** TBD. **Friendliness rating** TBD. **Parking** EU lot. **Bar** Full service. **Wine selection** Good. **Dress** Casual. **Disabled access** Good. **Hours** TBA.

SETTING AND ATMOSPHERE This indoor dining room is designed to appear like an open outdoor courtyard, set at perpetual twilight. Glowing lanterns float overheard, while sparkling neon lights in the shapes of dragons snake along the walls in this intimate and immersive dining environment.

HOUSE SPECIALTIES Japanese-, Chinese-, and Thai-inspired dishes, plus sake and Asian-inspired cocktails.

SUMMARY AND COMMENTS Located at the back of the park near the Helios Grand Hotel, and slightly less obvious to park-goers than the more front-and-center Atlantic, this restaurant features impeccable and dramatic theming you can only experience with a dining reservation.

Bob Marley—A Tribute to Freedom ★★★

JAMAICAN/CARIBBEAN **INEXPENSIVE–MODERATE** **QUALITY ★★★** **VALUE ★★★**
READER-SURVEY RESPONSES 86% 👍 14% 👎

CityWalk; ☎ 407-224-FOOD (3663)

Customers Locals and tourists. **Reservations** Accepted through Universal. **When to go** Early evening. **Entrée range** $15–$26. **Service rating ★★. Friendliness rating ★★★. Parking** Universal Orlando garage. **Bar** Full service. **Wine selection** Poor. **Dress** Casual. **Disabled access** Good. **Hours** Sunday–Thursday, 5 p.m.–midnight; Friday–Saturday, 5 p.m.–1 a.m.

SETTING AND ATMOSPHERE Set in a replica of reggae singer Bob Marley's Jamaican home, the building is filled with memorabilia and photos showcasing his career and life. Lots of lions, the colors of the Jamaican flag, and other Rastafarian influences pay tribute to the musician's career. Most of the area is open to the elements, and there's no air-conditioning, though there are shelters from the occasional rainstorm.

HOUSE SPECIALTIES Jerk-marinated chicken breast; Jamaican beef or vegetable patties; yucca fries; oxtail stew; curried chickpeas; stuffed peppers.

ENTERTAINMENT Live reggae band and DJ in courtyard nightly.

SUMMARY AND COMMENTS None of the food is spectacular or particularly adventurous, but it's worth a visit for the laid-back atmosphere. Feel free to get up and dance. Mobile Ordering is available for takeaway from the outdoor drink window.

The Bubba Gump Shrimp Co. Restaurant & Market ★★½

SOUTHERN/SEAFOOD **MODERATE** **QUALITY ★★★** **VALUE ★★½**
READER-SURVEY RESPONSES 87% 👍 13% 👎

CityWalk; ☎ 407-903-0044

Customers Tourists. **Reservations** Not accepted. **When to go** Anytime. **Entrée range** $18–$40. **Service rating ★★★. Friendliness rating ★★★★. Parking** Universal Orlando garage. **Bar** Full service. **Wine selection** Minimal. **Dress** Casual. **Disabled access** Good. **Hours** Sunday–Thursday, 11 a.m.–11 p.m.; Friday–Saturday, 11 a.m.–midnight.

SETTING AND ATMOSPHERE The movie that inspired the chain, *Forrest Gump*, plays on TVs throughout but without sound, just closed-captioning. Movie memorabilia decorates the wooden walls of this seafood shanty. License plates that say RUN FORREST RUN on one side and STOP FORREST STOP on another help signal a waiter when you need service, and waiters may ask you trivia questions from the movie.

HOUSE SPECIALTIES Fried, stuffed, or grilled shrimp (and shrimp cooked almost every other way); burgers; salads; grilled salmon; fried chicken; baby back ribs. A gluten-free menu is also offered.

SUMMARY AND COMMENTS The theme may seem a little cheesy, but this is a fun and festive atmosphere to bring the kids. The food is no worse than your average seafood chain (think Red Lobster without the cheese biscuits) and is not too spicy.

Confisco Grille ★★★

AMERICAN	MODERATE		QUALITY ★★★		VALUE ★★★
READER-SURVEY RESPONSES	82% 👍	18% 👎			

Islands of Adventure, Port of Entry; ☎ 407-224-4406

Customers Park guests. **Reservations** Accepted through Universal. **When to go** Anytime. **Entrée range** $18–$30. **Service rating** ★★★. **Friendliness rating** ★★★★. **Parking** Universal Orlando garage. **Bar** Full service. **Wine selection** Moderate. **Dress** Casual. **Disabled access** Good. **Hours** Daily, 11 a.m.–10 p.m. (varies with park closing).

SETTING AND ATMOSPHERE A way station on the road to Morocco, perhaps? Actually, it's meant to look like a customs house. Look for "smuggled goods," representing the park's various islands, decorating the lobby's upper level. You'll see giant dinosaur skeletons from *Jurassic Park,* golden urns from the Lost Continent, and even a wand from The Wizarding World of Harry Potter if you look hard enough.

HOUSE SPECIALTIES Spicy chicken wings or sweet-and-sour smoked ribs; hummus served with grilled pita bread; ahi tuna nachos; selection of salads; chicken, BLT, and banh mi sandwiches; noodle and fried rice bowls.

SUMMARY AND COMMENTS Confisco Grille isn't fine dining, but it does fine when you just can't stand in another line. Because of its varied menu of Mediterranean, Italian, Mexican, and Asian dishes, most people should find something to please them here. More-adventurous recommendations include Filipino-style sticky ribs, chilled soba noodle bowls with seared tuna sashimi, vegan "crab" cake, and Korean-style fried rice with your pick of protein; pass on the leathery pork belly. Several menu items can be made vegetarian- and vegan-friendly, and annual passholders get exclusive use of the **Navigator Club** dining room upstairs during select seasons. The adjoining **Backwater Bar** is a good spot to grab a cool sangria on a hot day.

The Cowfish Sushi Burger Bar ★★★★

AMERICAN/SUSHI	MODERATE		QUALITY ★★★★		VALUE ★★★½
READER-SURVEY RESPONSES	92% 👍	8% 👎			

CityWalk; ☎ 407-224-2690

Customers Locals and park guests. **Reservations** Accepted through Universal. **When to go** Early afternoon or late evening. **Entrée range** $12–$35. **Service rating** ★★½. **Friendliness rating** ★★★★. **Parking** Universal Orlando garage. **Bar** Full service. **Wine selection** Good. **Dress** Resort casual. **Disabled access** Good. **Hours** Sunday–Thursday, 11 a.m.–10 p.m.; Friday–Saturday, 11 a.m.–11 p.m.

SETTING AND ATMOSPHERE The Cowfish features colorful Pop Art displays (including a bug-eyed mascot out front for photo ops) and silly signage—be sure to check out the restrooms. Guests enter though the small lobby on the ground floor; all bars and seating—both indoors and out—are on the second and third floors. Young children will enjoy the touch-screen games and a make-your-own-fish app, which you can then watch swim in a virtual aquarium.

HOUSE SPECIALTIES Crab Rangoon dip, blackened tuna nachos, half-pound burgers, sushi and sashimi combos, fusion and Burgushi rolls and bento boxes, hand-spun milkshakes, specialty cocktails, and spiked shakes.

SUMMARY AND COMMENTS A one-of-a-kind dining concept that melds pan-Asian cuisine with the good ol' American burger, Cowfish's voluminous menu starts with familiar-sounding appetizers, such as Parmesan bacon truffle fries and tuna nachos. An extensive list of half-pound hormone-free hamburgers includes the standout Boursin Bacon Burger, with garlic-herb cheese and sautéed mushrooms. Traditional sushi selections range from chef combos of sashimi and nigiri to fusion makimono rolls; the premium tuna and salmon on Jen's Fresh Find roll is particularly flavorful.

Burgushi, the creative center of Cowfish's menu, offers sushi rolls made with Buffalo chicken, filet mignon, or barbecue pork. If you're still apprehensive, try a bento box, which brings a slider mini-burger, sushi roll, and several side dishes together on a Japanese TV dinner tray.

The extensive craft-cocktail list includes a bourbon-and-candied-bacon concoction and old-fashioned mules. Hand-spun milkshakes (nonalcoholic or spiked) headline the dessert menu, which also features yuzu-blueberry cheesecake.

We love the overall atmosphere, but the time it takes for a meal to come out of the undersized kitchen can be painfully slow. The wait can be long on a busy weekend, but the host will take your cell phone number when you check in, allowing them to text you when your table is ready.

Finnegan's Bar & Grill ★★★

IRISH	MODERATE	QUALITY ★★★	VALUE ★★★
READER-SURVEY RESPONSES	91% 👍	9% 👎	

Universal Studios Florida, New York; ☎ 407-363-8757

Customers Park guests. **Reservations** Accepted through Universal. **When to go** Anytime. **Entrée range** $17–$36. **Service rating** ★★★. **Friendliness rating** ★★★★. **Parking** Universal Orlando garage. **Bar** Full service. **Wine selection** Limited. Ireland isn't really known for its wines; good beer selection, though. **Dress** Casual. **Disabled access** Good. **Hours** Daily, 11 a.m.–park closing.

SETTING AND ATMOSPHERE Fashioned after an Irish bar in New York City, albeit one built as a movie set. Along with the requisite publike accoutrements—such as the tin ceiling and belt-driven paddle fans—are movie lights and half walls that suggest the back of scenery flats. Obligatory references to Guinness beer and New York City abound. The bar area is a popular gathering spot for locals and gets insanely busy during special events like Halloween Horror Nights.

HOUSE SPECIALTIES Shepherd's pie (beef or vegan); fish and chips; Guinness beef stew; bangers and mash; shrimp with boxty (potato pancakes); Irish coffee.

ENTERTAINMENT Singer/guitarist in the bar.

SUMMARY AND COMMENTS The food is modest, but the entertainment is fun and the beer is cold. Brew fans can happily explore six mixed draughts of international ales as they rest from the park. Add to that the fact that this is one of only two full-service spots in USF, and the average pub fare starts to look a bit more attractive.

The fish and chips, which come wrapped in "newspaper," are about the same as those served in The Wizarding World. The shepherd's pie is bland, but the potato-leek soup is good, and the fried potato–onion "web" is addictive. For entrées, burgers, sandwiches, salads, and Guinness stew are safe choices.

Galaxy Bowl ★★½

AMERICAN	INEXPENSIVE–MODERATE		QUALITY ★★½		VALUE ★★½
READER-SURVEY RESPONSES	74% 👍	26% 👎			

Cabana Bay Beach Resort; ☎ 407-503-4230

Customers Hotel guests. **Reservations** Accepted for parties of three or more through Resy; required for bowling. **When to go** Early afternoon or late evening. **Entrée range** $11–$28. **Service rating** ★★. **Friendliness rating** ★★★. **Parking** Universal Orlando garage or $53 for self-parking at hotel. **Bar** Full service. **Wine selection** Limited. **Dress** Casual. **Disabled access** Good. **Hours** Daily, noon–11 p.m. (bowling noon–11 p.m.; last lane-reservation time at 10:45 p.m.).

SETTING AND ATMOSPHERE Galaxy Bowl, on the second floor of the main Cabana Bay building directly above Starbucks, is the only full-service dining option inside the hotel. The 10-lane bowling alley is inspired by Hollywood Star Lanes, made famous in the film *The Big Lebowski*. The lanes are illuminated in trippy colors at night, and large projection screens broadcast sporting events.

HOUSE SPECIALTIES Cheese curds, chicken wings, salads, sandwiches, burgers, ribs, and loaded fries.

ENTERTAINMENT Bowling costs $22 per person ($20 before 5 p.m. Monday–Friday), including shoe rental, for 45 minutes of lane time with 1–3 bowlers or 75 minutes with 4–6; reservations required.

SUMMARY AND COMMENTS Galaxy Bowl has several tables where you can enjoy a meal before or after bowling, but you are not permitted to eat while sitting at a lane. The limited menu offers above-par greasy bowling alley grub, along with fast-food selections similar to dishes served downstairs in the Bayliner Diner. Draft beer is served in pitchers, and the list of specialty drinks is nearly as long as the food menu. There are Coke Freestyle machines for your refillable mugs. If you want the alcohol without the ambience of falling pins, the hotel lobby's **Swizzle Lounge** (open daily, 1 p.m.–midnight; hours subject to change) serves craft beers and classic cocktails, with a wide array of whiskeys.

Hard Rock Cafe ★★★

AMERICAN	MODERATE		QUALITY ★★★	VALUE ★★★
READER-SURVEY RESPONSES	90% 👍	10% 👎		

CityWalk; ☎ 407-351-7625

Customers Tourists. **Reservations** Accepted at cafe.hardrock.com/orlando or via OpenTable. **When to go** Afternoon or evening. **Entrée range** $19–$42. **Service rating** ★★★. **Friendliness rating** ★★. **Parking** Universal Orlando garage. **Bar** Full service. **Wine selection** Moderate. **Dress** Casual. **Disabled access** Good. **Hours** Daily, 11 a.m.–midnight.

SETTING AND ATMOSPHERE This is the biggest Hard Rock Cafe in the world (or in the Universe, as they like to say in this part of town). Shaped like the Roman Coliseum, the two-story dining room is a massive museum of rock art memorabilia. The circular center bar features a full-size pink 1959 Cadillac spinning overhead. If you need to be told that this is a noisy restaurant, you've never been to a Hard Rock Cafe before.

HOUSE SPECIALTIES Barbecue pork sandwich, charbroiled burgers, barbecue ribs, New York strip steak, hot fudge brownie, and milkshakes.

ENTERTAINMENT Rock-and-roll records and memorabilia, the biggest such collection on display anywhere in the Hard Rock chain. Ask at the check-in podium about free guided Vibe tours of the restaurant; if you're lucky, you may get a glimpse of the VIP-only John Lennon Room upstairs. Enjoy live music on the patio, 7–10 p.m. on most Fridays and Saturdays.

SUMMARY AND COMMENTS The best meals we've had here are when we order only appetizers (try the spicy Bangkok shrimp) or only desserts, and drinks. The entrées are average, and you'd be hard-pressed to differentiate them from anything you'd get at, say, Margaritaville. For vegans, the Impossible plant-based burger is nearly indistinguishable from the real thing. We like sitting at the bar, where service can be slow, but the snarky bartenders provide plenty of entertainment.

Hard Rock Cafe offers a 15% discount on food for Preferred and Premier annual passholders and military personnel with ID; 10% AAA discounts also apply. You can sign up for a Unity by Hard Rock membership at unity .hardrock.com to get additional offers and earn points on purchases (including alcohol). Be aware that admission to the adjoining Hard Rock Live concert hall is completely separate from the restaurant, though you can sometimes order food from the venue's bar.

Islands Dining Room ★★★½

PAN-ASIAN	MODERATE	QUALITY ★★★½	VALUE ★★★
READER-SURVEY RESPONSES	76% 👍	24% 👎	

Royal Pacific Resort; ☎ 407-503-3410

Customers Hotel guests. **Reservations** Accepted through Resy. **When to go** Breakfast or dinner. **Entrée range** Breakfast, $13–$21; dinner, $22–$48. **Service rating** ★★★. **Friendliness rating** ★★★. **Parking** $5 valet or free self-parking at hotel with validation. **Bar** Full service. **Wine selection** Average. **Dress** Casual. **Disabled access** Good. **Hours** *Breakfast:* Monday–Friday, 7–11 a.m.; Saturday–Sunday, 7 a.m.–noon; *dinner:* daily, 6–10 p.m.

SETTING AND ATMOSPHERE Pretty standard hotel dining room: big and open, and always spotless.

HOUSE SPECIALTIES Breakfast features waffles with mixed berries, Tahitian French toast à l'orange, and pancakes. Dinner options include stir-fry, fried rice, sticky-glazed ribs, and Korean bulgogi-style rib eye.

SUMMARY AND COMMENTS Breakfast here is a treat—the specialties are all tasty and (surprisingly) moderately priced; the morning buffet with custom omelets and smoked salmon costs $34 ($18 ages 3–9). At dinner, start with the chicken lettuce wraps, which are large enough to share. The all-you-can-eat Wok Experience, available every Friday and Saturday (plus select nights, seasonally) for $42 per person ($16 for kids), comes with a soup, salad, and dessert bar, along with bottomless bowls of made-to-order stir-fry; it's highly recommended by our resident gourmand Derek Burgan. A full plant-based menu is also available, but its noodle dishes tend to be bland; you're better off sticking with the Wok Experience, which offers tofu and vegan sauces. The à la carte steaks, ribs, and fried rice are good, but the teriyaki salmon is overwhelmed by its sweet honey glaze. Try the Hawaiian parfait of pineapple and white chocolate mousse for dessert.

Jake's American Bar ★★★

AMERICAN	MODERATE	QUALITY ★★★	VALUE ★★½
READER-SURVEY RESPONSES	80% 👍	20% 👎	

Royal Pacific Resort; ☎ 407-503-DINE (3463)

Customers Hotel guests. **Reservations** Accepted through Resy. **When to go** Early or late evening. **Entrée range** $15–$48. **Service rating** ★★★. **Friendliness rating** ★★★. **Parking** $5 valet or free self-parking at hotel with validation. **Bar** Full service. **Wine selection** Average. **Dress** Resort casual. **Disabled access** Good. **Hours** Daily, 11 a.m.–1 a.m. (kitchen closes 11 p.m.).

SETTING AND ATMOSPHERE Run-of-the-mill hotel bar and restaurant with a vaguely 1930s "Rick's Cafe" feel. The menu explains the backstory of Captain Jake McNally and his association with Royal Pacific Airways, continuing the overall theme of the resort, which centers on the golden age of travel.

HOUSE SPECIALTIES Homemade pretzel rods, hot wings, Mediterranean meze platter, pizzas, rib eye and frites, salmon with risotto, and grilled bacon-and-cheese sandwich.

ENTERTAINMENT Live music on select nights, 8–11 p.m.

SUMMARY AND COMMENTS This is a viable option if you're staying in the hotel, but as far as special meals go, this place doesn't deliver—and it really isn't meant to.
  Beer lovers will want to check out the four-sample flights, as well as the five-course pairing parties held periodically (visit theugseries.com/jakesbeer for Jake's Beer Dinner schedule). Jake's serves a limited late-night menu and is usually the only table-service restaurant at the resort serving hot food after 10 p.m.

Jimmy Buffett's Margaritaville ★★★

CARIBBEAN/AMERICAN	MODERATE	QUALITY ★★★	VALUE ★★★
READER-SURVEY RESPONSES	76% 👍	24% 👎	

CityWalk; ☎ 407-224-2155

Customers Local and tourist Parrot Heads. **Reservations** Accepted through Universal. **When to go** Early evening. **Entrée range** $19–$37. **Service rating** ★★★. **Friendliness rating** ★★★★. **Parking** Universal Orlando garage. **Bar** Full service. **Wine selection** Minimal. **Dress** Floral shirts and flip-flops. **Disabled access** Good. **Hours** Sunday–Thursday, 11 a.m.–10 p.m.; Friday–Saturday, 11 a.m.–11 p.m.

SETTING AND ATMOSPHERE A boisterous tribute to the chief Parrot Head, this two-story dining space has many large-screen TVs playing Jimmy Buffett music videos and scenes from his live performances. The focal point is a volcano that erupts occasionally, spewing margarita mix instead of lava.

HOUSE SPECIALTIES Cheeseburgers and margaritas, of course; volcano nachos; fish tacos; jambalaya; coconut shrimp; Key lime pie.

ENTERTAINMENT Live music on the porch early; a band plays on the inside stage during the late evening.

SUMMARY AND COMMENTS This is a relaxing, festive place, but it's not always worth the wait (especially if it's 2 hours, which it's been known to be). This place is wildly popular with Jimmy Buffett fans, who stand in line just to get on the wait list, so they can stand in line some more and wait for a table. The atmosphere, though, is like a taste of the beach without having to travel to the coast.
  The food is a mix of Floridian and Caribbean, so expect lots of seafood and Jamaican seasoning. The food is good, but not good enough for non-Buffett fans to make a special trip. If the line for a table is outrageous, see if you can sidle up to the bar for a margarita and appetizers, which is just as much—if not more—fun than actually having a full meal. None of the entrées, including the cheeseburger, will make you think you're in paradise, but fans don't seem to care.

The **Lone Palm Airport** tiki bar, across from the restaurant (home to Buffett's seaplane, the *Hemisphere Dancer*), is a great place to sit back with a drink and people-watch on CityWalk.

The Kitchen ★★★½

AMERICAN	MODERATE-EXPENSIVE		QUALITY ★★★★		VALUE ★★★
READER-SURVEY RESPONSES	94% 👍	6% 👎			

Hard Rock Hotel; ☎ 407-503-2430

Customers Tourists. **Reservations** Recommended through Resy. **When to go** Breakfast or dinner. **Entrée range** $18–$47. **Service rating** ★★★. **Friendliness rating** ★★★★. **Parking** $5 valet or free self-parking at hotel with validation. **Bar** Full service. **Wine selection** Good. **Dress** Casual. **Disabled access** Good. **Hours** Sunday–Thursday, 7 a.m.–10 p.m.; Friday–Saturday, 7 a.m.–11 p.m.

SETTING AND ATMOSPHERE With the appearance of a spacious kitchen in a rock megastar's mansion, The Kitchen features walls adorned with culinary-themed memorabilia from the Hard Rock Hotel's many celebrity guests. A colorful "kids' crib" adorned with beanbag chairs and TVs allows the adults to eat in peace.

HOUSE SPECIALTIES Breakfast choices include eggs Benedict, spinach-and-sausage frittata, and custom omelets. The lunch menu has salads, burgers, flatbreads, three-cheese mac and cheese, and sandwiches. At dinner, grilled sustainable salmon, bone-in tomahawk steaks, seared scallops, and vegan Bolognese are served. A gluten-free menu is available.

ENTERTAINMENT Rock stars occasionally visit to cook their specialties at the Chef's Table, so call ahead to see if any rock stars will be in the kitchen. Signed aprons and rock memorabilia hang on the walls. Magicians perform tableside on Wednesdays and Fridays, 6–10 p.m. On Mondays and Thursdays at Kids Can Cook, kids create their own pizzas or quesadillas. Enjoy live music during Sunday brunch, 10:30 a.m.–2 p.m.

SUMMARY AND COMMENTS Though we must admit our expectations weren't too high for this Hard Rock venture, we were pleasantly surprised with the food and service here. Though some entrées are expensive, the food is actually quite good, and the setting is pretty fun. Start with some wonderfully fluffy fresh-baked focaccia bread. The half-pound Kitchen burger is tasty, and quite a bargain compared with the humongous Kitchen Sink Cake. The luxurious lobster mac and cheese is a smart pick for shellfish fans, but skip the lamb unless you like your chops well-done. The $34 daily buffet breakfast ($18 for kids ages 3–9 and free for kids under 3; 7–11 a.m.) includes waffles or French toast, plus made-to-order omelets, scrambled eggs, bacon and sausage, and cinnamon rolls. The Kitchen offers happy hour specials all day on Sundays, and an "Acoustic Brunch" (10:30 a.m.–2 p.m.; $64 adults, $37 for kids ages 10–20, $20 for ages 3–9) adds smoked salmon, carving stations, and bottomless Bloody Marys and mimosas.

Lombard's Seafood Grille ★★★

SEAFOOD	MODERATE		QUALITY ★★★½		VALUE ★★★
READER-SURVEY RESPONSES	84% 👍	16% 👎			

Universal Studios Florida, San Francisco; ☎ 407-224-3613

Customers Park guests. **Reservations** Recommended through Universal. **When to go** Anytime. **Entrée range** $19–$37. **Service rating** ★★★. **Friendliness rating** ★★★.

Parking Universal Orlando garage. **Bar** Full service. **Wine selection** Good. **Dress** Casual. **Disabled access** Good. **Hours** Daily, 11 a.m.–9 p.m. (varies with park closing).

SETTING AND ATMOSPHERE Situated on the park's main lagoon, Lombard's looks like a converted wharf-side warehouse. The centerpiece of the brick-walled room is a huge aquarium with bubble glass windows, and a fish-sculpture fountain greets guests. Private dining rooms upstairs have balconies that overlook the park.

HOUSE SPECIALTIES Fried calamari, mahi-mahi tacos, fried fisherman's basket, lobster roll, rib eye steak, and fresh fish.

SUMMARY AND COMMENTS This is USF's San Francisco–inspired seafood restaurant, where the emphasis is on deep-fried favorites and daily fresh-fish specials. Lombard's has a casual focus, and unfortunately, so does the kitchen. The New England clam chowder is a standout, as is the shellfish-filled cioppino, and the lobster roll is loaded with tender tail and knuckle meat, but the tuna poké is oddly salsa-like, with a tomato-heavy garnish. Stick to the grilled or fried fish and you should be safe. There are arguably better food options in the park, but as one of only two full-service restaurants inside USF, it's your best choice for a quiet meal.

With two floors of seating, it's generally easy to get a table, even during the busier times. Only annual passholders may request to dine upstairs during select seasons.

Mama Della's Ristorante ★★★★

ITALIAN	MODERATE-EXPENSIVE		QUALITY ★★★★	VALUE ★★★★
READER-SURVEY RESPONSES	96% 👍	4% 👎		

Portofino Bay Hotel; ☎ 407-503-1432

Customers Hotel guests. **Reservations** Recommended through Resy. **When to go** Dinner. **Entrée range** $24–$46. **Service rating** ★★★★. **Friendliness rating** ★★★★. **Parking** $11 valet or free self-parking at hotel with validation. **Bar** Full service. **Wine selection** Good. **Dress** Nice casual. **Disabled access** Good. **Hours** Daily, 5–10 p.m.

SETTING AND ATMOSPHERE Just like being in the dining room of a Tuscan home, with hardwood floors, Provincial printed wallpaper, and wooden furniture. Check out the collection of chicken-themed tchotchkes on the walls.

HOUSE SPECIALTIES Veal piccata, pan-seared branzino, filet mignon with truffled potatoes, and lasagna.

ENTERTAINMENT Strolling musicians perform Italian American standards on select evenings.

SUMMARY AND COMMENTS This restaurant falls on the fancy scale somewhere between Bice and Trattoria del Porto. Traditional Italian food is served in a comfortable atmosphere conducive to a special meal but not quite as extravagant as its lavish neighbor, Bice. If you want food that's just as tasty but for (a bit) less dough, Mama Della's is a great choice.

Mythos Restaurant ★★★½

STEAK/SEAFOOD	MODERATE		QUALITY ★★★½	VALUE ★★★★
READER-SURVEY RESPONSES	92% 👍	8% 👎		

Islands of Adventure, The Lost Continent; ☎ 407-224-4534

Customers Park guests. **Reservations** Recommended through Universal. **When to go** Early evening. **Entrée range** $20–$38. **Service rating** ★★★½. **Friendliness rating** ★★★.

Parking Universal Orlando garage. **Bar** Full service. **Wine selection** Good. **Dress** Casual. **Disabled access** Good. **Hours** Daily, 11 a.m.–10 p.m. (varies with park closing).

SETTING AND ATMOSPHERE A grotto-like atmosphere suggests that you're eating in a cave. Large picture windows, framed by water cascading down from waterfalls on top of the restaurant, look out over the central lagoon to The Incredible Hulk Coaster. You can time your meal by coaster launchings.

HOUSE SPECIALTIES Fried calamari, meze platter, Greek salad, pan-roasted salmon, blue cheese–crusted pork, beef medallions, grilled cheese sandwich, bacon cheeseburger, pad Thai, and asparagus risotto with sea scallops.

SUMMARY AND COMMENTS Outside the restaurant is a sign proclaiming that Mythos was voted World's Best Theme Park Restaurant by visitors to the website themeparkinsider.com—an honor it has earned 10 times, most recently in 2022.

The food is well above average for theme park eats, and the setting provides a pleasant retreat. The spanakopita dip isn't far off from T.G.I. Friday's spinach dip, but the meze platter and jumbo prawns in tomato sauce are satisfying. Your best bets among the entrées are the cranberry pork chop (one of Seth's favorite entrées on property); the lamb burger; the Fork, Knife and Spoon Grilled Cheese (Derek Burgan's recommendation); or the beef medallions, which are equal in quality but less expensive than similar steaks at EPCOT. A Big Apple–based friend of the *Unofficial Guide* had this to say:

> *I had a beautiful piece of salmon at Mythos, and while the theme left something to be desired, everything it served was on par with what I would expect at a decent New York restaurant.*

Make an early reservation if you want to dine here on a busy day. During off-season, Mythos may close before dinnertime, as this reader discovered:

> *We were disappointed to find out that Mythos closed at 5 when the park closed at 7 p.m. Due to its popularity, only the Harry Potter area remained completely open until 7 p.m.*

NBC Sports Grill & Brew ★★½

AMERICAN/STEAK	MODERATE	QUALITY ★★½	VALUE ★★★
READER-SURVEY RESPONSES	78% 👍	22% 👎	

CityWalk ☎ 407-224-2690

Customers Sports fans. **Reservations** Accepted through Universal. **When to go** When the game is on. **Entrée range** $14–$33. **Service rating** ★★★. **Friendliness rating** ★★★½. **Parking** Universal Orlando garage. **Bar** Full service; more than 100 beers. **Wine selection** Average. **Dress** Casual. **Disabled access** Good. **Hours** Sunday–Thursday, 11 a.m.–10 p.m.; Friday–Saturday, 11 a.m.–11 p.m.

SETTING AND ATMOSPHERE NBC Sports Grill & Brew has nearly 100 big-screen TVs, so guests will have no problem ignoring their tablemates to watch the latest game. The decor is intended to evoke a luxury skybox (though it's more like sports bar industrial with dark concrete floors and exposed duct-work ceilings painted black), and the central show kitchen contains a signature open-flame kettle grill. Sadly, the giant steel fermenting tanks are only for show, as no brewing takes place on the premises. Bonus: Some dining tables are playable games (such as Foosball) with glass tops for the food. The exterior is distinguished by a supersize video screen that broadcasts games to all of CityWalk; during major events (like the Olympics), bleachers may be erected outside for alfresco viewing.

HOUSE SPECIALTIES Nachos, wraps, grilled wings, flatbreads, salads, ribs, steaks, and burgers.

SUMMARY AND COMMENTS With a large selection of burgers and beers, NBC Sports Grill & Brew is the go-to place at Universal to catch the latest game. The menu is surprisingly deep, and the open kitchen concept allows you to see the chefs in action. Beer lovers will be drawn to the large variety of selections (more than 100), including two brewed exclusively for the restaurant by Florida Beer Company, and a fresh firkin-contained ale that's hand-pumped from the cask.

As for the food, it's decent but not especially memorable. The slow-cooked birria-style chicken wings and Cajun deviled eggs are both pleasingly piquant (but not excessively spicy), the steaks and fresh fish sandwich are unexpectedly excellent, and the monster soft pretzel (served on its own stand with mustard and queso) has a cult following. Otherwise, stick to burgers and beer.

Orchid Court Lounge & Sushi Bar ★★★½

AMERICAN/ASIAN/SUSHI	MODERATE-EXPENSIVE	QUALITY ★★★½	VALUE ★★★
READER-SURVEY RESPONSES 90% 👍 10% 👎			

Royal Pacific Resort; ☎ 407-503-3200

Customers Hotel guests. **Reservations** Accepted through Resy. **When to go** Early or late evening. **Entrée range** $12–$80. **Service rating** ★★★. **Friendliness rating** ★★★. **Parking** $5 valet or free self-parking at hotel with validation. **Bar** Full service. **Wine selection** Average, but an excellent sake selection. **Dress** Resort casual. **Disabled access** Good. **Hours** Daily, 5 p.m.–1 a.m. (kitchen closes 11 p.m.).

SETTING AND ATMOSPHERE Located on the lobby level of the Royal Pacific Resort with gorgeous views of the pool and central reflecting fountain, the Orchid Court Lounge is filled with light and furnished in cool, contemporary colors. In the center of the lounge, you'll find a chandelier-crowned bar with both liquor and traditional sushi in see-through cases. Surrounding the four-sided bar, clusters of couches and armchairs form cozy seating areas.

HOUSE SPECIALTIES The sushi bar offers miso soup, seaweed salad, edamame, tuna *tataki, nigiri,* sashimi, makimono rolls, and cold and warm sake.

ENTERTAINMENT Live music on Friday and Saturday, 8–11 p.m.

SUMMARY AND COMMENTS The Orchid Court Lounge, which almost exclusively caters to guests staying at the Royal Pacific Resort, has sushi chefs who prepare fishy fare that falls (in terms of quality and creativity) somewhere between The Cowfish at CityWalk and Aventura's Urban Pantry. Most of the rolls are adequate executions of Japanese American standards—California, spicy tuna, shrimp tempura, and volcano—but their specialty maki rolls feature some unfortunate flavor combinations, like cilantro and jalapeno with escolar. Ordering nigiri à la carte can quickly add up; stick with staples like salmon, and definitely skip the overpriced frozen sea urchin. While combinations aren't cheap either, the big boats for up to four people break down to a decent value.

The Palm ★★★★

STEAK	VERY EXPENSIVE	QUALITY ★★★★	VALUE ★★½
READER-SURVEY RESPONSES 88% 👍 12% 👎			

Hard Rock Hotel; ☎ 407-503-7256

Customers Tourists. **Reservations** Recommended through OpenTable. **When to go** Dinner. **Entrée range** $34–$155. **Service rating** ★★★. **Friendliness rating** ★★★. **Parking** Free valet at hotel with validation. **Bar** Full service. **Wine selection** Very good. **Dress**

Resort, business casual, or smart casual; no sleeveless men's shirts. **Disabled access** Good. **Hours** Sunday, 5–9 p.m.; Monday–Saturday, 5–10 p.m.

SETTING AND ATMOSPHERE Despite the celebrity caricatures drawn on the wall, the restaurant exudes sophistication due to the dark woods and white table-cloths. The chain's flagship location is in New York, and the decor reflects this. Waiters wear long, white aprons.

HOUSE SPECIALTIES New York strip, bone-in rib eye, lamb chops, veal parmigiana, whole live lobster, Chilean sea bass, King salmon, and iceberg lettuce wedge salad.

SUMMARY AND COMMENTS The crowd here can get noisy, so The Palm may not be the best place for a romantic night out. However, if you're looking to celebrate with friends or family, it's a good, if very expensive, choice. The signature dry-aged prime steaks are fork-tender, and even the typically tasteless filets are full of flavor (thanks to parsley butter and hefty flakes of salt), but longtime fans have reported a decline in beef quality since Landry's Inc. bought the brand. Stick with the ginormous lobsters—which are impeccably prepared and entertainingly disassembled tableside—especially during summer discounts on three-course dinners featuring a 4-pounder split between two people. The side dishes are meant for sharing, and the creamed spinach is justly famous. A "Prime Time" happy hour offers discounted drinks at the bar Sunday–Friday, 4–6:30 p.m. If you dine here more than once a year, look into joining Landry's Select Club (landrysselect.com) for discounts and exclusive event invitations.

Pat O'Brien's Orlando ★★★

CAJUN	MODERATE		QUALITY ★★★½		VALUE ★★★½
READER-SURVEY RESPONSES	92% 👍	8% 👎			

CityWalk; ☎ 407-224-2106

Customers Tourists. **Reservations** Accepted through Universal. **When to go** Anytime. **Entrée range** $18–$25. **Service rating** ★★. **Friendliness rating** ★★★. **Parking** Universal Orlando garage. **Bar** Full service. **Wine selection** Modest. **Dress** Casual. **Disabled access** Good. **Hours** Daily, 5 p.m.–midnight. Piano bar open Friday and Saturday until 1 a.m.

SETTING AND ATMOSPHERE A fairly faithful rendition of the original Pat O'Brien's in New Orleans, from the redbrick facade to the fire-and-water fountain in the courtyard. The outdoor dining area is the most pleasant place to eat in cooler weather. Inside areas include a noisy "locals" bar and a dueling piano bar, featuring some of Orlando's most talented musicians.

HOUSE SPECIALTIES Shrimp gumbo, jambalaya, crawfish étouffée, and blackened redfish.

SUMMARY AND COMMENTS The food is surprisingly good and surprisingly affordable. Be careful about ordering a Hurricane, the restaurant's signature drink. Not only is it deceptively potent, but the price includes the souvenir glass—whether you want to keep it or not.

Strong Water Tavern ★★★½

CARIBBEAN	INEXPENSIVE-MODERATE		QUALITY ★★★★		VALUE ★★½
READER-SURVEY RESPONSES	83% 👍	17% 👎			

Sapphire Falls Resort; ☎ 407-503-5447

Customers Hotel guests. **Reservations** Accepted through Resy. **When to go** Evenings. **Entrée range** $12–$40. **Service rating** ★★★. **Friendliness rating** ★★★. **Parking** $5 valet or free self-parking at hotel with validation. **Bar** Full service with extensive rum selection. **Wine selection** Average. **Dress** Casual. **Disabled access** Good. **Hours** Sunday–Thursday, 4 p.m.–midnight; Friday–Saturday, 4 p.m.–1 a.m. (kitchen closes 11 p.m.).

SETTING AND ATMOSPHERE One of the largest lobby bars at any Universal Resort hotel, Strong Water Tavern—like the rest of Sapphire Falls Resort—fuses organically aged objects and sleek modern elements. This New World watering hole sports oversize vintage couches on which to sprawl, faux reclaimed rum barrels forming the ceiling on the inside, and a spectacular view over the hotel's signature waterfalls from the patio. A video display wall, which usually broadcasts sports or a loop of Universal advertisements, dominates one end of the room. The centerpiece of Strong Water Tavern is the massive marble bar, which features a designated seating area for rum-tasting experiences.

HOUSE SPECIALTIES Ceviche, arroz con pollo, ropa vieja, and rum cocktails.

ENTERTAINMENT Live music on Friday and Saturday, 8 p.m.–midnight.

SUMMARY AND COMMENTS We love almost everything about Strong Water Tavern—the contemporary Caribbean atmosphere, the variety of fresh ceviches, the potent cocktails—except for the prices. Drink prices are a bit steep but not unreasonable, considering the top-shelf ingredients. A couple mugs of the Tavern Grog will make you want to join the merchant marines, and the $21 tasting flight lets you sample three rums that normally retail at up to $25 per shot; don't order the over-proof Hamilton 151 if you plan on driving home. While those who enjoy authentic West Indian, Cuban, and Puerto Rican recipes will feel right at home, your *abuela* would never dream of charging this much for such tiny tapas-style servings. Periodic rum dinners feature an hors d'oeuvres reception, five culinary courses paired with craft rums, and an after-party with coffee and cigars; visit sapphirefalls.tix.com for details.

Toothsome Chocolate Emporium & Savory Feast Kitchen
★★★½

CHOCOHOLIC-AMERICAN	MODERATE	QUALITY ★★★½	VALUE ★★★
READER-SURVEY RESPONSES	85% 👍 15% 👎		

CityWalk; ☎ 407-224-FOOD (3663)

Customers Tourists and locals. **Reservations** Strongly recommended through Universal. **When to go** Dinner or late-evening dessert. **Entrée range** $15–$38. **Service rating** ★★½. **Friendliness rating** ★★★★. **Parking** Universal Orlando garage. **Bar** Full service with craft cocktails. **Wine selection** Modest. **Dress** Casual. **Disabled access** Good. **Hours** Sunday–Thursday, 10:30 a.m.–10 p.m.; Friday–Saturday, 10:30 a.m.–11 p.m.

SETTING AND ATMOSPHERE Looming across the CityWalk lagoon like Willy Wonka's summer home, Toothsome Chocolate Emporium & Savory Feast Kitchen is a whimsical steampunk-styled factory that's strongly inspired by Roald Dahl's crazed confectioner (closer to the Johnny Depp version than Gene Wilder). This multistory brick-faced wonderland with billowing smokestacks houses imaginative industrial contraptions (both physical and projected on large video screens) adorned with antique doodads. Much of the ground floor is devoted to a takeaway milkshake counter; a glassed-in kitchen where you can watch sweets being assembled; and a shop full of chocolates, candies, and steampunk souvenirs. Upstairs seating includes decadent semicircular booths and a private dining room; make sure to get a good look at the fiber-optic ceiling sculpture near the serpentine second-floor bar.

HOUSE SPECIALTIES Warm chocolate almond bread, baked Brie, pork belly sliders, salads, flatbreads, sandwiches, hamburgers, pasta, steaks, and all-day brunch with quiche and crepes. And of course, drinks, desserts, and milkshakes with lots and lots of chocolate.

ENTERTAINMENT Actors portraying proprietress Penelope Toothsome and her animatronic assistant Jacques roam the restaurant interacting with guests. Brush up on their backstory (found on the first page of the menu) before they arrive at your table for a more in-depth conversation.

SUMMARY AND COMMENTS Many (though not all) of the offerings include some form of cocoa, from the old-fashioned cocktails with chocolate bitters to the chocolate mole sauce served on the gnocchi (ask for it as an accompaniment with the brisket and mushroom meat loaf). Prices are moderate, and portions are big enough to share or take home leftovers. Be sure to save room for the dark chocolate mousse, which is richer than any we've tasted outside Paris.

Reactions to Toothsome are increasingly divided. Although many readers raved about Toothsome's atmosphere and food in its early days, this family from York, Pennsylvania, reflects the experiences of a growing number of guests:

> *We were sooo excited about trying Toothsome and stopped by for an evening meal the day we came in. It was the biggest disappointment of the trip—the service is worse than slow, the food was nothing special, and the shake was absolutely horrible.*

Even Toothsome's fans complain about the chronically understaffed restaurant's inattentive service, such this mom from Gurnee, Illinois:

> *We really like Toothsome, but the service was so slow. It took over 2 hours, and with three kids, that was just too long for them to sit still.*

Toothsome's signature milkshakes are also available to-go from a downstairs counter; their stiff price tags may be difficult to swallow, particularly since the shakes themselves are achingly sweet and not especially thick or large. But at least they are served in a souvenir Mason jar and crowned with an absurd mountain of toppings, such as an entire cupcake, brownie, or slice of Key lime pie. (Be warned that the sour ice cream used in some varieties lives up to its name.) Despite the mixed reviews, Toothsome is extremely popular; if you can't get a reservation, ask if you can sit at the second-floor bar.

Trattoria del Porto ★★★

ITALIAN	MODERATE		QUALITY ★★★	VALUE ★★
READER-SURVEY RESPONSES	89% 👍	11% 👎		

Portofino Bay Hotel; ☎ 407-503-1430

Customers Hotel guests. **Reservations** Suggested for dinner through Resy. **When to go** Breakfast or dinner. **Entrée range** Breakfast, $19–$25; lunch and dinner, $18–$48. **Service rating** ★★★. **Friendliness rating** ★★★. **Parking** $11 valet or free self-parking at hotel with validation. **Bar** Full service. **Wine selection** Average. **Dress** Resort casual. **Disabled access** Good. **Hours** Daily, 7 a.m.–10 p.m.

SETTING AND ATMOSPHERE Like an upscale kitchen in an elegant Italian home, the restaurant features tiled floors and big curved booths, with warm orange accents among the cool blue benches and clean white walls.

HOUSE SPECIALTIES At breakfast, Belgian waffles, steak and eggs, and customized omelets. Sandwiches and chicken wings for lunch. At dinner, caprese salads, burgers, steaks, pastas, and house-made desserts.

SUMMARY AND COMMENTS Where Mama Della's succeeds in not feeling like a hotel restaurant, Trattoria del Porto does not. The food is perfectly fine and moderately priced (relatively speaking). Omelets at breakfast can set you back more than $20, so opt instead for the buffet ($34 adults, $18 kids ages 3–9) offered in the mornings.

Vivo Italian Kitchen ★★★★

ITALIAN	MODERATE	QUALITY ★★★★		VALUE ★★★★½
READER-SURVEY RESPONSES	85% 👍	15% 👎		

CityWalk; ☎ 407-224-3663

Customers Locals and tourists. **Reservations** Accepted through Universal. **When to go** Dinner. **Entrée range** $14–$42. **Service rating** ★★★½. **Friendliness rating** ★★★½. **Parking** Universal Orlando garage. **Bar** Full service. **Wine selection** Good. **Dress** Casual. **Disabled access** Good. **Hours** Monday–Friday, 4–10 p.m.; Saturday–Sunday, 3–10 p.m.

SETTING AND ATMOSPHERE Sleek and contemporary without being stuffy, Vivo brings a touch of casual class to CityWalk's central crossroads. There are outdoor tables (with embedded chessboards) and a well-lit bar, along with plush semicircular booths surrounded by sinuous steel cages. But the real action is around the open kitchen; see if you can snag a seat at the food bar in front of the "tree" where fresh pasta is hung.

HOUSE SPECIALTIES Freshly made pasta, homemade mozzarella, pizza, salads, lasagna, chicken Marsala, and risotto.

SUMMARY AND COMMENTS Vivo is Universal's best Italian food outside Portofino Bay. The menu is filled with classic recipes prepared à la minute with the freshest ingredients, such as chicken piccata, veal parmigiana, spinach ravioli, and spaghetti Bolognese. Best of all, you can dine here for half the price of Bice, Mama Della's, or one of Disney's Signature restaurants.

Start with some hefty house-made meatballs or arugula salad with hand-pulled burrata, and ask for an extra basket of fresh-baked bread. Standout entrées include linguine with seasonal clams, black squid ink pasta with seafood, and lamb chops with risotto. On a cost-quality basis, this may be the best table-service meal you'll have on Universal property. If there's a long wait for a table, ask to eat at the bar.

Wantilan Luau ★★★★

HAWAIIAN	EXPENSIVE	QUALITY ★★★★		VALUE ★★★
READER-SURVEY RESPONSES	86% 👍	14% 👎		

Royal Pacific Resort; ☎ 407-503-DINE (3463)

Customers Tourists. **Reservations** Required through wantilanluau.eventbrite.com. **When to go** Dinner only. **Entrée range** Buffet: $114 adults, $53 children ages 3–9. (Prices include tax, fees, and gratuity for everyone, and mai tais, wine, and beer for guests age 21 and older.) **Service rating** ★★★. **Friendliness rating** ★★★★. **Parking** Free valet or free self-parking at hotel with validation. **Bar** Mai tais, wine, and beer included. **Wine selection** Limited. **Dress** Floral shirts, beachy casual. **Disabled access** Average. **Hours** Saturday; seating begins at 6 p.m., with registration starting 30 minutes before.

SETTING AND ATMOSPHERE Typical luau setting: tiki torches and wooden tables.

HOUSE SPECIALTIES Buffet includes pit-roasted suckling pig with spiced rum–soaked pineapple purée; Pacific catch of the day; Hawaiian chicken teriyaki; fire-grilled beef with mushrooms; and chicken fingers, mac and cheese, PB&J,

and pizza for kids. Dessert buffet has white chocolate mousse shots, passion fruit crème brûlée, and Kona coffee tarts.

ENTERTAINMENT Polynesian dancing, storytelling, hula dancers, and live music.

SUMMARY AND COMMENTS This is a fun diversion and a change of scenery from the other restaurants on Universal property. Though dinner is a bit expensive, it's among the best food of any dinner show in the area, and the entertainment is more energetic than Disney's now-defunct luau. Premium Seating gets you a souvenir tiki mug and a reserved table near the stage for an extra $23 per person. The check-in process can take a while, so send the rest of your party to watch the preshow on the nearby lawn while one member waits in line, but be sure to line up by the open-air venue's entrance before seating starts to get first crack at the buffet. The culinary star of the show is the roast pork, and the seared ahi tuna salad and cedar-plank roasted salmon are also excellent, but the bottomless mai tais are overpoweringly sweet. Food (with musical accompaniment) is served until 7:15 p.m., with the main show cranking up at 7. The hour-long entertainment features grass-skirted dancers paying tribute to the traditions of Hawaiian, Māori, and Tahitian cultures, climaxing in a dazzling display of fire twirling. This reader from Medford Lakes, New Jersey, wrote us saying the luau was a highlight of his Halloween trip:

> Very well done—very good food for a buffet and top-notch entertainment. A bit pricey, but highly recommended.

DINING *near* UNIVERSAL ORLANDO

AS WE'VE MENTIONED PREVIOUSLY, guests staying at Universal Orlando's on-site resorts may find their dining options a bit limited and expensive compared to the restaurants found at some Walt Disney World hotels. The flip side is that, while Disney's resorts are largely isolated from the outside world, Universal hotel guests have an array of off-property eateries only a few minutes' drive—or even walk—away. And if you don't feel like leaving your hotel room, most of these restaurants deliver through Uber Eats, Grubhub, DoorDash, and similar mobile services.

The closest off-site restaurants to Universal Orlando are found among the hotels along Major Boulevard, just east of the resort entrance on Kirkman Road. **Miller's Ale House** (5573 S. Kirkman Road, ☎ 407-248-0000, millersalehouse.com) is a popular after-hours hangout for Universal employees and serves the largest chicken nachos you'll ever see. Chefs at **Kobe Japanese Steakhouse & Sushi Bar** (5605 S. Kirkman Road, ☎ 407-248-1978, kobesteakhouse.com) perform at teppanyaki tables; ask about lunchtime, happy hour, and late-night specials. On the opposite side of Major Boulevard, you'll find a run-of-the-mill **T.G.I. Friday's** and **Tabla Restaurant** (5847 Grand National Dr., ☎ 407-248-9400, tablacuisine.com), an upscale Indian-Thai-Chinese restaurant tucked into the back of a Clarion Inn. A **Wendy's** and **Burger King** round out the block; more fast-food franchises,

Soupa Saiyan ramen bar (5689 Vineland Road, ☎ 407-930-3396, linktr.ee/soupasaiyan1), and **Carrabba's Italian Grill** are across the street on the north side of Vineland Road. Continue a few lights farther north, and you'll find a strip mall at the corner of Kirkman and Conroy Roads, housing **Bubbalou's Bodacious Bar-B-Que** (5818 Conroy Road, ☎ 407-295-1212, kirkman.bubbalous.com); **Oodle Ramen** (5812 Conroy Road, ☎ 407-286-6232, oodleorlando.kwickmenu .com); and **Sloppy Taco Palace** (4892 S. Kirkman Road, ☎ 407-574-6474, sloppytacoorlando.com), which lives up to its name.

Slightly farther afield, international treasures near Universal property along International Drive include **Aashirwad Indian Cuisine** (7000 S. Kirkman Road, ☎ 407-370-9830, aashirwadrestaurant.com); **Ichiban** sushi buffet (5529 International Dr., ☎ 407-930-8889, ichibanbuffet .com); **BoiBrazil Churrascaria** (5668 International Dr., ☎ 407-354-0260, boibrazil.com); **Thai Silk** (5532 International Dr., ☎ 407-226-8997, thaisilkorlando.com); **Nile Ethiopian Restaurant** (7048 International Dr., ☎ 407-354-0026, nileorlando.com); **Sushi Yama** (6748 Grand National Dr., ☎ 407-420-0666, sushiyamaorlando.com); **World's Magic Indonesian Restaurant** (7044 International Dr., ☎ 407-777-6763, worldsmagic restaurant.com); and, for late-night munchies, **Del Taco** (6855 Grand National Dr., ☎ 407-363-0738, deltaco.com).

If you take Universal Boulevard south past I-Drive and Sand Lake Road, you can access rear entrances for I-Drive restaurants without the traffic, ending up at the **Pointe Orlando** shopping and dining complex. Finally, take Turkey Lake Road south from Universal to Sand Lake Road, and turn right toward Restaurant Row for a plethora of upscale chain restaurants, including **Seasons 52, Morton's Steakhouse, Ocean Prime,** and many more.

If you want to take a drive to downtown Orlando or beyond in search of a fine meal, we can vouch for **The Ravenous Pig** (565 W. Fairbanks Ave., ☎ 407-628-2333, theravenouspig.com); **Kabooki Sushi** (7705 Turkey Lake Road, ☎ 407-776-2001; or 3122 E. Colonial Dr., ☎ 407-228-3839; kabookisushi.com); **Saigon Noodle & Grill** (101 N. Bumby Ave., ☎ 407-532-7373, sngbumby.com); **Pig Floyd's Urban Barbakoa** (1326 N. Mills Ave., ☎ 407-203-0866, pigfloyds.com); and **The Strand** (807 N. Mills Ave., ☎ 407-920-7744, strandorlando.com).

SHOPPING *at* UNIVERSAL ORLANDO

YOU'LL HAVE PLENTY OF OPPORTUNITIES at Universal Orlando to take home overpriced dust magnets (oops, *priceless mementos*) from your stay. And if you're staying on-site, you can charge them to your room using your hotel key card; just be prepared for the reckoning upon checkout.

If you return home and realize you forgot something, you can order a selection of Universal Orlando merchandise online at shop.universalorlando.com.

SHOPPING AT UNIVERSAL STUDIOS FLORIDA

AS KANG AND KODOS OBSERVE at the end of The Simpsons Ride, it's apparently a state law that every Universal attraction must end in (or near) a gift shop. Most of these have the typical T-shirts and toys tied to the experience you just exited, though a few have offerings of note.

The Universal Studios Store sits near the park's entrance: if you forgot to get a gift elsewhere in the park, you can probably find it here. Browse the selection of exclusive character-themed candy bars, including a Jurassic Park fossil bar with candy dino bones, Sponge-Bob's white chocolate bar with pineapple bits, and Donkey's maple-flavored waffle bar, but beware the bins of bulk candies at **Studio Sweets;** they are priced per quarter pound, and small bags can add up very quickly. Sitting across the street from the Studios Store, **UNI-VRS** sells exclusive seasonal collections of trendy clothing featuring classic characters. It adjoins the eye-poppingly adorable **Hello Kitty** shop, with clothing, housewares, and countless other Sanrio-sanctioned products displaying the Japanese character and her cartoon friends; and the **Betty Boop Store,** which stocks Boop-centric accessories and apparel, including nightgowns. These stores also stock a selection of Funko Pop figurines and Loungefly bags representing various Universal-affiliated franchises. **It's A Wrap** straddles the park exit, selling last season's souvenirs at discount prices. If you prepurchased a My Universal Photos package, stop in **On Location** to activate it or pick up prints.

In **Minion Land, Super Silly Stuff** at Despicable Me Minion Mayhem is decorated like the candy-colored amusement park from the film. You can access the Minion photo op at the attraction's postshow (when available) from the shop if the ride's queue is too long. **Evil Stuff,** at the exit of Villain-Con Minion Blast, stocks toys and souvenirs celebrating Despicable Me's bad guys, including replicas of the attraction's blaster and customized convention badges; check out the statues of Minions cosplaying as their favorite fiends. Across the street, **Bake My Day** carries character cupcakes, prepackaged sweets, and candy-themed souvenirs.

New York's postride shops are fairly pedestrian, though you'll find NBC apparel at **The Tonight Shop** and faux-Egyptian jewelry (plus creepy photo-ops) in Revenge of the Mummy's **Sahara Traders. Rosie's Irish Shop** has everything Emerald Isle expats (or just admirers) need, from coat of arms key chains to football club sweatshirts. Transformers' **Supply Vault** has pricey collectibles, as well as toy versions of the attraction's cybertronic stars. Directly across from the Transformers entrance sits **The Film Vault,** a movie nerd's nirvana with new products tied to vintage Universal films, from *Psycho* and *Scarface* to *Back* *to the Future* and *The Big Lebowski*. Nearby, the **Park Plaza Holiday Shop** sells hand-painted Universal ornaments, be it October or August.

Shopping in **San Francisco** is limited to the **San Francisco Candy Factory** (sadly, Ghirardelli is just a facade) and the **Custom Gear** gift shop at the exit of Fast & Furious: Supercharged, where you can pick out a personalized driver's license or dog tags.

The Wizarding World of Harry Potter—Diagon Alley is groaning with great shopping opportunities, including **Weasleys' Wizard Wheezes** (toys and candy), **Borgin and Burkes** (spooky stuff), **Madam Malkin's Robes for All Occasions** (clothing), **Magical Menagerie** (stuffed animals), **Sugarplum's Sweet Shop** (cakes and candy), **Globus Mundi** (travel-themed tchotchkes), and of course **Ollivanders** (wands). See page 213 for more Diagon Alley shopping details.

In **Springfield: Home of the Simpsons,** the **Kwik-E-Mart** has a great selection of *Simpsons* collectibles and exclusive candy bars, like the Krusty Klump (from the "Homer Badman" episode) and Farmer Billy's Choco-Bacon. **MIB Gear** in **World Expo** has a selection of superhero and anime collectibles, along with a kiosk for custom-printed cell phone cases.

Clothes and toys tied to characters from **DreamWorks Land** can be found in **High Five Hideaway,** a small outdoor kiosk that also sells light-up bubble wands that interact with the afternoon parade. The former KidZone's outskirts remains home to **SpongeBob StorePants,** where the big yellow guy himself holds court daily; adults will appreciate the snarky signs inside. **E.T. Toy Closet** has toys from that Spielberg classic and others, plus two adorable photo ops (one on a flying bicycle and the other in a closet full of toys) that are included with My Universal Photos packages.

Elsewhere in **Hollywood,** the **Five and Dime** stocks a small selection of apparel inspired by the ***Bourne Stuntacular,*** which exits through it, along with Universal Classic Monsters memorabilia for the *Horror Make-Up Show* next door. Note that in Universal's Hollywood, the **Brown Derby** is a rarely open kids' clothing and toy shop, not a restaurant.

Across from the Five and Dime sits the **Tribute Store,** a retail shop that rivals some attractions in immersive detail. The theme changes seasonally, celebrating Halloween in the fall, Christmas in the winter, and Mardi Gras in the spring; milestone anniversaries of classic Universal films like *Jurassic Park* have also been highlighted. No matter what the subject, take time to walk through the sumptuous decor and check out the delicious custom-made treats near the exit. (During some seasons, the Tribute store may be relocated to New York inside the Macy's facade near Revenge of the Mummy.)

Finally, **The NBC Media Center,** inside the Garden of Allah Villas between Hollywood and Dreamworks Land, is like a shop in reverse. Instead of spending money, you can volunteer to watch a video—often

Chris Eliopoulos

from a potential NBC TV series—and answer a survey in exchange for a Universal gift card. It isn't always available, and you may have to meet certain demographic qualifications, but you can make $20 or more in less than an hour. For guests on a tight schedule, this is a poor use of park time, but if you're a local or you're spending several days at Universal, it can be an interesting experience.

SHOPPING AT ISLANDS OF ADVENTURE

LIKE USF, IOA PLACES ITS BIGGEST RETAIL VENUE near the entrance; **Islands of Adventure Trading Company** in **Port of Entry** has selections from every area of the park, especially The Wizarding World. Next to it sits the open-air **Ocean Trader Market,** which sells exotic clothing and crafts. **Island Market and Export** has an open kitchen cooking fresh fudge (smells are free), along with self-scoop candy by the pound. For Grinch fans, the **Port of Entry Christmas Shoppe** celebrates the holiday season 365 days a year; there's even a section dedicated to Harry Potter–themed Yuletide gifts. **DeFoto's Expedition Photography** is this park's My Universal Photos headquarters, and **Port Provisions** is the last-chance gift discounter at the exit turnstiles.

The **Marvel Alterniverse Store** on **Marvel Super Hero Island** stocks Avengers toys and collectible figurines, while the **Comic Book Shop** has a good selection of current releases and trade-paperback classics.

The main drag of **Toon Lagoon** is made up of the **UOAP Lounge,** where annual passholders can chill out and recharge (see page 35), and **Toon Extra**—selling toys and apparel tied to characters no one under age 40 has heard of. **WossaMotta U** sells T-shirts and toys from more current cartoons like *The Secret Life of Pets* and *Trolls.*

Jurassic Park's post-splashdown shop **Jurassic Outfitters** specializes in beach towels (small wonder), and the Discovery Center's **Dinostore** sells semiprecious gems and semieducational toys. The gift kiosk at the exit of **Skull Island: Reign of Kong** is so small that it doesn't even have a name, though it does have some monkey mugs.

In **The Wizarding World of Harry Potter—Hogsmeade**, Honeydukes (candy), **Dervish and Banges** (toys, apparel), **Ollivanders** (wands), and **Filch's Emporium of Confiscated Goods** at the Forbidden Journey exit will sap your wallet as surely as a Dementor sucks souls. See page 259.

The diminished **Lost Continent** still has a few curiosities in its Arabian bazaar, such as a **heraldry shop** with fantasy-themed collectibles and a stall selling colorful clothing. **All Hallows Boutique,** next to The Mystic Fountain, sells spooky seasonal merchandise in a haunted house–like atmosphere. The "most eclectic" award goes to **Treasures of Poseidon,** where you can pick up a polo shirt, a scented candle, and a $20 pearl that's still inside a live oyster.

If you want a set of the Thing 1 and Thing 2 T-shirts you'll spot around Universal, **Cats, Hats and Things** at The Cat in the Hat ride exit in **Seuss Landing** is the spot. **Mulberry Street** has a small entrance door just for kids, but its limited edition prints and sculptures will appeal to adults. If your Theodor Geisel collection has any gaps, **All the Books You Can Read** can help fill it; plush pets are also up for adoption. And be warned: Upon exiting The High in the Sky Seuss Trolley Train Ride!, you may be forced to pass through **Snookers & Snookers Sweet Candy Cookers,** which is known to cause weight gain simply from staring at its case of fudge and candy apples.

MAGICAL MERCHANDISE

HERE'S DEREK BURGAN'S "Saturday Six" list of his favorite magic surprises to be found inside the wonderful shops of Harry Potter's Wizarding Worlds.

6. Professor Umbridge on a Unicycle at Weasleys' Wizard Wheezes (USF) The *Half-Blood Prince* film starts off with our favorite wizarding trio visiting Fred and George Weasley's new store in Diagon Alley. One of the whimsical items they see is a toy featuring the villainous Dolores Umbridge precariously balancing cauldrons of liquid while on a unicycle. At the Weasleys' store, you can not only see a life-size version of this toy working its way across a tightrope up above, but you can even buy a version to take home!

5. Vanishing Cabinet at Borgin and Burkes (USF) Also in *Half-Blood Prince*, Draco Malfoy uses vanishing cabinets to sneak Death Eaters into Hogwarts. In the back corner of the Borgin and Burkes location in Knockturn Alley, there is a vanishing cabinet. If you listen closely, you may just hear a little bird chirp.

4. Mirror at Madame Malkin's Robes For All Occasions (USF) While shopping for their favorite house's gear in Diagon Alley, Muggles can pose or pass by this magical contraption and get complimented on their attire (or possibly get some burning critique).

3. Snake at Magical Menagerie (USF) In Diagon Alley's Magical Menagerie, you can practice your Parseltongue on the snake in the window. You can watch the snake move, and if you get real close, you can even hear it hiss. Maybe you can impress your friends by translating what it is saying.

2. *Monster Book of Monsters* at Dervish and Banges (IOA) In *Prisoner of Azkaban*, Hagrid gets his chance at being a professor. One of the required texts is the *Monster Book of Monsters*, a book that spends most of its time attempting to attack anything around it. Don't worry—it has been locked up to protect guests from its occasional attacks!

1. Letter Stamped at Owl Post (IOA/USF) One of the best magical secrets of The Wizarding World is the ability to send regular Muggle mail via "owl." Visit the Owl Post with a letter or postcard and have it "postmarked" for free by the wizard or witch on hand, then put it in the drop box for delivery. Please note that standard Muggle mailing is used for all deliveries, so you'll have to affix a USPS postage stamp.

SHOPPING AT EPIC UNIVERSE

EPIC UNIVERSE OFFERS a whole new universe of additional shopping opportunities to Universal Orlando, beginning with its main retail location found within **Celestial Park,** named **Other Worlds Mercantile,** located to the left of the entrance. **Moonship Chocolates & Celestial Sweets** is an adjacent candy store. **Lens Flare** is the park's photo pickup location. To the right of the entrance you'll find **Various Emporia,** an apparel and accessories shop. **North Star Wintry Wonders** is the park's holiday store. And the **Nintendo Super Star Store** offers Super Nintendo World–branded merchandise, but without having to enter the land.

In **Super Nintendo World,** the **1-UP Factory** is the best spot to browse the largest collection of exclusive Super Nintendo World merchandise, including apparel, plush, toys, and collectibles. **Mario Motors** (the Mario Kart exit shop) offers a smaller collection but is the best place to find Mario Kart–related merch and specially packaged candies. And **Funky's Fly 'n Buy,** an outdoor kiosk, offers items specifically branded to Donkey Kong Country.

In **Dark Universe,** you'll find the largest retail option on the left side of the village street after entering; named **Pretorius' Scientific Oddities,** it includes the **Darkmoor Monster Makeup Experience** inside. The **Manor Storehouse** is the main ride's exit shop.

In **The Wizarding World of Harry Potter—Ministry of Magic,** you'll find **Cosme Acajor Baguettes Magique** (wands), **Les Galeries Mirifiques** (department store), **K. Ramelle** (sweets), **Mademoiselle Malkins** (robes), and **Tour en Floo** at the Ministry ride exit. See page 285 for details.

Find all your Viking gear and apparel in **How to Train Your Dragon— Isle of Berk** at **Viking Traders,** located within the center of land. Also here is the **How to Treat Your Dragon** sweets shop, with unique desserts made by dragons. **Hiccup's Work Shop** is the land's roller coaster's exit gift shop, featuring branded merchandise. **Toothless' Treasure** can be found near the land's theater show and features small interactive dragons you can adopt to access features within the land.

SHOPPING AT VOLCANO BAY

SHOPPING IS PROBABLY THE LAST THING on the minds of most guests splashing at the water park, unless they've forgotten some essential item. That explains why merchandise opportunities in Volcano Bay are minimal and mostly focused on beach apparel—hats, swimsuits, flip-flops—and accessories. **Waturi Marketplace,** next to the ice cream stand to the left of the park entrance, is the main gift store; it consists of two adjoining huts hocking clothing with the park logo, plus live plants and tiki tchotchkes. **Krakatoa Katy's,** a smaller outpost on the beach to the right of the main entrance, has a more limited selection of shirts, focusing instead on towels, bags, and collectible cups. Both locations stock sundries like sunscreen.

SHOPPING AT UNIVERSAL CITYWALK

CITYWALK (citywalk.com) comprises 30 acres in a relatively compact area between the two Universal theme parks. Its focus is on food and entertainment rather than high-dollar shopping sprees, so the limited store lineup is designed for casual browsing and impulse buys. A supersize **Universal Studios Store** occupies a large swath of the retail space on the right side of CityWalk heading toward Universal Studios Florida, offering one-stop shopping for all theme park souvenirs, including the best selection of Harry Potter and Super Nintendo products outside the parks. Across the plaza, the **Epic Universe Preview Center** is home to a massive model of the new park (download a free augmented reality camera app to make it come to life) and stocked with gear to get you ready for the upcoming expansion.

Up for some ink? CityWalk also has a branch of **Hart & Huntington Tattoo Company.** Finally, many of CityWalk's restaurants—including Bubba Gump, Margaritaville, Hard Rock Cafe, Bob Marley, and Pat O'Brien's—have merchandise shops, in case you want memories of your meal to live on forever in your closet.

SHOPPING AT UNIVERSAL ORLANDO RESORT HOTELS

EACH OF THE ON-SITE LOEWS HOTELS has a main store near the central lobby carrying sundries, souvenirs, and branded apparel. **Hard Rock Hotel's Rock Shop** carries hip brands such as Harajuku and English

Laundry, sells the bed and bath linens used in guest rooms, and even has a touch screen video wall with info on the hotel's rock memorabilia collection. At **Portofino Bay Hotel,** you'll find resort-specific items in **Le Memories de Portofino** and a full array of Universal merch in the harbor promenade's **Universal Studios Store,** along with snacks and sundries in **L'Ancora,** and resort wear and artwork at **Galleria Portofino. Toko Gifts** is a shop just inside the **Royal Pacific Resort**'s entrance that covers all the essentials, while **Treasures of Bali** by the pool carries beach gear and island wear. **Helios Grand Hotel** has a lobby gift shop located near the hotel's special entrance into Epic Universe, which features unique Helios-branded items in addition to the usual souvenirs and toiletries. **Cabana Bay Beach Resort,** which is among the cheaper hotels, actually has one of the best stores, with retro clothes, custom candy, and even Jack La-Lanne gear in the **Universal Studios Store. Sapphire Falls Resort, Aventura Hotel, Terra Luna** and **Stella Nova Resorts,** and **Endless Summer Resort** each has a **Universal Studios Store** of its own; while all have a good selection of sundries and theme park souvenirs, those hotels' branded merchandise isn't nearly as eye-catching as Cabana Bay's.

SHOPPING *near* UNIVERSAL ORLANDO

IF YOU'VE EXHAUSTED Universal Orlando's shopping venues and you want to venture off property, Central Florida's premier shopping experience is found only a couple exits east along I-4 at **The Mall at Millenia** (☎ 407-363-3555, mallatmillenia.com), anchored by **Bloomingdale's, Macy's,** and **Neiman Marcus.** Other stores include **Anthropologie, Burberry, Chanel, Coach, Gucci, Jimmy Choo, Kiehl's, Louis Vuitton, Lululemon, Tiffany & Co., Tory Burch, Urban Outfitters,** and **Versace.** Hours are Monday–Thursday, 11 a.m.–8 p.m.; Friday, 11 a.m.–9 p.m.; Saturday, 10 a.m.–9 p.m.; and Sunday, 11 a.m.–7 p.m.

The luxurious **Cinemark** movie theater (5150 International Dr., ☎ 407-352-1042, cinemark.com) and **Bass Pro Shops** (5156 International Dr., ☎ 407-563-5200, stores.basspro.com) are attached to The Auto Museum at Dezerland Park (☎ 321-754-1700, dezerlandpark .com/orlando), which used to be the Artegon Marketplace mall. **Gods & Monsters** (5421 International Dr., ☎ 407-270-6273, godmonsters .com), our favorite former Artegon fixture, relocated its comic books and sci-fi collectibles across the street, adding a retro arcade and postapocalypse-themed pub.

Finally, at the south end of International Drive is **Pointe Orlando** (9101 International Dr., ☎ 407-248-2838, pointeorlando.com), with a handful of stores. This complex gets a lot of its business from the convention center, less than a mile away, rather than from locals. Retail hours are daily, 11 a.m.–9 p.m. (Bars and restaurants stay open later.) I-Drive is the heart of Orlando's tourist district, jammed with hotels, discount stores, and endless traffic; locals generally avoid the area or use Universal Boulevard (on the south end) and Grand National Drive (on the north end) to dodge the worst of the congestion.

It definitely doesn't count as "near Universal," but hardcore collectors who have a car may want to make the 45-minute drive west on I-4 to the massive **Lakeland Antique Mall** (3530 US 98N, Lakeland; ☎ 863-603-3917; antiqueslakeland.com), where you can purchase props, costumes, and other castoffs from closed Universal attractions.

OUTLETS NEAR UNIVERSAL ORLANDO

AT MOST OUTLET STORES you'll save about 20% on desirable merchandise and up to 75% on last-season (or older) stock. Some stores in the outlet malls are full retail or sell a few brands at a 20% discount and the rest at full price.

Orlando Premium Outlets–International Drive (4951 International Dr., ☎ 407-352-9600, theugseries.com/orlandooutlets; open Monday–Saturday, 10 a.m.–9 p.m.; Sunday, 11 a.m.–7 p.m.; select holidays, 9 a.m.–11 p.m.), at the north end of I-Drive, features 180 of the world's hottest designers and brand names, among them **Dooney & Bourke, J. Crew, Kate Spade, Michael Kors, Movado, Saks Fifth Avenue OFF 5TH, St. John, Under Armour, Victoria's Secret,** and **White House Black Market.** There's even a **Disney's Character Warehouse,** where unsold Walt Disney World souvenirs go to die. You can reach the outlets by car (arrive early for any hope of free parking), taxi, or I-Ride Trolley (it's the first stop).

PART 11

UNIVERSAL ORLANDO CITYWALK

A SHOPPING, DINING, AND ENTERTAINMENT VENUE, City-Walk doubles as the entrance plaza for Universal Studios Florida and Islands of Adventure. Situated between the parking complex and the theme parks, CityWalk is heavily trafficked all day but truly comes alive at night. The complex is arranged in a crescent shape around the waterway that connects Universal's two original theme parks with the resort's on-site hotels. Along its streets, CityWalk offers a number of nightclubs to sample, and many of those entertainment and restaurant venues depend on well-known brand names. You'll find a **Hard Rock Cafe** and concert hall; **Jimmy Buffett's Margaritaville;** a **Bubba Gump Shrimp Co.;** a branch of New Orleans's famous **Pat O'Brien's** club; an **NBC Sports** bar; and a reggae club that celebrates the life and music of **Bob Marley.** Places that operate without big-name tie-ins include the **Red Coconut Club,** a lounge and nightclub; **Toothsome Chocolate Emporium,** a fanciful chocolate-themed restaurant; and **CityWalk's Rising Star,** a karaoke club with a live backup band.

Another CityWalk distinction is that most of the clubs are also restaurants, or alternatively, several of the restaurants are likewise clubs. Though there's a lot of culinary variety, restaurants and nightclubs are different animals. Room configuration, acoustics, intimacy, sight lines, and atmosphere—important considerations in a club—are not at all the same in a venue designed to serve meals. Though it's nice to have all that good food available, the club experience is somewhat dulled.

Red Coconut Club and CityWalk's Rising Star are more nightclub than restaurant, whereas Margaritaville is more restaurant than club. Bob Marley's and Pat O'Brien's are about half-and-half. The Hard Rock Cafe, Antojitos, Bigfire, Vivo, NBC Sports Grill & Brew, Toothsome Chocolate Emporium, and The Cowfish are restaurants, profiled in Part 10.

ARRIVING *and* PARKING

CITYWALK IS OPEN DAILY, 8 a.m.–midnight (until 2 a.m. during select seasons). CityWalk visitors park in the same garage as Universal park guests. Self-parking is free after 6 p.m. (except during Halloween and special events); prime and valet parking are also available. See Part 3 for detailed driving directions and parking information.

Universal Orlando on-site hotel guests can reach CityWalk using the same water taxis, buses, and walking paths that lead to the parks. The water taxi hub is located along the waterfront path before the bridge to Universal Studios Florida (USF). Guests walking from the Hard Rock and Portofino Bay Hotels enter CityWalk closest to USF near Hard Rock Cafe, while guests walking from the other hotels enter CityWalk near Jimmy Buffett's Margaritaville.

> *unofficial* **TIP**
> All unaccompanied minors under the age of 18 must leave CityWalk by 9 p.m. on Friday–Sunday nights, unless staying on-site or attending a ticketed event or movie.

As you enter CityWalk from the parking structure, you'll see a concierge kiosk beneath the escalator outside Starbucks, offering information, restaurant menus, and dining reservations. Guest Services, the restrooms, an ATM, and First Aid are all to your left, immediately past Cold Stone Creamery. None of CityWalk's clubs or restaurants currently levy a cover charge. All other shows and activities at CityWalk are separately ticketed and not included with any theme park admission.

CONTACTING CITYWALK

CONTACT CITYWALK GUEST SERVICES at ☎ 407-224-2691, or visit its website at citywalk.com/orlando. CityWalk personnel may not be up on individual club doings, so your best bet may be to contact specific clubs directly when you reach the Orlando area.

CITYWALK CLUBS

THE FOLLOWING NIGHTCLUB VENUES are mostly located along the elevated curving pathway that sits behind and above CityWalk's central plaza. At many of these venues, you must be 21 or older (passport or photo ID required) to enter after 10 p.m.

Bob Marley—A Tribute to Freedom

What it is Reggae restaurant and club. **Hours** Sunday-Thursday, 5 p.m.–midnight; Friday-Saturday, 5 p.m.–1 a.m. **Cuisine** Jamaican-influenced appetizers and main courses; Mobile Ordering available. **Entertainment** Live reggae bands and DJ in the outdoor gazebo nightly.

This club is a re-creation of Marley's home in Kingston, Jamaica, and contains a lot of interesting Marley memorabilia. The open-air courtyard is the center of action. Must be age 21 or older after 9 p.m.

continued on page 374

Universal Orlando CityWalk

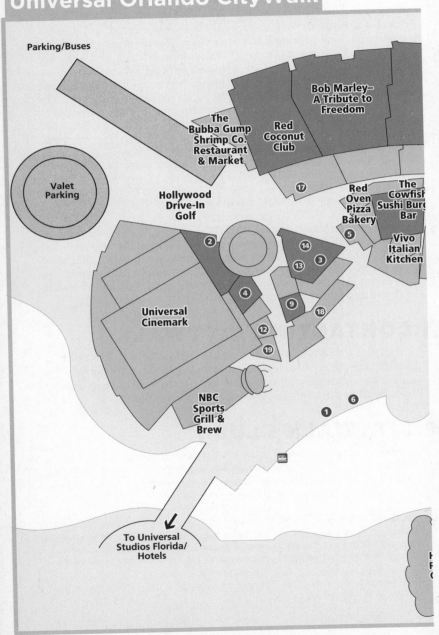

Parking/Buses

Valet
Parking

Hollywood
Drive-In
Golf

The
Bubba Gump
Shrimp Co.
Restaurant
& Market

Red
Coconut
Club

Bob Marley–
A Tribute to
Freedom

17

Red
Oven
Pizza
Bakery

The
Cowfish
Sushi Burg
Bar

5

Vivo
Italian
Kitchen

2

14

13

3

4

9

18

Universal
Cinemark

12

19

NBC
Sports
Grill &
Brew

1

6

To Universal
Studios Florida/
Hotels

H
F
C

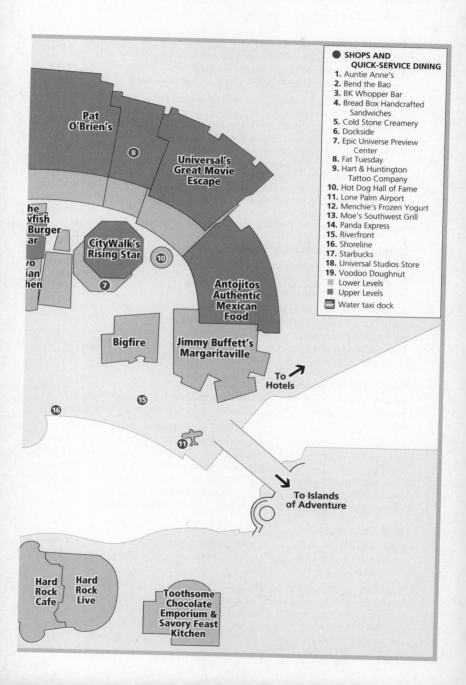

continued from page 371

CityWalk's Rising Star

What it is Karaoke club with live band and backup singers Wednesday–Sunday (Monday–Tuesday, sing to recorded tracks). **Hours** Sunday–Thursday, 7 p.m.–midnight; Friday–Saturday, 7 p.m.–1 a.m. **Cuisine** Pizza from Red Oven. **Entertainment** Karaoke.

With live musicians backing you up, you can pretend that you've hit the big time at this opulent karaoke. The good news is that, instead of a canned "tiny orchestra," Rising Star gives you a live host, plus a full live backing band and backup singers to perform with on select nights. The bad news is that the song list is rather short, with only a little more than 200 options instead of the thousands you may be used to back home. Even so, this is an extremely popular karaoke spot, so be sure to put in your selections as early in the evening as possible if you want to get on stage. If you're impatient, purchase VIP service to skip the queue and get dedicated service by emailing risingstar@universalorlando.com. While waiting your turn, you can get your courage up with one of its supersweet specialty cocktails; pizza delivery from Red Oven is available if stage fright makes you hungry. The club is normally restricted to those age 18 and up.

Jimmy Buffett's Margaritaville

What it is Key West–themed restaurant and club. **Hours** Sunday–Thursday, 11 a.m.–10 p.m.; Friday–Saturday, 11 a.m.–11 p.m. **Cuisine** Caribbean, Florida fusion, American. **Entertainment** Live rock and island-style music.

Margaritaville is a big place with three bars that turns into a nightclub after 10 p.m. Jimmy Buffett covers are popular (no surprise), as are island music and light rock. If you eat dinner here, you'll probably want to find another vantage point on nights when the band cranks up on the main stage around 9 p.m. There's always an acoustic guitarist strumming on the Porch of Indecision from 5 p.m. daily.

Pat O'Brien's Orlando

What it is Dueling-piano sing-along club and restaurant. **Hours** Sunday–Thursday, 5 p.m.–midnight; Friday–Saturday, 5 p.m.–1 a.m. **Cuisine** Cajun. **Entertainment** Dueling pianos and sing-alongs.

At this clone of the famous New Orleans club of the same name, a solo pianist starts playing a little after 5 p.m.; they are joined by a second pianist starting around 9 p.m. These are some of the most talented singing musicians in town and will happily handle nearly any request you throw at them (even—*gasp!*—Disney tunes) as long as you write your request on a generous gratuity. You can dine in the courtyard or on the terrace without paying a cover. You must be age 21 or older to hang out here after 10 p.m.

Red Coconut Club

What it is Modern lounge and nightclub. **Hours** Wednesday–Sunday, 5 p.m.–1 a.m.; hours vary seasonally. **Cuisine** No food, just booze. **Entertainment** Lounging and dancing, with live music or DJs on Friday and Saturday.

This nightspot is billed as a nightclub and ultra-lounge, advertising talk for "hip place to be seen." The eclectic mix of decor—part 1950s, part tiki—and three bars on two levels would make it a great latter-day hangout for the Rat Pack, if Frank and Dean happened to be resurrected in Orlando. There is a dance floor, and the bar serves signature martinis and mojitos. During seasonal celebrations, it may get dressed up as the Dead Coconut Club for Halloween, a voodoo-themed Mardi Gras bar, or the Green and Red Christmas club, all with wonderfully kitschy vintage decor and creative specialty cocktails.

CITYWALK ENTERTAINMENT

BEYOND THE CLUBS, CityWalk's attractions include an array of separately ticketed entertainment venues. Note that none of the following attractions are included in vacation packages or with park tickets.

UNIVERSAL CINEMARK 20 WITH XD

IF YOU WANT TO TAKE A BREAK from "riding the movies" inside Universal's parks and just want to watch one instead, the 20-screen Universal Cinemark at CityWalk has you covered. All 20 screens are outfitted with La-Z-Boy–like Luxury Loungers, featuring oversize cupholders and motorized footrests; the seats are quite comfy, but the upholstery is showing some wear and tear. All screens also have digital projection and surround sound, as well as stadium seating. An expansive snack bar serves hot foods (along with the usual overpriced cinema standards, including Coke Freestyle sodas) and alcohol.

The Cinemark's digital XD theater features a wall-to-wall screen, along with multichannel speakers and an advanced projector that generates 35 trillion colors. It's bigger than the standard screens and delivers more impact in 3-D films but isn't ginormous like the true IMAX screen at Pointe Orlando on I-Drive.

Tickets for showings starting after 6 p.m. (4 p.m. on Saturday, Sunday, and holidays) cost $12.50 for adults Sunday–Thursday and $13.75 Friday–Saturday; new releases cost 25¢ extra, 3-D and XD films cost $3.50 extra, and 3-D XD costs $6 extra. Matinees starting before 6 p.m. (4 p.m. on Saturday, Sunday, and holidays) are $10.25. Tickets for kids ages 1–11 and seniors age 62 and up cost $9 at all times. Universal seasonal and annual passholders (plus one guest) get $3 off regular prices after 6 p.m. On Discount Tuesday, all showings are just $5.50, or $5 for Cinemark Movie Rewards members (not valid on holidays or opening day of new films). Note that children under age 6 are not permitted to attend R-rated films after 6 p.m., thanks to Cinemark's distraction-free environment policy.

You can get reimbursed for standard self-parking at the Universal Orlando garage with the same-day purchase of two matinee movie tickets; be sure to bring your parking receipt with you to the box office before leaving the theater (see page 134 for details).

Visit theugseries.com/cinemark or use Cinemark's mobile app to see showtimes and buy tickets. Tickets can be retrieved from automated kiosks located inside the lobby. You can save the $1–$2 online service fee and get a free standard movie ticket each month, along with a 20% discount on concessions, by joining Cinemark's Movie Club for $13 (cinemark.com/movieclub).

UNIVERSAL'S GREAT MOVIE ESCAPE ROOM

OPENED IN LATE 2022 inside the space originally occupied by The Groove nightclub, Universal's first attempt at a permanent escape room comes from the same designers behind Halloween Horror Nights. For those unfamiliar with the genre, escape rooms are themed environments where small teams are tasked with solving a series of puzzles within a set time limit. Players must scour the room for clues, decode secret messages, and manipulate locks in order to achieve their goal before the hour is up. (Don't worry, you aren't literally locked inside the room, and can elect to escape at any time.)

Whereas most of the numerous escape rooms found throughout Central Florida feature generic settings and public-domain characters, Universal's Great Movie Escape Room shakes up the market with experiences based on two of the studio's most iconic franchises: *Back to the Future* and *Jurassic World*. In the latter, you are trainee geneticists reporting to your first day of work on Isla Nublar—which just happens to be the same day that all heck breaks loose in the park—and are tasked with securing DNA samples before escaping aboard a monorail. The former game (our favorite) features voice-overs by Christopher Lloyd as eccentric scientist Doc Brown, who recruits you to battle baddie Biff Tannen by visiting the Old West and "futuristic" 2015 using your own portable Flux Capacitor. Whether you choose to help restore the time-space continuum or brave rampaging raptors, you'll make your way through eight highly themed rooms and be immersed by authentic sets, sounds, and special effects straight from the silver screen.

Although some younger children enjoy escape rooms, the challenges are geared toward teens and adults, and some of the effects—especially during the dino-infested game—may be startling. The puzzles are designed to adjust to your group's size and skill level, so whether you solve the tasks quickly or get completely stumped, you'll still progress through your adventure at roughly the same pace, making this accessible for novices but ultimately unsatisfying for escape room veterans. Keep in mind that everything you need to solve the puzzles should be accessible without dismantling or destroying any scenery; escape rooms rely on observation and cooperation, not brute force.

Experiencing one of Universal's escape rooms will set you back $42–$64 per person, depending on what time and day you schedule, and there's no discount for playing both, although self-parking is included. If your group has fewer than 6 guests, you may be paired up with strangers to play; parties of 7 or 8 can book a private room for $256–$383. Tickets can be purchased in person at the venue or in advance online at theugseries.com/unimovieescape. Groups of more than 8 can book a private party by calling ☎ 407-224-8463. You don't need admission to enjoy a drink at the swanky lobby bar, which serves a superior "Smoke & Mirrors" old fashioned and coffee-pistachio martini. Although some puzzle solutions are randomized, these rooms don't have much repeatability once conquered, so if Universal's offering makes you eager for more, see page 31 for nearby alternatives.

CITYWALK STAGE

AT VARIOUS TIMES OF THE YEAR, Universal offers free concerts and DJ performances on a stage located in the plaza at CityWalk. The stage may be positioned in front of the water feature between Vivo and the Epic Universe Preview Center, or it may be located closer to the waterline at the bottom of the amphitheater. Performances are almost exclusively at night, though the space has been used for live tapings of morning talk shows, and there's normally no problem getting a view. The entertainment is usually free, but on New Year's Eve and a few other occasions, the entire area is reserved for those purchasing special-event tickets.

EPIC UNIVERSE PREVIEW CENTER

TO GET GUESTS HYPED ahead of Epic Universe's 2025 opening, the massive scale model Universal Creative made to plan the park was moved into the former Universal Legacy Store, making this hyperdetailed work of art (which required dozens of artisans and well over a million dollars to build) accessible to the general public. The model is a marvel to study with the naked eye, but download the free "Epic Universe Preview" app to see augmented reality animations of the upcoming attractions. There are also photo backdrops themed to each land, along with a selection of branded merchandise tied to each anticipated area.

HARD ROCK LIVE

ACROSS THE LAGOON from most of CityWalk, adjoining the Hard Rock Cafe and separate from the Hard Rock Hotel, this theater hosts concerts, contests, and various private events. Musical acts, both nationally known and up-and-coming, as well as stand-up comedians, appear regularly. Recent shows have run the gamut from Danny Ocean to The Psychedelic Furs, and from Lewis Black to Dino Ranch Live. Great acoustics, comfortable seating (for up to 3,000), and good sight lines make this the best concert venue in town.

The hours vary with live shows; performances usually begin 7–9:30 p.m. Ticket prices vary depending on the act, ranging from $24 to more than $200. There is a full liquor bar, and (depending on the event) you can order food from the restaurant's kitchen.

Floor viewing is from removable chairs, or sometimes standing-room only depending on the act, while guests in the VIP balcony can get cocktail service delivered to their leather armchairs. Premier and Preferred Annual passholders save $5 on tickets to the Classic Albums Live series, where talented studio musicians re-create records from the 1970s through 1980s note for note; their renditions of Queen and Pink Floyd are flawless.

Be sure to leave plenty of time for parking and security. You'll be inspected again before entering the venue, and the line can be agonizingly slow. Also note that there's normally no reentry allowed once you exit the venue.

For information and an events calendar, call ☎ 407-351-7625 or see hardrock.com/live/locations/orlando/calendar.aspx. To purchase tickets for an event at Hard Rock Live, call ☎ 407-351-LIVE (5483) or visit theugseries.com/hardrock. (*Warning:* Exorbitant service fees apply.)

HOLLYWOOD DRIVE-IN GOLF

SO THIS IS WHAT MONEY AND IMAGINATION CAN DO. On one edge of the CityWalk entertainment complex, these 18-hole courses are awash in elaborate settings, props, and even audio. The theme is a drive-in movie showing two features: *Invaders from Planet Putt* and *The Haunting of Ghostly Greens*. Players can choose a single (18 holes) or double (36 holes) feature.

The *Invaders from Planet Putt* course entertains with nonfrightening statues and props such as rocket ships and little green men; a pretend newspaper box shows the *Roswell* [New Mexico] *Register* of July 8, 1947, with the blaring headline UFO SIGHTINGS CONTINUE.

The *Haunting of Ghostly Greens* course features a giant spider, a graveyard, and a basement-lab scene. This course is particularly nice at night but may creep out younger golfers. At various holes, the sound effects are a mooing cow, a chain saw, and a ray gun.

The courses are quite easy, and the greens are in superb condition. We rank Hollywood Drive-In as the best minigolf in Orlando, along with Disney's Fantasia Gardens and Congo River in Kissimmee. Note that one of the courses is fully wheelchair accessible, while the other requires navigating some stairs.

Hollywood Drive-In is located at the entrance to CityWalk, between the Universal Cinemark and the valet parking loop. As you exit the parking garages and moving sidewalks, Hollywood Drive-In Golf is on your immediate right, down one level.

The course is open daily, 9 a.m.–midnight. For 18 holes, it costs $27 for adults and $24 for children ages 3–9. For 36 holes, it costs $47 for adults and $43 for children ages 3–9. All prices are $3 less before 6 p.m. Preferred and Power Annual Pass holders, Florida residents, military, adults age 62 and older, and AAA members all save 10% on 18 holes for up to five players; Premier Pass holders save 15%. You can purchase online at hollywooddriveingolf.com in advance, saving up to 10%, but online tickets aren't refundable if unused.

Before 6 p.m., you must pay the usual parking fee to play at Hollywood Drive-In, which drastically boosts the price of playing these courses if you aren't already visiting Universal Orlando.

Call ☎ 407-802-4848 or visit the website above for more information. You can download a free scorecard app for iOS and Android in preparation for your putting.

▌ APPENDIX

READERS' QUESTIONS TO THE AUTHORS

Question:

When you do your research, are you admitted to the parks for free? Do the Universal people know you're there?

Answer:

We pay the regular admission, and usually the Universal people don't know we're on-site. Similarly, both in and out of Universal Orlando, we pay for our own meals and lodging.

Question:

How often is The Unofficial Guide *revised?*

Answer:

We publish a new edition once a year in the late fall.

Question:

Where can I find information about what's changed at Universal Orlando in between published editions of The Unofficial Guide?

Answer:

We post important information online at theunofficialguides.com /universal-orlando-updates and touringplans.com.

Question:

Do you write each new edition from scratch?

Answer:

We do not. When it comes to a destination the size of Universal Orlando, it's hard enough to keep up with what's new. Moreover, we put a lot of effort into communicating the most useful information in the clearest possible language. For future editions, if an attraction or hotel hasn't changed, we're reluctant to tinker with its coverage for the sake of freshening the writing.

Question:

How many people have you surveyed for your age-group ratings regarding the attractions?

Answer:

Since the first *Unofficial Guide* containing Universal coverage was published in 1992, we've interviewed or surveyed thousands of Universal Orlando patrons. Even with such a large survey population, however, we continue to find that certain age groups are underrepresented. Specifically, we'd love to hear more from seniors about their experiences with coasters and other thrill rides.

READERS' COMMENTS

OUR READERS LOVE TO SHARE TIPS. An Iowa City, Iowa, couple offers this observation about being in touch with your feelings:

> We didn't build rest breaks into our plans but were willing to say, "OK, I'm just not having fun right now—we should leave the park," and go on to something else (like a water park, hotel pool, or shopping trip). This is a skill I would like to see more people develop. I can't count the number of people I saw who were obviously not having fun.

A Norwalk, Ohio, mom searched for happy feet:

> On the subject of footwear, support is just as important as comfort. On one trip I wore Keds—big mistake. My shins ached unbelievably before the end of the second day. From then on I was a die-hard tennis shoe girl, until I discovered FitFlops [go to fitflop.com for stores]. You get the support of a tennis shoe with the comfort of a flip-flop.

A woman from Mount Gretna, Pennsylvania, had some questions about theme park attire:

> There wasn't a section that addressed whether you could wear dresses on rides. Quite a few amusement parks have security straps or bars that come up between one's knees, making it very difficult and immodest to wear dresses or skirts. Many women want to wear dresses for convenience, comfort, or cultural/religious convictions. I was concerned as I was packing whether this would limit any rides I could get on. I was quite pleased that it did not.

A Columbia, Missouri, woman offers advice for wives with anxious husbands:

> A smartphone is the best thing in the world for keeping your husband busy in line. As long as mine had that phone, he could check email, check dinner plans, and take and send pictures of the kids to family back home. He never complained about waiting in line, ever.

All for the love of Mom, writes a woman from Haddon Heights, New Jersey:

> I was traveling with my mother, who has an artificial knee, a herniated disc, and bad feet. My mantra was, "Try not to kill your mother." Without the book, I would have undoubtedly come home an orphan.

Finally, a Somerville, Alabama, woman is succinct if nothing else:

> Everything, other than my husband, was perfect.

And so it goes. . . .

INDEX

EU = Epic Universe   **IOA** = Islands of Adventure
USF = Universal Studios Florida   **VB** = Volcano Bay

A

AAA member discounts, 40, 41
Aashirwad Indian Cuisine, 361
abbreviations, common, 19
accommodations. *See* hotels *or specific*
    establishment
admission
    annual passholders Early Park
        Admission (EPA), 57
    Early Park Admission (EPA), 53–57
    ticket savings from third-party vendors,
        40
    types and prices (table), 33
    Universal Orlando annual passes, 35–38
    to Universal Orlando, saving money,
        38–41
    to Volcano Bay, 295–300
adults
    attractions potentially problematic for
        (table), 185
    touring plans for, 240–241, 272, 288–289
Advance Dining Reservations, 304
AdventHealth Centra Care Dr. Phillips, 144
Airbnb, 105–106
airports, 127–128
Al-Alon/Alateen, 166
Alcoholics Anonymous, 166
All Hallows Boutique (**IOA**), 365
All the Books You Can Read (**IOA**), 365
Allegiant Air, 127
Amatista Cookhouse (Sapphire Falls), 79,
    90, 303, 340, 342
Amazing Adventures of Spider-Man, The
    (**IOA**), 245, 248
Animal Actors on Location! (**USF**), 220
animals, service, 160
Anker batteries, 147
Antojitos Authentic Mexican Food
    (CityWalk), 303, 340–341, 343
Apple Pay, 140
Apple Scooter, 159
apps
    See also specific app
    Uber, Lyft, 130
    Universal mobile, 22, 38
    Visitor Toll Pass smartphone, 120
Aquaria Bar (**EU**), 341
arrival
    early, 43

Early Park Admission (EPA), 53–57
    what to expect upon your (rope drop),
        51–53
arrival- and departure-day activities, 31
Astronomica splash pad (**EU**), 276
Atlantic restaurant (**EU**), 276, 303, 341, 343
ATMs (automated teller machines), 139
Atomic Tonic (Cabana Bay), 336
Attraction Tickets, 40
attractions
    See also specific attraction
    closures, 142
    at Islands of Adventure, 244–269
    potentially problematic for adults
        (table), 185
    replaced rides (table), 196
    small-child fright-potential tables,
        180–183
Attractions Assistance Pass (AAP), 165
Attractions Magazine, 22, 23
Auntie Anne's (**USF**), 317–318
authors, contacting the, 5
autism, 164
Auto Club South, 40
Aventura Hotel, 73, 80, 91–93, 114, 368
Avis car rentals, 41, 81, 135

B

baby swap, 60, 187–189
babysitting, 192
Bake My Day (**USF**), 362
Bambu (**VB**), 308, 332
Bar 17 Bistro (Aventura), 79, 93, 341, 342,
    343–344
Bar Moonshine (**EU**), 285
bathrooms, planning breaks, 50–51
batteries, 147
Bayliner Diner (Cabana Bay), 95, 308, 336
Beach Break Cafe (Surfside Inn), 336
Beach Pool, 86
BeachClub bar, 85
Beat Builders quartet (**USF**), 224
beer, wine, liquor, 155–156, 313
beignets, 218
Bend the Bao (CityWalk), 333
Best Price Mobility, 159
Best Western Plus Universal Inn, 113–114, 118
Betty Boop Store (**USF**), 362
Bice Ristorante (Portofino Bay), 79, 303,
    343–344

B (continued)

Bigfire (CityWalk), 303, 343, 345
Bite30, 41
BK Whopper Bar (CityWalk), 333
Blishen's Fire Whisky, 313
blisters, 144–145, 171–172
Blondie's (**IOA**), 324–325
Blue Dragon Pas-Asian Restaurant, The
  (**EU**), 276, 303, 342, 345–346
Blues Brothers Show, The (**USF**), 224
Bob Marley—A Tribute to Freedom
  (CityWalk), 303, 342, 346, 370, 371
BoiBrazil Churrascaria, 361
Borgin and Burkes (**USF**), 213, 363, 366
bottlenecks, avoiding, 44
Bourne Stuntacular, The (**USF**), 221, 363
Bowser Jr.'s lair (**EU**), 280
Bowser's Fortress (**EU**), 278
Bread Box Sandwiches (CityWalk),
  308, 333
Breakfast with The Grinch & Friends
  (**IOA**), 271
Brown Derby clothes and toys, 363
Bubba Gump Shrimp Co. Restaurant &
  Market (CityWalk), 303, 342, 343,
  346–347, 370
Bubbalou's Bodacious Bar-B-Que, 361
Bubblebee Man's Taco Truck (**USF**), 317
Bubbly Barrel, The (**EU**), 329
Budget car rentals, 41, 135
Buena Vista Rentals, 158–159
Bula Bar & Grille, 89
Burgan, Derek, 13, 270, 366
Burger Digs, The (**IOA**), 325
Burger King, 360
Burning Blade Tavern, The (**EU**), 281,
  329
Busch Gardens Tampa, 80–81
business centers, 80
Butterbeer, 310–312

C

CAA member discounts, 40
Cabana Bay Beach Resort, 73, 78, 79, 81,
  93–96, 114, 138, 368
Cabana Courtyard Pool, 95
cabanas and premium seating (**VB**), 294
Cafe 4 (**IOA**), 306, 307, 325
Cafe La Bamba (**USF**), 317–318
Cafe L'air la Sirene (**EU**), 308, 330
Camp Jurassic (**IOA**), 254–255
Captain America Diner (**IOA**), 307, 325
Carkitt Market (**USF**), 207
Caro-Seuss-el (**IOA**), 267

cars
  care, 143
  rental, 41, 81, 135
Carte Blanche, 140
Castle Hotel (Autograph Collection),
  114–115
castle tour, Harry Potter and the Forbidden Journey (**IOA**), 263
casts for broken bones, 159
Cat in the Hat, The (**IOA**), 267–268
Cats, Hats and Things (**IOA**), 365
celebration buttons, 146–147
Celestial Park (**EU**), 276–277, 366
Celestrina Warbeck and the Banshees
  (**USF**), 212
cell phones
  charging, 147–148
  service problems, 143
Central Park Crepes (**USF**), 318
character breakfast with The Grinch (**IOA**),
  271
characters. *See* Universal characters
Chargeback service, 143
charging cell phones, 147–148
charging stations (cars), 142–143
Checker Cab, 128
checks, personal and traveler's, 139
Chez Alcatraz (**USF**), 318
child swap, 68, 187–189
childcare, 192
children. *See* kids
Christmas in the Wizarding World (**USF**),
  238, 269–270
Cider, nonalcoholic, 312
Cinemark, 368
Cinemark 2D with XD, 375
CineSational: A Symphony Spectacular
  (**USF**), 225
Circus McGurkus Cafe Stoo-pendous
  (**IOA**), 326
City Cab, 128
City Snack Stands (**USF**), 318
CityWalk, 2, 14
  arrival, parking, 371
  ATMs (automated teller machines), 139
  clubs, 371, 374–375
  contacting, 371
  dining reservations, 304
  eating options, 303
  entertainment at, 375–378
  first aid, 148
  map, 9, 372–373
  overview, 370, 370–371
  plant-based dining, 305
  quick-service restaurants, 333–336
  shopping at, 367

stage, 377
Classic Albums Live concert tickets, 41
climate, 27–28
clip-out touring plans, 48, 395–416
clubs (CityWalk), 371, 374–375
"Coaster101 Podcast, The," 24
Coca-Cola Freestyle souvenir cups, 314
cognitive disabilities, planning guide, 164
Cold Stone Creamery (**USF**), 161, 317–318
Comfort Suites Near Universal Orlando
    Resort, 114, 115, 118
Comic Book Shop (**IOA**), 365
Comic Strip Cafe (**IOA**), 326
complaints, 146
concentrators, oxygen tanks, 164
condominiums, 106–110
Confisco Grille (**IOA**), 303, 342, 347
Constellation Carousel (**EU**), 277
conventions, trade shows, 26–27
Cosme Acajor Baguettes Magique (**EU**),
    285, 367
Cosmos Cafe and Market/Omega Cafe
    and Market (Stella Nova/Terra Luna),
    336–337
Costco Wholesale, 40
costs
    See also specific item, attraction, or
        establishment
    Cinemark 2D with XD, 375
    Early Park Admission (EPA), 71–72
    food on-site at Universal, 76–77
    Halloween Horror Nights (**USF**),
        231–232
    Hollywood Drive-in Golf (CityWalk), 378
    restaurants, 339
    Rock the Universe (**USF**), 227
    self-parking, 37–38
    stroller rental, 174–175
    Universal Express, 58–59
    VIP tours, 65–66
    weddings, 83
Cowfish Sushi Burger Bar, The (CityWalk),
    342, 343, 347–348
credit cards, 140
Croissant Moon Bakery (**IOA**), 326
Crowd Calendar, 21
cups, collectible souvenir, 313–315
currency exchange, 140
Curse of the Werewolf (**EU**), 281–282

D

Daisyroot Ale, 313
Dancing Dragons Boat Bar (**VB**), 308
Dark Arts at Hogwarts Castle, The
    (**IOA**), 266
Dark Forest Ale, 313

Dark Universe (**EU**), 273, 281–283, 366
Darkmoor (**EU**), 281
Darkmoor Monster Makeup Experience
    (**EU**), 281, 283, 366
Das Stakehaus (**EU**), 281, 308, 330
De Lacey's Cottage (**EU**), 330
DeFoto's Expedition Photography (**IOA**),
    152, 365
Del Taco, 361
dental needs, 144
Dervish and Banges toys, apparel (**IOA**),
    259, 365, 366
Despicable Me Minion Mayhem (**USF**), 18,
    198
Diagon Alley (**USF**), 207, 311
dietary restrictions, 160–161
dining
    See also restaurants or
        specific establishment
    cutting time at theme parks, 315–316
    dietary restrictions, 160–161
    discounts, 41
    dress code, 304
    fast food at Universal Orlando's parks,
        307–316
    Mobile Ordering, 68, 294, 310
    near Universal Orlando, 360–361
    plant-based, 305
    quick-service restaurants, 317–338
    reservations, 160–161, 304
    Universal character, 192
    at Universal Orlando generally, 302–306
Dinostore (**IOA**), 365
discounts
    for annual pass holders, 35–36
    hotels, 74
    military, 39
    resort, dining, entertainment, 41
Discover credit card, 140
Discover Universal blog, 22
Disney Character Warehouse, 369
Doc Sugrue's Desert Kebab House (**IOA**),
    326–327
Dockside Inn and Suites, 73, 97
DOCS (Doctors on Call Services), 144
Doctor Doom's Fearfall (**IOA**), 248
Donkey Kong Country (**EU**), 278
DoubleTree by Hilton Hotel at the Entrance
    to Universal Orlando, 114, 115, 118
Dr. Phillips Hospital, 144
Dragon Racer's Rally (**EU**), 285–286
Dragon Scale, 313
DreamWorks Imagination Celebration
    (**USF**), 218, 318
DreamWorks Land surprises (**USF**), 218

D *(continued)*

DreamWorks Land (**USF**), 196, 217–220, 363
dress code for dining, 304
Drhum Club Kantine, 90
drink ordering with Mobile Ordering, 310
drinks, refillable, 313–315
drugs and prescription medicine, 144
Drury Inn & Suites Near Universal Orlando Resort, 114, 115–116, 118
Dudley Do-Right's Ripsaw Falls (**IOA**), 13, 250–251
Duff Brewery (**USF**), 13, 319

E

early arrival, 43
Early Park Admission (EPA), 53–57, 272
ECV (electric conveyance vehicle) rentals, 158–159
Eisner, Michael, 5, 6, 13
electric vehicle charging stations, 79, 142–143
Emack & Bollo's ice cream shop, 84
Emack & Bollo's Marketplace (Hard Rock Hotel), 337
Endless Summer Resort, 73, 78, 79, 80, 96–99, 114, 118, 368
entertainment
  at CityWalk, 375–378
  in Diagon Alley (**USF**), 212
  discounts, 41
  in Hogsmeade (**IOA**), 265–266
  in Isle of Berk (**EU**), 287
Epic Universe (**EU**), 2, 30, 32–33, 70, 138, 143
  attraction height requirements (table), 187
  attractions, 276–287
  character-greeting locations, 191
  Family Services, 173
  live entertainment, 287–288
  map, 274–275
  overview, 7, 10, 273
  quick-service restaurants, 329–332
  restrooms, 160
  rope drop (arrival at), 52–53
  shopping at, 366–367
  small-child fright-potential table, 182–183
  touring plans, 288–289
Epic Universe Preview Center (CityWalk), 367, 377
E.T. Adventure (**USF**), 221–222
E.T. Toy Closet (**USF**), 363
Evil Stuff (**USF**), 362
Expedia, 104

Express Pass, 17
Express Unlimited Pass, 17

F

facilities tour, Jurassic World VelociCoaster (**IOA**), 256
Fairfield Inn & Suites Orlando Near Universal Orlando Resort, 114, 116, 118
family restrooms, 160
Family Services, 172–173
Fast & Furious: Supercharged (**USF**), 205–206
fast food at Universal Orlando's parks, 307–316
Fast Food Boulevard (**USF**), 302, 319
Fat Tuesday (**USF**), 317–318
Feasting Frog, The (**VB**), 308, 332
Filch's Emporium of Confiscated Goods (**IOA**), 260, 365
Film Vault, The (**USF**), 362–363
Finnegan's Bar and Grill (**USF**), 234, 303, 342, 348
Fire-Eater's Grill (**IOA**), 307, 327
first aid, 148, 172
First Aid Stations, 148
First Baptist Orlando, 155
fitness centers, 81
Five and Dime (**USF**), 363
Flavor by Loews program, 303
FlexPay service, 37
Flight of the Hippogriff (**IOA**), 18, 260
Florean Fortescue's Ice-Cream Parlour (**USF**), 307, 312, 319–320
Florida Dream Homes, 108
Floridays, 107
food
  See also dining, restaurants, *or specific restaurant*
  allergies, special requests, 305–306
  bringing your own, 141
  dietary restrictions, 160–161
  fast, at Universal Orlando's parks, 307–316
  groceries, 148–149
  saving money on, 316
foot care, footwear, 144–145, 171–172
Forbidden Forest (**IOA**), 259
Fountain of Fair Fortune (**USF**), 311, 320
Frankenstein Manor (**EU**), 281
free Express Passes, 17
Friends of Bill W., 166
Frog Choir (**IOA**), 265
Frosted Glacier overlook (**EU**), 280
FuelRod battery packs, 147–148
Funky's Fly 'n Buy (**EU**), 366
Fyre Drill (**EU**), 286

G

Galaxy Bowl (Cabana Bay Beach Resort), 95, 342, 349
Galleria Portofino (CityWalk), 368
Game Play cards (**USF**), 216
Game-O-Rama, 95
gamma tour, Incredible Hulk Coaster, The (**IOA**), 248
gasoline, 142–143
Gillywater, 312–313
Girl Scout Cookies, 322
glasses, 172
Glatt Kosher restaurant, 161
Globus Mundi (**USF**), 213, 363
Gods & Monsters, 368
God's House Orlando, 155
Google Pay, 140
Grand Liquors, 156
Greater Orlando Aviation Authority website, 127
Green Eggs and Ham Cafe (**IOA**), 307, 327
Grimmauld Place (**USF**), 207
Grinch character breakfast (**IOA**), 271
Grinchmas Who-liday Spectacular (**IOA**), 270
Gringotts Money Exchange (**USF**), 214
Gringotts Wizarding Bank Notes, 140–141, 214
Gringotts Wizarding Bank (**USF**), 207
groceries, 148–149
Guest Assistance Pass (GAP) entry cards, 165–166
Guest Services, 140, 143, 146, 176
guests
    international visitors, 166
    larger, 162–164
    with nonapparent disabilities, 164–166
    with special needs, 156–166

H

Häagen-Dazs (**USF**), 317
Haddock Paddock (**EU**), 287
Hagrid's Hut (**IOA**), 259
Hagrid's Magical Creatures Motorbike Adventure (**IOA**), 259, 260–261, 271
halal food, 161
Halloween Horror Nights (**USF**), 230–236
Halloween Nightmare Fuel dance show (**USF**), 235
Hard Rock Cafe (CityWalk), 85, 342, 349–350, 370
Hard Rock Hotel Orlando, 72, 73, 78, 80, 82, 83–85, 114, 136, 138
Hard Rock Hotel's Rock Shop, 367–368
Hard Rock Live, 377–378

Harry Potter and the Battle at the Ministry (**EU**), 283–284
Harry Potter and the Escape from Gringotts (**USF**), 208–209
Harry Potter and the Forbidden Journey (**IOA**), 7, 18, 259, 262–264
Hart & Huntington Tattoo Company (CityWalk), 367
headache relief, 144
hearing impairment, protection, 161, 172
height requirements, 185–189
Helios Grand Hotel, 73, 99–100, 114, 136, 138, 273, 303, 368
Helios Grand Hotel's club lounge, 82
Hello Kitty shop (**USF**), 362
Hemisphere Stage (**EU**), 287–288
heraldry shop (**IOA**), 365
Hiccup's Wing Gliders (**EU**), 286–287
Hiccup's Work Shop (**EU**), 367
Hideaway Bar & Grill (Cabana Bay), 336
High Five Hideaway (**USF**), 363
High in the Sky Seuss Trolley Train Ride!, The (**IOA**), 268
Hill, Jim, 22
Hillside Pool, 86
Hog's Head pub (**IOA**), 259, 307, 311, 327
Hogsmeade (**IOA**), 259, 311, 313
Hogwarts Always (**IOA**), 265–266
Hogwarts Castle (**IOA**), 259
Hogwarts Express (**IOA**), 33, 55, 209–210, 259, 263
Holiday Inn & Suites Across from Universal, 114, 116, 118
holidays
    at Islands of Adventure (**IOA**), 269–271
    at Universal Studios Florida (**USF**), 237–238
Hollywood (**USF**), 196, 220–223, 363
Hollywood Drive-in Golf (CityWalk), 41, 378
Hollywood Rip Ride Rockit (**USF**), 151, 200–202
Holy Family Catholic Community, 155
Honeydukes (**IOA**), 259, 365
Honu Slide (**VB**), 298
Hooligan's Grog & Gruel (**EU**), 330
Hopping Pot, The (**USF**), 311, 312, 320
Hot Dog Hall of Fame (CityWalk), 308, 334
hotel shopping, 104–106
hotels
    See also specific hotel
    accessibility, 75
    babysitting, in-room, 192
    best on-site rooms for families, 78
    check-in, checkout, 75
    club level, 82

H (continued)
hotels (continued)
   cribs, rollaway beds, 80
   fitness centers, 81
   how they compare (table), 114
   kids' activities, suites, 77, 79
   laundry, 81–82
   microwaves, refrigerators, 80
   pets, 75–76
   plant-based dining, 305
   pools, recreation, 77
   quick-service restaurants, 336–338
   reservations, cancellations, 74–75
   room ratings, 113–117
   rooms, getting what you want, 110,
     112–113
   seasonal rates, discounts, 73–74
   selecting, booking, 103–104
   smoking, 76
   10 best values, 118
   transportation and car rental, 80–81
   in Universal & I-Drive areas (map), 111
   Universal Orlando Resort hotel profiles,
     83–101
   walking to Universal Orlando from your,
     130–131
   weddings, 83
How to Train Your Dragon—Isle of Berk
   (EU), 276, 285–287, 367
Hyatt Place Across from Universal
   Orlando, 114, 116–117, 118

I
I-4 blues, 125–126
IBCCES Accessibility Card (IAC), 165
ice water, free, 316
Ichiban sushi, 361
Icon Park complex, 31
I-Drive Area Sneak Routes (map), 124
I-Drive hotels, 104
If I Ran the Zoo (IOA), 269
Ika Moana Slide (VB), 298
Imagination Celebration mural (USF), 218
immigration tour, Men in Black Alien
   Attack (USF), 215
Incredible Hulk Coaster, The (IOA), 151,
   248–249
infants, toddlers at the theme parks,
   172–173
Inside Universal, 22
inspection of brought items, 141–142
interactive experiences, entertainment in
   Isle of Berk (EU), 287
interactive Power-Up Bands and Key
   Challenges, 280–281

interactive wands, 211, 265, 284–285
International Board of Credentialing and
   Continuing Education Standards
   (IBCCES), 165
international visitors, 166
I-Ride Trolley, 132
Island Market and Export (IOA), 365
Islands Dining Room (Royal Pacific), 79,
   89, 303, 342, 350
Islands of Adventure (IOA)
   ATMs (automated teller machines), 139
   attraction height requirements (table),
     186
   attractions, 244–269
   beware of the wet, 242–243
   character-greeting locations, 191
   Early Park Admission (EPA), 55–56
   getting oriented at, 243–244
   lost and found, 143
   map, 8–9, 246–247
   overview, 7, 10, 242–243
   plant-based dining, 305
   quick-service restaurants, 324–329
   restrooms, 160
   rope drop (arrival at), 52
   shopping at, 365
   small-child fright-potential table,
     181–182
   special events, 269–271
   touring plans, 271–272
   UAOP lounge, 68
Islands of Adventure Trading Company
   (IOA), 144, 365
It's A Wrap (USF), 362

J
Jack LaLanne Fitness Center, 95
Jake's American Bar (Royal Pacific
   Resort), 79, 89, 342, 350–351
Japan Credit Bureau, 140
Jim Hill Media, 22
Jimmy Buffett's Margaritaville (CityWalk),
   303, 342, 351–352, 370, 374
Jurassic Outfitters (IOA), 365
Jurassic Park Discovery Center (IOA), 255
Jurassic Park (IOA), 243, 254–259, 260,
   365
Jurassic Park River Adventure (IOA), 13, 18,
   255–256
Jurassic World Kids' Suites, 88
Jurassic World VelociCoaster (IOA), 151,
   256–257

K
K. Ramelle sweet shop (EU), 285
Kabooki Sushi, 361

Kala & Tai Nui Serpentine Body Slides
  (**VB**), 296
Kang & Kodos' Twirl 'n' Hurl (**USF**), 216
Kayak, 105
kids
  age, when to visit, naps, 168–169
  babysitting, 192
  common issues, 171–173
  first aid, medication, 172
  height requirements, 185–189
  lost, 176–177
  quick-service meals, 308–310
  scary stuff, 178–185
  strollers, 173–176
  tattoos, temporary, 176
  touring plans for, 240–241, 272, 289
  at Universal Orlando generally, 167–171
  and Unofficial Guide touring plans, 171
  where to stay, 169–170
Kid's Nite Out, 192
Kids' Suites, 78–79, 90, 92
King Harold's Swamp Symphony (**USF**), 219
Kingdom Strollers, 174
Kitchen, The (Hard Rock Hotel), 84,
  342, 352
Knockturn Alley (**USF**), 207
Kobe Japanese Steakhouse & Sushi Bar,
  360
Kohola Reef Restaurant & Social Club
  (**VB**), 308, 332–333
Ko'okiri Body Plunge (**VB**), 299–300
Kopiko Wai Winding River (**VB**), 292, 298
Kosher Grill, 161
Krakatau (**VB**), 292, 295
Krakatau Aqua Coaster (**VB**), 292, 299
Krakatoa Katy's (**VB**), 144, 152, 367
Kubersky, Seth, viii, 4, 46, 311
Kunuku Boat Bar (**VB**), 308
Kwik-E-Mart (**USF**), 363

L
lagoon show, Halloween Horror Nights
  (**USF**), 236
Lakeland Antique Mall, 369
lanyards, souvenir, 61, 68, 149
larger guests, potentially problematic rides
  for, 162–164
laundry, 81–82
Lazy River Courtyard, 95
Le Cirque Arcanus (**EU**), 284
Le Gobelet Noir (**EU**), 330
Le Memories de Portofino, 368
Leaky Cauldron (**USF**), 207, 302, 307, 311,
  312, 320–321
Lee, Stan, 245
Lens Flare (**EU**), 152, 366

Les Galeries Mirifiques department store
  (**EU**), 285, 367
Lightning Lane, 17, 57–58
Lines app, 22–23
liquor, beer, wine, 155–156
live entertainment
  at Epic Universe (**EU**), 287–288
  at Universal Studios Florida (**USF**),
    224–226
lockers, 149–152, 294–295
lodging and sales tax, 71
Loews hotel chain, 70
Loews Portofino Bay Hotel. *See* Portofino
  Bay Hotel
Loews Royal Pacific Resort. *See* Royal
  Pacific Resort
Lombard's Seafood Grille (**USF**), 303, 343,
  352–353
London Taxi Hut (**USF**), 321
Lone Palm Airport, 352
Lord Voldemort's masked Death Eaters
  (**USF**), 213
lost kids, 176–177
lost and found, 143
Lost Continent, The (**IOA**), 243, 266–267,
  365
Louie's Italian Restaurant (**USF**), 321
Luna Overlook (**EU**), 276, 288
Lyft, 130
LYNX public bus system, 133

M
Madam Malkin's Robes for All Occasions
  (**USF**), 213, 363, 366
Mademoiselle Malkins robe shop (**EU**), 285
Magic of Christmas at Hogwarts (**IOA**),
  266
Magical Menagerie (**USF**), 213, 363, 366
Maku Round Raft Ride (**VB**), 296
Mall at Millenia, 368
Mama Della's Ristorante (Portofino Bay),
  79, 303, 343, 353
Mama Luna's Feline Fiesta (**USF**), 219
Mandara Spa, 41, 81, 84, 86
Manor Storehouse (**EU**), 366
maps
  CityWalk, 372–373
  Epic Universe, 274–275
  hotels in Universal & I-Drive areas, 111
  I-Drive Area Sneak Routes, 124
  Islands of Adventure (**IOA**), 246–247
  South Orlando, 122–123
  Universal Orlando, 8–9
  Universal Studios Florida (**USF**),
    194–195
  Volcano Bay (**VB**), 291

M *(continued)*
Mardi Gras live concerts (**USF**), 229–230
Mardi Gras (**USF**), 227–230
Marilyn Monroe and the Diamond Bellas (**USF**), 224
Mario Kart: Bowser's Challenge (**EU**), 278–279
Mario Motors (**EU**), 366
Marvel Alterniverse Store (**IOA**), 365
Marvel Character Dinner, 306
Marvel Comics, 244
Marvel Super Hero Island (**IOA**), 243, 244–250, 365
MasterCard, 140
Me Ship, *The Olive* (**IOA**), 251
Mead Hall (**EU**), 285, 308, 330–331
Mears Transportation Group, 128, 130, 131
Medical Concierge, 144
medical matters, 144–145, 148
medication for kids, 172
Mel's Drive-In (**USF**), 321
Men in Black Alien Attack (**USF**), 13, 214–215
Menchie's Frozen Yogurt (CityWalk), 308
Mess Tent, The (**IOA**), 328
Meteor Astropub (**EU**), 331
MIB Gear (**USF**), 363
military discounts, 39
Miller Ale House, 360
Mine-Cart Madness (**EU**), 279
Minion Cafe (**USF**), 302–303, 307, 322–323
Minion Land on Illumination Avenue (**USF**), 196, 197–198
Minion Land, Super Silly Stuff (**USF**), 362
Ministry of Magic (**EU**), 283
Mobil gas station, 142
Mobile Ordering, 68, 294, 310
mobility restrictions, 156–159
Moe's Southwest Grill (CityWalk), 334
Moe's Tavern (**USF**), 323
money
    See also discounts
    allocating, 32–41
    making the most of your, at Universal Orlando, 42–69
Monsters Unchained: The Frankenstein Experiment (**EU**), 281
Moonship Chocolates & Celestial Sweets (**EU**), 288, 366
Moose Juice, Goose Juice (**IOA**), 328
Morton's Steakhouse, 361
MouseSavers, 22, 38, 41, 130
Mulberry Street (**IOA**), 365
Music Corporation of America (MCA), 5, 6
Music Stage Plaza (**USF**), 200

Musica della Notte, 87
My Universal Photos, 68, 152–155, 365
Mystic Fountain (**IOA**), 267
Mythos Restaurant (**IOA**), 303, 343, 353–354

N
Natural Selections (**IOA**), 328
NBC Media Center (**USF**), 220, 363
NBC Sports Grill & Brew (CityWalk), 303, 342, 343, 354–355, 370
New Dutch Trading Co. (Sapphire Falls), 90, 337
New York (**USF**), 196, 200–205, 362
Nile Ethiopian Restaurant, 361
Nintendo Super Star Store (**EU**), 366
North Star Wintry Wonders (**EU**), 366

O
Oak and Star Tavern, The (**EU**), 331
Oasis Bar (Dockside Inn), 338
Ocean Prime restaurant, 361
Ocean Trader Market (**IOA**), 365
Oculus Nighttime Spectacular (**EU**), 288
Ohyah and Ohno Drop Slides (**VB**), 296
Ollivanders (**IOA**), 264
Ollivanders (**USF**), 210–212, 259, 363, 365
On Location photo shop (**USF**), 152, 362
1-Day Base Ticket, 32
1-Day Universal Express Plus Pass, 60
one-day touring, 42–44
One Fish, Two Fish, Red Fish, Blue Fish (**IOA**), 269
1-UP Factory store (**EU**), 278, 366
online travel agencies (OTAs), 104–105
Oodle Ramen, 361
operating hours, 32
Orange County Convention Center (OCCC), 26–27
Orbitz, 104
Orchid Court Lounge & Sushi Bar (Royal Pacific Resort), 89, 342, 343, 354–355
Orlando, South (map), 122–123
Orlando Business Journal, 22
Orlando Informer, 22
Orlando International Airport (MCO), 127–130
Orlando ParkStop Podcast, 24
Orlando Premium Outlets— International Drive, 369
Orlando Sentinel, 22
Orlando Stroller Rentals, 175
Orlando Theme Park News, 22
Orlando Ticket Connection, 40
"Orlando Tourism Report," 23–24
Orlando Weekly magazine, 22

Orlando's Magical Dining, 41
Other Worlds Mercantile (**EU**), 144, 366
outlets near Universal Orlando, 369
Owl Post (**IOA/USF**), 213, 259, 366
Owlery (**IOA**), 259
oxygen tanks, concentrators, 164

P

package delivery, 152
packing essentials, 141–142
Palm Restaurant, The (Hard Rock Hotel),
    79, 84, 303, 343, 355–356
Panda Express (CityWalk), 334
parades, 177, 225–226, 228–229, 238
Park Plaza Holiday Shop (**USF**), 363
parking
    at CityWalk, 371
    free self-parking, 68
    at quitting time, 69
    self-parking, 134
    at Universal Orlando, 79, 133–136
    valet parking, 135
Parkscope, 22
Park-to-Park admission, 34–35
Pat O'Brien's Orlando (CityWalk), 303,
    342, 355–356, 370, 374
Patisserie Matagot bakery (**EU**), 285
phone numbers at Universal Orlando
    (table), 24
photography, 68, 152–155, 365
Pier 8 Market (Dockside Inn), 337–338
Pig Floyd's Urban Barbakoa, 361
Pizza Moon (**EU**), 331
Pizza Predattoria (**IOA**), 328
Place Cachée (**EU**), 283
planning, gathering information, 21–24
podcasts, best Universal, 23–24
Pointe Orlando shopping & dining
    complex, 361, 368–369
popcorn, refillable drinks, 313–315
Popeye & Bluto's Bilge-Rat Barges (**IOA**),
    251–252
Poppy's Playground (**USF**), 220
Port of Entry Christmas Shoppe (**IOA**),
    365
Port of Entry (**IOA**), 243, 365
Port Provisions (**IOA**), 365
Portofino Bay Hotel, 72, 73, 78, 80, 81,
    85–87, 114, 138, 368
Portofino Club Lounge, 82
Po's Kung Fu Training Camp,
    featuring *Po Live!* (**USF**), 218–219
Power-Up Bands (**EU**), 278
Premier Annual Passes, 38
Premium Plus Internet, 80
Premium Scream Night (**USF**), 232

Presidential Suites, Sapphire Falls Resort,
    90
Pretorius' Scientific Oddities (**EU**), 281, 366
Priceline, 104
Prime Value hotels, 73
Princess Peach's Castle (**EU**), 278
private cabanas, 77
prosthetic limbs, 159
Pteranodon Flyers (**IOA**), 258
public transportation, 133
Publix groceries, 148
Puihi Round Raft Ride (**VB**), 296–297
Puka Uli Lagoon (**VB**), 297
Pumpkin Juice, Fizz, 312
Punga Racers (**VB**), 297

Q

Quality Quidditch Supplies (**USF**), 213
queues, 44–45
Quicksilver Tours & Transportation, 30,
    129–130
quitting time, 69

R

Race Through New York Starring Jimmy
    Fallon (**USF**), 202–203
rain
    and raingear, 145–146
    Universal Orlando climate (table), 28
Rainforest Village (**VB**), 292, 295–298
Raptor Encounter (**IOA**), 258–259
ratings, star. *See* star ratings
Ravenous Pig, The, 361
reader survey, 5
readers, comments from, 4–5, 380
reader's questions to authors, 379
Red Coconut Club (CityWalk), 370,
    374–375
Red Oven Pizza (CityWalk), 308, 335
Reef, The (**VB**), 292, 300
Regions bank, 139
religious services, 155
renting
    cars, 41, 81, 135
    strollers, 173–175
    wheelchairs, ECVs, 159–160
reservations
    See also Virtual Lines
    dining, 160–161
    private tours, 66
    Universal Orlando dining, 304
    Universal Orlando hotel, 74
restaurants
    See also specific restaurant
    at CityWalk (map), 372–373
    cost range, 339

R *(continued)*
restaurants *(continued)*
  at Epic Universe (map), 274–275
  fast food at Universal Orlando's parks,
    307–316
  full-service profiles, 339–360
  at Islands of Adventure (map), 246–247
  quick-service mini-profiles, 316–339
  reservations, 161–162, 304
  star ratings, 339
  at Universal Studios Florida (map),
    194–195
restrooms
  family, 160
  kid problems, 177
  at Volcano Bay (map), 291
Resy app, 304
Revenge of the Mummy (**USF**), 18,
  203–204
Richter's Burger Co. (**USF**), 323
rider swap, 60, 187–189
"Rider's Guide for Rider Safety & Guests
  with Disabilities," 156
RIP guided tour, Halloween Horror Nights
  (**USF**), 232
Rising Star karaoke club (CityWalk),
  370, 374
River Village (**VB**), 292, 298–299
Rix Flix, 22
Rock Royalty Lounge, 82
Rock the Universe (**USF**), 155, 226–227
room ratings, hotel, 113–117
rope drop (arrival at theme parks), 51–53
Rosen Shingle Creek, 114, 117
Rosie's Irish Shop (**USF**), 362
Royal Pacific Resort, 72–73, 87–89, 114, 368
Royal Pacific Resort Club Lounge, 82
Runamukka Reef (**VB**), 299

S
safety
  See also security
  "Rider's Guide for Rider Safety & Guests
    with Disabilities," 156
Sahara Traders (**USF**), 362
Saigon Noodle & Grill, 361
sales and lodging tax, 71, 141
Sal's Market Deli (Portofino Bay Hotel),
  308
San Francisco Candy Factory (**USF**), 363
San Francisco Pastry Company (**USF**), 323
San Francisco (**USF**), 196, 205–207, 363
Sanford International Airport (SFB), 127
Sapphire Falls Resort, 73, 80, 89–91,
  114, 368

Savory Feast Kitchen (CityWalk), 357–358
scary stuff for kids, 178–185
Schwab's Pharmacy (**USF**), 324
Scooter Bug, 159
Screamscape, 22
Scribbulus school supplies (**USF**), 213
"Season Pass, The," 24
Seasons 52 restaurant, 361
security
  at Orlando International Airport (MCO),
    127
  screenings at Universal Orlando,
    136–137
Sehlinger, Bob, viii, 4
self-parking, 134
seniors, touring plans for, 240, 272, 289
service animals, 160
Seuss, Dr. (Theodor Geisel), 267, 365
Seuss Landing (**IOA**), 243, 267, 365
Shakes Malt Shoppe (Cabana Bay), 336
Sheinberg, Sidney, 5–6
Sheraton Vistana Villages Resort Villas,
  I-Drive/Orlando, 114, 117, 118
shopping
  at CityWalk, 367
  at Diagon Alley (**USF**), 213–214
  at Epic Universe (**EU**), 366–367
  hotel, 104–106
  at Islands of Adventure (**IOA**), 365
  near Universal Orlando, 368–369
  at Universal Orlando, 361–368
  at Universal Orlando generally, 302–306
  at Universal Orlando hotels, 367–368
  at Universal Studios Florida (**USF**),
    362–364
  at Volcano Bay (**VB**), 367
  in the Wizarding World (**EU**), 285
Shrek's Swamp (**USF**), 219
Shrek's Swamp for Little Ogres (**USF**), 219
Shutterbutton's films, photos (**USF**),
  154, 213
shuttle service, 128–132, 131
Signature Collection resorts, 73
Simpsons Ride, The (**USF**), 13, 18, 216–217
single-rider lines, 63–64
Skull Island (**IOA**), 243, 252–254
Skull Island: Reign of Kong (**IOA**), 252–254,
  365
Sloppy Taco Palace, 361
smoking
  at Universal Orlando hotels, 76
  at Universal Orlando Resort, 155
Snookers & Snookers Sweet Candy
  Cookers (**IOA**), 365
social media feeds, best Universal Orlando,
  24

Soupa Saiyan ramen bar, 361
Southwest Orlando Jewish Congregation, 155
special events
    at Islands of Adventure (IOA), 269–271
    at Universal Studios Florida (USF), 226–238
spell-casting locations
    in Diagon Alley (USF), 211–212
    in Hogsmeade (IOA), 265
    in Ministry of Magic (EU), 284–285
Spit Fyre Grill (EU), 285, 331
SpongeBob StorePants (USF), 363
Springfield: Home of the Simpsons (USF), 196, 215–216, 363
star ratings
    hotel rooms, 113–117, 118
    restaurants, 339–340
Star Sui Bao (EU), 331
Starbucks, 92, 95, 98, 137
Starbucks (CityWalk), 335
Stardust Racers (EU), 151, 277
Stay More, Save More pricing structure, 74
Stella, Alicia, viii, 4, 20, 59, 201, 203, 205, 206, 210, 215, 216, 222, 244, 252, 257, 261, 265, 268, 279
Stella Nova and Terra Luna Resorts, 73, 100–101, 114, 118, 368
"Stella Says" sidebars, 20
Storm Force Accelatron (IOA), 249–250
Strand restaurant, The, 361
strollers
    in attractions, 157
    and attractions, 171
    overview, 173–176
Strong Water Tavern (Sapphire Falls), 79, 90, 303–304, 342, 356–357
Studio Audience Center, 197
Studio Sweets (USF), 362
Sugarplum's Sweet Shop (USF), 213, 312, 363
sunburn, sunglasses, 172
SunPass, 119
Sunset Lounge (Dockside Inn), 338
Super Nintendo World (EU), 273, 277–281, 366
Super Nintendo World store (CityWalk), 280
SuperStar Shuttle, 128, 131
Supply Vault (USF), 362
Surfside Inn and Suites, 73, 97
Sushi Yama, 361
Swamp Snacks & Troll Treats (USF), 324
Swizzle Lounge (Cabana Bay Beach Resort), 95, 349

T
Tabla Restaurant, 360
Tales of Beedle the Bard (USF), 213
Taniwha Tubes: Tonga & Raki (VB), 297
TapuTapu wristbands, 62, 292–294, 301
tattoos, temporary, 176
taxes, 71, 141
taxis, 129
TeAwa the Fearless River (VB), 292, 293, 297–298
technical rehearsals, 67
temperature, average daily by month (table), 28
Terra Luna Resort, 73, 100–101, 114, 118, 273, 368
Testa, Len, viii, 4
T.G.I. Friday's, 360
Thai Silk, 361
Theme Park Insider, 22
Theme Park Stop, viii
theme parks
    See also specific park
    operating hours, 32
    transportation between Universal resorts and, 137–138
    which one to visit, 30–31
Three Broomsticks (IOA), 259, 302, 307, 311, 312, 328–329
Thrills Taste Travels blog, 22
Thunder Falls Terrace (IOA), 307, 329
thunderstorms, 301
Tiffany Towncar Service, 129
Tiger Bar (EU), 345–346
time
    cutting dining time at theme parks, 315–316
    how much to allocate, 28–29
+time in Lines app, 23
timing your visit, 25–32
Toadstool Cafe (EU), 278, 308, 331–332
tobacco, 155
Today Cafe (USF), 307, 324
Toko Gifts (Royal Pacific), 368
toll roads, 119–120
Tonight Shop, The (USF), 362
Toon Extra toys, supplies (IOA), 365
Toon Lagoon (IOA), 243, 250–252, 365
Toothless' Treasure (EU), 287, 367
Toothsome Chocolate Emporium (City-Walk), 303, 342, 357–358, 370
Tot Tiki Reef (VB), 299
Tour en Floo gift shop (EU), 285
touring
    See also touring plans or specific tour
    free backstage tours, 66–67

T *(continued)*
touring *(continued)*
  nonexclusive, private, 65–66
  rainy-day, 145–146
  rules for successful, 42–44
  VIP tours, 64–66
Touring Plans, 22
touring plans
  choosing appropriate, 239–240
  clip-out, 48, 395–416
  Epic Universe (**EU**), 288–289
  generally, 45–46
  Islands of Adventure (**IOA**), 271–272
  for kids, 171
  overview, 46–51
  personalized tour-planning services, 46
  Universal Studios Florida (**USF**),
    238–241
  Volcano Bay (**VB**) strategy, 301
Touring Plans Crowd Calendar, 29
towels and lockers, 294–295
town car service, 129–130
trade shows, conventions, 26–27
Transformers: The Ride-3D (**USF**), 18,
  204–205
transportation
  between Universal resorts and the
    theme parks, 137–138
  shuttle service, 128–132, 131
  taxis, 129
Trattoria del Porto (Portofino Bay), 343,
  358–359
Travelocity, 104
Treasures of Bali (CityWalk), 368
Treasures of Poseidon (**IOA**), 365
Tribute Store (**USF**), 363
trip planner, online, 133
Triple, 313
Tripster, 40
Trivago, 105
Trolls Trollercoaster (**USF**), 218, 219–220
Tuk Tuk Market (Royal Pacific), 89, 338
Turbo Boost Treats (**EU**), 332
Turner Drugs, 144
Triwizard Spirit Rally, The (**IOA**), 265
2-Park, 3-Park Seasonal Annual Passes, 35

U
Uber, 130
Undercover Tourist, 40
Uni transponders, 119–120
Universal Aventura Hotel. *See* Aventura
  Hotel
Universal Cabana Bay Beach Resort. *See*
  Cabana Bay Beach Resort

Universal characters
  character dining, 192, 308–309
  greeting locations, 190–191
  and lost kids, 177
  Marvel Character Dinner, 306
  Meet the Monsters (**EU**), 283
  meeting, 189–191
Universal Cinemark, 41, 137, 375
Universal Endless Summer Resort.
  See Endless Summer Resort
Universal Epic Universe.
  See Epic Universe (**EU**)
Universal Express, 57–62, 293
Universal Helios Grand Hotel.
  See Helios Grand Hotel
Universal Islands of Adventure.
  See Islands of Adventure (**IOA**)
Universal Mega Movie Parade (**USF**),
  225–226
Universal mobile app, 22
Universal Orlando
  addresses, important (table), 23
  annual passes, 35–38
  benefits of staying on-site at, 71–72
  best hotels near, 110–117
  dining near, 360–361
  getting there, 119–133
  insider hacks, 67–68
  integrating vacation with WDW visit,
    29–30
  leaving, 138
  lexicon (glossary), 19
  making the most of your time, money,
    at, 42–69
  off-site lodging options, 103–110
  online websites, 22–23
  operating hours, 32
  overview, 5
  parking, 133–136
  phone numbers (table), 24
  quiet spots around, 68–69
  restaurants. *See* restaurants
  saving money on admission, 38–41
  shopping at, 361–368
  shopping near, 368–369
  vacation packages, 101–103
  vs. Universal Studios Hollywood (USH),
    17–18
  vs. Walt Disney World (WDW), 10–17,
    167–168
Universal Orlando CityWalk.
  See CityWalk
Universal Orlando gift cards, 141
Universal Orlando hotels
  See also specific hotel
  shopping at, 367–368

Universal Orlando Resort
  hotel profiles, 83–101
  hotel services, amenities, 76–83
  hotels generally, 72–76
  overview, 6–17
  plant-based dining, 305
  scary stuff, 178–185
  upcoming at, 19–20
Universal Orlando Vacations, 53, 101
Universal Orlando website, 22
Universal Orlando's Horror Make-Up Show
  (**USF**), 223
Universal Partner Hotel shuttle, 131
Universal Pay, 140
Universal Rewards Plus Visa Signature
  card, 140
Universal Rewards Visa, 140
Universal Service Center, 143
Universal Stella Nova and Terra Luna
  Resorts. *See* Stella Nova and Terra
  Luna Resorts
Universal Studios Florida (**USF**)
  ATMs (automated teller machines), 139
  attraction height requirements (table),
    186
  attractions, 197–223
  character-greeting locations, 190
  Early Park Admission (EPA), 55–56
  generally, 193
  getting oriented at, 193–197
  holidays at, 237–238
  live entertainment at, 224–226
  map, 9, 194–195
  overview, 6–7
  plant-based dining, 305
  quick-service restaurants, 317–324
  restrooms, 160
  rope drop (arrival at), 51–52
  secret entrance to, 197
  shopping at, 362–364
  small-child fright-potential table, 180–181
  special events at, 226–238
  touring plans, 238–241
  Visa cardholder lounge, 68
Universal Studios Hollywood (USH) vs.
  Universal Orlando, 17–18
Universal Studios Store (CityWalk), 90, 95,
  98, 144, 362, 367, 368
Universal uniforms, 176–177
Universal Vacation Planning Center, 79
Universal Vacation Services, 155
Universal Vacations, 75, 128–129
Universal Volcano Bay. *See* Volcano Bay
  (**VB**)
Universal's Great Movie Escape Room
  (CityWalk), 41, 376–377

Universal's Holiday Parade Featuring
  Macy's (**USF**), 238
Universal's mobile app, 310
Universal's official operating calendar, 142
UNIVRS clothing (**USF**), 362
Unlimited Universal Express, 59–60
Unmasking the Horror tour (**USF**), 232
"Unofficial Guide Newsletter," 21
*Unofficial Guide to Walt Disney World,
  The,* 3
"Unofficial" Guides, 1
Untrainable Dragon, The (**EU**), 287
UOAP Facebook group, 22
UOAP lounge (**IOA**), 35, 365
Urban Pantry Food Hall (Aventura Hotel),
  92, 308, 338
"UUOP: The Unofficial Universal Orlando
  Podcast," 23

V

vacation homes, 106–110
Vacation Rentals 411, 109
Vacation Rentals by Owner, 108–109
valet parking, 135–136
¡Vamos!—Báilalo (**USF**), 224
vaping, 155
Various Emporia (**EU**), 366
vegan food, 161
vehicle charging stations, 79
Velvet Bar, 84
Viking Traders (**EU**), 367
Viking Training Camp (**EU**), 287
Villa Pool, 86
Villain-Con Minion Blast (**USF**), 198–200
VIP tours, 64–66
Virtual Lines, 62–63, 292–294
vision impairment, 162
visit, timing your, 25–32
Visit Orlando website, 104, 109
Visitor Toll Pass, 120
Vista Cay developments, 107
Vivo Italian Kitchen (CityWalk), 303,
  343, 359
Volcano, The (**VB**), 292, 295
Volcano Bay (**VB**), 2
  admission, 34
  ATMs (automated teller machines), 139
  attraction height requirements (table),
    187
  attractions, 295–300
  Early Park Admission (EPA), 56
  first aid, 148
  getting oriented at, 292–295
  lost and found, 143
  map, 8, 291
  overview, 290–292

V *(continued)*
Volcano Bay *(continued)*
  parking, 135
  plant-based dining, 305
  quick-service restaurants, 332–333
  rainy-day touring, 145
  restrooms, 160
  rope drop (arrival at), 53
  shopping at, 367
  small-child fright-potential table, 183
  touring strategy, 300–301
  transportation to, 138
  Universal Express at, 60
  Virtual Lines, 62–63
Vol's Caverns (**VB**), 295
Voodoo Doughnut (CityWalk), 308,
  335–336

W

Walgreens, 144, 148, 156
Walt Disney World (WDW)
  getting to Universal Orlando from,
    130–131
  integrating Universal Orlando vacation
    with, 29–30
  mouse jabs, 13
  vs. Universal Orlando, 10–17, 167–168
wands, interactive, 211, 265
Wands by Gregorovitch (**USF**), 211
Wantilan Luau (Royal Pacific Resort), 89,
  342, 359–360
Wasserman, Lew, 5
water taxi service, 137–138
Watson Dental Care, 144
Waturi Beach (**VB**), 292, 300
Waturi Marketplace (**VB**), 152, 367
Wave Village (**VB**), 292, 294, 299–300
Waze traffic update app, 126
Weasleys' Wizard Wheezes (**USF**), 213,
  363, 366

weather, 27–28
websites
  See also specific website
  Universal Orlando, 22–23
  vacation homes, condos, 108–109
weddings, 83
Wells, Frank, 5
Wendy's, 360
Whakawaiwai Eats (**VB**), 308, 333
wheelchair accessibility, 156–159
wheelchair rentals, 158–159
Whole Foods Market, 148, 149
Wi-Fi
  free, 79–80
  service, 143
Wimpy's (**IOA**), 329
wine, beer, liquor, 155–156
Wiseacre's Wizarding Equipment (**USF**),
  214
Wizarding World of Harry Potter, The, 2, 7
Wizarding World of Harry Potter—Diagon
  Alley (**USF**), 7, 196, 207–214, 241, 363
Wizarding World of Harry Potter—
  Hogsmeade (**IOA**), 243, 259–266, 365
Wizarding World of Harry Potter—Ministry
  of Magic (**EU**), 273, 283–285, 367
Wizard's Brew, 313
World Expo (**USF**), 196, 214–215, 363
World's Magic Indonesian Restaurant,
  361
WossaMotta U toys, T-shirts (**IOA**), 365
Wyndham's Theatre (**USF**), 207

Y

Yellow Cab, 128
Yoshi's Adventure (**EU**), 280
Yoshi's Snack Island (**EU**), 332
YouTube, 22, 185

Universal Studios Florida

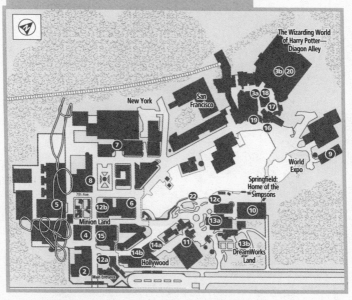

UNIVERSAL STUDIOS FLORIDA ONE-DAY TOURING PLAN FOR ADULTS

1. Buy admission in advance. Call ☎ 407-363-8000 or visit universalorlando.com the day before for the official opening time, and install Universal's app on your smartphone.

2. Arrive at USF 90–120 minutes before the official opening time if Early Park Admission is offered and you're eligible, or 30–45 minutes before opening if you're a day guest. Check Universal's app for daily showtimes.

3. Early-entry guests should visit Ollivanders (3a) and ride Harry Potter and the Escape from Gringotts (3b).

4. Before early entry ends, ride Despicable Me Minion Mayhem. Day guests should begin their tour here if the wait is 20 minutes or less; otherwise, skip it and try again later.

5. Ride Hollywood Rip Ride Rockit.

6. Experience Transformers: The Ride–3D.

7. Ride Revenge of the Mummy in New York.

8. Ride Race Through New York Starring Jimmy Fallon.

9. Experience Men in Black Alien Attack in World Expo.

10. Ride The Simpsons Ride in Springfield.

11. Ride E.T. Adventure near DreamWorks Land.

12. Eat lunch at TODAY Cafe (12a), Minion Cafe (12b), or Fast Food Boulevard (12c).

13. Work in *Animal Actors on Location!* (13a) and/or *Dreamworks Imagination Celebration* (13b) around lunch, according to the daily entertainment schedule.

14. See *Universal Orlando's Horror Make-Up Show* (14a) and *The Bourne Stuntacular* (14b) according to the daily entertainment schedule.

15. Experience Villain-Con Minion Blast, followed by Minion Mayhem (if you didn't ride it earlier).

16. Chat with the Knight Bus conductor and his shrunken head outside of Diagon Alley. Also look for Kreacher in the window of 12 Grimmauld Place, and dial MAGIC (62442) in the red phone booth.

17. See the *Celestina Warbeck and the Banshees* and/or *Tales of Beedle the Bard* shows.

18. See the wand ceremony at Ollivanders, and buy a wand if you wish.

19. Tour Diagon Alley. Browse the shops, explore the dark recesses of Knockturn Alley, and discover the interactive effects. If you're hungry, try the Leaky Cauldron or Florean Fortescue's Ice-Cream Parlour.

20. Ride Harry Potter and the Escape from Gringotts.

21. Revisit favorite attractions, or see any you skipped earlier, if time permits.

22. If it's scheduled, watch the evening lagoon show from Central Park (between Hollywood and Springfield).

Universal Studios Florida

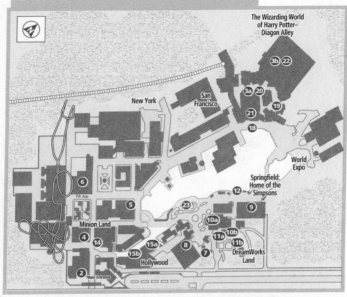

UNIVERSAL STUDIOS FLORIDA ONE-DAY TOURING PLAN
FOR FAMILIES WITH SMALL CHILDREN

1. Buy admission in advance. Call ☎ 407-363-8000 or visit universalorlando.com the day before for the official opening time, and install Universal's app on your smartphone.

2. Arrive at USF 90–120 minutes before the official opening time if Early Park Admission is offered and you're eligible, or 30–45 minutes before opening if you're a day guest. Check Universal's app for daily showtimes.

3. Early-entry guests should visit Ollivanders (3a) and experience Harry Potter and the Escape from Gringotts (3b). Use child swap or exit after the elevators if your child is under 42", or just enjoy Diagon Alley.

4. Before early entry ends, ride Despicable Me Minion Mayhem. Day guests should wait at the entrance until permitted to ride Despicable Me.

5. Experience Transformers: The Ride–3D if your kid can handle the noise and explosions.

6. Ride Race Through New York Starring Jimmy Fallon.

7. Enter DreamWorks Land to ride the Trolls Trollercoaster.

8. Ride E.T. Adventure.

9. Ride The Simpsons Ride in Springfield.

10. See *Animal Actors on Location* (10a) and *Dream-Works Imagination Celebration* (10b) according to the entertainment schedule. Get a snack on Fast Food Boulevard or in DreamWorks Land while you're waiting for the show to start.

11. Between shows, work in time at the Shrek's Swamp (11a) and Kung Fu Panda Training Camp (11b) play-grounds inside DreamWorks Land.

12. Try Kang & Kodos' Twirl 'n' Hurl.

13. Take a break from the park for at least 2 hours, depending on how late the park is open. If staying nearby, return to your room for a nap. Otherwise, take a rest at CityWalk or a resort hotel.

14. Return to the park and experience Villain-Con Minion Blast.

15. If your kids are brave, see *Universal Orlando's Horror Make-Up Show* (15a) and/or *The Bourne Stuntacular* (15b) according to the daily entertainment schedule.

16. Greet characters such as Shrek, SpongeBob, and the Transformers at locations shown in the app.

17. Watch the afternoon character parade (if scheduled) from the New York or Hollywood areas.

18. On your way into Diagon Alley, chat with the Knight Bus conductor and his shrunken head. Also look for Kreacher in the window of 12 Grimmauld Place, and dial MAGIC (62442) in the red phone booth.

19. See the *Celestina Warbeck and the Banshees* and/or *Tales of Beedle the Bard* shows.

20. See the wand ceremony at Ollivanders and buy a wand if you wish.

21. Tour Diagon Alley. If you're hungry, try the Leaky Cauldron or Florean Fortescue's Ice-Cream Parlour.

22. Ride Harry Potter and the Escape from Gringotts (if you didn't earlier). Use child swap or exit after the elevators if your child is under 42".

23. Revisit any favorite attractions, time permitting, and (if scheduled) watch the nighttime lagoon show from Central Park (between Hollywood and Springfield).

Universal Studios Florida

UNIVERSAL STUDIOS FLORIDA ONE-DAY TOURING PLAN FOR TWEENS

1. Buy admission in advance. Call ☎ 407-363-8000 or visit universalorlando.com the day before for the official opening time, and install Universal's app on your smartphone.

2. Arrive at USF 90–120 minutes before the official opening time if Early Park Admission is offered and you're eligible, or 30–45 minutes before opening if you're a day guest. Check Universal's app for daily showtimes.

3. Early-entry guests should visit Ollivanders (3a) and ride Harry Potter and the Escape from Gringotts (3b).

4. Before early entry ends, ride Despicable Me Minion Mayhem. Day guests should begin their tour here if the wait is 20 minutes or less; otherwise, skip it and try again later.

5. Ride Hollywood Rip Ride Rockit if your tween is brave and at least 51" tall.

6. Experience Transformers: The Ride–3D.

7. Ride Revenge of the Mummy in New York.

8. Ride Fast & Furious Supercharged in San Francisco.

9. Enter Diagon Alley and ride Harry Potter and the Escape from Gringotts (if you didn't earlier).

10. Experience Men in Black Alien Attack in World Expo.

11. Eat lunch at Minion Cafe (11a) or Fast Food Boulevard (11b).

12. Experience Villain-Con Minion Blast, followed by Minion Mayhem (if you didn't ride it earlier).

13. See *Universal Orlando's Horror Make-Up Show* (13a), *The Bourne Stuntacular* (13b), and/or *Animal Actors on Location!* (13c) according to the daily entertainment schedule.

14. Ride E.T. Adventure, then greet some characters in nearby DreamWorks Land.

15. Ride The Simpsons Ride in Springfield.

16. Try Kang & Kodos' Twirl 'n' Hurl if 50 or fewer people are in line.

17. Watch the afternoon character parade (if scheduled) from the New York or Hollywood areas.

18. Chat with the Knight Bus conductor and his shrunken head outside of Diagon Alley. Also look for Kreacher in the window of 12 Grimmauld Place, and dial MAGIC (62442) in the red phone booth.

19. See the *Celestina Warbeck and the Banshees* and/or *Tales of Beedle the Bard* shows.

20. See the wand ceremony at Ollivanders, and buy a wand if you wish.

21. Tour Diagon Alley. Browse the shops, explore the dark recesses of Knockturn Alley, and discover the interactive effects. If you're hungry, try the Leaky Cauldron or Florean Fortescue's Ice-Cream Parlour.

22. Revisit favorite attractions, or see any you skipped earlier, if time permits.

23. If it's scheduled, watch the evening lagoon show from Central Park (between Hollywood and Springfield).

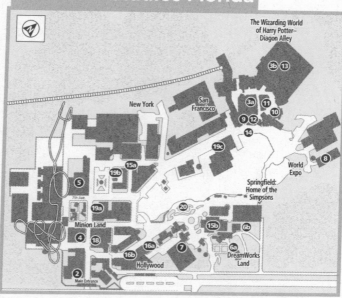

Universal Studios Florida

UNIVERSAL STUDIOS FLORIDA ONE-DAY TOURING PLAN FOR SENIORS

1. Buy admission in advance. Call ☎ 407-363-8000 or visit universalorlando.com the day before for the official opening time, and install Universal's app on your smartphone.

2. Arrive at USF 90–120 minutes before the official opening time if Early Park Admission is offered and you're eligible, or 30–45 minutes before opening if you're a day guest. Check Universal's app for daily showtimes. Rent a wheelchair or ECV if needed.

3. Early-entry guests should visit Ollivanders (3a) and ride Harry Potter and the Escape from Gringotts (3b). Exit after the elevators if you don't wish to experience a mild roller coaster. Or enjoy the rest of Diagon Alley.

4. Before early entry ends, hotel guests should exit Diagon Alley and then ride Despicable Me Minion Mayhem. Day guests should wait at the entrance until permitted to ride Despicable Me. Stationary seating is available on request.

5. Experience Race Through New York Starring Jimmy Fallon. If simulated motion bothers you, enjoy the preshow but exit before the ride.

6. Visit DreamWorks Land to see the *Imagination Celebration* (6a) and *Po Live!* (6b) shows.

7. Ride E.T. Adventure near DreamWorks Land.

8. Ride Men in Black Alien Attack in World Expo if you can tolerate some moderate spinning.

9. Have an early lunch at Leaky Cauldron.

10. See the *Celestina Warbeck and the Banshees* and *Tales of Beedle the Bard* shows.

11. See the wand ceremony at Ollivanders, and purchase a wand if you wish.

12. Tour Diagon Alley. Browse the shops, explore the dark recesses of Knockturn Alley, and discover the interactive effects. If you're still hungry, try Florean Fortescue's Ice-Cream Parlour.

13. Experience Harry Potter and the Escape from Gringotts (if you didn't earlier), and exit after the elevators if you don't wish to experience a mild roller coaster.

14. Chat with the Knight Bus conductor and his shrunken head. Also look for Kreacher in the window of 12 Grimmauld Place, and dial MAGIC (62442) in the red phone booth.

15. See *The Blues Brothers Show* (15a) and *Animal Actors on Location!* (15b) according to the daily entertainment schedule. If time is short, skip *Animal Actors*.

16. See *Universal Orlando's Horror Make-Up Show* (16a) and/or *The Bourne Stuntacular* (16b) according to the daily entertainment schedule.

17. Watch the afternoon character parade (if scheduled) from the New York or Hollywood areas.

18. Experience Villain-Con Minion Blast.

19. Have an early dinner inside the park at Minion Cafe (19a), Finnegan's Bar (19b), or Lombard's Seafood (19c).

20. Revisit any favorite attractions, time permitting, and (if scheduled) watch the evening lagoon show from Central Park (between Hollywood and Springfield).

Universal Islands of Adventure

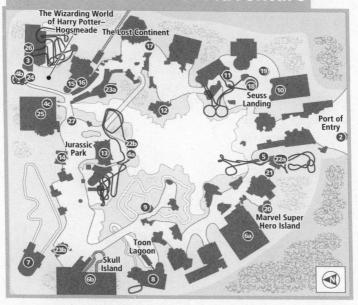

UNIVERSAL ISLANDS OF ADVENTURE ONE-DAY TOURING PLAN FOR ADULTS

1. Buy admission in advance. Call ☎ 407-363-8000 or visit universalorlando.com the day before for the official opening time, and install Universal's app on your smartphone.

2. Arrive at IOA 90–120 minutes before the official opening time if Early Park Admission is offered and you're eligible, or 30–45 minutes before opening if you're a day guest. Check Universal's app for daily showtimes.

3. Early-entry guests should ride Hagrid's Magical Creatures Motorbike Adventure in Hogsmeade only if they are at the front of the pack.

4. Early-entry guests may ride the Jurassic World VelociCoaster (4a) or Flight of the Hippogriff (4b), followed by Harry Potter and the Forbidden Journey (4c), if the posted wait is 15 minutes or less.

5. Guests without early entry should ride The Incredible Hulk Coaster first.

6. Ride The Amazing Adventures of Spider-Man. Day guests should start with Spider-Man (6a), followed by Skull Island: Reign of Kong (6b). Early-entry guests may ride Reign of Kong (6b) on their way to Spider-Man (6a) while walking from Jurassic Park. Both early-entry and day guests continue as follows.

7. Take the Jurassic Park River Adventure. Put your belongings in a pay locker here and leave them through the next two rides.

8. Ride Dudley Do-Right's Ripsaw Falls in Toon Lagoon.

9. Ride Popeye & Bluto's Bilge-Rat Barges. Retrieve your property from Jurassic Park.

10. Experience The Cat in the Hat in Seuss Landing.

11. Experience The High in the Sky Seuss Trolley Train Ride!

12. Eat lunch. A good sit-down choice is Mythos. Make reservations in Universal's app.

13. Explore the Jurassic Park Discovery Center.

14. Meet Blue at the Raptor Encounter.

15. See the *Frog Choir* or *Triwizard Spirit Rally* perform on the small stage outside Hogwarts Castle.

16. See the wand ceremony at Ollivanders and buy a wand if you wish.

17. Chat with the Mystic Fountain.

18. Enjoy the Caro-Seuss-el.

19. Ride One Fish, Two Fish, Red Fish, Blue Fish.

20. In Marvel Super Hero Island, ride Doctor Doom's Fearfall.

21. Ride Storm Force Accelatron.

22. Ride The Incredible Hulk Coaster (22a) or Jurassic World VelociCoaster (22b), whichever you did not ride earlier.

23. Have dinner at Three Broomsticks in Hogsmeade (23a) or Thunder Falls Terrace (23b) in Jurassic Park.

24. Ride Flight of the Hippogriff (if you haven't already).

25. Ride Harry Potter and the Forbidden Journey.

26. Ride Hagrid's Magical Creatures Motorbike Adventure after sunset, if possible.

27. Watch the last Hogwarts Castle light show of the night (if scheduled), or revisit any favorite attractions.

Universal Islands of Adventure

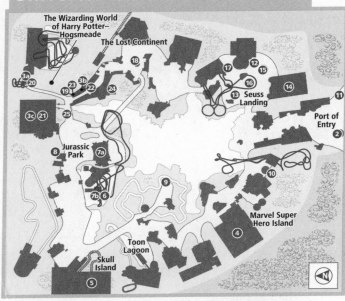

UNIVERSAL ISLANDS OF ADVENTURE ONE-DAY TOURING PLAN FOR FAMILIES WITH SMALL CHILDREN

1. Buy admission in advance. Call ☎ 407-363-8000 or visit universalorlando.com the day before for the official opening time, and install Universal's app on your smartphone.

2. Arrive at IOA 90–120 minutes before the official opening time if Early Park Admission is offered and you're eligible, or 30–45 minutes before opening if you're a day guest. Check Universal's app for daily showtimes. Rent a stroller if needed.

3. Early-entry guests should ride Flight of the Hippogriff (3a), see the wand ceremony at Ollivanders (3b), and tour the queue (but exit before boarding) at Harry Potter and the Forbidden Journey (3c).

4. Early-entry guests should exit Hogsmeade when early entry ends and head to Marvel Super Hero Island to ride The Amazing Adventures of Spider-Man.

5. Experience Skull Island: Reign of Kong if you dare.

6. Continue to Jurassic Park and get in line for Pteranodon Flyers if your child is 36–56 inches tall.

7. Let the kids explore the Jurassic Park Discovery Center (7a) and play in Camp Jurassic (7b).

8. Meet Blue at the Raptor Encounter.

9. Return to Toon Lagoon. Explore Me Ship, The Olive.

10. Ride Storm Force Accelatron in Marvel Super Hero Island on your way to the park exit.

11. Take a break from the park for at least 2 hours, depending on how late the park is open. If staying nearby, return to your room for lunch and a nap. Otherwise, take a rest at CityWalk or a resort hotel.

12. Return to the park. See the next scheduled show of *Oh! The Stories You'll Hear!* in Seuss Landing.

13. Explore If I Ran the Zoo while waiting for the show.

14. Ride The Cat in the Hat.

15. Ride One Fish, Two Fish, Red Fish, Blue Fish.

16. Enjoy the Caro-Seuss-el.

17. Ride The High in the Sky Seuss Trolley Train Ride.

18. Chat with the Mystic Fountain.

19. Enter The Wizarding World of Harry Potter–Hogsmeade, and see the *Frog Choir* or *Triwizard Spirit Rally* perform on the small stage outside Hogwarts.

20. Ride Flight of the Hippogriff (if you didn't earlier).

21. If you didn't already, walk through the queue of Harry Potter and the Forbidden Journey.

22. See the wand ceremony at Ollivanders if you didn't earlier, and buy a wand if you wish.

23. See the stage show you didn't see earlier. Snap a picture of the Hogwarts Express conductor, and explore the shops and interactive windows around Hogsmeade.

24. Have dinner at Three Broomsticks.

25. Watch the Hogwarts Castle light show (if scheduled), or revisit any favorite attractions.

Universal Islands of Adventure

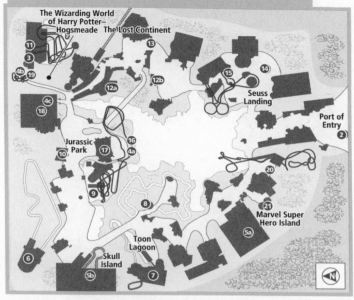

The Wizarding World of Harry Potter–Hogsmeade The Lost Continent

Seuss Landing

Port of Entry

Jurassic Park

Marvel Super Hero Island

Toon Lagoon

Skull Island

UNIVERSAL ISLANDS OF ADVENTURE ONE-DAY TOURING PLAN FOR TWEENS

1. Buy admission in advance. Call ☎ 407-363-8000 or visit universalorlando.com the day before for the official opening time, and install Universal's app on your smartphone.

2. Arrive at IOA 90–120 minutes before the official opening time if Early Park Admission is offered and you're eligible, or 30–45 minutes before opening if you're a day guest. Check Universal's app for daily showtimes.

3. Early-entry guests should ride Hagrid's Magical Creatures Motorbike Adventure in Hogsmeade only if they are at the front of the pack.

4. Early-entry guests may ride the Jurassic World VelociCoaster (4a) or Flight of the Hippogriff (4b), followed by Harry Potter and the Forbidden Journey (4c), if the posted wait is 15 minutes or less.

5. Guests without early entry should start with The Amazing Adventures of Spider-Man (5a) first, followed by Skull Island: Reign of Kong (5b). Early-entry guests may ride Reign of Kong (5b) on their way to Spider-Man (5a) while walking from Jurassic Park. Both early-entry and day guests continue as follows.

6. Take the Jurassic Park River Adventure. Put your belongings in a pay locker here and leave them through the next two rides.

7. Ride Dudley Do-Right's Ripsaw Falls in Toon Lagoon.

8. Ride Popeye & Bluto's Bilge-Rat Barges. Retrieve your property from Jurassic Park.

9. Dry off by running around Camp Jurassic.

10. Visit Blue at the Raptor Encounter if the wait is under 30 minutes.

11. Cross the bridge to Hogsmeade and ride Hagrid's Magical Creatures Motorbike Adventure.

12. Eat lunch at Three Broomsticks (12a) or Fire-Eater's Grill (12b).

13. Chat with the Mystic Fountain on your way through Lost Continent.

14. In Seuss Landing, ride One Fish, Two Fish, Red Fish, Blue Fish.

15. Experience The High in the Sky Seuss Trolley Train Ride!

16. Ride the Jurassic World VelociCoaster (51" minimum height) if you didn't earlier.

17. Explore the Jurassic Park Discovery Center.

18. Ride Harry Potter and the Forbidden Journey.

19. Ride Flight of the Hippogriff (if you haven't already).

20. In Marvel Super Hero Island, ride Storm Force Accelatron.

21. Ride Doctor Doom's Fearfall (52" minimum height).

22. Revisit any favorite attractions, then exit the park for dinner and entertainment in CityWalk.

Universal Islands of Adventure

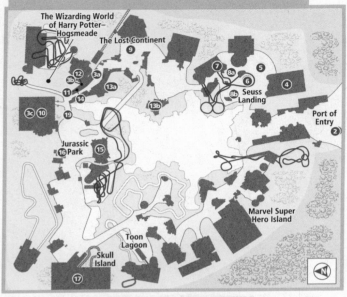

UNIVERSAL ISLANDS OF ADVENTURE
ONE-DAY TOURING PLAN FOR SENIORS

1. Buy admission in advance. Call ☎ 407-363-8000 or visit universalorlando.com the day before for the official opening time, and install Universal's app on your smartphone.

2. Arrive at IOA 90–120 minutes before the official opening time if Early Park Admission is offered and you're eligible, or 30–45 minutes before opening if you're a day guest. Check Universal's app for daily showtimes. Rent a wheelchair or ECV if needed.

3. Early-entry guests should explore the shops of Hogsmeade (3a), see the wand ceremony at Ollivanders (3b), and walk through the queue at Harry Potter and the Forbidden Journey (3c) (ask for the exit before boarding).

4. Exit Hogsmeade before early entry ends, and head to Seuss Landing to ride The Cat in the Hat. Guests without early entry should start at this step.

5. Ride One Fish, Two Fish, Red Fish, Blue Fish.

6. Enjoy the Caro-Seuss-el.

7. Ride The High in the Sky Seuss Trolley Train Ride!

8. See the next scheduled show of Oh! The Stories You'll Hear! (8a) and explore If I Ran the Zoo (8b) while waiting for the show.

9. Chat with the Mystic Fountain.

10. Enter Hogsmeade and walk through the queue of Harry Potter and the Forbidden Journey (if you didn't earlier).

11. See the Frog Choir or Triwizard Spirit Rally perform on the small stage outside Hogwarts.

12. See the wand ceremony at Ollivanders (if you didn't earlier), and buy a wand if you wish.

13. Have lunch at Three Broomsticks (13a) or Mythos (13b).

14. After lunch, see the stage show you didn't see earlier. Snap a picture of the Hogwarts Express conductor, and explore the shops and interactive windows around Hogsmeade. Make sure you sample (or at least smell) some sweets at Honeydukes.

15. Cross the bridge to Jurassic Park and see the exhibits in the Jurassic Park Discovery Center.

16. Meet Blue at the Raptor Encounter.

17. Ride Skull Island: Reign of Kong, or at least request a temple tour through its elaborate queue.

18. Walk counterclockwise around the park, paying attention to the quiet paths along the waterfront in each island.

19. Revisit any favorite attractions, or remain in Hogsmeade to watch the Hogwarts Castle light show (if scheduled). Or exit the park for an early dinner in CityWalk.

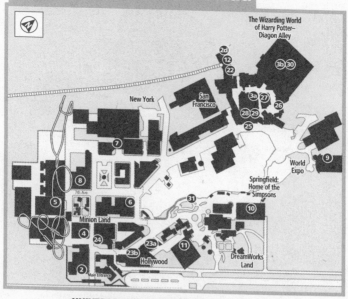

Universal Studios Florida

The Wizarding World
of Harry Potter–
Diagon Alley

New York

San Francisco

World Expo

Springfield:
Home of the
Simpsons

Minion Land

Hollywood

DreamWorks
Land

Main Entrance

7th Ave.

UNIVERSAL ORLANDO HIGHLIGHTS ONE-DAY/
TWO-PARK TOURING PLAN: PART ONE (Assumes: 1-Day Park-to-Park Ticket)

1. Buy admission in advance. Call ☎ 407-363-8000 or visit universalorlando.com the day before for the official opening time, and install Universal's app on your smartphone.

2. Arrive at USF 90–120 minutes before the official opening time if Early Park Admission is offered and you're eligible, or 30–45 minutes before opening if you're a day guest. Check Universal's app for daily showtimes. **Alternative:** If only IOA is open for Early Park Admission and you're eligible, arrive at IOA 90–120 minutes before official opening. Ride Hagrid's Magical Creatures Motorbike Adventure (**2a**), followed by Jurassic World Veloci-Coaster (**2b**) or Flight of the Hippogriff (**2c**). Then take the first Hogwarts Express (**2d**) of the morning to USF, and continue at the next step. **(See the next page for the map of the previous four steps.)**

3. Early-entry guests should head to Diagon Alley to visit Ollivanders (**3a**) and ride Harry Potter and the Escape from Gringotts (**3b**).

4. Return to the front of the park to ride Despicable Me Minion Mayhem. Day guests should begin here.

5. Ride Hollywood Rip Ride Rockit.

6. Experience Transformers: The Ride–3D.

7. Ride Revenge of the Mummy in New York.

8. Ride Race Through New York Starring Jimmy Fallon if the standby wait is short.

9. Ride Men in Black Alien Attack in World Expo.

10. Experience The Simpsons Ride in Springfield.

11. Ride E.T. Adventure near DreamWorks Land.

12. Ride Hogwarts Express to IOA. Have your park-to-park ticket ready.

Tour Islands of Adventure using Part Two of this plan (see next page); then return to USF and resume at step 23 below.

23. See *Universal Orlando's Horror Make-Up Show* (**23a**) and/or *The Bourne Stuntacular* (**23b**) according to the daily entertainment schedule.

24. Experience Villain-Con Minion Blast.

25. Chat with the Knight Bus conductor outside of Diagon Alley. Also look for Kreacher in the window of 12 Grimmauld Place and dial MAGIC (62442) in the red phone booth.

26. See *Celestina Warbeck and the Banshees* or *Tales of Beedle the Bard* in Diagon Alley.

27. See the wand ceremony at Ollivanders, and buy a wand if you wish.

28. Eat dinner at the Leaky Cauldron.

29. Tour Diagon Alley. Browse the shops, explore the dark recesses of Knockturn Alley, and discover the interactive effects.

30. Ride Harry Potter and the Escape from Gringotts.

31. If scheduled, watch the evening lagoon show from Central Park (between Hollywood and Springfield).

(continued on next page)

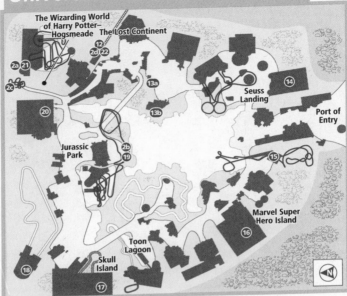

UNIVERSAL ORLANDO HIGHLIGHTS ONE-DAY/TWO-PARK
TOURING PLAN: PART TWO

(continued from previous page)

13. Break for lunch. We suggest Fire-Eater's Grill in Lost Continent (13a) for a quicker meal or Mythos (13b) for sit-down dining.

14. Ride The Cat in the Hat in Seuss Landing.

15. Ride The Incredible Hulk Coaster on Marvel Super Hero Island.

16. Ride The Amazing Adventures of Spider-Man.

17. Ride Skull Island: Reign of Kong.

18. Take the Jurassic Park River Adventure.

19. Ride the Jurassic World VelociCoaster.

20. Ride Harry Potter and the Forbidden Journey.

21. Experience Hagrid's Magical Creatures Motorbike Adventure.

22. Return to USF via Hogwarts Express, or walk back to the other park if the posted wait exceeds 20 minutes.

Resume Part One starting with step 23 (see previous page).

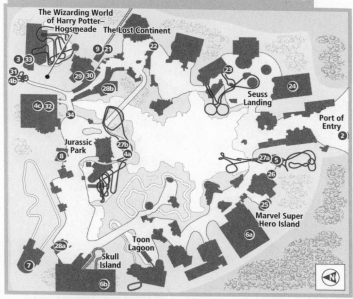

Universal Islands of Adventure

ALTERNATE UNIVERSAL ORLANDO HIGHLIGHTS ONE-DAY/TWO-PARK
TOURING PLAN: PART ONE *(Assumes: 1-Day Park-to-Park Ticket)*

1. Buy admission in advance. Call ☎ 407-363-8000 or visit universalorlando.com the day before for the official opening time, and install Universal's app on your smartphone.

2. Arrive at IOA 90–120 minutes before the official opening time if Early Park Admission is offered and you're eligible, or 30–45 minutes before opening if you're a day guest. Check Universal's app for daily showtimes.

3. Early-entry guests should ride Hagrid's Magical Creatures Motorbike Adventure in Hogsmeade only if they are at the front of the pack.

4. Early-entry guests may ride the Jurassic World VelociCoaster (**4a**) or Flight of the Hippogriff (**4b**), followed by Harry Potter and the Forbidden Journey (**4c**), if the posted wait is 15 minutes or less.

5. Guests without early entry should first ride The Incredible Hulk Coaster.

6. Ride The Amazing Adventures of Spider-Man. Day guests should start with Spider-Man (**6a**), followed by Skull Island: Reign of Kong (**6b**). Early-entry guests may ride Reign of Kong (**6b**) on their way to Spider-Man (**6a**) while walking from Jurassic Park. Both early-entry and day guests continue as follows.

7. Take the Jurassic Park River Adventure.

8. Meet Blue at the Raptor Encounter.

9. Ride Hogwarts Express to USF. Have your park-to-park ticket ready.

Tour Universal Studios Florida using Part Two of this plan (see next page); then return to IOA and resume at step 22 below.

22. Chat with the Mystic Fountain.

23. Experience The High in the Sky Seuss Trolley Train Ride! in Seuss Landing.

24. Experience The Cat in the Hat.

25. In Marvel Super Hero Island ride Doctor Doom's Fearfall.

26. Ride Storm Force Accelatron.

27. Ride The Incredible Hulk Coaster (**27a**) or Jurassic World VelociCoaster (**27b**), whichever one you did not ride earlier.

28. Eat dinner at Thunder Falls Terrace (**28a**) in Jurassic Park or Three Broomsticks (**28b**) in Hogsmeade.

29. See the *Frog Choir* or *Triwizard Spirit Rally* perform on the small stage outside Hogwarts Castle.

30. See the wand ceremony at Ollivanders and buy a wand if you wish.

31. Ride Flight of the Hippogriff (if you haven't already).

32. Ride Harry Potter and the Forbidden Journey.

33. Ride Hagrid's Magical Creatures Motorbike Adventure in Hogsmeade after sunset, if possible.

34. Watch the last Hogwarts Castle light show of the night (if scheduled), or revisit any favorite attractions.

(continued on next page)

Universal Studios Florida

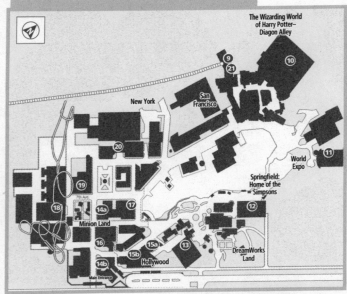

ALTERNATE UNIVERSAL ORLANDO HIGHLIGHTS ONE-DAY/TWO-PARK TOURING PLAN: PART TWO

(continued from previous page)

10. Enter Diagon Alley and ride Harry Potter and the Escape from Gringotts.

11. Ride Men in Black Alien Attack in World Expo.

12. Experience The Simpsons Ride in Springfield.

13. Ride E.T. Adventure near DreamWorks Land.

14. Break for lunch at Minion Cafe (**14a**) or Today Cafe (**14b**) near the front of the park.

15. See *Universal Orlando's Horror Make-Up Show* (**15a**) or *The Bourne Stuntacular* (**15b**) according to the daily entertainment schedule.

16. Experience Villain-Con Minion Blast.

17. Experience Transformers: The Ride-3D.

18. Ride Hollywood Rip Ride Rockit.

19. Ride Race Through New York Starring Jimmy Fallon if the standby wait is short.

20. Ride Revenge of the Mummy in New York.

21. Take a look around Diagon Alley before returning to IOA via Hogwarts Express, or walk back to the other park if the posted wait exceeds 20 minutes.

Resume Part One starting with step 22 (see previous page).

Universal Studios Florida

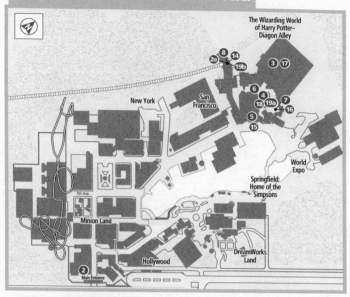

WIZARDING WORLD ONE-DAY/TWO-PARK TOURING PLAN: PART ONE
(Assumes: 1-Day Park-to-Park Ticket. Excludes: All non-Potter attractions.)

1. Buy admission in advance. Call ☎ 407-363-8000 or visit universalorlando.com the day before for the official opening time, and install Universal's app on your smartphone.

2. Arrive at USF 90–120 minutes before the official opening time if Early Park Admission is offered and you're eligible, or 30–45 minutes before opening if you're a day guest. Check Universal's app for daily showtimes. **Alternative:** If IOA is open for Early Park Admission and you're eligible, arrive at IOA's turnstiles 90–120 minutes before the official opening time (**2a**). Ride Hagrid's Magical Creatures Motorbike Adventure (**2b**) and then Flight of the Hippogriff (**2c**). Ride Harry Potter and the Forbidden Journey (**2d**) as well if you have time. Take the first Hogwarts Express of the morning to King's Cross Station (**2e**), and continue at the next step. (*See the next page for the map of the previous five steps.*)

3. Early-entry guests should ride Harry Potter and the Escape from Gringotts. If Gringotts isn't operating, enjoy the rest of Diagon Alley but don't get in line.

4. See the wand ceremony at Ollivanders, and buy a wand if you wish. Gringotts may have a long line by the time the park officially opens if Early Park Admission was offered, so day guests should begin with Ollivanders if the posted wait time for Gringotts is more than 30 minutes.

5. Have breakfast at the Leaky Cauldron or Florean Fortescue's Ice-Cream Parlour (hey, you're on vacation!).

6. Tour Diagon Alley. Browse the shops, explore the dark recesses of Knockturn Alley, and discover the interactive effects.

7. See either the *Tales of Beedle the Bard* or *Celestina Warbeck and the Banshees* shows.

8. Exit Diagon Alley and ride the Hogwarts Express from King's Cross Station to IOA. Have your park-to-park ticket ready.

Tour Islands of Adventure using Part Two of this plan (see next page); then return to USF and resume at step 15 below.

15. Chat with the Knight Bus conductor and his shrunken head. Also look for Kreacher in the window of 12 Grimmauld Place, and dial MAGIC (62442) in the red phone booth.

16. Reenter Diagon Alley and catch the *Carkit Market* show that you didn't see earlier.

17. Ride Harry Potter and the Escape from Gringotts.

18. Have dinner at the Leaky Cauldron, or just eat dessert from Florean Fortescue's Ice-Cream Parlour or Sugarplum's Sweet Shop.

19. Stay in Diagon Alley (**19a**) until closing time, enjoying the lagoon show's fireworks over Gringotts (when scheduled). Watch out for Death Eaters during the Halloween season. Alternatively, take Hogwarts Express (**19b**) back to IOA and watch the light show on Hogwarts Castle (**19c**) (performed seasonally).

(continued on next page)

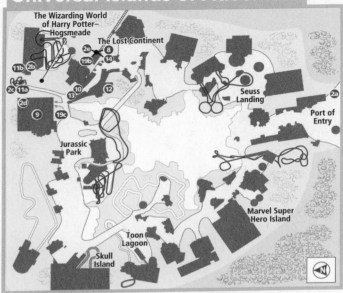

WIZARDING WORLD ONE-DAY/TWO-PARK TOURING PLAN: PART TWO

(Assumes: 1-Day Park-to-Park Ticket. Excludes: All non-Potter attractions.)

(continued from previous page)

9. Enter Hogsmeade and ride Harry Potter and the Forbidden Journey.

10. See the *Frog Choir* or *Triwizard Spirit Rally* perform on the small stage outside Hogwarts.

11. Ride Flight of the Hippogriff (11a), followed by Hagrid's Magical Creatures Motorbike Adventure (11b).

12. Have lunch at Three Broomsticks.

13. After lunch, see the stage show you didn't see earlier. Snap a picture of the Hogwarts Express conductor, and explore the shops and interactive windows around Hogsmeade. Make sure you sample (or at least smell) some sweets at Honeydukes.

14. Return to USF via Hogwarts Express.

*Resume Part One starting with step 15
(see previous page).*

Universal Islands of Adventure

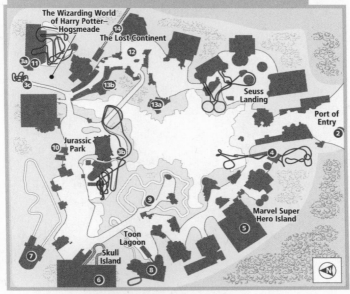

UNIVERSAL ORLANDO COMPREHENSIVE TWO-DAY/TWO-PARK
TOURING PLAN: DAY ONE
(Assumes: Multiday Park-to-Park Ticket)

1. Buy admission in advance. Call ☎ 407-363-8000 or visit universalorlando.com the day before for the official opening time, and install Universal's app on your smartphone.

2. Arrive at IOA 90–120 minutes before the official opening time if Early Park Admission is offered and you're eligible, or 30–45 minutes before opening if you're a day guest. Check Universal's app for daily showtimes.

3. Early-entry guests should ride Hagrid's Magical Creatures Motorbike Adventure in Hogsmeade (3a), followed by the Jurassic World VelociCoaster (3b) or Flight of the Hippogriff (3c) if the posted wait is 15 minutes or less.

4. Ride the Incredible Hulk Coaster in Marvel Super Hero Island. Guests without early entry should start at this step.

5. See The Amazing Adventures of Spider-Man.

6. Experience Skull Island: Reign of Kong.

7. Take the Jurassic Park River Adventure. Put your belongings in a pay locker here and leave them through the next two water rides.

8. Reverse course to ride Dudley Do-Right's Ripsaw Falls in Toon Lagoon.

9. Ride Popeye & Bluto's Bilge-Rat Barges. Now that you've achieved maximum soakage, retrieve your property from Jurassic Park.

10. Get your photo taken at the Raptor Encounter if the wait isn't overwhelming.

11. Ride Hagrid's Magical Creatures Motorbike Adventure if you didn't ride earlier.

12. Stop and chat with the Mystic Fountain in The Lost Continent.

13. Eat lunch at Mythos in Lost Continent (13a) or Three Broomsticks in Hogsmeade (13b).

14. After lunch, take the Hogwarts Express from Hogsmeade Station to USF, or walk to the other park if the posted wait exceeds 20 minutes. Have your park-to-park ticket ready.

(continued on next page)

Universal Studios Florida

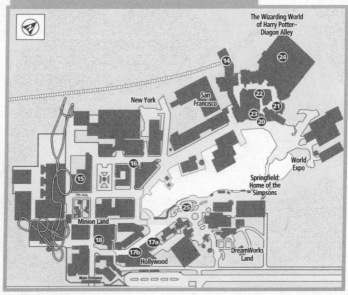

UNIVERSAL ORLANDO COMPREHENSIVE TWO-DAY/TWO-PARK TOURING PLAN:
DAY ONE *(continued)*
(Assumes: Multiday Park-to-Park Ticket)

(continued from previous page)

15. Ride Race Through New York Starring Jimmy Fallon if the wait is short.

16. Work in *The Blues Brothers Show* around your Jimmy Fallon ride according to the daily entertainment schedule.

17. See *Universal Orlando's Horror Make-Up Show* (**17a**) and *The Bourne Stuntacular* (**17b**) according to the daily entertainment schedule.

18. Experience Villain-Con Minion Blast.

19. Watch the afternoon character parade (if scheduled) from the New York or Hollywood areas.

20. On your way into Diagon Alley, chat with the Knight Bus conductor and his shrunken head. Also look for Kreacher in the window of 12

Grimmauld Place, and dial MAGIC (62442) in the red phone booth.

21. See the *Celestina Warbeck and the Banshees* or *Tales of Beedle the Bard* shows.

22. See the wand ceremony at Ollivanders, and buy a wand if you wish.

23. Tour Diagon Alley. Browse the shops, explore the dark recesses of Knockturn Alley, and discover the interactive effects. If you're hungry, try the Leaky Cauldron or Florean Fortescue's Ice-Cream Parlour.

24. Ride Harry Potter and the Escape from Gringotts.

25. Revisit any favorite attractions, time permitting, and (if scheduled) watch the evening lagoon show from Central Park (between Hollywood and Springfield).

(Day Two is on the next two pages.)

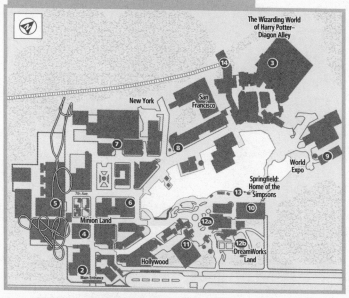

UNIVERSAL ORLANDO COMPREHENSIVE TWO-DAY/TWO-PARK
TOURING PLAN: DAY TWO
(Assumes: Multiday Park-to-Park Ticket) (Day One is on previous pages.)

1. Buy admission in advance. Call ☎ 407-363-8000 or visit universalorlando.com the day before for the official opening time, and install Universal's app on your smartphone.

2. Arrive at USF 90–120 minutes before the official opening time if Early Park Admission is offered and you're eligible, or 30–45 minutes before opening if you're a day guest. Check Universal's app for daily showtimes.

3. Early-entry guests should ride Harry Potter and the Escape from Gringotts. If Gringotts isn't operating, enjoy the rest of Diagon Alley but do not get in line.

4. Before early entry ends, hotel guests should exit Diagon Alley and ride Despicable Me Minion Mayhem. Day guests should wait at the entrance until permitted to ride Despicable Me.

5. Ride Hollywood Rip Ride Rockit.

6. Experience Transformers: The Ride-3D.

7. Ride Revenge of the Mummy in New York.

8. Experience Fast & Furious: Supercharged. Use the single-rider line or skip it if the standby wait time exceeds 20 minutes.

9. Walk past the London Waterfront to ride Men in Black Alien Attack in World Expo.

10. Ride The Simpsons Ride in Springfield.

11. Ride E.T. Adventure, then visit the characters in nearby DreamWorks Land.

12. Work in *Animal Actors on Location!* (12a) and *DreamWorks Imagination Celebration* (12b) around lunch (we recommend Fast Food Boulevard, Minion Cafe, or Today Cafe), according to the daily entertainment schedule.

13. Ride Kang & Kodos' Twirl 'n' Hurl if 50 or fewer people are in line.

14. Ride the Hogwarts Express from King's Cross Station to IOA. Have your park-to-park ticket ready.

(continued on next page)

412

Universal Islands of Adventure

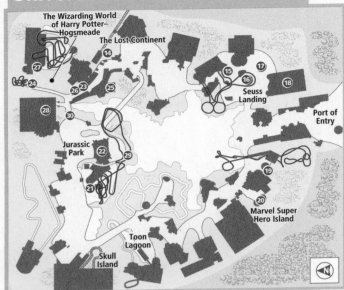

UNIVERSAL ORLANDO COMPREHENSIVE TWO-DAY/TWO-PARK TOURING PLAN:
DAY TWO *(continued)*
(Assumes: Multiday Park-to-Park Ticket)

(continued from previous page)

15. Ride The High in the Sky Seuss Trolley Train Ride! in Seuss Landing.

16. Enjoy the Caro-Seuss-el.

17. Ride One Fish, Two Fish, Red Fish, Blue Fish.

18. Experience The Cat in the Hat.

19. Cross through Port of Entry to Marvel Super Hero Island and ride Storm Force Accelatron.

20. While in Marvel, ride Doctor Doom's Fearfall.

21. Walk through Toon Lagoon to Jurassic Park and explore Camp Jurassic.

22. Check out the exhibits in the Jurassic Park Discovery Center.

23. Enter Hogsmeade and see the *Frog Choir* or *Triwizard Spirit Rally* perform on the small stage outside Hogsmeade.

24. Ride Flight of the Hippogriff.

25. Have dinner at Three Broomsticks.

26. After dinner, see the stage show you didn't see earlier. Snap a picture of the Hogwarts Express conductor, and explore the shops and interactive windows around Hogsmeade. Make sure you sample (or at least smell) some sweets at Honeydukes.

27. Try to ride Hagrid's Magical Creatures Motorbike Adventure around sunset.

28. Ride Harry Potter and the Forbidden Journey during the first Hogwarts Castle nighttime light show (performed seasonally).

29. Get in line for the Jurassic World VelociCoaster at least 30 minutes before the park closes.

30. Watch the last Hogwarts Castle light show of the night (if scheduled), or revisit any favorite attractions.

Epic Universe

UNIVERSAL EPIC UNIVERSE ONE-DAY TOURING PLAN FOR ADULTS

1. Buy admission well in advance to secure your desired day. Call ☎ 407-363-8000 or visit universalorlando.com the day before for the official opening time, and install Universal's app on your smartphone.

2. Plan to arrive at the Epic Universe parking lot or bus drop-off at least 60–90 minutes prior to opening.

3. Ride Harry Potter and the Battle at the Ministry at the back of the park first, while most guests are rushing to Super Nintendo World.

4. See the *Le Cirque Arcanus* show next, as all the headliner ride queues are likely full by now.

5. Explore the Parisian-style Wizarding shops, or purchase and utilize interactive wands before leaving the Wizarding World.

6. Go to Dark Universe next and head straight into Monsters Unchained: The Frankenstein Experiment. Use the single-rider option if possible.

7. Head back into Celestial Park for a ride on Constellation Carousel (7a) and/or Stardust Racers (7b), depending on your thrill level preference. (There will be another chance for these rides later if queues are too long.)

8. Break for lunch. Atlantic or Blue Dragon are full service options within this area, or dine at Oak and Star Tavern, Meteor Astropub, or Pizza Moon for quality quick-service options.

9. Enjoy the daytime fountain displays and atmospheric entertainment options in Celestial Park between worlds.

10. Watch *The Untrainable Dragon* at Isle of Berk, according to the daily performance schedule.

11. Take a ride on Hiccup's Wing Gliders before or after the show. (Skip Fyre Drill and Dragon Racer's Rally to save time unless they're important to you.)

12. Ride Mario Kart: Bowser's Challenge in Super Nintendo World, using single-rider if possible.

13. Purchase a Power-Up Band if you wish to partake in interactive experiences around Super Nintendo World.

14. Enjoy a Nintendo-themed snack or purchase a themed popcorn bucket while in this area.

15. Ride either Yoshi's Adventure (15a) or Mine-Cart Madness (15b).

16. Now that the sun is setting, head back to Dark Universe to ride Curse of the Werewolf and enjoy the spooky atmosphere while in the land.

17. Enjoy one last nighttime ride on the Stardust Racers roller coaster, which is a completely different experience at night.

18. Take in the nighttime fountain show and enjoy shopping within Celestial Park.

Epic Universe

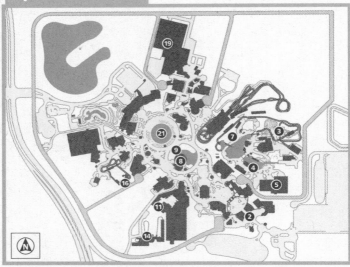

UNIVERSAL EPIC UNIVERSE ONE-DAY TOURING PLAN
FOR FAMILIES WITH SMALL CHILDREN

1. Buy admission well in advance to secure your desired day. Call ☎ 407-363-8000 or visit universalorlando.com the day before for the official opening time, and install Universal's app on your smartphone.

2. Plan to arrive at the Epic Universe parking lot or bus drop-off at least 60–90 minutes prior to opening.

3. If your children are brave enough, start your day with Hiccup's Wing Gliders at Isle of Berk.

4. Ride the Fyre Drill interactive boat ride in this area.

5. See *The Untrainable Dragon* show according to the daily performance schedule.

6. Meet Toothless and Hiccup after the show.

7. Explore the Viking Training Camp play area before heading out of Isle of Berk.

8. Ride Constellation Carousel in the center of the park.

9. Play in the Astronomica splash pad near the carousel.

10. Take a break from the park for at least 2 hours, depending on how late the park is open. If staying nearby, go back to the hotel for lunch and a nap.

11. Return to the park and ride Yoshi's Adventure at Super Nintendo World.

12. Meet Princess Peach, Toad, or Mario and Luigi in Super Mario Land.

13. Purchase a Power-Up Band to explore interactive areas and play games around Super Nintendo World as a family.

14. Ride Mine-Cart Madness if your child can handle its family-friendly thrills.

15. Meet Donkey Kong within the Donkey Kong Country mini-land.

16. Ride Curse of the Werewolf in Dark Universe, if you dare.

17. Meet the Monsters, and consider face paint to become one within Dark Universe, if your child is a fan of Frankenstein and his friends.

18. Explore interactive wand experiences and window displays within the Wizarding World.

19. Take a tour of the queue for Harry Potter and the Battle at the Ministry (but exit before boarding the ride).

20. Have dinner at one of the two restaurants within the Wizarding World, Pizza Moon in Celestial Park, or at Mead Hall within Isle of Berk (if everyone can handle the extra walking).

21. Watch the nighttime fountain show at the end of the night, or revisit any favorite or skipped attractions.

Epic Universe

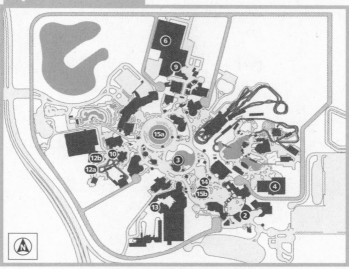

UNIVERSAL EPIC UNIVERSE ONE-DAY TOURING PLAN
FOR SENIORS

1. Buy admission well in advance to secure your desired day. Call ☎ 407-363-8000 or visit universalorlando.com the day before for the official opening time, and install Universal's app on your smartphone.

2. Plan to arrive at the Epic Universe parking lot or bus drop-off at least 60–90 minutes prior to opening.

3. Ride Constellation Carousel in the center of the park.

4. See *The Untrainable Dragon* show at Isle of Berk according to the daily show schedule.

5. Walk to the Wizarding World, but stop to see the large daytime fountain display near the back of the park on your way.

6. Take a tour of the queue for Harry Potter and the Battle at the Ministry (but exit before boarding the ride).

7. Explore interactive wand experiences and window displays within the Wizarding World.

8. Have lunch at one of the two Parisian-style cafes within the Wizarding World.

9. See the *Le Cirque Arcanus* show.

10. Explore the village streets of Dark Universe.

11. Meet the Universal Classic Monsters and other creepy characters inside Dark Universe.

12. Enjoy a drink or snack at The Burning Blade Tavern (12a) or De Lacey's Cottage (12b).

13. Ride Yoshi's Adventure in Super Nintendo World.

14. Spend time walking the gardens and bridges of Celestial Park, located between Super Nintendo World and Isle of Berk. You may catch entertainers performing within this area.

15. Stay for the nighttime fountain show (15a), stopping for dinner at Atlantic (15b), a full-service seafood restaurant, while you wait. Or revisit any favorite attractions before leaving for dinner at the I-Drive area.

Epic Universe

UNIVERSAL EPIC UNIVERSE ONE-DAY TOURING PLAN
FOR TWEENS

1. Buy admission well in advance to secure your desired day. Call ☎ 407-363-8000 or visit universalorlando.com the day before for the official opening time, and install Universal's app on your smartphone.

2. Plan to arrive at the Epic Universe parking lot or bus drop-off at least 60–90 minutes prior to opening.

3. Start with Harry Potter and the Battle at the Ministry at the back of the park.

4. See the *Le Cirque Arcanus* show.

5. Explore the Parisian-style Wizarding shops, or purchase and utilize interactive wands before leaving the Wizarding World.

6. Go to Dark Universe next and head straight into Monsters Unchained: The Frankenstein Experiment. Use the single-rider option if possible.

7. Ride Curse of the Werewolf.

8. Head back into Celestial Park for a ride on Constellation Carousel (8a) and/or Stardust Racers (8b), depending on your thrill level preference. (There will be another chance for these rides later if queues are too long.)

9. Break for lunch at The Oak and Star Tavern or Pizza Moon in Celestial Park, or Spit Fyre Grill in Isle of Berk.

10. Watch *The Untrainable Dragon* at Isle of Berk, according to the daily performance schedule.

11. Meet Hiccup and Toothless after the show if the wait is under 30 minutes.

12. Take a ride on Hiccup's Wing Gliders (12a) or Dragon Racer's Rally (12b).

13. Ride Mario Kart: Bowser's Challenge in Super Nintendo World, using single-rider if possible.

14. Ride either Mine-Cart Madness (14a) or Yoshi's Adventure (14b).

15. Purchase a Power-Up Band to partake in interactive experiences around Super Nintendo World.

16. Ride Stardust Racers (16a) at night, for special lighting effects, and Constellation Carousel (16b) if skipper earlier.

17. Revisit any favorite attractions if there is time before the nighttime fountain show in Celestial Park.